Lecture Notes in Artificial Intelligence   11509

Subseries of Lecture Notes in Computer Science

More information about this series at http://www.springer.com/series/1244

Leszek Rutkowski · Rafał Scherer ·
Marcin Korytkowski · Witold Pedrycz ·
Ryszard Tadeusiewicz · Jacek M. Zurada (Eds.)

Artificial Intelligence and Soft Computing

18th International Conference, ICAISC 2019
Zakopane, Poland, June 16–20, 2019
Proceedings, Part II

 Springer

Editors
Leszek Rutkowski
Częstochowa University of Technology
Częstochowa, Poland

Rafał Scherer
Częstochowa University of Technology
Częstochowa, Poland

Marcin Korytkowski
Częstochowa University of Technology
Częstochowa, Poland

Witold Pedrycz
University of Alberta
Edmonton, AB, Canada

Ryszard Tadeusiewicz
AGH University of Science and Technology
Kraków, Poland

Jacek M. Zurada
University of Louisville
Louisville, KY, USA

ISSN 0302-9743   ISSN 1611-3349 (electronic)
Lecture Notes in Artificial Intelligence
ISBN 978-3-030-20914-8   ISBN 978-3-030-20915-5 (eBook)
https://doi.org/10.1007/978-3-030-20915-5

LNCS Sublibrary: SL7 – Artificial Intelligence

This Springer imprint is published by the registered company Springer Nature Switzerland AG
The registered company address is: Gewerbestrasse 11, 6330 Cham, Switzerland

Preface

This volume constitutes the proceedings of the 18th International Conference on Artificial Intelligence and Soft Computing ICAISC 2019, held in Zakopane, Poland, during June 16–20, 2019. The conference was organized by the Polish Neural Network Society in cooperation with the University of Social Sciences in Łódź, the Institute of Computational Intelligence at the Częstochowa University of Technology, and the IEEE Computational Intelligence Society, Poland Chapter. Previous conferences took place in Kule (1994), Szczyrk (1996), Kule (1997), and Zakopane (1999, 2000, 2002, 2004, 2006, 2008, 2010, 2012, 2013, 2014, 2015, 2016, 2017 and 2018) and attracted a large number of papers and internationally recognized speakers: Lotfi A. Zadeh, Hojjat Adeli, Rafal Angryk, Igor Aizenberg, Cesare Alippi, Shun-ichi Amari, Daniel Amit, Plamen Angelov, Albert Bifet, Piero P. Bonissone, Jim Bezdek, Zdzisław Bubnicki, Andrzej Cichocki, Swagatam Das, Ewa Dudek-Dyduch, Włodzisław Duch, Pablo A. Estévez, João Gama, Erol Gelenbe, Jerzy Grzymala-Busse, Martin Hagan, Yoichi Hayashi, Akira Hirose, Kaoru Hirota, Adrian Horzyk, Eyke Hüllermeier, Hisao Ishibuchi, Er Meng Joo, Janusz Kacprzyk, Jim Keller, Laszlo T. Koczy, Tomasz Kopacz, Zdzisław Kowalczuk, Adam Krzyzak, Rudolf Kruse, James Tin-Yau Kwok, Soo-Young Lee, Derong Liu, Robert Marks, Evangelia Micheli-Tzanakou, Kaisa Miettinen, Krystian Mikołajczyk, Henning Müller, Ngoc Thanh Nguyen, Andrzej Obuchowicz, Erkki Oja, Witold Pedrycz, Marios M. Polycarpou, José C. Príncipe, Jagath C. Rajapakse, Šarunas Raudys, Enrique Ruspini, Jörg Siekmann, Andrzej Skowron, Roman Słowiński, Igor Spiridonov, Boris Stilman, Ponnuthurai Nagaratnam Suganthan, Ryszard Tadeusiewicz, Ah-Hwee Tan, Shiro Usui, Thomas Villmann, Fei-Yue Wang, Jun Wang, Bogdan M. Wilamowski, Ronald Y. Yager, Xin Yao, Syozo Yasui, Gary Yen, Ivan Zelinka, and Jacek Zurada. The aim of this conference is to build a bridge between traditional artificial intelligence techniques and so-called soft computing techniques. It was pointed out by Lotfi A. Zadeh that "soft computing (SC) is a coalition of methodologies which are oriented toward the conception and design of information/intelligent systems. The principal members of the coalition are: fuzzy logic (FL), neurocomputing (NC), evolutionary computing (EC), probabilistic computing (PC), chaotic computing (CC), and machine learning (ML). The constituent methodologies of SC are, for the most part, complementary and synergistic rather than competitive." These proceedings present both traditional artificial intelligence methods and soft computing techniques. Our goal is to bring together scientists representing both areas of research. This volume is divided into five parts:

- Various Problems of Artificial Intelligence
- Computer Vision, Image and Speech Analysis
- Bioinformatics, Biometrics and Medical Applications
- Agent Systems, Robotics and Control
- Data Mining

The conference attracted a total of 333 submissions from 43 countries and after the review process, 122 papers were accepted for publication.

I would like to thank our participants, invited speakers, and reviewers of the papers for their scientific and personal contribution to the conference.

Finally, I thank my co-workers Łukasz Bartczuk, Piotr Dziwiński, Marcin Gabryel, Marcin Korytkowski as well as the conference secretary, Rafał Scherer, for their enormous efforts to make the conference a very successful event. Moreover, I appreciate the work of Marcin Korytkowski, who was responsible for the Internet submission system.

June 2019   Leszek Rutkowski

Organization

ICAISC 2019 was organized by the Polish Neural Network Society in cooperation with the University of Social Sciences in Łódź and the Institute of Computational Intelligence at Częstochowa University of Technology.

ICAISC Chairs

Honorary Chairs

Hojjat Adeli, USA
Witold Pedrycz, Canada
Jacek Żurada, USA

General Chair

Leszek Rutkowski, Poland

Co-chairs

Włodzisław Duch, Poland
Janusz Kacprzyk, Poland
Józef Korbicz, Poland
Ryszard Tadeusiewicz, Poland

ICAISC Program Committee

Rafał Adamczak, Poland
Cesare Alippi, Italy
Shun-ichi Amari, Japan
Rafal A. Angryk, USA
Jarosław Arabas, Poland
Robert Babuska, The Netherlands
Ildar Z. Batyrshin, Russia
James C. Bezdek, Australia
Marco Block-Berlitz, Germany
Leon Bobrowski, Poland
Piero P. Bonissone, USA
Bernadette Bouchon-Meunier, France
Tadeusz Burczynski, Poland
Andrzej Cader, Poland
Juan Luis Castro, Spain
Yen-Wei Chen, Japan

Wojciech Cholewa, Poland
Kazimierz Choroś, Poland
Fahmida N. Chowdhury, USA
Andrzej Cichocki, Japan
Paweł Cichosz, Poland
Krzysztof Cios, USA
Ian Cloete, Germany
Oscar Cordón, Spain
Bernard De Baets, Belgium
Nabil Derbel, Tunisia
Ewa Dudek-Dyduch, Poland
Ludmiła Dymowa, Poland
Andrzej Dzieliński, Poland
David Elizondo, UK
Meng Joo Er, Singapore
Pablo Estevez, Chile

Raúl Rojas, Germany
Imre J. Rudas, Hungary
Enrique H. Ruspini, USA
Khalid Saeed, Poland
Dominik Sankowski, Poland
Norihide Sano, Japan
Robert Schaefer, Poland
Rudy Setiono, Singapore
Paweł Sewastianow, Poland
Jennie Si, USA
Peter Sincak, Slovakia
Andrzej Skowron, Poland
Ewa Skubalska-Rafajłowicz, Poland
Roman Słowiński, Poland
Tomasz G. Smolinski, USA
Czesław Smutnicki, Poland
Pilar Sobrevilla, Spain
Janusz Starzyk, USA
Jerzy Stefanowski, Poland
Vitomir Štruc, Slovenia
Pawel Strumillo, Poland
Ron Sun, USA
Johan Suykens, Belgium
Piotr Szczepaniak, Poland
Eulalia J. Szmidt, Poland
Przemysław Śliwiński, Poland

Adam Słowik, Poland
Jerzy Świątek, Poland
Hideyuki Takagi, Japan
Yury Tiumentsev, Russia
Vicenç Torra, Spain
Burhan Turksen, Canada
Shiro Usui, Japan
Michael Wagenknecht, Germany
Tomasz Walkowiak, Poland
Deliang Wang, USA
Jun Wang, Hong Kong, SAR China
Lipo Wang, Singapore
Paul Werbos, USA
Slawo Wesolkowski, Canada
Sławomir Wiak, Poland
Bernard Widrow, USA
Kay C. Wiese, Canada
Bogdan M. Wilamowski, USA
Donald C. Wunsch, USA
Maciej Wygralak, Poland
Roman Wyrzykowski, Poland
Ronald R. Yager, USA
Xin-She Yang, UK
Gary Yen, USA
Sławomir Zadrożny, Poland
Ali M. S. Zalzala, United Arab Emirates

Additional Reviewers

M. Baczyński
M. Blachnik
L. Bobrowski
P. Boguś
W. Bozejko
R. Burduk
J. ChandBansal
W. Cholewa
P. Ciskowski
M. Clerc
C. CoelloCoello
B. Cyganek
J. Cytowski
R. Czabański
I. Czarnowski

N. Derbel
L. Diosan
A. Dockhorn
W. Duch
S. Ehteram
B. Filipic
I. Fister
M. Fraś
M. Gavrilova
E. Gelenbe
M. Gorzałczany
G. Gosztolya
D. Grabowski
M. Grzenda
J. Grzymala-Busse

L. Guo
Y. Hayashi
F. Hermann
K. Hirota
A. Horzyk
J. Ishikawa
D. Jakóbczak
E. Jamro
A. Janczak
M. Jirina
W. Kamiński
E. Kerre
F. Klawonn
P. Klęsk
J. Kluska

A. Kołakowska

J. Konopacki

J. Korbicz

P. Korohoda

M. Korytkowski

M. Korzeń

J. Kościelny

L. Kotulski

Z. Kowalczuk

M. Kraft

M. Kretowska

D. Krol

B. Kryzhanovsky

A. Krzyzak

E. Kucharska

P. Kudová

J. Kulikowski

O. Kurasova

V. Kurkova

M. Kurzyński

J. Kwiecień

A. Ligęza

M. Ławryńczuk

J. Łęski

K. Madani

W. Malina

K. Malinowski

A. Materka

R. Matuk Herrera

J. Mazurkiewicz

V. Medvedev

M. Mernik

J. Michalkiewicz

S. Misina

W. Mitkowski

M. Morzy

P. Musilek

H. Nakamoto

G. Nalepa

M. Nashed

S. Nasuto

S. Osowski

A. Owczarek

E. Ozcan

M. Pacholczyk

W. Palacz

G. Papa

A. Parkes

A. Paszyńska

A. Piegat

V. Piuri

P. Prokopowicz

A. Przybył

A. Radzikowska

E. Rafajłowicz

E. Rakus-Andersson

Ł. Rauch

L. Rolka

A. Rusiecki

J. Sas

A. Sashima

R. Sassi

E. Sato-Shimokawara

R. Scherer

F. Scotti

C. Siemers

K. Skrzypczyk

E. Skubalska-Rafajłowicz

D. Słota

C. Smutnicki

A. Sokołowski

B. Strug

P. Strumiłło

P. Suganthan

J. Swacha

P. Szczepaniak

E. Szmidt

G. Ślusarczyk

J. Świątek

R. Tadeusiewicz

Y. Tanigaki

Y. Tiumentsev

K. Tokarz

S. Tomforde

H. Tsang

M. Vajgl

E. Volna

R. Vorobel

T. Walkowiak

L. Wang

T. Wang

Y. Wang

J. Wąs

M. Wojciechowski

M. Wozniak

M. Wygralak

R. Wyrzykowski

Q. Xiao

T. Yamaguchi

X. Yang

J. Yeomans

D. Zaharie

D. Zakrzewska

A. Zamuda

ICAISC Organizing Committee

Rafał Scherer (Secretary)

Łukasz Bartczuk

Piotr Dziwiński

Marcin Gabryel (Finance Chair)

Rafał Grycuk

Marcin Korytkowski (Databases and Internet Submissions)

Contents – Part II

Bioinformatics, Biometrics and Medical Applications

Data Mining

Various Problems of Artificial Intelligence

Agent Systems, Robotics and Control

Contents – Part I

Evolutionary Algorithms and Their Applications

Pattern Classification

Artificial Intelligence in Modeling and Simulation

Computer Vision, Image and Speech Analysis

Indoor Localization Using Cluster Analysis

Ramy Aboul Naga[1]($\boxtimes$)(iD), Rimon Elias[1](iD), and Amal El Nahas[2]

[1] German University in Cairo, Cairo, Egypt
{ramy.aboulnaga,rimon.elias}@guc.edu.eg
[2] British University in Egypt, Cairo, Egypt
amal.elnahas@bue.edu.eg

Abstract. One of the key requirements of context based systems and intelligent environments is a user's location. Numerous indoor localization solutions have been proposed. In this paper, we propose an enhancement to an already implemented indoor localization algorithm that utilizes the JUDOCA operator to linearly find a match to an input image within a geo-tagged dataset of pre-stored images. The proposed approach is based on k-medoids cluster analysis, which is used to compare distances calculated with the same JUDOCA operator used in the original algorithm in an attempt to enhance its execution time. The results showed that the proposed approach introduced an enhancement in the execution speed of around 10 times compared to the original approach.

Keywords: Correlation · Cluster analysis · Indoor localization ·
Intelligent environment · JUDOCA

1 Introduction

The growing need for location support systems emphasizes the importance of addressing the location-awareness problem. Identifying the user's location became a requirement that is demanded by most ubiquitous intelligent environments and systems. Intelligent environments consist of multiple intercommunicating wireless devices that process information about us and our surroundings. These devices may be stationary or mobile. Such environments depend greatly on the user's context, which translates to their location within the environment. This context defines how the functions provided by the environment are presented.

Localization can be classified into either indoor or outdoor. While outdoor localization is easily achieved using the Global Positioning System (GPS), accurate indoor localization is considered a topic of research.

In this paper, approaches attempting to solve the localization problem are discussed in Sect. 2. Section 2 discusses some related work. Our proposed solution is presented in Sects. 3 and 4 follows with the experimental results. Section 5 analyzes and discusses these results. Section 6 wraps up with a conclusion.

© Springer Nature Switzerland AG 2019
L. Rutkowski et al. (Eds.): ICAISC 2019, LNAI 11509, pp. 3–13, 2019.
https://doi.org/10.1007/978-3-030-20915-5_1

2   Literature Review

Indoor localization is crucial for many applications such as Augmented Reality. Various indoor localization techniques have been proposed which can be classified according to their precision, infrastructure dependencies, complexity, etc.

Beaconing technologies such as Infrared [13,22] and Ultrasound [18] are examples of techniques that require additional hardware. They use transmitters and receivers to locate a user based on proximity.

Another class of techniques includes localization using radio technology, images or videos. Radio-technology based localization focuses on WiFi [8,15]. By measuring the signal strength of multiple access points around the user, their location can be identified within a small area as demonstrated by the RADAR system [2] that compares the signal strength received by a user with a pre-constructed database of measured signal strengths at different locations. However, any alteration in the setup of the environment can impact the signal strength, resulting in inaccurate location estimations, which require recalibrating the system. The same approach was implemented using Bluetooth beacons, however, it experienced high delays during the discovery phase.

Recently, approaches that take advantage of the mobile phone sensors have been proposed in [26] and [4]. The user steps are counted and their direction is determined using the accelerometer and compass. Positioning is determined using Dead Reckoning which suffers from the fast accumulation of errors, requiring recalibration [4,16].

Image-based indoor localization techniques adopt the same approach as WiFi-based approaches, but rely on images. Locating a user is performed by matching the image of what they see with a database of geo-tagged images. No extra hardware is needed except for a digital camera, which all modern mobile phones are equipped with. What makes this approach promising is the recent advances in the field of computer vision that made image matching technology very accurate. However, current image matching algorithms are quite expensive in terms of delay.

In [19], color histograms, wavelet decomposition and shape matching were used, achieving more than 90% room-level accuracy and 80% meter-level accuracy.

[1] and [21] address the problem of large-scale visual place recognition by using convolutional neural network (CNN) and comparing input images with synthesized novel views respectively. Both approaches showed significant outperforming results in outdoor image location identification, and can theoretically be used indoor, but they present a load of complexity that is deemed unnecessary.

In [5], the JUDOCA operator presented in [7] is utilized to measure the similarity between an image and the images stored in the database, by detecting and comparing junctions.

The work in [24] uses a hashing-based image matching algorithm which is much more efficient in terms of energy consumption and computation cost.

2.1 Hashing

Several hashing techniques may be used to generate a unique hashed string for an image. This section explains the differences between these techniques and the results of using them are presented in Sect. 4.

Perceptual Hashing makes use of various features of the image. Perceptual hashes are considered almost identical if the features of their images are similar [11]. Perceptual hashes must be robust to account for geometrical transformations and yet be flexible to distinguish between dissimilar files. Perceptual Hashing relies on the Discrete Cosine Transform (DCT) function, which can compute a hash from frequency spectrum data that acts as a fingerprint, and is robust against minor rotation, blurring and compression, making it a good candidate for use in Perceptual Hashing. The low-frequency DCT coefficients are used to form the hash, as they are stable under image manipulations [10]. The DCT function is described in Eq. (1), where N is the number of pixels in the image, $f(x)$ gets the color value of the pixel x, and u ranges between 0 and $N - 1$.

$$F(u) = C(u) \sum_{x=0}^{N-1} f(x) \cos \left| \frac{\pi(2x+1)u}{2N} \right| \qquad C(u) = \begin{cases} \sqrt{\frac{1}{N}}, & \text{if } u = 0 \\ \sqrt{\frac{2}{N}}, & \text{otherwise} \end{cases} \qquad (1)$$

Block Hashing is a variation of the Perceptual Hashing algorithm [25]. It provides higher discriminability and lower complexity. Similar to Perceptual Hashing, it is robust to geometric distortions. Block Hashing generates hashes that are mathematically comparable and are near unique for resized versions of the image. Perceptual Hashing uses Lanczos interpolation [27], while Block Hashing works on non-overlapping blocks of the image and the median color value of their pixels, which is computationally less time consuming.

Average Hashing is another perceptual image similarity technique, the main idea of which is to use the average color of the image being processed to build a hash. Unlike the block mean value based method, it does not divide the image into blocks. This technique proved to be very promising in terms of speed and accuracy for finding perceptually similar images under limited resources devices like mobile phones [9].

Histogram Hashing. Histograms are invariant to geometric deformations [23]. The work done in [11], though, showed that the histogram based approach of hash generation would lead to a large number of false positives.

2.2 Feature Extraction and Detection

Feature extraction helps reduce the amount of resources required to describe a large set of data. These features are invariant to image transformations. A single feature is so distinctive that it can be correctly matched with high probability against a large database of features from many images [17].

Fig. 1. The junctions detected using the JUDOCA operator.

JUDOCA is an edge-based junction detector that can detect the location and orientation of junctions [7]. It was proposed to tackle indoor localization problems in [5], with a faster implementation tested in [6]. Figure 1 shows its output.

2.3 Distance Calculation

The generated hashes have to be compared using a subjective method that can be mathematically used to compare the similarity between images.

Hamming Distance. XORs the binary representation of the hashes, with the result having some bits set to 1, once for every time the corresponding bits of the hashes differ. The ratio of 1's to the total number of bits reflects a distance that is between 0 if the images are identical, and 1 if they are dissimilar.

Histogram Distance is done by comparing the values of the corresponding coefficients of the histograms using the sum of chi-squared test in Eq. (2), where $H(I_a, i)$ and $H(I_b, i)$ correspond to the frequency of the color value i for the input image and the image being compared from the dataset respectively.

$$d_{\text{hist}} = 1 - \frac{1}{2} \sum_{i=0}^{255} \frac{|H(I_a, i) - H(I_b, i)|^2}{H(I_a, i) + H(I_b, i)} \tag{2}$$

2.4 Cluster Analysis

Clustering, or cluster analysis, groups similar members of the dataset together, thus making them easier to be dealt with. It is well known in different fields [14]. Methods like centroid and medoid calculations are used to nominate a cluster representative that resembles an average of the features of all the members.

Objects in the same group or cluster are more alike compared to those in other clusters. Minimizing the intra-cluster distances ensures the homogeneity of the clusters, while maximizing the inter-cluster distances ensures their uniqueness.

Centroid- vs. Medoid-Based Clustering. In centroid-based clustering, clusters are represented by a mathematically-calculated vector, which may not map to an actual member of the cluster, as done in the k-means clustering algorithm [12]. The k-medoids algorithm differs in that it chooses the closest member of the cluster to the cluster's mathematical center [20]. When it comes to images, k-medoid clustering seems like the better fit. Thus, in the proposed enhanced algorithm, the k-medoid clustering is applied by choosing the image whose features resemble the features of the majority of the images near it, i.e. closest in distance to it. This will be further discussed in Sect. 3.1, specifically in **Stage IV** of the algorithm.

3   The Proposed Algorithm

The proposed algorithm is divided into a four-stage learning phase and a detection phase.

3.1   Learning Phase

The learning phase is a one-time process that is responsible for generating the clusters and constitutes to most of the execution time.

Stage I: Hash Generation. In this stage, the images are read and stored with some metadata needed by the following stage that differ depending on which of the hashing functions discussed in Sect. 2.1 was used.

Stage II: Distance Calculation. The metadata is used to calculate the cross-distance between all of the images of the dataset forming a "Distance Database". The distance function used corresponds to the hashing function applied. The database acts as a cache for the distances between any two images to avoid further calculations.

The Hamming distance discussed in Sect. 2.3 is used to calculate the distance between the images. In case the Normalized Histogram method discussed in Sect. 2.1 was used, the Histogram Distance method explained in Sect. 2.3 is used instead.

With regards to the JUDOCA-based approach, the sum of absolute differences (SAD) correlation is used to calculate the distances by forming and using triangular patches surrounding the junctions as in [5]. To further ensure the similarity of the junctions, they are compared on the pixel level after applying an affine transformation matrix A that is calculated using Eq. (3) to account for any geometrical transformations. (In this regard, a multi-edge junction is split into mutiple 2-edge junctions having the same location.) x_1 and y_1 represent the location of the 2-edge junction in the input image, and x_2, y_2, x_3 and y_3 represent the intersection of the two arms of the 2-edge junction with the circumference of a circle with radius r, whose center is at $[x_1, y_1]^{\mathrm{T}}$. x'_1, y'_1, x'_2, y'_2, x'_3 and y'_3 are the equivalent coordinates in the stored image. The junctions are correlated using their pixels' colors and compared against a threshold, t_{SAD}, that decides if the junction should be counted as a match. The correlated distance is calculated as the ratio of the number of the matching junctions to the total number of junctions.

$$a = \begin{bmatrix} x_1 \ y_1 \ 1 \\ x_2 \ y_2 \ 1 \\ x_3 \ y_3 \ 1 \end{bmatrix}^{-1} \qquad A = \begin{bmatrix} \left[a \ [x_1' \ x_2' \ x_3']^T \right]^T \\ \left[a \ [y_1' \ y_2' \ y_3']^T \right]^T \\ \left[a \ [1 \ 1 \ 1]^T \right]^T \end{bmatrix} \qquad (3)$$

Stage III: Clustering is based on how similar the images are, which is decided based on their distance that is compared against a threshold to tell if they are "close enough". Two approaches were tested to cluster the data.

Automatic clustering, which is the first approach, is a form of unsupervised learning that tries to find which cluster can accommodate a certain image by linearly comparing each of the images with the already clustered ones. The other approach clusters the images manually to avoid any incorrectly classified images.

Stage IV: Promotion. The main purpose of clustering the images of the dataset is to decrease the searching time. This stage attributes to this by promoting one of the members of each cluster to be its representative, by finding the member closest to the cluster's mathematical center. Having this will allow the input image to be compared with just this representative, instead of being compared with the individual members of each cluster. The approach used here is similar to how the local sensitive hashing works [3].

3.2 Detection Phase

This phase is concerned with locating an image, either by linearly finding a similar match from the dataset, or finding the best fitting cluster. The tagged geo-information of the match is used to locate the image. The input image undergoes the same stages of the learning phase to ensure its metadata is present.

The linear searching algorithm considers all of the images as its dataset. The cluster searching algorithm considers only the medoids of the clusters and when a matching medoid is found, the input image is said to belong to that medoid's cluster.

4 Experimental Results

The algorithm type, being linear (original approach) or clusters-based (proposed approach), is considered as an independent variable. The dependent variables found in the experiment setup were the average execution time and the accuracy. The original dataset in [5] was used. It is composed of 1233 images of different offices in a university building.

An image would be picked at random and used as input to both algorithms, then removed from the dataset. The results of both algorithms were compared to validate the results. The dataset is shuffled every iteration to ensure randomness.

The validation of the results was done using the Reference and Self verification methods. In the former, the results of the linear algorithm were used

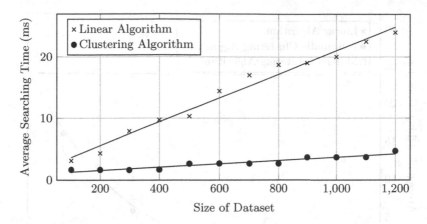

Fig. 2. Size of Dataset vs. Average Searching Time in Automatic Clustering, using a Distance Threshold of 0.76.

as reference. The number of times the clustering algorithm produced similar results to its linear counterpart was noted. In the latter, the input image was not removed and the times the match found was the input image itself, were noted.

The aim of the work done in this paper is to enhance the performance of the original searching algorithm [5]. The average searching time of the algorithm was measured and correlated with the distance threshold that achieved the most acceptable results. Figure 2 shows that the average searching time of the linear algorithm is proportional to the dataset size, which is directly affected by the distance threshold, while that of the clustering algorithm was unaffected when an adequate distance threshold was used, because the number of the generated clusters remains consistent regardless of the size of the dataset. An adequate distance threshold is one that when used, neither compromises the performance nor the quality of the algorithm.

It is necessary to relate the distance threshold to the average searching time. This will help pinpoint the best candidate for the value of the distance threshold that balances between the quality of the results of the algorithm and its performance. The graph in Fig. 3 demonstrates this relation.

The number of times the proposed algorithm succeeded in achieving the expected results was noted, as this reflects the accuracy of the algorithm, and is compared with the results of the original linear algorithm. Figure 4 shows the results of using the Automatic Clustering vs. Manual Clustering techniques discussed in Sect. 3.1, in terms of accuracy (% error) against different values for the distance threshold. The Manual Clustering technique shows better accuracy compared to its Automatic counterpart with varying values for the distance threshold and using the different hashing functions discussed in Sect. 2.1.

Figure 5 shows a sample of the output when the JUDOCA algorithm is set as the distance calculation algorithm, on a cluster generated using the Manual

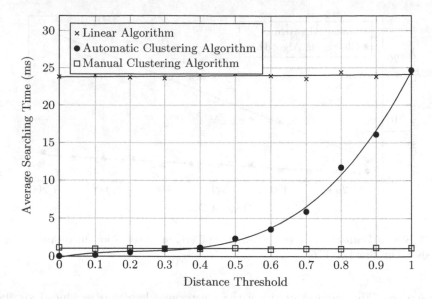

Fig. 3. Distance Threshold vs. Average Searching Time with a Dataset Size of 1233 images.

Clustering technique. Each of the images in the figure is tagged with its distance from the input image, d, and the searching time, t. Note that in this particular output of the enhanced proposed algorithm (b.2), the execution time t is 25 times less than that of the original linear algorithm (b.1).

5   Discussion

After reviewing the results above, it can be concluded that the cluster searching approach proposed by the work done in this paper is considered an enhancement to the original linear approach proposed in [5].

The proposed clustering analysis technique achieves results with an acceptable quality and accuracy compared to the original linear approach, and more specifically when the manual clustering method is used as shown in Fig. 4. This is done in a whole order of magnitude less time than the original approach. By superimposing the graphs in Figs. 3 and 4, the point of intersection between them was noticed to occur at a distance threshold of 0.76, which was noticed to be the value at which the most optimal results are achieved, in terms of both speed (searching time) and accuracy (% error). This was based on linear and polynomial regression, which was applied to the data points in Fig. 3.

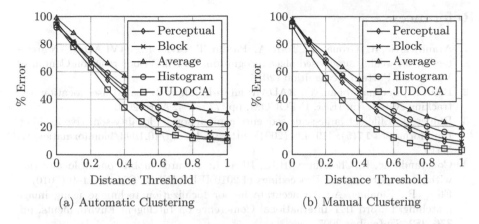

(a) Automatic Clustering   (b) Manual Clustering

Fig. 4. Distance Threshold vs. Error

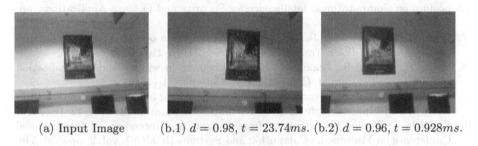

(a) Input Image   (b.1) $d = 0.98$, $t = 23.74ms$. (b.2) $d = 0.96$, $t = 0.928ms$.

Fig. 5. A sample run of the experiment using (b.1) The Original Linear Algorithm and (b.2) The JUDOCA-based Manual Clustering algorithm.

6 Conclusion

In this paper, we extended on the work done in [5]. A proposed cluster analysis approach was applied instead of linearly comparing each entry of the dataset as done in the original approach. Images with a similarity distance above a certain threshold were allocated to the same cluster. A member of each cluster was then promoted as its medoid, and used in the comparison process instead of the individual images comparison approach.

An experiment was conducted to test the validity of the new approach. The image matching process was divided into learning and detection phases. The output of the detection phase is the equivalent of what the original algorithm does. In order to measure the enhancement, two metrics were calculated. The first was the average searching time which was correlated with the distance threshold that achieved the most acceptable results. The second was measured by the times the algorithm succeeded in achieving the expected results.

The results showed that the clustering approach proposed by the work done in this paper is considered an enhancement to the original approach.

References

1. Arandjelović, R., Gronat, P., Torii, A., Pajdla, T., Sivic, J.: NetVLAD: CNN architecture for weakly supervised place recognition. In: IEEE Conference on Computer Vision and Pattern Recognition (2016)
2. Bahl, R., Padmanabhan, V.: RADAR: an in-building RF-based user location and tracking system. In: IEEE INFOCOM, pp. 775–784, April 2000
3. Buhler, J.: Efficient large-scale sequence comparison by locality-sensitive hashing. Bioinformatics **17**(5), 419–428 (2001). https://doi.org/10.1093/bioinformatics/17.5.419
4. Constandache, I., Choudhury, R.R., Rhee, I.: Towards mobile phone localization without war-driving. In: Proceedings of 2010 IEEE INFOCOM, pp. 1–9 (2010)
5. Elias, R., Elnahas, A.: An accurate indoor localization technique using image matching. In: 3rd IET International Conference on Intelligent Environments, pp. 376–382, September 2007
6. Elias, R., Elnahas, A.: Fast localization in indoor environments. In: IEEE Symposium on Computational Intelligence for Security and Defense Applications, pp. 1–6 (2009)
7. Elias, R., Laganiere, R.: JUDOCA: Junction detection operator based on circumferential anchors. IEEE Trans. Image Process. **21**(4), 2109–2118 (2012)
8. Farid, Z., Nordin, R., Ismail, M.: Recent advances in wireless indoor localization techniques and system. J. Comput. Netw. Commun. **1** (2013)
9. Farisa, S., Haviana, C., Kurniadi, D.: Average hashing for perceptual image similarity in mobile phone application. J. Telematics Informat. (JTI) **4**(1), 12–18 (2016)
10. Fridrich, J.: Robust bit extraction from images. In: Proceedings of International Conference on Multimedia Computing and Systems (ICMCS), vol. 2, pp. 536–540. IEEE, June 1999
11. Hadmi, A., Puech, W., Said, B., Ouahman, A.: Perceptual Image Hashing, Watermarking, vol. 2. InTech (2012)
12. Hartigan, J., Wong, M.: Algorithm AS 136: a k-means clustering algorithm. J. Roy. Stat. Soc. Ser. C (Appl. Stat.) **28**(1), 100–108 (1979)
13. Hopper, A., Harter, A., Blackie, T.: The Active Badge System. In: Proceedings of INTERACT 1993 and CHI 1993 Conference on Human Factors in Computing Systems, Amsterdam, The Netherlands, pp. 533–534 (1993)
14. Kaufman, L., Rousseeuw, P.: Finding Groups in Data: An Introduction to Cluster Analysis. Wiley Series in Probability and Statistics. Wiley, Hoboken (2009)
15. Ladd, A., Bekris, K., Rudys, A., Marceau, G., Kavraki, L., Wallach, D.: Roboticbased location sensing using wireless ethernet. In: Proceedings of the 8th Annual International Conference on Mobile Computing and Networking, Atlanta, GA, USA, pp. 227–238 (2000)
16. Li, F., Zhao, C., Ding, G., Gong, J., Liu, C., Zhao, F.: A reliable and accurate indoor localization method using phone inertial sensors. In: Proceedings of the 2012 ACM Conference Ubiquitous Computing, pp. 421–430 (2012)
17. Lowe, D.: Distinctive image features from scale-invariant keypoints. Int. J. Comput. Vis. **60**(2), 91–110 (2004)
18. Priyantha, N., Chakaborty, A., Balakrishnan, H.: The cricket location-support system. In: 6th ACM International Conference on Mobile Computing & Networking, pp. 32–43 (2000)

19. Ravi, N., Shankar, P., Frankel, A., Elgammal, A., Iftode, L.: Indoor localization using camera phones. In: Seventh IEEE Workshop Mobile Computing Systems Applications (WMCSA 2006 Supplement), p. 49, April 2006. https://doi.org/10.1109/WMCSA.2006.12

20. Sheng, W., Liu, X.: A hybrid algorithm for k-medoid clustering large data sets. In: Proceedings of the 2004 Congress Evolutionary Computation (IEEE Cat. No. 04TH8753), vol. 1, pp. 77–82, June 2004

21. Torii, A., Arandjelovic, R., Sivic, J., Okutomi, M., Pajdla, T.: 24/7 place recognition by view synthesis. IEEE Trans. Pattern Anal. Mach. Intell. 14, February 2017. https://hal.inria.fr/hal-01616660

22. Want, R., Hopper, A., Falcao, V., Gibbons, J.: The active badge location system. ACM Trans. Inf. Syst. **10**, 91–102 (1992)

23. Xiang, S., Kim, H., Huang, J.: Histogram-based image hashing scheme robust against geometric deformations. In: Proceedings of the 9th Workshop on Multimedia & Security, pp. 121–128. ACM, New York (2007)

24. Moon, Y., Noh, S., Park, D.: A camera-based positioning system using learning. In: Proceedings of the 29th IEEE International System-on-Chip Conference (SOCC), pp. 235–240 (2016)

25. Yang, B., Gu, F., Niu, X.: Block mean value based image perceptual hashing. In: International Conference on Intelligent Information Hiding and Multimedia, pp. 167–172 (2006)

26. Youssef, M., Yosef, M.A., El-Derini, M.: GAC: energy efficient hybrid GPS-accelerometer-compass GSM localization. In: Proceedings of 2010 IEEE Global Telecommunication Conference (GLOBECOM), pp. 1–5 (2010)

27. Zauner, C.: Implementation and benchmarking perceptual image hash functions. Master's thesis, Secure Information Systems, Hagenberg, Austria, July 2010

From Synthetic Images Towards Detectors of Real Objects: A Case Study on Road Sign Detection

Przemysław Klęsk[(✉)]

Faculty of Computer Science and Information Technology,
West Pomeranian University of Technology, ul. Żołnierska 49,
71-210 Szczecin, Poland
pklesk@wi.zut.edu.pl

Abstract. Large amounts of suitably marked images are required to feed a learning algorithm when building a detector. The process of collecting images and then marking locations of target objects in them is arduous. One could potentially speed up this process if real images for a given application were replaced by images generated synthetically, and coordinates of targets were simply imposed, rather then discovered manually. Despite the appeal of such an automatization, questions arise regarding the usefulness of systems built this way in real operating conditions. In particular, the obvious violation of i.i.d. principle might result in higher error rates at the testing stage.

In this paper we provide an experimental study of the above approach, taking up road sign detection as an example. We generate synthetic training scenes by laying road sign icons randomly over a set of backgrounds with additional perturbations (rotations, brightness changes, blurring, sharpening, noise). Ensemble learning is then carried out using a RealBoost algorithm with shallow decision trees. Haar-like features or Fourier moments constitute the direct input information extracted from images. In both cases we support the computations with suitable integral images. Accuracy of resulting detectors is finally tested on real images.

Keywords: Synthetic images · Road sign detection ·
Haar-like features · Fourier moments · Integral images · Boosting

1 Introduction

The success of machine learning applications d epends strongly on the amount and the quality of training data at disposal. In computer vision, and detection tasks in particular, large collections of images with suitably marked target objects are needed to feed a learning algorithm. Coordinates of bounding boxes surrounding the targets need to be registered both for training and testing data.

This work was financed by the National Science Centre, Poland. Research project no.: 2016/21/B/ST6/01495.

L. Rutkowski et al. (Eds.): ICAISC 2019, LNAI 11509, pp. 14–26, 2019.
https://doi.org/10.1007/978-3-030-20915-5_2

At the training stage these coordinates allow to crop the fragments with positive examples to learn from. At the testing stage the coordinates provide the ground truth information, which allows later to give a quantitative evaluation of an obtained classifier (detector). Namely, accuracy measures, such as: sensitivity, false alarm rate, AUC, F_1-score, etc., can be given. For industrial applications it is often expected that confidence intervals on the above characteristics are provided, so that users can know to what extent one can rely on a given detection system.

In some, non-frequent, cases it is possible to find an existing database with a suitably marked learning material. When no such source is at disposal, one is forced to mark the coordinates of targets *manually*. Needless to say, this process is arduous and can take weeks or even months—good-quality detectors typically need from about 10^4 to 10^5 positive examples to learn from[1].

Several ideas to automatize the process of data marking can be thought of. In particular, it seems tempting to replace real training images (i.e. acquired from the actual phenomenon of interest) with synthetic ones. By doing so, the coordinates of targets can be simply imposed. They do not have to be 'discovered' manually. Obviously, to generate synthetic images that mimic the phenomenon under study, one has to possess some sort of templates (or icons) representing the positive patterns to be detected. For example, when one aims to detect: company logos, vehicles (of a specific kind), characters (fonts), footprint shapes, palms, etc. then suitable templates can usually be provided, and attempts on synthetically trained detectors have already been presented in literature [2,9,10]. A particularly attractive application example can be found in [13] where Zhang and co-authors attempt to detect fires of wildland forests in bird's-eye-view videos. Synthetic smoke images are produced by inserting real or simulative smoke onto forest background to solve the lack of training data. Obviously, counter-examples to such approaches may also come to mind (e.g. detection of cancer tissues), where one can be sceptical about the usefulness of synthetic images.

In this context the elementary principle of machine learning ought to be reminded—the i.i.d. principle. It states that data examples are assumed to be *independent* and *identically distributed*. In other words, the probability distribution from which the data is drawn should be stationary. When a classifier is trained on synthetic data and then tested on real-life data, the i.i.d. principle is obviously violated (though the independence itself can hold). Simply speaking, the phenomenon under study is switched. Therefore, one should be well aware that higher error rates on testing data might be observed. In particular, generalization bounds compliant with the PAC[2] model do not have to hold [1,3,11].

In this paper we take up road sign detection as an example task. We limit our positive targets to **42 warning road signs** (yellow triangles with red borders), compliant graphically with Polish traffic regulations. Figure 1 shows a complete

---

[1] As regards the negative examples, they usually do not have to be processed manually. One can implement an automatic sampling procedure that picks negative windows on random e.g. from images containing no targets.

[2] Probably Approximately Correct.

icons of warning road signs   **backgrounds**

training examples   **synthetic training images**
positives   negatives

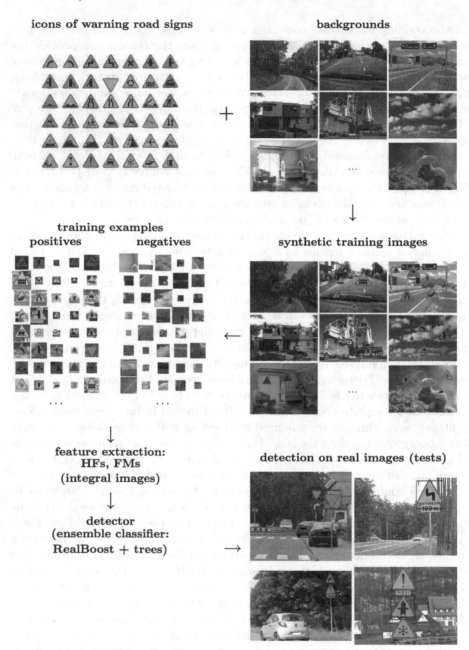

feature extraction:
HFs, FMs
(integral images)

detector
(ensemble classifier:
RealBoost + trees)

detection on real images (tests)

Fig. 1. High-level overview: detection of warning road signs based on machine learning from synthetic images. (Color figure online)

set of icons for those signs and gives a high-level intuition on the approach and experiments carried out. We generate synthetic training scenes by laying the icons randomly over a set of backgrounds with possible additional transformations (rotations, brightness changes, noise, blurring, sharpening)—details are given in Sect. 2. As the figure shows, we use several 'meaningful' backgrounds representing road views and landscapes, but we also do apply many unrealistic ones: in-door scenes, furniture, nature, etc. Cropped image fragments representing the targets (positives) together with randomly subsampled non-targets (negatives) are then subjected to feature extraction. For this purpose we apply Haar-like features (HFs) and Fourier moments (FMs)—those shall constitute the direct input information for the classifier. In both cases we support the computations with integral images and thereby we guarantee constant-time extraction of each feature. In the case of FMs we prepare two sets of integral images involving suitable trigonometric terms. For machine learning we apply boosting, using our version of the RealBoost algorithm with shallow decisions trees working as weak classifiers [7]. Details on feature extraction and learning are given in Sect. 3. Finally, in Sect. 4, we test accuracy of resulting detectors, distinguishing two groups of testing images: synthetic (again) and real. The first group is meant as a reference, because those images are produced according to the same probability distribution as the training data (i.i.d. principle preserved). The second group—real testing images—reflects to desired scenario, when one expects the synthetically trained detector to perform well in realistic conditions.

All necessary software has been programmed by us in C# language (learning algorithm, detection procedure, etc.), with key computational procedures (e.g. integral images, features extraction) implemented for efficiency in C++ as dll libraries. The part pertaining to the rendering of synthetic images has been implemented in Wolfram Mathematica 10.4 environment.

2   Synthetic Images and Transformations

Given a set of icons with road signs and a set of background images, the implemented procedure outputs the wanted number of images by laying roadsign icons at random locations and random sizes onto backgrounds, also picked on random. The implementation does not allow for location collisions (icons must not overlap). We use Mathematica built-in function `ImageCompose[...]` to render the final image. The following transformations can additionally take place:

- **small rotations of icons**—rotations within the angular range of $\pm 2.5°$ using `ImageRotate[...]` function, applied to icons only;
- **brightness changes**—no changes with probability $\frac{1}{2}$, otherwise either `Darker[...]` or `Lighter[...]` operation (each with nested probability $\frac{1}{2}$, mutually exclusive), applied to whole images;
- **blurring or sharpening**—no changes with probability $\frac{1}{2}$, otherwise either `Blur[...]` or `Sharpen[...]` operation (each with nested probability $\frac{1}{2}$, mutually exclusive), applied to whole images;

– **Gaussian or Poisson noise**—no changes with probability $\frac{1}{2}$, otherwise either `ImageEffect[...,{"GaussianNoise", 0.1}]` or `ImageEffect[...,{"PoissonNoise", 0.5}]` operation (each with nested probability $\frac{1}{2}$, mutually exclusive), applied to whole images.

Figure 2 illustrates the described transformations when applied separately to an image. Note that our probabilistic settings allow for images with mixtures of transformations into the data collection. About $\frac{1}{8}$ images shall remain plain, and similarly all other triplets of transformations (e.g. lighter + sharpened + Gaussian noise) take place with $\frac{1}{8}$ probability.

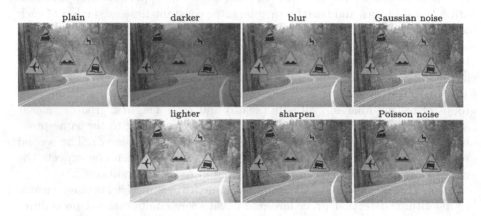

Fig. 2. A plain synthetic image and its versions with singular transformations.

3   Features and Learning Algorithm

3.1   Haar-Like Features and Fourier Moments Backed with Integral Images

Because of their computational demands, detection procedures favour fast features[3], in particular features that can be extracted in constant-time—$O(1)$. This means that the number of operations does not depend on the number of pixels in the analyzed image fragment (window). Commonly, the following constant-time features are applied by the community: Haar-like features (HFs), HOG features, and Local Binary Patterns (LBPs) [8,12]. It is not so well known that Fourier moments (FMs) of low orders can too be extracted in constant-time, provided that a collection of suitable integral images is prepared [5,6].

For our road sign detection experiments we purposely choose to apply HFs and FMs. HFs can be viewed as a representative from the group of descriptors

---

[3] An input image has to be scanned with a sliding window at several scales. Commonly, more than 10^4 window positions are checked for typical settings.

related to edges or edge-based patterns (HOG, LBP being the others). Shapes of our targets intuitively suggest that any edge-based descriptor should do well in the task. This is motivated by the presence of uniform colors and sudden step-like changes in road sign images. FMs constitute an alternate descriptor of different nature. Because of trigonometric functions standing behind the Fourier transform, FMs should potentially perform better for more smooth patterns (which is not the case here).

In the following paragraphs we remind very briefly the basics of Haar-like features and then devote more attention to Fourier moments calculated via integral images. In both cases, it will be convenient to explain the features mathematically in terms of *inner products* denoted by $\langle a, b \rangle = \sum \sum_{x,y} a(x,y)b(x,y)$, where a, b stand for any functions of two discrete variables.

Consider an image function $i(x, y)$ and its fragment spanning from (x_1, y_1) to (x_2, y_2). Haar-like features constitute a loose analogy to Haar wavelets and become generated from two-dimensional templates that can be placed at different locations and sizes within the image, see Fig. 3. Suppose $\psi_{\substack{x_1,y_1 \\ x_2,y_2}}$ represents a Haar-like feature function, generated from some template and imposed on the specified fragment. $\psi_{\substack{x_1,y_1 \\ x_2,y_2}}(x,y)$ yields: -1 whenever (x, y) pixel is in the black region, $+1$ for (x, y) in the white region, and 0 otherwise. Then, the Haar-like feature value can be calculated as follows:

$$h_{\substack{x_1,y_1 \\ x_2,y_2}} = \langle i, \psi_{\substack{x_1,y_1 \\ x_2,y_2}} \rangle / \left\| \psi_{\substack{x_1,y_1 \\ x_2,y_2}} \right\|^2, \tag{1}$$

where $\| \cdot \|$ stands form the norm of function; note that $\|a\|^2 = \langle a, a \rangle$. Because of ± 1 values in the basis function $\psi_{\substack{x_1,y_1 \\ x_2,y_2}}$, the inner product $\langle i, \psi_{\substack{x_1,y_1 \\ x_2,y_2}} \rangle$ expresses the difference between sums of pixel values under white and black regions. Therefore, HFs can be regarded as rough contours as indicated by templates.

Fig. 3. Common two-dimensional templates used to generate Haar-like features (left) and example of a diagonal feature overlaid on an image fragment (right).

The overall number of HFs that can be generated for training is typically controlled by two parameters: the number of scales[4] and the number of anchoring points to place them at. For example, with 5 templates (as shown in the figure), 7^2 scales (taking two axes into account) and using a 9×9 grid of anchoring points, one obtains $19\,845$ features in total.

---

[4] Templates can be scaled (stretched or squeezed) along either axis.

Extraction of each HF can be brought to constant-time complexity if the elementary integral image is prepared, namely: $ii(u,v) = \sum_{x=1}^{u} \sum_{y=1}^{v} i(x,y)$. To show this let us rewrite $\langle i, \psi_{x_1,y_1 \atop x_2,y_2} \rangle$ to the form

$$\sum_{\substack{r \text{ white} \\ \text{rectangle}}} \sum_{\substack{x_1(r) \leqslant x \leqslant x_2(r) \\ y_1(r) \leqslant y \leqslant y_2(r)}} i(x,y) - \sum_{\substack{r \text{ black} \\ \text{rectangle}}} \sum_{\substack{x_1(r) \leqslant x \leqslant x_2(r) \\ y_1(r) \leqslant y \leqslant y_2(r)}} i(x,y), \qquad (2)$$

where $(x_1(r), y_1(r))$ and $(x_2(r), y_2(r))$ are bounding coordinates of a rectangle r. Now, it is easy to see that any sum over a rectangle can be calculated using just 3 operations via the **growth** of the integral image (we skip r for simplicity):

$$\sum_{\substack{x_1 \leqslant x \leqslant x_2 \\ y_1 \leqslant y \leqslant y_2}} i(x,y) = ii(x_2,y_2) - ii(x_1-1,y_2) - ii(x_2,y_1-1) + ii(x_1-1,y_1-1) \equiv \underset{x_2,y_2}{\overset{x_1,y_1}{\Delta}}(ii).$$
$$(3)$$

It turns out that Fourier moments (FMs) can too be expressed in terms of growth operations but more integral images are required. Let us define a FM of order (k,l) in terms of the Hermitian inner product[5] as:

$$f_{x_1,y_1 \atop x_2,y_2}^{k,l} = \langle i, F_{x_1,y_1 \atop x_2,y_2}^{k,l} \rangle / \| F_{x_1,y_1 \atop x_2,y_2}^{k,l} \|^2 = \frac{1}{MN} \sum_{\substack{x_1 \leqslant x \leqslant x_2 \\ y_1 \leqslant y \leqslant y_2}} i(x,y) e^{-2\pi i \left(k \frac{x-x_1}{M} + l \frac{y-y_1}{N} \right)}, \quad (4)$$

where $M = x_2 - x_1 + 1$, $N = y_2 - y_1 + 1$, and $i = \sqrt{-1}$ is the imaginary unit (note the calligraphic difference from i).

To speed up calculations of (4) within a detection procedure, one can prepare **two sets of integral images**, denoted as $\{ii_{\cos}^{k,l}\}$, $\{ii_{\sin}^{k,l}\}$, related to cosine and sine functions, respectively, and constructed as follows:

$$ii_{\cos}^{k,l}(u,v) = \sum_{\substack{1 \leqslant x \leqslant u \\ 1 \leqslant y \leqslant v}} i(x,y) \cos\left(-2\pi \left(\frac{kx}{M} + \frac{ly}{N}\right)\right), \qquad (5)$$

$$ii_{\sin}^{k,l}(u,v) = \sum_{\substack{1 \leqslant x \leqslant u \\ 1 \leqslant y \leqslant v}} i(x,y) \sin\left(-2\pi \left(\frac{kx}{M} + \frac{ly}{N}\right)\right), \qquad (6)$$

where for the predefined maximum harmonic order n the indexes (k,l) iterate over the set:

$$\{(k,l): \ -n \leqslant k \leqslant -1, -n \leqslant l \leqslant n\} \cup \{(0,l): \ -n \leqslant l \leqslant -1\} \cup \{(0,0)\}. \quad (7)$$

The full set of indexes $-n \leqslant k,l \leqslant n$ is not necessary due to the symmetry property $\overline{f_{...}^{-k,-l}} = \overline{f_{...}^{k,l}}$ as FMs for opposed indexes are complex conjugates.

---

[5] $\langle a,b \rangle = \sum \sum_{x,y} a(x,y)\overline{b}(x,y)$, where $\overline{b}$ denotes the complex conjugate of b.

Now, the following constant-time formulas for real and imaginary parts of FMs can be given:

$$\mathrm{Re}\left(f^{k,kl}_{\substack{x_1,y_1\\x_2,y_2}}\right) = \frac{1}{MN}\left(\cos\phi\underset{\substack{x_1,y_1\\x_2,y_2}}{\Delta}\left(ii^{k,l}_{\cos}\right) - \sin\phi\underset{\substack{x_1,y_1\\x_2,y_2}}{\Delta}\left(ii^{k,l}_{\sin}\right)\right), \qquad (8)$$

$$\mathrm{Im}\left(f^{k,kl}_{\substack{x_1,y_1\\x_2,y_2}}\right) = \frac{1}{MN}\left(\sin\phi\underset{\substack{x_1,y_1\\x_2,y_2}}{\Delta}\left(ii^{k,l}_{\cos}\right) + \cos\phi\underset{\substack{x_1,y_1\\x_2,y_2}}{\Delta}\left(ii^{k,l}_{\sin}\right)\right), \qquad (9)$$

where $\phi = 2\pi\left(kx_1/M + ly_1/N\right)$. It is possible to check that either of the formulas includes 21 operations in total: 8 additions (or subtractions), 8 multiplications, 3 divisions, and 2 trigonometric functions.

The number of FMs that can be extracted from an image fragment for a given n is $2n^2 + 2n + 1$ (again, due to the complex conjugacy). We remark that both real and imaginary parts can be used as separate features for learning and detection, which leads to roughly[6] twice as many features. Similarly, the needed number of integral images, it is equal to the double of $2n^2 + 2n + 1$, since required are two kinds of integral images, related to cosine and sine functions, for each (k, l) pair. More details on constant-time FMs can be found in [5,6].

3.2 Learning Algorithm: RealBoost + Trees

We have chosen boosted decision trees to be our classifiers. To train them we applied our variant of the RealBoost algorithm, proposed in [7] (see there for details). Shortly speaking, the algorithm produces an ensemble of shallow decision trees (512 trees with at most 16 terminals each for our road signs experiments), grown using Gini index. To speed up learning, our algorithm imposes a restriction on possible splits in the trees. This is done by a binning mechanism, which allows to avoid sorting of data points for each feature and leads to linear complexity of split selection. Responses of tree terminals (leaves) are real-valued and calculated according to the logit transform [4]:

$$\frac{1}{2}\log\frac{P(y = +1|\mathbf{x})}{P(y = -1|\mathbf{x})}. \qquad (10)$$

After preliminary experimentations we have decided to allow (as an option) to extend the training data with so-called **hard negatives**, see Fig. 4e. They are examples of windows cropped randomly from 'whereabouts' of actual targets but *not* properly centered on them and of slightly different sizes. The motivation for this option was the presence of erroneous nested positive detections in initial results caused by specific triangular shapes of our patterns and their internal similarity. Unwanted smaller windows were sometimes detected lying inside actual targets, see Fig. 4ab.

---

[6] The moment of order zero is a real number: $\mathrm{Im}\,f^{0,0}_{...} = 0$.

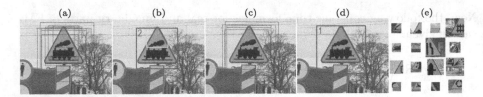

Fig. 4. Examples of: erroneous nested positive detection, resulting in bad grouping with a false alarm (a → b), correct detections and grouping (c → d), hard negatives prepared as additional training examples (e).

4   Experiments

The following naming scheme is used in reports of results. 'P'/'T' labels pertain respectively to detectors trained on plain or transformed synthetic images (Sect. 2). The presence of 'HN' label in a name indicates that hard negatives have been included in the training set. 'HFs'/'FMs' labels indicate the type of features applied. In final experiments, 10 125 HFs or 2 401 FMs have been given to disposal of the learning algorithm. The number of FMs was smaller in order to stick to low harmonic orders of moments and avoid preparing too many integral images. We shall also inform about the number of features selected to the resulting ensembles of trees in the course of the learning algorithm. For example, the label T+HN+FMs (1 846) informs that the learning was based on: synthetic images with transformations (T), with hard negatives included (HN), using Fourier moments (FMs) as the direct input information, and that 1 846 features out of the total of 2 401 was selected to the ensemble. Table 1 gathers all important details and settings about the experimental setup.

We start reporting the results by visual examples—detections on real images returned by the best variant of detector T+HFs (3 948) found during experiments. Figure 5 presents correct outcomes, whereas Fig. 6 shows examples of mistakes.

ROC curves describing detectors on test synthetic images are presented in Fig. 7. To distinguish the curves better logarithmic scale has been imposed on FAR axis and sensitivity ranges adjusted. It can be observed that HFs-based detectors surpassed the ones based on FMs. Also, it is possible to see that detectors trained on transformed images (right-hand-side) were in general better than their counterparts trained on plain images—note the difference in range along the sensitivity axis.

The most interesting are detection results obtained from a batch procedure executed on **100 real test images**. Due to the density of our sliding-window scan, the total of over **16.7 million windows** has been checked within that procedure. Results are presented in the right part of Table 2, where we report sensitivity, FAR and overall accuracy. For the two last measures (FAR, accuracy) we additionally make a distinction between a result calculated *per window* and *per image*. Obviously, the former is more optimistic quantitatively due to the very large number of windows. The latter is more pessimistic and reflects better

Table 1. Setup and data sizes for road sign detection experiments.

Quantity/parameter	Value	Additional information
Synthetic train data		
No. of images	2 000	5 warning road signs implanted per image
No. of positive examples	10 000	Window examples with road signs cropped automatically
No. of negative examples	100 000	Imposed quantity, negative examples subsampled from backgrounds
No. of hard negative examples (HN)	20 000	(Optional) windows cropped randomly from whereabouts of positives but not centered on them
Detection procedure (scanning with a sliding window)		
Image height	480	Before detection, images scaled to the height 480, keeping original height: width proportion
No. of detection scales	8	Images scanned with 8 different sizes of window
Window growing coefficient	1.2	Window widths and heights increase by ≈20% per scale
Smallest window size	48 × 48	Targets smaller than ≈10% of image height not to be detected
Largest window size	172 × 172	Targets larger than ≈36% of image height not to be detected
Window jumping coefficient	0.05	Window jumps equal to ≈5% of its width and height
Synthetic test data		
No. of images	200	5 warning road signs implanted per image
No. of positive examples	1 000	Window examples with road signs cropped automatically
No. of negative examples	33 438 997	No. of windows implied by settings of detection procedure (ran on 200 synthetic test images)
No. of negative examples subsampled for ROC curves	1 000 000	For the purposes of plot generation
Real test data		
No. of images	100	
No. of positive examples	120	
No. of negative examples	16 716 538	No. of windows implied by settings of detection procedure (ran on 100 real test images)

Fig. 5. Examples of correct detections by the best detector T+HFs (3 948).

Fig. 6. Examples of errors (one misdetection and three false alarms) produced by the best detector T+HFs (3 948). Note: in the third image the bottom-right-most sign is correctly not detected, the object does not represent a valid warning road sign.

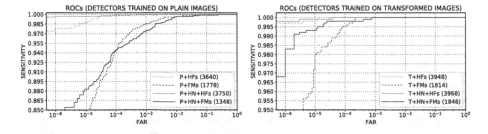

Fig. 7. ROC curves for 'synthetic' road sign detectors (logarithmic FAR axis).

Table 2. Accuracy measures of detectors on test data (best variant in dark gray).

name / description	tests on synthetic images				tests on real images			
	sensiti-vity	FAR per image	FAR per window	accuracy per window	sensiti-vity	FAR per image	FAR per window	accuracy per window
P+HFs (3 640)	.896	.235	$14.1 \cdot 10^{-7}$	.99999548	.775	.090	$5.38 \cdot 10^{-7}$	.99999785
P+FMs (1 778)	.616	.130	$3.89 \cdot 10^{-7}$	.99999881	.275	.010	$0.60 \cdot 10^{-7}$	.99999474
P+HN+HFs (3 750)	.962	.355	$21.2 \cdot 10^{-7}$	.99999674	.875	.160	$9.57 \cdot 10^{-7}$	.99999815
P+HN+FMs (1 348)	.782	.145	$8.67 \cdot 10^{-7}$	.99999671	.617	.120	$8.37 \cdot 10^{-7}$	.99999641
T+HFs (3 948)	.944	.120	$7.18 \cdot 10^{-7}$	.99999761	.917	.050	$2.99 \cdot 10^{-7}$	.99999910
T+FMs (1 814)	.865	.265	$15.8 \cdot 10^{-7}$	.99999438	.580	.130	$7.78 \cdot 10^{-7}$	.99999623
T+HN+HFs (3 968)	.980	.160	$9.57 \cdot 10^{-7}$	.99999844	.917	.120	$7.18 \cdot 10^{-7}$	.99999868
T+HN+FMs (1 846)	.934	.220	$13.2 \cdot 10^{-7}$	.99999671	.808	.120	$7.18 \cdot 10^{-7}$	.99999791

the experience of a detector user. The variant **T+HFs** turned out to provide the **best detector** yielding **91.7% sensitivity** and only **5%** of **false alarms** per image. The overall per-window accuracy for this detector was 99.99991%.

5   Conclusions

Our experimental study shows that classifiers trained on synthetic images can be successfully applied as detectors of road signs. Despite the violation of i.i.d. principle, properties of best classifiers were translated with insignificant changes from synthetic training data onto real-life test data.

In particular, the study indicates that additional transformations (perturbations) on images can improve results, even though our procedure synthesizing the images was simple. No special effort was made to mimic very natural conditions, e.g. a variety of many unrealistic backgrounds was allowed into the training data.

As expected, Haar features, which are naturally suited to describe patterns with strong edges, surpassed Fourier moments in this particular application.

References

1. Anthony, M., Bartlett, P.: Neural Network Learning: Theoretical Foundations. Cambridge University Press, Cambridge (2009)
2. Bera, A., Klęsk, P., Sychel, D.: Constant-time calculation of zernike moments for detection with rotational invariance. IEEE Trans. Pattern Anal. Mach. Intell. **41**(3), 537–551 (2019)
3. Cherkassky, V., Mulier, F.: Learning from Data, 2nd edn. Wiley, Hoboken (2007)
4. Friedman, J., Hastie, T., Tibshirani, R.: Additive logistic regression: a statistical view of boosting. Ann. Stat. **28**(2), 337–407 (2000)
5. Klęsk, P., Kapruziak, M., Olech, B.: Fast extraction of 3D fourier moments via multiple integral images: an application to antitank mine detection in GPR C-Scans. In: Chmielewski, L.J., Datta, A., Kozera, R., Wojciechowski, K. (eds.) ICCVG 2016. LNCS, vol. 9972, pp. 206–220. Springer, Cham (2016). https://doi.org/10.1007/978-3-319-46418-3_19

6. Klęsk, P.: Constant-time fourier moments for face detection—can accuracy of haar-like features be beaten? In: Rutkowski, L., Korytkowski, M., Scherer, R., Tadeusiewicz, R., Zadeh, L.A., Zurada, J.M. (eds.) ICAISC 2017. LNCS (LNAI), vol. 10245, pp. 530–543. Springer, Cham (2017). https://doi.org/10.1007/978-3-319-59063-9_47

7. Klęsk, P., Godziuk, A., Kapruziak, M., Olech, B.: Fast analysis of C-Scans from ground penetrating radar via 3D Haar-like features with application to landmine detection. IEEE Trans. Geosci. Remote Sens. **53**(7), 3996–4009 (2015)

8. Korytkowski, M., Rutkowski, L., Scherer, R.: Fast image classification by boosting fuzzy classifiers. Inf. Sci. **327**, 175–182 (2016)

9. Montserrat, D., et al.: Logo detection and recognition with synthetic images. Electronic Imaging **7**, 337-1–337-7 (2018). Imaging and Multimedia Analytics in a Web and Mobile World 2018

10. Rozantsev, A., Lepetit, V., Fua, P.: On rendering synthetic images for training an object detector. Comput. Vis. Image Underst. **137**, 24–37 (2015)

11. Vapnik, V.: Statistical Learning Theory: Inference from Small Samples. Wiley, New York (1998)

12. Viola, P., Jones, M.: Rapid object detection using a boosted cascade of simple features. In: Conference on Computer Vision and Pattern Recognition, CVPR 2001, pp. 511–518. IEEE (2001)

13. Zhang, Q., et al.: Wildland forest fire smoke detection based on faster R-CNN using synthetic smoke images. Procedia Eng. **211**, 441–446 (2018). 2017 8th International Conference on Fire Science and Fire Protection Engineering (ICFSFPE 2017)

Enhanced Local Binary Patterns
for Automatic Face Recognition

Pavel Král[1,2]([✉]), Antonín Vrba[1], and Ladislav Lenc[1,2]

[1] Department of Computer Science and Engineering, Faculty of Applied Sciences,
University of West Bohemia, Pilsen, Czech Republic
[2] NTIS - New Technologies for the Information Society, Faculty of Applied Sciences,
University of West Bohemia, Pilsen, Czech Republic
{pkral,llenc}@kiv.zcu.cz

Abstract. This paper presents a novel automatic face recognition approach based on local binary patterns. This descriptor considers a local neighbourhood of a pixel to compute the feature vector values. This method is not very robust to handle image noise, variances and different illumination conditions. We address these issues by proposing a novel descriptor which considers more pixels and different neighbourhoods to compute the feature vector values. The proposed method is evaluated on two benchmark corpora, namely UFI and FERET face datasets. We experimentally show that our approach outperforms state-of-the-art methods and is efficient particularly in the real conditions where the above mentioned issues are obvious. We further show that the proposed method handles well one training sample issue and is also robust to the image resolution.

Keywords: E-LBP · Enhanced local binary patterns ·
Face recognition · Local binary patterns · LBP

1 Introduction

Automatic face recognition (AFR) consists in person identification from digital images using a computer. This field has been intensively studied during the past a few decades and its importance is constantly growing particularly due to the nowadays security issues.

It has been proved that local binary patterns (LBP) are an efficient image descriptor for several tasks in computer vision field including automatic face recognition [1]. It considers a very small local neighbourhood of a pixel to compute the feature vector values. The individual values are then computed using the differences between intensity values of the central and surrounding pixels.

In this paper, we propose a novel image descriptor called *Enhanced local binary patterns (E-LPB)*. This method improves the original LBP operator by considering larger central area and larger neighbourhood to compute the feature

© Springer Nature Switzerland AG 2019
L. Rutkowski et al. (Eds.): ICAISC 2019, LNAI 11509, pp. 27–36, 2019.
https://doi.org/10.1007/978-3-030-20915-5_3

vector values. These properties keep more information about the image structure and can compensate some noise, image variance issues and the differences between train/test images. This method of computation of the LBP operator considering more points has, to the best of our knowledge, never been done before and it is thus the main contribution of this paper.

The proposed method is evaluated on two standard corpora, UFI [2] and FERET [3] face datasets. UFI dataset is chosen to show the results in real conditions where the images are noisy, vary in the pose and are illuminated differently. FERET corpus is used in order to show the results of one training sample issue. In this case, we have only one image for training. Therefore it is not possible to improve the results by training step as presented for instance in [4] and we focus thus rather on the descriptor itself.

2   Related Work

Methods based on local binary patterns generally use LBP histograms computed in rectangular regions [1]. The concatenated histograms create face representation vectors which are then compared using a distance metric. Uniform local binary patterns are an interesting LBP extension [5] which reduces the histogram size to 59. Ojala et al. [6] further use a circular neighbourhood created by a number of points P placed on a circle with a diameter R. This LBP variant is denoted as $LBP_{P,R}$.

Li et al. [7] propose dynamic threshold local binary pattern (DTLBP). They use the mean value of the neighbouring pixels and also the maximum contrast between the neighbouring points to compute the feature vector. Another LBP extension are local ternary patterns (LTP) [8] which uses three states to capture the differences between the central pixel and the neighbouring ones.

Local derivative patterns (LDP) are proposed in [9]. The difference from the original LBP is that it uses the features of higher order. Davarzani et al. [10] propose a weighted and adaptive LBP-based texture descriptor. This approach successfully handles some issues of the previously proposed LBP-based approaches such as invariance to scaling, rotation, viewpoint variations and non-rigid deformations.

Elongated binary patterns [11] are another variant of the LBP using an elliptical instead of circular neighbourhood. The main advantage of this modification is that it retains better structural information in the images. Jin et al. [12] propose improved local binary patterns (ILBP). This method compares the intensities of neighbourhood pixels against the local mean pixel intensity (instead of the intensity of the central pixel).

Another interesting LBP adaptation proposed by Li et al. is extended local binary patterns [13]. This method introduces two different and complementary feature types (pixel intensities and differences).

The previously described methods were oriented to the modification of the LBP operator itself, however creation of the feature vector and recognition procedure remain usually similar. Both tasks are significantly improved by

Lenc and Kral [14] by automatic identification of the important facial points using Gabor wavelets and k-means clustering algorithm. Lei et al. [4] further propose a learning step to improve the results of the LBP operator when more gallery images available.

3   Enhanced Local Binary Patterns for Face Recognition

3.1   Local Binary Patterns

The original LBP [6] operator uses a 3×3 square neighbourhood centred at a given pixel. The algorithm assigns either 0 or 1 value to the 8 neighbouring pixels by Eq. 1.

$$N_i = \begin{cases} 0 \text{ if } g_i < g_c \\ 1 \text{ if } g_i \geq g_c \end{cases} \tag{1}$$

where N_i is the binary value assigned to the neighbouring pixel $i \in \{1, .., 8\}$, g_i denotes the gray-level value of the neighbouring pixel i and g_c is the gray-level value of the central pixel. The resulting values are then concatenated into an 8 bit number. Its decimal representation is used to create the feature vector.

3.2   Enhanced Local Binary Patterns (E-LBP)

We extend the original LBP operator by computing the feature values from point-sets instead of the isolated points. We also consider different sizes of the neighbourhood of the central area. This concept can handle several LBP issues:

- LBP has small spatial support, therefore it cannot properly detect large-scale textural structures;
- It loses local textural information, since only the signs of differences of neighbouring pixels are used;
- It is sensitive to noise, because the slightest fluctuation above or below the value of the central pixel is treated as equivalent to a major contrast between the central pixel and its surroundings.

The proposed algorithm is depicted in Fig. 1 and simultaneously described next. Let G_{N_i} be a set of neighbouring pixel intensities with its central pixel C_{N_i} (the closest left/top pixel is used as the central one in the case of the neighbourhoods of the even size). Let G_C be a set of central pixel intensities with its central pixel C_C and let r be a distance between the central pixels C_{N_i} and C_C. We calculate the representative values for these sets as average values of the pixel intensities belonging to these sets: $g_i' = mean(G_{N_i})$, $i \in \{1, .., 8\}$ and $g_C' = mean(G_C)$.

The feature vector is then created in a similar way as in the case of the original LBP operator using g_i' and g_C' values instead of g_i and g_c, respectively (see Sect. 3.1).

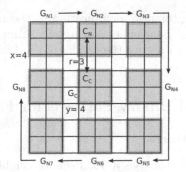

Fig. 1. Scheme of E-LBP$_{4,4,3}$ operator (i.e. x $=$ 4, y $=$ 4, r $=$ 3)

Note that it is possible to consider several point-set topologies of different sizes to capture different texture information, however in this paper we use only the square shapes of the sizes 2 × 2, i.e. 4 points and 3 × 3 points, i.e. 9 points.

The proposed operator is further denoted as E-LBP$_{x,y,r}$, where $x \in \{4, 9\}$ represents the neighbouring pixel-set topology, $y \in \{4, 9\}$ is the central pixel-set topology and r is the distance between the central pixels C_N and C_C, which is hereafter called *E-LBP range*.

3.3   Face Modelling and Recognition

We compute LBP values in all points of the face image. The image is then divided into a set of square cells lying on a regular grid. Feature vectors are computed for each cell as a histogram of the E-LBP values. Every cell is then represented by one feature vector of the size 256. As many other LBP based face recognition methods, we concatenate the feature histograms into one feature vector to create the face model. We use a histogram intersection distance with 1-NN classifier for the face recognition.

4   Evaluation

4.1   Experimental Set-Up and Corpora

We used OpenCV[1] toolkit for implementation of our models to realize the following experiments. The face databases used for evaluation of our approach are briefly described next.

UFI Dataset. Unconstrained facial images (UFI) dataset [2] contains face images of 605 persons extracted from real photographs and is mainly dedicated for face recognition in real conditions. In the following experiments, we use *Cropped images* partition. Figure 2 (left) shows two images of one individual from this partition with recognition results of our method.

---

[1]   http://opencv.org/.

FERET Dataset. FERET dataset [3] contains 14,051 images of 1,199 individuals. We use *fa* set for training while *fb* set for testing of the proposed method which represents 1195 of different individuals to recognize. Note that only one image per person/set is available therefore we address the one training sample problem. For the following experiments, the faces are cropped according to the eye positions and resized to 130×150 pixels. Figure 2 (right) shows two example images of one person from the FERET database with recognition results obtained by the proposed approach.

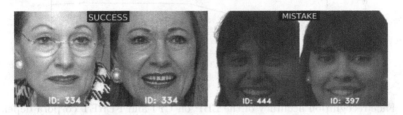

Fig. 2. Example images of one person from the UFI (left, correct recognition) and FERET (right, recognition error) datasets

4.2 Optimal Cell Size of the Proposed Approach

The cell size (see Sect. 3.3) is one important parameter of the whole approach. This value should be set correctly to obtain a good recognition accuracy. However, it does not influence the E-LBP operator itself and it should depend mainly on the image resolution. We thus set this value experimentally using original LBP operator.

The results of this experiment are depicted in Fig. 3 for UFI and FERET corpora. This figure shows that the recognition accuracies are increasing and from the value of 10 they remain almost constant for both corpora. Therefore, we chose this value for the following experiments.

4.3 Optimal Range of the Proposed Operator

E-LBP range (see Sect. 3.2) is another important parameter of the proposed method. It defines the distance between the individual point-sets to compute the feature vector values and it also influences significantly the recognition results. Therefore, we determine its optimal value for both corpora in the second experiment (see Fig. 4 for UFI and Fig. 5 for FERET dataset). We can thus summarize:

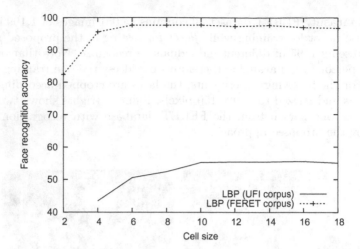

Fig. 3. Face recognition accuracy of the LBP on UFI and FERET corpora depending on the cell size.

- The optimal E-LBP range is 5 for both corpora;
- The best topology is E-LBP$_{4,9}$ for both corpora;
- The results of E-LBP$_{4,4}$ are almost similar to E-LBP$_{4,9}$;
- Proposed E-LBP operator significantly outperforms the baseline LBP in these two cases on both corpora;
- The behaviour of this operator on both corpora is consistent (similar progress).

We conclude that the proposed E-LBP operator is very robust and we also assume that it should perform well on other corpora using these settings.

4.4   Image Resolution Evaluation

Another important requirement is the robustness to the different image resolution. It is beneficial to keep the high recognition score also when image resolution is changing. Therefore, we report in Fig. 6 the dependence of the recognition accuracy on the image resolution. The image resolution varies from 96×96 to 256×256 and we use both corpora for this experiment.

This figure shows that the proposed E-LBP approach is robust against the image resolution on both corpora. The recognition accuracy is higher than the baseline LBP$_{8,2}$ operator, except for the 96 × 96 case. We can thus conclude that the proposed operator is not suitable for images in very small resolution.

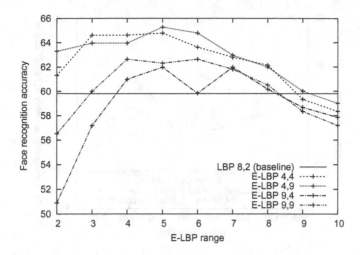

Fig. 4. Face recognition accuracy of the proposed method on UFI dataset depending on the E-LBP range

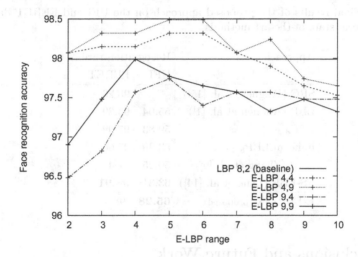

Fig. 5. Face recognition accuracy of the proposed method on FERET dataset depending on the E-LBP range

4.5 Final Results

Table 1 compares the performance of the proposed method against several other state-of-the-art algorithms. It demonstrates that the proposed approach is efficient particularly in the real conditions (i.e. UFI dataset), where it outperforms the standard LBP by 10% and the previous best method by 2% in absolute value. This method also achieves competitive recognition rate on FERET dataset (one training sample issue).

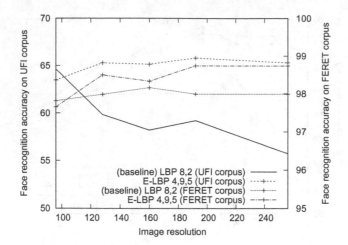

Fig. 6. Face recognition accuracy of the proposed method compared to the baseline $LBP_{8,2}$ operator depending on the image resolution on UFI and FERET corpora

Table 1. Final results of the proposed approach on the UFI and FERET databases against several state-of-the-art methods

Approach	Recognition rate [%]	
	UFI	FERET
SRC (Wagner et al. [15])	-	95.20
LBP (Ahonen et al. [1])	55.04	93.89
$LBP_{8,2}$	59.83	97.99
uniform $LBP_{8,2}$	53.39	97.66
LDP (Zhang et al. [9])	50.25	97.4
FS-LBP (Lenc et al. [14])	63.31	**98.91**
$E\text{-}LBP_{4,9,5}$ (proposed)	**65.28**	98.5

5   Conclusions and Future Work

This paper introduced a novel face recognition approach based on LBP. We proposed an original image descriptor which considers more pixels and different neighbourhoods to compute the feature vector. We evaluated this method on the standard UFI and FERET face datasets.

We experimentally showed that our approach outperforms a number of other state-of-the-art methods ($LBP_{8,2}$ included) and its capabilities are particularly evident in the real conditions when images can be noisy, vary in the pose and are illuminated differently. We also demonstrated that the proposed approach is robust to the image resolution. This was demonstrated on the UFI dataset, where we obtained recognition accuracy 65.28%, which represents the increase by 2% over the other best method.

The first perspective consists in evaluation of different point-set topologies (see Sect. 3.2) to compute the feature vector. Then, we will modify the matching method as suggested in [14]. We also would like to evaluate the proposed method on some other corpora and also on other tasks (e.g. texture classification or object recognition) to demonstrate its robustness and applicability to other domains.

Acknowledgment. This work has been supported by Cross-border Cooperation Program Czech Republic - Free State of Bavaria ETS Objective 2014-2020, project no. 211 - Modern Access to Historical Sources.

References

1. Ahonen, T., Hadid, A., Pietikäinen, M.: Face recognition with local binary patterns. In: Pajdla, T., Matas, J. (eds.) Computer Vision - ECCV 2004. ECCV 2004 Lecture Notes in Computer Science, vol. 3021, pp. 469–481. Springer, Heidelberg (2004). https://doi.org/10.1007/978-3-540-24670-1_36
2. Lenc, L., Král, P.: Unconstrained facial images: database for face recognition under real-world conditions. In: Lagunas, O.P., Alcántara, O.H., Figueroa, G.A. (eds.) MICAI 2015. LNCS (LNAI), vol. 9414, pp. 349–361. Springer, Cham (2015). https://doi.org/10.1007/978-3-319-27101-9_26
3. Phillips, P.J., Wechsler, H., Huang, J., Rauss, P.: The FERET database and evaluation procedure for face recognition algorithms. Image Vis. Comput. **16**(5), 295–306 (1998)
4. Lei, Z., Pietikäinen, M., Li, S.Z.: Learning discriminant face descriptor. IEEE Trans. Pattern Anal. Mach. Intell. **36**(2), 289–302 (2014)
5. Ojala, T., Pietikäinen, M., Harwood, D.: A comparative study of texture measures with classification based on featured distributions. Pattern Recogn. **29**(1), 51–59 (1996)
6. Ojala, T., Pietikainen, M., Maenpaa, T.: Multiresolution gray-scale and rotation invariant texture classification with local binary patterns. IEEE Trans. Pattern Anal. Mach. Intell. **24**(7), 971–987 (2002)
7. Li, W., Fu, P., Zhou, L.: Face recognition method based on dynamic threshold local binary pattern. In: Proceedings of the 4th International Conference on Internet Multimedia Computing and Service, pp. 20–24. ACM (2012)
8. Tan, X., Triggs, B.: Enhanced local texture feature sets for face recognition under difficult lighting conditions. IEEE Trans. Image Process. **19**(6), 1635–1650 (2010)
9. Zhang, B., Gao, Y., Zhao, S., Liu, J.: Local derivative pattern versus local binary pattern: face recognition with high-order local pattern descriptor. IEEE Trans. Image Process. **19**(2), 533–544 (2010)
10. Davarzani, R., Mozaffari, S.: Robust image description with weighted and adaptive local binary pattern features. In: 22nd International Conference on IEEE Pattern Recognition (ICPR), 2014, pp. 1097–1102 (2014)
11. Liao, S., Chung, A.C.S.: Face recognition by using elongated local binary patterns with average maximum distance gradient magnitude. In: Yagi, Y., Kang, S.B., Kweon, I.S., Zha, H. (eds.) ACCV 2007. LNCS, vol. 4844, pp. 672–679. Springer, Heidelberg (2007). https://doi.org/10.1007/978-3-540-76390-1_66
12. Jin, H., Liu, Q., Lu, H., Tong, X.: Face detection using improved LBP under Bayesian framework. In: Third International Conference on Image and Graphics (ICIG 2004), pp. 306–309. IEEE (2004)

13. Liu, L., Zhao, L., Long, Y., Kuang, G., Fieguth, P.: Extended local binary patterns for texture classification. Image aVis. Comput. **30**(2), 86–99 (2012)
14. Lenc, L., Král, P.: Local binary pattern based face recognition with automatically detected fiducial points. Integr. Comput.-Aided Eng. **23**(2), 129–139 (2016)
15. Wagner, A., Wright, J., Ganesh, A., Zhou, Z., Mobahi, H., Ma, Y.: Toward a practical face recognition system: robust alignment and illumination by sparse representation. IEEE Trans. Pattern Anal. Mach. Intell. **34**(2), 372–386 (2012)

Novel Texture Descriptor Family
for Face Recognition

Pavel Král[1,2] and Ladislav Lenc[1,2(✉)]

[1] Department of Computer Science and Engineering, Faculty of Applied Sciences,
University of West Bohemia, Pilsen, Czech Republic
[2] NTIS - New Technologies for the Information Society, Faculty of Applied Sciences,
University of West Bohemia, Pilsen, Czech Republic
{pkral,llenc}@kiv.zcu.cz

Abstract. This paper presents a novel image descriptor family. The
shaped local binary patterns are an extension of the popular local binary
patterns (LBPs). It takes into consideration larger neighbourhoods of the
central pixel. The main novelty is that this descriptor allows using varying shapes of the neighbourhood instead of just one point. This property ensures better robustness and gives the opportunity to fine-tune the
descriptor for a given task. We evaluate the descriptor on the face recognition task in the frame of an application for recognition of real-world
face images. The results on two standard face corpora show improved
performance over the basic LBP method.

Keywords: Face recognition · FERET · Image descriptor ·
Local binary patterns · LBP · S-LBP · UFI

1 Introduction

Image descriptors are utilized for creation of image representations in many tasks
such as object detection or recognition, image annotation, etc. The properties
of the descriptors are crucial for the success of the classifiers that are based
upon representations created this way. In this work we concentrate on the face
recognition task where many successful descriptor based methods are used.

The descriptor usually captures certain properties of the processed image
such as colour, shape or texture. The proposed *Shaped local binary patterns (S-
LBP)* belongs to the family of texture descriptors and is based on local binary
patterns (LBP) [1]. It was designed in order to better describe the local image
patches and to ensure robustness to noise in the images. It allows to use several
topologies (shapes) for which an average is computed and is used for comparison with the central pixel. The other parameters of the method are range and
neighbours. These parameters define the radius of the circle and the number of
neighbouring points respectively.

The descriptor is tested on two face recognition corpora, namely FERET
and UFI. Both datasets possess different characteristics which allows a thorough
evaluation of the method.

© Springer Nature Switzerland AG 2019
L. Rutkowski et al. (Eds.): ICAISC 2019, LNAI 11509, pp. 37–47, 2019.
https://doi.org/10.1007/978-3-030-20915-5_4

2   Related Work

The original LBP operator was proposed in [8]. It was used for texture classification and is basically a variant of the texture unit [13]. Its computation is
based on a small local neighbourhood of a given pixel. The central pixel is compared with 8 neighbouring ones. The resulting code is a number in range 0 to
255. Ahonen et al. [1,2] first found its usefulness for the face recognition task
and achieved very good results on FERET dataset. These publications started
a boom of local descriptors coming out of the LBP method.

A simple extension was proposed in [11]. It is called local ternary patterns
(LTP) and utilizes a threshold and a three-level division for the resulting codes. It
is then split into two binary codes and is treated as two separate LBP channels.
It outperformed the results of LBP mainly on face corpora with challenging
illumination conditions.

Another variant is dynamic threshold LBP (DTLBP) [6]. It takes into consideration the mean value of the neighbouring pixels and also the maximum
contrast between the neighbouring points. It is stated there that this variation
is less sensitive to noise than the original LBP method. The recognition rates
reported on the Yale B database outperform both LBP and LTP.

Completed LBP (CLBP) [3] utilizes the sign of the difference between the
central and the neighbouring pixels as well as its magnitude. It results in three
codes that are fused to create the final representation. The approach proved
better performance on the texture classification task then LBP.

Another type of descriptor was proposed in [16]. The local derivative patterns (LDP) construct features of higher order compared to the first order LBP.
It showed better capabilities mainly on face recognition task with varying illumination.

Three- and Four-patch LBP variations were proposed in [14]. The codes are
constructed by comparison of three or four patches respectively. The more sophisticated computation brings better robustness. The algorithm works very well on
face recognition using the LFW dataset.

More information about texture descriptors is available in [7].

3   Face Recognition Using S-LBP

In this section we describe the methodology of using the S-LBP descriptor for
face recognition.

3.1   Local Binary Patterns

Local binary patterns algorithm is used as a baseline for comparison with the
proposed method. We briefly describe next the circular version of the LBP,
because our methods extends this LBP variant and it also represents a stronger
baseline compared to the original square LBP operator.

The operator is denoted as $LBP_{P,R}$ where P is the number of neighbouring points used for calculation and R is the radius of the circle on which the points lie. The values of points that are placed in the pixel centres are computed using a bilinear interpolation. The value of the operator is computed by Eq. 1.

$$LBP_{P,R} = \sum_{p=0}^{P-1} s(g_p - g_c)2^p, S(x) = \begin{cases} 0 \text{ if } x < 0 \\ 1 \text{ if } x \geq 0 \end{cases} \tag{1}$$

where g_p denotes the points on the circle and g_c is the central point. Figure 1 illustrates the computation of $LBP_{8,2}$ operator.

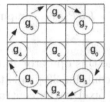

Fig. 1. Computation of $LBP_{8,2}$ operator.

3.2 Shaped Local Binary Patterns

The S-LBP operator is based on the LBP computation. It was developed to increase the robustness of the resulting descriptors by incorporating more pixels in the neighbourhood for the computation. This concept should ensure that more information about the local patch is preserved in the operator computed in the given central point. The main difference from the circular LBP is that S-LBP computes an average value of the pixels in the neighbourhood of the pixel lying on the circle. This value is then used for comparison with the central pixel.

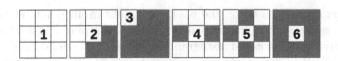

Fig. 2. Six different S-LBP shapes.

We propose 6 different shapes of the neighbourhood as depicted in Fig. 2. The number placed in the central pixel denotes the specific S-LBP topology. The grey region is used for computation of the average value.

S-LBP descriptor is then defined as $S - LBP_{(N,r,S)}$, where N is the number of neighbours, r is the S-LBP range (radius of the circle) and S defines the shape topology $S \in [1; 2; 3; 4; 5; 6]$. The shape number 1 represents the basic circular LBP where only one point is used for comparison.

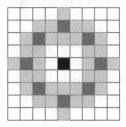

Fig. 3. $S - LBP_{(8,3,5)}$ computation.

Figure 3 shows an example of this operator in configuration $S - LBP_{(8,3,5)}$. In this case the neighbourhood contains 32 pixels that are used for computation of the S-LBP value. The black pixel is the central one. Grey pixels lie on the circle with radius 3 and the light grey ones are the pixels in the neighbourhood (defined by shape 5) that are used for averaging.

S-LBP as well as original LBP can use either all patterns or only so called uniform patterns. The uniformity is evaluated according to the binary notation of the code. The pattern is uniform if it contains at most two transitions from 0 to 1 or vice versa. In the case of methods with 8 points, the number of uniform patterns is 58. It thus reduces the space from 256 to 59 (the 59th pattern is used for all non-uniform patterns). It has been shown that the majority of patterns occurring in the images are uniform [2]. The reduction of the number of patterns thus causes only small information loss but can highly improve the speed of the algorithm.

3.3 Face Representation and Recognition

The representation is based on the operator values in all points of the image. The S-LBP values of the image pixels are thus computed first. The feature vectors are created as so called histogram sequences [17] as follows. The image is uniformly divided to non-overlapping square regions (*cells*) of a given size. The cell size is an important parameter of the whole approach. Then the histogram of S-LBP values is computed for each region. Resulting n histograms are then concatenated to one large vector which represents the image. The histogram sequence constructed this way ensures that parts of the image are compared to corresponding parts of the other image.

The classification is performed using the nearest neighbour (1-NN) classifier. It finds, using some distance function, the most similar image in the gallery (training) set. The label of the most similar image is then used for the classified image. We utilize the histogram intersection (HI) [10] metric in this work, because it proved the best performance in the preliminary experiments. The HI is computed according to Eq. 2.

$$HI(H_1, H_2) = \sum_{i=1}^{n} H_1(i) - \min(H_1(i), H_2(i)) \tag{2}$$

H_1 and H_2 are the compared histograms and n is the size of the histograms.

4 Evaluation

4.1 Experimental Set-Up and Corpora

UFI Dataset. Unconstrained facial images (UFI) dataset [4] contains face images of 605 persons extracted from real photographs and is mainly dedicated to face recognition in real conditions. In this work, we use the cropped partition where faces are already extracted from the photographs. The resolution of the images is 128×128 pixels. Figure 4 shows three example images from this corpus.

Fig. 4. Three example images from UFI face database.

FERET Dataset. FERET dataset [9] contains 14,051 images of 1,199 individuals. In this paper, we use *fa* set as the gallery (training) set while *fb* is used for testing. Only one image per person is available in each set. For the following experiments, the faces are cropped according to the eye positions and resized to 130×150 pixels. Figure 5 shows three example images from FERET database.

Fig. 5. Three example images from FERET face database.

4.2   Analysis of the Algorithm Parameters

The proposed algorithm has several important parameters that influence the final classification result. The following sections are thus dedicated to the analysis of these parameters in order to identify the optimal configuration for the automatic face recognition task on both corpora.

Cell Size. Cell size is a crucial parameter for the face representation stage while it determines the size and properties of the resulting feature vector. However, its value does not influence the S-LBP operator itself. We assume that it should be more or less independent on the used operator and depends mainly on the image resolution and character. Therefore, we first set this value experimentally using the standard $LBP_{8,1}$ operator. Figure 6 shows the influence of cell value on the classification accuracy on FERET (left) and UFI datasets.

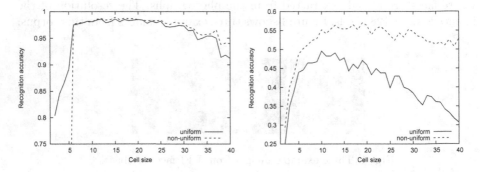

Fig. 6. Impact of the cell size on the classification accuracy tested with $LBP_{8,1}$ operator on FERET (left) and UFI datasets.

This figure shows that the proposed algorithm is relatively robust to this parameter and the range of suitable values for FERET is rather wide. The results on UFI show that the appropriate choice of this parameter is crucial for a sufficient recognition score. Optimal value of this parameter using UFI dataset lies within the interval $[10; 15]$.

In the following experiment (see Fig. 7), we would like to confirm our assumption that this parameter is rather independent on the operator used. Therefore, we analyze the impact of the cell size with the novel S-LBP[1] operator on the UFI corpus. This experiment shows that the optimal value of this parameter is also, as in the previous case, in interval $[10; 15]$ points. Therefore, we confirm our assumption that this parameter is rather independent on the operator used. This experiment also shows that the influence of the cell size on the recognition score is much larger in unconstrained settings where the images vary significantly.

---

[1] We used $S - LBP_{8,5,6}$ configuration.

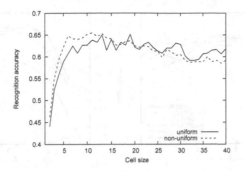

Fig. 7. Impact of the cell size on the classification accuracy tested with $SLBP_{8,5,6}$ operator on UFI dataset.

Based on the above experiments, we propose to use the cell size of 13 pixels in the following experiments while it brings a good recognition score in all cases. This value guarantees large enough cells to handle small shifts and rotations in the image while preserving sufficient amount of details with reasonable computational costs.

S-LBP Range and Shape. The S-LBP range specifies the radius of the circle on which the points are considered. It means that this value influences mainly the size of the features that are captured by the operator. This experiment demonstrates the dependence of classification accuracy on this parameter. The number of neighbours is fixed and set to 8 in all cases. We used both UFI and FERET datasets for this experiment.

Figure 8 illustrates this dependence for all proposed S-LBP shapes (shape 1 is equivalent to basic circular LBP) on both FERET (left) and UFI corpora. The best results on FERET are obtained using the shape number 6 combined with the range size of 2. The best performing combination for UFI is also shape 6 but with range 7. This difference can be explained by higher variations among images in the UFI dataset. The results indicate that the behaviour of this parameter is very consistent for all shapes. Moreover, all of them outperform the basic LBP operator. We can conclude that larger range values are suitable mainly for more challenging real-world datasets.

Based on this experiment, we suggest using the shape 6 which gives the best results for both datasets and the range 5 which is a compromise between the two best performing values (7 and 2). This configuration will be used for the following experiments. This choice was done to show the robustness of our operator.

Number of Neighbours. The last important parameter of the S-LBP method is the number of neighbours. Therefore, we analyze the dependence of the recognition rate on the number of neighbours on both corpora.

The results of this experiment are shown in Fig. 9. The depicted curves have analogical behaviour for both datasets. We can observe that the numbers of

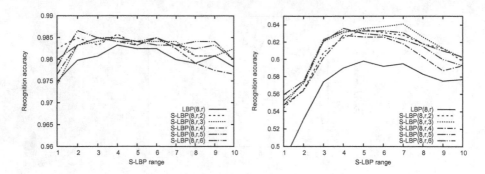

Fig. 8. Performance of the proposed S-LBP shapes depending on the S-LBP range using FERET (left) and UFI corpora.

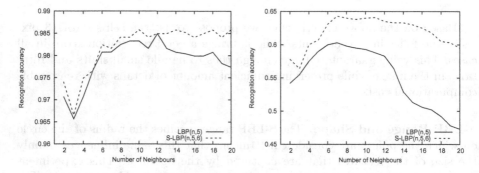

Fig. 9. Performance of the proposed S-LBP method depending on the number of neighbours using FERET (left) and UFI corpora; tested with shape 6 and range 5. Compared with results for LBP with radius 5.

neighbours in intervals $[8; 13]$ and $[7; 12]$ are sufficient for reaching a good accuracy on FERET and UFI datasets respectively. Further increasing of this value leads to very long feature vectors and slows down the computation. Based on this results, we propose to use the average value of 10 neighbours.

4.3   Comparison of Uniform and Non-uniform Versions

The uniform variant of the proposed operators can bring better results with a decrease of computation costs. Therefore, we further analyze the differences in the behaviour of non-uniform and uniform patterns (see Table 1).

This table shows that in both cases the non-uniform operators outperform the uniform variant. This is particularly evident in the case of the standard S-LBP$_{8,1}$ operator. For the proposed S-LBP$_{10,5,6}$, the decrease of accuracy is only very small. We also show the times needed for the evaluation on the UFI corpus. The results show that the computation time is roughly one order higher for the non-uniform patterns. These results show a clear advantage of the proposed method over the basic LBP.

Table 1. Comparison of $LBP_{8,1}$ and $S\text{-}LBP_{10,5,6}$ descriptors with uniform and non-uniform patterns on UFI dataset.

Approach	Recognition rate [%]	Time [s]
$LBP_{8,1}$ uniform	49.10	153
$LBP_{8,1}$ non-uniform	56.36	549
$S\text{-}LBP_{10,5,6}$ uniform	64.79	458
$S\text{-}LBP_{10,5,6}$ non-uniform	**65.62**	3332

4.4 Final Results

Table 2 summarizes the results obtained on both UFI and FERET corpora. It allows comparison of the proposed method with several other approaches.

Table 2. Final results of the proposed approach on the UFI and FERET databases in comparison with several state-of-the-art methods.

	Recognition rate [%]	
Approach	UFI	FERET
SRC (Wagner et al. [12])	-	95.20
LGBPH (Yao et al. [15])	-	97.00
LBP (Ahonen et al. [1])	55.04	93.89
$LBP_{8,2}$	59.83	97.99
LDP (Lenc et al. [4])	50.25	97.4
FS-LBP (Lenc et al. [5])	63.31	**98.91**
$S\text{-}LBP_{10,5,6}$ (proposed)	**65.62**	98.4

This table shows that the proposed S-LBP operator outperforms all methods on the UFI dataset. The best achieved result on FERET is competitive with the best reported accuracy. It must be noted that the previous best reported result on UFI uses a more complicated feature extraction method which is much slower than the proposed method. The results also indicate that the newly developed descriptor is particularly suitable for the challenging real-word images present in the UFI dataset where the performance gains are more noticeable.

5 Conclusions and Future Work

This paper described a novel local descriptor family called S-LBP. It allows using more points creating different shapes for comparison with the central pixel. The computation ensures better robustness and has the ability to hold more information in the resulting representation.

The descriptor has been tested on the face recognition task utilizing two standard corpora. It achieved a new state-of-the art result on the UFI dataset and significantly outperformed basic LBP variants. A competitive result was obtained on the fb partition of the standard FERET dataset. The best obtained accuracies are 65.6% and 98.4% on UFI and FERET respectively.

The method has been tested on the face recognition task, however it may be used also in other tasks such as image annotation, etc. The possible future work is thus evaluation of this descriptor on other tasks.

Acknowledgment. This work has been partly supported by the project LO1506 of the Czech Ministry of Education, Youth and Sports.

References

1. Ahonen, T., Hadid, A., Pietikäinen, M.: Face recognition with local binary patterns. In: Pajdla, T., Matas, J. (eds.) ECCV 2004. LNCS, vol. 3021, pp. 469–481. Springer, Heidelberg (2004). https://doi.org/10.1007/978-3-540-24670-1_36
2. Ahonen, T., Hadid, A., Pietikainen, M.: Face description with local binary patterns: application to face recognition. IEEE Trans. Pattern Anal. Mach. Intell. **28**(12), 2037–2041 (2006)
3. Guo, Z., Zhang, L., Zhang, D.: A completed modeling of local binary pattern operator for texture classification. IEEE Trans. Image Process. **19**(6), 1657–1663 (2010)
4. Lenc, L., Král, P.: Unconstrained facial images: database for face recognition under real-world conditions. In: Lagunas, O.P., Alcántara, O.H., Figueroa, G.A. (eds.) MICAI 2015. LNCS (LNAI), vol. 9414, pp. 349–361. Springer, Cham (2015). https://doi.org/10.1007/978-3-319-27101-9_26
5. Lenc, L., Král, P.: Local binary pattern based face recognition with automatically detected fiducial points. Integr. Comput.-Aided Eng. **23**(2), 129–139 (2016). https://doi.org/10.3233/ICA-150506
6. Li, W., Fu, P., Zhou, L.: Face recognition method based on dynamic threshold local binary pattern. In: Proceedings of the 4th International Conference on Internet Multimedia Computing and Service, pp. 20–24. ACM (2012)
7. Nanni, L., Lumini, A., Brahnam, S.: Survey on LBP based texture descriptors for image classification. Expert Syst. Appl. **39**(3), 3634–3641 (2012)
8. Ojala, T., Pietikainen, M., Harwood, D.: Performance evaluation of texture measures with classification based on kullback discrimination of distributions. In: 1994 Proceedings of the 12th IAPR International Conference on Pattern Recognition. Vol. 1-Conference A: Computer Vision & Image Processing, vol. 1, pp. 582–585. IEEE (1994)
9. Phillips, P.J., Wechsler, H., Huang, J., Rauss, P.: The FERET database and evaluation procedure for face recognition algorithms. Image Vis. Comput. **16**(5), 295–306 (1998)
10. Smith, J.R.: Integrated spatial and feature image systems: retrieval, analysis and compression. Ph.D. thesis, Columbia University (1997)
11. Tan, X., Triggs, B.: Enhanced local texture feature sets for face recognition under difficult lighting conditions. IEEE Trans. Image Process. **19**(6), 1635–1650 (2010)

12. Wagner, A., Wright, J., Ganesh, A., Zhou, Z., Mobahi, H., Ma, Y.: Toward a practical face recognition system: robust alignment and illumination by sparse representation. IEEE Trans. Pattern Anal. Mach. Intell. **34**(2), 372–386 (2012)
13. Wang, L., He, D.C.: Texture classification using texture spectrum. Pattern Recogn. **23**(8), 905–910 (1990)
14. Wolf, L., Hassner, T., Taigman, Y., et al.: Descriptor based methods in the wild. In: Workshop on Faces in 'Real-Life' Images: Detection, Alignment, and Recognition (2008)
15. Yao, B., Ai, H., Ijiri, Y., Lao, S.: Domain-partitioning rankboost for face recognition. In: 2007 IEEE International Conference on Image Processing, ICIP 2007, vol. 1, p. I-129. IEEE (2007)
16. Zhang, B., Gao, Y., Zhao, S., Liu, J.: Local derivative pattern versus local binary pattern: face recognition with high-order local pattern descriptor. IEEE Trans. Image Process. **19**(2), 533–544 (2010)
17. Zhang, W., Shan, S., Gao, W., Chen, X., Zhang, H.: Local Gabor binary pattern histogram sequence (LGBPHS): a novel non-statistical model for face representation and recognition. In: 2005 Tenth IEEE International Conference on Computer Vision, ICCV 2005, vol. 1, pp. 786–791. IEEE (2005)

Video Sequence Analysis Using Local Binary Patterns for the Detection of Driver Fatigue Symptoms

Andrzej Majkowski, Marcin Kołodziej, Dariusz Sawicki,
Paweł Tarnowski, Remigiusz J. Rak$^{(\boxtimes)}$, and Adam Kukiełka

Warsaw University of Technology, Warsaw, Poland
remigiusz.rak@ee.pw.edu.pl

Abstract. Fatigue is one of the important causes of car accidents. Analysis of falling asleep while driving helps to explain many of the most tragic events. To minimize the tragic consequences of falling asleep at the wheel, solutions were developed that allow early detection of fatigue symptoms. The article presents a system for the detection of symptoms of driver fatigue, based on an analysis of an image recorded by a camera. Two symptoms, that is slow blinking and yawning, are detected. To detect the symptoms of fatigue, cascade classifiers based on Local Binary Patterns were implemented. The classifiers were trained with the use of the OpenCV library. The system was tested on a collection of movies taken from the YawDD database. Conducted tests confirmed the correctness of the developed method. The impact of external factors, that could affect the effectiveness of the solution, was also analyzed. The system is able to correctly detect fatigue symptoms with an average accuracy of 99%. This result is comparable to the best published solutions.

Keywords: Fatigue detection · Image processing · Image understanding · Vision system

1 Introduction

1.1 Motivation

It is widely known that professional car drivers are particularly vulnerable to the effects of fatigue [1]. Fatigue and falling asleep while driving are important causes of car accidents. This problem is analyzed in many countries [2, 3]. According to the Central Police Headquarters [4], sleep and fatigue accounted for around 2% of all accidents in 2017 in Poland (67 people were killed and 888 injured).

Fatigue is most often defined as an internal state, causing a decrease in the ability to work, which is the result of previously undertaken effort. This leads to reduced ability to act in the sphere of both physiological and mental processes. The symptoms of driver fatigue include [1]:

- longer reaction time,
- hesitation, worse attention,

© Springer Nature Switzerland AG 2019
L. Rutkowski et al. (Eds.): ICAISC 2019, LNAI 11509, pp. 48–57, 2019.
https://doi.org/10.1007/978-3-030-20915-5_5

- deterioration of visual perception,
- problems with information processing and short-term memory,
- a decrease in the level of vigilance and efficiency in driving.

In order to minimize the tragic consequences of falling asleep while driving, solutions have been developed that react immediately after the detection of fatigue and instruct the driver to make a stop. Researchers and car makers are constantly striving to create an effective fatigue early-warning system.

1.2 The Aim of the Article

The aim of the research presented in this article is to describe a vision system which is able to detect driver fatigue in changing lighting conditions. The system identifies signs of fatigue, which include: slow blinking and yawning. To detect the above mentioned symptoms of fatigue, cascade Local Binary Patterns (LBP) classifiers were implemented, trained with the use of the OpenCV library v.3.4. The created system was tested on a collection of movies from a Yawning Detection Dataset (YawDD) [5].

2 Materials

Two sets of images were used to train cascade classifiers [6]. The first contained images of the detected object, while the second set consisted of images not related to the object. In the case of cascade classifiers, the following rule applies: the more images representing the detected object that are used at the training stage, the better. Of great importance is also the variety of images depicting the detected object, which include variable lighting conditions, different object positions and even skin colors. It is recommended that a set consisting of several thousand images representing the detected object should be used to train cascade classifiers [7, 8]. In this research we used:

- 7,000 images containing faces – for facial detection,
- 3,000 images of open eyes – for detection of open eyes,
- 2,000 images of closed eyes – for detection of closed eyes,
- 3,000 images of yawning people – for yawning detection,
- 45,000 images that did not contain classified objects.

The largest challenge was to collect 7,000 images containing human faces. This was achieved thanks to a database containing 4,000 images provided by researchers from the University of California San Diego [9], combined with a database of images taken from [10]. After reviewing the collected database, we managed to select 3,000 pictures showing people with open eyes. The images needed to train the cascade classifiers of closed eyes were taken from the database mentioned in [10]. This collection of images was made available by researchers from the University of Aeronautics and Astronautics in Nanjing and can be used for research purposes. The biggest problem turned out to be the collection of 3,000 photos of yawning people. For this purpose, three videos from the YouTube portal were used [11–13].

Images that do not contain classified objects were taken from movies made by the authors. Each frame from the movie was saved to disk, then the images were copied and rotated left and right. As a result of this procedure, the database of images that did not contain classified objects was enlarged three-fold and contained approximately 45,000 pictures.

The fatigue detection system was tested for its effectiveness and resistance to changing lighting conditions. For this purpose, the YawDD database was used [5]. The database consists of a set of movies showing drivers. We chose 16 recordings with male drivers representing different ethnic groups; some wearing glasses. The recordings were made in variable lighting conditions. Individual recordings consisted of scenes reflecting driving, conversations and yawning while driving. The movies were shot in 640 × 480 pixels, in a 24-bit RGB color space at 30 frames per second and recorded in AVI format.

3 Methods

3.1 Feature Extraction

In the OpenCV library there are two types of features on which classifiers operate: Haar-like features (H-lf) [14] and Local Binary Patterns (LBP) [15]. Differences between cascade classifiers based on H-lf and LBP features are very significant. Haar-like features are characterized by high accuracy and precision of detection; however, they are much slower in operation than LBP. In addition, the time to train a classifier based on H-lf can be up to a week, while training a classifier that uses local binary patterns may take only several minutes. We decided to use cascade LBP classifiers for facial, open and closed eyes and yawning detection.

The term LBP should be understood as a type of video descriptor used to describe the content of an image or movie. Binary patterns represent elemental features such as shape, color, and texture. The feature vector is determined according to a specific algorithm. In the first step, the examined area of an image is divided into cells (e.g., 16 × 16 pixels). Then, every pixel in the cell is compared to each of its eight neighbors, chosen around a circle. If the neighbor value is lower than the value of the tested pixel, then it is marked as 0. If the neighbor value is greater than or equal to the value of the currently tested pixel, then it is marked as 1. In order to improve the algorithm's operation, it is possible to use a variable circle diameter and a variable number of neighbors. Examples of circles used to define the area and calculations of local binary patterns are shown in Fig. 1.

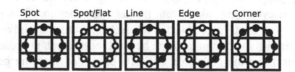

Fig. 1. Examples of different circles in the LBP algorithm.

The set of zeros and ones in a given cell determines the eight-bit number. Next, we calculate the histogram of these numbers (features). The histogram takes the form of a 256-dimensional feature vector describing the given cell. The combination of these vectors into one new vector results in obtaining a vector of features, calculated for the whole of the studied area. The prepared set can be used by cascade classifiers to detect objects in the image.

3.2 Algorithm

A block diagram of proposed driver fatigue detection algorithm is shown in Fig. 2.

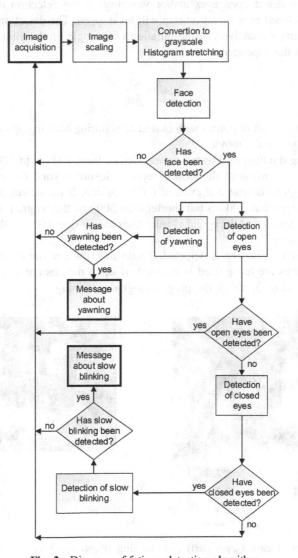

Fig. 2. Diagram of fatigue detection algorithm

First, a video file is opened. Then, the first frame from the recording is taken. In order to speed up the process of image processing, the frame resolution is halved. The image is scaled to 320 × 240 pixels. In addition, only every second frame of the film is analyzed.

Cascade classifiers work on images in shades of gray, so the frame is transformed into a grayscale image. Such images are more resistant to changes in lighting, also the matrices holding brightness values of individual pixels are much smaller. In order to improve image brightness, the histogram stretching operation [16] is performed.

Detection of symptoms of fatigue begins with the driver's face detection. In addition, the top and bottom part of the face are separated. This operation reduces the time needed for further image analysis. Then in the area of the recognized face, cascade classifiers try to detect open eyes and/or yawning. If the detection of open eyes is successful, the closed-eyes detection step will be skipped. The detection of closed eyes (Fig. 3, left) starts the analysis of the duration of a single blink. Blink duration bd is calculated from the dependence (1):

$$bd = \frac{fce}{fps} \tag{1}$$

where, fce – the number of frames with closed eyes during blinking, fps – the number of frames per second in the movie.

The blinking duration of a rested person ranges from 100 ms to 300 ms [17]. This means that any extension of duration of eyelid closure beyond those values can be considered a sign of fatigue and even of falling asleep. If the detected eyelid closing time bd lasts longer than 300 ms but shorter than 500 ms, the program will signal slow blinking. If the duration of the eyelid closure lasts longer than 500 ms, the program will detect falling asleep.

Simultaneously, yawning is detected. To do this, the number of frames on which wide-open mouths are recognized is counted. If open mouths are detected on 5 consecutive frames (Fig. 3, right), the program signals yawning.

Fig. 3. Detection of closed eyes (left) and yawning (right) using an image taken from the YawDD database (Abtahi et al. [5]).

4 Results

Our system was tested on 90-s fragments from 16 movies from the YawDD database. The results of slow blink detection are presented in Table 1.

Table 1. The results of slow blink detection.

Rec. No.	Number of slow blinks	TP	TN	FP	FN
1	–	–	–	–	–
2	3	0	357	0	0
3	–	–	–	–	–
4	4	4	356	0	0
5	–	–	–	–	–
6	–	–	–	–	–
7	1	0	359	0	1
8	–	–	–	–	–
9	3	2	357	0	1
10	–	–	–	–	–
11	4	1	356	0	3
12	3	1	357	0	2
13	2	1	358	0	1
14	2	2	358	0	0
15	2	2	358	0	0
16	1	1	359	0	0

Table 2. Effectiveness of slow blink detection.

Rec No.	ACC	PPV	TPR	TNR
1	–	–	–	–
2	1	0	0	1
3	–	–	–	–
4	1	1	1	1
5	–	–	–	–
6	–	–	–	–
7	0.99	0	0	1
8	–	–	–	–
9	0.99	1	0.67	1
10	–	–	–	–
11	0.99	1	0.25	1
12	0.99	1	0.33	1
13	0.99	1	0.5	1
14	1	1	1	1
15	1	1	1	1
16	1	1	1	1
Mean	**0.99**	**0.80**	**0.58**	**1**

The program processes a sequence of images at the speed of 8 frames per second, and each recording lasts 90 s. As our program processes only every second frame, the maximum number of events in each of the movies is 360. Empty cells in tables mean that the searched event did not occur. Table 1 presents the number of slow blinking events and true positive, true negative, false positive and false negative indicators.

Table 2 presents statistical measures of slow blink detection: accuracy – ACC, precision – PPV, sensitivity – TPR, specificity – TNR. The overall accuracy of slow blink detection is 0.99. Different lighting conditions resulted in an average precision of 0.8. For most recordings, it was 1. The reason for such a distribution of results may be false detections of the open eyes classifier, which recognizes closed eyes as open. The average sensitivity of the classification is also low, as it is only 0.58. This means that, on average, 58% of all true correct results are detected. Again, the reason for this may be false classification of objects during the detection of open eyes. On the other hand, slow blinking was not detected at times when it does not occur.

The results of yawning detection are shown in Table 3. Assuming that the yawning lasts for 10 successive frames of the recording, the calculated number of events is 72 for a 90-second recording. Table 3 presents the number of yawning events and true positive, true negative, false positive and false negative indicators.

In most of the tested recordings, the algorithm correctly recognized and communicated the yawning events. Movies in which yawning was not detected, were made in difficult lighting conditions. In addition, in many cases yawning was not detected, because the classifier of face detection was unable to recognize the face in the image. This was due to the wrong angle of the driver's position in relation to the camera lens, so that the image was not recorded from a perpendicular direction.

Table 3. The results of yawning detection.

Rec No.	Number of yawns	TP	TN	FP	FN
1	3	3	69	0	0
2	3	0	69	0	3
3	3	3	69	0	0
4	3	3	69	0	0
5	3	1	69	0	2
6	3	3	69	0	0
7	3	3	69	0	0
8	2	2	70	0	0
9	3	2	69	0	1
10	3	3	69	0	0
11	3	3	69	0	0
12	4	4	68	0	0
13	3	0	69	0	3
14	2	2	70	0	0
15	2	1	70	0	1
16	3	0	69	0	3

Table 4. Effectiveness of yawning detection.

Rec No.	ACC	PPV	TPR	TNR
1	1	1	1	1
2	0.96	0	0	1
3	1	1	1	1
4	1	1	1	1
5	0.97	1	0.33	1
6	1	1	1	1
7	1	1	1	1
8	1	1	1	1
9	0.99	1	0.67	1
10	1	1	1	1
11	1	1	1	1
12	1	1	1	1
13	0.96	0	0	1
14	1	1	1	1
15	0.99	1	0.5	1
16	0.96	0	0	1
Mean	**0.99**	**0.81**	**0.72**	**1**

The results contained in Table 4 can definitely be described as satisfactory. The yawning classification was performed with very high accuracy – 0.99. In addition, 81% of all the detected yawning events were correctly recognized as actual occurrences of yawning. Averaged sensitivity of detection was 0.72. It is also worth noting that in none of the recordings was yawning detected in moments when it actually did not occur.

5 Discussion

In the literature, many studies can be found in which the authors tried to detect fatigue using various methods. In [18] fatigue detection was based on the eye tracking system. The average effectiveness of fatigue detection was 88.9%. However, the test database only consisted of 4 recordings that were recorded in good lighting conditions, which in turn does not reflect the full effectiveness of the solution.

In the solution described in [19], face detection was based on the transformation of the image to the YCbCr color space, followed by the observation of Cb and Cr components. Using the transformation and operations on the images, the current eye condition is determined. The authors assumed that if the eyes are closed for 5 consecutive frames, the application signals fatigue. For testing purposes, the authors used a database consisting of 150 photos of drivers. The effectiveness of the algorithm was as follows: face detection: 99.3%, eye detection: 99.3%, fatigue detection: 96%

In [20], the authors decided to use cascade classifiers based on H-lf for face and eye detection. The presented solution was tested on the basis of 6 movies. People on the recordings were between 23 and 38 years of age, of both sexes and one wore glasses. The average accuracy of fatigue detection was 99.45%, while the average precision was 90.5%.

In [21], the authors performed fatigue detection based on an observation of the driver's eye condition. From the area of the face, a horizontal fragment containing the eyes was cut out. The image was then subjected to a binarization operation. In this way, an image consisting of white and black fields was obtained. The distinction between open eyes and closed eyes consisted in counting white fields defining open eyes, for which the number of white fields is 4 (2 fields defining the eyeballs and 2 fields defining the eyebrows). If their number was less than four, that meant that the driver's eyes were closed. The tests were carried out on a group of 10 people under normal lighting conditions. However, the camera was placed at a distance of 35 cm from the driver's face. Such lens alignment could hinder driving. The achieved fatigue detection accuracy was 99.5%.

Table 5 summarizes the results obtained using our proposed algorithm under good lighting conditions, also for intermediate stages, i.e. face detection, open and closed eyes detection, and open mouth detection. The accuracy of fatigue symptoms detection was 99% and precision 80.5%. Bad lighting conditions and large changes in the angle of image registration, drastically reduce the quality of the system.

Table 5. Fatigue detection results.

Detected object	Accuracy	Precision
Face	96.4%	100%
Open eyes	92.3%	96.6%
Closed eyes	94.1%	95.6%
Open mouths	93.8%	100%
Yawning	98.9%	81.2%
Slow blinking	99.8%	80%

6 Conclusions

The article presents a system for the detection of driver fatigue symptoms based on the analysis of a recorded image. For detection of the face, eyes and yawning, we used a cascade classifier based on LBP vision descriptors. The process of cascade classifier training required the creation of a very large training database.

For the system to function properly, it is necessary to ensure good lighting conditions and a proper camera position in relation to the driver. The system is able to correctly detect symptoms of fatigue with an accuracy of 99%. Referring the obtained results to similar solutions of other authors, it can be stated that the created system is characterized by a good quality of fatigue detection.

Acknowledgements. This paper has been based on the results of a research project carried out within the framework of the fourth stage of the National Programme "Improvement of safety and working conditions" partly supported in 2017–2019 within the framework of research and development by the Ministry of Labour and Social Policy. The Central Institute for Labour Protection – National Research Institute is the Programme's main coordinator.

References

1. Łuczak, A., Zużewicz, K.: Zmęczenie kierowców a bezpieczeństwo pracy. Bezp. Pr. Nauka Prakt. nr **4**, 20–23 (2006)
2. Osh in figures: Annex to Report: Occupational Safety and Health in the Road Transport sector: An Overview. European Agency for Safety and Health at Work (2011)
3. National Sleep Foundation. http://sleepfoundation.org/
4. Symon, E.: Wypadki drogowe w Polsce w 2017 roku. Wydział Opiniodawczo-Analityczny Biura Ruchu Drogowego Komendy Głównej Policji, Warszawa (2018)
5. Abtahi, S., Omidyeganeh, M., Shirmohammadi, S., Hariri, B.: YawDD: a yawning detection dataset. In: Proceedings of the 5th ACM Multimedia Systems Conference, pp. 24–28. ACM, New York (2014)
6. Bradski, G., Kaehler, A.: The OpenCV Library. Dr Dobb's J. Softw. Tools **25**, 120–125 (2000)
7. Lienhart, R., Kuranov, A., Pisarevsky, V.: Empirical analysis of detection cascades of boosted classifiers for rapid object detection. In: Michaelis, B., Krell, G. (eds.) DAGM 2003. LNCS, vol. 2781, pp. 297–304. Springer, Heidelberg (2003). https://doi.org/10.1007/978-3-540-45243-0_39
8. Shen, C., Wang, P., van den Hengel, A.: Optimally Training a Cascade Classifier. arXiv: 1008.3742 Cs (2010)
9. The MPLab GENKI Database. http://mplab.ucsd.edu. Accessed 12 Dec 2018
10. Song, F., Tan, X., Liu, X., Chen, S.: Eyes closeness detection from still images with multi-scale histograms of principal oriented gradients. Pattern Recogn. **47**, 2825–2838 (2014)
11. Youtube: megamayd: yawning. https://www.youtube.com/watch?v=o1sOuj3UOcs&t=1s. Accessed 12 Dec 2018
12. Youtube: AsapSCIENCE: The Yawn-O-Meter (How Long Can You Last?). https://www.youtube.com/watch?v=AJXX4vF6Zh0&t=2s. Accessed 12 Dec 2018
13. Youtube: BuzzFeedVideo: Can You Watch This Without Yawning? https://www.youtube.com/watch?v=M3QYDtSbhrA. Accessed 12 Dec 2018
14. Viola, P., Jones, M.: Rapid object detection using a boosted cascade of simple features. In: Proceedings of the 2001 IEEE Computer Society Conference on Computer Vision and Pattern Recognition, CVPR 2001, p. I (2001)
15. Ahonen, T., Hadid, A., Pietikäinen, M.: Face recognition with local binary patterns. In: Pajdla, T., Matas, J. (eds.) ECCV 2004. LNCS, vol. 3021, pp. 469–481. Springer, Heidelberg (2004). https://doi.org/10.1007/978-3-540-24670-1_36

16. Im, J., Jeon, J., Hayes, M.H., Paik, J.: Single image-based ghost-free high dynamic range imaging using local histogram stretching and spatially-adaptive denoising. IEEE Trans. Consum. Electron. **57**, 1478–1484 (2011)

17. Friedrichs, F., Yang, B.: Camera-based drowsiness reference for driver state classification under real driving conditions. In: 2010 IEEE Intelligent Vehicles Symposium, pp. 101–106 (2010)

18. Horng, W.-B., Chen, C.-Y., Chang, Y., Fan, C.-H.: Driver fatigue detection based on eye tracking and dynamic template matching. In: 2004 IEEE International Conference on Networking, Sensing and Control, pp. 7–12 (2004)

19. Fazli, S., Esfehani, P.: Tracking eye state for fatigue detection. Presented at the International Conference on Advances in Computer and Electrical Engineering (ICACEE 2012) (2012)

20. AL-Anizy, G.J., Nordin, M.J., Razooq, M.M.: Automatic driver drowsiness detection using haar algorithm and support vector machine techniques. Asian J. Appl. Sci. **8**, 149–157 (2015)

21. Singh, A., Kaur, J.: Driver fatigue detection using machine vision approach. In: 2013 3rd IEEE International Advance Computing Conference (IACC), pp. 645–650 (2013)

Randomness of Shares Versus
Quality of Secret Reconstruction
in Black-and-White Visual Cryptography

Arkadiusz Orłowski and Leszek J. Chmielewski[✉]

Department of Informatics, Warsaw University of Life Sciences – SGGW,
ul. Nowoursynowska 159, 02-776 Warsaw, Poland
{arkadiusz_orlowski,leszek_chmielewski}@sggw.pl
http://www.wzim.sggw.pl

Abstract. Standard Naor-Shamir visual cryptography scheme is modified in a way that allows sampling from all possible 16 two-by-two tiles for generating shares. Such a procedure makes shares not only looking random but simply being random in the statistical sense. Of course there is a price to pay in the form of slightly deteriorated quality of the reconstructed secret. In this paper we try to find a reasonable compromise between the randomness of shares and the quality of the secret reconstruction.

Keywords: Visual cryptography · Randomness · Testing

1   Introduction

In our recently published paper [6] we have presented a generalization of the Naor-Shamir black-and-white visual cryptography scheme [3,4] in such a way that the images used for coding the secret image not only contain no information on the secret when observed separately, but also are random themselves, which makes the process of transferring information invisible to any third party. This is done at a cost of accepting some level of errors in the decoded image. These errors do not make it impossible to see the secret, however.

The basic idea in visual cryptography is to represent any single pixel in the secret image with a square, usually 2×2 pixels, in each of the images used to encode the secret. If black and white images are considered, there exist 16 different squares like this. Naor and Shamir used six of them. In [6], in addition to using all the 16 squares, also two other subsets of possible squares were considered, and the results for a very small number of random realizations of the encoding images were presented. In the present paper we broaden the analysis to all reasonable subsets of squares, and present the results for a large number of random realizations, so that some more general observations can be made and some new, constructive conclusions can be drawn on the randomness of the

© Springer Nature Switzerland AG 2019
L. Rutkowski et al. (Eds.): ICAISC 2019, LNAI 11509, pp. 58–69, 2019.
https://doi.org/10.1007/978-3-030-20915-5_6

Fig. 1. The possible 16 tiles of size 2×2 with their indexes.

process of transferring and decoding the images in the visual cryptography processes. In particular, it will be shown that there exist two subsets of squares for which the encoding images pass a basic randomness test, and that the questions of generating the coding images in a random way and checking their randomness require special attention. Among others, we shall make an observation that an image generated in a random way according to the rules required by its future use does not guarantee that it is a set of random pixels in the general sense.

The remaining part of this paper is organized as follows. In Sect. 2 the basic concepts of visual cryptography are reminded. The concept of accepting some imperfections in the decoded images by using more tiles in the coding process than in the classic approach are outlined in Sect. 3. In Sect. 4 the randomness of the images in which the secret image is encoded is studied. In the last Section some conclusions are given and the future research is outlined.

2   Classic Coding

Let us briefly recall the methodology of visual encryption and its basic notions which we shall use in this paper. The general assumption is that the decryption can be performed without the use of a computer, but only by observing an image with a naked eye. Therefore, any computations on the images are excluded, which means that the only admissible pixel-wise operation made on the coded images is the AND operation.

The image to be encoded is binary (one bit/pixel). It is called the *secret*. The secret is encoded in two images called the *shares*. Any one of them contains no information on the secret, but when overlaid on one another they reveal the view of the secret to the human eye. This is called the *decoding*. In general, each pixel of the secret corresponds to a square of $n \times n$ pixels, called the *tile*, in each share. In our case, as it was in the classic works by Naor and Shamir [3,4], it is $n = 2$, so the shares as well as the decoded image have the number of pixels two times larger in each direction than the secret (the size of images can be the same if the pixels are two times smaller). In the coding process, one share called the *basic share* is generated according to some rules, independently of the secret, and the other share called the *coding share* is the function of the first share and the secret. A tile in the basic share will be called the *basic tile*, and the one in the coding share – the *coding tile*. All possible 2×2 tiles are shown in Fig. 1.

The *encoding* process consists in that a coding tile is set to equal to the respective basic tile if the corresponding pixel in the secret is white, and it is set to the negative of the basic tile if the corresponding pixel in the secret is black.

The *decoding* process consists in precisely overlapping the two shares on each other, so that the corresponding basic and coding tiles overlap each other, down to the pixel accuracy. As a result, in the consequence of the encoding rule, the following appears. In each black pixel of the secret, any basic tile is overlaid over the coding tile which is its negative, so the result is totally black. An example is when the coding tile no. 2 (Fig. 1) is overlapped on its negative, tile 15. In each white pixel of the secret, any basic tile is overlaid on itself, so the result is either totally black (tile 1), totally white (tile 16) or partly white (remaining 14 tiles). In the majority of cases, the result is at least partly white.

In the classic coding-decoding scheme by Naor and Shamir only the tiles having two white and two black pixels are used (tiles 4, 6, 7, 10, 11 and 13, Fig. 1). In that scheme, the number of white and black pixels is always equal in the basic as well as in the coding share. According to the decoding rule just outlined, each black pixel in the secret is transformed to an entirely black tile, and each white pixel is transformed into a half-white tile. In consequence, for the human eye, a black and white image is transformed into a black and gray image, and the secret can be easily seen. An example is shown in Fig. 2.

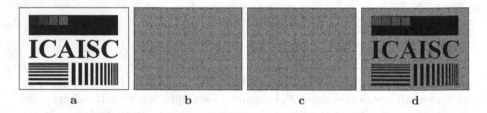

Fig. 2. Example of a secret image (a), two shares generated with classic coding (b, d), and the decoded image (c). Black frames used to better show size, esp. of image a. To be viewed in magnification.

3   Coding with More Tile Types

In the Naor-Shamir scheme, the gray part of the decoded image is 2/4 white in a uniform way. In [6] it has been noticed that this is not the only possibility, and that an image can be decoded in a visually acceptable way also when a white pixel is transformed into a tile which is white in 1/4 or 3/4 pixels, and even the presence of a small number of 0/4 white, that is, totally black tiles, among those representing the white pixels in the secret, can be accepted in the decoded image due to the ability of the human eye to recognize a partly damaged image.

This gave rise to a concept of *decoding errors* presented in [6]. Let us take as the reference the classic coding in which a white pixel of the secret is decoded as a 2/4 white tile. A 1/4 white decoding will be called the −1 pixel error, and a 3/4 white decoding – the +1 pixel error. Accordingly, the 0/4 white decoding is the −2 pix error, and the 4/4 white one – the +2 pix error. The −2 pix error is the most undesirable one, while both +1 and +2 pix errors are expected to

Table 1. Codings used in considered publications. Citation [T] refers to this paper.

No.	Tiles used	Possible errors	Name in [T]	Name in [6]	Paper
1	4, 6, 7, 10, 11, 13	none	classic	classic	[3,4,6], [T]
2	all	±2 pix, ±1 pix	random	random	[6], [T]
3	2–16	+2 pix, ±1 pix	–	near-random 1	[6]
4	2–15	±1 pix	1 pix error	near-random 2	[6], [T]
5	as in classic plus 1, 16	±2 pix	2 pix error	–	[T]

hinder the visibility of the secret to the least extent. No errors are possible in the black regions of the secret.

The types of errors present in the coding depend on which subset of the set of 16 tiles shown in Fig. 1 are used in the basic share. In [6] we have investigated the Naor-Shamir coding, called there the *classic* coding, the *random* coding with all the 16 tiles, and the coding without the ±2 pixel errors, called the *near-random 2* coding, with all the tiles except 1 and 2. Note that we did not consider the coding with the classic tiles plus the tiles 1 and 16. Using such tiles would exclude the ±1 pix errors but will leave ±2 pix errors, which might seem unreasonable. We shall see further that this coding has some interesting properties.

Let us now make a remark on the coding without only −2 pix errors, found in [6] to cause an immediate leakage of information that the coding is performed. In this coding, all the tiles except the tile number 1 were used. The leakage took place due to that in the basic share the tile 1 is missing, and in the coding share the frequency of appearance of tiles 1 and 16 is approximately half of that of other tiles. Therefore, additionally, the shares are statistically different. This suggests obeying the recommendation that if any tile is included in the set used in the coding, then its negative tile should also be included. Let us call this recommendation the *negative tiles* recommendation. Here, we shall consider only the sets of tiles which obey the negative tiles recommendation.

In this paper, some of the codings will be named according to the errors they admit. The codings are listed in Table 1. In this paper we shall consider the codings with numbers 1, 2, 4 and 5. Examples of images decoded with these codings, and their errors, for the image of Fig. 2, are shown in Fig. 3. The errors are visualized with a diverging color palette for the five classes: −2 pix, −1 pix, no error, +1 pix and +2 pix decoding errors. The palette was adapted from the colorblind-safe, printer-friendly palette generated with the www.ColorBrewer. org software [1]. In this palette, denoted in [1] as BrBG, the negative errors are represented by shades of brown and the positive ones by shades of turquoise. Here, this palette was adapted to show the most severe −2 pix errors more clearly by replacing dark brown with dark red, and by showing the error-free pixels in white.

The decoded images are not as clear as that in Fig. 2c, but it can be noticed that the patterns are still visible, perhaps except for the one or two finest checkerboards in the black field, not very clearly represented in Fig. 2c either.

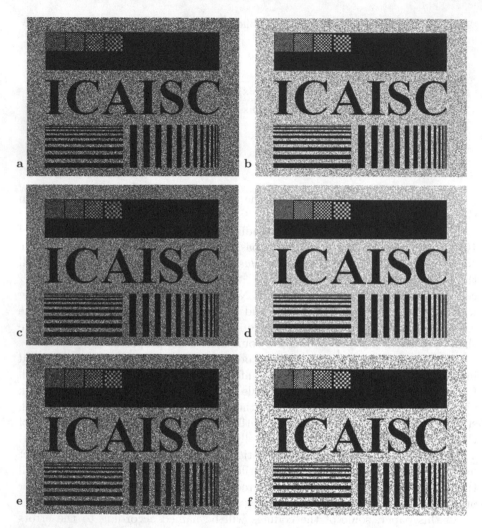

Fig. 3. Examples of images decoded with the variants of the method shown in Table 1 for the image of Fig. 2. (a, c, e) Images coded with codings: (a) classic, (c) 1 pix error, (e) 2 pix error. (b, d, f) Errors of decoded images, respectively, shown with colors: dark red (■): −2 pix error; beige (■): −1 pix error; turquoise (■): +1 pix error; teal (■): +2 pix error. (Color figure online)

4   Randomness

4.1   Test Image

In our considerations on the randomness of the shares we shall refer to numerical experiments made for an example image shown in Fig. 4, designed so that the result of decoding could be estimated by eye. For this, a fragment of text

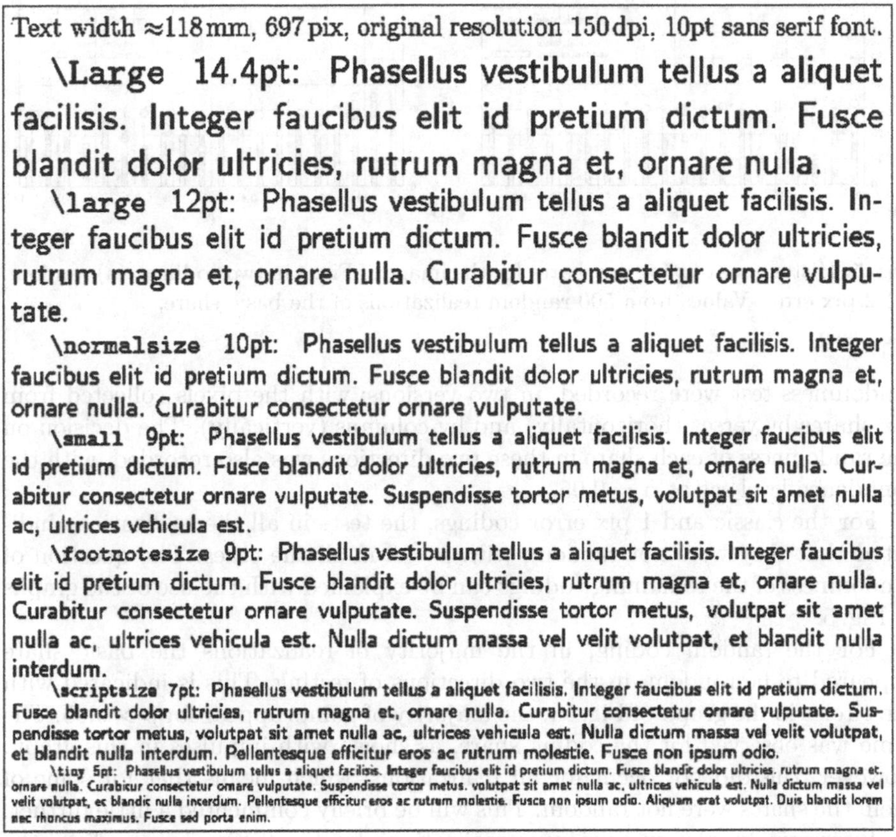

Text width ≈118 mm, 697 pix, original resolution 150 dpi, 10pt sans serif font.

\Large 14.4pt: Phasellus vestibulum tellus a aliquet facilisis. Integer faucibus elit id pretium dictum. Fusce blandit dolor ultricies, rutrum magna et, ornare nulla.

\large 12pt: Phasellus vestibulum tellus a aliquet facilisis. Integer faucibus elit id pretium dictum. Fusce blandit dolor ultricies, rutrum magna et, ornare nulla. Curabitur consectetur ornare vulputate.

\normalsize 10pt: Phasellus vestibulum tellus a aliquet facilisis. Integer faucibus elit id pretium dictum. Fusce blandit dolor ultricies, rutrum magna et, ornare nulla. Curabitur consectetur ornare vulputate.

\small 9pt: Phasellus vestibulum tellus a aliquet facilisis. Integer faucibus elit id pretium dictum. Fusce blandit dolor ultricies, rutrum magna et, ornare nulla. Curabitur consectetur ornare vulputate. Suspendisse tortor metus, volutpat sit amet nulla ac, ultrices vehicula est.

\footnotesize 9pt: Phasellus vestibulum tellus a aliquet facilisis. Integer faucibus elit id pretium dictum. Fusce blandit dolor ultricies, rutrum magna et, ornare nulla. Curabitur consectetur ornare vulputate. Suspendisse tortor metus, volutpat sit amet nulla ac, ultrices vehicula est. Nulla dictum massa vel velit volutpat, et blandit nulla interdum.

\scriptsize 7pt: Phasellus vestibulum tellus a aliquet facilisis. Integer faucibus elit id pretium dictum. Fusce blandit dolor ultricies, rutrum magna et, ornare nulla. Curabitur consectetur ornare vulputate. Suspendisse tortor metus, volutpat sit amet nulla ac, ultrices vehicula est. Nulla dictum massa vel velit volutpat, et blandit nulla interdum. Pellentesque efficitur eros ac rutrum molestie. Fusce non ipsum odio.

\tiny 5pt: Phasellus vestibulum tellus a aliquet facilisis. Integer faucibus elit id pretium dictum. Fusce blandit dolor ultricies, rutrum magna et, ornare nulla. Curabitur consectetur ornare vulputate. Suspendisse tortor metus, volutpat sit amet nulla ac, ultrices vehicula est. Nulla dictum massa vel velit volutpat, ec blandic nulla incerdum. Pellentesque efficitur eros ac rutrum molestie. Fusce non ipsum odio. Aliquam erat volutpat. Duis blandit lorem nec rhoncus maximus. Fusce sed porta enim.

Fig. 4. Image for testing the readability of text after the decoding (see text). A frame used to show the size.

from *Lorem ipsum* [2] was used. The text was typeset with the MiKTEX implementation [7] of the LATEX typesetting system [5]. The dimensions of the image were such that the letters in normal size have actual 10 points. The smallest font available – tiny – presents some difficulty in reading, while the largest font used is easy to read. Sans serif font was used to avoid unnecessary details. The image has resolution 150 dpi, so it can be properly reproduced even on paper. The 256-level gray image of the page taken from the screen was thresholded at 230 to receive a 1-bit image. The threshold represented a subjective optimum between maximum clarity of letters and minimum spurious links between them.

4.2 Results for Four Codings

For this image, the coding and decoding were performed with each of the four codings previously presented, with 500 random realizations of the basic share. For each realization, decoding errors for four codings, and the p-value in the

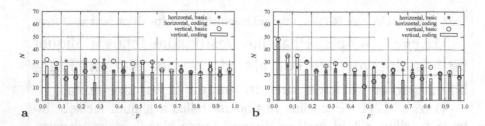

Fig. 5. Histograms of p for the shares for the image of Fig. 4 in two codings: (a) random, (b) 2 pix error. Values from 500 random realizations of the basic share.

randomness test were recorded, in two versions: with the pixels collected from the shares by verses (horizontally) and by columns (vertically). The decision on the randomness of each share in these two directions was also recorded, with the confidence level set at $\alpha = 0.05$.

For the classic and 1 pix error codings, the tests in all the realizations indicated that they were not random, with $p = 0$ in all the cases. The question of randomness of the remaining codings can be explained with the use of the graphs in Fig. 5.

For the random coding, in the majority of realizations the basic share appeared to be random, in the two directions of testing. This is indicated with the circles in the graph of Fig. 5a: the majority of points appear for $p > 0.05$. The same was observed for the coding share, as shown with impulses in this graph. However, this did not occur for all realizations, which means that for some of them the shares were not random. This will be briefly commented a little further.

Interestingly, also in numerous realizations for the 2 pix error coding, the results were random, as shown with graphs in Fig. 5b. Also in this case, this concerned only some of the realizations. Their number was smaller than in the case of random coding, but still much larger than the number of nonrandom realizations. This seems to indicate that adding the tiles that generate the most noxious errors, which in itself seems to be unreasonable, brought as a side-effect the randomness of shares, or at least it made it possible to generate the shares having the randomness property.

4.3   Nonrandomness of Some Results

Let us consider the observation that among the basic shares generated as random, some failed the randomness test. Also, some coding shares failed this test. All the possible combinations of randomness and nonrandomness between the shares were observed: in a largest number of nonrandomness cases the basic and coding shares were both nonrandom; in less numerous cases the basic share was random and the coding share was nonrandom; in the least frequent cases the basic share was nonrandom and the coding share was random. However, the number of observations was far too small to state whether this observation was significant. The phenomenon itself seems to be also random.

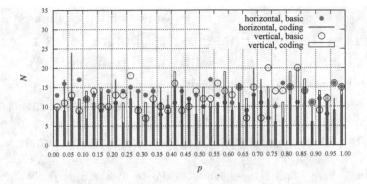

Fig. 6. Histogram of p for the shares for the image of Fig. 4, in the random coding. Basic share was generated by separately drawing, from a uniform distribution, the rows and columns for pixels to be set white. Result for 500 random realizations shown.

Three remarks can be made on the apparent nonrandomness of theoretically random images. First, the coding share is generated in the way of randomly drawing the tiles from the set of acceptable tiles (see Table 1), and not by drawing the pixel values at random. This was the consequence of programming the basic share generator in a uniform way for all the four codings. Second, a pseudo-random generator from Matlab [8] was used, while in the case of cryptography, and especially visual cryptography where large volumes of data are used, this is generally not a sufficient solution. Third, the randomness test used was the `runstest()` function from Matlab, which is not the optimal test to be used in cryptography. In this test the null hypothesis is that the set is random, so it can only be shown that it is untypical for a random distribution.

What concerns the first remark, a test was made with the same image and with direct random image generation for the random coding. The basic share was generated from an initially zero-valued binary image by separately drawing, from a uniform distribution, the indexes of the row and the verse of a pixel, and setting it to 1, if it was not 1 already. Exactly a half of all the pixels of the image were set to 1 in this way. The final result of testing the two shares in the random coding performed for 500 such realizations is shown in Fig. 6. The bins of the histogram were two times finer than in the preceding tests, to look at the data more precisely. The total number of realizations with $p < 0.05$ was 29, versus 19 in the previously used version of generating the basic share. The more advanced random generation of the basic share did not reduce the number of cases of its final nonrandomness. This seems to indicate that there is an indirect relation between generating a random image according to some rules required by the application and the randomness of the set of its pixels.

In relation to the second remark it can be said that it is possible to apply a better generator; moreover, it is possible to test the randomness and to use the images which pass the test and exclude the images which fail.

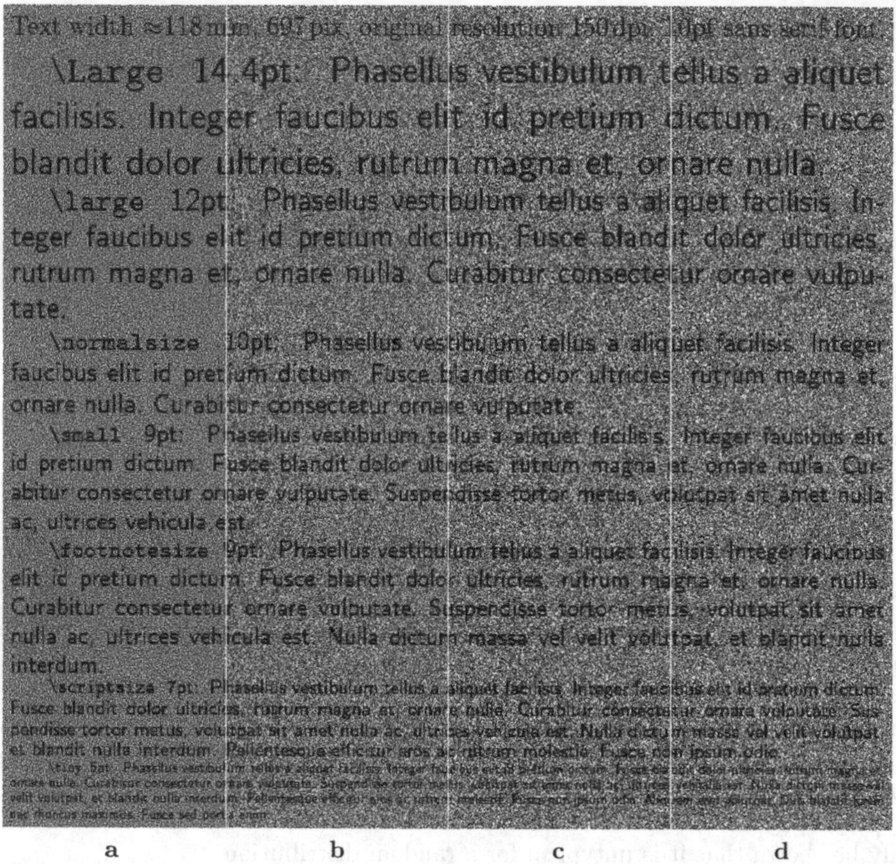

a   b   c   d

Fig. 7. Results of decoding the image of Fig. 4 with the four codings shown in one image, in parts: (a) classic, (b) 1 pix error, (c) random, (d) 2 pix error.

What concerns the second and third remark, the experiments with professional random number generators and randomness tests will be the subject of our further research.

4.4 Quality of the Decoded Images

Let us now examine the results of decoding with the four coding methods considered, shown in Fig. 7. It can be observed that the border between the text easily readable and difficult to read goes between the 7 and 5 pt fonts for the classic coding, and between the 9 and 7 pt fonts for all the remaining codings. The use of other codings than the classic one reduces the visual quality of the decoded image, but the extent of such reduction is limited, so the successful use of the truly random codings remains possible.

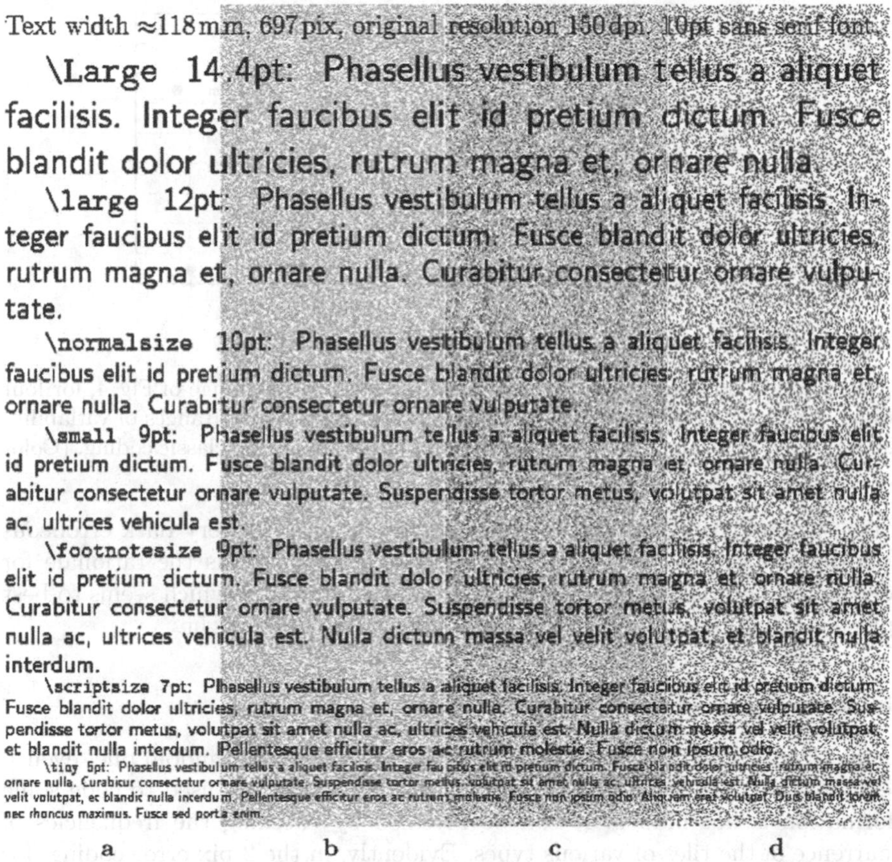

Text width ≈118 mm, 697 pix, original resolution 150 dpi. 10pt sans serif font.

\Large 14.4pt: Phasellus vestibulum tellus a aliquet facilisis. Integer faucibus elit id pretium dictum. Fusce blandit dolor ultricies, rutrum magna et, ornare nulla.

\large 12pt: Phasellus vestibulum tellus a aliquet facilisis. Integer faucibus elit id pretium dictum. Fusce blandit dolor ultricies, rutrum magna et, ornare nulla. Curabitur consectetur ornare vulputate.

\normalsize 10pt: Phasellus vestibulum tellus a aliquet facilisis. Integer faucibus elit id pretium dictum. Fusce blandit dolor ultricies, rutrum magna et, ornare nulla. Curabitur consectetur ornare vulputate.

\small 9pt: Phasellus vestibulum tellus a aliquet facilisis. Integer faucibus elit id pretium dictum. Fusce blandit dolor ultricies, rutrum magna et, ornare nulla. Curabitur consectetur ornare vulputate. Suspendisse tortor metus, volutpat sit amet nulla ac, ultrices vehicula est.

\footnotesize 9pt: Phasellus vestibulum tellus a aliquet facilisis. Integer faucibus elit id pretium dictum. Fusce blandit dolor ultricies, rutrum magna et, ornare nulla. Curabitur consectetur ornare vulputate. Suspendisse tortor metus, volutpat sit amet nulla ac, ultrices vehicula est. Nulla dictum massa vel velit volutpat, et blandit nulla interdum.

\scriptsize 7pt: Phasellus vestibulum tellus a aliquet facilisis. Integer faucibus elit id pretium dictum. Fusce blandit dolor ultricies, rutrum magna et, ornare nulla. Curabitur consectetur ornare vulputate. Suspendisse tortor metus, volutpat sit amet nulla ac, ultrices vehicula est. Nulla dictum massa vel velit volutpat, et blandit nulla interdum. Pellentesque efficitur eros ac rutrum molestie. Fusce non ipsum odio.

\tiny 5pt: Phasellus vestibulum tellus a aliquet facilisis. Integer faucibus elit id pretium dictum. Fusce blandit dolor ultricies, rutrum magna et, ornare nulla. Curabitur consectetur ornare vulputate. Suspendisse tortor metus, volutpat sit amet nulla ac, ultrices vehicula est. Nulla dictum massa vel velit volutpat, et blandit nulla interdum. Pellentesque efficitur eros ac rutrum molestie. Fusce non ipsum odio. Aliquam erat volutpat. Duis blandit lorem nec rhoncus maximus. Fusce sed porta enim.

a   b   c   d

Fig. 8. Errors of decoding the image of Fig. 4 with four codings, shown in one image: (a) classic (no errors), (b) 1 pix error, (c) random, (d) 2 pix error. Colors as in Fig. 2.

The errors made in the codings are shown in Fig. 8. It is clear that the result from the classic coding is visually the best. However, it is not clear how the results of the remaining codings could be sequenced according to the decreasing visual quality. Some objectivity can be introduced to this problem with the use of graphs of the numbers of various types of decoding errors with the four methods, shown in Fig. 9. There are no errors with the classic method (green empty points). The 2 pix error coding introduces some ±2 pixel errors (red empty triangles) which reduces the number of errorless pixels by roughly 25%. A small number of ±2 pix errors results from the small number of only black or only white tiles in the set of tiles which are randomly drawn to form the basic shares. With the 1 pix error coding and the random coding the numbers of errorless pixels are the smallest, while the distributions of errors are similar.

When showing the mere numbers of errors, as in the graphs in Fig. 9, the visual conspicuity of errors of various types is not taken into account, although it is important as far as recognition of details is considered. Our subjective obser-

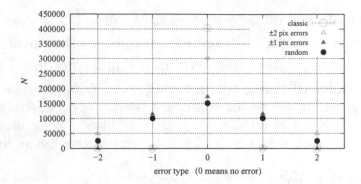

Fig. 9. Numbers of decoding errors and errorless pixels in the image of Fig. 4, for four codings, averaged for 500 random realizations of the basic share. Ranges of variability are small w.r.t. the values, so they have been marked only for the classic coding. (Color figure online)

vation suggests that the presence of only very bright and very dark erroneous spots deteriorates the image to the largest extent. This was the rationale for ordering the decoded images in the sequence used in Fig. 7, which seems to best represent the decreasing quality of the images from left to right.

4.5 Secretness of the Coding Activity

Finally, let us remark that in any coding except the truly random one, even if the shares pass the randomness test, the fact that they are used to code some information is not hidden. It can be revealed by checking the frequencies of occurrence of the tiles of various types. Evidently, in the 2 pix error coding, for example, the tiles 2, 3, 5, 8, 9, 12, 14 and 15 will be missing. As noted in [6], only in the truly random coding the frequencies of all the tile types are nonzero and close to equal, as it should be in a truly random image.

5   Conclusions

We have considered the codings with the use of all the reasonable subsets of tiles possible to be used in the visual coding of black-and-white (one bit) images, from the point of view of the types of errors made in the decoding process (reasonable means those taking into account the *negative tiles* recommendation, which means that if a specific tile is used, then its negative tile should be used also). These were the *classic* coding scheme, for which it was assumed that no decoding errors are made, the ±1 *pixel error* coding, the ±2 *pixel error* coding, and the *random* coding, in which all the ±1 pixel and ±2 pixel errors can be made. We have shown that, besides the *random* coding scheme, there exists one more scheme in which both the basic and the coding share can pass the randomness test. This is the ±2 *pixel error* scheme, in which beside the tiles used in the *classic* coding by Naor and Shamir, also the entirely black and entirely white tiles are used.

We have found that it can happen that an image, randomly generated to be used as the basic share in the coding process, and the respective coding share, can fail to pass the randomness test. This was observed on the basis of a set of 500 random realizations of the basic shares, for each of the four codings considered. As a partial solution it can be proposed to test the shares for randomness before using them to convey the information, and to use only those which appear truly random.

As a general result, it can be confirmed that in purely visual cryptography, where the message is decrypted without the use of a computer, but only by superimposing the shares and examining them by a human eye, it is possible to convey the information in the shares which are truly random. Under the assumption that the tile used to code one pixel is 2×2, this can be done in at least two specific ways: with the *random* coding and with the ± 2 *pixel error* coding. The prize that is paid for this randomness is some deterioration of the quality of the secret image transferred, and the intensity of deterioration seems to be larger in the ± 2 *pixel error* coding than that in the *random* coding, but this is the result of a subjective estimation. In both cases, this deterioration is at the level which can be considered acceptable, provided that the level of detail in the secret image is not too high. The images used in the experiments contained text typeset with fonts of various sizes so that its readability in the decoded image could be easily examined by eye.

In this preliminary study, the general-purpose random number generator and randomness test were used, which is clearly not the optimal solution. Experiments with more advanced cryptographic random number generators and tests of randomness are planned as the future research.

References

1. Brewer, C.A. (2019). http://www.ColorBrewer.org. Accessed 1 Feb 2019
2. Lorem Ipsum (2019). http://www.lipsum.com. Accessed 1 Feb 2019
3. Naor, M., Shamir, A.: Visual cryptography II: improving the contrast via the cover base. In: Lomas, M. (ed.) Security Protocols 1996. LNCS, vol. 1189, pp. 197–202. Springer, Heidelberg (1997). https://doi.org/10.1007/3-540-62494-5_18
4. Naor, M., Shamir, A.: Visual cryptography. In: De Santis, A. (ed.) EUROCRYPT 1994. LNCS, vol. 950, pp. 1–12. Springer, Heidelberg (1995). https://doi.org/10.1007/BFb0053419
5. Oetiker, T., Partl, H., Hyna, I., Schlegl, E.: The not so short introduction to LaTeX 2ε (2018). https://www.latex-project.org
6. Orłowski, A., Chmielewski, L.J.: Generalized visual cryptography scheme with completely random shares. In: Proceedings of the 2nd International Conference on Applications of Intelligent Systems APPIS 2019. ACM International Conference Proceedings Series, Association for Computing Machinery, Las Palmas de Gran Canaria, Spain, 7–9 January 2019 (2019). https://doi.org/10.1145/3309772.3309805
7. Schenk, C.: MiKTeX Manual (2019). https://miktex.org
8. The MathWorks, Inc.: MATLAB. Natick, MA, USA (2018). https://www.mathworks.com

Control of Dissolving Cytostatics Using Computer Image Analysis

Pawel Rotter[✉] and Wiktor Muron

Department of Automatic Control and Robotics,
AGH University of Science and Technology,
al. A. Mickiewicza 30, 30-059 Krakow, Poland
rotter@agh.edu.pl

Abstract. In this paper we present the concept and prototype of a visual inspection system for the control of dissolving cytostatics. It is a part of a broader system for the automatic preparation of cytostatics. The idea consists in rotating the vessel, stopping it, and analysing a sequence of images while the particles in the solution are still moving. We proposed 30 descriptors of the variability of statistical properties of image noise. We used PCA for the reduction of space dimensionality, and cross-validation to optimise the parameters of the method and to assess its performance. Our approach allows us to detect undissolved powder, even if the size of its particles is comparable with pixel size.

Keywords: Machine vision · Image processing · Visual inspection · Cytostatics · Vision-based powder detection

1 Introduction

Cytostatics are a group of highly toxic medicines used in cancer chemotherapy. They are provided to hospitals in the form of powder or liquid concentrate, which must be dissolved in a sterile environment. The process of preparation is expensive because of the requirements for high sterility and accuracy, and the risk of negative effects on personnel if the procedures are not strictly followed. Any mistake can be extremely dangerous to a patient's life [1].

In recent decades, the improved performance of computer vision methods has enabled the use of automatic visual inspection in many processes that were previously controlled by people [2]. Nevertheless, cytostatics are prepared manually and there have been few attempts at automation. One of the main reasons for this is the need for constant and precise control of the process. Personnel must decide when stirring can be stopped, by looking at the content of the phial. Machine vision, like any artificial intelligence system, is never deterministic and reliability of such solutions cannot be formally proved [3]. Therefore, appearance-based control to establish whether the phial or plastic bag is free of impurities that could be dangerous for the patients is carried out manually, and this step has not been automated even in the few solutions in which dispensing is done by robots [4]. On the other hand, the long-term exposure of the medical staff involved in the manual preparation of cytostatics brings a number of adverse health effects [5, 6], even despite strict measures such as sanitary lock, laminar flow cabinet and protective clothing including double protective gloves.

© Springer Nature Switzerland AG 2019
L. Rutkowski et al. (Eds.): ICAISC 2019, LNAI 11509, pp. 70–79, 2019.
https://doi.org/10.1007/978-3-030-20915-5_7

In this article we present the concept and prototype of a visual inspection system for the control of dissolving cytostatics. It is one part of a prototype robotic system for the automated preparation of cytostatic drugs, developed at AGH-University of Science and Technology in Krakow.

2   General Concept of the System and Hardware Prototype

Our prototype system is designed as a closed cabinet. The front-end consists of a set of drawers, in which staff can put cytostatic concentrates in phials (see Fig. 1a).

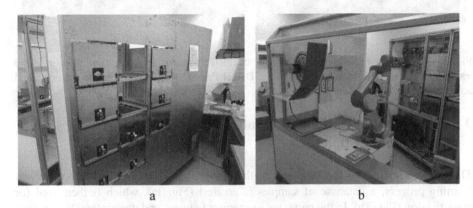

a   b

Fig. 1. Universal Robots UR5 robotic arm, used in our prototype

Within the cabinet, a robotic arm operates, able to reach both a stand with the concentrates in plastic bags (Fig. 1b) and the visual inspection station (Fig. 2). In our prototype we used the Universal Robots UR5 arm.

Our image analysis system is looking for the undissolved powder and any other impurities in the cytostatic solution. The idea consists in rotating the vessel, stopping it, then taking a sequence of images while the particles in the solution are still moving, and analysing them. There are two kinds of vessels used in the production of cyto-statics: glass phials and plastic bags. In the first case, rapid rotation and making the vessel still are easily done by the robotic arm; however, the second case is more problematic. For this purpose, we designed the "carousel" – a stand with a transparent wheel, rotated by an electromagnetic drive placed inside, shown in Fig. 2. In the initial solution, a plastic bag was put on the wheel, which therefore had to be placed at a slight angle to prevent the bag from sliding. In the current version, staff initially place plastic bags into frames which match a metal framework fixed to the wheel, as shown in Fig. 2b. The object is backlit by the illuminator in our prototype SAH7 1886. The visual inspection process starts with the robotic arm placing a phial or a bag in the frame onto the framework. The wheel is rotated 180° and a video sequence is taken. Detection of impurities and undissolved powder based on statistical analysis of the video sequence taken directly after rotation is described in the next section.

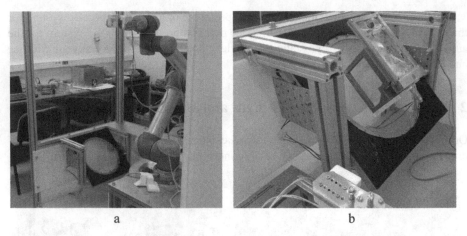

a   b

Fig. 2. The stand for rotating plastic bags, with electromagnetic drive for rapid rotation of the transparent wheel. We thank the team of Dr. Daniel Prusak, which produced the rotating stand according to our specifications

3 The Proposed Method for Statistical Analysis of Differential Images

The general scheme of the proposed method is presented in Fig. 3. In a supervised learning process, a database of samples is created (Fig. 3a), which is then used for classification (Fig. 3b). In the paper we use terms: features and descriptors. By features

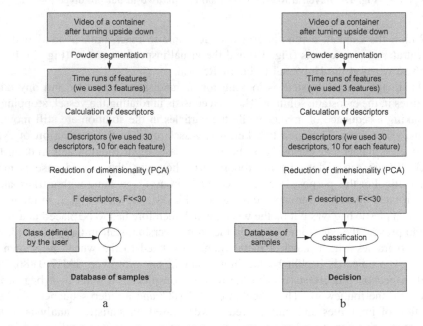

a   b

Fig. 3. Scheme of the proposed method: (a) learning (b) classification based on the database of samples saved during the learning process

we mean the values describing the basic characteristics of image noise at a given moment, while descriptors are values that characterise how these features change over time. The details of each stage are described in the subsequent sub-chapters.

3.1 Powder Segmentation

The first problem is segmentation of the powder, i.e. extracting it from the background, including the irregularities of the container's surface. A natural solution is based on motion: in our system the container is moved by the robot arm and then stabilised. After a short while, when oscillation of the container has stopped but the powder particles are still in motion, they can be distinguished from the background based on differential images.

The same method is used for the detection of any small particles in the solution, which could be dangerous for a patient. For this purpose, we consider not only bottles but also plastic bags, so we designed a stand, presented in Fig. 2. The built-in electromagnetic drive enables the rapid 180° rotation of the transparent wheel with a bag attached. The illuminator provides strong backlighting.

The differential image is generated as the difference between the current image frame and the background image, which is calculated from several previous frames. We used the popular background generation method based on the Mixture of Gaussians (MoG) method [7].

The next step is extraction of noise, which is our case is the source of information about undissolved powder. Figure 4 shows a diagram of noise extraction.

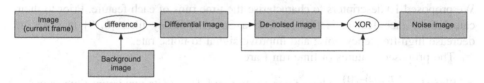

Fig. 4. Noise extraction scheme proposed in our algorithm

3.2 Features

A straightforward approach based on detecting and counting of particles cannot be applied because the powder particles are very small, and after rapid movement of the container a large number of small air bubbles are generated, which move in the liquid along with the powder. Powder particles can be confused both with the image noise and with the air bubbles. Also, the size of a single particle is often smaller than a pixel in the image. We propose analysis of the trajectories of the selected statistical properties of noise in the Region of Interest (ROI) for differential images after moving a container.

We selected three features for further analysis:

- Feature 1: the ordinate of the centre of gravity of noise
- Feature 2: the amount of noise, calculated as the number of pixels classified as noise in the noise image
- Feature 3: the moment of inertia of noise

The above features characterise the behaviour of noise in the image during several seconds after turning the container upside down. Based on the time charts, we will infer whether undissolved powder is still present in the liquid and whether there are impurities in the solution. In other words, we will classify a sample into one of the following three classes:

- *Impurities*: the solution contains impurities or a powder that presents different behaviour than the powder used for training the system
- *Powder*: the solution contains undissolved medicine in the form of a powder which is moving downward after turning the container
- *Bubbles*: the solution is clear, and after turning the container, the only moving objects are the air bubbles. They move upwards and disappear when they reach the surface

In Table 1 we present 10 examples of time series of each of the three selected features for each class. Let us note that the behaviour of these runs varies within the same class. This means that classification cannot be based on a simple rule-based algorithm and it is necessary to use machine learning methods to find appropriate descriptors that could discriminate classes correctly. The idea presented in the following chapters consists in proposing a relatively large number of descriptors (thirty) and then using Principal Component Analysis (PCA) to find their linear combinations that demonstrate the highest variability across different samples.

3.3   Descriptors

We proposed 10 descriptors to characterise the time runs of each feature. Prior to their calculation, each feature is filtered with a Savitzky-Golay filter [8, 9] in order to decrease high-frequency noise and improve signal-to-noise rate.

The proposed features of time run f are:

- $Slope1 = \frac{f(T_{max}/2)-f(1)}{T_{max}/2}$, where f is a feature and T_{max} is its maximum time range
- $Slope2 = \frac{f(T_{max})-f(T_{max}/2)}{T_{max}/2}$
- Linear approximation error (mean square error of linear regression)
- Average value of feature f over the entire time range
- Variance of f
- Maximum value of f
- Minimum value of f
- Mean of beginning – mean of first N values of f (in experiments $N = 50$)
- Mean of end – mean of last N values of f
- Slope = $(f(T_{max}) - f(1))/T_{max}$

Table 1. Time charts of the three selected features that characterise the behaviour of noise in the image after turning the container. Experiments were done for different kinds of containers

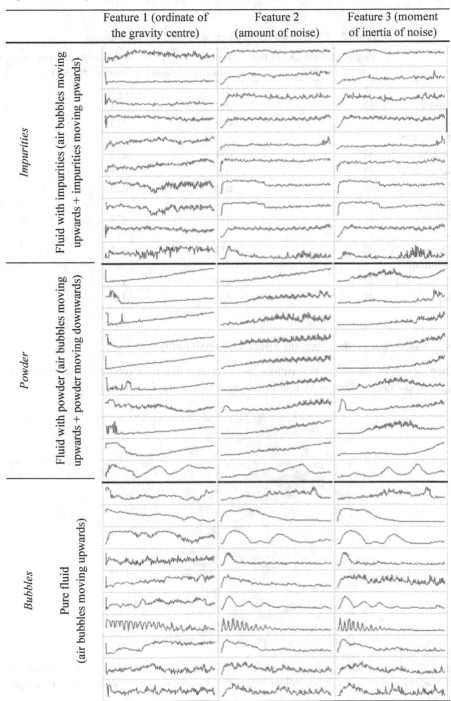

Since we defined three features, and for each feature we calculate the 10 descriptors listed above, the total number of descriptors is 30, see Table 2.

Table 2. Numeration of 30 descriptors used for calculations

	Feature 1 (ordinate of the gravity centre)	Feature 2 (amount of noise)	Feature 3 (moment of inertia of noise)
Slope 1	d1	d11	d21
Slope 2	d2	d12	d22
Linear approx. error	d3	d13	d23
Average	d4	d14	d24
Variance	d5	d15	d25
Maximum value	d6	d16	d26
Minimum value	d7	d17	d27
Mean of beginning	d8	d18	d28
Mean of end	d9	d19	d29
Slope	d10	d20	d30

3.4   Reduction of the Decision Space Dimensionality

When designing the set of descriptors, we expected that they would be correlated and highly redundant, which is visible in the correlation matrix (Fig. 5).

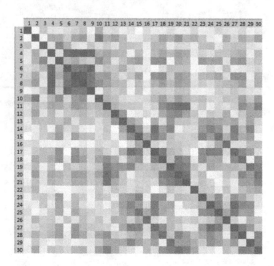

Fig. 5. Correlation matrix for the set of descriptors d1–d30. Blue colour denotes positive and red – negative correlation. White colour means that descriptors are not correlated (Color figure online)

For the reduction of the decision space dimensionality we used Principal Component Analysis (PCA) [10, 11]. The idea of the method is to find linear combinations of descriptors (decision variables), which are less numerous but allow effective discrimination of observations. In Table 3 we present the first nine principal components of data and their variability. The first component includes almost one third of variability, while the first three components account for almost 70 per cent.

Table 3. First nine principal components and their variability

Principal component	F1	F2	F3	F4	F5	F6	F7	F8	F9	...
Eigenvalue	9.75	7.40	3.62	2.16	1.49	1.38	1.34	0.97	0.62	...
Variability (%)	32.49	24.67	12.06	7.21	4.96	4.59	4.46	3.22	2.08	...
Cumulative variability (%)	32.49	57.16	69.22	76.43	81.40	85.99	90.45	93.67	95.75	...

4 Optimisation of Parameters and the Experimental Results

For classification we chose the K-nearest neighbours algorithm [12]. Optimisation of the parameters and verification of our algorithm were based on a cross-validation method, which exploits all available data both for learning and for testing, but the learning set and the testing set never intersect, so estimation is not biased [13]. There are several variants of this method, so the version appropriate to purpose should be selected [14]. For the selection of parameters of our algorithm we used k-fold cross-validation with k = 3. This means that all available samples are divided into k equal subsets, with all classes equally (or approximately equally) represented in each subset. In i-th round, i = 1,.., k, the i-th set is left for validation and other k-1 subsets are used for training.

In a series of experiments, we used a generalised classification error of 3-fold cross-validation to observe how the classification error depends on the values of the following preliminary video processing parameters:

- The number of frames of the recording; we worked at a constant framerate of 180 fps, so this parameter determines the length of the recording
- The number of frames removed from the beginning of the recording: our background model is based on the Mixture of Gaussians algorithm, and the initial part of the recording (which starts immediately after rotation of the vessel) should be removed in order to generate the correct background model
- The size of the Savitzky-Golay filter, used for smoothing time runs of features

Based on experiments, we set the following values of preliminary image processing parameters: the number of frames = 325, the number of frames removed = 25, the size of the Savitzky-Golay filter = 49.

The details of how the classification quality depends on the values of the above parameters are included in the monograph with project results [15].

In the second series of experiments we observed classification error as a function of classification parameters:

- The number of principal components M (dimensionality of observation vectors after reduction),
- The number of nearest neighbours K in the K-NN algorithm.

The results are presented in Table 4.

Table 4. Classification errors for the cross-validation method for different values of parameters M and K.

K \ M	2	3	4	5	6	7	10	15
1	13.3%	6.7%	10.0%	3.3%	10.0%	3.3%	6.7%	6.7%
3	6.7%	3.3%	3.3%	3.3%	6.7%	6.7%	6.7%	3.3%
5	6.7%	10.0%	3.3%	3.3%	10.0%	6.7%	13.3%	3.3%
7	6.7%	6.7%	3.3%	3.3%	3.3%	6.7%	6.7%	6.7%
9	10.0%	6.7%	6.7%	13.3%	6.7%	3.3%	6.7%	3.3%

Values M = 4–5 and K = 3–7 (dashed rectangle in Table 4) yield the smallest classification errors. We selected M = 5 and K = 5. For these parameter values we achieved a classification error of 3.3%.

5   Conclusions

In this paper we have presented the idea and prototype development of a system for the control of the process of dissolving cytostatic drugs based on computer vision. Undissolved powder is detected based on analysis of a video taken directly after rotation of the vessel, when the powder and any other impurities are in motion, so they can be segmented from the background. The size of single particles is often smaller than one pixel, and they can be indistinguishable from image noise. Therefore, our algorithms are based on statistical analysis of time runs of selected noise properties.

We have proposed three features that characterise noise at a single moment, and 10 descriptors characterising the time runs of each feature (yielding a total number of 30 highly correlated descriptors) for each feature. We used the PCA method for the reduction of dimensionality of the descriptor space. For the classification of samples in the reduced descriptor space we used the K-nearest neighbours algorithm. The method was optimised and tested using three-fold cross-validation. After finding the optimal values for parameters of preliminary video processing, dimensionality of the reduced descriptor space and the number of nearest neighbours in the K-nearest neighbours algorithm, we achieved a classification error at the level of 3.3%. This error rate is sufficient for taking the decision to stop stirring, but the final product must undergo manual, visual inspection.

Acknowledgments. This work was supported by the National Centre for Research and Development (NCBiR) within the Applied Research Programme, research grant PBS1/A9/1/2012.

References

1. Lagarce, F.: Centrally prepared cytotoxic drugs: what is the purpose of their quality control? Pharm. Technol. Hosp. Pharm. **2**(1), 29–33 (2017)
2. Bogue, R.: Imaging technology opens up new robotic applications. Ind. Robot: Int. J. **38**(4), 343–348 (2011). https://doi.org/10.1108/01439911111132021
3. Tadeusiewicz, R.: How intelligent should be system for image analysis? In: Kwasnicka, H., Jain, L.C. (eds.) Innovations in Intelligent Image Analysis. Studies in Computational Intelligence, vol. 339, pp. V–X. Springer, Heidelberg (2011)
4. Chen, W.H., Shen, L.J., Guan, R.J., Wu, F.L.: Assessment of an automatic robotic arm for dispensing of chemotherapy in a 2500-bed medical center. J. Formos. Med. Assoc. **112**(4), 193–200 (2013)
5. Ensslin, A.S., et al.: Biological monitoring of hospital pharmacy personnel occupationally exposed to cytostatic drugs: urinary excretion and cytogenetics studies. Int. Arch. Occup. Environ. Health **70**(3), 205–208 (1997)
6. Sessink, P.J.M.: Environmental contamination with cytostatic drugs: past, present and future. Saf. Consid. Oncol. Pharm. **2011**(Fall), 3–5 (2011)
7. Zivkovic, Z., Heijden, F.: Efficient adaptive density estimation per image pixel for the task of background subtraction. Pattern Recogn. Lett. **27**(7), 773–780 (2006)
8. Savitzky, A., Golay, M.J.E.: Smoothing and differentiation of data by simplified least squares procedures. Anal. Chem. **36**(8), 1627–1639 (1964). https://doi.org/10.1021/ac60214a047
9. Schafer, R.W.: What is a Savitzky-Golay filter? IEEE Signal Process. Mag. **28**(4), 111–117 (2011). https://doi.org/10.1109/MSP.2011.941097
10. Jolliffe, I.T.: Principal Component Analysis. Springer Series in Statistics. Springer, New York (2002). https://doi.org/10.1007/b98835
11. Abdi, H., Williams, L.J.: Principal component analysis. Wiley Interdisc. Rev.: Comput. Stat. **2**, 433–459 (2010)
12. Russ, J.C.: The Image Processing Handbook. CRC Press, Boca Raton (2011)
13. Refaeilzadeh, P., Tang, L., Liu, H.: Cross-validation. In: Özsu, M.T., Liu, L. (eds.) Encyclopedia of Database Systems. Springer, Boston (2009). https://doi.org/10.1007/978-0-387-39940-9
14. Kohavi, R.: A study of cross-validation and bootstrap for accuracy estimation and model selection. In: Proceedings of International Joint Conference on AI 1995, pp. 1137–1145
15. Rotter, P., Muron, W.: Algorytmy wizyjnego systemu sterowania i kontroli dla zautomatyzowanego procesu przygotowywania leków cytostatycznych (Algorithms for vision-based control and inspection system for automated process of cytostatics' preparation). NOT Rzeszów - Naczelna Organizacja Techniczna (2016)

Brassica Napus Florescence Modeling Based on Modified Vegetation Index Using Sentinel-2 Imagery

Michał Słapek[1] , Krzysztof Smykała[1] ,
and Bogdan Ruszczak[1,2]

[1] QZSolutions, Ozimska 72A, 45-310 Opole, Poland
{mslapek,ksmykala}@qzsolutions.pl
[2] Opole University of Technology, Prószkowska 76, 45-758 Opole, Poland
b.ruszczak@po.opole.pl

Abstract. The paper aims to discuss the difficulties with vegetation indices determined using satellite imagery of Brassica napus crops. Data used in the study was registered by Sentinel-2 satellite. Differential evolution method was used for vegetation model fitting for numerous monitored fields. In specific cases that procedure allowed to determine parameters even with a very limited number of clear images. Crop vegetation modeling using only NDVI (Normalized Differential Vegetation Index) or solely on EVI (Enhanced Vegetation Index) is often problematic while these indices are not resistant to imagery issues caused by clouds and cloud shadows registered on earth surface. To overcome the limitations of those indices the novel index MSVI (Maxima Standardized Vegetation Index) was proposed. Robust regression was used to find its optimal parameters for individual fields. To verify the presented methodology a set of satellite images of Grudziądz area (northern Poland) for the period 1st to 25th of May 2018 was used, with 6373 fields of Brassica napus that were analyzed. According to the conducted experiments, the median value of absolute error of the florescence date estimated using the proposed methodology was only 0.421 days and was significantly lower to those calculated using conventional indices: NDVI or EVI - 1.191 and 14.128 days respectively.

Keywords: Image processing · Sentinel-2 · Satellite imagery ·
Differential evolution · Regression analysis ·
Normalized Difference Vegetation Index · Enhanced Vegetation Index ·
Crops modeling · Brassica napus

1 Brassica Napus Florescence Study Using Vegetation Indexes and Satellite Imagery

Widely available spectral satellite imagery allows on-going monitoring of many phenomena taking place on Earth. One of the industries that extensively use this type of data is agriculture. Access to the current information about large areas allows to conduct studies for the state of crops and to observe the progress of their vegetation.

© Springer Nature Switzerland AG 2019
L. Rutkowski et al. (Eds.): ICAISC 2019, LNAI 11509, pp. 80–90, 2019.
https://doi.org/10.1007/978-3-030-20915-5_8

The following paper covers the results of plants vegetation observations on the example of Brassica napus. That species is an oily plant and its cultivation is important for agricultural and food processing sectors, for fuel industry as a source of second-generation biofuel [1] as well as for apicultural sector [2]. In each of these cases, the information on the crop growth progress and the occurrence of its key moments, such as flowering or harvest phase, are valuable. Therefore, the study of vegetation change of Brassica napus during the season is the subject of this paper and other works as well [3].

Obtaining the information on all crops and their dynamics and providing their analysis for a large area requires the use of a data source that can satisfy such demand. According to the suggestions of many researchers, a valuable data source for plants' appearance mapping may be satellite imagery. Missions carried out by European Space Agency (ESA) using the Sentinel-2 satellite system [4, 5] or images from Landsat-8 system serves by National Aeronautics and Space Administration (NASA) [6] are useful for such applications.

The further described experiment is based on the images taken by MultiSpectral Instrument (MSI) installed on Sentinel-2 (tandem satellite containing Sentinel-2A and Sentinel-2B). Depending on the spectral wavelength (band), this device can register 13 spectral bands with 19–242 nm of spectral resolution. The following (Table 1) presents a summary of the bands used in this study to determine the value of various vegetation indices. Additionally, the values of the cloud band (CLD) were used for initial verification of the examined parts of images. Data with high cloud coverage were eliminated from the calculations due to their low usability.

Table 1. Sentinel-2 spectral imagery channels used in experiments.

Sentinel-2 channel or map name	Sentinel-2A		Sentinel-2B		Spatial resolution [m]
	Central wavelength [nm]	Bandwidth [nm]	Central wavelength [nm]	Bandwidth [nm]	
Band 2 – BLUE	496.6	98	492.1	98	10
Band 4 – RED	664.5	38	665	39	10
Band 8 – NIR	835.1	145	833	133	10
Band 10 – CLD – cloud map	–	–	–	–	20, resampled to 10

Source: [7]

According to grasslands spectral characteristic the reflection increases between 680–750 nm. Red and blue light is absorbed by plants in photosynthesis process, but part of green light and most of the near-infrared spectrum is reflected. Normalized Difference Vegetation Index (NDVI) was proposed based on that relationships by Rouse Jr. et al. in 1973 [8]. It could be applied to compute spectral resolution vegetation mask [6] and is calculated with the following formula:

$$NDVI = \frac{(NIR - RED)}{(NIR + RED)} \tag{1}$$

where: *NIR* – pixel values stored in channel 8 referring surface reflectance infrared, *RED* – channel 4 representing the reflectance values in the red-light spectrum.

Enhanced Vegetation Index (EVI) is an example of another often-used index, implemented also in this study. The indicator allows to determine plants condition. This is done by enhancing vegetation signal on areas with high biomass, better monitoring of the canopy background and reduction of the atmosphere aerosol influence. EVI was proposed by Liu et al. [9] in 1995 and can be expressed as follows [10]:

$$EVI = G \cdot \frac{(NIR - RED)}{(NIR + C_1 \cdot RED - C_2 \cdot BLUE + L)} \tag{2}$$

where: *NIR* – pixel values recorded by MSI (Sentinel-2) on band 8 and corresponding to near-infrared reflectance of the ground, *RED* – band 4 representing the reflectance values in the red light spectrum and *BLUE* – band 2 for blue light spectrum; C_1 and C_2 – atmosphere aerosol resistance parameters, *L* canopy background adjustment value and *G* - enhancement value.

During EVI computation, using according to MODIS instructions [10], following values of its parameters were applied: $L = 1$; $C_1 = 6$; $C_2 = 7.5$; $G = 2.5$.

2   Vegetation Modelling Using Differential Evolution

The vegetation curve is used to model the progress of vegetation. This curve can be used to describe the state of vegetation based on observed values of vegetation indices and values of NDVI and EVI can be used for modeling. Such curve should allow inference even when there are many observations missing for a field that is being modeled. This may be the case if the quality of images is not sufficient, what is not so rare for satellite imagery.

The vegetation curve function assigns the expected index value to each date. The vegetation curve is based on the trigonometric function cosine. However, in one season (year) the curve is not periodic. Hence we introduced base(x) function, which is based on cosine:

$$\mathrm{base}(x) = \begin{cases} \cos(\pi(x+1)) & \text{for} - 1 \leq x \leq 1 \\ 1 & \text{otherwise} \end{cases} \tag{3}$$

A transformed curve is described as:

$$\mathrm{curve}_\theta(x) = \mathrm{min\_value} + \mathrm{half\_height} + \mathrm{half\_height} \cdot \mathrm{base}\left(\frac{x - \mathrm{min\_arg}}{\mathrm{half\_width}}\right) \tag{4}$$

The transformed curve is parametrized by vector θ, which consists of:

- min_arg – the value of x, which the minimum is attained for. Thus: min_arg = $\text{argmin}_x \text{curve}_\theta(x)$.
- min_value – minimum attained by the curve. Thus min_value = $\text{min}_x \text{curve}_\theta(x)$.
- half_height – half of the curve height.
- half_width – half of the curve width.

It is worth noting that maximum value of the curve is: $\text{max}_x \text{curve}_\theta(x) =$ min_value $+ 2 \cdot$ half_height.

2.1 Curve Fitting Procedure

The assumption was made that $D \in \mathbb{N}$ days of observations and for each day $d \in \{1, 2, \ldots, D\}$, there are $P \in \mathbb{N}$ pixels of observations. Each day has a date $x_d \in \mathbb{R}$ assigned. The value x_d is defined as a number of days from the reference date that has been arbitrarily chosen, in this case: 14 May 2018. For each $p \in \{1, 2, \ldots, P\}$ let $y_{dp} \in \mathbb{R}$ denote the observed value of a p-th pixel of a day d.

Let:

$$\tilde{y}_{dp}(\theta) = \text{curve}_\theta(x_d) \tag{5}$$

denote predicted index value for the p-th pixel of the d-th day.

Total loss is defined as mean absolute error:

$$L(\theta) = \frac{1}{DP} \sum\nolimits_{d=1}^{D} \sum\nolimits_{p=1}^{P} |\tilde{y}_{dp}(\theta) - y_{dp}| \tag{6}$$

The best fitted curve is defined as the one to which the lowest loss is attained:

$$\hat{\theta} = \text{argmin}_\theta L(\theta) \tag{7}$$

The first attempt to determine the curve parameters for each analyzed field example was the optimization using the Broyden-Fletcher-Goldfarb-Shanno minimization algorithm. That was not successful hence a large number of local minima, and similar limitations were reported also in [11]. Instead of that method, it was solved using the *differential evolution* algorithm, described in [12], and implemented in *scipy.optimize* package. This approach was found less susceptible to local minima.

2.2 Results Interpretation

While considering the curve, fitted using the procedure described above, one could use it to find out the exact florescence date. If one add min_arg days to reference date, could get a date of the least intensive chlorophyll. The beginning and the end of brassica napus florescence can be established by adding the values min_arg $\pm$ half_width to the reference date. It is worth noting that for some scenarios min_arg $\pm \alpha \cdot$ half_width for chosen $0 < \alpha < 1$ might result with better curve fit.

Figure 1 presents the vegetation curve fitted to NDVI values of sample field from the analyzing dataset. As it is depicted there, it is possible to fit the vegetation curve and predict Brassica napus florescence date even for a limited sample series, containing a few days only.

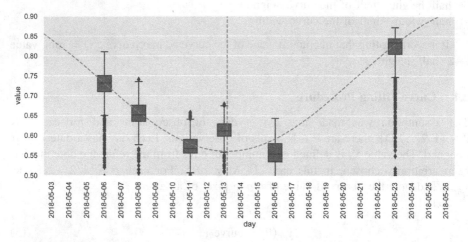

Fig. 1. NDVI values in May 2018 and fitted vegetation curve for the Brassica napus exemplary field in the area of Grudziądza.

3   Vegetation Indexes Limitations Regarding Various Overcast and Cloud Shadows

Although vegetation modeling using NDVI and EVI is popular, it has some limitations. For instance, NDVI is not resistant to image artifacts like clouds and cloud shadows or leaf canopy shadow [13]. Another main disadvantage of NDVI in remote sensing applications based on satellite data is the fact that final output is influenced by natural conditions, like canopy background reflectance or atmosphere aerosol, according to [13]. To a certain extent, the solution to that technological challenge is the Enhanced Vegetation Index (EVI) [9].

Those difficulties were also confirmed in the presented study. Several limitations related to inference based only on NDVI or EVI were noted during the experiments. Analyses of Sentinel imagery revealed that NDVI values were incorrect in case of parts of images containing cloudy areas. The index values calculated for crops using EVI were not very sensitive to cloudiness, however in that case incorrect values were caused by cloud shadows. Examples of these phenomena on analyzed Sentinel-2 images are presented in Fig. 2.

On the other hand, it was observed that NDVI values were not affected by shadows covering the image of the crop. Therefore, it was considered reasonable to combine the results of both indices in the analysis. However, in order to compare determined NDVI and EVI values, the indices should be standardized, as their expected results are obtained in two different scales (the relation between EVI and NDVI values I depicted on Fig. 3).

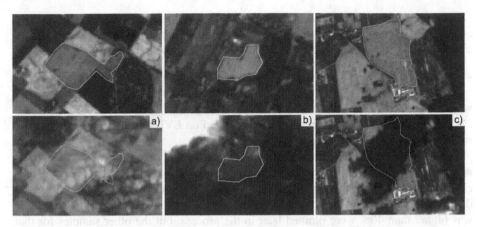

Fig. 2. Selected fragments of analyzed satellite imagery without anomalies and with some problematic cases of: (a) clouds; (b) both light shadows and clouds (c) dark shadows

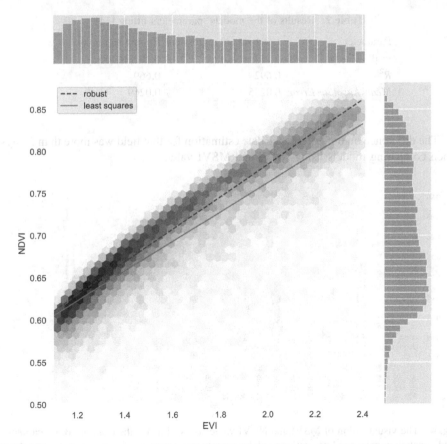

Fig. 3. The relation between EVI and NDVI distribution for analyzed fields data, with regression lines, highlighted.

Based on the preliminary experiments, for the unification of the image of the analyzed vegetation, an aggregation index for both discussed indicators was proposed – maxima standardized vegetation index (MSVI). It could be expressed as follows

$$MSVI = \max(NDVI, \alpha \cdot EVI + \beta) \tag{8}$$

where:
- α, β – parameters of linear transformation applied on EVI, which gives results on the same scale as NDVI for analyzed images.

The use of the MSVI allows to avoid of most restrictions of both indices (NDVI and EVI) occurring on images that contain small clouds or small shadows and full-cloud images. The last-mentioned issue is handled by removing these images from the dataset at preprocessing stage by using CLD band. Crops images samples where CLD was higher than 40% were omitted later in the process, but the other samples for that field from other dates were analyzed separately to be checked against this criterion (Table 2).

Table 2. Results of the models' parameters fitting [14]

Parameter	Least square regression	Robust regression
α; β	0.174; 0.414	0.192; 0.400
R^2	0.692	0.669
Mean Absolute Error	0.0285	0.0269

The difference on the florescence date estimation for that field was more than 2 days when comparing models using NDVI and MSVI values.

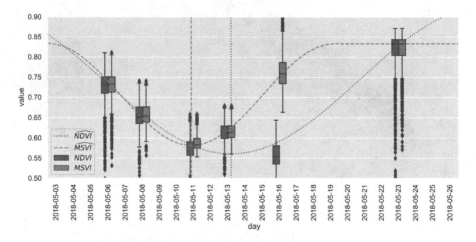

Fig. 4. The visualization of MSVI and NDVI values (box plot) for the example Brassica napus field vegetation, with fitted vegetation models (curves) and florescence dates (vertical lines). Note that the dotted lines refer to the NDVI and dashed to the MSVI

On the chart (Fig. 4) the adjusted models for a selected Brassica napus field were presented. The closer look at the images reveals there were small clouds registered over that field on 16 May 2018. Those anomalies were large enough to disturb NDVI values and to hinder vegetation curve fit.

4 Method Verification and Results Overview

The following experiment was performed to evaluate the presented vegetation modeling methodology on the dataset of labeled satellite images. There were 6373 Brassica napus instances locations provided for the images registered in 2018, between 1 and 25 of May, by Sentinel-2. During that period 10 images of tile 33UYV (the area of $10\,000\ \mathrm{km}^2$) were collected. This set was used to model the three vegetation indices and estimate florescence dates. Subsequently carefully marked image fragments for all consecutive days were also classified, to provide the information of clouds and cloud shadows occurrence. On the preprocessing stage, the samples with the cloud level higher than 40% were excluded, as they did not provide any information about vegetation on that area. Figure 5 provides an overview of the analyzed imagery with labeled Brassica napus fields.

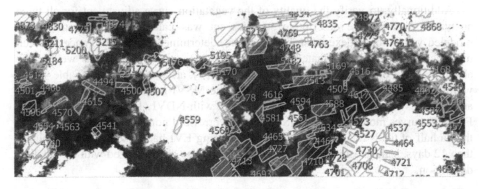

Fig. 5. The imagery taken by Sentinel-2 on 23 May 2018 for Grudziądz neighborhood with Brassica napus fields locations reference information.

Two tests were performed in order to verify the florescence date estimations using NDVI, EVI and MSVI for randomly drawn samples of fields with different anomalies (various cloudiness and shadowing levels) with the defined florescence dates g_i. For each of tested algorithm ($v_{\mathrm{NDVI}}, v_{\mathrm{EVI}}, v_{\mathrm{MSVI}}$) the sample errors were computed as follows:

$$\epsilon_{\mathrm{NDVI},i} = v_{\mathrm{NDVI},i} - g_i \tag{9}$$

$$\epsilon_{\mathrm{EVI},i} = v_{\mathrm{EVI},i} - g_i \tag{10}$$

$$\epsilon_{\mathrm{MSVI},i} = v_{\mathrm{MSVI},i} - g_i \tag{11}$$

It was later checked if those error distributions are significantly different for modeling only with NDVI or only with EVI to those modeled using MSVI. With the assumptions that $\epsilon_{NDVI,i}$, $\epsilon_{EVI,i}$, $\epsilon_{MSVI,i}$ are independent and normally distributed, the Brown–Forsythe tests [15] were performed to test the hypothesis that with the significance level $\alpha = 5\%$, variances of those distributions are significantly different. The test hypothesis and the results could be found in the Table 3. For the drawn sample tests were passed, and both hypothesis – regarding modeling using NDVI and EVI only, were found significantly different to the modelling of florescence date using the proposed MSVI index.

Table 3. Tested hypothesis and results

Parameter	Test for NDVI	Test for EVI
H_0	$Var[\epsilon_{NDVI}] = Var[\epsilon_{MSVI}]$	$Var[\epsilon_{EVI}] = Var[\epsilon_{MSVI}]$
H_1	$Var[\epsilon_{NDVI}] \neq Var[\epsilon_{MSVI}]$	$Var[\epsilon_{EVI}] \neq Var[\epsilon_{MSVI}]$
Test statistic F	5.418275	21.496576
p-value	0.025071	0.000037

Additionally, to verify the quality of the vegetation curve adjustment for all three analyzed scenarios the descriptive statistics set was calculated. The statistics for modeled vegetation indexes distribution errors, determined as the difference between reference date and the estimated florescence date ($\epsilon_{NDVI}, \epsilon_{EVI}, \epsilon_{MSVI}$), as well as the absolute values of those errors ($|\epsilon_{NDVI}|, |\epsilon_{EVI}|, |\epsilon_{MSVI}|$), are provided in the Table 4. It is worth noting that the mean absolute error for the MSVI model was only 0.533 days, and that was a much better result in comparison with NDVI (1.49) and EVI (12.501). For 95% curves modelled using MSVI absolute error did not exceed 1.391 days. More than a half of fields analyzed using the curves using EVI had an absolute error bigger than 12 days. Values estimated using the MSVI are also characterized with the smallest dispersion.

Table 4. Descriptive statistics for modeled vegetation indexes distribution errors, calculated for all errors in two ways: for its observed errors values and absolute values

Parameter	$\epsilon_{(EVI,i)}$	$|\epsilon_{(EVI,i)}|$	$\epsilon_{(NDVI,i)}$	$|\epsilon_{(NDVI,i)}|$	$\epsilon_{(MSVI,i)}$	$|\epsilon_{(MSVI,i)}|$
Mean	3.329	12.501	−0.311	1.490	−0.145	0.533
Std	17.179	11.944	2.333	1.793	0.786	0.584
5%	−23.800	0.023	−2.432	0.071	−1.069	0.008
25%	−0.612	0.985	−1.191	0.314	−0.434	0.126
50%	0.985	14.128	−0.071	1.191	−0.002	0.421
75%	19.362	23.106	1.144	1.924	0.184	0.570
95%	24.980	27.458	1.924	2.695	1.099	1.391

5 Conclusion

The paper presents the Brassica napus vegetation condition analysis based on the modeling of this process characteristic. This was done using vegetation indices values that were calculated using Sentinel-2 imagery and vegetation curves fitted with differential evolution. The study revealed difficulties in the analysis of satellite images that are frequently affected by overcast and contain small clouds and their shadows on the ground. As a solution to that the MSVI was proposed, that is the index that allows to significantly reduce mentioned disruptions occurring while processing satellite imagery.

In addition, the procedure of modeling of flowering phases using differential evolution was provided, to allow simultaneous and efficient analysis of many crops in vast areas with plenty of fields.

The analysis provided in the article was limited to the Brassica napus crops modeling only, because the information of best precision regarding its exact locations and vegetation course was available. However, the presented modeling procedure is also expected to be valid for other crops, and that is planned to be examined in the following research. As it was suggested by other authors [3, 16, 17], such approach to vegetation curves modeling can also be used for later classification of individual crops in satellite images. That could be done by comparing their vegetation curves at different moments of vegetation.

Acknowledgments. Słapek, Smykała and Ruszczak were supported by European Regional Development Fund grant no.: RPOP.01.01.00-16-0056/16-00.

References

1. Basili, M., Rossi, M.A.: Brassica carinata-derived biodiesel production: economics, sustainability and policies. Italian case. J. Cleaner Prod. **191**, 40–47 (2018). https://doi.org/10.1016/j.jclepro.2018.03.306
2. Szczęsna, T., Rybak-Chmielewska, H., Waś, E., Kachaniuk, K., Teper, D.: Characteristics of Polish unifloral honeys. I. Rape honey (Brassica napus L. var. oleifera Metzger). J. Apic. Sci. **55**(1), 111–119 (2011)
3. Wang, N., et al.: Flowering time variation in oilseed rape (Brassica napus L.) is associated with allelic variation in the FRIGIDA homologue BnaA.FRI.a. J. Exp. Botany **62**(15), 5641–5658 (2011). https://doi.org/10.1093/jxb/err249
4. Peschechera, G., Fratino, U.: Calibration of CLAIR model by means of Sentinel-2 LAI data for analysing wheat crops through Landsat-8 surface reflectance data. In: Gervasi, O., et al. (eds.) ICCSA 2018. LNCS, vol. 10964, pp. 294–304. Springer, Cham (2018). https://doi.org/10.1007/978-3-319-95174-4_24
5. Sakowska, K., Juszczak, R., Gianelle, D.: Remote sensing of grassland biophysical parameters in the context of the Sentinel-2 satellite mission. J. Sens. **2016** (2016). https://doi.org/10.1155/2016/4612809
6. Modica, G., Pollino, M., Solano, F.: Sentinel-2 imagery for mapping cork oak (*Quercus suber* L.) distribution in Calabria (Italy): capabilities and quantitative estimation. In: Calabrò, F., Della Spina, L., Bevilacqua, C. (eds.) ISHT 2018. SIST, vol. 100, pp. 60–67. Springer, Cham (2019). https://doi.org/10.1007/978-3-319-92099-3_8

7. European Space Agency: MultiSpectral Instrument (MSI) Overview (2018). earth.esa.int/web/sentinel/technical-guides/sentinel-2-msi/msi-instrument

8. Rouse, J.W., Haas, R.H., Schell, J.A., Deering, D.W.: Monitoring the vernal advancement and retrogradation (green wave effect) of natural vegetation. Prog. Rep. RSC 1978-1, Remote Sensing Center, Texas A&M University, College Station, nr E73-106393, 93 (NTIS No. E73-106393) (1973)

9. Liu, H.Q., Huete, A.: Feedback based modification of the NDVI to minimize canopy background and atmospheric noise. IEEE Trans. Geosci. Remote Sens. 33(2), 457–465 (1995)

10. TBRS team, MODIS Vegetation Indices, The University of Arizona (2002). tbrs.arizona.edu

11. Saputroa, D.R.S., Widyaningsih, P.: Limited memory Broyden-Fletcher-Goldfarb-Shanno (L-BFGS) method for the parameter estimation on geographically weighted ordinal logistic regression model (GWOLR). In: AIP Conference Proceedings, vol. 1868 (2017). https://doi.org/10.1063/1.4995124

12. Storn, R., Price, K.: Differential evolution - a simple and efficient heuristic for global optimization over continuous spaces. J. Global Opt. 11, 341–359 (1997)

13. Xue, J., Su, B.: Significant remote sensing vegetation indices: a review of developments and applications. J. Sens. 2017 (2017). https://doi.org/10.1155/2017/1353691

14. Rousseeuw, P.J., Leroy, A.M.: Robust Regression and Outlier Detection. Wiley, Hoboken (2003)

15. Brown, M.B., Forsythe, A.B.: Robust tests for equality of variances. J. Am. Stat. Assoc. 69, 364–367 (1974). https://doi.org/10.1080/01621459.1974.10482955

16. Belgiua, M., Csillik, O.: Sentinel-2 cropland mapping using pixel-based and object-based time-weighted dynamic time warping analysis. Remote Sens. Environ. 204 (2018). https://doi.org/10.1016/j.rse.2017.10.005

17. Garroutte, E.L., Hansen, A.J., Lawrence, R.L.: Using NDVI and EVI to map spatiotemporal variation in the biomass and quality of forage for migratory elk in the greater yellowstone ecosystem. Remote Sens. 8(5) (2016). https://doi.org/10.3390/rs8050404s

Ensemble of Classifiers Using CNN and Hand-Crafted Features for Depth-Based Action Recognition

Jacek Trelinski and Bogdan Kwolek[✉]

AGH University of Science and Technology, 30 Mickiewicza, 30-059 Krakow, Poland
{tjacek,bkw}@agh.edu.pl
http://home.agh.edu.pl/~bkw/contact.html

Abstract. In this paper, we present an algorithm for action recognition that uses only depth maps. At the beginning we extract features describing the person shape in single depth maps. For each class we train a separate one-against-all convolutional neural network to extract class-specific features. The actions are represented by multivariate time-series of such CNN-based frame features for which we calculate statistical features. For the non-zero pixels representing the person shape in each depth map we calculate handcrafted features. For time-series of such handcrafted features we calculate the statistical features. Afterwards, handcrafted features that are common for all actions and CNN-based features that are action-specific are concatenated together resulting in action feature vectors. For each action feature vector we train a multiclass classifier with one-hot encoding of output labels. The prediction of the action is done by a voting-based ensemble operating on such one-hot encoding outputs. We demonstrate experimentally that on UTD-MHAD dataset the proposed algorithm outperforms state-of-the-art depth-based algorithms and achieves promising results on MSR-Action3D dataset.

Keywords: Convolutional neural networks · Ensemble · Action classification

1 Introduction

The aim of the Human Action Recognition (HAR) is to automatically recognize what kind of action is performed in the image or depth map sequence. This is really a hard problem due to a lot of challenges involved in HAR. These challenges include: variation in human shape, differences in human motion, self-occlusions, cluttered backgrounds, varying illumination conditions, and viewpoint variations [1]. There are many different ways in which action can be done. Research on action recognition focuses on processing conventional RGB image sequences and then extracting handcrafted features. Compared to RGB image sequences the depth maps deliver range information and are less sensitive to varying illumination conditions. However, most current approaches to action

© Springer Nature Switzerland AG 2019
L. Rutkowski et al. (Eds.): ICAISC 2019, LNAI 11509, pp. 91–103, 2019.
https://doi.org/10.1007/978-3-030-20915-5_9

recognition on data delivered by depth sensors are based on skeleton modality or on handcrafted features [2], which in many scenarios provide insufficient discriminative power. In recent decade, local features methods were the most successful in action recognition. Those methods are based on feature detectors and model the local neighborhood of detected points of interest. The advantage of such approaches is that they do not require sophisticated techniques for joint detection (i.e. skeleton detection) as a pre-processing step. One of the drawbacks of methods relying on local features is that they usually ignore spatio-temporal layout of detected features.

In a typical algorithm for action recognition we can distinguish three main steps: feature extraction, quantization/dimension reduction and classification. Designing both effective and efficient feature set for action recognition on depth map sequences is not an easy task [3]. The main difficulty is that in contrast to color images the depth maps do not have as much texture as color ones. Usually, they are too noisy alike spatially and temporally to apply gradient operators both in space and time. Last but not least, the recognition is typically realized on depth maps acquired by a single sensor. Since body parts undergo occlusions, the robustness of global feature-based methods can be poor [3]. In order to cope with challenges mentioned above, various features that are semi-local, highly discriminative and robust to occlusions have been developed [4].

Because of noisy character of depth maps that limits applying local differential operators, the number of depth map-based sequential approaches, which achieved competitive results in comparison to depth-maps or depth-maps space-time volume approaches is limited [5]. Since the skeleton data is one of the most natural features for modeling action dynamics, the most successful approaches utilize skeleton information [6]. A method called Histogram of 3D Joint Locations (HOJ3D) [7] that encodes spatial occupancy information with regard to the skeleton root is a representative method for such approaches. The HOJ3D features are computed on action depth sequences, projected by LDA and then clustered into posture visual words to represent the prototypical poses of actions. The temporal evolutions of such visual words are modeled by discrete HMMs.

In this work, we present an algorithm for action recognition that is based on depth maps only. At the beginning we extract features describing the person shape in single depth maps. For each action class we train a separate one-against-all convolutional neural network in order to extract class-specific features. The actions are represented by multivariate time-series of such CNN-based frame features for which we determine statistical features. For non-zero pixels representing the person shape in each depth map we calculate handcrafted features. For time-series of such handcrafted features we determine the statistical features. Next, handcrafted features that are common for all classes and CNN-based features that are class-specific are concatenated together resulting in action feature vectors. For each action feature vector we train a multi-class logistic regression classifier with one-hot encoding of output labels. Action classification is performed by a voting-based ensemble operating on such one-hot encoding outputs. We demonstrate experimentally that on the UTD-MHAD dataset the proposed algorithm outperforms state-of-the-art algorithms and achieves promising results on the MSR-Action3D dataset.

2   Relevant Work

As noticed in a recently published survey [2], among datasets utilized in evaluation of action recognition algorithms, the MSR-Action3D dataset is the most popular and widely used benchmark data. For the MSR-Action3D dataset, most of the studies follow the evaluation setting of Li et al. [8], in which twenty actions are divided into three subsets AS1, AS2, AS3, each having eight actions. For each subset, the tests T1, T2 and CST are usually performed. In most papers the classification accuracy better than 90% in the first two tests is reported. In the third test, however, the recognition performance is generally far lower. It follows from here that many of these methods do not have good generalization capabilities when unlike performer is performing the action, even in identical conditions and environment. As an example, the algorithm of Li et al. achieves 74.7% classification accuracy in the CST test, whereas 91.6% and 94.2% accuracies were obtained in tests T1 and T2, respectively.

As already mentioned, approaches based on the joint features achieve far better classification performance in comparison to methods relying on depth maps or points clouds [6]. However, skeleton-based methods are not applicable for applications, where skeleton data is not accessible [9]. Since our method is based on depth modality only, below we discuss only depth-based approaches to action recognition.

In [10], depth images were projected onto three orthogonal planes and then accumulated in order to generate Depth Motion Maps (DMMs). Afterwards, the histograms of the oriented gradients (HOGs) computed from DMMs were employed as feature descriptors. A method proposed in [11] does not utilize the skeletal joints information. Random occupancy pattern (ROP) features were extracted from depth map sequences and a sparse coding was utilized to encode such features. In a method proposed in [12], the depth map sequence is divided into a spatiotemporal grid. Subsequently, a simple feature called global occupancy pattern is determined, where the number of the occupied pixels is stored for each grid cell. In [13] depth cuboid similarity features (DCSF) are built around the local spatio-temporal interest points (STIPs), which are extracted from depth map sequences. A method proposed in [14] does not require a skeleton tracker and determines a histogram of oriented 4D surface normals (HON4D) in order to capture complex joint shape-motion cues at pixel-level. In contrast to method proposed in [10], the temporal order of the events in the action sequences is encoded and not ignored. A recently proposed method [9] employs three projection views to capture motion cues and then uses LBPs to determine compact feature representation. In a more recent method [15], recognition of human action from depth maps is done using weighted hierarchical depth motion maps (WHDMM) and three-channel deep convolutional neural networks (3DConvNets).

3   The Method

Having on regard that in currently available datasets for depth-based action recognition the amount of data (depth map sequences) is insufficient to train deep models with good generalization capabilities, we propose to use CNNs operating on single depth maps (pairs of consecutive frames) to extract informative features. The main difference between our approach and other approaches is that instead of training CNNs/LSTMs on depth map sequences we train a set of CNNs on single depth maps to extract considerable number of features. In the proposed approach, a CNN is trained for each class to extract class-specific features. The class-specific models that were trained for action classification are used as feature extractors by removing the softmax output layer (which outputs class scores). A separate CNN is trained for each action class to distinguish between this class and all remaining classes, like in one-vs-all approach to multi-class classification. This means that each action-specific CNN is trained to predict if the considered depth map belongs to the class for which the CNN is trained or to one of the remaining classes. Each CNN is trained on single depth maps belonging to the considered class and depth maps sampled from the remaining classes. Since the number of single depth maps in all depth maps sequences is considerable it is possible to train CNNs without overfitting and with good generalization capabilities. In our approach the features are extracted using the outputs from the penultimate layer consisting of one hundred neurons. This means that the size of the feature vector extracted by each action-specific CNN is equal to one hundred, and the number of 100-element vectors is equal to the number of the actions. Since the number of frames in depth maps sequences representing the actions is different, the lengths of multivariate time-series are usually not identical.

In the proposed approach the input depth maps have size 64×64 pixels. The input of convolutional neural network is a $4 \times 64 \times 64$ tensor consisting of two consecutive depth maps, and orthogonal projection of the input depth map onto xz and yz planes [16]. This means that aside the frontal depth maps we also employ side-view and top projections of the depth maps. The convolutional layer C1 consists of sixteen 5×5 convolutional filters that are followed by a subsampling layer. The next convolutional layer C2 operates on sixteen feature maps of size 15×15. It consists of sixteen 5×5 convolutional filters that are followed by a subsampling layer. It outputs sixteen feature maps of size 2×2. The next fully connected layer FC consists of one hundred neurons. At the learning stage, the output of the CNN is a softmax layer with number of neurons equal to two. Every action-specific network has been learned on depth maps from training parts of depth map sequences. After the training, the layers before the softmax have been employed to extract shape features.

The actions are represented by multivariate time-series of CNN-based features. For each time-series composed of class-specific CNN-based features we calculate three statistical features: average, standard deviation and skewness. The motivation of using skewness was to include a parameter describing asymmetry in random variable's probability distribution with respect to a normal distribution. This means that each action is described by a $3 \times 100 = 300$ element vector describing statistically the multivariate time series of CNN-based features.

Aside from the CNN-based features for each frame we calculate handcrafted features. At the beginning the depth map is projected onto two orthogonal planes to determine side-view and top projections of the depth map. Given that pixels with non-zero values represent the performer on depth maps, only pixels with non-zero values are utilized in calculation of handcrafted features. The following features are calculated on such three depth maps: area ratio (single value for axes x, y, z), standard deviation (axes x, y, z), skewness (axes x, y, z), correlation (xy, xz and zy axes). This means that the number of handcrafted features describing a single depth map is equal to ten. Every realization of action is described by a multivariate time-series of length equal the number of frames and dimension equal to ten.

For each action realization that is represented by a time-series of handcrafted features the following statistical features are calculated:

1. average
2. std
3. skewness
4. number of local minimas in a time series
5. number of local maximas in a time series
6. location of global maximum in a time series (as part of time-series length)
7. location of global minimum in a time series (as part of time-series length)
8. mean change ($\frac{1}{n-1} \sum_{i=1}^{n-1} \frac{|f_{i+1}-f_i|}{f_i}$, f_i denotes feature value in frame i)
9. difference between the average and the median

The features mentioned above were grouped into the following feature collections: I - (1, 2, 3), II - (4, 5), III - (6, 7), IV - (8), V - (9). In order to determine the discriminative power of the handcrafted features we performed evaluations of action classification using the following feature sets: I, I+II+III, I+II+III+IV, I+II+III+V and I+II+III+IV+V. For the mentioned feature sets the number of handcrafted features was equal to: 30, 70, 80, 80 and 90, respectively. The CNN-based features that are action-specific and handcrafted features that are common for all actions were concatenated together resulting in action feature vectors. This means that class-specific feature vectors of size 300 that are extracted by CNNs were concatenated with handcrafted feature vectors of size dependent of the used feature set. More details are in Sect. 4.

For each action feature vector we train a multi-class classifier with one-hot encoding of output labels. The prediction of the action is done by a voting-based ensemble operating on such one-hot encoding outputs. Thanks to training a CNN for each class the features extracted by the CNNs are uncorrelated and thus provide sufficient diversity for the ensemble. What is more, handcrafted features describing individual depth maps are uncorrelated with CNN-based features and thus introduce the diversity for the ensemble.

4   Empirical Results and Discussion

The proposed framework has been evaluated on two publicly available benchmark datasets: MSR-Action3D dataset [8] and UTD-MHAD dataset [16]. The
datasets were chosen due to their frequent use as benchmark data by action
recognition community. In all experiments and evaluations, 557 sequences of
MSR-Action3D dataset were investigated. Half of the subjects were used as
training data and the rest of the subjects has been considered as test subset. In
the discussed classification setting, half of the subjects are used for the training,
and the rest for the testing, which is different from evaluation protocols based
on AS1, AS2 and AS3 data splits and averaging the classification accuracies
over such data splits. It is worth mentioning that the classification performances
achieved in the utilized setting are lower in comparison to classification performances that are achieved on AS1, AS2, AS3 setting due to bigger variations
across the same actions performed by different subjects. The cross-subject evaluation scheme [13,15] has been applied in all evaluations. This scheme is different
from the scheme utilized in [7], in which more subjects were in the training
subset.

The UTD-MHAD dataset consists of 27 different actions performed by 8
subjects (4 females and 4 males). Each performer repeated each action 4 times.
All actions were performed in an indoor environment with fixed background.
The dataset was collected using Kinect sensor and a wearable inertial sensor. It
includes 861 data sequences.

At the beginning we evaluated the discriminative power of handcrafted features on UTD-MHAD dataset. A multi-class linear SVM has been trained on
statistical features of time-series consisting of handcrafted features. The evaluation has been performed for feature sets discussed in Sect. 3. The value of C
parameter of a linear SVM has been determined in a grid search. As we can
observe in Table 1, the best results were achieved for I+II+III+IV+V feature
set. We considered also a logistic regression-based multi-class classifier, but the
best classification accuracy was about five percent worse in comparison to classification accuracy achieved by the linear SVM.

Table 1. Recognition performance on UTD-MHAD dataset that was achieved by SVM
using handcrafted features.

f. set	f. num.	Accuracy	Precision	Recall	F1-score
I	30	0.6884	0.7143	0.6884	0.6752
I+II+III	70	0.7419	0.7615	0.7419	0.7350
I+II+III+IV	80	0.7531	0.7748	0.7531	0.7531
I+II+III+V	80	0.7535	0.7792	0.7535	0.7501
I+II+III+IV+V	90	0.7744	0.7923	0.7744	0.7718

Table 2 shows recognition performance that has been obtained by the ensemble on UTD-MHAD dataset. The class-specific CNN-based features were concatenated with common handcrafted features and then used to train class-specific multi-class logistic regression classifiers. In a second option, Recursive Feature Elimination (RFE) algorithm has been executed to select the most informative CNN-based features, which were then concatenated with the handcrafted features and then used to train class-specific multi-class logistic regression classifiers. The first row presents results that were achieved by the ensemble using only CNN-based features. In the next rows there are results achieved on the basis of CNN-based features that were concatenated with handcrafted features. The next two rows in discussed table present results that have been achieved using the I feature set, which was concatenated with CNN-based features. In the following groups of two rows there are shown results that were obtained by I+II+III, I+II+III+IV, I+II+III+V and I+II+III+IV+V feature sets, respectively. In each group of two rows, the first row depicts results without selection of the most informative features, whereas the second row in each group demonstrates results achieved on the basis of the most informative features, concatenated with the handcrafted features. The number of features utilized by the classifiers is shown in the third column. The values in the remaining columns illustrate the accuracies, precisions, recalls and F1-scores that were obtained using the discussed above feature sets. As we can observe, the best results were obtained using both handcrafted features and deep features, and feature selection by RFE. In general, the use of RFE leads to better results for a given feature set. The resulting feature vectors are about twice shorter in comparison to feature vectors not processed by RFE, which in turn leads to better generalization. As we can observe, owing to the use of handcrafted features the classification accuracy has been improved from 61.6% to 83%. On the other hand, the best classification

Table 2. Recognition performance on UTD-MHAD dataset that was achieved by the ensemble.

f. set	f. sel.	f. num.	Accuracy	Precision	Recall	F1-score
-	-	300	0.6163	0.6259	0.6163	0.6040
I	-	330	0.7163	0.7359	0.7163	0.7101
I	RFE	130	0.7535	0.7724	0.7535	0.7510
I+II+III	-	370	0.7674	0.7741	0.7674	0.7580
I+II+III	RFE	170	0.7953	0.8044	0.7953	0.7897
I+II+III+IV	-	380	0.7860	0.8010	0.7860	0.7755
I+II+III+IV	RFE	180	0.8209	0.8314	0.8209	0.8167
I+II+III+V	-	380	0.7860	0.8010	0.7860	0.7755
I+II+III+V	RFE	180	0.8070	0.8256	0.8070	0.7981
I+II+III+IV+V	-	390	0.7953	0.8083	0.7953	0.7885
I+II+III+IV+V	RFE	190	0.8302	0.8398	0.8302	0.8250

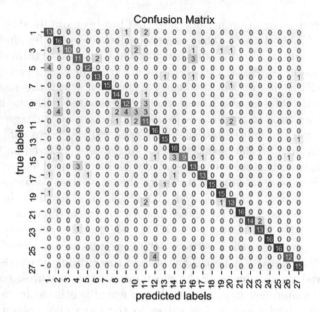

Fig. 1. Confusion matrix obtained by the ensemble on UTD-MHAD dataset.

accuracy on the basis of only handcrafted features was equal to 77.4%, see also Table 1.

Figure 1 depicts the confusion matrix that was determined on the basis of results achieved by the ensemble on the UTD-MHAD dataset.

Table 3 presents the recognition performance of the proposed method compared with the state-of-the-art methods. Most of current methods for action recognition on UTD-MHAD dataset are based on skeleton data. It is worth noting that methods based on skeleton modality usually achieve better results in comparison to methods relying on depth data only. Despite the fact that our method is based on depth modality, we evoked the recent skeleton-based methods to show that it outperforms many of them. The methods based on depth data have wide range applications since not all sensors or cameras delivering depth modality have support for skeleton extraction. Our method is considerably better than the WHDMM+3DConvNets method that employs weighted hierarchical depth motion maps (WHDMMs) and three 3D ConvNets. The WHDMMs are employed at several temporal scales to encode spatiotemporal motion patterns of actions into 2D spatial structures. In order to provide sufficient amount of training data, the 3D points are rotated and then used to synthesize new exemplars. In contrast, our algorithm operates on class-specific CNN features that are concatenated with handcrafted features. The improved performance of our method may suggest that the proposed method has better viewpoint tolerance in comparison to depth-based algorithms, including [15].

Table 3. Comparative recognition performance of the proposed method with recent algorithms on MHAD dataset.

Method	Modality	Accuracy [%]
JTM [17]	Skeleton	85.81
SOS [18]	Skeleton	86.97
Cov3DJ [19]	Skeleton	85.58
Kinect & inertial [16]	Skeleton	79.10
ELC-KCSVD [20]	Skeleton	76.19
Struct. body [21]	Skeleton	66.05
Struct. part [21]	Skeleton	78.70
Struct. joint [21]	Skeleton	86.81
Struct. SzDDI [21]	Skeleton	89.04
WHDMMs + ConvNets [15, 21]	Depth	73.95
Proposed method	Depth	**83.02**

Table 4 presents results that were achieved on MSR-Action3D dataset by a multi-class linear SVM operating only on the handcrafted features. As we can notice, the best classification accuracy has been achieved on the basis of I+II+III+V feature set. We considered also a multi-class logistic regression classifier, but it turned out that the best classification accuracy was about four percent worse in comparison to classification accuracy achieved by the linear SVM classifier.

Table 5 shows the recognition performance that was achieved on the basis of different feature sets on MSR-Action3D dataset. As we can observe, the best results were achieved on the basis of I+II+III+IV handcrafted feature set that was concatenated with CNN-based features, and which were selected by the RFE algorithm. The accuracy that was achieved using I+II+III+IV+V feature set is identical, but precision is worse. The RFE-based feature elimination decreases the number of CNN-based features and the results on the reduced feature subsets are better. The results presented in Tables 2 and 5 were achieved by ensemble

Table 4. Recognition performance on MSR-Action3D dataset that was achieved by SVM using handcrafted features.

f. set	f. num.	Accuracy	Precision	Recall	F1-score
I	30	0.8109	0.8232	0.8109	0.7948
I+II+III	70	0.8182	0.8270	0.8182	0.8102
I+II+III+IV	80	0.7927	0.8049	0.7927	0.7883
I+II+III+V	80	0.8400	0.8440	0.8400	0.8420
I+II+III+IV+V	90	0.8036	0.8134	0.8036	0.7922

consisting of multi-class logistic classifiers with one-hot encoding of output labels. We considered also multi-class logistic classifiers and multi-class SVMs with probabilistic outputs, which were then used to determine the ensemble output. However, the results were not better.

Table 5. Recognition performance on MSR-Action3D dataset that was achieved by the ensemble.

f. set	f. sel.	f. num.	Accuracy	Precision	Recall	F1-score
-	-	300	0.8000	0.8098	0.8000	0.7883
I	-	330	0.8982	0.9092	0.8982	0.8690
I	RFE	130	0.8545	0.8761	0.8545	0.8491
I+II+III	-	370	0.8727	0.8812	0.8727	0.8671
I+II+III	RFE	170	0.8945	0.8977	0.8945	0.8827
I+II+III+IV	-	380	0.8691	0.8827	0.8691	0.8578
I+II+III+V	RFE	180	0.8836	0.8944	0.8836	0.8740
I+II+III+V	-	380	0.8873	0.8920	0.8873	0.8770
I+II+III+IV	RFE	180	0.9055	0.9204	0.9055	0.8945
I+II+III+IV+V	-	390	0.8836	0.8941	0.8836	0.8712
I+II+III+IV+V	RFE	190	0.9055	0.9095	0.9055	0.8955

Table 6 illustrates the classification performance of the proposed method in comparison to previous depth-based methods on the MSR-Action3D dataset. The classification performance of the proposed framework has been determined using the cross-subject evaluation [22], where subjects 1, 3, 5, 7, and 9 were employed for training and subjects 2, 4, 6, 8, and 10 were utilized for testing. As we can notice, the proposed method achieves better classification accuracy in comparison to recently proposed method [17], and it has worse performance in

Table 6. Comparative recognition performance of the proposed method with recent algorithms on MSR-Action3D dataset.

Method	Split	Modality	Accuracy[%]
3DCNN [17]	Split II	Depth	84.07
Depth motion maps [10]	Split II	Depth	88.73
PRNN [18]	Split II	Depth	94.90
Range sample [24]	Not shown	Skeleton	95.62
WHDMM+CNN [23]	Split I	Depth	100.00
S DDI [21]	Split I	Depth	100.00
Proposed method	Split I	Depth	**90.6**

comparison to recently proposed methods [18,21,23]. One of the main reasons for this is limited amount of training samples in the MSR-Action3D dataset. In order to cope with such a limitation, Wang et al. generated synthesized training samples on the basis of 3D points. This means that the discussed algorithm is not based on depth maps only. Comparing the results from Tables 3 and 6 we can notice that the classification performances achieved by the WHDMM algorithm on UTD-MHAD dataset are worse in comparison to results achieved by the proposed algorithm.

The proposed method has been implemented in Python using Theano and Lasagne deep learning frameworks. The Lasagne library is built on top of Theano. The values of the initial weights in CNNs networks were drawn randomly from uniform distributions. The binary cross-entropy loss function has been used in the minimization. The CNN networks were trained using SGD with momentum. Much computations were performed on a PC computer equipped with an NVIDIA GPU card. The source code of the proposed algorithms is freely available[1].

5   Conclusions

In this work a method for action recognition on depth map sequences has been proposed. Due to considerable amount of noise in depth maps that prevent applying local differential operators, the number of depth maps-based sequential approaches is limited and most of the approaches are skeleton-based. We demonstrated experimentally that the proposed algorithm can achieve superior results in comparison to results achieved by state-of-the-art algorithms, including recently proposed deep learning-based algorithms. The method has been evaluated on two widely employed benchmark datasets and compared with state-of-the-art methods. We demonstrated experimentally that on challenging MSR-Action3D and UTD-MHAD datasets the proposed method achieves superior results or at least comparative results in comparison to results achieved by recent methods.

Acknowledgment. This work was supported by Polish National Science Center (NCN) under a research grant 2017/27/B/ST6/01743.

References

1. Aggarwal, J., Ryoo, M.: Human activity analysis: a review. ACM Comput. Surv. **43**(3), 16:1–16:43 (2011)
2. Liang, B., Zheng, L.: A survey on human action recognition using depth sensors. In: International Conference on Digital Image Computing: Techniques and Applications, pp. 1–8 (2015)
3. Aggarwal, J., Xia, L.: Human activity recognition from 3D data: a review. Pattern Recognit. Lett. **48**, 70–80 (2014)

---

[1] https://github.com/tjacek/DeepActionLearning.

4. Chen, L., Wei, H., Ferryman, J.: A survey of human motion analysis using depth imagery. Pattern Recognit. Lett. **34**(15), 1995–2006 (2013)
5. Ye, M., Zhang, Q., Wang, L., Zhu, J., Yang, R., Gall, J.: A survey on human motion analysis from depth data. In: Grzegorzek, M., Theobalt, C., Koch, R., Kolb, A. (eds.) Time-of-Flight and Depth Imaging. Sensors, Algorithms, and Applications. LNCS, vol. 8200, pp. 149–187. Springer, Heidelberg (2013). https://doi.org/10.1007/978-3-642-44964-2_8
6. Lo Presti, L., La Cascia, M.: 3D skeleton-based human action classification. Pattern Recognit. **53**(C), 130–147 (2016)
7. Xia, L., Chen, C.C., Aggarwal, J.: View invariant human action recognition using histograms of 3D joints. In: CVPR Workshops, pp. 20–27 (2012)
8. Li, W., Zhang, Z., Liu, Z.: Action recognition based on a bag of 3D points. In: IEEE International Conference on Computer Vision and Pattern Recognition - Workshops, pp. 9–14 (2010)
9. Chen, C., Jafari, R., Kehtarnavaz, N.: Action recognition from depth sequences using depth motion maps-based local binary patterns. In: 2015 IEEE Winter Conference on Applications of Computer Vision, pp. 1092–1099 (2015)
10. Yang, X., Zhang, C., Tian, Y.L.: Recognizing actions using depth motion maps-based histograms of oriented gradients. In: Proceedings of the 20th ACM International Conference on Multimedia, pp. 1057–1060. ACM (2012)
11. Wang, J., Liu, Z., Chorowski, J., Chen, Z., Wu, Y.: Robust 3D action recognition with random occupancy patterns. In: Fitzgibbon, A., Lazebnik, S., Perona, P., Sato, Y., Schmid, C. (eds.) ECCV 2012. LNCS, pp. 872–885. Springer, Heidelberg (2012). https://doi.org/10.1007/978-3-642-33709-3_62
12. Vieira, A.W., Nascimento, E.R., Oliveira, G.L., Liu, Z., Campos, M.F.M.: STOP: space-time occupancy patterns for 3D action recognition from depth map sequences. In: Alvarez, L., Mejail, M., Gomez, L., Jacobo, J. (eds.) CIARP 2012. LNCS, vol. 7441, pp. 252–259. Springer, Heidelberg (2012). https://doi.org/10.1007/978-3-642-33275-3_31
13. Xia, L., Aggarwal, J.: Spatio-temporal depth cuboid similarity feature for activity recognition using depth camera. In: IEEE International Conference on Computer Vision and Pattern Recognition, pp. 2834–2841 (2013)
14. Oreifej, O., Liu, Z.: HON4D: histogram of oriented 4D normals for activity recognition from depth sequences. In: IEEE International Conference on Computer Vision and Pattern Recognition, pp. 716–723 (2013)
15. Wang, P., Li, W., Gao, Z., Zhang, J., Tang, C., Ogunbona, P.: Action recognition from depth maps using deep convolutional neural networks. IEEE Trans. Hum.-Mach. Syst. **46**(4), 498–509 (2016)
16. Chen, C., Jafari, R., Kehtarnavaz, N.: UTD-MHAD: a multimodal dataset for human action recognition utilizing a depth camera and a wearable inertial sensor. In: 2015 IEEE International Conference on Image Processing (ICIP), pp. 168–172, September 2015
17. Wang, P., Li, W., Li, C., Hou, Y.: Action recognition based on joint trajectory maps with convolutional neural networks. Knowl.-Based Syst. **158**, 43–53 (2018)
18. Hou, Y., Li, Z., Wang, P., Li, W.: Skeleton optical spectra-based action recognition using convolutional neural networks. IEEE Trans. Circuits Syst. Video Technol. **28**(3), 807–811 (2018)
19. Hussein, M.E., Torki, M., Gowayyed, M.A., El-Saban, M.: Human action recognition using a temporal hierarchy of covariance descriptors on 3D joint locations. In: Proceedings of the Twenty-Third International Joint Conferences on Artificial Intelligence, IJCAI 2013, pp. 2466–2472. AAAI Press (2013)

20. Zhou, L., Li, W., Zhang, Y., Ogunbona, P., Nguyen, D., Zhang, H.: Discriminative key pose extraction using extended LC-KSVD for action recognition. In: 2014 International Conference on Digital Image Computing: Techniques and Applications (DICTA), pp. 1–8 (2014)
21. Wang, P., Wang, S., Gao, Z., Hou, Y., Li, W.: Structured images for RGB-D action recognition. In: 2017 IEEE International Conference on Computer Vision Workshops (ICCVW), pp. 1005–1014 (2017)
22. Wu, Y.: Mining actionlet ensemble for action recognition with depth cameras. In: IEEE International Conference on Computer Vision and Pattern Recognition, pp. 1290–1297 (2012)
23. Wang, P., Li, W., Gao, Z., Zhang, J., Tang, C., Ogunbona, P.O.: Action recognition from depth maps using deep convolutional neural networks. IEEE Trans. Hum.-Mach. Syst. **46**(4), 498–509 (2016)
24. Lu, C., Jia, J., Tang, C.: Range-sample depth feature for action recognition. In: IEEE International Conference on Computer Vision and Pattern Recognition, pp. 772–779 (2014)

Gamification of Eye Exercises for Evaluating Eye Fatigue

Mindaugas Vasiljevas[1]($\boxtimes$), Robertas Damaševičius[1], Dawid Połap[2], and Marcin Woźniak[2]

[1] Department of Software Engineering, Kaunas University of Technology, 51368 Kaunas, Lithuania
{mindaugas.vasiljevas, robertas.damasevicius}@ktu.lt
[2] Institute of Mathematics, Faculty of Applied Mathematics, Silesian University of Technology, 44100 Gliwice, Poland
{dawid.polap, marcin.wozniak}@polsl.pl

Abstract. Extensive use of computer and mobile devices places large burden on our eyes. To tackle the symptoms of digital eye strain and improve eyesight, the use of eye exercises are suggested. However, few people do eye exercising as it is considered boring. In this paper we apply a serious game approach to eye exercising. We developed a PacMan style game to promote horizontal and vertical eye movements. Eye and game performance characteristics are collected during the game and used to evaluate the onset of eye fatigue during the game. The damped oscillation model is applied to observe the learning and fatigue effects. Analysis of data collected during game sessions from 14 subjects is presented.

Keywords: Gamification · Serious game · Gaze tracking · Eye fatigue

1 Introduction

Overuse of smartphones and other electronic devices have become almost an epidemic. In 2017, internet users spent an average of 223 min. per day on mobile devices, an increase from 188 daily min. in 2016 [1]. US adults average daily time spent with major media (mostly digital and TV) exceeded 12 h in 2017 [2]. This represents a major burden on our eyes. Eye fatigue has been attributed to computer usage for academic or entertainment purposes or social networking among university students. An over exposure to blue violet light emitted by cellphone screens can lead to a greater risk of macular degeneration which is a leading cause of blindness [4]. The use of smartphones while lying in the dark may lead to transient smartphone blindness (TSB). Smartphone use is a risk factor for the dry eye syndrome that results in ocular discomfort, visual disturbances, with potential damage to the eye [6]. The problem is especially acute for children as 97% of children suffering from dry eye disease reported using their smartphones for an average of 3.2 h a day [7].

Eye exercises have been recommended by medical doctors to prevent vision problems and eye diseases such as hyperopia and myopia [8], reduce eye fatigue [9], and improve visual acuity. Active pursuit eye movements while focusing on moving

L. Rutkowski et al. (Eds.): ICAISC 2019, LNAI 11509, pp. 104–114, 2019.
https://doi.org/10.1007/978-3-030-20915-5_10

visual stimuli were found to be move efficient than exercising using static visual displays [11]. If practiced faithfully every day, eye exercises can improve accuracy and letter recognition [12], and may actually help to delay the need for glasses or contact lenses for some people. However, eye exercises usually are not performed regularly or at all, because these exercises are considered to be boring [13]. Another well known problem is that people, especially children, do not know how to perform eye exercises correctly [14]. Serious games [15] have been proposed as an attractive mean to engage people in performing useful activities such as learning [16] through an accomplishment of certain in-game tasks. For example, 4.00% of the apps in the Apple iTunes Store are intended for use in eye care [17]. Examples of such games are games for treating amblyopia (lazy eye) [18], or a First Person Shooter (FPS) game for visual rehabilitation of patients with mild visual impairment [19].

The onset of eye fatigue has been detected using the fixation qualitative score that represents the distance between the gaze fixation sites and the stimulus [20], while in [22] eye blink rate was used, and in [23] the number and duration of fixations, blink duration, eye movement distance and average saccade length were used. Other important role play data extraction [5, 10] and decision support methods [3, 21]. In our previous research, we have investigated gaze fatigue while using eye blinking for text entry [24] and applied the Banister's model [25]. Here we present a gamification of eye exercises using a PacMan style game. We describe a model for evaluating changes in eye performance, and present the results from our experiments.

2 Method

In the subsequent subsections, we describe the design of the game, gaze metrics used for evaluation of performance, our gaze fatigue model and the methods used for processing and analyzing data obtained from the game.

2.1 Design of Game

The aim of the game is to promote horizontal and vertical saccadic movements of eye, which are a part of vision therapy used to improve eyesight [26]. The exercise task usually consists of alternating horizontal and vertical eye movements performed over an extended period of time [12]. As the exercise task is boring and people usually quickly lose interest in performing it regularly, we have implemented the gamification of an eye exercise in a form of a computer game, in which the movement of a main character is controlled by gaze using the gaze tracking equipment.

The idea of the game is based on a widely known Pac-Man game, which is a type of maze chase games. The player navigates Pac-Man through a maze containing resources (dots), and adversaries (ghosts). The goal of the game is to collect the dots while avoiding the ghosts. We have implemented a simpler version of the game, in which the player has to move vertically or horizontally in the maze and collect pills. There are two modes of the game: simple mode and timed mode. While playing in simple mode, in order to win, the player needs to collect all pills in the maze. In timed mode, the aim is to collect as many as possible pills in a specified period of time. When a specific pill is taken, it will appear after some time in the same place. Note that while the aim of the game is to collect pills, the desired eye movements are achieved by navigating in the maze. We have modelled the game mechanics of each mode using the Machinations diagrams [27] presented in Fig. 1. The developed game is easy to play and implements the principles of effective human-computer interaction outlined in [28]: strive for consistency (a familiar graphics and game mechanics from well-known Pac-Man game is used), informative feedback (score is counted to reflect game actions), and support internal locus of control (the player initiates the action).

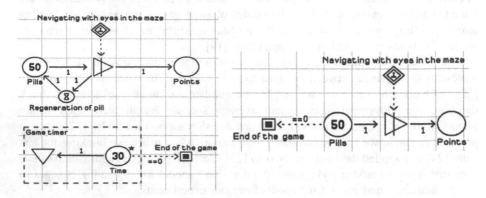

Fig. 1. Game mechanics (in Machinations [27]) of timer mode (left) and simple mode (right)

The interface of the game is presented in Fig. 2, left. The movements of the main character are restricted by the walls of the game maze. The character of the game (represented by blue point) is controlled by eye movements of the player. The control principles are represented abstractly in Fig. 2, right. The area around the game character is divided in four equal sectors, defined by 90° wide angle sectors from the starting point, which coincides with the game character. Each of the sectors represents the directions of movement. When the gaze landing site of the player is captured at the specific sector, the game character moves at the direction specified by that sector.

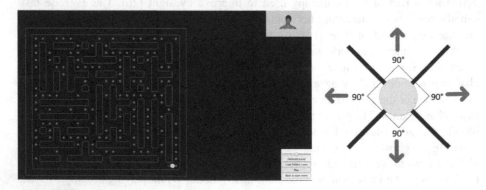

Fig. 2. Screenshot of game with main character (left) and control of main character (right) (Color figure online)

2.2   Evaluation of Eye Performance

During the course of the game the following eye and game performance characteristics are collected:

- Direction, amplitude and velocity of saccadic movements;
- Distribution of the number of turns while navigating in the maze.

The saccadic characteristics are further analyzed using the statistical and linear regression methods. The game characteristics are analyzed by fitting the collected data to the proposed eye fatigue model.

2.3   Eye Fatigue Model

Two major factors influence the cognitive performance of the player during the game: learning, which represents the improvement of characteristics due to practice and mastery of control, and fatigue, which represents the decrease of abilities to perform game action due to eye muscular and mental fatigue. To evaluate the effects of fatigue and performance recovery on the capability to perform tasks by gaze, we have adopted a well known model of damped oscillation. A damped oscillation wave is an exponentially decaying sinusoidal wave whose amplitude of oscillation diminishes over time. This model represents the effects of long-term fatigue interrupted by short-time recovery of the performing abilities of biological structures such as eyeball controlling muscles. The model can be considered as a generalization of Fitness-Fatigue models such as the Banister model, which expressed the muscular adaptation to physical training as a sum of two exponential functions representing a positive effect (fitness) and a negative effect (fatigue) on sports performance [29].

We describe the adopted model of the change of game performance characteristic f over time t as follows:

$$f(t) = Ae^{-\lambda t} \times \cos(wt + \phi) \tag{1}$$

here A is the initial amplitude of the amplitude, λ is the damping factor, w is angular frequency, and ϕ is the initial phase angle. Note that if the damping factor is positive, the performance decreases due to fatigue, whereas in case of negative damping the performance increases due to the learning effect. To represent the data graphically, we use the phase space plots [30], which show the value of $f(t)$ vs. $f(t+1)$.

2.4   Preprocessing of Data and Fitting to the Model

To analyze the change of player performance during the game, we considered the temporal distribution of the number of successful number of turns while travelling in a maze. Each turn requires that a user performs a saccadic movement of an eye in the horizontal or vertical direction, which is the serious aim of the game. The game is started in the timed mode and the number of new turns is registered every 20 s. As the resulting time serious is very rugged and is poorly handled by model fitting algorithms, the smoothing of the time series is performed. Here we used the Empirical Mode

Decomposition (EMD) based denoising method [31]. First, the time series is decomposed into independent components (modes) representing variability of the time series at different frequency scales. Then the first mode of the signal with a highest frequency of oscillation is considered as a noise and is subtracted from the original time series. The resulting time series is used for fitting to model described by Eq. (1) and finding its coefficients using The Levenberg–Marquardt fitting algorithm. The reliability of fitting is evaluated using the odd-even reliability test by correlating scores on the odd-numbered items with scores on the even-numbered items.

2.5   Analysis of Saccadic Velocity and Directional Distribution

We use circular statistics to analyze the distribution of saccade velocity and movement direction over time and direction. We analyze the data during the first half and second half of the game session. The results, represented as Wind Rose plots, are used for comparison to detect the effects of eye fatigue. We also use linear regression to validate the trends observed in the data.

3   Experiments and Results

Fourteen healthy subjects (7 males and 7 females), aged 21–42, participated in the experiment. All subjects filled an informed consent form and the principles of the Helsinki declaration were adhered to. The subjects were asked to play game in a timed mode for 15 min. In order to capture eye movements and control the main character of the game by the gaze of the player, Tobii Eye Tracker 4C device was used. See a photo of a subject playing a game in Fig. 3.

Fig. 3. Sample playing the game

Our method requires that the time series of the game performance measure, first, must be smoothed to allow successful model fitting. To validate the used EMD-based denoising method, we compared it with other popular smoothing methods (moving mean, Savitzky-Golay and median filters) using time series smoothness characteristics (standard deviation, standard deviation of derivative, standard deviation of normalized derivative, number of sign changes, path length and cumulative jerk).

We used smoothness results to rank smoothing methods and performed the Nemenyi test to check if the differences between methods are statistically significant. The results of the Nemenyi test demonstrating suitability and superiority of the EMD-based smoothing method over other smoothing (filtering) methods for pre-processing the game performance time series are shown in Fig. 4. Note that 5 out of 6 tests ranked the EMD-based smoothing method as the best one for smoothing game data.

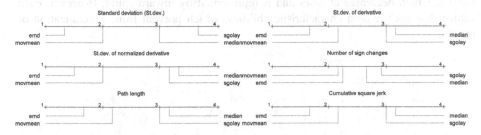

Fig. 4. Results of Nemenyi test comparing EMD-based smoothing method with moving mean, Savitzky-Golay and median filters when preprocessing the game performance time series

Next, the game performance data was fitted to damped oscillation wave model (Eq. 1). The results of model fitting for all subjects are given in Table 1. The overall reliability of model fitting using the odd-even test was 0.82 ± 0.08 (mean $\pm$ std. dev.). Interestingly, we noted a strong $r = 0.82$ positive correlation between amplitude and damping factor. That means that good starters usually have faster fatigue rates, whereas

Table 1. Model parameters of each subjects according to damped oscillation wave model

Subject no.	Coefficients of the model				Odd-even reliability
	Amplitude	Damping factor	Angular frequency	Phase	
1	7.6393	0.0317	−0.5407	−2.0307	0.8945
2	4.7579	0.0348	0.2657	0.5575	0.8046
3	11.5454	0.0248	12.1409	1.1401	0.8823
4	15.1602	0.0667	0.3611	−2.9749	0.7480
5	4.1099	0.0114	−0.7830	0.8002	0.9819
6	2.6943	0.0011	−1.1269	−2.4147	0.7095
7	1.5840	−0.0862	−0.2036	−1.1776	0.7852
8	0.5918	−0.0933	−0.4659	1.7690	0.8982
9	6.2494	−0.0060	0.5168	0.8993	0.7780
10	0.3761	−0.1147	0.3136	2.3527	0.7217
11	7.1254	−0.0062	−0.1551	−2.8604	0.7979
12	1.9880	−0.0483	−0.3842	−0.8683	0.8071
13	8.4314	0.0404	0.8598	−1.1648	0.9275
14	1.6275	−0.0571	0.2378	2.0307	0.8512

slow starters have less fatigue and even improve their game performance during playing. The model parameters can be used to categorize players according to their playing behavior into learners (with negative damping factor) and fatiguers (with positive damping factor).

Figure 5 represents changes in game performance using phase space plots. They show how the abilities to play are influenced by two processes: learning, which improves abilities and is represented by outward spiral in the phase space plot, and fatigue, which decreases abilities and is represented by inward spiral. However, each subject has his/her own characteristic abilities, which prevent from generalization of results.

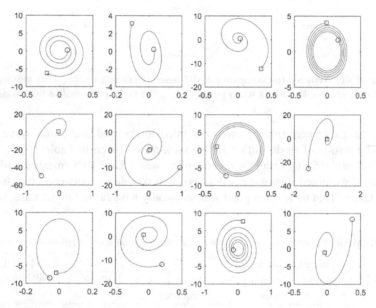

Fig. 5. Phase space plots of game performance characteristic fitted to damped oscillation model (□ - begin of game, ○ - end of game)

The results of changes in saccade velocity and spatial distribution (see an example in Fig. 6) show that saccade velocity decreases in time while spatial distribution of gazes becomes blurred and less focused on the main control axes (i.e., horizontal, W-E, and vertical, N-S) of the game indicating both the loss of ability to follow the game and the loss of accuracy in control.

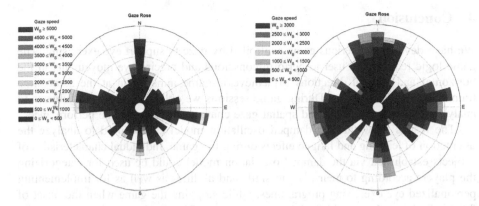

Fig. 6. Changes in saccade velocity and distribution during the game (Subject 5): first half (left) and second half (right)

To validate the claim, we have calculated the comparison operator

$$C(\Delta t) = \sum_{\Delta t=1}^{\Delta t_{max}} [v(t + \Delta t) < v(t)], \tag{2}$$

here $[\cdot]$ is the Iverson bracket operator, v is saccade velocity, Δt is time difference, and Δt_{max} is the largest time difference.

Then we performed the linear regression of C with respect to Δt as $C = b_0 + b_1 \Delta t$ for all subjects. The negative trend (i.e., decrease of saccade velocity) was confirmed for all subjects with $b_1 = -0.53 \pm 0.09$ and mean linear regression model correlation of 0.98. The values of Pearson correlation for each subject are presented in Fig. 7.

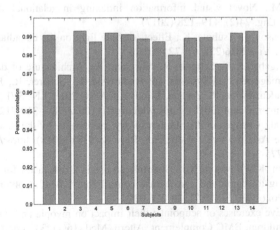

Fig. 7. Pearson correlation values confirming negative trend in saccade velocity

4 Conclusion

We have developed a serious game controlled by gaze to support eye exercising. The game logic requires the user to perform conscious and precise eye movements in the horizontal and vertical directions to achieve in-game aims while at the same time training the ocular muscles. During game sessions we collected data from subjects to analyze changes in temporal and spatial gaze characteristics and game performance.

The results show that the damped oscillation model can be used to analyze the interaction of learning and fatigue effects during the game. Individual characteristics of subjects established via the damped oscillation model could be used for categorizing the players according to their playing skills and abilities as well as for implementing personalized eye exercising programmes, while stopping the game when the onset of fatigue is detected to avoid further strain on eyes. The results are supported by the temporal and directional analysis of saccade velocity, which indicates the reduction of saccade velocity and gaze movement accuracy during the game due to eye fatigue.

Acknowledgement. The Authors would like to acknowledge contribution to this research from the "Diamond Grant 2016" No. 0080/DIA/2016/45 funded by the Polish Ministry of Science and Higher Education.

References

1. Statista: the statistics portal: Daily time spent on mobile by Millennial internet users worldwide from 2012 to 2017 (in minutes) (2018). https://www.statista.com/statistics/283138/millennials-daily-mobile-usage/
2. eMarketer: US Adults Now Spend 12 Hours 7 Minutes a Day Consuming Media (2017). https://www.emarketer.com/Article/US-Adults-Now-Spend-12-Hours-7-Minutes-Day-Consuming-Media/1015775
3. Korytkowski, M.: Novel visual information indexing in relational databases. Integr. Comput.-Aided Eng. **24**(2), 119–128 (2017)
4. Tosini, G., Ferguson, I., Tsubota, K.: Effects of blue light on the circadian system and eye physiology. Mol Vis. **2016**(22), 61–72 (2016)
5. Grycuk, R., Najgebauer, P., Scherer, R., Siwocha, A.: Architecture of database index for content-based image retrieval systems. In: Rutkowski, L., Scherer, R., Korytkowski, M., Pedrycz, W., Tadeusiewicz, R., Zurada, J. (eds.) ICAISC 2018. LNCS (LNAI), vol. 10842, pp. 36–47. Springer, Cham (2018). https://doi.org/10.1007/978-3-319-91262-2_4
6. Inomata, T., et al.: Changes in distribution of dry eye disease by the new 2016 diagnostic criteria from the Asia dry eye society. Sci. Rep. **8**(1918) (2018). https://doi.org/10.1038/s41598-018-19775-3
7. Moon, J.H., Kim, K.W., Moon, N.J.: Smartphone use is a risk factor for pediatric dry eye disease according to region and age: a case control study. BMC Ophthalmol. **16**(1), 188 (2016). https://doi.org/10.1186/s12886-016-0364-4
8. Lin, Z., et al.: Eye exercises of acupoints: their impact on myopia and visual symptoms in Chinese rural children. BMC Complement. Altern. Med. **16**(1), 349 (2016). https://doi.org/10.1186/s12906-016-1289-4
9. Kim, S.: Effects of yogic eye exercises on eye fatigue in undergraduate nursing students. J. Phys. Ther. Sci. **28**(6), 1813–1815 (2016). https://doi.org/10.1589/jpts.28.1813

10. Gabryel, M.: The bag-of-words methods with pareto-fronts for similar image retrieval. In: Damaševičius, R., Mikašytė, V. (eds.) ICIST 2017. CCIS, vol. 756, pp. 374–384. Springer, Cham (2017). https://doi.org/10.1007/978-3-319-67642-5_31
11. Kerkhoff, G., Keller, I., Ritter, V., Marquardt, C.: Repetitive optokinetic stimulation induces lasting recovery from visual neglect. Restor. Neurol. Neurosci. **24**(4–6), 357–369 (2006)
12. Di Noto, P., Uta, S., DeSouza, J.F.X.: Eye exercises enhance accuracy and letter recognition, but not reaction time, in a modified rapid serial visual presentation task. PLoS ONE **8**(3), e59244 (2013). https://doi.org/10.1371/journal.pone.0059244
13. Xiaoxiao, W., Jingjing, W.: Investigation and analysis on health care knowledge attitude and behavior of university students for myopia. Chin. Gen. Nurs. **9**, 2257 (2011)
14. Kang, M., et al.: Chinese eye exercises and myopia development in school age children: a nested case-control study. Sci. Rep. **6**, 28531 (2016). https://doi.org/10.1038/srep28531
15. Wouters, P., van Nimwegen, C., van Oostendorp, H., van Der Spek, E.D.: A meta-analysis of the cognitive and motivational effects of serious games. J. Educ. Psychol. **105**(2), 249–265 (2013). https://doi.org/10.1037/a0031311
16. Danevicius, E., Maskeliunas, R., Damaševicius, R., Polap, D., Woźniak, M.: A soft body physics simulator with computational offloading to the cloud. Inf. (Switzerland) **9**(12), 318 (2018). https://doi.org/10.3390/info9120318
17. Rodin, A., Shachak, A., Miller, A., Akopyan, V., Semenova, N.: Mobile apps for eye care in Canada: an analysis of the iTunes store. JMIR mHealth uHealth **5**(6), e84 (2017). https://doi.org/10.2196/mhealth.7055
18. Nabin, P.: Smartphone applications for amblyopia treatment: a review of current apps and professional involvement. Telemed. e-Health **24**(10) (2018). https://doi.org/10.1089/tmj.2017.0220
19. Wu, G., et al.: New software, "OKN-dot Test" for visual rehabilitation for eye patients. Invest. Ophthalmol. Vis. Sci. **55**(13), 2569 (2014)
20. Lohr, D.J., Abdulin, E., Komogortsev, O.V.: Detecting the onset of eye fatigue in a live framework. In: Eye Tracking Research and Applications Symposium (ETRA), vol. 14, pp. 315–316 (2016). https://doi.org/10.1145/2857491.2884058
21. Gabryel, M.: Data analysis algorithm for click fraud recognition. In: Damaševičius, R., Vasiljevienė, G. (eds.) ICIST 2018. CCIS, vol. 920, pp. 437–446. Springer, Cham (2018). https://doi.org/10.1007/978-3-319-99972-2_36
22. Thilanka, L.G.A., Ekanayake, Y., Weerasinghe, A.R.:. Personalized eye fatigue detection for mobile users. In: 16th International Conference on Advances in ICT for Emerging Regions, ICTer 2016, pp. 296–303 (2017). https://doi.org/10.1109/icter.2016.7829934
23. Wang, Y., et al.: Eye fatigue assessment using unobtrusive eye tracker. IEEE Access **6**, 55948–55962 (2018). https://doi.org/10.1109/ACCESS.2018.2869624
24. Vasiljevas, M., Gedminas, T., Ševčenko, A., Jančiukas, M., Blažauskas, T., Damaševičius, R.: Modelling eye fatigue in gaze spelling task. In: 2016 IEEE 12th International Conference on Intelligent Computer Communication and Processing, ICCP 2016, pp. 95–102 (2016). https://doi.org/10.1109/iccp.2016.7737129
25. Hellard, P., Avalos, M., Lacoste, L., Barale, F., Chatard, J., Millet, G.P.: Assessing the limitations of the banister model in monitoring training. J. Sports Sci. **24**(5), 509–520 (2006). https://doi.org/10.1080/02640410500244697
26. Brunyé, T.T., Mahoney, C.R., Augustyn, J.S., Taylor, H.A.: Horizontal saccadic eye movements enhance the retrieval of landmark shape and location information. Brain Cogn. **70**, 279–288 (2009). https://doi.org/10.1016/j.bandc.2009.03.003
27. Dormans, J.: Simulating mechanics to study emergence in games. In: Artificial Intelligence in the Game Design Process, vol. 2, no. 6.2, p. 5-2 (2011)

28. Shneiderman, B., Plaisant, C.: Designing the User Interface - Strategies for Effective Human-Computer Interaction, 5th edn. Addison-Wesley, Boston (2010)
29. Calvert, T.W., Banister, E.W., Savage, M.V.: A systems model of the effects of training on physical performance. SMC Syst. Man Cybern. 2, 94–102 (1976)
30. Damasevicius, R., Martisius, I., Jusas, V., Birvinskas, D.: Fractional delay time embedding of EEG signals into high dimensional phase space. Electron. Electr. Eng. 20(8), 55–58 (2014). https://doi.org/10.5755/j01.eee.20.8.8441
31. Damasevicius, R., Vasiljevas, M., Martisius, I., Jusas, V., Birvinskas, D., Wozniak, M.: BoostEMD: an extension of EMD method and its application for denoising of EMG signals. Electron. Electr. Eng. 21(6), 57–61 (2015). https://doi.org/10.5755/j01.eee.21.6.13763

Bioinformatics, Biometrics and Medical Applications

Raw G-Band Chromosome Image Segmentation Using U-Net Based Neural Network

Emrecan Altinsoy[1]($\boxtimes$), Can Yilmaz[1], Juan Wen[2], Lingqian Wu[2],
Jie Yang[1], and Yuemin Zhu[3]

[1] School of Electronic, Information and Electrical Engineering,
Shanghai Jiao Tong University, Shanghai 200240, China
{emrecanaltinsoy,montagnard,jieyang}@sjtu.edu.cn
[2] Center for Medical Genetics, School of Life Sciences, Central South University,
Changsha 410078, China
{juanwen,wulingqian}@sklmg.edu.cn
[3] Creatis, INSA Lyon, Villeurbanne, France
zhu@creatis.insa-lyon.fr

Abstract. Chromosome analysis plays an important role in investigating one's genetic disorders and abnormalities. Many works are done on automating this operation for decades. Segmentation of chromosomes is the first step of this process, and it is essential for the next step which is classification. However, it is not an easy task due to a very noisy background, the presence of other cells and the variation of chromosome structures. In this paper, we propose a raw G-band chromosome image segmentation method using U-net based convolutional neural network. To this end, we constructed a raw G-band chromosome dataset which consists of 40 images. In order to prevent over-fitting, we implemented augmentations on the training and the validation set images. The trained model achieved 96.97% dice score. The experimental results showed that, the convolutional neural network can provide satisfying results, especially with highly noisy images.

Keywords: Raw G-band chromosome image · Segmentation · U-net ·
Convolutional neural network · Deep learning

1 Introduction

Chromosomes are considered the main genetic information carriers. Every healthy individual has 46 chromosomes in total, 22 pairs of non-sex and two sex chromosomes. Analyzing the quantity and the structure of these chromosomes helps us to investigate one's genetic disorders (e.g. Down syndrome and

This research is partly supported by NSFC, China (No: 61572315), Committee of Science and Technology, Shanghai, China (No. 17JC1403000) and 973 Plan, China (No. 2015CB856004).

© Springer Nature Switzerland AG 2019
L. Rutkowski et al. (Eds.): ICAISC 2019, LNAI 11509, pp. 117–126, 2019.
https://doi.org/10.1007/978-3-030-20915-5_11

Turner syndrome) and genetic abnormalities [3]. It is difficult to differentiate the chromosomes under a light microscope. Therefore, scientists developed different staining methods (bandings), which are used to color different parts of the chromosomes, in order to display their structural details. These bandings make the chromosome identification easier and more reliable. The most known ones are G-banding, Q-banding, R-banding, and C-banding. G-band images are obtained by using Giemsa dye, which reacts differently for each nucleic acid base pairs. It leads to a set of bright or dark gray bands throughout the chromosomes. Today, G-banding is the most used method for karyotyping.

Thanks to the improvements in computer science in the last 30 years, the use of computers on chromosome analysis is now achievable. Automated chromosome analysis has been studied by many researchers. Preprocessing and segmentation of chromosomes from the background pixels are the first step for an automated solution and necessary for the next steps, which are the classification of chromosomes and karyotyping. However, it is a challenging task for several reasons: a very noisy background, the presence of other cells and the variation of chromosome structures.

Otsu thresholding method [11] was used by Ji [5]. However, using a global threshold value caused losses on the bright chromosome parts and the chromosome satellites. To cope with this issue, Ji [6] and Stanley [15] proposed a local re-thresholding method. This method consists of two steps. Firstly, Otsu thresholding is applied on the whole image. Secondly, the objects are separated from the segmented image using connected components and then applied a second Otsu thresholding on each object. Grisan et al. [4] presented locally adaptive thresholding for the segmentation of Q-band chromosome images. The images are divided into small squares, 100 pixels by 100 pixels, and Otsu thresholding was applied on each square. Then, the squares are resized to the original image size using bilinear interpolation to obtain a pixel-wise map. Sugapriyaa et al. [16] adopted this method and applied it on G-band metaphase images. Lerner [9], Cao et al. [1] and Soumya [14] employed clustering based segmentation methods for the chromosome and background separation, such as K-means clustering and fuzzy C-means clustering algorithm. Poletti et al. [12] implemented and compared the performance of different thresholding methods on Q-band chromosome images in their review paper. As observed in the article, adaptive and region based thresholding methods provided better results compared to global thresholding methods. Yilmaz et al. [17] cleared the background pixels of G-band chromosome images by implementing a thresholding method based on the peak value of the image histogram. Afterward, the interphase cells were removed using their characteristics and Gaussian filter was applied to obtain clear chromosome borders. Unlike the others, in [17] raw images are used. Most of the works carried in this field need human interaction to achieve good results. In addition, the used images are preprocessed: the chromosomes are already separated from the background pixels and the noise is reduced or removed.

In this paper, we introduced a U-net [13] based neural network for segmentation of raw G-band chromosome images. First, we created the dataset with the images taken from Renji Hospital. For the purpose of improving the segmentation results and to prevent over-fitting, we implemented augmentations on the images in the dataset. For the evaluation of the model, Jaccard distance loss and dice coefficient loss are employed as metrics, since these metrics provide a better evaluation for the instance segmentation processes. Finally, we compared the segmentation results with the local adaptive thresholding results.

2   Method

2.1   Dataset and Data Augmentation

For the experiments, the dataset is created with the images taken from Renji Hospital. It consists of 40 raw G-band chromosome images, 25 images for the training set, 5 images for the validation set and 10 images for the test set. The images are all in the same resolution, 1200×1600 pixels. However, it is reduced to 480×640 pixels to be able to train the model with the available GPU memory. The training set and validation set images are labeled manually. Raw G-band chromosome image and its mask are shown in Fig. 1.

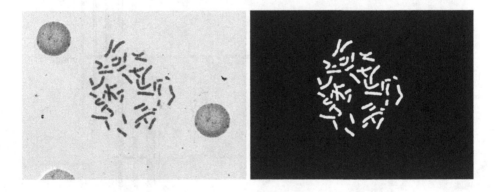

Fig. 1. Raw G-band chromosome image and its mask.

Since the images in the dataset are not various and not numerous enough to obtain satisfactory results and to prevent over-fitting, augmentations are used to increase the number of images in the training set and in the validation set up to 3500 and 700, respectively. The summary of the applied augmentation methods are given in Table 1.

2.2   U-Net Based Neural Network

Segmentation of medical images has constraints due to its characteristics, such as detailed patterns, unclear object boundaries, among others. Long et al. [10] proposed to use skip connections which combine two convolutional layers (encoding

Table 1. Summary of applied augmentations

Method	Range
Rotation	±45°
Horizontal flip	50% chance
Vertical flip	50% chance
Width shift	5% of the total width
Height shift	5% of the total height
Shear intensity	10° in the counter-clockwise direction
Zoom	±10%

and decoding layers) to generate better segmentation results. Drozdzal et al. indicated that skip connections can be used on biomedical images [2]. Ronneberger et al. [13] also adopted this idea and proposed the original U-net architecture for biomedical image segmentation.

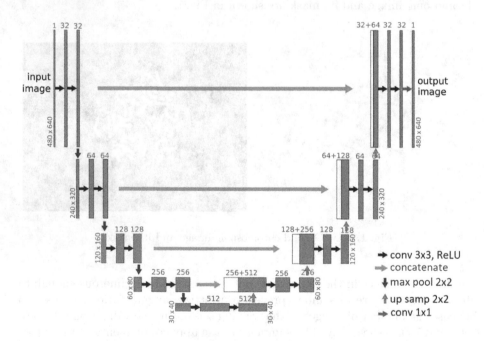

Fig. 2. U-net architecture

Original U-net model [13] is symmetrical fully convolutional neural network and it consists of two parts which are down-sampling (left side) and up-sampling (right side). In total the network has 9 convolutional blocks and each block consists of two convolutional layers with 3 × 3 kernel size. On the down-sampling part, each convolutional block is followed by a max pooling layer with 2×2 pool size. After every max pooling layer, the size of the feature maps is divided by two and the number of feature maps is duplicated by two. On the up-sampling part, before every convolutional block, there is an up-sampling layer with the size of 2×2. The output of the up-sampling layers concatenates with the corresponding feature maps from the down-sampling part. Unlike the down-sampling part, after every convolutional block, the size of the feature maps is duplicated by two and the number of feature maps divided by two. All convolutional layers use ReLU as an activation function, except the last one which uses sigmoid function.

In this study, the U-net architecture (Fig. 2) is used with several changes:

- The number of the feature maps are half of the original U-net architecture to be able to train the model with the available GPU memory.
- Input and Output image sizes are changed to 480×640.
- Since the number of future maps is large compared to the number of images in the training dataset, to avoid over-fitting dropout layer is added after 4th (before the max pooling layer) and 5th convolutional blocks.
- Adam optimizer [8] is used instead of stochastic gradient descent optimizer.
- Jaccard distance loss [7] and dice similarity coefficient are used for the evaluation of the model.

2.3   Evaluation Metrics

Jaccard Index. In biomedical image segmentation, binary cross-entropy is not a good indicator for the evaluation. Instead, the Jaccard index, also known as intersection over union score (IoU), is widely used. It measures the similarity between ground truth and predicted masks. It is defined as the intersection of the masks divided by the union of the masks and it returns a value between 0 and 1.

$$Jacc = \frac{|M_{pred} \cap M_{truth}|}{|M_{pred} \cup M_{truth}|} = \frac{|M_{pred} \cap M_{truth}|}{|M_{pred}| + |M_{truth}| - |M_{pred} \cap M_{truth}|}$$

$$= \frac{\text{True Positive}}{\text{Union}} \qquad (1)$$

where M_{pred} is the vector of predicted mask and M_{truth} is the vector of ground truth mask.

As mentioned before, for the evaluation of the model, Jaccard distance loss [7] is used. Jaccard distance measures the dissimilarity between ground truth and the predicted masks, and it can be derived as

$$1 - Jacc = \frac{|M_{pred} \setminus M_{truth}| + |M_{truth} \setminus M_{pred}|}{|M_{pred} \cup M_{truth}|}$$

$$= \frac{\text{False Positive} + \text{False Negative}}{\text{Union}} \qquad (2)$$

Dice Similarity Coefficient. Dice similarity coefficient (DSC) is the other metric widely employed in instance segmentation problems. It calculates the spatial overlap between the predicted mask and the ground truth mask. It is defined as two times the intersection of the ground truth and the predicted masks divided by the sum of the masks (Eq. 3) and it returns a value between 0 and 1.

$$DSC = \frac{2 \times |M_{pred} \cap M_{truth}|}{|M_{pred}| + |M_{truth}|}$$

$$= \frac{2 \times \text{True Positive}}{\text{False Positive} + \text{False Negative} + (2 \times \text{True Positive})} \qquad (3)$$

3 Experiments

3.1 Training

The model is implemented with Keras. As mentioned earlier, Adam optimizer [8] is adopted for the model weights estimation. The beginning learning rate is set to 0.0001, batch size is set to 2 and the number of epochs is set to 100. Keras callback functions are used during the training. The learning rate is multiplied by 0.2 when the loss metric stopped improving for two epochs. On the 22nd epoch, the training was stopped, because the loss metric had not been improved for the last 5 epochs. At the end of the training, the lowest Jaccard distance loss recorded on the 17th epoch as 0.0589. The dice similarity coefficient was recorded as 96.97%. Learning curves of Jaccard distance loss and dice similarity coefficient are shown in Fig. 3.

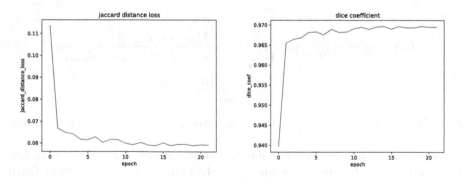

Fig. 3. Jaccard distance loss and dice similarity coefficient learning curves

3.2 Results

The trained model is tested on several images. It takes around 0.25 s to segment one image. Segmentation results are depicted in Fig. 4. As it can be observed, the proposed method also clears the interphase cells with the background pixels. Besides, the chromosome boundaries are almost completely preserved.

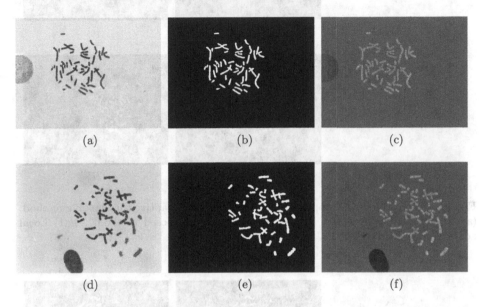

(a)   (b)   (c)

(d)   (e)   (f)

Fig. 4. Segmentation results. (a) (d) Raw G-band chromosome images, (b) (e) The predicted masks, (c) (f) Overlayed predicted masks

The proposed method is compared with the local adaptive thresholding method. The comparison results of the two methods are shown in Figs. 5 and 6. When the G-band chromosome image is not very noisy, both methods provide satisfying results. However, the proposed method produces clearer chromosome borders than the local adaptive thresholding method. When the input image is highly noisy, the local adaptive thresholding method provides very poor results. On the contrary, the proposed method segments the chromosomes with very small errors. The segmentation errors are marked with red ellipses in Fig. 6b and e.

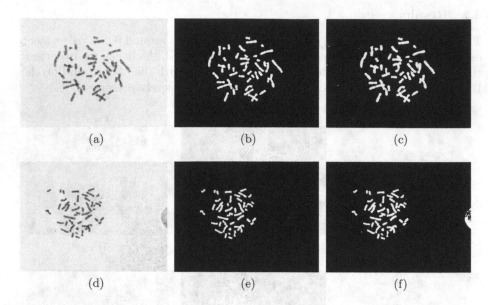

Fig. 5. Comparison of the proposed method and locally adaptive thresholding method. (a) (d) Original images, (b) (e) Predictions of the proposed method, (c) (f) Local adaptive thresholding results

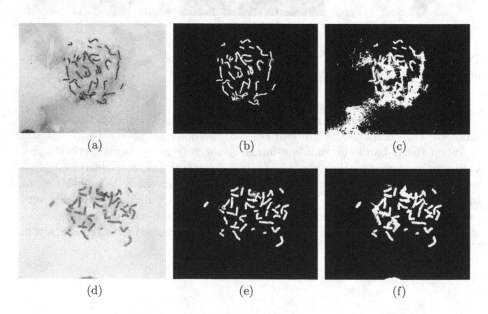

Fig. 6. Comparison of the proposed method and locally adaptive thresholding method. (a) (d) Original highly noisy images, (b) (e) Predictions of the proposed method, (c) (f) Local adaptive thresholding results

4   Conclusion

In this paper, we presented a segmentation method for raw G-band chromosome images using U-net based convolutional neural network. The trained model achieved a 96.97% dice score. The experimental results showed that the convolutional neural network provides satisfying results for the segmentation task. Furthermore, the proposed method segmented highly noisy images with small errors compared to local adaptive thresholding method. The residual errors occured due to lack of image variety in the dataset. For this reason, in the future, we plan to increase the quantity and the diversity of the images in the dataset. Additionally, we intend to increase the segmentation accuracy by using multi-class labels, such as chromosomes, interphase cells, and background masks, instead of using single class mask input.

References

1. Cao, H., Wang, Y.P.: Segmentation of M-FISH images for improved classification of chromosomes with an adaptive fuzzy C-means clustering algorithm. In: 2011 IEEE International Symposium on Biomedical Imaging: From Nano to Macro, pp. 1442–1445. IEEE (2011)
2. Drozdzal, M., Vorontsov, E., Chartrand, G., Kadoury, S., Pal, C.: The importance of skip connections in biomedical image segmentation. In: Carneiro, G., et al. (eds.) LABELS/DLMIA-2016. LNCS, vol. 10008, pp. 179–187. Springer, Cham (2016). https://doi.org/10.1007/978-3-319-46976-8_19
3. Graham, J., Piper, J.: Automatic karyotype analysis. In: Gosden, J.R. (ed.) Chromosome Analysis Protocols. MIMB, pp. 141–185. Springer, Cham (1994). https://doi.org/10.1385/0-89603-289-2:141
4. Grisan, E., Poletti, E., Ruggeri, A.: Automatic segmentation and disentangling of chromosomes in Q-band prometaphase images. IEEE Trans. Inf. Technol. Biomed. 13(4), 575–581 (2009)
5. Ji, L.: Intelligent splitting in the chromosome domain. Pattern Recognit. 22(5), 519–532 (1989). https://doi.org/10.1016/0031-3203(89)90021-6
6. Ji, L.: Fully automatic chromosome segmentation. Cytom.: J. Int. Soc. Anal. Cytol. 17(3), 196–208 (1994)
7. Kayalibay, B., Jensen, G., van der Smagt, P.: CNN-based segmentation of medical imaging data. arXiv preprint arXiv:1701.03056 (2017)
8. Kingma, D.P., Ba, J.: Adam: a method for stochastic optimization. arXiv preprint arXiv:1412.6980 (2014)
9. Lerner, B.: Toward a completely automatic neural-network-based human chromosome analysis. IEEE Trans. Syst. Man Cybern. Part B (Cybern.) 28(4), 544–552 (1998)
10. Long, J., Shelhamer, E., Darrell, T.: Fully convolutional networks for semantic segmentation. In: Proceedings of the IEEE Conference on Computer Vision and Pattern Recognition, pp. 3431–3440 (2015)
11. Otsu, N.: A threshold selection method from gray-level histograms. IEEE Trans. Syst. Man Cybern. 9(1), 62–66 (1979). https://doi.org/10.1109/TSMC.1979.4310076

12. Poletti, E., Zappelli, F., Ruggeri, A., Grisan, E.: A review of thresholding strategies applied to human chromosome segmentation. Comput. Methods Programs Biomed. **108**(2), 679–688 (2012)
13. Ronneberger, O., Fischer, P., Brox, T.: U-Net: convolutional networks for biomedical image segmentation. In: Navab, N., Hornegger, J., Wells, W.M., Frangi, A.F. (eds.) MICCAI 2015. LNCS, vol. 9351, pp. 234–241. Springer, Cham (2015). https://doi.org/10.1007/978-3-319-24574-4_28
14. Soumya, D., Arya, V.: Chromosome segmentation using k-means clustering. Int. J. Sci. Eng. Res. **4**(9), 937–940 (2013)
15. Stanley, R.J., Keller, J.M., Gader, P., Caldwell, C.W.: Data-driven homologue matching for chromosome identification. IEEE Trans. Med. Imaging **17**(3), 451–462 (1998)
16. Sugapriyaa, T., Kaviyapriya, P., Gomathi, P.: Segmentation and extraction of chromosomes from G-band metaphase images. Indian J. Sci. Technol. **11**(18) (2018)
17. Yilmaz, I.C., Yang, J., Altinsoy, E., Zhou, L.: An improved segmentation for raw G-band chromosome images. In: The 2018 5th International Conference on Systems and Informatics, pp. 944–950. IEEE (2018)

Hybrid Ant Fuzzy Algorithm for MRI Images Segmentation

Alexander Bozhenyuk[1] , Samer El-Khatib[1] , Janusz Kacprzyk[2] ,
Margarita Knyazeva[1(✉)] , and Sergey Rodzin[1]

[1] Southern Federal University, Nekrasovskiy Street, 44, 347928 Taganrog, Russia
{avb002,srodzin}@yandex.ru, samerel_khatib@mail.ru,
margarita.knyazeva@gmail.com
[2] Systems Research Institute Polish Academy of Sciences,
Newelska 6, 01-447 Warsaw, Poland
janusz.kacprzyk@ibspan.waw.pl

Abstract. Image segmentation is the process of subdividing an image
into regions that are consistent and homogeneous in some characteristics. Image segmentation is indeed a vital process in the early diagnosis
of abnormalities and treatment planning. The segmentation algorithms
are applied to extract the anatomical structures and anomalies from
medical images. Segmentation of Magnetic Resonance Imaging (MRI)
requires a lot of time when it is performed by medical specialists. The
task of automation of recognition is topical in case the correct evaluation
is given. The different types of segmentation algorithms are discussed
in this paper. It is true that there is no universal algorithm for medical image segmentation, wherein, the choice depends upon the image
modality, characteristics of region of interest and application. There is
neither a single segmentation model for all medical image modalities nor
all methods are efficient for a specific medical image modality. In image
processing and computer vision, segmentation is still a challenging problem in many real time applications and hence more research work is
required. The Hybrid Ant Fuzzy Algorithm (HAFA) for the segmentation of MRI is considered in this paper. The parameters of the HAFA
are examined for different groups of MRI images. Medical images from
OsiriX set and real patient pictures were used to test the algorithm.
The experimental results show that the proposed algorithm has good
performance and accuracy in comparison to analogues.

Keywords: Magnetic resonance imaging · Image segmentation ·
Fuzzy c-means · Ant colony optimization

1 Introduction

Modern medical diagnostics are impossible without processing medical images.
Medical images of magnetic resonance imaging (MRI) are complex and variable.

This work has been supported by the Ministry of Education and Science of the Russian
Federation (Project part, State task 2.918.2017).

L. Rutkowski et al. (Eds.): ICAISC 2019, LNAI 11509, pp. 127–137, 2019.
https://doi.org/10.1007/978-3-030-20915-5_12

They are used to distinguish pathological tissues from normal tissues. Nowadays, millions of medical images are regularly produced and analyzed in medical centers. One of the most difficult tasks in image processing is segmentation. All subsequent processing steps, such as classification, image retrieval and identification, directly depend on the results of segmentation [1]. Segmentation based on MRI data is very important but at the same time it is a time-consuming task if it is performed manually by medical specialists. Therefore, there is a need for computer analysis of image to facilitate diagnosis. The task of automation MRI recognition is an actual task, provided that proper evaluation. The main difficulty of the segmentation process is the presence of additional factors that are inherent in MRI data, namely: variety of the areas of interest in size and position, overlapping tumors with normal tissue, deforming and abnormal geometry of healthy tissues, background variability, noise and artifacts in the images [2].

In this paper we consider a hybrid ant fuzzy algorithm (HAFA) for segmentation 2D magnetic resonance images.

2   Methods of Image Segmentation

Segmentation is the process of dividing the original image of $W \times H$ size into K segments in such a way that they differ as much as possible from each other and represent objects of the original image. Segmentation is an important part of automated image recognition systems. It is widely used in studies devoted to intellectual analysis of data, decision making, and machine learning. Segmentation of MRI is used to diagnose many diseases. Numerous publications are devoted to the segmentation problem [3–11]. The rising levels of awareness about benefits of early diagnosis and affordability of advanced healthcare services due to the rising economic stability of the population are the chief reasons behind this.

An extensive review of the algorithms for the segmentation of medical images is presented in [12]. In extension, this literature review indeed paves an ample platform to the researchers for better understanding of various segmentation techniques and its characteristics for medical images. There are two main classes of segmentation algorithms: automatic and interactive. In automatic segmentation, user participation is not required. In interactive segmentation, additional information is required from the user. The most well-known algorithms for automatic segmentation are k-means algorithm, Histogram thresholding, Image domain or Region Based Techniques, Neural network based techniques, Fuzzy Techniques, Hybrid techniques, etc. [13,14]. Among the interactive methods, the best results are obtained by graph algorithms [15]. However, there is no universal algorithm for segmenting MRI images.

The k-means algorithm involves rapid cluster analysis by isolating K segments (clusters), which are located at the maximum distance from each other. The algorithm guarantees the convergence, but the run time depends on the initial set of segments. The drawbacks of the algorithm are: sensitivity to the noise; the speed of its operation decreases with large amounts of data; number of segments must be pre-specified [16].

One of the best graph algorithms is the Normalized Cut algorithm and its modifications [17]. Most of the graph cutting algorithms have the complexity $O(J)$, but they require considerable memory to store distance matrices of size $J \times J$, where J is the number of pixels. Therefore, it is difficult to apply them to high-dimensional images. The problem of constructing algorithms for segmenting the entire image based on graph clustering with acceptable memory and speed requirements remains relevant.

The neural network approach [18] for solving the image segmentation problem is not entirely appropriate. In this approach operator participation and preliminary image processing are required. Different initial conditions for MRI lead to different end results of segmentation. The training of the neural network is realized on the basis of random selection, and as a result, the resulting weight coefficients for the output neurons depend on the input sequence. The completion of the learning process is not based on rigorous optimization mathematical models. Although it is impossible to exclude the use of neural networks as part of an integrated system of image segmentation. There is a fuzzy algorithm for c-means (FCM) image segmentation [19], which shows good accuracy characteristics, but its results depend on the specificity of the images. The solution is obtained as a result of multiple iterations of the algorithm, which can complicate the segmentation process in real time.

One of the best population-type algorithms is the genetic algorithm (GA) for segmentation. It is a search method that uses evolution operators, such as selection, crossover, and mutation [20]. At the beginning, an initial population of chromosomes is randomly generated, each of which represents a variant of the solution. Then the fitness function of each chromosome is calculated and, according to it, a new population of the fittest individuals is created using crossover and mutation. For each population, segment centers are recalculated using the best chromosome from the current population. New centers are obtained, and the algorithm continues to work until it reaches the stopping criterion. The genetic algorithm does not guarantee finding the optimal solution, but it can show good results compared to other segmentation algorithms. There are examples of successful application of the ant colony (ACO) algorithm for the MRI segmentation [21]. The idea of the ant algorithm is to simulate the behavior of ants associated with their ability to quickly find the shortest path from an anthill to a food source and adapt to changing conditions, finding a new optimal path. During the movement, the ant leaves the pheromone on its way, and this information is used by other ants to select the path. Ants dynamically cluster an image into independent segments that include only similar pixels.

None of the algorithms is ideal, it is necessary to use hybrid segmentation, which is composed of different algorithms.

3   Hybrid Ant Fuzzy Algorithm (HAFA) for Segmentation

A distinctive feature of the proposed hybrid ant fuzzy algorithm is the use of the c- means algorithm for recalculating the center of each segment and applying a superposition of several optimality criteria for the resulting solutions, taking into account both the color and geometric characteristics of the image. The image can be either color or halftone, with different initial conditions (noise, high contrast, fuzziness). The algorithm can be used in interactive or automatic.

Control parameters for setting the algorithm are the following variables: K – the number of segments to divide the original image into; m – number of ants that perform the segmentation; n_0 – the maximum number of iterations in the algorithm to find the solution; α – parameter that controls the degree of influence of the pheromone level; β – parameter that controls the membership function of the pixel to a certain segment.

The main idea of the algorithm is as follows. At the first step of the algorithm, the values of the number of segments K are set and their centers are initialized. On the second step, the membership function for each pixel of the image belonging to a certain cluster is determined. The membership function is inversely proportional to the distance between the pixel, the center of the segment and the variable τ, which represents the level of pheromone:

$$\mu_i(X_n) = \frac{[\tau_i(X_n)]^a \times [\eta_i(X_n)]^\beta}{\sum\limits_{j=0}^{K} [\tau_j(X_n)]^a \times [\eta_j(X_n)]^\beta}, \tag{1}$$

where $\mu_i(X_n)$ is membership degree of the pixel X_n belonging to segment i; $\tau_i(X_n)$ - information about pheromone; $\eta_i(X_n)$ - a heuristic variable about the belonging of the pixel $\mu_i(X_n)$ to the segment i. Heuristic variable $\eta_i(X_n)$ is calculated by the following equation:

$$\eta_i(X_n) = \frac{b}{CDist(X_n, CC_i) \times PDist(X_n, PC_i)}, \tag{2}$$

where CC_i is the i-th spectral center; PC_i - i-th spatial center of the segment; $CDist(X_n, CC_i)$ is a distance between (X_n, CC_i) the pixel color characteristics; $PDist(X_n, PC_i)$ - Euclidean distance between (X_n, PC_i) according to the location of the pixel in the image; b - constant that is used to balance the values ν and θ. In Eq. (2) color and geometric information are used simultaneously. The values of $CDist$ and $PDist$ are defined as:

$$CDist(X_n, CC_i) = Int(X_n) - Int(CC_i)$$

where $Int(X_n)$ is the intensity of the pixel X_n; $Int(CC_i)$ is the intensity of the pixel CC_i;

$$PDist(X_n, PC_i) = \sqrt{(X_n x - PC_i x)^2 + (X_n y - PC_i y)^2}$$

where $X_n x$ is the x-coordinate of the pixel X_n; $PC_i x$ is the x-coordinate of the pixel PC_i; $X_n y$ is the y-coordinate of the pixel X_n; $PC_i y$ is the y-coordinate of the pixel PC_i.

The objective function (fitness function) is important for the bioinspired ant method. Different target functions are used in ant methods [22–26], which have their advantages and disadvantages. To solve the problem of image segmentation, the following set of rules is used as a criterion for finding the optimal solution in the proposed ant method:

1. $\max \left(\sum\limits_{i=1..m} \sum\limits_{k=1..K-1} \sum\limits_{j=k+1..K} CDist(C_k, C_j) \right)$ - the maximum of the sum of the color distances between the center of the segments for all ants, where $CDist$ is the color distance between two pixels, C_k is the center of segment k;

2. $\min \left(\sum\limits_{i=1..m} \sum\limits_{k=1..K} \sum\limits_{p=1..S_k} PDist(C_k, X_p) \right)$ - the minimum value of the sums of the geometrical distances between the centers of the segments and the pixels in the segment, where S_k is the number of pixels in the segment k, $PDist(C_k, X_p)$ is the Euclidean distance between C_k and X_p;

3. $\min \left(\sum\limits_{i=1..m} \sum\limits_{k=1..K} \sum\limits_{p=1..S_k} CDist(C_k, X_p) \right)$ - the minimum value of the sum of the color distances between the center of the segments and the pixels in the segment, where $CDist(C_k, X_p)$ is the color distance between C_k and X_p.

The target function for the ant mi is as follows:

$$f_1(m_i) = \sum_{k=1..K-1} \sum_{j=k+1..K} CDist\,(C_{m_ik}, C_{m_ij}) \rightarrow \max, \tag{3}$$

$$f_2(m_i) = \sum_{k=1..K-1} \sum_{p=1..S_{m_ik}} PDist\,(C_{m_ik}, C_{m_ip}) \rightarrow \min, \tag{4}$$

$$f_3(m_i) = \sum_{k=1..K-1} \sum_{p=1..S_{m_ik}} CDist\,(C_{m_ik}, C_{m_ip}) \rightarrow \min, \tag{5}$$

Next, a multicriteria problem is solved by the method of linear scalarization (additive convolution):

- we determine the coefficients of importance (weight) c_i for each of the objective functions $f_1(m_i)$, $f_2(m_i)$, $f_3(m_i)$;
- we replace the signs of functions in order to move from the minimization task to the maximization task;
- we perform the normalization of objective functions by the formula:

$$\tilde{f}_r(m_i) = \frac{f_r(m_i) - f_r^{\min}}{f_r^{\max} - f_r^{\min}}, r = 1, 2, 3$$

- we construct an additive objective function.

Since there is no information on the importance of functions $f_1(m_i)$, $f_2(m_i)$, $f_3(m_i)$ we set $c_r = 1/3$ $(r = 1, 2, 3)$.

The minimization problem can be turned into a task to search for a maximum by changing the sign of the functions $f_2(m_i)$, $f_3(m_i)$ inverse. This is due to the fact that the function $(-f)$ reaches its maximum value at those points where the function f takes the smallest value. This means that the conditions [f → min] and [(−f) → max] are equivalent.

Then the additive objective function has the form:

$$f = \frac{1}{3}\widetilde{f_1}(m_i) - \frac{1}{3}\widetilde{f_2}(m_i) - \frac{1}{3}\widetilde{f_3}(m_i), \tag{6}$$

After the best solution is chosen, the value of the pheromone level is updated. The level of pheromone is determined proportionally to the minimum distance between each pair of cluster centers and inversely proportional to the distance between each pixel and its center. Thus, the value of the pheromone level increases with the increase in the distance between the cluster centers, as well as the compactness of the pixels in the cluster. Under the same conditions, the membership degree of the pixel to the cluster is increased. The proposed level of pheromone is updated according to the following equation:

$$\tau_i(X_n) \leftarrow (1-\rho)\tau_i(X_n) + \sum_i \Delta\tau_i(X_n), \tag{7}$$

where ρ is the evaporation coefficient $0 \leq \rho \leq 1$, which affects the previously established level of pheromone. Due to this coefficient, the influence of later priority decisions is strengthened, and the influence of earlier decisions is weakened. The parameter $\Delta\tau_i(X_n)$ in Eq. (7) is the difference in pheromone level, compared to the previous best solution. In other words, this is the evaporation of pheromone, which is calculated according to the following equation:

$$\Delta\tau_i(X_n) = \begin{cases} \frac{Q \times Min(k')}{AvgCDist(k',i) \times AvgPDist(k',i)}, \\ 0, \end{cases} \tag{8}$$

where Q is a positive constant, which is determined by the amount of pheromone added by the ants; $Min(k')$ is the minimum of the color distances between each two cluster centers, found by the ant k' (the most successful ant); $AvgCDist(k',i)$ is the mean value of the color distances and $AvgPDist(k',i)$ is the average value of the spatial Euclidean distances between each pixel and the centers (color and spatial) for the most successful ant.

The level of pheromone at the initial stage is set to 1. After calculating and updating the pheromone level, the segment centers are updated by recalculating the average pixel value in each segment. The c-means procedure splits a set of pixels into a specified number of fuzzy sets. The characteristic of the splitting is the usage of a fuzzy U with elements u_{ij} that determine the membership degree of the i-th element of the original set of pixels to the j-th segment. Segments are described by their centers and the task of minimizing the function of Bezdek [27] with the selected fuzzification parameter is solved. The procedure continues until the values of the segment center are changed significantly. The process of clustering is performed by m ants, each of which ultimately finds its own individual solution. After the ants segmented the image, the best solution is selected for the current iteration. Pheromone level is increased for better solution and cluster centers are updated. Thus, at each iteration, each of the m ants finds an individual solution, which is corrected by the overall best solution found by all the ants. This is repeated until a solution is found that satisfies all the given conditions. Segmentation is terminated when the stopping criterion is fulfilled. As the stop criterion the algorithm uses the limitation on maximum number of iterations $n_0 \leq 30$, or there are no changes for the cluster centers after 3 iterations.

The following HAFA pseudocode is presented below:

1. Initialize the main parameters of the method: the value of the pheromone level is equal to 1; the number of clusters – K; the number of ants – m; the maximum number of iterations – n_0.
2. Initialize m ants for K randomly selected cluster centers.
3. Let each ant connect each pixel Xn to one of the clusters i randomly, with membership function $\mu_i(X_n)$ according to the expression (1).
4. Calculate the new centers of clusters. If the new centers coincide with the previous centers, then go to 5, if not, go to 3.
5. Keep the best solution from all found by m ants according to the expressions (3), (4), and (6).
6. Update the level of pheromone for each pixel according to expressions (7) and (8).
7. Correct the overall best solution based on the individual solutions found for each ant.
8. If the stop criterion is fulfilled, then go to 9, if not, go to 3.
9. The overall best solution is found.

The convergence of the HAFA algorithm is guaranteed, that is, in any case we get the optimal solution. However, the convergence time is not defined, since the algorithm depends on the initial parameters, which are selected based on experiment results. An important property of the HAFA algorithm is preserving diversity: even after a large number of iterations, many solutions are simultaneously investigated, as a result of which there are no long time delays in local extremes.

4   Experimental Result

The effectiveness of the proposed algorithm HAFA depends on the parameters of its configuration: $m, n_0, \tau_0, \alpha, \beta$. The number of ants m affects the computational complexity of the algorithm. With a small value of the number of iterations n_0, the algorithm can "not be in time" to find the optimal solution. The initial concentration of pheromone τ_0, the degree of pheromone influence α and the membership degree of the pixel to be in a cluster β also influence the speed of solution search and convergence to the optimum. Experimental studies were held to evaluate the algorithm using the developed software application. Set of medical MRI images provided by company OsiriX [28], as well as pictures of real patients were used in the algorithm test. The plan of experiments included the following steps: evaluation of the quality of the algorithm, determining its optimal parameters for automatic and interactive segmentation, examining the effect of scaling the original image and the possibility of the algorithm for segmentation of color images. The proposed algorithm was tested with the help of the developed software application: 400 images were taken from the OsiriX benchmark, pictures of real patients, a number of artificial images, as well as the pictures from Berkeley complex structured images benchmarks [29]. The study provided for modeling the behavior of the method with various variants of parameters in order to determine the influence of the initial parameters on the overall convergence of the method, the number of iterations, the closeness of the solution found to the optimal one, and the degree of identity of the result of processing the reference image. The HAFA algorithm was compared with algorithms of segmentation c-means, $ACO - k$-means, and Magic Wand. The parameters for the mentioned above algorithms are given in papers [30–32]. Elements of the matrix were calculated as follows: the reference image is superimposed on the result of segmentation. Then the difference is calculated. The formula for calculations is as follows:

$$P_{pres} = \frac{N - D}{N} \times 100\%$$

where N is the total number of pixels, D is the number of pixels that differ from the reference. Table 1 shows the results of comparison of segmentation accuracy for good quality images, noisiness images, contrast images and fuzzy images, respectively.

Table 1. Results of comparison of segmentation accuracy

Algorithm	Image type			
	Good quality	Noisiness	Contrast	Fuzzy
c-means	79	55	66	52
$ACO - k$-means	95	81	90	60
Magic Wand	90	72	80	60
HAFA	95	90	95	64

As can be seen the proposed hybrid algorithm performance is better than the segmentation results of the c-means, $ACO - k$-means and Magic Wand algorithms, which confirms the idea of the applicability of the ant colony method for the medical images segmentation.

5   Conclusion

Rapid and accurate detection of pathologies on MRI images is a complex problem. The problem of automating the recognition of pathologies while ensuring the correct evaluation is topical. Hybrid ant colony algorithm - fuzzy c-means (HAFA) for the segmentation of MRI images was proposed in this paper. This method differs from the known ones using the fast cluster analysis for recalculating the center of each segment and applying a superposition of several optimality criteria for the resulting solutions taking into account different characteristics of the image. Parameters of the HAFA algorithm for various groups of MRI images were examined. Images from the OsiriX collection and real patient pictures were used to test the algorithm. The experimental results demonstrate the advantage and confirm the prospects of using the developed algorithm HAFA in digital processing of medical images for solving segmentation problem. The HAFA algorithm is recommended to be used for segmentation of noisy and contrast MRI images with increased requirements for recognition accuracy. As a further research idea the method can be modified to solve the problem of color and 3D image segmentation. Exploring the capabilities of software and GPU implementation are also the issues to be considered in the future research process.

References

1. Pratt, W.: Introduction to Digital Image Processing. CRC Press, New York (2013)
2. Asha, A., Victor, S., Lourdusamy, A.: Feature extraction in medical image using ant colony optimization: a study. Int. J. Comput. Sci. Eng. **3**(2), 714–721 (2011)
3. Bajwa, G., Gill, H.: Medical image segmentation based on PSO-PFC. Int. J. Comput. Appl. **126**(10), 33–37 (2015)
4. Christ, M., Sivagowri, S., Babu, P.: Segmentation of brain tumors using meta heuristic algorithms. Open J. Commun. Softw. **1**(1), 1–10 (2014)
5. Harikumar, R., Kumar, B.: Performance analysis of medical image segmentation and edge detection using MEM and PSO algorithms. Appl. Math. Inf. Sci. **9**(6), 3235–3243 (2015)
6. Maksoud, E.A.A., Elmogy, M., Al-Awadi, R.M.: MRI brain tumor segmentation system based on hybrid clustering techniques. In: Hassanien, A.E., Tolba, M.F., Taher Azar, A. (eds.) AMLTA 2014. CCIS, vol. 488, pp. 401–412. Springer, Cham (2014). https://doi.org/10.1007/978-3-319-13461-1_38
7. Nasab, N., Fatehi, M.: Automatic cerebral magnetic resonance image segmentation using artificial neural network. J. Multidiscip. Eng. Sci. Technol. (JMEST) **4**(2), 6713–6719 (2017)
8. Patil, D., Patil, S.: Brain image segmentation by ant colony optimization in brain tumor diagnosis. Int. J. Adv. Res. Comput. Sci. Softw. Eng. **5**(6), 273–276 (2015)
9. Rajput, V., Tiwari, N., Ramaiya, M.: Brain MRI segmentation using canny edge detection technique. Int. Adv. Res. J. Sci. Eng. Technol. **4**(2), 108–113 (2017)
10. Rezaee, V., Tavakoli, M.: Cancerous masses segmentation by using heuristic ant colony algorithmsin medical images. J. Image Graph. **2**(2), 128–135 (2014)
11. Saxena, V., Shrivastava, S.: Brain tumor detection and classification using segmentation in MRI. Int. J. Eng. Sci. Comput. **7**(9), 14867–14869 (2017)
12. Kumar, S., Lenin, F., Muthukumar, S., Kumar, A., Varghese, S.: A voyage on medical image segmentation algorithms. Biomed. Res. 1–12 (2017). Special Issue

13. Gonzalez, R., Woods, R.: Digital Image Processing. Prentice Hall, Upper Saddle River (2007)
14. Jayaraman, S., Esakkirajan, S., Veerakima, T.: Digital Image Processing. McGraw-Hill, New Delhi (2009)
15. Rother, C., Kolmogorov, V., Blake, A.: GrabCut - interactive foreground extraction using iterated graph cuts. In: Proceedings of the 30th Annual Conference on Computer Graphics and Interactive Techniques SIGGRAPH, vol. 23, no. 3, pp. 309–314 (2004)
16. Hatamloua, A., Abdullahb, S., Nezamabadi, H.: A combined approach for clustering based on K-means and gravitational search algorithms. Swarm Evol. Comput. **6**, 47–52 (2012)
17. Shi, J., Malik, J.: Normalized cuts and image segmentation. IEEE Trans. Pattern Anal. Mach. Intell. **22**(8), 888–905 (2000)
18. Kaur, A., Randhawa, Y.: Image segmentation with artificial neural networks along with updated JSEG algorithm. IOSR J. Electron. Commun. Eng. (IOSR-JECE) **9**(4), 1–13 (2014)
19. Gupta, S., Kaur, P.: Medical image segmentation using fuzzy-C means for MRI images. IOSR J. Electron. Commun. Eng. (IOSR-JECE), 35–40 (2015). National Conference on Advances in Engineering, Technology and Management (AITM 2015)
20. Aswathy, S., Devadhas, G.G., Kumar, S.: MRI brain tumor segmentation using genetic algorithm with SVM classifier. IOSR J. Electron. Commun. Eng. (IOSR-JECE), 22–26 (2017). http://www.iosrjournals.org/iosrjece/papers/Conf.17009-2017/Volume-1/5.%2022-26.pdf
21. Devos, A., et al.: Does the combination of magnetic resonance imaging and spectroscopic imaging improve the classification of brain tumours? In: 26th Annual International Conference (IEMBS 2004), pp. 407–410 (2004)
22. Bingiaz, A., Abbasi, A.: Segmentation and edge detection based on modified ant colony optimization for Iris image processing. J. Artif. Intell. Soft Comput. Res. **3**(2), 133–141 (2014)
23. Feng, Y., Wang, Z.: Ant colony optimization for image segmentation. In: Feng, Y. (ed.) Ant Colony Optimization - Methods and Applications, pp. 263–286 (2011). http://www.academia.edu/1458125/Ant_colony_optimization_for_image_segmentation
24. Mendhule, V., Soni, D., Sharma, A.: Interactive image segmentation using combined MRF and ant colony optimization. Int. J. Eng. Comput. Sci. **4**(6), 12281–12288 (2015)
25. Saatchi, S., Hung, C.: Swarm intelligence and image segmentation. In: Swarm Intelligence, Focus on Ant and Particle Swarm Optimization, pp. 163–179. Itech Education and Publishing, Vienna (2007)
26. Zhou, J., Hu, D.: Applications of improved ant colony optimization clustering algorithm in image segmentation. TELKOMNIKA **13**(3), 955–962 (2015)
27. Bezdek, J., Ehrlich, R., Full, W.: FCM: the fuzzy c-means clustering algorithm. Comput. Geosci. **10**(2–3), 191–203 (1984)
28. OsiriX Medical system. http://www.osirix-viewer.com
29. The Berkeley Segmentation Dataset and Benchmark. http://www.eecs.berkeley.edu/Research/Projects/CS/vision/bsds
30. Catherine, A., James, G.: Finding the number of clusters in a data set. J. Am. Stat. Assoc. **98**(463), 750–763 (2003)

31. El-Khatib, S., Rodzin, S., Skobtcov, Y.: Investigation of optimal heuristical parameters for mixed ACO-k-means segmentation algorithm for MRI images. In: Proceedings of the Conference on Information Technologies in Science, Management, Social Sphere and Medicine, vol. 51, pp. 216–221 (2016)

32. Finnell, A.: How to implement a magic wand tool (2007). http://losingfight.com/blog/2007/08/28/how-to-implement-a-magic-wand-tool/

Narrow Band-Based Detection of Basal Ganglia Subterritories

Konrad A. Ciecierski[(✉)](iD)

Research and Academic Computer Network, Warsaw, Poland
konrad.ciecierski@gmail.com

Abstract. Basal Ganglia (BG) are functional areas within human brain that are target for various deep brain stimulation (DBS) surgeries. During DBS surgery a permanent stimulating electrode is placed within selected part of the BG. One of the methods of localization of the selected part of the BG is based upon analysis of recordings obtained from BG using thin neurosurgical microelectrodes. This paper shows method for obtaining the minimal frequency ranges required for detection of the STN (*Subthalamic Nucleus*) area of the BG as well as frequencies that can be used for detection of another BG area denoted as SNr (*Substantia Nigra pars reticulata*). The recorded signal is analyzed in separate 100 Hz bands to find a subset of them that provides good basis for classification of recordings. It is shown that already a continuous block of five such bands is sufficient to discriminate STN recordings with both sensitivity and specificity above 0.92. It is also shown that results obtained from some of those bands, show distinct differences between signals obtained from STN and SNr.

Keywords: Band filtering · Classification · AdaBoost · Basal Ganglia · STN · SNr

1 Introduction

During the Deep Brain Stimulation (DBS) surgery, the goal is the precise placement of the stimulating electrode [3] in patient's brain. In case of Basal Ganglia, the DBS target is often only few millimeters across [6]. As the wrong placement of the stimulating electrode within the BG can cause very severe adverse effects [5] it is very important to have an exact stareotactic localization of the target of the surgery.

There are two main approaches to localization of the target of the DBS surgery. First one is based solely on medical imaging techniques (Computer Tomography (CT) and Magnetic Resonance Imaging (MRI)) while the second one is based upon analysis of data obtained from microelectrodes.

This paper applies to data obtained with the second approach. To obtain precise information about localization of the target of the surgery, first its expected localization is obtained using imaging data from CT and MRI. Then during

© Springer Nature Switzerland AG 2019
L. Rutkowski et al. (Eds.): ICAISC 2019, LNAI 11509, pp. 138–148, 2019.
https://doi.org/10.1007/978-3-030-20915-5_13

surgery, a set of very thin neurosurgical electrodes is advanced through the brain towards the expected target. Typically this set consists of up to five parallel electrodes. Electrodes are advanced in steps until they traverse the target of the surgery. In case of DBS surgery for Parkinson's Disease, the target is the STN and electrodes are advanced until they traverse its ventral border. Electrodes are not advanced further than to the SNr as doing so might result in permanent damage to the optic nerve [3]. Typically from location that is few millimeters dorsal to the target, at each step the electrodes record the neurophysiological activity of the surrounding brain tissue. The step between adjacent recording depths depends on the selected target and neurosurgeon's choice but in most cases is 1000 μm or smaller [3].

As shown in [7] there are many approaches to identification of the recordings there were recorded within the STN. Those approaches concentrate mainly on spiking activity and/or background activity that is present in recorded signals. Paper in [7] that shows the best sensitivity and specificity in finding the STN recordings [1], uses many features for classification, both derived from spiking activity and background noise. This paper among others attributes uses power of the signal extracted from two frequency bands, first one below 500 Hz and second one between 500 Hz and 3 KHz. While the results shown in [1] prove that those two bands together with other signal based attributes are sufficient for good discrimination of the signals that originated within STN, there is no in depth explanation why those two bands were chosen. While they were chosen with accordance to the medical knowledge and expertise, it is shown in this paper, that it is possible to select just five 100 Hz wide frequency bands to discriminate STN recordings according to their power with results better than obtained from mentioned two wide frequency bands.

2   Materials and Methods

All results found in this paper are based upon 18349 DBS recordings acquired during 175 neurosurgicla procedures. Each recording is at least 5 s long and is sampled with 24 KHz. All recordings come from DBS surgeries for treatment of Parkinson's Disease. Recordings were originally labeled according to surgical protocols into two classes. Recordings registered within *Subthalamic Nucleus* were labeled as STN while all others have label MISS. 3693 recordings (20%) have label STN while 14646 (80%) are labeled as MISS.

2.1   Power of the Signal in Given Frequency Band

Lets assume that for each recording with n samples

$$rec = \{x_0, ..., x_{n-1}\} \tag{1}$$

the

$$bpf(rec, f_b.f_e) \tag{2}$$

denotes recording 1 filtered with band pass filter passing only frequencies between f_b Hz and f_e Hz. The normalized power of the recording rec in frequency band between f_b Hz and f_e Hz is then given by

$$npwr(rec, f_b.f_e) = \frac{24000 * \sum_{x \in bpf(rec, f_b.f_e)} x^2}{n - szc(rec)} \tag{3}$$

where $szc(rec)$ is the count of samples zeroed in rec during the artifact removal phase. For comparability, the artifact removal process has been done in a way described in [1].

2.2 Power Based Attributes

Let's define now for each recording rec, a set of 30 attributes such that

$$a_j(rec) = npwr(rec, 100 * j, 100 * (j+1)) \quad for \; j = 0...29 \tag{4}$$

Electrode Level Normalization. Attributes $a_0 \ldots a_{29}$ do need further normalization. Each recording electrode might have slightly different electrical properties, also the recording device can be configured in many different ways. This is why to maintain comparability between recording registered by different electrodes, the normalization at the electrode level is required. Let's assume that during single pass of an electrode e_i following ordered collection of m recordings has been acquired:

$$(rec_{i,0}, \; rec_{i,1}, \; rec_{i,2}, \; rec_{i,3}, \; rec_{i,4}, ..., rec_{i,m-1}) \tag{5}$$

Let for electrode e_i and attribute a_j be defined set

$$B_{i,j} = \{a_j(rec_{i,k}) : \; k = 0...4\} \tag{6}$$

Let's now remove from the $B_{i,j}$ set its minimum and maximum.

$$BR_{i,j} = B_{i,j} \setminus (min(B_{i,j}) \cup max(B_{i,j})) \tag{7}$$

In the context of electrode e_i the base value of attribute a_j is then

$$b_{i,j} = mean(BR_{i,j}) \tag{8}$$

and finally, normalized value of attribute a_j for recording $rec_{i,k}$ is

$$an_j(rec_{i,k}) = \frac{a_j(rec_{i,k})}{b_{i,j}} \tag{9}$$

Normalization according to the first few depths can be safely done as the recording typically starts well more than 5 mm above the expected location of the target structure. Exclusion of the smallest and largest values, minimizes influence of the variance of the attribute during the first five depths.

3   Evaluation and Interpretation

Remark: For simplicity in the following classification results, instead of referring to the attribute an_j that gives normalized power for the band $100 * j \sim 100 * (j+1)$ Hz, description of this band itself is used. That is, for example, by results basing on band $1600 \sim 1700$ Hz it is meant, that those result base on attribute an_{16}.

All classification results presented in this paper were obtained using Matlab R2018. Classifications have all been made using classifier AdaBoostM1 with 500 trees, minimal leaf size 5 and learning rate 0.1. All presented results have been obtained using 10-fold cross validation schema [2]. AdaBoost has been chosen as it is particularly well suited for imbalanced data [4,8].

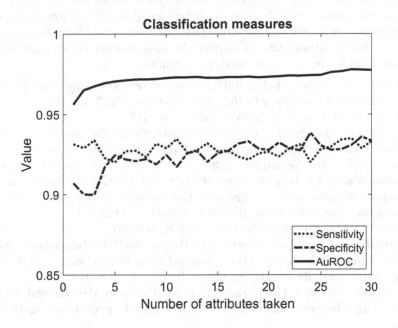

Fig. 1. Clafficication measures according to number of attributes taken

Set of all 30 attributes has been in the first step sorted according to their influence on of Area under ROC (AuROC) value using Matlab's function *rankfeatures*. The change in sensitivity, specificity and AuROC values as following attributes are added to the classification pool, can be seen on Fig. 1.

From Fig. 1 it can be immediately seen, that the AuROC value increases with first five attributes after which its increase slows down. It becomes particularly interesting when one is to look which of attributes were taken as the first five (see Table 1). Those five attributes cover continuous frequency range $1500 \sim 2000$ Hz. According to rank given by the AuROC value influence one can observe that frequency range taken, starts with 1600 ~ 1700 Hz to subsequently steadily grow in a continuous fashion.

Considering only 100 Hz wide frequency bands between 1500 and 2000 Hz (see distinction in Table 1) one obtains sensitivity 0.92, specificity 0.93 and AuROC 0.97. For comparison, results obtained using method from [1] with two frequency bands (<500 Hz, 500 ~ 3000 Hz) are inferior with sensitivity 0.92, specificity 0.86 and AuROC 0.95.

Values provided in Table 1 for sensitivity, specificity and AuROC were obtained as averages from 10-fold cross validation run ten times (n = 100). Confidence Intervals provided in this paper have all been calculated with confidence 95%.

Quite informative is also the contents of the Table 2. One can readily see that for all frequency bands (i.e. all attributes) the ranges Q1–Q3 for MISS and STN class do not overlap. The Confidence Intervals do not overlap either. Also what one can notice is that fraction of outliers has distinctively lower values for frequencies between 1500 and 2000 Hz. This can be observed both for the MISS and STN classes. Above directly implies the classification results that can be obtained using a selected single band, for example:

For attribute an_0 i.e. band below 100 Hz results are exceptionally poor. Classifier assigned almost all recordings to the MISS class (see Fig. 2a). Sensitivity 0.0049, Specificity 1.0000, AuROC 0.5517.

For attribute an_1 i.e. band between 100 Hz and 200 Hz the results are already much better than for frequencies below 100 Hz. Still quality of classification is not good (see Fig. 2b). Sensitivity 0.8015, Specificity 0.7721, AuROC 0.8253.

For attribute an_{16} i.e. band between 1600 Hz and 1700 Hz the results of classification are of good quality. Using only this single band one can obtain both sensitivity and specificity above the 0.9 threshold (see Fig. 2c). Sensitivity **0.9315**, Specificity **0.9071**, AuROC **0.9563**.

For attribute an_{29} i.e. band between 2900 Hz and 3000 Hz classification results are good but clearly inferior to those obtained from 1600 Hz and 1700 Hz range (see Fig. 2d). Sensitivity 0.9004, Specificity 0.8941, AuROC 0.9391.

One can generalize that the farther given band is from 1600 Hz and 1700 Hz band, the larger becomes the fraction of outliers and the poorer are classification results.

3.1 Statistical Analysis of Classification Results

To test that classifiers whose results are shown in Table 1 differ in a significant way, the two-sample Kolmogorov-Smirnov test [10] has been made. Test shows if addition of subsequent frequency ranges, changes the distribution of sensitivity, specificity and AuROC in a significant way. The null hypothesis is that addition of subsequent frequency range does not affect the distribution. P-value below 0.05 is considered as the indicator that significant change in distribution has occurred [9]. As one can see in Table 3, only in two cases, the distribution of one of the measures (sensitivity) was not affected by the increase of the frequency range.

Table 1. Classification measures change according to bands considered

Frequency band (Hz)	Sensitivity μ	Sensitivity CI	Specificity μ	Specificity CI	AuROC μ	AuROC CI
2500 ~ 2600	0.931	(0.929, 0.934)	0.907	(0.906, 0.908)	0.956	(0.955, 0.958)
2400 ~ 2500	0.929	(0.926, 0.932)	0.900	(0.896, 0.904)	0.965	(0.964, 0.966)
2300 ~ 2400	0.934	(0.930, 0.938)	0.900	(0.897, 0.903)	0.968	(0.966, 0.969)
2200 ~ 2300	0.923	(0.919, 0.927)	0.917	(0.915, 0.919)	0.970	(0.969, 0.970)
2100 ~ 2200	0.920	(0.915, 0.925)	0.925	(0.921, 0.928)	0.971	(0.970, 0.972)
2000 ~ 2100	0.927	(0.924, 0.930)	0.922	(0.920, 0.924)	0.971	(0.970, 0.972)
1900 ~ 2000	0.927	(0.923, 0.932)	0.921	(0.917, 0.925)	0.972	(0.971, 0.973)
1800 ~ 1900	0.923	(0.918, 0.929)	0.922	(0.919, 0.926)	0.972	(0.971, 0.973)
1700 ~ 1800	0.932	(0.928, 0.935)	0.919	(0.917, 0.921)	0.972	(0.971, 0.973)
1600 ~ 1700	0.929	(0.925, 0.933)	0.925	(0.923, 0.927)	0.973	(0.972, 0.974)
1500 ~ 1600	0.935	(0.930, 0.939)	0.917	(0.915, 0.920)	0.973	(0.972, 0.974)
1400 ~ 1500	0.926	(0.923, 0.929)	0.926	(0.924, 0.928)	0.973	(0.972, 0.974)
1300 ~ 1400	0.928	(0.924, 0.931)	0.927	(0.925, 0.929)	0.973	(0.972, 0.974)
1200 ~ 1300	0.932	(0.928, 0.936)	0.920	(0.917, 0.923)	0.973	(0.972, 0.974)
1100 ~ 1200	0.927	(0.923, 0.931)	0.926	(0.924, 0.928)	0.973	(0.972, 0.974)
1000 ~ 1100	0.927	(0.924, 0.931)	0.927	(0.925, 0.929)	0.973	(0.972, 0.974)

Table 2. Quartiles and outliers fraction for frequency bands

F. band (Hz)	MISS						STN					
	Q1	Q2	Q3	Outliers	μ	CI	Q1	Q2	Q3	Outliers	μ	CI
< 100	0.152	0.901	2.514	0.115	4.957	(4.152, 5.763)	0.285	1.722	6.893	0.135	25.625	(16.577, 34.674)
100 ～ 200	0.874	1.026	1.391	0.114	1.420	(1.383, 1.457)	2.024	3.403	6.073	0.070	5.209	(4.998, 5.420)
200 ～ 300	0.895	1.042	1.489	0.117	1.520	(1.489, 1.551)	2.659	4.374	7.509	0.076	6.558	(6.307, 6.808)
300 ～ 400	0.910	1.052	1.560	0.116	1.564	(1.533, 1.596)	3.263	5.072	8.552	0.076	7.478	(7.211, 7.745)
400 ～ 500	0.926	1.058	1.578	0.113	1.543	(1.517, 1.570)	3.488	5.339	8.517	0.076	7.353	(7.124, 7.582)
500 ～ 600	0.938	1.071	1.599	0.113	1.541	(1.517, 1.564)	3.707	5.547	8.673	0.068	7.327	(7.119, 7.534)
600 ～ 700	0.943	1.075	1.613	0.108	1.541	(1.518, 1.564)	3.877	5.778	8.768	0.065	7.346	(7.154, 7.538)
700 ～ 800	0.953	1.081	1.618	0.108	1.535	(1.513, 1.557)	4.065	5.930	8.925	0.059	7.460	(7.269, 7.651)
800 ～ 900	0.961	1.092	1.612	0.107	1.524	(1.503, 1.544)	4.207	6.031	8.996	0.053	7.469	(7.284, 7.654)
900 ～ 1000	0.967	1.097	1.611	0.103	1.509	(1.490, 1.527)	4.276	6.067	8.896	0.054	7.386	(7.208, 7.563)
1000 ～ 1100	0.970	1.101	1.604	0.100	1.496	(1.478, 1.514)	4.262	6.089	8.817	0.050	7.281	(7.112, 7.450)
1100 ～ 1200	0.973	1.103	1.591	0.099	1.484	(1.465, 1.503)	4.231	6.026	8.625	0.049	7.137	(6.975, 7.300)
1200 ～ 1300	0.975	1.103	1.574	0.097	1.463	(1.445, 1.481)	4.198	5.918	8.479	0.047	6.954	(6.798, 7.110)
1300 ～ 1400	0.977	1.101	1.554	0.094	1.436	(1.421, 1.452)	4.106	5.826	8.187	0.045	6.736	(6.588, 6.884)
1400 ～ 1500	0.977	1.098	1.534	0.093	1.411	(1.397, 1.425)	4.036	5.680	7.885	0.044	6.512	(6.370, 6.654)
1500 ～ 1600	0.977	1.094	1.515	0.090	1.388	(1.375, 1.401)	3.919	5.529	7.707	0.041	6.301	(6.165, 6.437)
1600 ～ 1700	0.976	1.091	1.499	0.089	1.369	(1.356, 1.382)	3.833	5.370	7.482	0.041	6.102	(5.972, 6.232)
1700 ～ 1800	0.976	1.088	1.477	0.089	1.353	(1.341, 1.366)	3.726	5.244	7.261	0.039	5.932	(5.806, 6.057)
1800 ～ 1900	0.975	1.083	1.460	0.090	1.339	(1.327, 1.351)	3.625	5.099	7.095	0.036	5.768	(5.646, 5.890)
1900 ～ 2000	0.975	1.079	1.444	0.090	1.326	(1.314, 1.337)	3.515	4.947	6.839	0.038	5.612	(5.494, 5.730)
2000 ～ 2100	0.974	1.076	1.429	0.090	1.313	(1.302, 1.324)	3.401	4.814	6.615	0.039	5.455	(5.341, 5.569)
2100 ～ 2200	0.973	1.071	1.409	0.092	1.300	(1.289, 1.311)	3.312	4.702	6.419	0.041	5.299	(5.189, 5.409)
2200 ～ 2300	0.971	1.066	1.391	0.094	1.287	(1.277, 1.298)	3.230	4.577	6.231	0.039	5.149	(5.043, 5.255)
2300 ～ 2400	0.970	1.061	1.374	0.095	1.275	(1.265, 1.285)	3.142	4.427	6.074	0.039	5.003	(4.901, 5.106)
2400 ～ 2500	0.968	1.059	1.359	0.096	1.264	(1.254, 1.274)	3.057	4.304	5.886	0.040	4.857	(4.759, 4.956)
2500 ～ 2600	0.968	1.055	1.343	0.099	1.253	(1.243, 1.263)	2.963	4.160	5.699	0.041	4.708	(4.613, 4.803)
2600 ～ 2700	0.966	1.050	1.331	0.101	1.242	(1.232, 1.251)	2.876	4.018	5.522	0.040	4.557	(4.466, 4.648)
2700 ～ 2800	0.965	1.046	1.318	0.102	1.230	(1.221, 1.240)	2.779	3.889	5.338	0.041	4.409	(4.321, 4.496)
2800 ～ 2900	0.963	1.042	1.301	0.104	1.219	(1.210, 1.228)	2.684	3.756	5.173	0.040	4.263	(4.180, 4.347)
2900 ～ 3000	0.962	1.039	1.284	0.107	1.208	(1.199, 1.216)	2.611	3.636	4.988	0.041	4.124	(4.043, 4.204)

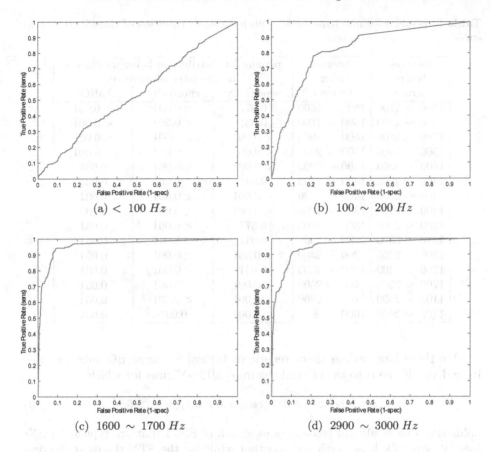

Fig. 2. ROC plots for classification based on different bands

3.2 Properties of SNr Recordings

The recordings were originally labeled into two classes i.e. those recorded within *Subthalamic Nucleus* are labeled as STN while all others have label MISS. One can however easily divide the MISS class further. Lets take out from the MISS class all of the recordings that were recorded last i.e. recording recorded at most ventral depths and put them into new class MISS-V. From [3,6], one must expect that at least some of them have been recorded in the SNr. Distribution of an_3 and an_4 values in classes MISS, MISS-V and STN can be seen on Fig. 3. One can notice that while as expected Q1–Q3 ranges of MISS-V and STN do not overlap also the Q3 of the MISS-V class is much bigger than Q3 of the MISS class. That means that in the MISS-V class, one can find values much larger than those in MISS class (see also the Q2 values).

Table 3. p-values for null hypothesis of unchanging distribution of classification measures

interval before increase	interval after increase	p-value for distribution being unaffected by the interval increase		
		sensitivity	specificity	AuROC
$1600 \sim 1700$	$1600 \sim 1800$	0.677	< 0.001	< 0.001
$1600 \sim 1800$	$1500 \sim 1800$	0.031	< 0.001	< 0.001
$1500 \sim 1800$	$1500 \sim 1900$	< 0.001	< 0.001	< 0.001
$1500 \sim 1900$	$1500 \sim 2000$	< 0.001	< 0.001	< 0.001
$1500 \sim 2000$	$1400 \sim 2000$	< 0.001	< 0.001	0.031
$1400 \sim 2000$	$1400 \sim 2100$	0.031	< 0.001	0.031
$1400 \sim 2100$	$1400 \sim 2200$	< 0.001	< 0.001	0.031
$1400 \sim 2200$	$1300 \sim 2200$	< 0.001	< 0.001	0.031
$1300 \sim 2200$	$1300 \sim 2300$	0.677	< 0.001	0.031
$1300 \sim 2300$	$1200 \sim 2300$	0.031	< 0.001	0.031
$1200 \sim 2300$	$1200 \sim 2400$	< 0.001	< 0.001	0.031
$1200 \sim 2400$	$1200 \sim 2500$	0.031	< 0.001	0.031
$1200 \sim 2500$	$1100 \sim 2500$	< 0.001	< 0.001	0.031
$1100 \sim 2500$	$1100 \sim 2600$	< 0.001	< 0.001	0.031
$1100 \sim 2600$	$1000 \sim 2600$	< 0.001	0.031	0.031

Are those large values characteristic or typical for some BG substructure? Indeed yes. If one is to take recordings from MISS-V class for which

$$an_2(rec) > 7 \wedge an_3(rec) > 6 \wedge an_4(rec) > 6 \qquad (10)$$

holds true one would get recordings as shown of Fig. 4 that are typical for SNr (see [3] page 87). It is worth noticing that while for the STN the most discriminating were frequencies around $1600 \sim 1700$ Hz, for the SNr the characteristic ones were in $200 \sim 500$ Hz range. It is important distinction as those two structures are – depending on patient – separated only by single millimeters or even adjacent [3,6]. In most DBS surgeries distinction between them is important as only the STN is used as the DBS target. SNr detection is important from the point of the safety of the surgery, during DBS surgery for Parkinson's Disease upon detection of the SNr, electrodes are advanced no further as doing so might result in permanent damage to other critical brain structures.

All of the recordings detected using Formula 10 were clearly of the SNr origin. From this one might infer a hypothesis that recordings located ventral to the STN that satisfy this formula are deemed to be recorded within the SNr. It however is not certain at this time that implication goes both ways. That is, it is not certain that all of the SNr recording do satisfy Formula 10. Verification of this requires manual recheck of all recordings and labeling by hand those recorded within SNr. This is necessary as the detection of the SNr is not always noted in surgical protocols.

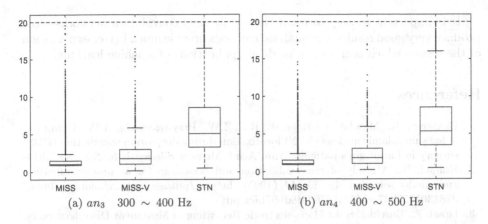

(a) an_3 $300 \sim 400$ Hz

(b) an_4 $400 \sim 500$ Hz

Fig. 3. Box plots

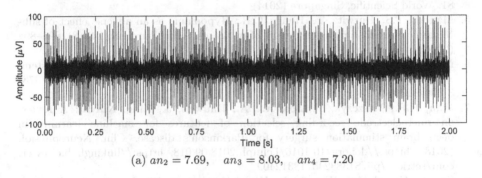

(a) $an_2 = 7.69$, $an_3 = 8.03$, $an_4 = 7.20$

Fig. 4. SNr recording

4   Conclusions

It has been shown that narrow band approach to classification of recordings acquired during DBS surgeries provides results that are better than in case of bands that are 500 Hz wide or wider. Use of relatively narrow bands allows one to find ranges that are good for discrimination of STN recordings (frequencies around $1600 \sim 1700$ Hz band) and also for detection of SNr recordings ($200 \sim 500$ Hz bands). While detection of SNr does require further work, it is worth noticing here that bands characteristic for STN and SNr do not overlap. Moreover, also in frequency bands used for SNr detection (see Fig. 3) the Q1–Q3 ranges of MISS-V and STN do not intersect. Use of narrow bands with other attributes reflecting for example distribution of amplitude would certainly improve the results even further than presented here – sensitivity and specificity of over 0.92.

It is important to keep in mind that while deep convolution networks often produce very good results, the analytic methods provide much better explanation of the results which is crucial in medical applications of machine learning.

References

1. Ciecierski, K., Mandat, T., Rola, R., Raś, Z.W., Przybyszewski, A.W.: Computer aided subthalamic nucleus (STN) localization during deep brain stimulation (DBS) surgery in Parkinson's patients. Ann. Acad. Medicae Silesiensis **5**, 275–283 (2014)
2. Kohavi, R.: A study of cross-validation and bootstrap for accuracy estimation and model selection. In: IJCAI (1995). https://pdfs.semanticscholar.org/0be0/d781305750b37acb35fa187febd8db67bfcc.pdf
3. Israel, Z., Burchiel, K.J.: Microelectrode Recording in Movement Disordersurgery. Thieme, Stuttgart (2011)
4. Lior, R., et al.: Data Mining with Decision Trees: Theory and Applications, vol. 81. World Scientific, Singapore (2014)
5. Mandat, T.S., Hurwitz, T., Honey, C.R.: Hypomania as an adverse effect of subthalamic nucleus stimulation: report of two cases. Acta Neurochir. **148**(8), 895–898 (2006)
6. Nieuwenhuys, R., Voogd, J., Van Huijzen, C.: The Human Central Nervous System: A Synopsis and Atlas. Springer, Heidelberg (2007). https://doi.org/10.1007/978-3-540-34686-9
7. Wan, K.R., Maszczyk, T., See, A.Q.A., Dauwels, J., King, N.K.K.: A review on microelectrode recording selection of features for machine learning in deep brain stimulation surgery for Parkinson's disease. Clin. Neurophysiol. (2018). https://doi.org/10.1016/j.clinph.2018.09.018. https://linkinghub.elsevier.com/retrieve/pii/S1388245718312409
8. Sun, Y., Kamel, M.S., Wong, A.K., Wang, Y.: Cost-sensitive boosting for classification of imbalanced data. Pattern Recognit. **40**(12), 3358–3378 (2007). https://doi.org/10.1016/J.PATCOG.2007.04.009. https://www.sciencedirect.com/science/article/abs/pii/S0031320307001835
9. Blackwelder, W.C.: "Proving the null hypothesis" in clinical trials. Control. Clin. Trials **3**(4), 345–353 (1982). https://www.sciencedirect.com/science/article/pii/0197245682900241
10. Young, I.T.: Proof without prejudice: use of the Kolmogorov-Smirnov test for the analysis of histograms from flow systems and other sources. J. Histochem. Cytochem. **25**(7), 935–941 (1977). https://doi.org/10.1177/25.7.894009

Realizations of the Statistical Reconstruction Method Based on the Continuous-to-Continuous Data Model

Robert Cierniak[1]($\boxtimes$), Jarosław Bilski[1], Piotr Pluta[1], and Zbigniew Filutowicz[2,3]

[1] Institute of Computational Intelligence, Czestochowa University of Technology, Armii Krajowej 36, 42-200 Czestochowa, Poland
robert.cierniak@iisi.pcz.pl
[2] Information Technology Institute, University of Social Science, 90-113 Lodz, Poland
[3] Clark University, Worcester, MA 01610, USA

Abstract. The presented paper describes a successfully parallel implementation of the statistical reconstruction method based on the continuous-to-continuous model using both CPU and GPU hardware approaches. Data were obtained from a commercial computer tomography device which were saved in DICOM standard file. The implemented reconstruction algorithm is formulated taking in two consideration the statistical properties of signals obtained by x-ray CT and the continuous-to-continuous data model. During our experiments, we tested the speed of the implemented algorithm and we optimized it in terms of the critical parameter which is very important regarding the potential use of this solution in clinical practice.

Keywords: Image reconstruction from projections ·
Statistical iterative reconstruction algorithm · Computer tomography

1 Introduction

The main challenge in x-ray computed tomography is to improve the resolution of reconstructed images and/or decrease the x-ray dose absorptions by a patient during examination, while maintaining the quality of the CT images obtained, and therefore this is a barrier to the development of this wildly-spread medical imaging technique. It is why the statistical reconstruction methods are being so intensively developed. In the statistical approach, signal processing is adaptive to the statistic of measurements present in a given image technique and in this way, we can reduce the dose absorbed by a patient during an examination (see e.g. in [1,2]). This paper presents our investigations on this challenge. We present hire results obtained using implementations of statistical reconstruction algorithm based on a continuous-to-continuous data model. Because the time is a crucial parameter in medical practice, it is very important to perform a whole reconstruction procedure in a limited time, i.e. within a few seconds. To make this

© Springer Nature Switzerland AG 2019
L. Rutkowski et al. (Eds.): ICAISC 2019, LNAI 11509, pp. 149–156, 2019.
https://doi.org/10.1007/978-3-030-20915-5_14

time as short as possible we strived to implement as parallel realizations of this algorithm using a multi-thread assembler working on AVX512 vector registers and a few different GPUs accelerators.

2   Statistical Reconstruction Algorithm

Our reconstruction method is based on the well-know maximum-likelihood (ML) estimation [3–5]. In most cases, the objective in those solutions is devised according to a discrete-to-discrete (D-D) data model. However, this scheme has some very serious drawbacks, namely: the statistical reconstruction procedure based on this methodology necessitates simultaneous calculations for all the voxels, in the range of the reconstructed 3D image, the size of the forward model matrix $\mathbf{A}$ is huge, and this makes it often necessary to calculate them in every iteration of the reconstruction algorithm. In this case, the reconstruction problem is extremely ill-conditioned, and it is necessary to introduce an *a priori* term (often referred to in the literature as a regularization term) into the objective, and this leads to the use of the MAP model. We propose here an optimization formula which is consistent with the C-C data model, in the following form:

$$
\mu_{\min} = \arg\min_{\mu} \left(\int_x \int_y \left(\int_{\bar{x}} \int_{\bar{y}} \mu\left(\bar{x},\bar{y}\right) \cdot h_{\Delta x, \Delta y} d\bar{x} d\bar{y} - \tilde{\mu}\left(x,y\right) \right)^2 dx dy \right), \quad (1)
$$

where $\tilde{\mu}(x,y)$ is an image obtained by way of a back-projection operation, obtained theoretically in the following way:

$$
\tilde{\mu}\left(x,y\right) \approx \int_0^{2\pi} \int_{-\beta_{max}}^{\beta_{max}} p^h\left(\beta, \alpha^h, z_k\right) \frac{R_{fd}}{\sqrt{R_{fd}^2 + z_k^2}} int_L\left(\Delta\beta\right) d\beta d\alpha, \quad (2)
$$

where $p^h(\beta, \alpha_\psi^h, z_k)$ are measurements carried out using a spiral cone-beam scanner, R_{fd} is the SDD (Source-to-Detector Distance), and the coefficients $h_{\Delta i, \Delta j}$ can be pre-calculated according to the following relation:

$$
h_{\Delta x, \Delta y} = \int_0^{2\pi} int\left(\Delta x \cos\alpha + \Delta y \sin\alpha\right) d\alpha, \quad (3)
$$

and $int(\Delta s)$ is an interpolation function.

The presence of a shift-invariant system in the optimization problem implies that this system is much better conditioned than the least squares problems present in the referential approach [6]. It is necessary for a computer implementation of the above C-C model to discretization Eqs. (1)–(3). After the process of discretization Eqs. (1)–(3) can be presented in the following form (4)–(6)

$$
\mu_{\min} = \arg\min_{\mu} \left(\Delta_{xy}^2 \sum_i \sum_j \left(\Delta_{\bar{x}\bar{y}}^2 \sum_{\bar{i}} \sum_{\bar{j}} \mu(\bar{x}_i, \bar{y}_j) h_{\Delta i, \Delta j} - \tilde{\mu}(x_i, y_j) \right) \right) \quad (4)
$$

where: $\Delta_{x,y}$, is a distance between pixels in a reconstruction image; $\Delta_i = |\bar{i} - i|$, $\Delta_j = |\bar{j} - j|$, are distances between pixels in the reconstruction images in the x and y directions, respectively; $\tilde{\mu}(x_i, y_j)$ is a discrete form of an image obtained by the way of back-projection operation, obtained in the following way:

$$\tilde{\mu}(x_i, y_j) \approx \Delta_\alpha \Delta_\beta \sum_\psi \sum_l p^h(\beta_l, \alpha_\psi^h, z_k) \frac{R_{fd}}{\sqrt{R_{fd}^2 + z_k^2}} int_{lin}(\Delta\beta) \qquad (5)$$

where $p^h(\beta_l, \alpha_\psi^h, z_k)$ are measurements carried out using a real spiral cone-beam scanner (see e.g. [7]); R_{fd} is the SDD (Source-to-Detector Distance); Δ_α is an angular raster between angles of projections; Δ_β is an angular distance between the radiations detectors in columns of the detector area; $int_{lin}\Delta\beta$ is a linear interpolation function; (k, l) indicates a positions of a given detector in the detector area; and the coefficients $h_{\Delta i, \Delta j}$ can be pre-calculated according to the following relations:

$$h_{\Delta i, \Delta j} = \Delta_\alpha \sum_\psi int(\Delta_i \cos\psi * \Delta_\alpha + \Delta_j \sin\psi * \Delta_\alpha) \qquad (6)$$

The most important thing in this approach is the possibility of an implementation of the fast fourier transform (FFT) algorithm to solve optimization problem (4) in an iterative procedure. The main aim of our paper is to present the acceleration of the performers of the calculations regarding this application of FFT using its parallel realizations (see e.g. [8]).

The conception of full 3D reconstructions algorithm proposed in this paper is based on one of the principal reconstruction methods devised for the cone-beam spiral scanner, i.e. the generalized FDK approach to the reconstruction problem.

The statistical reconstruction algorithm formulated by us consists of two steps, namely: a back-projection operation represented by relation 5 and an iterative reconstruction procedure described to formula 4. The whole statistical reconstruction algorithm, including of implementation of the FFT, proposed by us is the depicted in Fig. 1.

3   Results of Reconstruction Images

In Fig. 2, we present the reconstructed image obtained using the presented here method.

The above showed result demonstrates that the algorithm works properly, and the reconstructed image contains a lot of details while minimizing the noise overhead. Thanks to this solution, it will be possible to see a potential threat to the patient's life or reduce the dose of x-ray radiation in order to obtain the same quality of the diagnostic images in comparison to the existing reconstruction methods.

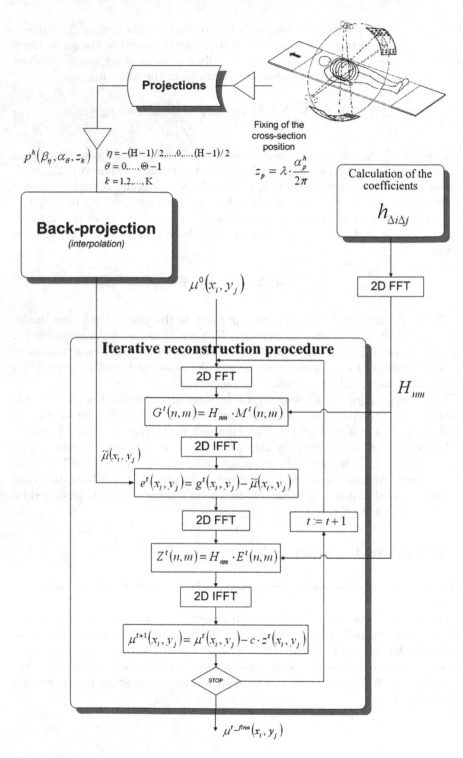

Fig. 1. An image reconstruction algorithm for the cone-beam computer tomograph

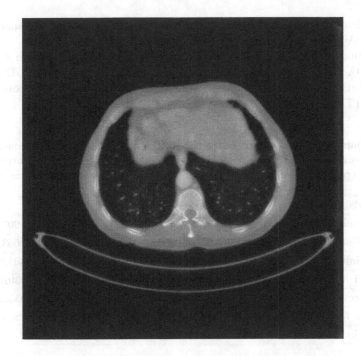

Fig. 2. Reconstructed images from the cone-beam computer tomograph with spiral pitch 0.6 after 20000 iterations.

4   Hardware Description and Time Results

Here we present our results regarding the time of the performance of the reconstruction process which is required to receive the result presented in Sect. 3. Our hardware platform is a computer with processor Intel i9-7900X BOX, mainboard ASUS TUF X299 MARK 2, LGA 2066, X299, with 32 GB RAM DDR4/3200 MHz. This equipment is managed by the operating system: Microsoft Windows 10 professional 64 bit. On this system is running our program which we describe in Sect. 2.

In Table 1, we show time result for the application which is working only on CPU. This version of the application is developed in Assembler which uses special vector registers (AVX 512), which are available only in top models of mainstream Intel's processors, or in servers processors which are very expensive compared to mainstream processors. The discrepancy between standard deviation varies with CPU because the operating system takes some of the resources to maintain the computer.

In Table 2, we show time result for the application which is working only on GPU accelerators. We could compare those accelerators, and draw conclusions that the program is very stable about the time of performance because the deviation is extremely small. Additionally, the application it is very susceptible to parallelization because the time of the one iteration is getting the smaller the more CUDA Cores are assembled in GPU Accelerator.

The situation can be much better in future Graphics Cards which will have more CUDA cores. The border of its is approximate 130 thousand CUDA cores, so it is about 25 square more than today have the best graphics card from Nvidia Company (Titan V).

Table 1. Obtained results regarding the time of the performance of the reconstruction procedure using a multi-threading CPU, i.e. Intel i9-7900X (10-cores, 20-threads). An application created in the assembler programming language with multithreading.

Threads:	4	8	10	16	20
Avg. time 30000 [ms]	63 724,36	33 571,42	29 836,34	30 532,14	27 905,62
Avg. time 20000 [ms]	42 482,91	22 380,95	19 890,89	20 354,76	18 603,75
Avg. time 10000 [ms]	21 241,45	11 190,47	9 945,45	10 177,38	9 301,87
Time/1 iteration [ms]	2,124145	1,119047	0,994545	1,017738	0,930187
HT effectiveness	-	-	-	0,909468	0,935290
Median for 30000	63 694	33 542,5	29 800	30 566	27 854
Deviation std.	135,69	117,32	217,58	193,88	391,76

Table 2. Obtained results regarding the time of the performance of the reconstruction procedure using different models of GPU accelerator. An application created in the CUDA programming language.

GPU	MSI GTX 1050	ASUS GTX 1080 Ti	nVidia Titan V
Avg. time 30000 [ms]	2 562 175,10	49 699,71	28 858,40
Avg. time 20000 [ms]	170 845,28	33 132,52	19 224,48
Avg. time 10000 [ms]	85 467,24	16 593,00	9 616,75
Time/1 iteration [ms]	8,540583	1,656657	0,961947
Median for 30000	256 229,55	49 703,68	28 861,24
Deviation std.	0,160806	0,310476	0,010239

5   Conclusion

We have shown that the statistical approach to the image reconstruction problem based on the continuous-to-continuous data model, which was originally formulated for scanners with parallel beam geometry, can be also utilized in helical CT scanners. Computer simulations have been performed, which prove that our reconstruction method is very fast, mainly thanks to the use of an FFT algorithm. The computational complexity for the proposed reconstruction algorithm is proportional to $8I^2 \log_2(2I)$, wherein it is approximate I^4 operations for the referential approach based on the discrete-to-discrete data model. Thanks to the parallel implementations of the proposed method, the whole reconstruction procedure takes about 7 s regarding a single image, what is absolutely acceptable from the clinical point of view (the obtained images are with satisfactory quality with strongly suppressed noise). It is worth to note that for the referential reconstruction method doctors obtain the first diagnostic CT images after 10–90 min. However, computational intelligence can find their application in reconstruction techniques (see e.g. in [9–19]).

Acknowledgments. This work was partly supported by The National Centre for Research and Development in Poland (Research Project POIR.01.01.01-00-0463/17).

References

1. Cierniak, R.: A new approach to image reconstruction from projections problem using a recurrent neural network. Int. J. Appl. Math. Comput. Sci. **183**(2), 147–157 (2008)
2. Cierniak, R.: A new approach to tomographic image reconstruction using a Hopfield-type neural network. Int. J. Artif. Intell. Med. **43**(2), 113–125 (2008)
3. Sauer, K., Bouman, C.: A local update strategy for iterative reconstruction from projections. IEEE Trans. Signal Process. **41**(3), 534–548 (1993)
4. Cierniak, R.: Neural network algorithm for image reconstruction using the grid-friendly projections. Australas. Phys. Eng. Sci. Med. **34**, 375–389 (2011)
5. Cierniak, R.: An analytical iterative statistical algorithm for image reconstruction from projections. Appl. Math. Comput. Sci. **24**(1), 7–17 (2014)
6. Cierniak, R., Lorent, A.: Comparison of algebraic and analytical approaches to the formulation of the statistical model-based reconstruction problem for X-ray computed tomography. Comput. Med. Imaging Graph. **52**, 19–27 (2016)
7. Cierniak, R.: A three-dimentional neural network based approach to the image reconstruction from projections problem. In: Rutkowski, L., Scherer, R., Tadeusiewicz, R., Zadeh, L.A., Zurada, J.M. (eds.) ICAISC 2010. LNCS (LNAI), vol. 6113, pp. 505–514. Springer, Heidelberg (2010). https://doi.org/10.1007/978-3-642-13208-7_63
8. Cierniak, R., Bilski, J., Smolag, J., Pluta, P., Shah, N.: Parallel realizations of the iterative statistical reconstruction algorithm for 3D computed tomography. In: Rutkowski, L., Korytkowski, M., Scherer, R., Tadeusiewicz, R., Zadeh, L.A., Zurada, J.M. (eds.) ICAISC 2017. LNCS (LNAI), vol. 10245, pp. 473–484. Springer, Cham (2017). https://doi.org/10.1007/978-3-319-59063-9_42
9. Chu, J.L., Krzyżak, A.: The recognition of partially occluded objects with support vector machines, convolutional neural networks and deep belief networks. J. Artif. Intell. Soft Comput. Res. **4**(1), 5–19 (2014)
10. Bas, E.: The training of multiplicative neuron model artificial neural networks with differential evolution algorithm for forecasting. J. Artif. Intell. Soft Comput. Res. **6**(1), 5–11 (2016)

11. Chen, M., Ludwig, S.A.: Particle swarm optimization based fuzzy clustering approach to identify optimal number of clusters. J. Artif. Intell. Soft Comput. Res. 4(1), 43–56 (2014)
12. Aghdam, M.H., Heidari, S.: Feature selection using particle swarm optimization in text categorization. J. Artif. Intell. Soft Comput. Res. 5(4), 231–238 (2015)
13. El-Samak, A.F., Ashour, W.: Optimization of traveling salesman problem using affinity propagation clustering and genetic algorithm. J. Artif. Intell. Soft Comput. Res. 5(4), 239–245 (2015)
14. Miyajima, H., Shigei, N., Miyajima, H.: Performance comparison of hybrid electromagnetism-like mechanism algorithms with descent method. J. Artif. Intell. Soft Comput. Res. 5(4), 271–282 (2015)
15. Bologna, G., Hayashi, Y.: Characterization of symbolic rules embedded in deep DIMLP networks: a challenge to transparency of deep learning. J. Artif. Intell. Soft Comput. Res. 7(4), 265–286 (2017)
16. Notomista, G., Botsch, M.: A machine learning approach for the segmentation of driving maneuvers and its application in autonomous parking. J. Artif. Intell. Soft Comput. Res. 7(4), 243–255 (2017)
17. Rotar, C., Iantovics, L.B.: Directed evolution - a new metaheuristc for optimization. J. Artif. Intell. Soft Comput. Res. 7(3), 183–200 (2017)
18. Chang, O., Constante, P., Gordon, A., Singana, M.: A novel deep neural network that uses space-time features for tracking and recognizing a moving object. J. Artif. Intell. Soft Comput. Res. 7(2), 125–136 (2017)
19. Liu, H., Gegov, A., Cocea, M.: Rule based networks: an efficient and interpretable representation of computational models. J. Artif. Intell. Soft Comput. Res. 7(2), 111–123 (2017)

Classification of Transposable Elements by Convolutional Neural Networks

Murilo H. P. da Cruz[1]([✉]), Priscila T. M. Saito[1,2], Alexandre R. Paschoal[1], and Pedro H. Bugatti[1]

[1] Bioinformatics Graduation Program (PPGBIOINFO),
Department of Computing, Federal University of Technology - Parana (UTFPR),
Cornelio Procopio, Brazil
murilocruz@alunos.utfpr.edu.br, {psaito,paschoal,pbugatti}@utfpr.edu.br
[2] Institute of Computing, University of Campinas (UNICAMP),
Campinas, Brazil

Abstract. The correct classification of transposable elements (TEs) present in the genomes is crucial to understand the real role and the consequences of these elements on the organisms. Here we present a method that classifies TEs by training a CNN to label them in classes, orders and superfamilies. Unlike previous works in the literature, the proposed method does not search for similarities to classify the sequences or use traditional machine learning classifiers. Instead of that, it automatically extracts features and classify the sequences by the CNN itself. We performed an extensive experimental evaluation, analyzing our proposed method under different scenarios. It was capable to classify TEs' sequences from various datasets in 9 different superfamilies and obtained an accuracy of 94%. We also present comparisons between the proposed method and other state-of-the-art classification tools (PASTEC, REPCLASS and TECLASS), our method presents very promising results, outperforming PASTEC and REPCLASS.

Keywords: Classification · Convolutional Neural Networks · Deep learning · Transposable Elements

1 Introduction

Transposable Elements (TEs), also called transposons, are elements present in the genomes of most eukaryotes. They can move to different regions of the genomes. This transposition can cause a variety of effects on the organisms. For example, regulation of inflammatory response and controlling the developmental switch from fetal to adult globin and prolactin expression during pregnancy are some of the regulatory activities related to TEs on humans [3].

In [16] the authors proposed a unified classification system for eukaryotic transposable elements. It groups similar elements into 4 hierarchical divisions, such as: classes, subclasses, orders and superfamilies. For each level of hierarchy, elements grouped in the same category (i.e. same class, subclass, order and

© Springer Nature Switzerland AG 2019
L. Rutkowski et al. (Eds.): ICAISC 2019, LNAI 11509, pp. 157–168, 2019.
https://doi.org/10.1007/978-3-030-20915-5_15

Table 1. Categories (class, subclass, order and superfamily) for the classification of eukaryotic transposable elements.

Class	Subclass	Order	Superfamily
Class I (retrotransposons)		LTR	Copia
			Gypsy
			Bel-Pao
			Retrovirus
			ERV
		DIRS	DIRS
			Ngaro
			VIPER
		PLE	Penelope
		LINE	R2
			RTE
			Jockey
			L1
			I
		SINE	tRNA
			7SL
			5S
Class II (DNA transposons)	Subclass 1	TIR	Tc1-Mariner
			hAT
			Mutator
			Merlin
			Transib
			P
			PiggyBac
			PIF-Harbinger
			CACTA
		Crypton	Crypton
	Subclass 2	Helitron	Helitron
		Maverick	Maverick

superfamily) share similarities. The hierarchical division and the categories of Wicker's proposed classification system can be observed on Table 1. To study these elements on the organisms, it is necessary to know which category an element belongs. This is achieved by the classification of these elements' sequences.

There are approaches in the literature that try to classify these sequences. TECLASS [2] classifies TEs into DNA transposons, long terminal repeats (LTRs), long interspersed nuclear elements (LINEs), and short interspersed nuclear elements (SINEs). To do so, it uses support vector machines (SVM) to classify these sequences based on oligomer frequencies. This method achieved an accuracy of about 90%–97% for DNA transposons and LTRs sequences, and 75% of accuracy for LINEs and SINEs classification.

The PASTEC method [7] uses hidden Markov models (HMMs) profiles and homology search by tblastx, blastx and blastn to search for similarities and structural features, and then to classify TE sequences into their respective order. This method can classify TE sequences into retrotransposon (class I), LTR, dictyostelium intermediate repeat sequence (DIRS), penelope-like element (PLE), large retrotransposon derivative (LARD), terminal-repeat retrotransposon in miniature (TRIM), LINE, SINE, DNA transposon (class II), terminal inverted repeat (TIR), miniature inverted-repeat transposable elements (MITE), Crypton, Maverick and Helitron. It can also distinguishes between host genes, simple sequence repeat (SSR), and ribossomal DNA (rDNA), which are other repetitive sequences.

The REPCLASS method [5] classifies TEs by homology search (via tblastx and Repbase sequences), structural features and by target site duplication (TSD) search. This method classifies TEs into retrotransposon, DNA transposon, LTR, LINE/SINE, and Helitron.

All these methods use homology based on search and structural features, like terminal repeats, tRNA, polyA signals, SSR, and protein coding domains. These features depend on the amount and diversity of sequences on a database to achieve good homology search results (for similarity search and protein domain or structural feature search).

Our approach proposes a method that uses a convolutional neural network (CNN) as an automatic feature extractor and classifier. It does not search for homology or structural features directly. The CNN can learn the representation for the TE sequences. Then, through this learning process, it classifies the sequences into categories of superfamilies.

Some superfamilies slightly differ in terms of structural features (i.e. order of protein coding domains). This presents a challenge for homology-based classification and even for structural feature-based classification systems. By using a representation learning method (i.e. CNN), our approach can correctly classify TEs into a great variety of superfamilies, including very likely superfamilies as Copia and Gypsy.

The inspiration for the proposed method comes from the use of CNN on natural language processing (NLP) systems, such as [9]. Clearly, genome sequences are different from natural languages, but it is a kind of language, one which encodes genes in the midst of apparently meaningless sequences. Besides, to the best of our knowledge, this is the first attempt to apply CNNs to solve the TEs' classification problem.

This paper is organized as follows: Sects. 2 and 3 present the basic concepts regarding transposable elements and convolutional neural networks, respectively. Section 4 presents the proposed CNN for classification of the TE sequences. Section 5 details the experiments and discuss the results. Section 6 presents the conclusions.

2 Transposable Elements

Transposable elements are mostly present in the genomes of eukaryotes, especially in genomes of plants which more than 80% of the genome can be composed of TEs. These elements are sequences that can be transposed to other regions of the genome by copying itself to other regions or by excision from the current location and insertion into another location. These two types of transposition represent the classes from Wicker's classification system, class I (retrotransposons) and class II (DNA transposons), respectively. The retrotransposons perform copy-paste like transpositions, and DNA transposons perform cut-paste like transpositions.

The elements are further classified into different orders, which group elements that share the same transposition mechanism or the same sequence structure. The elements of the same order are divided into different superfamilies, which the protein coding domains and their order can be different. Table 1 shows the orders of each class and the superfamilies of each order.

The transposition action of TEs can produce great effects on the organisms, such as: the regulatory activities described in [3] and phenotype instability, usually observed in plants. These effects occur because TEs can move into a gene region or other region that will affect the gene transcription. Then, it will not produce certain proteins and cause the mentioned effects.

The correct identification and classification of these elements are highly important to study the effects of these elements on organisms and how they work. Once well understood, the TE's processes could be used to regulate the gene expression of certain genes.

3 Convolutional Neural Networks

Convolutional Neural Networks (CNNs) are deep learning algorithms. Usually, it presents more than one convolutional layer and flat fully-connected hidden layers. It can be applied to speech recognition, visual object recognition, object detection, and many other applications [11].

CNNs try to learn possible representations for the data. Based on this learning process, it can perform classification, detection or other tasks. Basically, the CNN applies a feature extraction step by the convolutional layers and a classification and/or detection step by the flat fully-connected layers [6].

The algorithm is composed by convolutional layers that apply filters (kernels) to the input data. Each layer tries to filter some abstraction from the input data. For example, when applied on image classification tasks, the first layer filters simple shapes, like straight lines, border lines and edges. The next layers detect more abstracted shapes, like squares and circles. This process of abstraction continues until the last convolutional layer. If the model that are being applied poses enough convolutional layers, it should be able to learn well the last abstraction step. In an image classification problem this step performs the correct association of an image and its corresponded label [6].

Another possible layer for the CNN model is the pooling layer, usually applied after a convolutional layer. This layer reduces the dimension of convolutional layers' outputs. To do so, it applies measures of central tendency, such as: mean, median or mode, or by applying a max function [6,11].

The pooling layer consists of a kernel with certain width and height that is applied throughout the entire layer's input in a sliding window manner. Like the convolutional layer, the pooling layer also can skip certain amount of units (i.e. a stride can be defined). On images, the application of pooling layers provides tolerance to some transformations, such as rotation and small translations [6,11]. On sequences, it can learn to be invariant to single nucleotide polymorphisms (SNPs) on the sequences and translations.

The other most common layer of a CNN is the fully-connected layer, which is basically a flat artificial neural network with hidden layers [6,11]. The convolutional and pooling layers are designed to perform the feature extraction, and the fully-connected layer is designed to perform the classification or detection tasks. This layer is applied after the convolutional and pooling layers and it is responsible to produce the output of the model given some input. The last fully-connected layer in a traditional CNN architecture have the same number of neurons as the number of classification labels [6,11].

The basic CNN is the union of a series of convolutional layers followed by pooling layers and then, by a fully-connected layer. The convolution consists of applying a weighted sum with weights from a convolution kernel and the values on the input data (for the first convolutional layer) or the previous layer's output (for the other convolutional layers) [6,11].

The kernel usually consists of a matrix with fixed width and height that is applied throughout the whole input data (with respect to the layer). It is applied like a sliding window filter throughout the data. This filter has a stride of a certain value, which represents the amount of units that will be skipped after each convolution operation [6,11].

After applying the weighted sum, the results are passed to an activation function. This function maps the weighted sum to a restricted range of values, for instance, between 0 and 1 (or between −1 and 1). There are many activation functions that can be used to produce the convolutions' outputs, like ReLU, sigmoid, hyperbolic tangent, and many others [6,11].

Each convolutional layer can have more than one feature detection map. Each map represents the filtered input data by the respective applied convolution kernel. CNN learns what are the best weights for the kernels. These weights are learned by an optimization algorithm that tries to minimize the error between the model's output and the desired output.

4   Proposed Method

We proposed a new method for classification of TEs. Unlike literature works, the proposed method does not classify the sequences of the TEs based on similarities, or through traditional machine learning (ML) process (e.g. considering

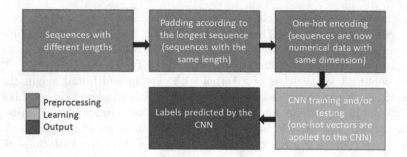

Fig. 1. Pipeline of the proposed method.

handcrafted features). Our method automatically extracts features and classify the sequences by training a CNN (end-to-end). Figure 1 illustrates the pipeline of our proposed method.

CNN and many other ML methods require that all inputs have numerical values of the same dimension. Biological sequences can present different lengths. To satisfy this same dimension requirement, all sequences shorter than the longest sequence are padded with a background symbol (i.e. a symbol different from any other possible symbol found on the sequences).

To transform the sequence values into numerical values, we applied the one-hot encoding transformation to the input sequences. This transformation maps each possible symbol into a specific position in a binary array. For each sequence symbol the mapping task is performed in a way that only the respective nucleotide position is set to "on" value and the others to "off" value. An example of this transformation can be observed on Fig. 2. Because of all these mandatory conditions, the cornerstone of our method is the proposed pre-processing module.

		Sequence																
	A	C	G	T	A	C	A	G	N	G	A	C	T	T	A	T	A	...
A	1	0	0	0	1	0	1	0	0	0	1	0	0	0	1	0	1	...
C	0	1	0	0	0	1	0	0	0	0	0	1	0	0	0	0	0	...
G	0	0	1	0	0	0	0	1	0	1	0	0	0	0	0	0	0	...
T	0	0	0	1	0	0	0	0	0	0	0	0	1	1	0	1	0	...
N	0	0	0	0	0	0	0	0	1	0	0	0	0	0	0	0	0	...

One-hot vector

Fig. 2. One-hot encoding transformation example.

For the implementation of the CNN, we considered a simple architecture. It is composed by 2 pairs of convolutional and pooling layers and a fully-connected layer. However, our method can be easily extended to different state-of-the-art CNNs. It is not bounded to a specific CNN structure (same sequence and/or number and type of layers).

To address the TEs' sequence classification problem the kernel size and strides for pooling and convolutional layers must be defined in a way that the last sliding window fits perfectly on the end of the input data (i.e. the last sliding window should end on the last input's element). Our pre-processing module also transforms the sequences according to this condition.

Our CNN model intends to classify TE sequences from a dataset, which is composed by sequences from several datasets and different species. Here, the CNN architecture is proposed to classify the sequences into the superfamily level. However, it is very flexible and can be modified to classify different superfamilies. It can also be easily modified to classify TEs by orders or classes simply by changing the sequences of the dataset and the architecture (like the number of the last fully-connected layer).

To the best of our knowledge, this is the first time that CNNs are applied and modified to the TE classification problem. Our method encodes the domain knowledge through the pre-processing module that we proposed to the TEs problem. After pre-processing we can apply any state-of-the-art CNN architecture to solve the TEs classification. We believe that this can open new ways to cope with the problem.

5   Experiments and Results

5.1   Dataset Description

The dataset is composed by sequences from the datasets: DPTEdb [12], PGSB [14], Repbase [8], RiTE [4], SPTE [17], TEfam[1] and TREP [15]. DPTEdb [12] is a dataset composed by sequences of TEs from 8 different plant species. PGSB [14] is also composed by plant sequences.

RepBase [8] is one of the most famous TE database. It comprises different repetitive sequences of eukaryotic species (which most of them tend to be transposable element sequences). The RiTE [4] database presents sequences from 11 species from the Oryza genre and a specie related to the *Leersia perrieri*.

SPTE [17] is another plant species TE database, and comprises sequences from the species *Populus trichocarpa*, *Populus euphratica* and *Salix suchowensis*. The TEfam (See footnote 1) database is composed by sequences from two mosquitoes species, *Aedes aegypti* and *Anopheles gambiae*.

The TREP [15] database consists of various plants, bacteria, and fungi repetitive sequences and some animals repetitive sequences. When available, the whole sequences were obtained, instead of just the TE consensus sequences.

5.2   Scenarios

Initially, to evaluate the effectiveness of our method on TE classification tasks, $344,925$ sequences were obtained, divided into 29 different superfamilies. Some superfamilies have less than $2,000$ sequences, and were not used to train or

---

[1] https://tefam.biochem.vt.edu/tefam/index.php.

test the model. Then, we used 9 superfamilies, Copia, Gypsy, Bel-Pao, L1, Tc1-Mariner, hAT, Mutator, PIF-Harbinger and Helitron to train and test the model. These 9 classes are balanced in a way that at least 3,000 sequences from each class are randomly selected. We considered all sequences from the classes that have more than 2,000 but less than 3,000. Only the class Bel-Pao does not present more than 3,000 sequences. Table 2 shows the final number of sequences for each class.

Therefore, in our experiments, we used 26,778 sequences from 9 different superfamilies. From this dataset, 80% of the sequences are randomly selected to compose the training set and the other 20% is selected to compose the test set.

Table 2. Distribution of samples for each superfamily.

Superfamily	Samples
Copia	3,000
Gypsy	3,000
Bel-Pao	2,778
L1	3,000
Tc1-Mariner	3,000
hAT	3,000
Mutator	3,000
PIF-harbinger	3,000
Helitron	3,000

In a second scenario, we performed comparisons between the proposed method and other literature methods (PASTEC, REPCLASS and TECLASS). To do so, the A. thaliana consensuses from Repbase update version 15.09 were obtained and classified based on the sequence's class (i.e. DNA transposon and retrotransposon) and the sequence's order (i.e. LTR, LINE, TIR). In this scenario, we trained our method considering only sequences from the DPTE database.

5.3   Implementation Details

To corroborate our method we used a simple CNN architecture with 3 hidden layers. The first one is a convolution layer with 64 kernels and stride = 6. Second is also a convolution, but with 32 kernels and stride = 1. The third one comprises an average pooling layer with kernel = 20 and stride = 20. Finally, we used a fully connected layer with $p_{os} * c_{2f}$ units where p_{os} is the pooling's output size and c_{2f} is the number of kernels on the second convolution layer. After layer we applied the rectified linear unit (ReLU) activation function.

Our method is trained end-to-end and as loss function we used the cross-entropy over all labeled samples. To optimize the loss function we applied the

Adam optimizer [10] with a learning rate $= 10^{-3}$. To avoid overfitting problems and vanishing gradients we defined a dropout of 0.5. We used a batch size $= 64$. Our method was implemented using Tensorflow [1].

5.4 Results

The results for the first scenario can be observed on Tables 3 and 4. Table 3 shows the average accuracy, error rate and f1-score obtained by the CNN for the classification of TEs. Table 4 presents the average of accuracy, error rate, precision, recall and f1-score for each superfamily of TEs. These metrics are calculated according to [13]. In addition, Fig. 3 illustrates a confusion matrix from one of the cross-validation folds. Based on these results (Tables 3, 4 and Fig. 3), it is possible to note that the proposed method is capable to obtain good results, specially a high accuracy rate. Then, it can be applied to solve TE classification problems.

Table 3. Results obtained by CNN for the classification of TEs.

Metric	Value
Accuracy	0.94
Error rate	0.06
F-score (micro)	0.73

Table 4. Results obtained by CNN for each superfamily of TEs.

Superfamily	Accuracy	Error	Precision	Recall	F1-score
Bel-Pao	0.96	0.05	0.77	0.82	0.79
Copia	0.91	0.09	0.60	0.46	0.50
Gypsy	0.88	0.12	0.46	0.43	0.44
hAT	0.93	0.07	0.70	0.69	0.69
L1	0.95	0.05	0.79	0.74	0.76
Tc1-Mariner	0.95	0.05	0.75	0.81	0.78
Mutator	0.96	0.04	0.81	0.82	0.82
PIF-Harbinger	0.93	0.07	0.66	0.75	0.70
SINE	0.97	0.03	0.86	0.85	0.85

The results obtained by our method and the state-of-the-art methods on the A. thaliana's TE classification can be observed on Table 5. The proposed method obtained better accuracy than PASTEC and REPCLASS for the classification

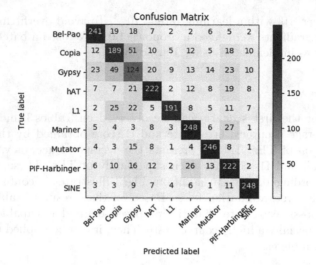

Fig. 3. Confusion matrix from one of the cross-validation folds.

based on class. Our method also obtained a better accuracy than PASTEC for the order classification.

TECLASS presented a slightly better accuracy because it not only considered sequences from the same dataset (i.e. Repbase), but also from the same specie (A. thaliana's TE) for training and testing phases. Considering our method, in this experiment, we trained it with sequences from other species obtained from the DPTE database, and tested against the Repbase sequences. Hence, TECLASS tries to solve a trivial problem (uses the same dataset to train and test) when compared with our proposed method. For future investigations, the CNN could be trained with different sequences from A. thaliana's TEs in order to improve the obtained results.

Table 5. Results obtained by our approach and other state-of-the-art approaches (PASTEC, REPCLASS and TECLASS) from the A. thaliana's TE classification.

Metric	Proposed	PASTEC	REPCLASS	TECLASS
Accuracy (class)	0.951	0.807	0.836	0.984
Accuracy (order)	0.827	0.714	0.855	0.975

6 Conclusions

The proposed method shows that it can be applied to TEs sequences classification and can obtain good results with a considerable amount of classes. It was able to classify 9 different superfamilies, which can be considered a challenge, given that the superfamilies from the same order tend to be very similar. Our method was also capable to classify sequences from A. thaliana's TEs by using sequences from different species, and could obtain better results than other methods from the literature. Besides, it can be easily applied using different state-of-the-art CNN architectures.

Acknowledgements. The authors thank Prof. Dr Douglas Silva Domingues and Ms. Daniel Longhi Fernandes Pedro for all the comments in this work. This work has been supported by CNPq (grants #372528/2018-0, #431668/2016-7, #422811/2016-5); CAPES; Araucaria Foundation; SETI; PPGBIOINFO; and UTFPR.

References

1. Abadi, M., et al.: TensorFlow: a system for large-scale machine learning. In: Proceedings of the Conference on Operating Systems Design and Implementation, pp. 265–283. USENIX Association (2016)
2. Abrusán, G., Grundmann, N., DeMester, L., Makalowski, W.: TEclass: a tool for automated classification of unknown eukaryotic transposable elements. Bioinformatics **25**(10), 1329–1330 (2009). https://doi.org/10.1093/bioinformatics/btp084
3. Chuong, E.B., Elde, N.C., Feschotte, C.: Regulatory activities of transposable elements: from conflicts to benefits. Nat. Rev. Genet. **18**, 71–86 (2016)
4. Copetti, D., et al.: RiTE database: a resource database for genus-wide rice genomics and evolutionary biology. BMC Genomics **16**(1), 538 (2015)
5. Feschotte, C., Keswani, U., Ranganathan, N., Guibotsy, M.L., Levine, D.: Exploring repetitive DNA landscapes using repclass, a tool that automates the classification of transposable elements in eukaryotic genomes. Genome Bioloyand Evol. **1**, 205–220 (2009). https://doi.org/10.1093/gbe/evp023. https://www.ncbi.nlm.nih.gov/pubmed/20333191
6. Goodfellow, I., Bengio, Y., Courville, A.: Deep Learning. MIT Press (2016)
7. Hoede, C., et al.: PASTEC: an automatic transposable element classification tool. PLOS ONE **9**(5), 1–6 (2014). https://doi.org/10.1371/journal.pone.0091929
8. Jurka, J., Kapitonov, V.V., Pavlicek, A., Klonowski, P., Kohany, O., Walichiewicz, J.: Repbase update, a database of eukaryotic repetitive elements. Cytogenet. Genome Res. **110**(1–4), 462–467 (2005)
9. Kim, Y.: Convolutional neural networks for sentence classification. CoRR abs/1408.5882 (2014). http://arxiv.org/abs/1408.5882
10. Kingma, D.P., Ba, J.: Adam: a method for stochastic optimization. In: International Conference on Learning Representations, pp. 1–15 (2015)
11. LeCun, Y., Bengio, Y., Hinton, G.: Deep learning. Nature **521**, 436–444 (2015). https://doi.org/10.1038/nature14539
12. Li, S.F., et al.: DPTEdb, an integrative database of transposable elements in dioeciousplants. Database (Oxford) **2016**, 1–10 (2016). https://doi.org/10.1093/database/baw078. https://www.ncbi.nlm.nih.gov/pubmed/27173524
13. Sokolova, M., Lapalme, G.: A systematic analysis of performance measures for classification tasks. Inf. Process. Manag. **45**(4), 427–437 (2009). https://doi.org/10.1016/j.ipm.2009.03.002. http://www.sciencedirect.com/science/article/pii/S0306457309000259

14. Spannagl, M., et al.: PGSB PlantsDB: updates to the database framework for comparative plant genome research. Nucleic Acids Res. **44**(D1), D1141–D1147 (2016). https://doi.org/10.1093/nar/gkv1130. https://www.ncbi.nlm.nih.gov/pubmed/26527721
15. Wicker, T., Matthews, D.E., Keller, B.: TREP: a database for triticeae repetitive elements. Trends Plant Sci. **7**(12), 561–562 (2002)
16. Wicker, T., et al.: A unified classification system for eukaryotic transposable elements. Nat. Rev. Genet. **8**, 973–982 (2007). https://doi.org/10.1038/nrg2165
17. Yi, F., Jia, Z., Xiao, Y., Ma, W., Wang, J.: SPTEdb: a database for transposable elements in salicaceous plants. Database **2018**(bay024), 1–8 (2018)

Human Cognitive State Classification Through Ambulatory EEG Signal Analysis

Sumanto Dutta(✉), Sumit Hazra, and Anup Nandy

Machine Intelligence and BioMotion Research Lab,
Department of Computer Science and Engineering,
National Institute of Technology Rourkela, Rourkela, Odisha, India
sumanto.nitrkl@gmail.com, sumhaz15@gmail.com, nandy.anup@gmail.com
http://www.nitrkl.ac.in/

Abstract. Human cognitive state classification using Electroencephalogram (EEG) signal is one of the dynamic exploring regions in emerging smart machine systems. It motivates to build estimator for revealing the human cognitive behaviours for different environments. In this work, we present an operational human cognitive behaviour detection system based on ambulatory EEG signal analysis. A novel event driven environment is created using external stimuli to collect those signals. They are captured using 14 channel Emotiv neuro-headset. Mel-Frequency Cepstral Coefficients (MFCC) is a very popular feature extraction method in acoustic signal processing. In spite of it's popularity, it has not been explored much when it comes to EEG signals. This paper proposes a novel technique of applying MFCC feature extraction method for ambulatory EEG signals and the results are found to be promising. Besides other feature extraction methods such as: Power Spectral Density (PSD), Discrete Wavelet Transformation (DWT) are used to extract intrinsic features from EEG signal. A statistical technique, Fisher Discriminant Ratio (FDR) is applied on them to evaluate the robustness of each feature. A higher FDR value is observed from MFCC features which demonstrate its discriminative power during classification. Different machine learning techniques such as Probabilistic neural network (P-NN), k-nearest neighbor (kNN), multi-class support vector machine (MCSVM) are applied for training, testing and validating the extracted features. A comparative analysis is discussed for each classifier coupled with each feature. It is found that P-NN with MFCC feature produces the maximum accuracy of 92.61% amongst all the remaining classifiers.

Keywords: Electroencephalogram (EEG) ·
Mel-Frequency Cepstral Coefficients (MFCC) ·
Fisher Discriminant Ratio (FDR) ·
Probabilistic neural network (P-NN)

© Springer Nature Switzerland AG 2019
L. Rutkowski et al. (Eds.): ICAISC 2019, LNAI 11509, pp. 169–181, 2019.
https://doi.org/10.1007/978-3-030-20915-5_16

1   Introduction

Mini Mental State Examination (MMSE) proposed by (Folstein [4]) is useful in approximating the cognitive impairment with recording of cognitive change. Examination consists of questionnaires, tasks, pictures logically representing a diverse mental domain and functionality. As there is no standard method which quantify mental state this method is very popular and act as the benchmark for many studies. Conventionally, EEG is a usual non-intrusive process in neuroscience and cognitive science. It is used for observing and evaluating different states of mind. Different applications are developed for sleep, recall investigation, epilepsy observation, attention deficit hyperactivity disorder (ADHD) based on the property of EEG (Thakor et al. [15]). The growing accessibility of EEG systems as a low price wearable gadgets, generated a new variety of devices for non-medicinal usage. For example, even though fastened EEG device are being utilized in gaming since many years, wireless EEG devices are currently used for brain-computer interfaces (BCI's) (Amores et al. [1], Bashivan et al. [3]). Besides, these devices can also be functional to discreetly control innovative situation based applications like house illumination systems or augmented reality backgrounds. Several situation-based applications have used EEG to rise road safety by measuring and computing driver's fatigue. (Jap et al. [6]) made use of ratios of EEG spectral features to approximate sleepiness. Another investigation proposed driver-fatigue recognition and computation procedures using features of EEG (Kar et al. [8]) which are entropy based. Measures beyond the evaluation of sleepiness and fatigue are the acknowledgement of another state of mind based on EEG data (Muller et al. [13]), as well as the study of mental performance (Klimesch et al. [10]) or attention (Kelly et al. [9]). Various assessments use graphical arousal that need a discrete visual impetus in order to part it from the normal EEG signal. Moreover, these were conducted under precise clinical conditions and with prominent EEG systems. For the understanding of difficult cognitive processes, situation shall be as genuine as possible (Hasson et al. [5]).

So far as discussed in the literature, numerous pattern-recognition systems were established for non-ambulatory EEG signals. Mental state classification for EEG using existing feature extraction methods such as high-order statistics (HOS), PSD and wavelet transform has already been worked upon previously. Combining inter-subject situations for performance assessment requires different subject records for training and testing data. This poses a challenge for the spontaneous approaches established. The approaches due to the variation in information spreading in the training and test data when information of numerous subjects are joined together. The contribution of this research work is aimed at overcoming the change in information spreading in inter-subject situations. The ambulatory EEG dataset is created using a novel event-driven environment. Also, a novel method of MFCC feature extraction for ambulatory EEG signals is proposed in this research work. Previous works focused and used existing feature extraction methods. MFCC's ability to capture the working mechanism of the signal, makes it a very popular feature extraction method in acoustic signal processing especially for audio signals. Thus, clearly bearing testimony to the fact that it has not been exploited much for ambulatory EEG signals. So MFCC is being implemented in our work for cepstral coefficient extraction which are used as features for this work. Hence clarifying it's use for EEG signal analysis. FDR is applied to it to evaluate the robustness and discriminative power of the feature. Different machine learning techniques are applied and classification is done to find out different human cognitive states.

This paper is organized as follows: Sect. 2 deals with Proposed Methodology, Sect. 3 is about Results Analysis and Discussion, Sect. 4 is for Comparative study with previous work, Conclusion and Future Work is discussed in Sect. 5.

2   Proposed Methodology

2.1   Experimental Set-Up for Data Acquisition

External stimuli are collected from different sources. Some of them are as follows: Geneva affective picture database (GAPED), pictures from various resources on the internet, psycho physiological experiments from different books and other materials. Mental states such as EOS (Emotion Oriented State), TOS (Thinking Oriented State), MOS (Memory Oriented State) and Simple Regular Oriented State (SROS) are generated from the external stimuli. Twenty subjects contribute for the experimental data collection fully confirming with the NIT Rourkela, IRB guidelines. All subjects are physically fit, and provided their written consent to the protocol used for our proposed work. The demographic information of all participants are presented in Table 1.

Table 1. Demographic characteristics of subjects. Data has been presented as Mean ± SD, M = male, F = female.

Variable	Values
Age (years)	23.3 ± 2.412
Gender	19 M/01 F
Education (years)	16.7 ± 1.159

2.2   EEG Data Collection Procedure

In our experiment we use a emotive neuro headset for capturing brain signals for different psychological states. The proposed protocol used in this experiment is shown in Fig. 1. It has four sessions with an interval of 5–10 min between the sessions. Each of the sessions has four different walking speeds with video clips displayed for 15–30 s between the trials depending on different cognitive states. The subjects are asked to position themselves on the treadmill in the created environmental contexts in the laboratory itself. They are asked to wear

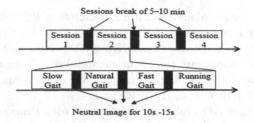

Fig. 1. The proposed EEG data collection protocol

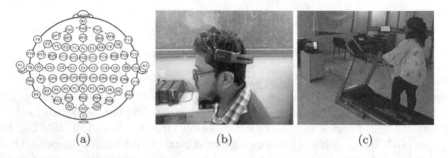

(a)   (b)   (c)

Fig. 2. (a) The international 10–20 system electrode scheme [7]. (b) Subject wearing the Emotiv Epoch+ 14 channel headset. (c) Experimental setup

the Emotiv headset and to walk in all the four specified speed levels 1.5, 3, 5 and 6.5 km/h respectively. The interval between the trial sessions allows the participants to relax during the experiment. All sessions of the protocol is for a duration of 30 min approximately. Their EEG signals corresponding to different cognitive states are collected and are processed further. To obtain a good mental state data, the subjects are instructed to rest before the start of the experiment and focus on the external stimuli. The data acquired are passed through the digitization process via wireless technology. It utilizes a proprietary USB dongle for communication using the 2.4 GHz band. The following Fig. 2a illustrates the electrode scheme of the international 10–20 system. Figure 2b shows the subject wearing the Emotiv Headset. The experimental setup is illustrated in Fig. 2c. The experimental sessions are carried out under dim lighted environment, to avoid visual disturbances, following our proposed protocol.

The sequence of steps followed for our experiment is shown in Fig. 3. The collected raw EEG data are pre-processed using FFT (Fast Fourier Transform) and bandpass filtering. It gives a cleaner signal with reduced levels of noise, increased clarity and accuracy. The Independent Component Analysis (ICA) technique was applied to remove artifacts like eye blink, eye movement from signal, to get a better processed EEG data in terms of it's depth. ICA is also used to select best channels among 14 channels for more promising results. Three feature extraction (PSD, DWT, MFCC) methods are used to extract feature from processed EEG data. FDR is applied on them to evaluate the robustness of each feature. The best feature is selected having higher FDR values. Positive negative and neutral classes are considered for each of the mental states and assigned to each features. Then different machine learning techniques are applied to classify human cognitive states.

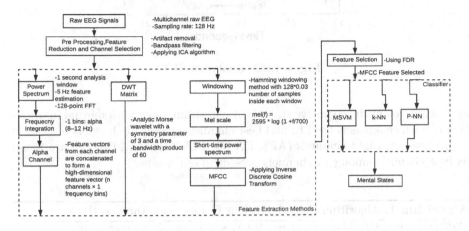

Fig. 3. Proposed methodology

2.3   Pre-processing

The raw data signals obtained are pre-processed using FFT (Fast Fourier Transform) where 0.16 Hz first order high-pass filter is used to remove the background signal. The data collected for each of the simulated walking conditions are then merged into one data set for each subject. Thus, giving cleaner signals with reduced levels of noise and increased clarity and accuracy. Most of the signals after FFT application undergoes a significant refining and are processed further. Noisy channels are identified using similar methods and thresholding channels by standard deviation and correlation between neighboring channels. Removal of artifacts is a necessary step to get more insights of EEG data after it is cleaned. Figure 4 shows EEG signal after FFT is applied on raw EEG signal. ICA is performed on EEG data using Algorithm 1 to remove artifacts like eye blinking and eye movements. Decrease in the amount of input features is further encouraged by the restricted data acquirement and handling abilities of the hardware. While gathering depths from the EEG channels and then projecting their joint feature vector, certain factors are essential for consideration. Hardware restrictions, the expensive cost of gathering and handling each extra EEG channel signal beyond the ability of the hardware are such factors. They compel us to emphasize on finding the significant channels that give most valuable information for precise

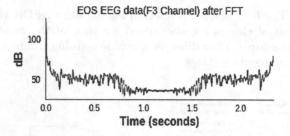

Fig. 4. EEG signal after FFT

approximation of the cognitive state. ICA algorithm along with mutual information of each channels is used to find best channels among 14 channels of Emotiv
neuro-headset. Eight channels (AF3, F7, F3, FC5, O1, O2, FC6, F8) are found
as best channels among 14 channels present in our headset.

Algorithm 1. Algorithm for Independent Component Analysis (ICA)

INPUT: A = Prewhitened matrix of size MXN, where each column represents
an N − dimensional sample
OUTPUT: W = Unmixing matrix of size NXQ , where each column
projects A onto Q independent component.
S = Independent components matrix, with M columns
representing a sample with Q dimensions.

Assumption: As Hyvarinen states that the functions $f(u) = u.e^{\frac{-u^2}{2}}$ and
$$f'(u) = (1 - u^2).e^{\frac{-u^2}{2}}$$

1: **procedure** ICA(A)
2:     $w_i = Random\ vector\ of\ length\ N$
3:     **while** w_i changes **do**
4:         $w_i = \frac{1}{M}.A.f(w_i^T.A)^T - \frac{1}{M}.A.f'(w_i^T.A)^T.w_i$
5:         $w_i = w_i - (\sum_{j=1}^{i-1} w_i^T.w_j.w_j^T)^T$
6:         $w_i = \frac{w_i}{||w_i||}$
7:     **end while**
8:     $W = w_i$
9:     $S = W^T.A$
10:     Return S
11: **end procedure**

2.4   Feature Extraction

In this work, three feature extraction methods are carried out namely: Mel Frequency Cepstrum Coefficients, PSD and Discrete Wavelet Transform for classifying different cognitive states. After pre processing of raw EEG signal and
channel selection using ICA, different feature extraction methods are applied to
extract MFCC, PSD and DWT features from pre processed EEG signal.

(i) To create Mel-frequency Cepstrum with a sampling rate of 128 Hz, firstly frequency spectrum is sliced into windows using hamming windowing method with fs * 0.03(in our case 385) number of samples inside each window. Overlapping samples between adjacent windows are decided as fs * 0.02(in our case 256). Then spectrum is changed into Mel scale [14] using (1).

$$mel(f) = 2595 * \log_{10}(1 + \frac{f}{700}) \tag{1}$$

Then, short time power spectrum $|f(w)|^2$ found via (2).

$$\theta(M_i) = \ln[\sum_{i=1}^{n} |X(i)|^2 H_k(i)], k = 1, 2, ...m \tag{2}$$

where $M_i = i^{th}$ critical band total energy, n= framelength, $X(i)$ = DFT signal, $H_k(i)$ is the critical band filter at the ith coefficient, lastly MFCC found by applying Inverse Discrete Cosine Transform (IDCT) using (3).

$$c_k = \sum_{i=1}^{n} \theta(M_i)\cos(\frac{m(i-0.5)\pi}{n}), m = 1, 2, ...p \tag{3}$$

where c_k denotes the kth MFCC, p is number of mel-scale cepstral coefficients and n = Number of triangular bandpass filters.

(ii) The range of a signal called spectrum, exhibits the amount of power contained in each of it's spectral components. In PSD, the whole average power in the signal is equivalent to the total area covered. It is always a positive value and symmetrical in nature. The total power of the EEG signal is splited and integrated over its entire one sided frequency domain, in our case it is $(0, 128)$ in the time range using (4) where $S(n)$ = DFT signal and t_1 and t_2 are time period and F_n = Frequency.

$$\int_0^{F_s} PSD(k)dk = \int_0^{F_s} \frac{2|S(n)|^2}{t_2 - t_1}dk \tag{4}$$

(iii) In DWT, the two types of functions that is scaling function and wavelet function are accompanied with lowpass and highpass filters to find the corresponding DWT coefficients. Firstly, the signal X[n] is given to a highpass filter G[n] and a lowpass filter H[n]. It results in two halves of original signal one from highpass filter and other from low pass filter. Adhering to the Nyquist's theorem 50% i.e. half of the samples can be rejected after filtering process. Now signal has a maximum frequency of f/2 not f Hz. It shows that the original signal is subsampled by a factor of 2. This is expressed using (5) where $y_h[i]$ and $y_l[i]$ are the outputs of the highpass and lowpass filters, respectively.

$$y_h[i] = \sum_n X[n] \cdot G[-n+2i], y_l[i] = \sum_n X[n] \cdot H[-n+2i] \qquad (5)$$

Using this method we find DWT coefficient matrix which uses the mother wavelet as the Morse wavelet. It has a symmetry parameter of 3 and a time-bandwidth product of 60.

3   Result Analysis and Discussion

The EEG movement artifact signals are processed offline. Also initial analysis using all of the electrodes are carried out. Eventually we focus our analysis on eigth electrodes of Emotiv Epoc+ 14 channel headset. These electrodes are spatially distributed over the head at certain specified positions based on result given by ICA algorithm. Correlation at various stages of analysis shows that it differs for artifact data than for non artifact data and also data during walking is much similar to cognitive walking. It is illustrated in Fig. 5. FDR is applied using (5)(6) on different features and it is found that $MFCC > PSD > DWT$ with values 0.92, 0.75, 0.67 respectively with respect to our data set and our procedure.

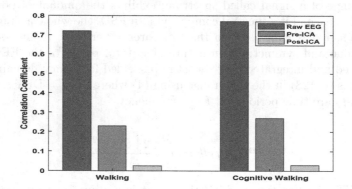

Fig. 5. Correlation at various stages of analysis for the EEG data for simple walking, walking with a cognitive task

$$J(W) = \frac{|S'_B|}{|S'_W|} \qquad (6)$$

$$S'_B = W^t S_B W, \ S'_W = W^t S_W W \qquad (7)$$

where W is a transformation matrix, S_B is between-class scatter matrix and S_W is within-class matrix.

So, MFCC is taken into consideration for further classification. Different Multi Class classifiers P-NN, kNN with k = 5, Multi-Class SVM with Radial Basis function in our case are trained, tested in (80:20) pattern and validated using 10-fold cross validation on extracted features. MFCC showed better result for each classifier techniques and an overall accuracy of 92.61% is attained in P-NN classifier. Figure 6 shows plot of accuracy versus feature and statistical measures of P-NN. Table 2 shows different statistical measures for P-NN clas-

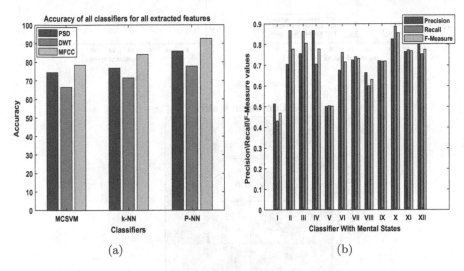

(a)   (b)

Fig. 6. (a) Accuracy plot of classifier v/s features. (b) Plot of statistical measures of P-NN

Table 2. Different statistical measures for different classifier for different feature extraction method

		MFCC				PSD				DWT			
		EOS	TOS	SROS	MOS	EOS	TOS	SROS	MOS	EOS	TOS	SROS	MOS
		Accuracy - 92.6083 %				Accuracy - 85.8564 %				Accuracy - 77.7085 %			
P-NN	Precision	0.936	0.923	0.924	0.920	0.919	0.849	0.873	0.794	0.862	0.804	0.783	0.689
	Recall	0.912	0.936	0.920	0.934	0.866	0.874	0.822	0.875	0.762	0.753	0.764	0.829
	F-measure	0.924	0.929	0.922	0.927	0.892	0.861	0.847	0.833	0.809	0.778	0.774	0.752
		Accuracy - 84.1528 %				Accuracy - 76.7908 %				Accuracy - 71.4568 %			
k-NN	Precision	0.874	0.856	0.846	0.794	0.779	0.822	0.770	0.710	0.734	0.658	0.734	0.716
	Recall	0.830	0.877	0.818	0.837	0.790	0.808	0.794	0.688	0.696	0.691	0.781	0.670
	F-measure	0.851	0.866	0.832	0.815	0.784	0.815	0.782	0.699	0.714	0.674	0.757	0.692
		Accuracy - 78.4016 %				Accuracy - 74.4404 %				Accuracy - 66.5009 %			
MCSVM	Precision	0.720	0.826	0.764	0.799	0.513	0.704	0.755	0.866	0.500	0.675	0.725	0.663
	Recall	0.718	0.886	0.773	0.753	0.431	0.866	0.863	0.705	0.504	0.761	0.740	0.599
	F-measure	0.719	0.855	0.768	0.775	0.468	0.777	0.805	0.777	0.502	0.715	0.732	0.630

178   S. Dutta et al.

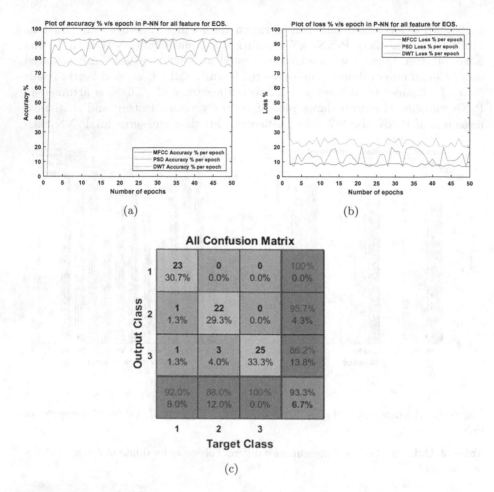

Fig. 7. (a) Plot of accuracy % v/s epoch in P-NN. (b) Plot of loss % v/s epoch in P-NN. (c) Confusion matrix for P-NN classifier using MFCC.

sifier. From Table 2 it is clearly inferred that P-NN is among best classifier to classify different mental states using MFCC's. Figure 7a and b shows Accuracy for testing data per epoch is more for MFCC than PSD and DWT and it is constant at each epoch. Model loss plot shows that our classifier fits data well for MFCC feature than other two extracted features. Figure 7c shows confusion matrix of P-NN using MFCC feature for each class. This figure shows overall confusion matrix which depicts performance of P-NN using MFCC feature at every step.

Figure 8a depicts the error histogram of P-NN for the training, validation and testing steps. This figure clearly states that the data fitting errors are distributed around zero error within a reasonable range. Figure 8b shows cross entropy performance graph for P-NN classifier using MFCC for each class, this figure shows measures of error between output and target output for training, testing and validation steps. In Fig. 8b best validation performance is 0.1136 at epoch 12 curve. Figure 9 shows receiver operating characteristic (ROC) curve for overall ROC curve. This figure shows the analytical facility of a P-NN using MFCC for evaluating the quality of classification in different phases. From this figure we can infer that curves for one verses all class shows better performance as curves are situated near top left corner of roc.

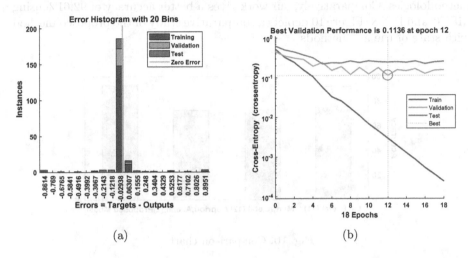

(a)   (b)

Fig. 8. (a) Error histogram for P-NN classifier using MFCC. (b) Cross entropy performance graph for P-NN classifier using MFCC.

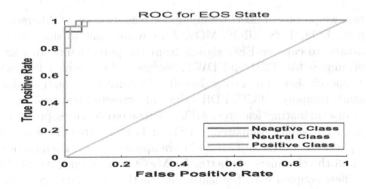

Fig. 9. ROC curve for P-NN (one versus all class of EOS)

4   Comparative Analysis

All previous studies implemented binary classification where as our work considers multi class classification. An essential observation is that previous papers applied old, popularly known methods for the extraction of features. In contrary, we present a new feature extraction method namely MFCC for EEG. It is inferred from the previous studies that the overall accuracy to classify different cognitive states by (Lin, Fu-Ren, et al. [11]) was 91.8% using decision tree, SVM and ANN classifiers respectively. Also, (Mert, Ahmet, et al. [12]) achieved an accuracy of 72.87% using k-NN, ANN whereas (Appriou, Aurlien et al. [2]) reported an accuracy of 72.7% using FBCSP, Riemmanian geometry and CNN methodologies. Comparatively, our work gives a better accuracy of 92.61% using MFCC and P-NN. Figure 10 depicts a comparative study of the proposed method with state of the art methods.

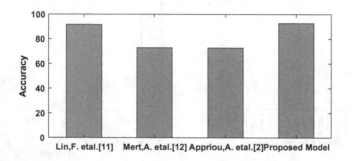

Fig. 10. Comparison chart

5   Conclusion and Future Work

In this paper, we propose a novel technique for classification of different psychological states : EOS, TOS, SROS, MOS. An environment to simulate different states is created to capture EEG signals from the participants. In contrary to popular techniques like PSD and DWT, we use MFCC which is much more advanced in speech signal processing domain. We consider a small window range of EEG signals to apply MFCC. FDR values of extracted features are found to select most discriminating features. MFCC extracted features produce significantly higher FDR values compared to PSD or DWT. Three different classification techniques P-NN, kNN and MCSVM are applied to extracted features. Performance of all the classifiers are better for MFCC extracted features. Amongst all the classifiers coupled with the feature extraction methods, an overall accuracy of 92.61% is achieved for PNN using MFCC. It is found to be the best one. Future work involves mental state modelling using Bayesian network technique in order to establish a relationship among possible environment effects on various cognitive states.

Acknowledgement. This work is sponsored by SERB, DST (Department of Science and Technology, Govt. Of India) for the Project file no. ECR/2017/000408. We would like to extend our sincere gratitude to the students of Department of Computer Science and Engineering, NIT Rourkela for their uninterrupted co-operation and consented participation for data collection.

References

1. Amores, J., Benavides, X., Maes, P.: PsychicVR: increasing mindfulness by using virtual reality and brain computer interfaces. In: Proceedings of the 2016 CHI Conference Extended Abstracts on Human Factors in Computing Systems, p. 2. ACM (2016)
2. Appriou, A., Cichocki, A., Lotte, F.: Towards robust neuroadaptive HCI: exploring modern machine learning methods to estimate mental workload from EEG signals. In: Extended Abstracts of the 2018 CHI Conference on Human Factors in Computing Systems, p. LBW615. ACM (2018)
3. Bashivan, P., Rish, I., Heisig, S.: Mental state recognition via wearable EEG. arXiv preprint arXiv:1602.00985 (2016)
4. Folstein, M.F., Folstein, S.E., McHugh, P.R.: "Mini-mental state": a practical method for grading the cognitive state of patients for the clinician. J. Psychiatr. Res. 12(3), 189–198 (1975)
5. Hasson, U., Honey, C.J.: Future trends in neuroimaging: neural processes as expressed within real-life contexts. NeuroImage 62(2), 1272–1278 (2012)
6. Jap, B.T., Lal, S., Fischer, P., Bekiaris, E.: Using EEG spectral components to assess algorithms for detecting fatigue. Expert Syst. Appl. 36(2), 2352–2359 (2009)
7. Jasper, H.H.: The ten-twenty electrode system of the international federation. Electroencephalogr. Clin. Neurophysiol. 10, 370–375 (1958)
8. Kar, S., Bhagat, M., Routray, A.: EEG signal analysis for the assessment and quantification of driver's fatigue. Transp. Res. Part F: Traffic Psychol. Behav. 13(5), 297–306 (2010)
9. Kelly, S.P., Lalor, E.C., Finucane, C., McDarby, G., Reilly, R.B.: Visual spatial attention control in an independent brain-computer interface. IEEE Trans. Biomed. Eng. 52(9), 1588–1596 (2005)
10. Klimesch, W.: EEG alpha and theta oscillations reflect cognitive and memory performance: a review and analysis. Brain Res. Rev. 29(2–3), 169–195 (1999)
11. Lin, F.R., Kao, C.M.: Mental effort detection using EEG data in e-learning contexts. Comput. Educ. 122, 63–79 (2018)
12. Mert, A., Akan, A.: Emotion recognition from EEG signals by using multivariate empirical mode decomposition. Pattern Anal. Appl. 21(1), 81–89 (2018)
13. Müller, K.R., Tangermann, M., Dornhege, G., Krauledat, M., Curio, G., Blankertz, B.: Machine learning for real-time single-trial EEG-analysis: from brain-computer interfacing to mental state monitoring. J. Neurosci. Methods 167(1), 82–90 (2008)
14. O'shaughnessy, D.: Speech Communication: Human and Machine. Universities Press (1987)
15. Thakor, N.V., Sherman, D.L.: EEG signal processing: theory and applications. In: He, B. (ed.) Neural Engineering, pp. 259–303. Springer, Boston (2013). https://doi.org/10.1007/978-1-4614-5227-0_5

Generalizations of Aggregation Functions for Face Recognition

Paweł Karczmarek[1]([⊠]), Adam Kiersztyn[1], and Witold Pedrycz[2,3,4]

[1] Institute of Computer Science, Lublin University of Technology,
ul. Nadbystrzycka 36B, 20-618 Lublin, Poland
pawel.karczmarek@gmail.com, adam.kiersztyn.pl@gmail.com
[2] Department of Electrical and Computer Engineering, University of Alberta,
Edmonton, AB T6R 2V4, Canada
wpedrycz@ualberta.ca
[3] Department of Electrical and Computer Engineering, Faculty of Engineering,
King Abdulaziz University, Jeddah 21589, Saudi Arabia
[4] Systems Research Institute, Polish Academy of Sciences, Warsaw, Poland

Abstract. The problem of aggregation of the classification results is one of the most important task in image recognition or decision-making theory. There are many approaches to solve this problem as well as many operators and algorithms proposed such as voting, scoring, averages, and more advanced ones. In this paper, we examine the well-known existing and recently introduced to the practice of classification tasks generalizations of aggregation functions. Moreover, we introduce a few operators which have not been presented in the literature of the subject. The findings of this paper can shed a new light onto the theory of face recognition and help build advanced ensembles of classifiers.

Keywords: Classifiers aggregation · Pre-aggregation functions ·
Face recognition · Choquet integral · Generalized Choquet integral

1 Introduction

One of the most interesting problems in the field of classification methods is building efficient ensembles of classifiers. It can be realized using aggregation techniques. The advantage of this kind of methods is their increased accuracy expressed via the recognition rate. Moreover, they can be effectively used when there are more than a single source of evidence. In case of face recognition those could be the presence of the images taken from various cameras or separate consideration of various regions of a face as a classifiers. A shortcoming may be the time of realization of an aggregation-based methods since all the considered classification processes are executed separately. Furthermore, modern sophisticated aggregation functions can be relatively time consuming. Of course, the proper choice of the aggregation operator is pivotal here. The well-known conditions

© Springer Nature Switzerland AG 2019
L. Rutkowski et al. (Eds.): ICAISC 2019, LNAI 11509, pp. 182–192, 2019.
https://doi.org/10.1007/978-3-030-20915-5_17

regarding the n-argument aggregation functions $f : [0,1]^n \to [0,1]$ come in the form [8]

$$f(0,0,\ldots,0) = 0, \tag{1}$$

$$f(1,1,\ldots,1) = 1, \tag{2}$$

and

$$f(\mathbf{x}) \le f(\mathbf{y}) \quad \text{for} \quad \mathbf{x} \le \mathbf{y}. \tag{3}$$

The most important results related to the aggregation methods were presented in [9] (4 facial regions and a method based on scoring and template matching strategy), [39] (Eigenfaces [41] for different face parts), [16] (majority rule and RBF neural networks), [17] (T-norms), [14] (utility functions), [2] (a three-valued logic with an aggregation mechanism built with fuzzy sets). However, the most successful and efficient ones seem to be the methods based on fuzzy measure and fuzzy (granular) models [4,19–23,25,27–29,37]. The general concept and in-depth analysis of many aggregation methods can be found, among others, in [3,6,11,42].

In the series of works [10,15,31–36] proposed were many generalizations of the aggregation functions, among them a concept of a so-called **r**-increasing function, i.e., the function $f : [0,1]^n \to [0,1]$ that for all points $(x_1, x_2, \ldots, x_n)$ and some $a > 0$ fulfills the condition

$$f(x_1, x_2, \ldots, x_n) \le f(x_1 + ar_1, x_2 + ar_2, \ldots, x_n + ar_n), \tag{4}$$

where $r_1, r_2, \ldots, r_n$ are the elements of some vector **r**. Furthermore, the authors proved that if $T : [0,1]^2 \to [0,1]$ fulfills the conditions $T(x,y) \le x$, $T(x,1) = x$, and $T(0,y) = 0$, T is increasing over $[0,1]$, and if for the arbitrary fuzzy measure g on the sets A_i one builds the function of the form

$$Ch_T \int h \cdot g(T) = \sum_{i=1}^{n} T(h(x_i) - h(x_{i+1}), g(A_i)), \tag{5}$$

with the assumption that

$$h(x_{n+1}) = 0, \tag{6}$$

and $h(x_i)$, $i = 1, \ldots, n$, is non–increasing sequence for some function h, then Ch_T is **r**-increasing for some **r** and its value is in-between the minimum and maximum of the parameters $x_1, x_2, \ldots, x_n$. This property can lead us to realization of many efficient generalizations of Choquet-like integrals for the aggregation purposes.

The main objective of this study is to comprehensively compare the above-mentioned generalizations of the Choquet integral in an application to the face classification problem when the particular classifiers are focused on the parts of face or the classic face recognition methods are applied to the whole faces. Moreover, we propose a new generalization of the Choquet integral which construction is inspired by the numerical schemes of solving differential equations. Some introductory results of this paper were covered in the monograph [19]. It is worth stressing that these generalizations and augmentations have not been studied in the existing literature.

The paper is organized as follows. In Sect. 2 we briefly present the compared generalizations of the Choquet integral. Section 3 contains the experimental results. The conclusions and future work directions are presented in Sect. 4.

2   Generalizations of Choquet Integral

Recall that if X is a set and $P(X) = 2^X$ is a family of its all subsets then fuzzy measure is a set function such that

$$g(\emptyset) = 0, \tag{7}$$

$$g(X) = 1, \tag{8}$$

$$g(A) \leq g(B), \quad A \subset B, \quad A, B \in P(X), \tag{9}$$

and

$$\lim_{n \to \infty} g(A_n) = g\left(\lim_{n \to \infty} A_n\right) \tag{10}$$

for any increasing set sequence $\{A_n\}$, $n = 1, 2, \ldots$. Sugeno λ-fuzzy measure is a realization of the above measure with the following requirement:

$$g(A \cup B) = g(A) + g(B) + \lambda g(A) g(B), \quad \lambda > -1, \tag{11}$$

where A and B are disjoint sets. If $A_i = \{x_1, \ldots, x_n\}$ and $A_{i+1} = \{x_1, \ldots, x_{n+1}\}$ then

$$g(A_{i+1}) = g(A_i) + g_{i+1} + \lambda g(A_i), \tag{12}$$

where

$$g_i = g(\{x_i\}), \quad i = 1, \ldots, n. \tag{13}$$

Next, assume that the values of some function h, namely $h(x_i)$, $i = 1, \ldots, n$, form a non-increasing sequence and $h(x_{n+1}) = 0$ then Choquet integral is defined as follows

$$Ch = \sum_{i=1}^{n} (h(x_i) - h(x_{i+1}) g(A_i)). \tag{14}$$

Possible generalizations are above-mentioned Ch_T (5) and

$$Ch_F = \min\left(\sum_{i=1}^{n} T(h(x_i) - h(x_{i+1}), g(A_i)), 1\right) \tag{15}$$

(see [31,35]),

$$Ch_C = \sum_{i=1}^{n} (T(h(x_i), g(A_i)) - T(h(x_{i+1}), g(A_i))) \tag{16}$$

(see [32]) and C_{min} with minimum in the place of T (T is any t-norm) under the integral [15]. Our six new proposals are

$$Ch_{TC} = \sum_{i=1}^{n} (T(h(x_i), g(A_i)) - T(h(x_{i+1}), g(A_i)) \\ +T(h(x_i) - h(x_{i+1}), g(A_i))), \tag{17}$$

$$Ch_{Tmin} = \sum_{i=1}^{n} T(\min(h(x_i), g(A_i)) - \min(h(x_{i+1}), g(A_i)), g(A_i)), \tag{18}$$

$$Ch_{Tmin2} = \sum_{i=1}^{n} T(\min(h(x_i), g(A_i)), \min(h(x_{i+1}), g(A_i))), \tag{19}$$

$$Ch_{minT} = \sum_{i=1}^{n} \min(T((h(x_i), g(A_i))), T(h(x_{i+1}), g(A_i))), \tag{20}$$

$$Ch_{Diff} = \sum_{i=1}^{n} T(h(x_{i-1}) - h(x_{i+1}), g(A_i)), \tag{21}$$

$$Ch_{Diff2} = \sum_{i=1}^{n} T(h(x_{i-1}) + h(x_{i+1}) - h(x_i), g(A_i)). \tag{22}$$

Note that the function T can be substituted, for instance, by any t-norm. These operations are simple generalizations of Choquet integral inspired by numerical methods and the formulas used in numerical integration where various averaging functions are used. The intuitive explanation is that we are interested in possibly averaged value of the function h in some interval of interest.

3 Experimental Results

In the series of experiments with Choquet-like integrals, we have used the model of aggregation described in the well-known works [28,29]. We do not recall its description because of space constraints.

Here, we report on the summarized results of coming out of 27 experiments using the following commonly considered datasets of images: AT&T [5], FERET [40], Labeled Faces in the Wild [18], MUCT [38], PUT [26], and Yale [43]. The first of the sets is a good alternative to verify the methods of aggregation since it is easy to preprocess the images, i.e., scaling, cropping, histogram equalization, etc. The partition of the facial region (see, e.g., [19]) eyebrows, eyes, nose, mouth, left and right cheek and the methods such as Eigenfaces with Euclidean, cosine, and Canberra distances, Fisherfaces [7] with the same three kinds of distances were tested. Again, the 6 above methods for the extended regions of eyes, nose, mouth, and the whole face, three versions (3, 5, and 7 pixels blocks) of Multi-scale Block Local Binary Pattern [12,30], Full Ranking [13], Chain Code-Based Local Descriptor [24] were verified. Finally, the whole face images only, but with many various methods like Eigenfaces, Fisherfaces, Local Binary Pattern [1], MB-LBP, Full Ranking, CCBLD were examined. In case of FERET dataset we have tested Fisherfaces method (with 3 various norms) for the 6 facial subregions (eyes, eyebrows, nose, mouth, left and right cheeks) and the whole face-based methods (Eigenfaces, Fisherfaces, LBP, MBLBP, and CCBLD). The dataset of Yale images were examined with CCBLD and two kinds of MBLBP (5 and 7 px blocks). LFW images were used to evaluate the aggregation of CCBLD, LBP, and MBLBP results. Finally, for PUT and MUCT we have used Eigenfaces, Fisherfaces, CCBLD, LBP, and MBLBP. The fuzzy measure densities were obtained in the same way as reported in [19]. Different kinds of classifiers are shown in Fig. 1.

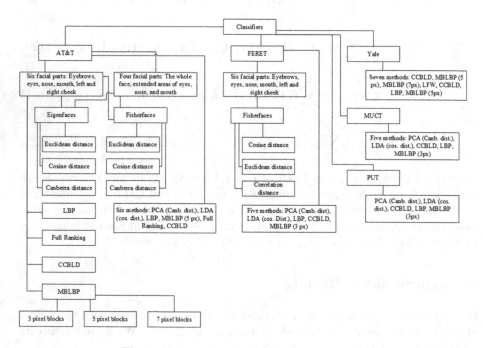

Fig. 1. Various classifiers used in experiments

Table 1 shows that our proposal, namely Choquet-like integral denoted by Ch_{TC} hits the classic Choquet integral in 22 of 27 cases of the experiments. It means that in 22 of 27 series of experiments it produces better results for specific t-norms T and their parameters. However, Ch_T, Ch_F and Ch_C give very similar results. Moreover, the latter function has produced the best global results in 11 of 27 series of experiments. It is worth noting that the best of the results obtained with the generalizations of Choquet integral was better then the recognition rate obtained with the Choquet integral by 2.9%.

In Tables 2, 3, 4 and 5 presented are the values of the parameters of 25 functions T standing under the integral sign in the above formulas for generalized Choquet integrals and for which the final results of classification were better than the classification using classic Choquet integral, i.e., the classfication rates were higher. These 25 functions are detailed in the monograph [3][p. 72, Table 2.6]. However, the best average value over all the 27 series of experiments was obtained with an application of the following t-norm:

$$T_\alpha\left(x,y\right) = xy/\left(1 + (1 - x)^\alpha\left(1 - y\right)^\alpha\right)^{1/\alpha} \tag{23}$$

for $\alpha = 7.4$.

Table 1. The summary of results

Number of	Ch_T	Ch_F	Ch_C	Ch_{min}	Ch_{TC}	Ch_{Tmin}	Ch_{minT}	Ch_{Diff}	Ch_{Diff2}
Results better than Ch	21	21	21	0	22	3	3	4	1
Global best result	2	2	11	0	9	1	1	3	0

Table 2. The scope of the parameters of the t-norms (see [3]) for which the particular function generalizing Choquet integral produced better result than the original Choquet integral operator. AT&T dataset

Index of t-norm family	Ch_T	Ch_F	Ch_C	Ch_{TC}	Ch_{Tmin}	Ch_{minT}
6	0.1	0.1	-	0.1	0.1	0.1
12	0.2	0.1	0.2	0.2	0.2	0.2
16	-	-	0.1	-	-	-
23	-	-	-	9.8	-	-

Table 3. The scope of the parameters of the t-norms for which the particular function generalizing Choquet integral produced better result than the original Choquet integral operator. FERET dataset

Index of t-norm family	Ch_{TC}	Ch_{Diff}
3	-	0.2
5	-	[0.3, 0.5]
6	-	1.2
14	-	-0.1
16	0.1	-
20	-	[-0.6, -0.3]

Table 4. The scope of the parameters of the t-norms for which the particular function generalizing Choquet integral produced better result than the original Choquet integral operator. LFW dataset

T-norm	Ch_T	Ch_F	Ch_C	Ch_{TC}	Ch_{Tmin}, Ch_{minT}	Ch_{Diff}	Ch_{Diff_2}
1	-	-	-	-	-	-	$[-0.2, -0.1]$
3	-	-	-	-	$[-10, -7]$	-	$[-10, -5.9]$
4	-	-	-	-	0.6	-	0.6
5	-	-	-	-	$[-5.8, -4.6]$	-	$[-5.8, -3.6]$
6	-	-	-	-	0.2	-	-
7	-	-	2.5	$[2, 2.3]$	-	2.5	-
8	-	-	-	0.7	-	-	-
9	1.6	1.6	-	-	$[1.4, 1.7]$	-	$[1.4, 2.8], [6.8, 7.2]$
11	-	-	-	1	-	-	-
13	-	-	-	$[0.4, 0.5]$	-	-	-
14	-9.9	-	-	-	-	$[-9.9, -9.8]$	-
15	-	-	-	-	0.2	-	$[0.2, 0.3]$
17	-	-	-	-	-	-	$[2, 2.1]$
20	-	-	-	-	$[-10, -8.5]$	-	$[-9.9, -6.4]$
23	9.5	9.5	-	-	9.5	-	9.5
24	-	-	-	-	-	-	$[2.3, 2.4], 2.6$
25	0.4	0.4	-	2.5	0.4	-	$[0.3, 0.4]$

Table 5. The scope of the parameters of the t-norm for which the particular function generalizing Choquet integral produced better result than the original Choquet integral operator. MUCT dataset

T-norm ID	Ch_T, Ch_F	Ch_C	Ch_{TC}	Ch_{Diff}
1	$[0.1, 0.4]$	$-0.8, -0.1,$ $[0.1, 1]$	$-0.8, [0.1, 1.4],$ $[4, 4.1]$	$[1.1, 9.4]$
2	-	$[1.2, 1.3],$ $[2.5:3.1]$	1.2	$[4.4, 10]$
3	$[-0.7, -0.1],$ $[0.2 : 0.4]$	$[-5.8, -5.1],$ $[-4.6, -3.3],$ $[-0.2, -0.1],$ $[0.1, 1]$	$[-2.6, -0.2],$ $[0.2, 1]$	-
4	$0.9, [1.1, 1.2]$	$[0.6, 0.7], 0.9,$ $[1.1, 1.7]$	$0.9, [1.2, 2.7]$	$[1.5, 10]$
5	$[-1.1, 0.1],$ $[0.3, 0.4], 0.6$	$[-9.9, -9.5,]$ $[-0.4, -0.2],$ $[0.2, 4.3]$	$[-7.7, -7.4],$ $[-6.7, -6.5],$ $[-5.9, -5.7],$ $[-4.5, -0.3],$ $[0.4, 0.5],$ $[0.7, 0.8],$ $[1.1, 4.9],$ $[5.2, 5.7]$	$[2.6, 2.7],$ $[2.9, 3.1],$ $[3.5, 10]$

(*continued*)

Table 5. (*continued*)

T-norm ID	Ch_T, Ch_F	Ch_C	Ch_{TC}	Ch_{Diff}
6	$[0.7 : 0.9], 1.1$	$[0.6, 0.9],$ $[1.1, 2.5]$	$[0.6, 0.9],$ $[1.2, 6]$	$[2, 10]$
7	-	$[0.5, 0.6]$	0.5	-
8	-	$[1.3, 1.4],$ $[4.4, 10]$	$[1.4, 1.5]$	-
10	$0.1, [1.3, 1.4],$ $[1.8, 10]$	$[2.2, 10]$	$[0.1, 10]$	-
11	-	0.6	0.6	-
12	$[0.4, 0.7]$	$[0.6, 1]$	$[0.4, 1.2]$	$[1.1, 6.9]$
14	-0.1	0.6	0.6	-
15	$[0.8, 0.9],$ $[1.1, 1.9]$	$0.9, [1.1, 3.1]$	$[0.6, 0.9],$ $[1.1, 3.5]$	$[2.8, 10]$
16	$[0.3, 0.5]$	$[0.5, 1.1]$	$[0.1, 1.6]$	$0.1, [1.1, 10]$
17	-	$1.1, [1.8, 2.1]$	$[2.4, 3.5]$	$[2, 10]$
18	$[0.1, 0.8]$	-	-	-
20	$[-2.8, -1.2],$ $[-0.9, -0.8],$ $[-0.6, -0.5],$ $-0.3, -0.1,$ $[0.1, 0.6]$	$[-1.6, -1.2],$ $[-0.8, -0.1],$ $[0.1, 5.2]$	$[-9.9, -7.1],$ $-5.2,$ $[-4.6, -1.4],$ $[-0.8, -0.6],$ $[-0.4, -0.2], 0.1,$ $0.2, [0.4, 7.8]$	$[4.4, 10]$
22	-	-	$0.1, [0.4, 0.8]$	$0.1, 0.3, [0.5, 3.7]$
23	$[0.1, 0.3]$	$[0.1, 0.4]$	$[0.1, 0.9]$	$[0.5, 0.6], [0.8, 1.3]$
24	-	$1.1, [2, 2.9]$	$[3.9, 5.8]$	$[2.4, 10]$
25	-	1.4	1.4	-

4 Conclusions and Future Studies

In the study, we have presented the results of in-depth analysis of various forms of generalizations of Choquet integral, e.g. by the modification of the formula under the integral sign. We have studied both the recent formulas presented in literature and our new proposals. The results have shown that the proper choice of the integrand and its parameters may significantly improve the final accuracy of the aggregation of the classifiers based on nearest-neighbor algorithm. Future studies may focus on an application of Choquet-like integrals to the aggregation od deep learning-based classifiers or implementing the optimization methods to find the most optimal values of Choquet-like integral's parameters.

Acknowledgements. The authors are supported by National Science Centre, Poland (grant no. 2014/13/D/ST6/03244). Support from the Canada Research Chair (CRC) program and Natural Sciences and Engineering Research Council is gratefully acknowledged (W. Pedrycz).

References

1. Ahonen, T., Hadid, A., Pietikäinen, M.: Face recognition with local binary patterns. In: Pajdla, T., Matas, J. (eds.) ECCV 2004. LNCS, vol. 3021, pp. 469–481. Springer, Heidelberg (2004). https://doi.org/10.1007/978-3-540-24670-1_36

2. Al-Hmouz, R., Pedrycz, W., Daqrouq, K., Morfeq, A.: Development of multimodal biometric systems with three-way and fuzzy set-based decision mechanisms. Int. J. Fuzzy Syst. **20**, 128–140 (2018)

3. Alsina, C., Frank, M.J., Schweizer, B.: Associative Functions. Triangular Norms and Copulas. World Scientific, New Jersey (2006)

4. Anderson, D.T., Scott, G.J., Islam, M.A., Murray, B., Marcum, R.: Fuzzy choquet integration of deep convolutional neural networks for remote sensing. In: Pedrycz, W., Chen, S.-M. (eds.) Computational Intelligence for Pattern Recognition. SCI, vol. 777, pp. 1–28. Springer, Cham (2018). https://doi.org/10.1007/978-3-319-89629-8_1

5. AT&T Laboratories Cambridge. [online] The Database of Faces. http://www.cl.cam.ac.uk/research/dtg/attarchive/facedatabase.html. Accessed 11 July 2018

6. Baczyński, M., Bustince, H., Mesiar, R.: Aggregation functions: theory and applications. Fuzzy Set. Syst. **324**, 325 (2017)

7. Belhumeur, P.N., Hespanha, J.P., Kriegman, D.J.: Eigenfaces vs. fisherfaces: recognition using class specific linear projection. IEEE Trans. Pattern Anal. Mach. Intell. **19**, 711–720 (1997)

8. Beliakov, G., Pradera, A., Calvo, T.: Aggregation Functions: A Guide for Practitioners. Springer, Heidelberg (2007). https://doi.org/10.1007/978-3-540-73721-6

9. Brunelli, R., Poggio, T.: Face recognition: features versus templates. IEEE Trans. Pattern Anal. Mach. Intell. **15**, 1042–1052 (1993)

10. Bustince, H., et al.: Pre-aggregation functions: definition, properties and construction methods. In: 2016 IEEE International Conference on Fuzzy Systems (FUZZ-IEEE), pp. 294–300 (2016)

11. Calvo, T., Mayor, G., Mesiar, R.: Aggregation Operators. New Trends and Applications. Physica-Verlag, Heidelberg (2014)

12. Chan, C.-H., Kittler, J., Messer, K.: Multi-scale local binary pattern histograms for face recognition. In: Lee, S.-W., Li, S.Z. (eds.) ICB 2007. LNCS, vol. 4642, pp. 809–818. Springer, Heidelberg (2007). https://doi.org/10.1007/978-3-540-74549-5_85

13. Chan, C.H., Yan, F., Kittler, J., Mikolajczyk, K.: Full ranking as local descriptor for visual recognition: a comparison of distance metrics on s_n. Pattern Recognit. **48**, 1328–1336 (2015)

14. Dolecki, M., Karczmarek, P., Kiersztyn, A., Pedrycz, W.: Utility functions as aggregation functions in face recognition. In: 2016 IEEE Symposium Series on Computational Intelligence (SSCI), Athens, pp. 1–6 (2016)

15. Dimuro, G.P., Lucca, G., Sanz, J.A., Bustince, H., Bedregal, B.: CMin-Integral: a choquet-like aggregation function based on the minimum t-norm for applications to fuzzy rule-based classification systems. In: Torra, V., Mesiar, R., De Baets, B. (eds.) AGOP 2017. AISC, vol. 581, pp. 83–95. Springer, Cham (2018). https://doi.org/10.1007/978-3-319-59306-7_9

16. Haddadnia, J., Ahmadi, M.: N-feature neural network human face recognition. Image Vis. Comput. **22**, 1071–1082 (2004)

17. Hu, X., Pedrycz, W., Wang, X.: Comparative analysis of logic operators: a perspective of statistical testing and granular computing. Int. J. Approx. Reason. **66**, 73–90 (2015)
18. Huang, G.B., Ramesh, M., Berg, T., Learned-Miller, E.: Labeled faces in the wild: a database for studying face recognition in unconstrained environments. University of Massachusetts, Amherst, Technical report 07–49 (2007)
19. Karczmarek, P.: Selected problems of face recognition and decision-making theory. Lublin University of Technology Press, Lublin (2018)
20. Karczmarek, P., Kiersztyn, A., Pedrycz, W.: An evaluation of fuzzy measure for face recognition. In: Rutkowski, L., Korytkowski, M., Scherer, R., Tadeusiewicz, R., Zadeh, L.A., Zurada, J.M. (eds.) ICAISC 2017. LNCS (LNAI), vol. 10245, pp. 668–676. Springer, Cham (2017). https://doi.org/10.1007/978-3-319-59063-9_60
21. Karczmarek, P., Kiersztyn, A., Pedrycz, W.: Generalized Choquet integral for face recognition. Int. J. Fuzzy Syst. **20**, 1047–1055 (2018)
22. Karczmarek P., Kiersztyn, A., Pedrycz W.: On developing Sugeno fuzzy measure densities in problems of face recognition. Int. J. Mach. Intell. Sens. Sig. Process. **2**, 80–96 (2017)
23. Karczmarek, P., Pedrycz, W., Kiersztyn, A., Dolecki, M.: A comprehensive experimental comparison of the aggregation techniques for face recognition. Irani. J. Fuzzy Syst. (in press)
24. Karczmarek, P., Pedrycz, W., Kiersztyn, A., Dolecki, M.: An application of chain code-based local descriptor and its extension to face recognition. Pattern Recognit. **65**, 26–34 (2017)
25. Karczmarek, P., Pedrycz, W., Reformat, M., Akhoundi, E.: A study in facial regions saliency: a fuzzy measure approach. Soft Comput. **18**, 379–391 (2014)
26. Kasiński, A., Florek, A., Schmidt, A.: The PUT face database. Image Process. Commun. **13**, 59–64 (2008)
27. Kurach, D., Rutkowska, D., Rakus-Andersson, E.: Face classification based on linguistic description of facial features. In: Rutkowski, L., Korytkowski, M., Scherer, R., Tadeusiewicz, R., Zadeh, L.A., Zurada, J.M. (eds.) ICAISC 2014. LNCS (LNAI), vol. 8468, pp. 155–166. Springer, Cham (2014). https://doi.org/10.1007/978-3-319-07176-3_14
28. Kwak, K.-C., Pedrycz, W.: Face recognition using fuzzy integral and wavelet decomposition method. IEEE Trans. Syst. Man. Cybern. B Cybern. **34**, 1666–1675 (2004)
29. Kwak, K.-C., Pedrycz, W.: Face recognition: a study in information fusion using fuzzy integral. Pattern Recognit. Lett. **26**, 719–733 (2005)
30. Liao, S., Zhu, X., Lei, Z., Zhang, L., Li, S.Z.: Learning multi-scale block local binary patterns for face recognition. In: Lee, S.-W., Li, S.Z. (eds.) ICB 2007. LNCS, vol. 4642, pp. 828–837. Springer, Heidelberg (2007). https://doi.org/10.1007/978-3-540-74549-5_87
31. Lucca, G., de Vargas, R.R., Dimuro, G.P., Sanz, J.A., Bustince, H., Bedregal, B.R.C.: Analysing some t-norm-based generalizations of the Choquet integral for different fuzzy measures with an application to fuzzy rule-based classification systems. In: ENIAC 2014, Encontro Nac. Intelig. Artificial e Computacional. SBC, São Carlos, pp. 508–513 (2014)
32. Lucca, G., et al.: CC-integrals: Choquet-like copula-based aggregation functions and its application in fuzzy rule-based classification systems. Knowl.-Based Syst. **119**, 32–43 (2017)

33. Lucca, G., Sanz, J.A., Dimuro, G.P., Bedregal, B., Bustince, H.: Pre-aggregation functions constructed by CO-integrals applied in classification problems. In: Proceedings of IV CBSF, pp. 1–11 (2016)

34. Lucca, G., Sanz, J.A., Dimuro, G.P., Bedregal, B., Bustince, H., Mesiar, R.: CF-integrals: a new family of pre-aggregation functions with application to fuzzy rule-based classification systems. Inf. Sci. **435**, 94–110 (2018)

35. Lucca, G., et al.: The notion of pre-aggregation function. In: Torra, V., Narukawa, Y. (eds.) MDAI 2015. LNCS (LNAI), vol. 9321, pp. 33–41. Springer, Cham (2015). https://doi.org/10.1007/978-3-319-23240-9_3

36. Lucca, G., et al.: Preaggregation functions: construction and an application. IEEE Trans. Fuzzy Syst. **24**, 260–272 (2016)

37. Melin, P., Felix, C., Castillo, O.: Face recognition using modular neural networks and the fuzzy Sugeno integral for response integration. Int. J. Intell. Syst. **20**, 275–291 (2005)

38. Milborrow, S., Morkel, J., Nicolls, F.: The MUCT landmarked face database. In: Pattern Recognition Association, South Africa (2010)

39. Pentland, A., Moghaddam, B., Starner, T.: View-based and modular eigenspaces for face recognition. In: Proceedings of 1994 IEEE Computer Society Conference on Computer Vision and Pattern Recognition, CVPR 1994, pp. 84–91 (1994)

40. Phillips, P.J., Wechsler, J., Huang, J., Rauss, P.: The FERET database and evaluation procedure for face recognition algorithms. Image Vis. Comput. **16**, 295–306 (1998)

41. Turk, M., Pentland, A.: Eigenfaces for recognition. J. Cogn. Neurosci. **3**, 71–86 (1991)

42. Yager, R.R., Kacprzyk, J.: The oRdered Weighted Averaging Operators: Theory and Applications. Springer, New York (2012)

43. Yale Face Database. [online]. http://vision.ucsd.edu/content/yale-face-database. Accessed 6 Apr 2017

Epileptic Seizure Detection Based on ECoG Signal

Marcin Kołodziej[1], Andrzej Majkowski[1], Remigiusz Jan Rak[1(✉)], Paweł Tarnowski[1], and Andrzej Rysz[2]

[1] Warsaw University of Technology, Warsaw, Poland
remigiusz.rak@ee.pw.edu.pl
[2] Medical University of Warsaw, Warsaw, Poland

Abstract. The article presents a system for detection of epileptic seizures with the use of automatic ECoG signal analysis. Features in the form of signal energy in nine different signal subbands were used. Next algorithms of feature selection (SFS, SBS) and classification (LDA, QDA) were performed. The developed algorithm was tested on signals taken from the ECoG database, containing signals recorded during epileptic seizures and without seizures. The proposed method is characterized by relatively low computational complexity and satisfactory accuracy of classification - up to 98%.

Keywords: Epileptic seizure detection · Electrocorticography ·
Linear discriminant analysis · Quadratic discriminant analysis ·
Sequential forward/backward selection

1 Introduction

1.1 What Is Epilepsy?

Epilepsy is a disease that affects 1–2% of the population. During the epileptic seizure the pathological synchronous activity starts at a small brain area, within the gray matter and then spreads to its immediate vicinity, recruiting more and more parts of the brain neural network. In the case of generalized epilepsy, the synchronous neural firing can affect the whole cortex. In the case of focal epilepsy only parts of it, the so-called epileptogenic area is affected [1]. A major symptom of epilepsy is unexpected seizures, during which the patient loses control over both, mind and body. This is dangerous not only for the patient and also for the environment (especially if the patient is driving a car, passing the street, etc.). Some patients use drugs that effectively reduce seizures. However, drugs do not help in 20–40% of the cases.

There is still a clear demand for automated algorithms for detection of epileptic seizures. Such algorithms can be used to control neurostimulation devices that are used to prevent the propagation of epileptic seizures in drug resistant epilepsy [2]. An example of such a system is RNS (NeuroPace) device approved in 2013 by the American Food and Drug Administration (FDA). Thanks to electrical brain stimulation just before the epileptic seizure a reduction of repeatability of seizures by 50% is obtained [3]. Critical in this case, is the precise detection of the onset of an epileptic

© Springer Nature Switzerland AG 2019
L. Rutkowski et al. (Eds.): ICAISC 2019, LNAI 11509, pp. 193–202, 2019.
https://doi.org/10.1007/978-3-030-20915-5_18

seizure. The issue of false seizure detections is equally important. So-called "false alarms" cause unnecessary stimulations of the brain, which significantly increase the discomfort of the patient and lead to a reduction in the life of the batteries used.

A study on brain discharges related to epilepsy was launched in 1970, and it has since been a subject of intense research to date [4]. The widespread use of computer techniques had a significant impact on the attempt to detect these discharges. Very often, in the discussions about epileptic discharges, reference is made to EEG signals, which of course are similar to electrocorticographic (ECoG) signals. The analysis of EEG and ECoG signals, in the context of epilepsy, usually covers three separate issues: prediction of epileptic seizures, detection of the beginning of the seizures, and iden-tification of the channels on which the discharges occur [5, 6]. Numerous algorithms have been proposed for the detection of epilepsy based on frequency analysis [7], time–frequency and wavelet analysis [8], artificial neural networks [9, 10], SVM classifiers [11], and data-mining tools [12]. Conventional time and frequency signal analysis was used in the works [13–15]. Much attention has been paid to quantitative description and dynamics of signals [16, 17]. Also, mutual correlation [18], Lapunov exponents [19, 20], and Kolmogorov entropy [21] were often used.

1.2   The Goal of the Investigations

The aim of the research was to develop a relatively simple method, with a low com-putational complexity, for the effective detection of epileptic seizures. Ultimately, the proposed method is to be implemented in a dedicated RNS stimulator and operate in on-line mode. The ECoG signals recorded in clinical conditions, before and during epileptic seizures were used [22]. As features, energy in the nine frequency subbands was used. The sequential feature selection algorithms were used in the feature selection process (sequential forward selection - SFS and sequential backward selection - SBS). In the classification process, discriminant algorithms such as linear discriminant analysis (LDA) and quadratic discriminant analysis (QDA) were implemented [23, 24]. The algorithms were tested using a tenfold cross validation (10-CV) test.

2   Materials

2.1   Description of the Research Material

The database material included in [22] was used in our experiments. ECoG signals from 5 patients were registered, all of whom had achieved complete seizure control after resection of one of the hippocampal formations, which was therefore correctly diagnosed to be the epileptogenic zone. All ECoG signals were recorded with the same 128-channel amplifier, using an average common reference. After 12 bit analog-to-digital conversion, the data were written continuously onto the disk, at a sampling rate of 173.61 Hz. Figure 1 presents sample 3-second signal recordings. The first two drawings (a and b) present the ECoG signal recorded during normal brain activity, two subsequent drawings (c and d) present the ECoG signal recorded during an epileptic seizure. We can observe an increase in the amplitude of the ECoG signal during an epileptic seizure. The nature of the signal waveform also changes. The database contains one hundred "A" examples which were recorded from within the epileptogenic zone (but not during an epileptic seizure), and one hundred "B" examples containing seizure activity.

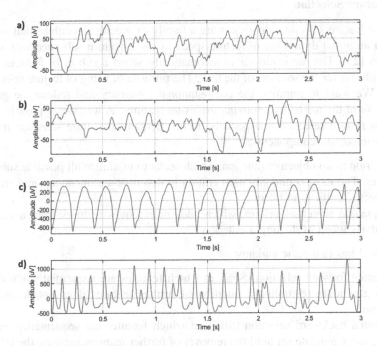

Fig. 1. Examples of registered ECoG signals in the database. (a), (b) – signals recorded during normal brain activity, (c), (d) – signals recorded during an epileptic seizure.

3   Methods

3.1   Preprocessing and Feature Extraction

The data used in our experiment contains 100 examples for each set A and B. Recorded ECoG signals were filtered using a 4th-order Butterworth filter set. After filtering we obtained signals in the following subbands:

1. Delta (0÷4 Hz);
2. Theta (4÷8 Hz);
3. Alpha (8÷12 Hz);
4. Beta (12÷32 Hz);
5. Alpha-Theta (5÷9 Hz);

6. Gamma (32÷80 Hz);
7. Alpha Low (8÷10 Hz);
8. Alpha High (10÷12 Hz);
9. iEEG/EEG (0.1÷60 Hz);

For each of the registered signals, the energy in these frequency subbands was calculated. In this way, each signal was described by a set of 9 features. So we created the matrix of features [9 features × 200 examples].

3.2   Feature Selection

Sequential feature selection algorithms are a family of greedy algorithms that are used to reduce an initial dimension of feature space to some feature subspace with smaller dimension [25]. The motivation is to automatically select a subset of features that is most significant for the solution of the task. The purpose of using of feature selection is twofold. We want to improve the computational efficiency and reduce the generalization error of the model by removing irrelevant features. A wrapper approach such as sequential feature selection is especially useful. Sequential feature selection methods have two important components:

1. A criterion as an objective function, which seeks to minimize all possible subsets of features. The most commonly used criteria in that case are: mean squared error and incorrect classification factor.
2. A sequential search algorithm, which adds or removes features from a subset of candidates when evaluating a criterion.

The method has two basic variants:

1. Sequential forward selection (SFS), in which features are sequentially added to an empty candidate set until the addition of further features does not decrease the criterion.
2. Sequential backward selection (SBS), in which features are sequentially removed from a full candidate set until the removal of further features increase the criterion.

3.3   Classification

In our experiments we used two classifiers: Linear Discriminant Analysis (LDA) and Quadratic Discriminant Analysis (QDA) [26]. LDA is a kind of discriminant function for dimensionality reduction in the preprocessing step for pattern-classification. The goal is to project a dataset onto a lower-dimensional space with good class-separability in order to avoid overfitting and also reduce computational costs. In LDA approach, in addition to finding the component axes that maximize the variance of processed data (like in PCA), we are looking for the axes that maximize the separation between classes. So that it can be successfully used for a multi-class classification task.

QDA holds the same assumptions like LDA. It is a general discriminant function with a quadratic decision boundaries which can be used to classify datasets with two or more classes. QDA has more predictability power than LDA but it needs to estimate the covariance matrix for each classes.

Tenfold cross validation (10-CV) test was used as a measure of the classification accuracy [7, 27]. In 10-CV test, the original set is randomly partitioned into 10 equal sized subsets. Of the 10 subsets, a single subset is retained as the validation data for testing the model, and the remaining 9 subsets are used as training data. The cross-validation process is then repeated 10 times, with each of the 10 subsets used exactly once as the validation data. The 10 results from the folds are then averaged to produce a single estimation.

4   Results

4.1   Classification Using the Energy in Selected Frequency Subbands

A classification of the signals from the set "A" (free of seizures) and the signals from the set "B" (containing seizure activity) was performed. The classification was performed for one feature that is the energy of the ECoG signal in the selected frequency subband. The LDA and QDA classifiers and the 10-CV test were used. The results of the classification are shown in Table 1.

Table 1. Results of ECoG signal classification accuracy

	EEG	Delta	Theta	Alpha	Beta	Gamma	Alpha low	Alpha high	Alpha theta
LDA	0.76	0.71	0.81	0.78	0.69	0.70	0.76	0.77	0.81
QDA	0.82	0.67	0.86	0.87	0.93	0.81	0.81	0.91	0.86

The best classification accuracy results were obtained for Theta (0.81), Alpha Theta (0.81) frequency subbands for LDA classifier and for Beta subband (0.93) for QDA classifier.

4.2   Classification with the Use of SFS Algorithm

Again, a classification of the signals from both sets ("A" and "B") was performed. ECoG signal energy in subbands were used as features.

Table 2. Stages of the SFS algorithm.

	EEG	Delta	Theta	Alpha	Beta	Gamma	Alpha low	Alpha high	Alpha theta	[CA]
1	−	−	−	−	+	−	−	−	−	0.92
2	−	+	−	−	+	−	−	−	−	0.94
3	−	+	−	+	+	−	−	−	−	0.95
4	−	+	+	+	+	−	−	−	−	0.97
5	−	+	+	+	+	−	−	−	+	0.97
6	−	+	+	+	+	+	−	−	+	0.98
7	−	+	+	+	+	+	+	−	+	0.98
8	−	+	+	+	+	+	+	+	+	0.98
9	+	+	+	+	+	+	+	+	+	0.97

The QDA classifier was used in conjunction with the sequential forward selection (SFS) method. The 10-CV test was used. Classification accuracy (CA) for individual stages of the SFS algorithm are shown in Table 2. The "+" mark means that the feature was selected in a particular stage of the algorithm. The best classification results for the first (1) stage of the SFS algorithm was obtained for the Beta band (0.92). For the stage (6) the best results was obtained by selecting subbands: Delta, Theta, Alpha, Beta, Gamma, Alpha Theta (0.98).

4.3   Classification with the Use of SBS Algorithm

In the next experiment, QDA classifier was used in conjunction with the sequential backward selection (SBS) method. Classification accuracy (CA) for individual stages of the SBS algorithm are shown in Table 3. The "+" mark means that the feature was selected in a particular stage of the algorithm. The best classification result – 0.98 was obtained for 8, 7, 6, 5 selected features (Table 3).

Table 3. Stages of the SBS algorithm.

	EEG	Delta	Theta	Alpha	Beta	Gamma	Alpha low	Alpha high	Alpha theta	[CA]
9	+	+	+	+	+	+	+	+	+	0.96
8	–	+	+	+	+	+	+	+	+	0.98
7	–	–	+	+	+	+	+	+	+	0.98
6	–	–	+	+	–	+	+	+	+	0.98
5	–	–	+	+	–	–	+	+	+	0.98
4	–	–	+	–	–	–	+	+	+	0.97
3	–	–	–	–	–	–	+	+	+	0.95
2	–	–	–	–	–	–	–	+	+	0.94
1	–	–	–	–	–	–	–	+	–	0.91

5   Discussion

Figure 2 presents ECoG signal recorded during epileptic seizure and the same signal after applying subband filters (Delta, Theta, Alpha, Beta, Gamma). The highest signal energy was obtained for Theta and Beta bands and the lowest for the Delta, Alpha and Gamma bands. However, the largest values of energy do not determine the usefulness of the feature for the purposes of classification.

The statistical significance (p-value) between the groups of features obtained for seizure and without seizure was calculated. For each of the feature (that is energy in the Delta, Theta, Alpha, Beta, Gamma, Alpha Low, Alpha High, Alpha Theta and EEG subbands) a statistically significant difference $p < 0.0001$ was obtained.

The obtained classification results (Tables 1, 2 and 3) are satisfactory. The best classification accuracy was 0.98. It should be noted that the 10-CV test draws the division of training/testing data, therefore the accuracy obtained may be slightly different for each run of the algorithm. However, this does not prevent the estimation of the accuracy of the classification and the indication of the best set of features.

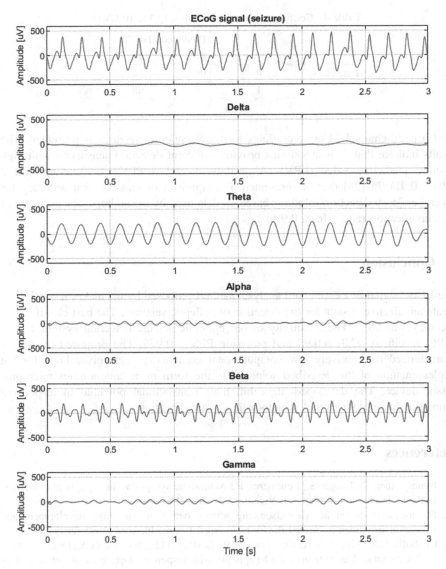

Fig. 2. Registered signal during an epileptic seizure, and the same signal after filtration in the Alpha, Beta, Gamma, Delta, Theta bands.

The eight, best features, that is energies in subbands: Delta Theta Alpha, Beta Gamma Alpha, Low Alpha High, Alpha Theta were used to assess the effectiveness of seizure detection system. The QDA classifier and the 10-CV test were used. Table 4 presents a confusion matrix (0-lack of seizure, 1-seizure).

Based on the confusion matrix sensitivity TPR = 0.96, specificity TNR = 0.98 and precision PPV = 0.979 for the epileptic seizure detection system were calculated. Similar results were obtained in works [2, 28]. In [2] a summary in which the authors

Table 4. Confusion matrix (8 features, QDA, 10-CV).

		Predicted class	
		0	1
True class	0	96	4
	1	2	98

used a multi-channel ECoG recordings to detect epileptic seizures is presented. The results indicate that their algorithms provide sufficient detection sensitivity with high positive predictive value (PPV) (Algorithms 1 and 3 PPV = 0.99, Algorithm 2 PPV = 0.97). In [28] there is presented a comparison of classification accuracy for several epilepsy detection solutions based on data used by the authors. The accuracy of the classification ranges from 0.9 to 1.

6 Conclusion

The ECoG signal processing and analysis method proposed by us, makes it possible to create an effective system for the detection of epileptic seizures. The best classification accuracy was 98%. The sensitivity of our epileptic seizure detection system TPR = 0.96, specificity TNR = 0.98 and precision PPV = 0.979. The proposed method is characterized by relatively low computational complexity. This gives hope for the implementation of the described solution, in the form of an autonomous microprocessor device. The developed algorithm have translational potential in responsive neurostimulation devices and in automatic seizure detection.

References

1. Baumgartner, C., Lurger, S., Leutmezer, F.: Autonomic symptoms during epileptic seizures. Epileptic Disord. Int. Epilepsy J. Videotape **3**, 103–116 (2001)
2. Baldassano, S.N., et al.: Crowdsourcing seizure detection: algorithm development and validation on human implanted device recordings. Brain **140**, 1680–1691 (2017)
3. Chabolla, D.R., Murro, A.M., Goodman, R.R., Barkley, G.L., Worrell, G.A., Drazkowski, J. F.: Treatment of Mesial temporal lobe epilepsy with responsive hippocampal stimulation by the RNSTM neurostimulator. Presented at the Annual meeting of the American Epilepsy Society (2006)
4. Bozek-Juzmicki, M., Colella, D., Jacyna, G.M.: Feature-based epileptic seizure detection and prediction from ECoG recordings. In: Proceedings of IEEE-SP International Symposium on Time-Frequency and Time-Scale Analysis, pp. 564–567 (1994)
5. Gotman, J.: Automatic detection of seizures and spikes. J. Clin. Neurophysiol. Off. Publ. Am. Electroencephalogr. Soc. **16**, 130–140 (1999)
6. McGrogan, N., Prof, S., Tarassenko, L.: Neural Network Detection of Epileptic Seizures in the Electroencephalogram (1999)
7. Harner, R.: Automatic EEG spike detection. Clin. EEG Neurosci. **40**, 262–270 (2009)
8. Dümpelmann, M., Elger, C.E.: Automatic detection of epileptiform spikes in the electrocorticogram: a comparison of two algorithms. Seizure **7**, 145–152 (1998)

9. Webber, W.R., Litt, B., Wilson, K., Lesser, R.P.: Practical detection of epileptiform discharges (EDs) in the EEG using an artificial neural network: a comparison of raw and parameterized EEG data. Electroencephalogr. Clin. Neurophysiol. **91**, 194–204 (1994)
10. Wilson, S.B., Turner, C.A., Emerson, R.G., Scheuer, M.L.: Spike detection II: automatic, perception-based detection and clustering. Clin. Neurophysiol. **110**, 404–411 (1999)
11. Fan, J., Shao, C., Ouyang, Y., Wang, J., Li, S., Wang, Z.: Automatic seizure detection based on support vector machines with genetic algorithms. In: Wang, T.-D., et al. (eds.) Simulated Evolution and Learning, pp. 845–852. Springer, Berlin Heidelberg (2006). https://doi.org/10.1007/11903697_106
12. Exarchos, T.P., Tzallas, A.T., Fotiadis, D.I., Konitsiotis, S., Giannopoulos, S.: EEG transient event detection and classification using association rules. IEEE Trans. Inf Technol. Biomed. **10**, 451–457 (2006)
13. Srinivasan, V., Eswaran, C., Sriraam, N.: Artificial neural network based epileptic detection using time-domain and frequency-domain features. J. Med. Syst. **29**, 647–660 (2005)
14. Polat, K., Güneş, S.: Classification of epileptiform EEG using a hybrid system based on decision tree classifier and fast Fourier transform. Appl. Math. Comput. **187**, 1017–1026 (2007)
15. Übeyli, E.D., Güler, İ.: Features extracted by eigenvector methods for detecting variability of EEG signals. Pattern Recognit. Lett. **28**, 592–603 (2007)
16. Iasemidis, L.D., Sackellares, J.C.: REVIEW: Chaos theory and epilepsy. Neurosci. **2**, 118–126 (1996)
17. Kannathal, N., Acharya, U.R., Lim, C.M., Sadasivan, P.K.: Characterization of EEG–a comparative study. Comput. Methods Programs Biomed. **80**, 17–23 (2005)
18. Lerner, D.E.: Monitoring changing dynamics with correlation integrals: case study of an epileptic seizure. Phys. Nonlinear Phenom. **97**, 563–576 (1996)
19. Rysz, A., Swiderski, B., Cichocki, A., Osowski, S.: Epileptic seizure characterization by Lyapunov exponent of EEG signal. COMPEL Int. J. Comput. Math. Electr. Electron. Eng. **26**, 1276–1287 (2007)
20. Srinivasan, V., Eswaran, C., Sriraam, N.: Approximate entropy-based epileptic EEG detection using artificial neural networks. IEEE Trans. Inf Technol. Biomed. **11**, 288–295 (2007)
21. Schwab, M., Schmidt, K., Witte, H., Abrams, M.: Investigation of nonlinear ECoG changes during spontaneous sleep state changes and cortical arousal in fetal sheep. Cereb. Cortex **1991**(10), 142–148 (2000)
22. Andrzejak, R.G., Lehnertz, K., Mormann, F., Rieke, C., David, P., Elger, C.E.: Indications of nonlinear deterministic and finite-dimensional structures in time series of brain electrical activity: dependence on recording region and brain state. Phys. Rev. E: Stat., Nonlin, Soft Matter Phys. **64**, 061907 (2001)
23. Patel, K., Chua, C., Fau, S., Bleakley, C.J.: Low power real-time seizure detection for ambulatory EEG. In: 2009 3rd International Conference on Pervasive Computing Technologies for Healthcare, pp. 1–7 (2009)
24. Starzacher, A., Rinner, B.: Evaluating KNN, LDA and QDA classification for embedded online feature fusion. In: 2008 International Conference on Intelligent Sensors, Sensor Networks and Information Processing, pp. 85–90 (2008)
25. Aha, D.W., Bankert, R.L.: A comparative evaluation of sequential feature selection algorithms. In: Fisher, D., Lenz, H.-J. (eds.) Learning from Data: Artificial Intelligence and Statistics V, pp. 199–206. Springer, New York (1996). https://doi.org/10.1007/978-1-4612-2404-4_19

26. Izenman, A.J.: Linear Discriminant Analysis. In: Izenman, A.J. (ed.) Modern Multivariate Statistical Techniques: Regression, Classification, and Manifold Learning, pp. 237–280. Springer, New York (2008). https://doi.org/10.1007/978-0-387-78189-1

27. Kohavi, R.: A study of cross-validation and bootstrap for accuracy estimation and model selection. Presented at the (1995)

28. Orosco, L., Garces, A., Laciar, E.: Review: a survey of performance and techniques for automatic epilepsy detection. J. Med. Biol. Eng. 33, 526–537 (2013)

A Computational Model of Myelin Excess for Patients with Post-Traumatic Stress Disorder

Jelmer Langbroek🆔, Jan Treur$^{(\boxtimes)}$🆔,
and S. Sahand Mohammadi Ziabari🆔

Social AI Group, Vrije Universiteit Amsterdam,
De Boelelaan 1105, Amsterdam, The Netherlands
jelmerlangbroek@gmail.com, j.treur@vu.nl,
sahandmohammadiziabari@gmail.com

Abstract. The brain is the central organ of stress and controls the adaptation to stressors, while it perceives what is potentially threatening and determines the behavioral and physiological responses. Post-traumatic stress disorder (PTSD) is a mental health disease in which an individual has been exposed to a traumatic event that involves actual or imminent death or serious injury, or threatens the physical integrity of the self or others. The effects on the brain caused by stress for people with PTSD are the main subject of this paper. A literature research was conducted to see how stress affects the brain and how regions of the brain are distorted by an excess of myelin, which is formed by oligodendrocytes, in people with PTSD. Network-Oriented Modeling perspective is proposed as an alternative way to address complexity. This perspective takes the concept of network and the interactions within a network as a basis for conceptualization and structuring of any complex processes. It appears myelin, and the oligodendrocytes which produce the myelin can have altering effects in the brain of patients with PTSD. The fear response is increased significantly and the forming and retrieval of memories is also disrupted. As the effect of myelin is decreased in the model, the effects are also decreased. The main purpose of this paper is providing insight into what the effects of myelin excess might be for patients with PTSD, and simulating these effects to make these insights easily accessible.

Keywords: Network-Oriented Modeling · PTSD · Stress · Myelin

1 Introduction

The brain is the central organ of stress and controls the adaptation to stressors, while it perceives what is potentially threatening and determines the behavioral and physiological responses. In addition, the brain is a target of stress. Stressful experiences change the architecture, gene expression and function through internal neurobiological mechanisms in which circulating hormones play a role [8].

The effects of stress on an individual's health is a widely researched area, in which it is mostly found that stress causes a negative impact on health. In most recent research

© Springer Nature Switzerland AG 2019
L. Rutkowski et al. (Eds.): ICAISC 2019, LNAI 11509, pp. 203–215, 2019.
https://doi.org/10.1007/978-3-030-20915-5_19

the subject is not if stress affects health, but is focused more on causes of stress, for whom and what type of stressors cause the effect of stress on health [1].

Stress is often seen as a negative phenomenon, but stress has played an important role in our survival as a species. Animals and even plants have a stress response, however, the stress response can cause harm if not controlled properly [11]. Different individuals experience stress in different ways. Symptoms vary from an anxious or depressed mood, anger, irritability to the digestive system or skin complains.

Stress plays an important role in our lives as it both negatively and positively effects our physical and mental health. Prolonged stress can cause mental health problems such as burnout, depression and post-traumatic stress disorder [5]. According to [12] and stress disrupts normal brain functioning by interrupting connectivity between different brain regions.

The effects on the brain caused by stress for people with PTSD are the main subject of this paper. Some network-oriented models for PTSD have been published [14–21]. Literature research will be conducted to see how stress effects the brain and how regions of the brain are distorted in people with PTSD. The interruptions in connections in the brain will be displayed in a model using network-oriented modeling as proposed by [13]. Network-Oriented Modeling perspective is proposed as an alternative way to address complexity. This perspective takes the concept of network and the interactions within a network as a basis for conceptualization and structuring of any complex processes. Network- Oriented Modeling is not considered here as modeling of networks, but modeling any (complex) processes by networks.

2 Underlying Biological and Neurological Principles

Stress can also come from the inside. For example, when someone has fear and is uncertain. For example, if you do not have enough money to pay the rent [4]. Stressors can be real or perceived. Moreover, stressors are not only dependent on the subject, but also have a clear dynamic in time (recurring, short-term or long-term) and can vary in intensity (or at least in the perception of the individual). That is, stressors can be mild and relatively harmless or result from major events and can have immediate and/or long-lasting effects on the well-being of the person. Therefore, it is fundamentally inevitable that most people will feel stressed from time to time [7].

Stress will almost always find a way to show itself as a physical condition such as fatigue, headaches or muscular tension. Stress is not always seen as a cause for physical problems at first. As people are unaware of the effects stress can have on their body and mind. They then tend to have the symptoms treated rather than the cause [3].

According to [9] there are three types of stress. eustress, neustress, and distress. Eustress is a positive kind of stress which involves positive emotions. For example, meeting your favorite artist. Mostly situations in which eustress occurs are considered enjoyable and are not a threat. Neustress is either good or bad. For example, news of an earthquake somewhere in a remote area. Distress is a negative variant of stress. Distress, in turn, is divided into two types: acute stress and chronic stress. Acute stress occurs suddenly, is quite intense but lasts for a short period of time. Chronic stress can last for a prolonged period of time but is mostly less intense.

We can label a stressful experience as good, tolerable or toxic, depending on the degree to which a person has control over a particular stressor and has supportive systems and resources to deal with it. Meeting the demands imposed by stressful experiences can lead to growth, adaptation, and beneficial forms of learning that promote resiliency and good health. In contrast, other stressful experiences can promote proliferation of recursive neural, physiological, behavioral, cognitive and emotional changes that increase the vulnerability to poor health and premature death from various chronic medical conditions [6].

According to [8] the brain adapts to stress and can sometimes be even named as resilient towards stress. [7] highlight evidence that the brain is the central mediator and target of stress resiliency and vulnerability processes. They emphasize that the brain determines what is threatening, and therefore what is stressful to the individual. The brain regulates the physiological, behavioral, cognitive, and emotional responses for an individual in order to cope with a certain stressor. The brain changes in its plasticity both adaptively and maladaptively as a result of coping with stressful experiences.

Research in both humans and animal models has begun to identify morphological correlates of functional changes. These include altered cell fate in cortical and subcortical structures, dendritic and synaptic reorganization and glial remodeling. The emerging view is that stress causes a dislocation syndrome, which disrupts transmission and integration of information critical to orchestrating appropriate physiological and behavioral responses [12].

In Research done by [10] in the field of fundamental science and functional neuroimaging has helped identify three brain regions that may be involved in the pathophysiology of PTSD: the amygdala, medial prefrontal cortex and hippocampus. The amygdala is involved in the assessment of threat-related stimuli and biologically relevant ambiguity and is necessary for the process of anxiety conditioning. Given that people with PTSD are hypervigilant with regard to a potential threat in the environment and that they show a relatively increased acquisition of conditioned fear in the laboratory, many researchers have the hypothesis that the amygdala is hyperreactive in people with PTSD. Functional neuroimaging studies have provided evidence for amygdala hyper reactivity in PTSD.

Research by [2] has shown a difference in the gray versus white matter ratio between healthy people and patients with PTSD. Gray matter in the brain is composed mainly of neurons and glia-cells. Neurons store and process information and glia-cells support the neurons. White matter is mostly composed of axons, which form a network of fibers to connect the neurons. White matter is called white because of the white fatty sheath of myelin coating that insulates the nerves and accelerates the transmission of the signals between the cells. The research by [2] focused on the cells in the brain that can produce myelin to see if a connection could be found between stress and the proportion of white brain matter to grey. Research was done on the hippocampus area of the brain within adult rats. The general belief as to stem cells is that they would only become neurons or astrocyte cells which are a type of glial cells. But the neural stem cells seemed to behave differently. Under stress, the cells became oligodendrocytes which are another type of glial cells which produce myelin. These cells also help to form the synapses, the communication tools with which nerve cells can exchange information. As can be inferred from these findings, chronic stress can cause more myelin-producing cells and fewer neurons. Communication in the brain can be disrupted by this imbalance and could lead to problems. This also might mean that people with stress disorders, such as PTSD, have alterations in their brain connectivity. This can lead to a stronger connection between the hippocampus and the amygdala (the area that processes the fight-or-flight reaction).

The most effective way to treat PTSD is with trauma-focused psychotherapy. This type of treatment focuses on the memory of the traumatic event or its meaning (United States Department of Veterans Affairs, 2017). There are also some types of medication, but most of this only help in reducing symptoms. Anti-depressants for example help the patient feel less depressed, but the cause of these feelings is not removed. In this article excess of myelin is proposed as a negative result caused by PTSD. There seems to be no medication yet to reduce the amount of myelin. There is also no medication which can cause fewer oligodendrocytes to form, the type of cells that produce myelin. There are some medications which can do the opposite, generate more myelin-producing cells. It seems the only way to reduce the excess myelin is to undergo psychotherapy.

3   The Adaptive Temporal-Causal Network Model

First, the Network-Oriented Modelling approach used to model this process is briefly explained. As discussed in detail in [13, Chap. 2] this approach is based on temporal-causal network models which can be represented at two levels: by a conceptual representation and by a numerical representation. A conceptual representation of a temporal-causal network model in the first place involves representing in a declarative manner states and connections between them that represent (causal) impacts of states on each other, as assumed to hold for the application domain addressed. In reality, not all causal relations are equally strong, so some notion of the *strength of a connection* is used. Furthermore, when more than one causal relation affects a state, some way to *aggregate multiple causal impacts* on a state is used. Moreover, a notion of *speed of change* of a state is used for timing of the processes. These three notions form the defining part of a conceptual representation of a temporal-causal network model:

- **Strength of a connection** $\omega_{X,Y}$. Each connection from a state X to a state Y has a *connection weight value* $\omega_{X,Y}$ representing the strength of the connection, often between 0 and 1, but sometimes also below 0 (negative effect) or above 1.
- **Combining multiple impacts on a state** $c_Y(..)$. For each state (a reference to) a *combination function* $c_Y(..)$ is chosen to combine the causal impacts of other states on state Y.
- **Speed of change of a state** η_Y. For each state Y a *speed factor* η_Y is used to represent how fast a state is changing upon causal impact.

Combination functions can have different forms, as there are many different approaches possible to address the issue of combining multiple impacts. Therefore, the Network-Oriented Modelling approach based on temporal-causal networks incorporates for each state, as a kind of label or parameter, a way to specify how multiple causal impacts on this state are aggregated by some combination function. For this aggregation a number of standard combination functions are available as options and a number of desirable properties of such combination functions have been identified; see [13, Chap. 2, Sects. 2.6 and 2.7]. In Fig. 1 the conceptual representation of the temporal-causal network model is depicted. A brief explanation of the states used is shown in Table 1.

Table 1. Explanation of the states in the model

X_1	srs_s	Sensory representation state of extreme fear
X_2	ps_{fear}	Preparation state for extreme fear
X_3	fs_{fear}	State of fear
X_4	cs	Control state for regulating the fear response (located in the prefrontal cortex)
X_5	myelin	State which represents the fatty sheet around axons and helps to increase the speed of impulses along fibers. It also insulates, so the electrical current cannot leave the axon
X_6	sr_i	Sensory input: This can be any kind of sensory input, such as visual, audio, smell
X_7	sm	Sensory memory: The sensory memory holds input after it is perceived for less than a second. Thus, this information has to be recalled immediately or else it decays
X_8	stm	Short-term memory: The short-term memory can hold input from seconds to a minute. This allows for rehearsal, which can lead to information to be stored from short-term to long-term memory
X_9	ltm	Long-term memory: The long-term memory can store large quantities of information and hold these for a long period of time. It is quite unmeasurable, as some information decays after a period of time
X_{10}	cs_m	Control state memory: The connection between long-term and short-term memory is mostly controlled by the hippocampus which in this case is the control state for memory

Figure 1 is a visual representation of the basic model. The myelin has an effect on the connection between the control state and both ps_{fear} and fs_{fear}, as stated before the myelin excess can cause a disruption in connectivity between the hippocampus and the prefrontal cortex. The prefrontal cortex moderates/controls the fear responses. States ps_{fear} and fs_{fear} thus cannot be decreased properly. Also because of the increase between the hippocampus and the amygdala, caused by the excess myelin, the fear responses connection increases over time.

In this model the connections have a certain weight. These can both be negative or positive. These amounts can have a big effect (when the amount is near 1 or −1 for negative effects) or a smaller effect (when the amount is near 0). In this case for example it is clear that ps_{fear} and FSfear have a small negative effect on cs. The values for these connections are based on the literature study. The small negative effect occurs because the control state will not be able to have a control effect on ps_{fear} and fs_{fear}.

These states are implemented in a visual model (Fig. 2). As an individual perceives a certain sensory input (sr_i), which can be visual, auditory or any other kind that uses

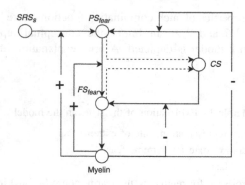

Fig. 1. Visual representation of the fear model

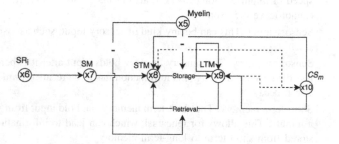

Fig. 2. Visual representation of the memory model

the human senses, this is stored in the Sensory memory (sm). The sensory memory can only store information for a very short period of time (less than a second), after this, it either decays or stays present in the short-term memory (stm). In the state sm the information can be stored a few seconds to a minute, which allows for rehearsal which in turn can lead to storage in the long-term memory (ltm). Information can also be transferred from stm to ltm without rehearsal. The ltm can store information up to a lifetime, but can also suffer from decay.

When an individual tries to access information stored in the LTM, the information will be retrieved from the ltm to the stm allowing the individual to 'work' with the information. The state stm is also referred to as working memory, which in turn is split up into three different parts. For this research the simpler stm is used to ensure the model is not too comprehensive.

With the retrieval and storage of information from stm to ltm and ltm to stm formation and elimination of axons and synapses is critical. If any disruptions occur, the forming of new memories and the retrieval of former memories can be corrupted. There is evidence that myelin inhibits synapse formation and reduces plasticity in the central nervous system, that oligodendrocytes inhibit axon growth cones, and that oligodendrocytes precursor cells are repulsive for growing axons. Thus, one consequence of excessive myelin, particularly in the hippocampus, can very well be a reduced ability to learn and remember. Which is shown in Fig. 2 by the negative

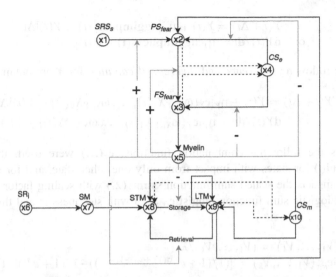

Fig. 3. Visual representation of the combined model

arrows towards the connections between stm and ltm. The ltm also has a connection to itself which will lead to a more persistent connection.

This visual model is converted into Table 2. Again, the effects can both be negative or positive. These amounts can have a big effect (when the amount is near 1 or −1 for negative effects) or a smaller effect (when the amount is near 0). The amounts are based on the literature on how well the brain stores and retrieves memories. Also, all connections are implemented in the table where Hebbian learning, state-connection amplification and the positive or negative effect of myelin come into play.

The conceptual representation was transformed into a numerical representation as follows [13, Chap. 2]:

- at each time point t each state Y in the model has a real number value in the interval [0, 1], denoted by $Y(t)$
- at each time point t each state X connected to state Y has an impact on Y defined as $\textbf{impact}_{X,Y}(t) = \omega_{X,Y}X(t)$ where $\omega_{X,Y}$ is the weight of the connection from X to Y
- The *aggregated impact* of multiple states X_i on Y at t is determined using a *combination function* $\textbf{c}_Y(..)$:

$$\textbf{aggimpact}_Y(t) = \textbf{c}_Y(\textbf{impact}_{X_1,Y}(t), \ldots, \textbf{impact}_{X_k,Y}(t))$$
$$= \textbf{c}_Y(\omega_{X_1,Y}X_1(t), \ldots, \omega_{X_k,Y}X_k(t))$$

where X_i are the states with connections to state Y
- The effect of $\textbf{aggimpact}_Y(t)$ on Y is exerted over time gradually, depending on speed factor η_Y:

$$Y(t + \Delta t) = Y(t) + \eta_Y[\mathbf{aggimpact}_Y(t) - Y(t)]\Delta t$$
$$\text{or} \quad \mathbf{d}Y(t)/\mathbf{d}t = \eta_Y[\mathbf{aggimpact}_Y(\mathbf{t}) - Y(t)]$$

- Thus, the following *difference* and *differential equation* for Y are obtained:

$$Y(t + \Delta t) = Y(t) + \eta_Y[\mathbf{c}_Y(\omega_{X_1,Y}X_1(t), \ldots, \omega_{X_k,Y}X_k(t)) - Y(t)]\Delta t$$
$$\mathbf{d}Y(t)/\mathbf{d}t = \eta_Y[\mathbf{c}_Y(\omega_{X_1,Y}X_1(t), \ldots, \omega_{X_k,Y}X_k(t)) - Y(t)]$$

For states the following combination functions $\mathbf{c}_Y(\ldots)$ were used, the identity function $\mathbf{id}(.)$ for states with impact from only one other state, and for states with multiple impacts the scaled sum function $\mathbf{ssum}_\lambda(\ldots)$ with scaling factor λ, and the advanced logistic sum function $\mathbf{alogistic}_{\sigma,\tau}(\ldots)$ with steepness σ and threshold τ.

$$\mathbf{id}(V) = V$$
$$\mathbf{ssum}_\lambda(V_1, \ldots, V_k) = (V_1, \ldots, V_k)/\lambda$$
$$\mathbf{alogistic}_{\sigma,\tau}(V_1, \ldots, V_k) = [(1/(1 + e^{-\sigma(V_1 + \ldots + V_k - \tau)})) - 1/(1 + e^{\sigma\tau})](1 + e^{-\sigma\tau})$$

Here first the general Hebbian Learning is explained. In a general example model considered it is assumed that the strength ω of such a connection between states X_1 and X_2 is adapted using the following Hebbian Learning rule, taking into account a maximal connection strength 1, a learning rate $\eta > 0$ and a persistence factor $\mu \geq 0$, and activation levels $X_1(t)$ and $X_2(t)$ (between 0 and 1) of the two states involved. The first expression is in differential equation format, the second one in difference equation format:

$$d\omega(t)/dt = \eta[X_1(t)X_2(t)(1 - \omega(t)) - (1 - \mu)\omega(t)]$$
$$\omega(t + \Delta t) = \omega(t) + \eta[X_1(t)X_2(t)(1 - \omega(t)) - (1 - \mu)\omega(t)]\Delta t$$

4   Example Simulation

An example simulation of this process is shown in Figs. 2 and 3. The connection weight parameters are shown in Tables 2 and 3.

Table 2. Connection weights for the example simulation for the fear model

Connection weights		X_1 srs_s	X_2 ps_{fear}	X_3 fs_{fear}	X_4 cs	X_5 myelin
X_1	srs_s	1	0.7			
X_2	ps_{fear}			0.5	0.6	
X_3	fs_{fear}				0.4	1
X_4	cs		−0.2	−0.2		
X_5	myelin					

The memory model will be a representation of how the myelin producing oligo-dendrocytes effect the encoding and retrieval of memories from the short-term memory to the long-term memory and vice versa.

Table 3. Connection weights for the example simulation of memory model

Connection weights		X_6 sr_i	X_7 sm	X_8 stm	X_9 ltm	X_{10} cs_m
X_6	sr_i	1	1			
X_7	sm			0.8		
X_8	stm				0.9	0.4
X_9	ltm			0.85	0.3	0.5
X_{10}	cs_m			0.6	0.7	

Figure 4 is a representation of the effect of myelin excess on the fear response. This scenario shows how two connection becomes stronger and two others become weaker. The control state (X_4) is getting less grip on the situation. As long as the fear response cannot be controlled, the symptoms of PTSD will not be reduced.

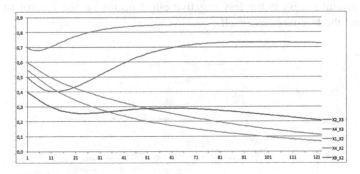

Fig. 4. Simulation result for the effect of myelin excess on the fear response

Figure 5 shows the connections between ltm and stm and vice versa. Both con-nections decrease over time, which indicates that the storage and retrieval of memories within a patient with PTSD and myelin excess is getting worse. Since myelin inhibits synapse formation and reduces plasticity in the central nervous system, oligodendro-cytes inhibit axon growth cones, and oligodendrocytes precursor cells are repulsive for growing axons. And the formation and elimination of axons and synapses are critical for learning and memory. Patients with PTSD tend to have problems with their memory. Forming new memories is often disrupted, and the retrieval of memories can also be a problem.

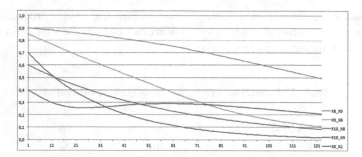

Fig. 5. Simulation results for the memory connections

For the memory model, the myelin effect is also lowered accordingly. Again, this results in a much less dramatic negative effect on the retrieval and forming of memories. Figures 6 and 7 show the simulation of this lowered myelin effect. Here it is shown that both the memory retrieval is and the formation of memories is moving towards a more steady value.

In Fig. 6 the influence of myelin excess on the fear response and the forming and retrieving of memories is simulated. From 1 and −1 the effect is now 0.3 and −0.3 for a positive and negative effect receptively. The result is shown in Fig. 6. It seems that the initial effects are still present, but in a far less dramatic way. This may indicate, the lower the myelin excess is the less negative effect occurs on the control of the fear response and the fear response itself.

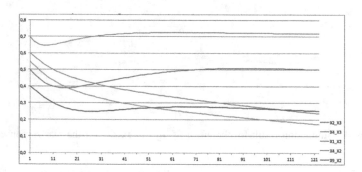

Fig. 6. Simulation results for decreased myelin effects on fear

For the memory model the myelin effect is also lowered accordingly. Again, this results in a much less dramatic negative effect on the retrieval and forming of memories. Figure 7 shows the simulation of this lowered myelin effect. Here it is shown that both the memory retrieval is and the formation of memories are moving towards more steady value.

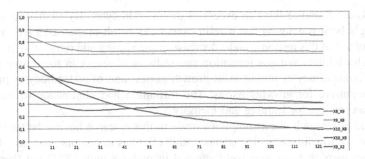

Fig. 7. Simulation results for decreased myelin effects on memory

An overview of the result of the simulation of both models combined is shown in Fig. 8. The decreased effect of myelin in the combined model is shown in Fig. 9.

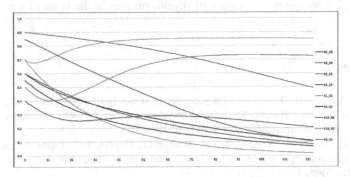

Fig. 8. Simulation results for the combined model

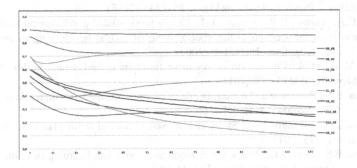

Fig. 9. Simulation results for decreased myelin effect in the combined model

5   Conclusion

The network-oriented modeling technique is used in this thesis as a way to simulate certain scenarios for patients with PTSD. This resulted in the formation of a computational model. It appears myelin, and the oligodendrocytes which produce the myelin can have altering effects in the brain of patients with PTSD. When under stress, patients with PTSD are found to form an excess of oligodendrocytes. By simulating what the effects might be it was found that myelin excess can result in increased fear response, reduced control of this response and a decrease in the storing and retrieval of memories. Since myelin inhibits synapse formation and reduces plasticity in the central nervous system, oligodendrocytes inhibit axon growth cones, and oligodendrocytes precursor cells are repulsive for growing axons. The formation and elimination of axons and synapses are critical for learning and memory.

For further research, the assumptions made in this research have to be tested. More research on the myelin excess in patients with PTSD has to be done. Not only fear and memory are parts that are negatively affected in patients with PTSD but there might also be more which is influenced by the growth of myelin-producing oligodendrocytes. When the effects of the myelin are proven, the medical field tries to manipulate the oligodendrocytes, and maybe form some type of drug that can suppress the effects. Also, it might be interesting to see if psychotherapy, which is proven to decrease PTSD symptoms, also decreases the amount of myelin present in the brain of a patient with PTSD.

References

1. Carr, D., Umberson, D.: The social psychology of stress, health, and coping. In: DeLamater, J., Ward, A. (eds.) Handbook of Social Psychology, pp. 465–487. Springer, Dordrecht (2013). https://doi.org/10.1007/978-94-007-6772-0_16
2. Chao, L.L., Tosun, D., Woodward, S.H., Kaufer, D., Neylan, T.C.: Preliminary evidence of increased hippocampal myelin content in veterans with posttraumatic stress disorder. Front. Behav. Neurosci. **9**, 333 (2015)
3. Hamm, J.M., Perry, R.P., Chipperfield, J.G., Stewart, T.L., Heckhausen, J.: Motivation-focused thinking: buffering against stress-related physical symptoms and depressive symptomology. Psychol. Health **30**(11), 1326–1345 (2015)
4. Lewis, C.A., Turton, D.W., Francis, L.J.: Clergy work-related psychological health, stress, and burnout: an introduction to this special issue of mental health, religion and culture. Mental Health Relig. Cult. **10**(1), 1–8 (2007)
5. Marin, M.-F., et al.: Chronic stress, cognitive functioning and mental health. Neurobiol. Learn. Mem. **96**(4), 583–595 (2011)
6. McEwen, B.S.: Protective and damaging effects of stress mediators: central role of the brain. Dialogues Clin. Neurosci. **8**(4), 367 (2006)
7. McEwen, B.S., Gianaros, P.J.: Stress-and allostasis-induced brain plasticity. Annu. Rev. Med. **62**, 431–445 (2011)
8. McEwen, B.S., Gray, J.D., Nasca, C.: Recognizing resilience: Learning from the effects of stress on the brain. Neurobiol. Stress **1**, 1–11 (2015)
9. Seaward, B.L.: Managing Stress. Jones & Bartlett Publishers (2013)
10. Shin, L.M., Rauch, S.L., Pitman, R.K.: Amygdala, medial prefrontal cortex, and hippocampal function in PTSD. Ann. N. Y. Acad. Sci. **1071**(1), 67–79 (2006)
11. Sousa, N.: The dynamics of the stress neuromatrix. Mol. Psychiatry **21**(3), 302–312 (2016)
12. Sousa, N., Almeida, O.F.: Disconnection and reconnection: the morphological basis of (mal) adaptation to stress. Trends Neurosci. **35**(12), 742–751 (2012)
13. Treur, J.: Network-Oriented Modeling: Addressing Complexity of Cognitive. Affective and Social Interactions. Springer, Cham (2017). https://doi.org/10.1007/978-3-319-45213-5

14. Treur, J., Mohammadi Ziabari, S.S.: An adaptive temporal-causal network model for decision making under acute stress. In: Nguyen, N.T., Pimenidis, E., Khan, Z., Trawiński, B. (eds.) ICCCI 2018. LNCS (LNAI), vol. 11056, pp. 13–25. Springer, Cham (2018). https://doi.org/10.1007/978-3-319-98446-9_2

15. Mohammadi Ziabari, S.S., Treur, J.: Computational analysis of gender differences in coping with extreme stressful emotions. In: Proceedings of the 9th International Conference on Biologically Inspired Cognitive Architecture (BICA2018), Czech Republic. Elsevier (2018)

16. Mohammadi Ziabari, S.S., Treur, J.: A modeling environment for dynamic and adaptive network models implemented in Matlab. In: Proceedings of the 4th International Congress on Information and Communication Technology (ICICT2019), 25–26 February 2019. Springer, London (2019)

17. Mohammadi-Ziabari, S.S., Treur, J.: Integrative biological, cognitive and affective modeling of a drug-therapy for a post-traumatic stress disorder. In: Fagan, D., Martín-Vide, C., O'Neill, M., Vega-Rodríguez, M.A. (eds.) TPNC 2018. LNCS, vol. 11324, pp. 292–304. Springer, Cham (2018). https://doi.org/10.1007/978-3-030-04070-3_23

18. Mohammadi Ziabari, S.S., Treur, J.: An adaptive cognitive temporal-causal network model of a mindfulness therapy based on music. In: Tiwary, U.S. (ed.) IHCI 2018. LNCS, vol. 11278, pp. 180–193. Springer, Cham (2018). https://doi.org/10.1007/978-3-030-04021-5_17

19. Mohammadi Ziabari, S.S., Treur, J.: Cognitive modeling of mindfulness therapy by autogenic training. In: Satapathy, S.C., Bhateja, V., Somanah, R., Yang, X.-S., Senkerik, R. (eds.) Information Systems Design and Intelligent Applications. AISC, vol. 863, pp. 53–66. Springer, Singapore (2019). https://doi.org/10.1007/978-981-13-3338-5_6

20. Mohammadi Ziabari, S.S., Treur, J.: A temporal cognitive model of the influence of methylphenidate (ritalin) on test anxiety. In: Proceedings of the 4th International Congress on Information and Communication Technology (ICICT2019), 25–26 February 2019. Springer, London (2019)

21. Mohammadi Ziabari, S.S.: An adaptive temporal-causal network model for stress extinction using fluoxetine. In: Proceedings of the 15th International Conference on Artificial Intelligence Applications and Innovations (AIAI 2019), Crete, Greece, 24–26 May 2019 (2019)

On Machine Learning Approach for the Design of Pharmaceutical Technology of Tablets: Acetyl Salicylic Acid with Atorvastatin

Vasyl Martsenyuk[1]([✉])(iD), Taras Hroshovyi[2](iD), Oksana Trygubchak[2](iD),
and Aleksandra Klos-Witkowska[1](iD)

[1] Department of Computer Science and Automatics, University of Bielsko-Biala,
43-309 Bielsko-Biala, Poland
vmartsenyuk@ath.bielsko.pl
[2] Ternopil State Medical University, Ternopil 46001, Ukraine

Abstract. The objective of this work is to offer an approach of application of machine learning (ML) in the problem of design of pharmaceutical technology of tablets, which basically consists of choosing qualitative and quantitative content of the corresponding excipients, enabling us necessary values of pharmaceutical and technological characteristics. At the first stage, we choose technology and qualitative content of tablets, including filler, acidity regulator, disintegrant, binder and stabilizer. After selecting excipients ensuring some acceptable values of output variables for tablets, at the second stage, the problem of optimization of some objective variable is considered subject to quantitative content of excipients. An example, which is devoted to the development of a technology of tablets of acetylsalicylic acid with atorvastatin is considered.

Keywords: Machine learning · Pharmaceutical technology ·
Neural network · R · Tablets

1 Introduction

In pharmaceutical research tasks a large number of experiments taking into account several factors and their combinations are required. Special experiment plans can be very useful, which are based on combinatorial configurations. Applying special plans (e.g., using a second-order Latin cube), the problem can be solved using fewer experiments [4,6]. In this case, the experimental material obtained will meet all requirements. Tasks of this type are typical for a large number of research areas. This is the search for new drugs, fertilizers, feed, construction materials, alloys, lubricating oils, and many other mixtures. Experiment planning and analysis are an important branch of statistical methods,

Supported by University of Bielsko-Biala.

which are designed to detect and verify causal relationships between input variables (factors) and output (responses).

The *objective* of this work is to offer an approach of application of ML in the problem of design of pharmaceutical technology of tablets, which basically consists of choosing qualitative and quantitative content of the corresponding excipients (auxiliary substances), enabling us necessary values of pharmaceutical and technological characteristics.

"Tablets may be defined as the solid unit dosage form of medicament or medicaments with or without suitable excipients and prepared either by molding or by compression. It includes a mixture of active substances and excipients, usually in powder form, pressed or compacted from a powder into a solid dose. The excipients can include diluents, binders or granulating agents, glidants (flow aids) and lubricants to ensure efficient tableting; disintegrants to promote tablet break-up in the digestive tract; sweeteners or flavors to enhance taste; and pigments to make the tablets visually attractive or aid in visual identification of an unknown tablet" [2].

Currently, there are two main methods of producing tablets. They are the direct compression of substances and granulation.

The method of direct compression has several advantages. It allows you to achieve high productivity, significantly reduce the time of the technological cycle by eliminating a number of operations and stages, eliminate the use of several equipment items, reduce production areas, and reduce energy and labor costs. The direct compression makes it possible to obtain tablets from moisture, thermolabile and incompatible substances. Nowadays, however, less than 20% of tablets are obtained by this method. It follows from the fact that the majority of medicinal substances do not possess the properties providing their direct compression. These properties include the isodiametric shape of crystals, good flowability (fluidity) and compressibility, low adhesiveness to the compression tool of the tablet machine.

Granulation is directed enlargement of particles, i.e. it is the process of turning a powdered material into grains of a certain size. Granulation is necessary to improve the flowability of the tableting mass, which occurs as a result of a significant decrease in the total surface of the particles when they stick together into granules and, therefore, a corresponding reduction in friction that occurs between these particles during movement. The stratification of a multi-component powder mixture usually occurs due to the difference in particle sizes and the specific gravity values of the medicinal and auxiliary components included in its composition. This separation is possible with various kinds of vibrations of the tablet machine or its funnel. The stratification of the tableted mass is a dangerous and unacceptable process, in some cases causing an almost complete separation of the component with the highest specific gravity from the mixture and violation of its dosage. Granulation prevents this danger since particles of various sizes and specific densities stick together in its process. The resulting granulate, subject to the equality of the sizes of the resulting granules, acquires a fairly constant bulk density. The strength of the granules also plays an important role, i.e., strong granules are less prone to abrasion and have better flowability.

The currently existing methods of granulation are divided into the following main types: dry granulation; wet granulation or extrusion granulation; structural granulation.

2 General Scheme of Design of Tablet Technology with the Help of ML

The general scheme of ML is based on the application of neural networks. Namely, if there is only one hidden layer and only one output unit, then the set of all implemented neural networks with N hidden units is

$$\mathcal{R}_n^{(N)}(\psi) = \left\{ h(x) : \mathbb{R}^n \to \mathbb{R} | h(x) = \sum_{j=1}^{N} \beta_j (w_j^\top x - \theta_j) \right\},$$

where ψ is the common activation function of the hidden units and $^\top$ denotes transpose, output units are always assumed to be linear [7].

Assume we consider some active pharmaceutical ingredient (API or medicament) P^1.

Stage 1. Choice of Technology and Qualitative Content. In general case, we start tablet design from investigating the possibility of application of the direct compression. For this purpose we consider some excipients (auxiliary substances), including filler A, acidity regulator B, disintegrant C, binder D and stabilizer E. We note that from viewpoint of ML we have the following categorical variables and their values corresponding to certain excipients

$$A \in \{a_1, a_2, \ldots, a_{n_A}\}, \quad B \in \{b_1, b_2, \ldots, b_{n_B}\}, \quad C \in \{c_1, c_2, \ldots, c_{n_C}\},$$

$$D \in \{d_1, d_2, \ldots, d_{n_D}\}, \quad E \in \{e_1, e_2, \ldots, e_{n_B}\}.$$

Here n_A, n_B, n_C, n_D, $n_E \in \mathbb{N}$ are the quantities of different fillers, acidity regulators, disintegrants, binders and stabilizers, respectively, which are considered in the tablet design.

When developing ML model we consider the tuples of input variables in the following binary form

$$\{a_1, a_2, \ldots, a_{n_A}, b_1, b_2, \ldots, b_{n_B}, c_1, c_2, \ldots, c_{n_C}, d_1, d_2, \ldots, d_{n_D}, e_1, e_2, \ldots, e_{n_B}\} \in \mathbb{B}^n,$$

where $n = n_A + n_B + n_C + n_D + n_E$, $\mathbb{B}^n = \{(b_1, b_2, \ldots, b_n) | b_i \in \{0, 1\}, i = \overline{1, n}\}$. Each tuple of input variables $\mathcal{E}_i$, $i = \overline{1, p}$ ($p \in \mathbb{N}$ is the number of experiments) corresponds to the certain experiment implying the application of corresponding excipients.

As a rule after mixing active ingredient with excipients, we get a powder with some properties with respect to compression. If the powder (as a tablet mass)

---

[1] It can be some complex of ingredients, as it is shown in Sect. 3.

can be compressed we produce tablets through direct compression, otherwise, we apply granulation at first.

In any case we should investigate the pharmaceutical and technological indices of granules (in case of granulation) $y_i \in \mathbb{R}$, $i = \overline{1,6}$ (see Table 1), tablet mass $y_i \in \mathbb{R}$, $i = \overline{7,12}$ (see Table 2) and tablets $y_i \in \mathbb{R}$, $i = \overline{13,15}$ (see Table 3), which are considered as output variables in ML algorithms.

For example, in case of compressible tablet mass we consider y_i, $i = \overline{7,12}$ as outputs, in case of preliminary application of granulation we need y_i, $i = \overline{1,6}$ and then we observe y_i, $i = \overline{7,12}$. Finally, we get tablets, which are characterised by the variables $y_i \in \mathbb{R}$, $i = \overline{13,15}$.

After fulfilling p experiments, which are described by the binary matrix of input variables $\mathcal{E} \in \mathbb{B}^{p \times n}$ and real-valued matrix of output variables $Y = (y_i^j) \in \mathbb{R}^{p \times 15}$, we construct 15 neural networks $h_i \in \mathcal{R}_n^{(N)}$, $i = \overline{1,16}$ corresponding pharmaceutical and technological indices y_i, $i = \overline{1,15}$.

Table 1. Output variables for granulate

Denotion	Meaning	Units
y_1	Humidity of the granulate	%
y_2	Bulk density of the granulate	g/ml
y_3	Density after shrinkage of the granulate	g/ml
y_4	Carra index of granulate	%
y_5	Flow of granulate	c/100 g
y_6	Angle of slope of the granulate	°

Table 2. Output variables for tablet mass

Denotion	Meaning	Units
y_7	Bulk density of the tablet mass	g/ml
y_8	Density after shrinkage of the tablet mass	g/ml
y_9	Carra index of tablet mass	%
y_{10}	Pill weight	c/100 g
y_{11}	Slope of the tablet mass	°
y_{12}	Homogeneity of mass	%

Stage 2. Quantitative Optimization. After selecting excipients ensuring some acceptable values of output variables for tablets y_i, $i = \overline{13,15}$ there appears the problem of optimization of some objective variable y_{i^*}, $i^* \in \overline{13,15}$. Namely, let us assume we have selected some values a_{i^*}, b_{j^*}, c_{k^*}, d_{l^*}, e_{m^*}, $i^* \in \overline{1,n_A}$,

Table 3. Output variables for tablets

Denotion	Meaning	Units
y_{13}	Resistance to crushing	N
y_{14}	Erasure	%
y_{15}	Decomposition	Min

$j^* \in \overline{1, n_B}$, $k^* \in \overline{1, n_C}$, $l^* \in \overline{1, n_D}$, $m^* \in \overline{1, n_E}$, characterizing excipients. The goal is to search the quantities of excipients enabling us the optimal[2] value of an index y_r, $r \in \overline{13, 15}$.

We offer the following approach. We consider five levels for each of the excipients a_{i*}, b_{j*}, c_{k*}, d_{l*}, e_{m*}, determining the corresponding concentrations. We denote them as

$$l_1^{a_{i*}}, l_2^{a_{i*}}, \ldots, l_5^{a_{i*}}, l_1^{b_{i*}}, l_2^{b_{i*}}, \ldots, l_5^{b_{i*}}, l_1^{c_{i*}}, l_2^{c_{i*}}, \ldots, l_5^{c_{i*}},$$

$$l_1^{d_{i*}}, l_2^{d_{i*}}, \ldots, l_5^{d_{i*}}, l_1^{e_{i*}}, l_2^{e_{i*}}, \ldots, l_5^{e_{i*}},$$

The choice of values for levels of concentrations depends on concrete substances and is a sort of art.

When developing ML model we consider the tuples of input variables in the following binary form

$$\{l_1^{a_{i*}}, l_2^{a_{i*}}, \ldots, l_5^{a_{i*}}, l_1^{b_{i*}}, l_2^{b_{i*}}, \ldots, l_5^{b_{i*}}, l_1^{c_{i*}}, l_2^{c_{i*}}, \ldots, l_5^{c_{i*}},$$

$$l_1^{d_{i*}}, l_2^{d_{i*}}, \ldots, l_5^{d_{i*}}, l_1^{e_{i*}}, l_2^{e_{i*}}, \ldots, l_5^{e_{i*}}\} \in \mathbb{B}^{25}$$

Each tuple of input variables $\mathcal{E}'_i$, $i = \overline{1, p'}$ ($p' \in \mathbb{N}$ is the number of experiments) corresponds to the certain experiment implying application of excipients a_{i*}, b_{j*}, c_{k*}, d_{l*}, e_{m*} at given levels of concentrations. y_r is considered as output variable in ML algorithm.

After fulfilling p_r experiments, which are described by the binary matrix of input variables $\mathcal{E}_r \in \mathbb{B}^{p_r \times 25}$ and vector of output variables $Y_r = (y_{jr}) \in \mathbb{R}^{p_r}$, we construct neural network $h_r \in \mathcal{R}_{25}^{(N)}$, corresponding pharmaceutical (or technological) index y_r.

At last, we apply the optimization algorithm (e.g., genetic algorithm) for the objective function given by neural network h_r. As a result we get some optimal solution

$$\{l_{j*}^{a_{i*}}, l_{j*}^{b_{i*}}, l_{j*}^{c_{i*}}, l_{j*}^{d_{i*}}, l_{j*}^{e_{i*}}\} \in \mathbb{B}^5$$

resulting to the optimal value of y_r[3].

---

[2] Without loss of generality we look for minimal value.

[3] Without loss of generality we choose unique index j^* for all excipients, which it can be reached by reordering levels.

3 Application for Tablets of Acetyl Salicylic Acid with Atorvastatin

In the following example, we demonstrate the application of the general scheme presented above for the design of tablets based on atorvastatin.

The release of active ingredient and poor flowability of the tablet mass requires optimization. Therefore, the decision is made to combine atorvastatin with poor flowability with a solution in granules, which improves flowability.

In the literature, atorvastatin calcium is described as an unstable substance and many approaches are proposed for obtaining a stable pharmaceutical form of atorvastatin. If necessary, the problem can be solved by obtaining atorvastatin calcium only in crystalline form (see WO 97/3958 and WO 97/3959) [3] and only in amorphous form (see WO 97/3960, WO 01/42209 and P-9900271) [8,10], respectively, before entering it into a formulation requiring an additional operation in which 5–10% of the substance is lost. Therefore, 10.36 mg of atorvastatin calcium powder per tablet should be used for the obtaining of 10 mg of atorvastatin to the dosage form.

The solubility of various forms of atorvastatin calcium and, accordingly, its solubility can also be solved at the drug level by adding to the formulation a basic or buffering agent (see WO 00/35425 (D2), WO 94/16693 (D1 (WL8))) [9], which increases the bioavailability of atorvastatin by increasing its solubility and dissolution rate in aqueous solutions. To obtain a stabilized amorphous substance, a combination of methods described in WO 01/42209, P-9900271 and WO 01/42209 can be used. An additional argument in favor of this solution is the fact that atorvastatin calcium is an expensive substance.

The researchers found that the solubility of atorvastatin calcium in aqueous solutions is significantly improved with pH values equal to pKa+1 or higher. At the same time, the difference between the solubility of atorvastatin calcium in the crystalline and amorphous form becomes insignificant. The value of pKa of the final carboxyl group of atorvastatin is 4.5. To increase the pH of the aqueous solution to the desired range of values, the pharmaceutical formulation may contain a substance B adjusting the pH of 0.2–2.0 mmol, preferably 0.4–1.2 mmol. Accordingly, the best adjusting substances are metal oxides, inorganic or organic bases, salts of organic or inorganic acids and alkaline earth metals, in particular, magnesium oxide, alkaline phosphate buffers, in particular, sodium phosphate and hydrophosphate, and organic amines, in particular, tris (hydroxymethyl) methylamine.

Mills and co-authors of U.S. Patent No. 5686104 state that the pharmaceutical composition may contain an inorganic base of calcium, magnesium, aluminum, or lithium salt. Examples of such salts include calcium carbonate, calcium hydroxide, magnesium carbonate, magnesium hydroxide, magnesium silicate, magnesium aluminate, aluminum hydroxide or lithium hydroxide [N 5686104]. In addition, U.S. Patent No. US20040247673 states that since adding alkaline earth metal salts can affect the bioavailability of atorvastatin, this is necessary to ensure that it is added to atorvastatin when wet granulation of the composition (see US20040247673). Among buffering agents, WO 00/35425 describes sodium or potassium citrate, sodium phosphate, sodium sulfate, sodium carbonate or magnesium, sodium ascorbinate, sodium benzoate, sodium carbonate or potassium bicarbonate, lauryl sulfate, or a mixture of such buffers (see WO 00/35425).

To enhance the disintegration of granules you can add a leavening agent C. US20040247673 states that some disintegrators may be harmful to atorvastatin stability, for example, croscarmellose sodium (see US20040247673).

WOO 1/76566 describes a stabilized pharmaceutical composition of atorvastatin calcium and an effective stabilizing amount of an amido group or an amino group comprising a polymeric compound from the group consisting of polyvinylpyrrolidone, crosslinked polyvinylpyrrolidone, copolymers of vinylpyrrolidone and vinyl acetate and polynocycline (see WOO 1/76566).

The binders D may be selected from the group consisting of starch, gelatin, dextrin, maltodextrin, natural and synthetic gums such as Arabic gum, alginic acid, sodium alginate, guar gum, Irish moss extract, ghatti gum, husks mucus, carboxymethyl cellulose, methyl cellulose, hydroxyethyl cellulose, hydroxypropyl cellulose, hydroxypropylmethylcellulose, polyvinylpyrrolidone, wigum, arabogalactans and the like and their mixture. Typically, the number of binders may vary from about 0.5% to about 10% by weight of the composition.

Increased stability can be achieved by introducing an additional stabilizer of E. An additional stabilizer includes antioxidants selected from the group consisting of butylated hydroxyanisole, butylated hydroxytoluene, DL-alpha-tocopherol, propyl ghalate, octyl gallate, ethylenediaminetetraacetate, ascorbil palmitate, acetylcysteine, ascorbic acid, sodium ascorbate, fumaric acid, lecithin, and the like, and their mixtures. The number of antioxidants can vary from about 0.001% to about 0.01% by weight, preferably 0.009%.

In most of the cases, the stabilizer includes tromethamine, antioxidants, and sodium lauryl sulfate. Sodium levels of lauryl sulfate may range from 1% to 2% by weight of the composition.

Given the fact that atorvastatin is characterized by high lyophilicity, this requires the addition of surfactants. A classic example is a polysorbate (Twin 80), but it is incompatible with phenol, salicylates. Therefore, poloxamer 338 was investigated as a stabilizer.

Fillers A that can be used include micro-cellulose, mannitol, dextritis, dextrin, dextrose, fructose, lactose, lactitol, maltitol, maltodextrin, maltose, and the like. Mostly the filler is the micro-cellulose. For wet granulation commercially available is micro-cellulose 101.

For the reasonings given above, the studied excipients were grouped by functional purpose (see Table 4).

When receiving the granules, 10.36 g of the atorvastatin calcium was mixed with 18.55 g of MCC 101 and there were added 22 g of the substance from the group A, 33 g from B and 7.5 g from C. The substances D and E were added to 27.76 g of purified water. The powder mixture was moistened with the resulting solution, passed through a sieve with a hole diameter of 2 mm and dried at 85 °C. The dried granules were calibrated through a sieve with a diameter of holes of

Table 4. Excipients to be considered in tablets of acetyl salicylic acid with atorvastatin design

Variable	Corresponding excipient
a_1	Lactose monohydrate (Pharmattose 200M)
a_2	Sorbitol (Parteck SI 150)
a_3	Mannit (Parteck Delta M)
b_1	Magnesium carbonate
b_2	Calcium carbonate
b_3	Calcium dihydrogen phosphate
c_1	Corn starch
c_2	Sodium croscarmellose
c_3	Crospovidone XL-10
d_1	PVP (Kollidone 17 PF)
d_2	PVP (plasdone K 90)
d_3	PVP (plasdone K 25)
d_4	PVP (plasdone K 30)
d_5	PVP (Pladdon S630)
d_6	Gipromeloz E 5
d_7	Gipromeloz E 15
d_8	Klucel EXF
d_9	Hydroxypropylmethylcellulose acetose succinate (Shin-Etsu AS-MF)
e_1	Magnesium aluminosilicate (neusilin US2)
e_2	Silicon dioxide anhydrous colloid (aerosil 200)
e_3	Sodium stearyl fumarate
e_4	Sodium lauryl sulfate
e_5	Potato starch
e_6	Potato starch pregelatinised (Starch 1500)
e_7	PEG 4000
e_8	PEG 8000 (macrogol)
e_9	Poloxamer 338

1 mm and tested twice with respect to the pharmaceutical and technological parameters. 92 g of granulate was added with 75 g of acetyl salicylic acid and the following excipients: 1 g of citric acid, 21 g of MCC 102, 10 g of starch of corn. 1 g of calcium stearate was used for flushing. Each series of tablet mass was tested twice in all metrics according to pharmacopoeial requirements. Biconvex tablets with a diameter of 8 mm and an average weight of 0.2 g were pressed.

3.1   Implementation of the Neural Network Modeling in R

Calculations were implemented in RStudio (version 1.1.456). Nowadays it one of the most effective ways to apply ML algorithms for practical tasks [5].

"Binarization" of input data, which were primarily stored in data frame `df`, was implemented with help of R code[4]

```
flags = data.frame(Reduce(cbind,
                          lapply(levels(df$A),
                          function(x){(df$A == x)*1})
                   )) # transforming levels of A to binary values
names(flags) = levels(df$A) # names of columns corresponding to
                            # levels of A
df = cbind(df, flags) # binding binary columns
```

In case of atorvastatin tablets we have $n = 27$ binary input variables corresponding to different excipients. We consider the results of $p = 270$ experiments.

Hence, names of all binarized input variables in the form of string, which can be used in ML formula, are obtained in the following way

```
inputvariables = paste(c(paste(levels(df$A),collapse = " + "),
                         paste(levels(df$B),collapse = " + "),
                         paste(levels(df$C),collapse = " + "),
                         paste(levels(df$D),collapse = " + "),
                         paste(levels(df$E),collapse = " + ")),
                         collapse = " + ")
```

Neural network construction is implemented within package `neuralnet` with help of the following function

```
net_y15 = neuralnet(paste("y15 ~ ", inputvariables), df,
                    hidden = c(18), threshold = 0.01)
```

Here we construct neural network for the output variable y_{15} on the basis of 27 binary input variable. We consider one hidden layer containing 18 neurons[5] The neural network obtained is presented on Fig. 1.

We applied cross-validation for building the predictive model. It implies repeating K times of the following process [1]: 1. The train-test splitting in the ratio of 90% of training tuples. 2. Fitting the model to the train set. 3. Testing the model on the test set. 4. Calculating the prediction error.

When we let $K = 30$ for the amount of cross validation steps then we get the mean value of MSE equal to 3.65e-05 (see Fig. 2).

---

[4] It is example of code for input variable A.

[5] The quantity of 18 neurons (i.e. 2/3 of the quantity of input variables) was chosen experimentally with the aim to reach the smallest mean-squared error (MSE).

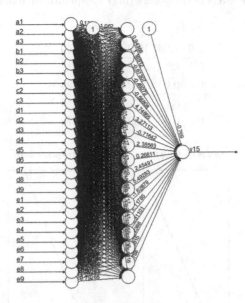

Fig. 1. Neural network for predicting variable y_{15} on the basis of excipients for design of tablets containing atorvastatin. The black lines show the connections between each layer and the weights on each connection while the blue lines show the bias term added in each step (Color figure online)

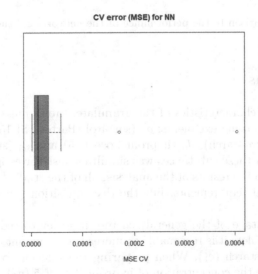

Fig. 2. MSE as a result of procedure of cross validation for design of atorvastatin tablets

Table 5. The levels of excipients (mg) for quantitative optimization

l_1^{c1}	l_2^{c1}	l_3^{c1}	l_4^{c1}	l_5^{c1}
5.0	7.03	10.0	12.97	15.0
l_1^{d6}	l_2^{d6}	l_3^{d6}	l_4^{d6}	l_5^{d6}
0	0.05	0.12	0.19	0.24
l_1^{e5}	l_2^{e5}	l_3^{e5}	l_4^{e5}	l_5^{e5}
0	0.36	0.89	1.42	1.78

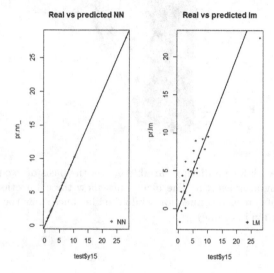

Fig. 3. Visual comparison to the performance of the network and the linear model on the test set

4   Conclusions

The best values of characteristics of the granulate, tablet mass and tablets are provided by the following excipients: a_2 (sorbitol (Parteck SI 150)), b_2 (calcium carbonate), c_1 (corn starch), d_6 (hypromellose E 5) and e_5 (starch potatoes). The combination of these substances was simultaneously investigated in the 5th series. According to the results of the analysis, all of the studied parameters met the pharmacopoeial requirements, but the decomposition (on average 11 min) should be reduced.

In the second stage of the general scheme, in order to reduce the time of disintegration of tablets it is reasonable to increase the amount of disintegrating substance of corn starch (c_1). When preparing the solution for moisture, it is necessary to reduce the concentration of hypromellose E 5 (d_6) and increase the content of potato starch (e_5). The quantities of these substances were studied at 5 levels (see Table 5).

As a result of application of genetic algorithm we obtained the minimal value of y_{15} at the levels $l_4^{c_1}$, $l_1^{d_6}$ and $l_5^{e_5}$ respectively. Such quantitative content of excipients in tablets corresponds to experiments entirely [11,12].

We compared the application of neural network with a linear model. By visually inspecting the plot (see Fig. 3) we can see that the predictions made by the neural network are (in general) more concentrated around the line (a perfect alignment with the line would indicate an MSE of 0 and thus an ideal perfect prediction) than those made by the linear model (LM).

References

1. Fitting a neural network in R; neuralnet package—datascience+. https://datascienceplus.com/fitting-neural-network-in-r/. Accessed 02 July 2019
2. Tablet (pharmacy) - Wikipedia. https://en.wikipedia.org/wiki/Tablet_(pharmacy). Accessed 02 July 2019
3. Bavec, S., Kerc, J., Mateja, S.: Pharmaceutical formulation comprising atorvastatin calcium, March 2011
4. Benzel, I., Hordiienko, O., Hroshovyi, T., Benzel, L., Pokryshko, O.: Obtaining of geranium sanguineum phytoextracts and study of their anti-microbial properties. Int. J. Green Pharm. (IJGP) **12**(02), 142–147 (2018)
5. Burger, S.: Introduction to Machine Learning with R: Rigorous Mathematical Analysis. O'Reilly Media, Incorporated (2018). https://books.google.pl/books?id=UYW0swEACAAJ
6. Demchenko, V., Groshovyi, T.: Optimization of tablet-production technology. Farmatsevtychnyi zhurnal **48**(4), 37–40 (1993)
7. Hornik, K.: Approximation capabilities of multilayer feedforward networks. Neural Netw. **4**(2), 251–257 (1991)
8. Kerc, J., Mateja, S., Bavec, S.: Pharmaceutical formulation comprising atorvastatin calcium, September 2002
9. Kerc, J., Mateja, S., Bavec, S.: Atorvastatin calcium in pharmaceutical formulation, its composition and atorvastatin calcium-containing pharmaceutical prescription, April 2005
10. Pflaum, Z.: Process for the preparation of amorphous atorvastatin, September 2003
11. Trygubchak, O.V., Voytkova, L.S.: Trend analysis of combined drugs creation (for example acetylsalicylic acid). J. Pharm. Pharmacol. **3**(10), 451–462 (2015). https://doi.org/10.17265/2328-2150/2015.10.002
12. Tryhubchak, O.V.: The study of the assortment of drugs of acetylsalicylic acid in combination with statin. Socìalna farmacìâ v ohoronì zdorovâ **4**(3), 80–86 (2018). https://doi.org/10.24959/sphhcj.18.127

On an Approach of the Solution of Machine Learning Problems Integrated with Data from the Open-Source System of Electronic Medical Records: Application for Fractures Prediction

Vasyl Martsenyuk[1]([⊠])(iD), Vladyslav Povoroznyuk[2](iD), Andriy Semenets[3](iD), and Larysa Martynyuk[4](iD)

[1] Department of Computer Science and Automatics, University of Bielsko-Biala, 43-309 Bielsko-Biala, Poland
vmartsenyuk@ath.bielsko.pl
[2] D.F. Chebotarev Institute of Gerontology of NAMS of Ukraine, Kyiv 04074, Ukraine
[3] Department of Medical Informatics, Ternopil State Medical University, Ternopil 46001, Ukraine
[4] Department of Emergency Medical Care, Ternopil State Medical University, Ternopil 46001, Ukraine

Abstract. The purpose of the work is to develop mathematical and software background for the development of ML models in medical research, which is based on the application of open-source EMR systems and ML tools. The flowchart includes basic steps of ML model development, including import and preparing the clinical data, the statement of task, the choice of method (learner), setting its parameters and model assessment. The problems dealing with dimension reduction which arise often in medical research are highlighted and solved with the help of modified principal component analysis (PCA) method. We analyze the problem of export-import data from EMR system and offer the ways of its solution within the most known open-source systems (OpenEMR and OpenMRS). The special attention is paid to the application of free open-source software in ML in medical research with the purpose of development of methodologies of prophylaxis and treatment. As an example, we consider the problem of development of classifier for fractures prediction where we describe all the presented steps of ML model development. With the help of benchmark of learners in the package `mlr` we compare different methods of ML when applying them in medical research.

Keywords: Machine learning · PCA · Classification · EMR system · mlr

---

Supported by University of Bielsko-Biala.

L. Rutkowski et al. (Eds.): ICAISC 2019, LNAI 11509, pp. 228–239, 2019.
https://doi.org/10.1007/978-3-030-20915-5_21

1   Introduction

Nowadays, machine learning (ML) in medical research is one of the tools for analysis of experimental data and clinical observations, as well as language, by means of which the obtained results are presented. This is not the only task of ML in medicine. Mathematical apparatus of ML is widely used for diagnostic purposes, solving classification problems and the search for new patterns with help of prediction, for the formulation and checking of new scientific hypotheses. The use of ML algorithms assumes knowledge of basic methods and stages of data analysis: their sequence, necessity and sufficiency. The proposed paper does not focus on the detailed representation of formulas that make up ML methods, but on their essence and rules of application in case of the open-source electronic medical record (EMR) systems.

The solutions for healthcare, which are based on open-source software has been actively developed for the last decade along with the commercial ones [1,3,8]. The most widely used open-source EMR systems are WorldVistA[1], OpenEMR[2] and OpenMRS[3] [3,4]. Prospects for open-source and free EMR software in developing countries, or countries with financial problems have been considered by Aminpour, Fritz, Reynolds and others [3,4,8]. The approaches to implementing open-source EMR systems, especially OpenEMR, OpenMRS and OpenDental, in Ukrainian healthcare system have been studied, as well as methods of integrating these EMR systems with other medical-purpose software have been developed by authors during last few years [5–7,9,10].

The purpose of the work is to develop mathematical and software background for the development of ML models in medical research, which is based on the application of open-source EMR systems and ML tools.

2   Material and Method

2.1   Mathematical Description

Mathematically, the problems of machine learning in medical research[4] are based on the following data. We have a set D containing N tuples. Depending on the task, certain sets of tuples will be used for training, testing or prediction. Each ith tuple $(a_1^i, a_2^i, \ldots, a_p^i, c^i)^\top$ consists of input data $(a_1^i, a_2^i, \ldots, a_p^i)^\top$ (we call them attributes) and output data c^i, which is the class attribute. Let row vector $a_j = (a_j^1, a_j^2, \ldots, a_j^N)$ presents the values of jth attribute of all N tuples. Attributes $a_1, \ldots, a_p$ can accept both numeric and categorical values. The class attribute C accepts one of K discrete values: $c \in \{1, \ldots, K\}$.

The purpose is to predict, using some predictor, the value of the class attribute C based on the attribute values $a_1, \ldots, a_p$. It should maximize the

---

[1] http://worldvista.org/.

[2] http://www.open-emr.org/.

[3] http://openmrs.org/.

[4] Here we are bounded with machine learning in traditional meaning, i.e., we do not consider data like images or signals, which are covered by deep learning algorithms.

accuracy of prediction of the class attribute, namely the probability $P\{c = c^*\}$ for arbitrary $c^* \in \{1, \dots, K\}$.

The first problem to solve in real medical research is the reduction of the dimension $p \in \mathbb{N}$. For this purpose, we offer the following modification of the method of principal component analysis (PCA). It includes the following steps.

Input data: $A = \{(a_1^i, a_2^i, \dots, a_p^i, c^i)^\top\}_{i=1}^N$

Output data: principle components together with attributes

1. Transform all categorical attributes encoding them as a set of boolean inputs, each representing one category with 0 or 1. We can generate columns with category flags automatically. As a result we get numerical matrix $X = \{(x_1^i, x_2^i, \dots, x_{p_1}^i, c^i)^\top\}_{i=1}^N \in \mathbb{R}^{p_1+1 \times N}$.

2. Calculate mean values for rows: $\bar{x}_i = \frac{1}{N} \sum_{j=1}^N x_i^j$, $i = \overline{1, p_1}$.

3. Calculate variances $\text{Var}(x_i)$, $i = \overline{1, p_1}$. Let $\text{Var}(X) = \sum_{i=1}^{p_1} \text{Var}(x_i)$ be total variance (sum of the sample variances).

4. Calculate matrix of deviations: $X' = \{x_j^i - \bar{x}_i\}_{i=\overline{1,p_1}, j=\overline{1,N}} \in \mathbb{R}^{p_1 \times N}$.

5. Calculate covariance matrix $C = \frac{1}{p_1} X'(X')^\top \in \mathbb{R}^{p_1}$.

6. Calculate eigenvalues of matrix C: $\lambda_1 \le \lambda_2 \le \cdots \le \lambda_{p_1}$.

7. Calculate eigenvectors of C. Consider eigenvectors w_{p_1} and $w_{p_1-1} \in \mathbb{R}^{p_1}$ corresponding to λ_{p_1} and λ_{p_1-1} correspondingly. We get two the first principle components as $\text{PC1} = X^\top w_{p_1}$ and $\text{PC2} = X^\top w_{p_1-1}$. Calculate variances $\text{Var}(\text{PC1})$ and $\text{Var}(\text{PC2})$. Hence we get the percentages of explained variance corresponding to the first two components. Namely, they are $\text{ExplainedVar}(\text{PC1}) := \frac{\text{Var}(\text{PC1})}{\text{Var}(X)}$ and $\text{ExplainedVar}(\text{PC2}) := \frac{\text{Var}(\text{PC2})}{\text{Var}(X)}$ respectively.

8. Order the values in eigenvectors w_{p_1} and w_{p_1-1} in decreasing order of their absolute values. For this goal we apply permutations $\pi(w_{p_1})$ and $\pi(w_{p_1-1})$[5]. Then we return names of the first $\text{ExplainedVar}(\text{PC1}) * 100\%$ attributes in permutation $\pi(w_{p_1})$ and the first $\text{ExplainedVar}(\text{PC2}) * 100\%$ attributes in permutation $\pi(w_{p_1-1})$.

As a result of reduction of dimension we get some numerical matrix $X^{\text{red}} = \{(x_1^i, x_2^i, \dots, x_{p_2}^i, c^i)^\top\}_{i=1}^N \in \mathbb{R}^{p_2+1 \times N}$, where $p_2 \le p_1$. Then these data may be used as training ones for series of ML problems.

Note, that the steps 1, 7 and 8 are the modifications of the traditional PCA algorithm. Firstly, at step 1 we transform all categorical attributes, which are widely used in medical research, to boolean inputs. Secondly, when considering two principal components, which are traditionally used for plane presentation of training

---

[5] We use the denotion $\pi(x)$ for the permutation ordering the vector x in decreasing order of absolute values of its elements.

sets, we offer an approach to choose some reduced quantity of attributes for further investigation (e.g., development of ML model). This quantity is related to the number of variations explained.

The last assumption allows for reducing really the dimension of ML problems in medical research.

2.2 Development of ML Model

Our approach is based on the development of the ML model. Here we mean general flowchart allowing us to get ML solver with possibilities of accurate, sensible and stable results.

Due to scheme offered in Fig. 1 we start from importing and preparing (feature engineering, filling gaps, normalization) data gathered in EMR systems. The ways which are possible to import datasets from EMR systems are described in Subsect. 2.3. We note that the choice of open-source EMR systems as compared with commercial ones is crucial since it enables us to have open access to clinical data, which can be processed and selected for further steps of ML.

In a real application, as it is shown in Sect. 3, we deal with a lot of attributes. Only a few of them can be significant for ML problems. So, it is natural to try to reduce the dimension leaving the attributes with the biggest variances.

Then we should determine the task itself in terms of ML. It can be a regression, classification, ranking, etc. Further, we select the corresponding method (learner) of the solution. The most important is to choose parameters for the methods. It affects the model accuracy.

The last steps (starting from the selection of method) can be repeated in order to get the most effective model. Facilities of current programming tools allow us even to compare different methods using corresponding benchmarks which are developed with respect to certain tasks.

The model of ML presented above agrees entirely with **mlr** package which is demonstrated in Sect. 3.

2.3 The Problem of Exporting-Importing Data from Open-Source EMR System

The problem of import of training, testing and predicting datasets from EMR system into a machine-learning environment is not so trivial due to a series of reasons both programmatic and legislative and ethics. There are the following basic approaches to access a patient's medical record data in a typical EMR system:

- with help of native remote access API of EMR system (REST/XMLRPC/ SOAP);
- using standardized HL7 data formats;
- using general data formats (XML/CSV).

Here we present some details of the application of the approaches mentioned above for two the most widely used open-source EMR systems: OpenEMR and OpenMRS.

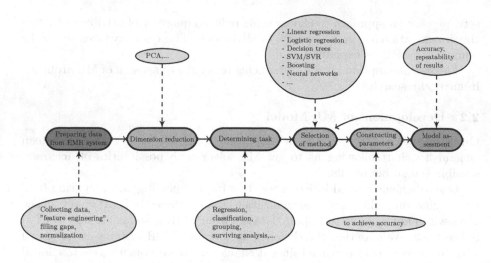

Fig. 1. Development of machine learning model for medical research

When considering native remote access APIs of commercial EMR systems we note lack of technological tools (especially - remote access APIs). Even free open-source EMR systems have a few remote access APIs with limited capabilities. For example, OpenEMR offers single native remote access API implemented. Despite it has been developed in 2013, Master Mobility App[6] is still useful and fully functional one.

OpenMRS implements remote access to internal API through REST protocol using custom REST Module[7]. OpenMRS API specification is accessible[8].

Unfortunately, despite a long period of development and application, even mainstream and widely-used EMR systems (both, commercial and free open-source ones) have limited or partial support of HL7 capabilities. For example, OpenEMR has a few built-in features to deal with HL7.

OpenMRS provide more possibilities, including bi-directional HL7 data processing using custom modules: Sockethl7listener Module[9] accepts and processes import of HL7 (version 2.x only) messages; Export CCD Module[10] provides export of patient's medical data record summary in HL7-vesion-3.x-compatible CCD format; HL7Query Module[11] supports export of patient data in form of HL7 version 2.x messages also (only ORUR01 in current version) using custom module.

Despite mentioned above problems regarding the level of implementations, there are sufficient arguments for adoption and usage of HL7-compatible data

---

[6] https://github.com/oemr501c3/openemr-api.

[7] https://wiki.openmrs.org/display/docs/REST+Module.

[8] https://psbrandt.io/openmrs-contrib-apidocs/.

[9] https://wiki.openmrs.org/display/docs/sockethl7listener.

[10] https://wiki.openmrs.org/display/docs/Export+CCD.

[11] https://wiki.openmrs.org/display/docs/HL7Query+Module.

formats for development of ML-oriented information systems. Availability and active development of a large number of free and open-source HL7 parsers for different programming languages is one of such reasons.

It is important to note that the batch export of multiple patients' medical records from the EMR system is rarely supported (especially in case of commercial systems). When considering open-source EMR systems, then OpenEMR has few built-in features to export data in custom formats: export of single patient's data record into ASTM-compatible CCR XML-based data format is available (under Parient's Reporting section); separate Form documents and Lab data records can be exported as PDF (rarely – XML or CSV); each single-selected patient's demographics data record can be exported as XML dataset; multiple (selected) patients' demographics data records could be exported as CSV file using Batch Communication Tool (Fig. 2).

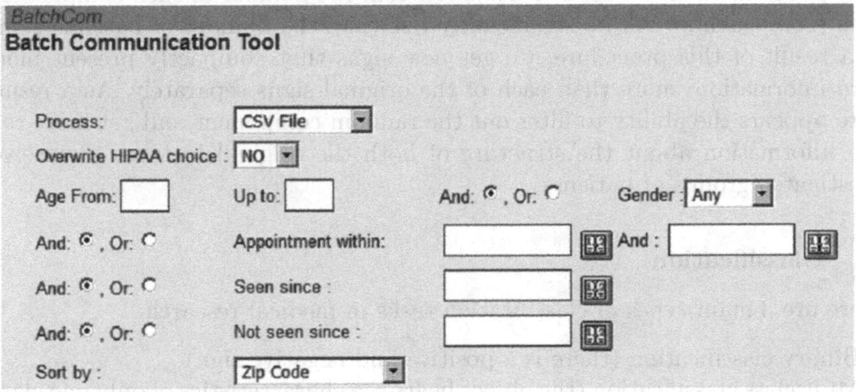

Fig. 2. Batch export of multiple records into CSV in OpenEMR.

So, the establishment of interoperability and data exchanging between different EMR systems is an important problem [2]. It leads to development not only mentioned above international standards but also special platforms and frameworks. Among dozens of solutions, we pay our attention to OpenEHR which is an open domain-driven platform for developing flexible e-health systems[12]. Another way for interoperability has been proposed by NextGen Healthcare[13] with their NextGen Connect (formerly Mirth Connect) open-source tool[14]. For the reasons given, we conclude that an effective way to get training, testing and predicting datasets from the EMR system is export-import of medical data records into XML-compatible formats. Such file is partially or even completely CCR/CCD (CDA) compatible - depending on the level of adoption of international standards by particular EMR system that the researcher is dealing with.

---

[12] https://www.openehr.org/.

[13] https://www.nextgen.com/.

[14] https://svn.mirthcorp.com/connect/.

At the same time, XML data files has been natively converted and parsed using dozens of libraries (e.g., in Python or R).

2.4 Reduction of Dimension

In medical research, there is always a large total number of relations studied. However, many of them will not be statistically significant, and in the absence of clinical significance, they are not necessarily taken into account and interpreted. How much will be valuable from the point of view of the objectives of the study of relationships? It is impossible to assume in advance. As a rule, only 5–25% of all possible connections are statistically and clinically significant.

Moreover, many indicators may have dependencies between themselves. Using them as an initial subset of indices, we can state and solve the problem of constructing on their basis more complex, integrated features using e.g. principal component analysis (PCA). Wherein the number of such complex features (components) will be significantly less than the number of baseline signs. As a result of this procedure, we get new signs that compactly present much more information, more than each of the original signs separately. As a result, there appears the ability to filter out the random component and get more reliable information about the structure of both the original features themselves investigated groups of patients.

2.5 Classification

There are 3 main types of classification tasks in medical research.

1. Binary classification (there is a positive and negative sign)
2. Multiclass classification (the object bears the characteristics of only one class)
3. Multilabel classification (the object has signs of several classes at the same time).

Consider 3 examples, one for each type of a task.

1. Determining whether a person has a certain disease X. 1 - a person is sick, 0 - a person is healthy.
2. Identification of a single disease among diseases A, B, C, D, E.
3. Determining several diseases among A, B, C, D, E.

The algorithms for classification (like the induction of decision trees on nodes) automatically divide the values of numerical attributes a_j into two intervals: $a_j \leq y_j$, $a_j > y_j$ and the categorical attributes a_k are divided into two subsets: $a_k \in S_k$, $a_k \notin S_k$.

The partitioning of numerical attributes is based, as a rule, on measures on the basis of entropy, or the Gini index. The partitioning process is recursively repeated while there is an improvement in prediction accuracy. The last step involves removing the nodes to avoid overfitting the model. As a result, we must get a set of rules that go from root to each terminal node, contain inequalities for numerical attributes and the inclusion conditions for categorical attributes.

3   Experimental Research

Our experimental research is dealing with predicting fractures for middle-aged women which is an actual clinical and prophylactic problem nowadays.

We consider data of clinical and laboratory investigations of 1469 women, which were primarily stored in OpenEMR system. The most important group of signs are the results of bone densitometry. At whole, we have $p = 182$ indices. After removing gaps in dataset 1242 tuples left.

Patients were grouped into three groups with respect to the availability of fractures. For this purpose, we use the class attribute "Fractures" with the following categorical values: 1 - none fractures, 2 - peripheral fractures, 3 - vertebral fractures.

Applying reduction of dimension with help of method PCA, we consider two principle components. Namely, PC1 has 43.4% of explained variance, PC2 - 12.5%. That is, these two components are able to explained 55.9% variance of data. The results of PCA are displayed in Fig. 3. Due to approach offered in Subsect. 2.1, propotionally to the percentages ExplainedVar(PC1) and ExplainedVar(PC2) we choose 8 attributes, which are based on PC1 and 2 attributes taking into account PC2. Namely, they are "Weight", "TOTAL_Fat", "RIGHT_TOTAL_Fat_g", "LEFT_TOTAL_Fat_g", "RIGHT_TOTAL_Total_Mass_kg", "LEFT_TOTAL_Total_Mass_kg", "TOTAL_Tissue_g", "RIGHT_TOTAL_Tissue_g" for ExplainedVar(PC1) and "Weight", "TOTAL_Fat" for ExplainedVar(PC2). All considered attributes are numerical ones and after reduction of dimension we consider $p_1 = 8$ attributes mentioned above. In Fig. 4 we can analyze PC1-PC2 plane with respect to ellipsoids representing three groups of patients of predicted fractures. Reducing dimension we see here the attributes with the biggest variances together with their directions with respect to patients' groups.

Development of the ML model was implemented in R free software environment with the help of **mlr** package.

Following Fig. 1 we determine ML task. In our case it is classification problem with respect to class attribute "Fractures". In terms of **mlr** package it can be described as

```
task = makeClassifTask(id = "fractures_classification",
                       data = df1, target = "Fractures")
```

The next step is to choose a method to solve the ML task. We create "learner" for this purpose. Package **mlr** allows us to create a benchmark of learners

```
lrns <- makeLearners(c("lda","rpart", "C50","rFerns",
                     "randomForestSRC"), type = "classif")
```

Here benchmark include 5 methods that we would like to apply for classification task. Namely, linear discriminant analysis (lda), rpart, C5.0, random ferns and random forest

```
comparison <- benchmark(tasks = task, learners = lrns,
                        resampling = cv5)
```

Here we determine ML task, learners (methods) and resampling strategy.

As a result, we get ML model in which 5 different methods are used. The results of the performance of the methods with the help of measure mmce are presented in Fig. 5. We see that the most accurate model with respect to the assessment of the quality of the prediction is based on random forest technique, the "worst" one is with the help of ferns.

The decision tree induced on the basis of attributes of reduced dimension is shown in Fig. 6. Here only 5 attributes were included with the usage shown in Table 1.

Table 1. Attribute usage for decision tree in Fig. 6

Name of attribute	Usage
RIGHT_TOTAL_Tissue_g	100.00%
RIGHT_TOTAL_Fat_g	14.05%
RIGHT_TOTAL_Total_Mass_kg	14.05%
TOTAL_Fat	11.19%
TOTAL_Tissue_g	2.61%

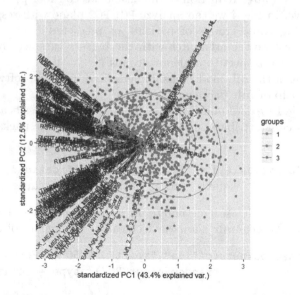

Fig. 3. Data in PC1-PC2 plane. Arrows show "rotations" of attributes in PC1-PC2 plane.

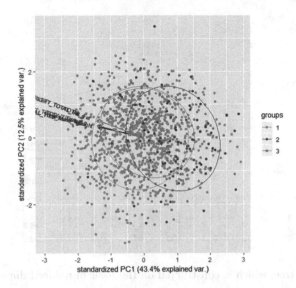

Fig. 4. Data in `PC1-PC2` plane. Arrows show the reduction of dimension and "directions" of changes in patients group.

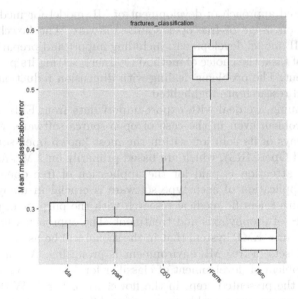

Fig. 5. Comparison of performance measures for different classification methods: lda, rpart, C50, rFerns, randomForestSRC.

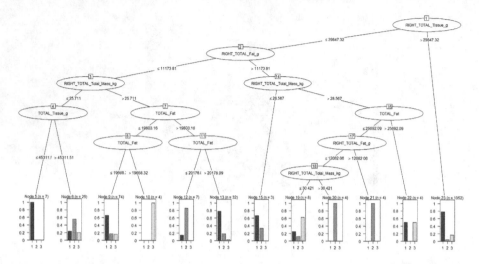

Fig. 6. Decision tree, which is constructed on the basis of reduced dimension of data.

4 Conclusions

Here we presented approach of development of ML model for medical research which is based on usage of free open-source software. The flowchart includes basic steps of ML model development, including import and preparing the data, the statement of task, the choice of method (learner), setting its parameters and model assessment. The problems dealing with dimension reduction which arise often in medical research are highlighted.

In the beginning, we deal with export-import data from EMR system. It is not a trivial problem even in the case of open-source software. we analyze it and offer the ways of its solution within the most known open-source systems (OpenEMR and OpenMRS), which are based primarily on XML-formats.

The special attention is paid for the application of free open-source software in ML. Application of such type software is crucial in many cases dealing primarily with scientific medical research with the purpose of development of methodologies of prophylaxis and treatment. The approach which uses data from the open-source EMR system that in the sequel will be used as the training and testing datasets in free ML environment is promising. As an example, we consider the problem of development of classifier for fractures prediction where we describe all the presented steps in the flowchart of Fig. 1. With the help of benchmark of learners we are able to compare different methods of ML when applying them in medical research.

References

1. List of open-source health software. https://en.wikipedia.org/wiki/List_of_open-source_health_software#Electronic_health_or_medical_record. Accessed 12 Nov 2017
2. Almeida, J., Frade, S., Cruz-Correia, R.: Exporting data from an openEHR repository to standard formats. Procedia Technol. **16**, 1391–1396 (2014). https://doi.org/10.1016/j.protcy.2014.10.157. http://www.sciencedirect.com/science/article/pii/S2212017314003843, cENTERIS 2014 - Conference on ENTERprise Information Systems/ProjMAN 2014 - International Conference on Project MANagement/HCIST 2014 - International Conference on Health and Social Care Information Systems and Technologies
3. Aminpour, F., Sadoughi, F., Ahamdi, M.: Utilization of open source electronic health record around the world: a systematic review. J. Res. Med. Sci.: Off. J. Isfahan Univ. Med. Sci. **19**(1), 57 (2014)
4. Fritz, F., Tilahun, B., Dugas, M.: Success criteria for electronic medical record implementations in low-resource settings: a systematic review. J. Am. Med. Inform. Assoc. **22**(2), 479–488 (2015)
5. Martsenyuk, V., Semenets, A.: on code refactoring for decision making component combined with the open-source medical information system. In: Pejaś, J., El Fray, I., Hyla, T., Kacprzyk, J. (eds.) ACS 2018. AISC, vol. 889, pp. 196–208. Springer, Cham (2019). https://doi.org/10.1007/978-3-030-03314-9_18
6. Martsenyuk, V., Vakulenko, D., Vakulenko, L., Kłos-Witkowska, A., Kutakova, O.: Information system of arterial oscillography for primary diagnostics of cardiovascular diseases. In: Saeed, K., Homenda, W. (eds.) CISIM 2018. LNCS, vol. 11127, pp. 46–56. Springer, Cham (2018). https://doi.org/10.1007/978-3-319-99954-8_5
7. Martsenyuk, V., Semenets, A.: System elektronicznych zapisów medycznych dla wspomagania decyzji z wykorzystaniem Google Application Engine (GAE). Studia Ekonomiczne **308**, 157–172 (2016)
8. Reynolds, C., Wyatt, J.: Open source, open standards, and health care information systems. J. Med. Internet Res. **13**(1), e24 (2011)
9. Semenets, A.: On organizational and methodological approaches of the emr-systems implementation in public health of Ukraine. Med. Inform. Eng. **2013**(3), 35–42 (2013). https://doi.org/10.11603/mie.1996-1960.2013.3.1742
10. Semenets, A.: About experience of the patient data migration during the open source EMR-system implementation. Med. Inform. Eng. **2014**(1), 28–37 (2014). https://doi.org/10.11603/mie.1996-1960.2014.1.3756

Energy Consumption Analysis of the Nussinov RNA Folding Implementations

Marek Palkowski[✉]

Faculty of Computer Science and Information Systems,
West Pomeranian University of Technology in Szczecin,
Zolnierska 49, 71210 Szczecin, Poland
mpalkowski@wi.zut.edu.pl
http://www.wi.zut.edu.pl

Abstract. An energy consumption analysis of the Nussinov RNA folding algorithm implementations is discussed in this paper. We consider
parallel and cache-efficient Nussinov codes generated automatically by
the Traco and PluTo optimizing compilers and the manual implementation known as Transpose (Li et al.). The experimental study presents
the times and power consumption of optimized code using the modern
Intel i7 processor with 12 threads. We apply the Intel RAPL technique to
measure energy on the processor socket, cores, and RAM. The access to
the Linux kernel energy events is provided by the *perf* tool. We analyze
the power consumption in terms of the execution times of the Nussinov
codes for various RNA sequences lengths and number of threads.

Keywords: Computational biology · The Nussinov algorithm ·
RNA folding · Transpose · Intel RAPL · Power consumption

1 Introduction

Optimization of molecular biology programs is a current challenging task
for developers and researchers. Intensive-computing bioinformatics algorithms
solved within the dynamic programming cores such as RNA folding or DNA
sequences alignment have many parallel and cache-efficient implementations.
These codes can be also successfully optimized with the source-to-source compilers based on the polyhedral model [10,14].

In this paper, we focus on the commonly known classic Nussinov algorithm for
RNA folding. We study power consumption and time execution of the Nussinov
implementations. We consider parallel and cache efficient Nussinov triply-nested
loop nests generated automatically by the Traco [2] and PluTo [4] optimizing
compilers and the manual implementation known as *Transpose* introduced by Li
et al. [8].

The polyhedral Traco and PluTo compilers improve locality of input codes by
means of loop tiling. TRACO extracts 3-d rectangular tiles of the Nussinov loop
nest and corrects them applying the exact transitive closure of a dependence

© Springer Nature Switzerland AG 2019
L. Rutkowski et al. (Eds.): ICAISC 2019, LNAI 11509, pp. 240–249, 2019.
https://doi.org/10.1007/978-3-030-20915-5_22

graph [14]. PluTo is based on affine transformation framework but tiles only two outermost loop nests of the Nussinov algorithm. The Traco and PluTo parallelize tiles using the loop skewing transformation. *Transpose* is a manual approach that stores cells copies in the unused left-lower triangle of the Nussinov array and changes the column major order to the row order in the Nussinov array to optimize code locality. Diagonal scanning of the Nussinov array cells is applied to parallelize the *Transpose* codes.

The rest of the paper is organized as follows. Section 2 introduces the Nussinov algorithm. Section 3 explains the manual *Transpose* technique and loop tiling transformations implemented within the TRACO and PluTo compilers. Section 4 outlines related work. Section 5 presents the results of experiments and demonstrates that optimized codes are dramatically faster and energy-efficient than the original one for the modern Intel i7 processor. This section discusses the following factors: time of code execution, energy consumption measured on processor socket and its cores, and RAM. We apply the *perf* tool to access to the kernel energy events provided by the Intel RAPL (Running Average Power Limit) [6]. We discuss and compare these factors within the studied Nussinov RNA folding implementations. The last section presents conclusions and future work.

2 Nussinov RNA Folding Algorithm

Nussinov made one of the first attempts at folding RNA in a computationally efficient way as the base pair maximization approach in 1978 [11]. An RNA sequence is a chain of nucleotides from the alphabet G (guanine), A (adenine), U (uracil), C (cytosine). Given an RNA sequence $x_1, x_2, ..., x_n$, the Nussinov algorithm solves the problem of RNA non-crossing secondary structure prediction by means of computing the maximum number of base pairs for subsequences $x_i, ..., x_j$, starting with subsequences of length 1 and building upwards, storing the result of each subsequence in a dynamic programming array.

Let N be a $n \times n$ Nussinov matrix and $\sigma(i, j)$ be a function which returns 1 if (x_i, x_j) match and $i < j - 1$, or 0 otherwise, then the following recursion $N(i, j)$ (the maximum number of base-pair matches of $x_i, ..., x_j$) is defined over the region $1 \leq i \leq j \leq n$ as

$$N(i,j) = max(N(i+1, j-1) + \sigma(i,j), \max_{1 \leq j \leq n}(N(i,k) + N(k+1, j))) \quad (1)$$

and zero elsewhere [18].

The equation leads directly to the C/C++ code with triple-nested loops presented in Listing 1. [10].

This algorithm is an example of "nonserial polyadic dynamic programming" (NPDP). The term "nonserial polyadic" stands for family of dynamic programming codes exposing non-uniform data dependences, which is more difficult to be optimized [9].

Listing 1. Nussinov loop nest.

```
for (i = N-1; i >= 0; i--) {
 for (j = i+1; j < N; j++) {
  for (k = 0; k < j-i; k++) {
   S[i][j] = MAX(S[i][k+i] + S[k+i+1][j], S[i][j]); //s0
  }
  S[i][j] = MAX(S[i][j], S[i+1][j-1] + can_pair(RNA,i,j));//s1
 }
}
```

3   Parallel and Cache Efficient Nussinov RNA Folding Implementations

On modern architectures, memory latency and bandwidth have become a major limiting factor in achieving good performance. The cost of moving data from main memory is orders of magnitude higher than the cost of computation. This disparity between communication and computation costs has prompted a paradigm shift in algorithm design [10].

To perform energy analysis we chose three parallel and cache-efficient implementations of the Nussinov RNA folding. The first two ones are generated by means of the Traco and PluTo compilers. Both compilers are automatic code optimization tools based on the polyhedral model. The tools transform C programs from source to source for coarse-grained parallelism and data locality simultaneously with the OpenMP pragmas. To achieve cache-efficient code, loop tiling is used.

Tiling is a very important iteration reordering transformation for both improving data locality and extracting loop nest parallelism. Tiling for improving locality groups loop nest statement instances in a loop nest iteration space into smaller blocks (tiles) allowing reuse when the block fits in local memory.

The Traco compiler uses tile correction algorithm to tile affine loop nests which is based on the transitive closure of program dependence graphs [3]. First, rectangular tiles are formed, then they are corrected to establish tiling validity. Tile statements which are dependence destinations are moved to lexicographically greater tiles containing dependence sources. Next, tiled loops are skewed to obtain the parallel code.

It is worth to note that the TRACO tiled code does not have dependence cycles between tiles and loop tiling is independent of the parallelism method. The algorithm is able to tile non-fully permutable loops with non-uniform and negative data dependences which are exposed for NPDP codes [14].

The core transformation framework of the PluTo scheduling algorithms mainly works by finding affine transformations for efficient tiling [4]. The PluTo performs outer (communication-free), inner, or pipelined parallelization. The target code is also optimized for locality and made amenable for auto-vectorization. PluTo uses commonly known transformations as loop permutation or fusion to eliminate negative dependences and to find solutions of affine equations. The

Listing 2. The *Transpose* C/C++ code [8]

```
for(diag=2; diag<=N-1; diag++){
#pragma omp parallel for private(_max, t, col)
 for(row=0; row<=N-diag-1; row++){
   col = diag + row;
   _max = S[row+1][col-1]+can_pair(RNA,row,col)
   for(k=row; k <=col-1; k++){
     t = S[row][k] + S[k+1][col];
     _max = MAX(_max, t);
   }
   S[row][col] = _max;
   S[col][row] = _max;
 }
}
```

classic PluTo algorithms are limited by non-uniform dependences and cycles in inter-tile dependence graphs. Hence, PluTo is not able to tile the innermost loop nest of the Nussinov algorithm [10]. The result code is limited to the skewed loop nests where only two outermost loop bounds are tiled.

Li et al. proposed a cache-efficient manual transformation of the Nussinov loop nests. The original RNA folding algorithm uses the only upper (right) triangle of the Nussinov matrix. The authors proposed to write cell copies to the unused lower (left) triangle and change column order of reading to the cache-efficient row order. Diagonal scanning makes this code parallel. The OpenMP pragmas (parallel for) [12] are inserted manually. The listing 2 represents the Li's modifications for the Nussinov algorithm C/C++ code [8].

4 Related Work

A number of authors have developed theoretical approaches to optimizing the Nussinov loop nests, e.g. [1,5,7,17].

Wonnacott et al. introduced 3-d tiling of "mostly-tileable" loop nests of RNA secondary-structure prediction codes in paper [18]. For mostly-tileable loop nests, the number of "problematic" iterations grows with the tile size, but not with the problem size, whereas the number of non-problematic iterations grows with the problem size, i.e., the loop nest iteration space is dominated by non-problematic iterations. Unfortunately, the paper does not consider any parallel code, tiling is represented with the serial code.

Mullapudi and Bondhugula presented dynamic tiling for the Zuker's optimal RNA secondary structure prediction [10]. 3-d iterative tiling for dynamic scheduling is calculated by means of reduction chains. Operations along each chain can be reordered in order to eliminate cycles in an inter-tile dependence graph. Their approach involves the dynamic scheduling of tiles, rather than the generation of a static schedule.

Zhao et al. improved the *Transpose* method and performed the experimental study of the energy-efficient codes. Their benchmarking shows that depending on the studied computational platform and programming language, either *ByRow* or *ByBox* give best run time and energy performance. As a result, using the same amount of memory, the algorithms proposed by Zhao et al. can solve problems up to 40% larger than those solvable by *Transpose*. To our best knowledge, authors do not present multi-threaded implementations, hence we do not consider this approach in our analysis.

In paper [13], runtime scheduling of the RNA secondary structure prediction for parallel machines is discussed. Although the algorithm does not require the transitive closure calculation, it is limited only to program loops with known parameters during compilation time. The approach does not also improve code locality for the Nussinov algorithm.

5 Experimental Study

To carry out experiments, we used a machine with a processor Intel i7-8700 (3.2 GHz, 4.6 GHz in turbo, 6 cores, 12 threads, 12MB Cache) and 16 GB RAM. The optimized codes were compiled by means of the GNU C++ Compiler 8.1 (*gcc*). All programs were compiled with the -O3 flag of optimization.

Energy consumption was measured with RAPL in Joules. The Intel RAPL provides a set of counters providing energy and power consumption information for recent (Sandy Bridge and later) Intel processors. RAPL is rather a software power model than an analog power meter [6]. This software power model estimates energy usage by using hardware performance counters and I/O models.

The i7 processors have one packages which contains multiple cores (Fig. 1). Each core typically has hyper-threading, which means it contains two logical CPUs. The part of the i7 package outside the cores includes the last level cache, the memory controller and the integrated GPU. RAM energy is separate from the processor.

In the experimental study, we measure time executions and three power events: package, cores and RAM by means of the *perf_event* [16] interface dedicated to the Linux 3.14 based systems or newer. The *perf* tool requires root privileges to collect energy measurements.

Experiments were carried out for ten RNA sequences lengths of the problem defined with parameter N. For test data, we used randomly generated RNA sequences. Papers [8,14,19] discussed that code performance of the Nussinov RNA folding depends on the length of the sequence and not its content.

We chose tile sizes $[1 \times 128 \times 16]$ for the tile correction and $[16 \times 16 \times 1]$ for the PluTo code as the best ones according to the research conclusions in paper [15]. Untiling the outermost loop allows us to minimize the correction of tiles and leave them in the original rectangular form.

Table 1 shows the time and energy performance of the tile correction method compared to the original code. The best results were obtained for the all available 12 threads.

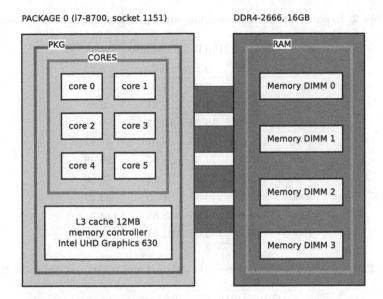

Fig. 1. RAPL energy measurements from Linux on i7-8700

Table 1. Execution time (in seconds) and energy consumption (in Joules) of the original and tiled code for RNA sequence length 5000.

N	Original	Tile correction (Traco)				
Threads	1	1	2	4	8	12
Time (s)	114.55	69.93	37.29	21.69	18.62	17.12
Package (J)	3421.7	2289.9	1586.2	1248.7	1211.8	1111.4
Cores (J)	2802.1	1903.8	1371.1	1115.8	1096.6	1005.6
RAM (J)	137.1	107.7	85.9	72.9	65.9	60.2

Table 2 presents execution times for optimized codes for RNA sequence lengths from 1000 to 10000. The tile correction code is the fastest for RNA folding with 3000 nucleotides in sequences and more.

The tiling correction code is the most energy-efficient and it corresponds to the time execution results. Tiling correction and *Transpose* allow us to save approximately more than 80% energy on the package (Table 3) and cores (Table 4) of the i7 processor for the longest sequences.

The PluTo time and energy results are worse because of the lack of the innermost loop tiling. The energy consumption of the PluTo code is close to the original code energy demand.

Table 5 presents the energy consumption of the optimized codes measured on RAM. Tile correction intensively minimizes the number of RAM references and its RAM energy consumption is approximately 85% than the original code

Table 2. Execution time of the original and optimized codes (in seconds).

N	Original	PluTo	Transpose	Traco
1000	0.36	0.10	0.09	0.22
2000	4.71	0.98	1.07	1.19
3000	18.93	4.46	4.41	3.80
4000	52.09	15.24	10.94	9.06
5000	114.55	36.89	21.97	17.12
6000	237.89	74.51	38.57	29.28
7000	395.16	133.93	61.83	46.56
8000	608.29	240.35	91.15	69.29
9000	1447.14	648.94	138.86	114.2
10000	2121.90	786.00	191.51	174.21

Table 3. Package power consumption of the original and optimized codes (in Joules).

N	Original	PluTo	Transpose	Traco
1000	10.3	6.9	6.4	12.9
2000	125.8	68.7	72.5	78.5
3000	526.3	291.4	287.1	246.8
4000	1565.5	990.6	710.8	588.6
5000	3421.7	2388.8	1426.6	1111.4
6000	7095.6	4728.8	2503.4	1901.4
7000	11286.3	8486.7	4012.8	3022.5
8000	17925.4	15109.2	5915.7	4497.4
9000	42251.9	38465.7	9011.3	7414.5
10000	61954.2	47700.1	12415.3	11295.9

and 25% lower than *Transpose* which refers to the both left and right triangles of the Nussinov matrix.

Summing up, we noted significant energy saving of the tile correction approach in comparison to the original Nussinov algorithm code. We observed also that this method successfully reduces the time of execution as well as energy consumption on multi-core processors and RAM in comparison to the related approaches. Traco to minimize cache-misses calculates tile bounds and array addresses using arithmetic operations including integer divisions. However, the overhead of these calculations does not limit us to achieve satisfactory energy performance.

Table 4. Cores power consumption of the original and optimized codes (in Joules).

N	Original	PluTo	Transpose	Traco
1000	8.4	6.4	5.9	11.8
2000	100.4	63.3	65.7	71.7
3000	423.7	265.8	258.8	224.1
4000	1282.6	898.0	640.3	533.2
5000	2802.1	2161.3	1285.0	1005.6
6000	5811.9	4263.7	2255.1	1719.5
7000	9148.3	7645.1	3614.7	2732.0
8000	14627.6	13591.2	5328.0	4064.8
9000	34052.2	34305.7	8125.6	6698.9
10000	50062.8	42684.6	11202.5	10220.6

Table 5. RAM power consumption of the original and optimized codes (in Joules).

N	Original	PluTo	Transpose	Traco
1000	0.2	0.1	0.1	0.1
2000	5.0	1.4	4.4	2.4
3000	23.0	9.4	18.9	11.1
4000	65.5	47.6	47.6	29.9
5000	137.1	125.5	95.5	60.2
6000	269.2	270.5	167.1	106.0
7000	467.2	503.9	267.4	172.3
8000	739.6	928.5	397.4	257.4
9000	2942.0	2710.0	576.1	428.1
10000	3927.1	3256.7	791.5	608.4

6 Conclusion

In this paper, we presented energy consumption for the Nussinov RNA secondary structure prediction codes optimized with Traco and PluTo compilers and *Transpose* transformation. We demonstrated that tile correction produces the most energy-efficient as well as the time execution shortest codes.

In the future, we are going to study the energy consumption of optimized codes for other RNA folding approaches like the Zuker algorithm and MEA on other Intel platforms like i9 or Xeon Phi. We plan also to improve or develop new tiling strategies dedicated to the bioinformatics NPDP programs with $O(n^4)$ computational complexity.

References

1. Almeida, F., Andonov, R., Gonzalez, D., Moreno, L.M., Poirriez, V., Rodriguez, C.: Optimal tiling for the RNA base pairing problem. In: Proceedings of the Fourteenth Annual ACM Symposium on Parallel Algorithms and Architectures, SPAA 2002, pp. 173–182. ACM, New York (2002)
2. Bielecki, W., Palkowski, M.: A parallelizing and optimizing compiler - TRACO (2013). http://traco.sourceforge.net
3. Bielecki, W., Palkowski, M.: Tiling of arbitrarily nested loops by means of the transitive closure of dependence graphs. Int. J. Appl. Math. Comput. Sci. (AMCS) **26**(4), 919–939 (2016)
4. Bondhugula, U., Hartono, A., Ramanujam, J., Sadayappan, P.: A practical automatic polyhedral parallelizer and locality optimizer. SIGPLAN Not. **43**(6), 101–113 (2008)
5. Frid, Y., Gusfield, D.: An improved Four-Russians method and sparsified Four-Russians algorithm for RNA folding. Algorithms Mol. Biol. **11**(1), 22 (2016). https://doi.org/10.1186/s13015-016-0081-9
6. Intel Corporation: Intel® 64 and IA-32 Architectures Software Developer's Manual, Volume 3B: System Programming Guide, Part 2, September 2016. https://www.intel.com/content/dam/www/public/us/en/documents/manuals/64-ia-32-architectures-software-developer-vol-3b-part-2-manual.pdf
7. Jacob, A.C., Buhler, J.D., Chamberlain, R.D.: Rapid RNA folding: analysis and acceleration of the Zuker recurrence. In: 2010 18th IEEE Annual International Symposium on Field-Programmable Custom Computing Machines (FCCM), pp. 87–94 (2010)
8. Li, J., Ranka, S., Sahni, S.: Multicore and GPU algorithms for Nussinov RNA folding. BMC Bioinf. **15**(8), S1 (2014). https://doi.org/10.1186/1471-2105-15-S8-S1
9. Liu, L., Wang, M., Jiang, J., Li, R., Yang, G.: Efficient nonserial polyadic dynamic programming on the cell processor. In: 25th IEEE International Symposium on Parallel and Distributed Processing, IPDPS 2011, Anchorage, Alaska, USA, 16–20 May 2011 - Workshop Proceedings, pp. 460–471 (2011)
10. Mullapudi, R.T., Bondhugula, U.: Tiling for dynamic scheduling. In: Rajopadhye, S., Verdoolaege, S. (eds.) Proceedings of the 4th International Workshop on Polyhedral Compilation Techniques, Vienna, Austria, January 2014
11. Nussinov, R., Pieczenik, G., Griggs, J.R., Kleitman, D.J.: Algorithms for loop matchings. SIAM J. Appl. Mat. **35**(1), 68–82 (1978)
12. OpenMP Architecture Review Board: OpenMP application program interface version 4.0 (2013). http://www.openmp.org/mp-documents/OpenMP4.0.0.pdf
13. Palkowski, M.: Finding free schedules for RNA secondary structure prediction. In: Rutkowski, L., Korytkowski, M., Scherer, R., Tadeusiewicz, R., Zadeh, L.A., Zurada, J.M. (eds.) ICAISC 2016. LNCS (LNAI), vol. 9693, pp. 179–188. Springer, Cham (2016). https://doi.org/10.1007/978-3-319-39384-1_16
14. Palkowski, M., Bielecki, W.: Parallel tiled Nussinov RNA folding loop nest generated using both dependence graph transitive closure and loop skewing. BMC Bioinf. **18**(1), 290 (2017)
15. Palkowski, M., Bielecki, W.: Tuning iteration space slicing based tiled multi-core code implementing Nussinov's RNA folding. BMC Bioinf. **19**(1), 12 (2018)
16. de Melo, A.C.: The new linux 'perf' tools. Technical report, Linux Kongress, Georg Simon Ohm University Nuremberg/Germany (2010)

17. Tan, G., Feng, S., Sun, N.: Locality and parallelism optimization for dynamic programming algorithm in bioinformatics. In: SC 2006 Conference, Proceedings of the ACM/IEEE, p. 41 (2006)
18. Wonnacott, D., Jin, T., Lake, A.: Automatic tiling of "mostly-tileable" loop nests. In: IMPACT 2015: 5th International Workshop on Polyhedral Compilation Techniques, at Amsterdam, The Netherlands (2015)
19. Zhao, C., Sahni, S.: Cache and energy efficient algorithms for Nussinov's RNA folding. BMC Bioinf. **18**(15), 518 (2017)

Behavior-Based Emotion Recognition Using Kinect and Hidden Markov Models

Aleksandra Postawka[✉][iD]

Department of Computer Engineering,
Wroclaw University of Science and Technology, Wrocław, Poland
aleksandra.postawka@pwr.edu.pl

Abstract. According to the literature review the autistic children behavior is strictly connected to their emotions. Moreover, it is repeatable and – although it is understandable only for their caregivers – it seems to be predictable. We state a hypothesis supported by the literature's findings that it should be possible to describe autistic child's behavior using the statistic models. However, every autistic person is different and therefore the model should be developed individually for each of them. We present a preliminary research on behavior-based emotion recognition and methods for behavior model estimation by using Hidden Markov Models. The behavior model may be created for any combination of following types of events: body positions, activities based on position changes, activities based on hand movements. The conducted experiments provide very satisfactory results. The major conclusion is to use the complex events such as activities.

Keywords: Autism · Emotion recognition · Hidden Markov Models ·
Skeleton tracking · Microsoft Kinect 2.0

1 Introduction

Children diagnosed with Autism Spectrum Disorder (ASD) cannot express their feelings and emotions in the way which is typical for the rest of community. Seach *et al.* [1] showed that they manifest significantly less facial expressions and body language than other people. Moreover, the autistic child's facial expressions, similarly to gestures and tone of the voice, rarely correspond to their real feelings [2,3]. However, despite the fact that the emotions are not expressed in the typical way, they do have an effect on person's behavior [1]. For example, autistic child's caretakers learn to identify their emotions and needs over time. In contrast, they are unable to understand the behavior in the case of foreign children with ASD [4]. Each autistic person is different, needs individual approach and expresses their emotions in a very individual way. Nearly half of autistic people population experiences the self-injurious behavior which can be manifested in various ways: hitting the head, biting own hands or excessive skin scratching [5]. The aggressive and self-injurious behavior occur mostly in the case of children with communication problems [1].

© Springer Nature Switzerland AG 2019
L. Rutkowski et al. (Eds.): ICAISC 2019, LNAI 11509, pp. 250–259, 2019.
https://doi.org/10.1007/978-3-030-20915-5_23

The majority of applications which solve the emotion recognition problem are based on facial expressions tracking and microexpressions detection. Probably the best known expert and authority in this area of knowledge is Ekman [6]. A number of publications appeared as a result of the EmotiW challenge – the participants dealt with emotion recognition based on the video recordings [7, 8]. Several methods for the emotion recognition problem are based on speech analysis [9–11]. The different approach was presented in [12] – the emotions were recognized as interactions between a couple of people. The authors underline that the mutual body orientation may be strongly connected to emotions. The algorithms used for emotion recognition are based on i.a. deep learning [7,9,10] and continuous Hidden Markov Models [11]. To the best of author's knowledge there is a lack of research on emotion recognition with algorithms based on a behavior model created from long term observation sequences.

Unfortunately, procedures which can be found in the mentioned publications may not be suitable for emotion recognition in the case of people with autism. This results from the following observations [4]:

- emotions are expressed in a very individual way and therefore it is probably impossible to create a general behavior model,
- autistic children rarely express their emotions through nonverbal communication in a natural way – even if a child uses facial expressions they apply only to extremes of emotions and the child needed to learn principles of nonverbal communication (these skills were not developed naturally),
- children with autism may learn some gestures, however they tend to reduce the gestures complexity to a bare minimum – the movements may change in time.

In this paper a novel approach based on the behavior model has been applied to the emotion recognition problem. According to the literature review the autistic children behave in the way which is strictly connected to their emotions. Moreover, their behavior is repeatable and logical (although understandable only for their caregivers), thus it should be possible to model it by statistical models. However, each autistic person is different and therefore the model should be adapted individually.

The Hidden Markov Models [13] have been used for behavior modeling and emotion recognition. It should be noted that the caregivers of low-functioning autistic children do not see their emotions directly but they interpret the children mood based on some observations. These observations correspond to children behavior, which is comprised of various events. This is a fundamental reason for using the statistical models in which states (emotions) are observed by the observation symbols (events).

A preliminary research on behavior-based emotion recognition is presented and developed methods for behavior model estimation are proposed. The models may be created for any combination of following types of events: body positions, activities based on position changes or activities based on hand movements.

Data are obtained from the second version of Micosoft Kinect sensor. One of the most important advantages of this approach is respecting the observed person's privacy as only the skeleton coordinates are considered – we are aiming at research on autistic people thus this feature extremely matters. Several algorithms from our previous research were used: body position recognition [14] and activities recognition. The activities may be based on the hand movements [15] or on body position changes [16]. The application also provides the capability of the real-time recognition and some potentially dangerous activities detection [17] which are applied in order to distinguish the autism self-injurious behavior and similar normal activities (where the same movement trajectory is used). Such a behavior may have a great influence on emotion recognition.

The paper is organized as follows. Section 2 presents the system outline and its dependencies. Section 3 includes the Hidden Markov Models notation. Section 4 describes the basic methods and algorithms. In Sect. 5 the results obtained from the conducted experiments are presented. Section 6 contains the overall conclusions and plans for the future.

2   System Overview

The emotion recognition system is composed of four basic modules which have been presented in Fig. 1. Additionally the diagram includes the most important elements developed in our previous research.

One of the most important components is the *data collection* module. The element is responsible for long term child observations and storing collected data into a file. For this task the module uses some recognition data from different parts of the system (not being a subject of this research): the body position ID and the IDs of the recognized activities. The body position ID is recognized for each frame. The recognized activities ID's are written to the observation file only in the case of detecting the new complete activity. Each new recognized activity is reported once. There are two types of activities modeled in the system: activities based on position changes and activities based on hand movements. A few hand activity models describe the single hand movements and the others describe both hands movements. The activities may be easily added to or removed from the system. During the research there was a set of 10 activities of the first type and 19 activities of the second type. There were also some activities marked as potentially dangerous which were meant for autism self-injurious behavior. The frames and (optionally) recognized events are saved into the long term observation file.

The complete list of body positions and activities modeled in the system is presented in Table 1. The body positions are listed in the left column and the activities based on these positions changes are placed in the middle. The activities based on hand movements are contained in the column on the right. The potentially dangerous activities are emphasized.

In the learning phase the observation file is manually divided into parts which are labeled with emotion IDs. The prepared data may be used as a learning set or test set.

The learning set is further used in the *learning* module in order to estimate the HMM behavior model's parameters. For this purpose we use the algorithms described in Sect. 4. At the very beginning the combination of tracked events have to be chosen: body positions, activities based on positions or activities based on hand movements. This is the key operation and has a great impact on the emotion recognition quality. The decision is made twice – before the model estimation and at the beginning of each experiment. However, in each experiment the model with appropriate settings has to be used (the number and type of observations has to coincide).

The test set is used in experiments conducted in the *test* module. In each iteration the component communicates with the *emotion recognition* module which estimates the emotional state's ID. The emotion is calculated based on the behavior HMM model (with specified events settings) and the time window with defined number of historic observations (read from the long term observation files). In the test module the estimated emotion ID is compared to the manually assigned label. The algorithms may be also used for the real-time emotion recognition – in such a case the history is saved based on the live observations and there is no human verification.

3   Notation

The following notation will be used for the Hidden Markov Models:
$\lambda = \{A, B, \pi\}$ - the complete parameter set for HMM,
N - the number of states,
M - the number of observation symbols,
T - the length of observation sequence,
$S = \{s_i\} : i \in \{1 \ldots N\}$ - the set of states,

Table 1. The list of body positions and activities modeled in the system

Body positions	Body position changes	Hand activities
Standing	Standing → Sitting (chair)	Right arm twisting forward
Sitting (chair)	Sitting (chair) → Standing	Right arm twisting backward
Kneeling	Standing → Kneeling	Raising and lowering right hand
Bending	Kneeling → Standing	Left arm twisting forward
Lying	Standing → Bending → Standing	Left arm twisting backward
On all fours	Sitting (chair) → Bending → Sitting (chair)	Raising and lowering left hand
Sitting (ground)	Sitting (ground) → Lying	Both hands twisting forward
	Lying → Sitting (ground)	Both hands twisting backward
	Sitting (ground) → Standing	Raising and lowering both hands
	Standing → Sitting (ground)	Clapping hands
		Clapping hands over the head
		Crawl forward
		Crawl backward
		Touching the head with right hand
		Touching the head with left hand
		Touching the head with both hands
		Hitting the head with right hand
		Hitting the head with left hand
		Hitting the head with both hands

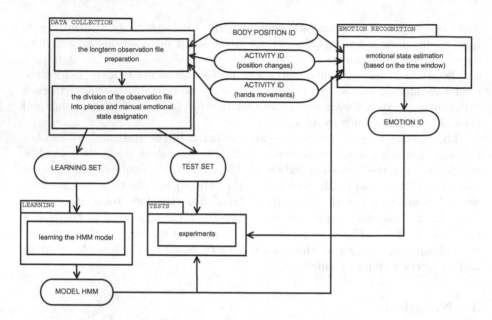

Fig. 1. The scheme of the emotion recognition system

$V = \{v_i\} : i \in \{1 \dots M\}$ - the set of observation symbols,
$A = \{a_{ij} : i, j \in \{1 \dots N\}\}$ - the state transition matrix,
$B = \{b_{ij} : i \in \{1 \dots N\}, j \in \{1 \dots M\}\}$ - the probability distribution matrix for observed symbols,
$\pi = \{\pi_i, i \in \{1 \dots N\}\}$ - initial state distribution vector,
$O = \{O_t\} : t \in \{1 \dots T\}$ - observation sequence,
$E = \{e_t\} : t \in \{1 \dots T\}$ - the sequence of estimated states.

4   Methods

In this paper methods based on Hidden Markov Models and long term observations were used to model behavior. Further the model is used in the emotion recognition problem. The model may be created for one or more of the following events:

- body position,
- activity based on the body position changes,
- activity based on the hand movements.

The positions are recognized for each frame obtained from the Kinect device, while the activities are registered only in the case of new complete activity detection [17]. The data set (long term observation files) is divided into pieces corresponding to emotions considered in the system and the emotional state IDs are manually assigned to them. The file parts order remains unchanged.

The emotional state IDs are mapped into HMM states s_i, $i \in \{1, \ldots, N\}$. The event IDs (positions, activities) are mapped into the HMM observation symbols v_k, $k \in \{1, \ldots, M\}$ (the consecutive natural numbers). Based on the learning set, an ordered list of pairs ($\{HMM\ observation\ symbol\ O_t = v_k\}$; $\{emotional\ state\ e_t = s_i\}$)is created. Each element from the list is numbered in accordance with its order $t \in \{1, \ldots, T\}$. Using this observation list the behavior model is created.

In the learning phase the emotional states are known (assigned by a child's caretaker), thus the learning algorithm can be simplified to some events counting:

- $A[i][j]$ is proportional to the number of such events that the observed person was in the i-th emotional state at time t and he/she was in the j-th emotional state at time $t + 1$,
- $B[i][j]$ is proportional to the number of occurrences of the j-th HMM observational symbol in the i-th emotional state,
- $\pi[i]$ is proportional to the number of occurrences of the i-th emotional state.

The vectors $A[i]$ and $B[i]$ are normalized for each i value and the vector π is also normalized.

There is only one learning sequence, therefore the initial state distribution vector π is filled in with probability values proportional to the number of occurrences of corresponding states. It may be also filled in with the equal values $\frac{1}{N}$.

Formally the model parameters are calculated using Eqs. (1)–(6).

$$
f_A(i, j, t) = \begin{cases} 1 \text{ if } e_t = s_i \wedge e_{t+1} = s_j \\ 0 \text{ otherwise} \end{cases} \tag{1}
$$

$$
\underset{i \in \{1, \ldots, N\}}{\forall}\ \underset{j \in \{1, \ldots, N\}}{\forall}\ A[i][j] = \frac{\sum\limits_{t \in \{1, \ldots, T\}} f_A(i, j, t)}{\sum\limits_{k \in \{1, \ldots, N\}} \sum\limits_{t \in \{1, \ldots, T\}} f_A(i, k, t)} \tag{2}
$$

$$
f_B(i, j, t) = \begin{cases} 1 \text{ if } e_t = s_i \wedge O_t = v_j \\ 0 \text{ otherwise} \end{cases} \tag{3}
$$

$$
\underset{i \in \{1, \ldots, N\}}{\forall}\ \underset{j \in \{1, \ldots, M\}}{\forall}\ B[i][j] = \frac{\sum\limits_{t \in \{1, \ldots, T\}} f_B(i, j, t)}{\sum\limits_{k \in \{1, \ldots, M\}} \sum\limits_{t \in \{1, \ldots, T\}} f_B(i, k, t)} \tag{4}
$$

$$
f_\pi(i, t) = \begin{cases} 1 \text{ if } e_t = s_i \\ 0 \text{ otherwise} \end{cases} \tag{5}
$$

$$\underset{i\in\{1,...,N\}}{\forall}\ \pi[i] = \frac{\displaystyle\sum_{t\in\{1,...,T\}} f_\pi(i,t)}{\displaystyle\sum_{k\in\{1,...,N\}}\sum_{t\in\{1,...,T\}} f_\pi(k,t)} \qquad (6)$$

The obtained HMM behavior model is further used in the experiments. Based on the model and the time window defined for the hictorical events the actual emotional state is estimated. For this purpose the Viterbi algorithm [13] is used – the last decoded state is the estimated emotional state.

5   Experiments

The experiments were conducted in order to determine if Hidden Markov Models are suitable for emotion recognition based on the behavior model. The developed model described observed person's behavior in three emotional states: calm, nervous, angry/aggressive. For each of these states some illustrative behavior have been registered by an healthy adult. It has been assumed, that:

– the calm person usually sits on the chair, however it is possible for them to stand, walk or bend,
– the nervous person very often stands up and walk around the room,
– the angry person sits on the chair very rarely and sometimes the movements characteristic only for this state occur (during this experiments the existing activity – hitting the head – has been used in order to model some self-injurious behavior).

A few changes of mood in different order were recorded so as to enable the transitions between the states. The graphical interpretation for the obtained transition matrix is presented in Fig. 2.

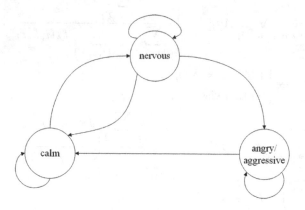

Fig. 2. The graphical interpretation for the transition matrix A obtained in all described experiments

The experiments were conducted for three different types of events:

- body positions and all activities recognized in the system,
- body positions,
- all activities recognized in the system.

In all experiments the emotional state was estimated for the time window including 1000 historical observations. The window width was chosen arbitrarily. A better emotional state estimation should be obtained with wider time window. However, along with each observation rises also the time needed for computations – the Viterbi algorithm computational complexity is $O(N^2T)$. The chosen observation number is a compromise between the accuracy and computation time.

The detailed information about the particular experiments is presented below.

5.1   Emotion Recognition Based on Body Positions and Activities

The aim of this experiment was to check the usefulness of the behavior model based on recognized body positions and detected activities of all types for the emotion recognition purposes. In total there are 36 possible HMM observation symbols in this test. In the experiment all available types of events were used.

The comparison of emotional states IDs (learnt ID and the estimated one) resulted in the coincidence rate at 65.36%. It has been noticed that for the sequence of the same recognized position (observation symbol) the decoded state always tends to the one with the symbol probability distribution having this symbol at the highest probability value. It becomes a problem because of the high sampling rate provided by the Kinect device and calculation of the position for each single frame. The number of recognized positions is nearly the same as the number of all observations. Nevertheless, the recognized emotional states rate is quite high.

5.2   Emotion Recognition Based on Body Positions

The aim of this experiment was to check the usefulness of the behavior model based on recognized body positions for the emotion recognition purposes. In this experiment only the 7 body positions recognized in the system were used.

The comparison of emotional states IDs (learnt ID and the estimated one) resulted in the coincidence rate at 65.29%. The result is a little bit worse than in the previous experiment (Sect. 5.1) where additionally the activities were used. Although the difference is insignificant, the experiment suggests that using the activities may improve the recognition rate. Therefore the experiment for emotion recognition based only on activities has been conducted (Sect. 5.3).

The experiment does not rule out the possibility that the lower sampling rate would improve the position based emotion recognition. This remark is connected with the time window width.

5.3   Emotion Recognition Based on Activities

The aim of this experiment was to check the usefulness of the behavior model based on recognized activities of all types for the emotion recognition purposes. In total there are 29 possible HMM observation symbols in this test. In the experiment only the activities were used.

The activities are detected much less often than body positions, thus in this experiment the number of HMM observations was much lower than in previous experiments (Sects. 5.1 and 5.2).

The comparison of emotional states IDs (learnt ID and the estimated one) resulted in the coincidence rate at 92.63%. In comparison to the experiments where the body positions have been used, the score is significantly higher.

The results obtained in this experiment are very satisfactory and they drive to the conclusion that the model creation should be based on new recognized activities. Moreover, the activities that occur only in particular states (for example, in this experiment the activity *Hitting the head* occurred only in the *angry/aggressive state*) may significantly improve the emotion recognition quality. However, these are only the preliminary research results thus any further conclusions cannot be made at this moment. The number of experiments has to be increased and the experiments have to be conducted for real data – for experiments described in this paper the data have been recorded by an actor who was told to behave in a particular way.

6   Conclusions and Future Work

The emotions are usually reflected in human behavior, except for the situation when the person attempts to hide them. In the case of autistic children the expressed emotions are always real. Unfortunately, their individual way of emotion expression is completely incomprehensible for the community. However, according to the literature it seems that these behaviors are repeatable and in a certain sense – rational. This observation became an inspiration for investigation into the emotion recognition problem using the statistical models.

In this paper the preliminary research on behavior-based emotion recognition was presented. The behavior model may be created for various types of events: body positions and activities based on position changes or hand movements. The developed methods described in this paper use the Hidden Markov Models.

A few experiments have been conducted in order to evaluate the model usefulness for the emotion recognition purposes. The preliminary results are very satisfactory. The experiments reveal that the most promising approach is the one using the complex events such as activities.

However, the emotion recognition problem is a very complex issue and needs much more attention. The experiments are very time consuming and they also require the cooperation with psychologist or psychiatrist who knows the autistic child really well. Such a research should be carried out in the future.

Acknowledgment. This work was supported by the statutory funds of the Faculty of Electronics 0401/0140/18, Wroclaw University of Science and Technology, Wroclaw, Poland.

References

1. Seach, D., Lloyd, M., Preston, M.: Supporting Children with Autism in Mainstreem Schools. The Questions Publishing Company Ltd. (2003). ISBN 83-60215-17-0
2. American Psychiatric Association: Diagnostic and Statistical Manual of Mental Disorders, 4th edn. American Psychiatric Publishing Inc., Washington (2013)
3. Autism (in Polish). http://dajmiczas.pl/autyzm/
4. Ricks, D.M., Wing, L.: Language, communication, and the use of symbols in normal and autistic children. J. Autism Child. Schizophr. **5**(3), 191–221 (1975)
5. Endelson, S.M., Johnson, J.B.: Autoaggressive behaviors in autism. The reasons and procedures. Wydawnictwo Harmonia (2018). (in Polish)
6. Ekman, P., Friesen, W.V.: Unmasking the Face. A Guide to Recognizing Emotions from Facial Clues. Institute for Study of Human Knowledge (2015)
7. Kahou, S.E., et al.: EmoNets: multimodal deep learning approaches for emotion recognition in video. J. Multimodal User Interfaces **10**(2), 99–111 (2016)
8. Dhall, A., Ramana Murthy, O.V., Goecke, R., Joshi, J., Gedeon, T.: Video and image based emotion recognition challenges in the wild: EmotiW 2015. In: Proceedings of the 2015 ACM on International Conference on Multimodal Interaction, pp. 423–426 (2015)
9. Trigeorgis, G., et al.: Adieu features? End-to-end speech emotion recognition using a deep convolutional recurrent network. In: 2016 IEEE International Conference on Acoustics, Speech and Signal Processing (ICASSP), pp. 5200–5204 (2016)
10. Han, K., Yu, D., Tashev, I.: Speech emotion recognition using deep neural network and extreme learning machine. In: INTERSPEECH-2014, no. September, pp. 223–227 (2014)
11. Schuller, B., Rigoll, G., Lang, M.: Hidden Markov model-based speech emotion recognition. In: 2003 IEEE International Conference on Acoustics, Speech, and Signal Processing (ICASSP 2003), vol. 2, pp. 401–404 (2003)
12. Manzi, A., Fiorini, L., Limosani, R., Dario, P., Cavallo, F.: Two-person activity recognition using skeleton data. IET Comput. Vis. **12**, 27–35 (2017)
13. Rabiner, L., Juang, B.: An introduction to hidden Markov models. IEEE ASSP Mag. **3**(January), 4–16 (1986)
14. Postawka, A., Śliwiński, P.: A kinect-based support system for children with autism spectrum disorder. In: Rutkowski, L., Korytkowski, M., Scherer, R., Tadeusiewicz, R., Zadeh, L.A., Zurada, J.M. (eds.) ICAISC 2016. LNCS (LNAI), vol. 9693, pp. 189–199. Springer, Cham (2016). https://doi.org/10.1007/978-3-319-39384-1_17
15. Postawka, A.: Exercise recognition using averaged hidden Markov models. In: Rutkowski, L., Korytkowski, M., Scherer, R., Tadeusiewicz, R., Zadeh, L.A., Zurada, J.M. (eds.) ICAISC 2017, Part II. LNCS (LNAI), vol. 10246, pp. 137–147. Springer, Cham (2017). https://doi.org/10.1007/978-3-319-59060-8_14
16. Postawka, A., Rudy, J.: Lifelogging system based on averaged hidden Markov models: dangerous activities recognition. Comput. Sci. **19**(3), 257–278 (2018)
17. Postawka, A.: Real-time monitoring system for potentially dangerous activities detection. In: Proceedings of the 22nd International Conference on Methods and Models in Automation and Robotics (MMAR), pp. 1005–1008. IEEE Xplore Digital Library (2017)

Case-Based Reasoning for Context-Aware Solutions Supporting Personalised Asthma Management

Mario Quinde[1,2](✉) [ID], Nawaz Khan[1] [ID], and Juan Carlos Augusto[1] [ID]

[1] Research Group on Development of Intelligent Environments,
Middlesex University, London, UK
MQ093@live.mdx.ac.uk, {N.X.Khan,J.Augusto}@mdx.ac.uk
[2] University of Piura, Piura, Peru
Mario.Quinde@udep.pe

Abstract. Context-aware solutions have the potential to address the personalisation required for implementing asthma management plans. However, they have limitations to aid people with asthma when their triggers and symptoms are poorly known or changing. Case-Based Reasoning can address these limitations as it can effectively deal with personal constraints in problems that involve evolving context adaptation. This research work proposes to use Case-Based Reasoning together with Context-Aware Reasoning to aid the personalisation of asthma management plans at specific stages of the condition when the triggers and symptoms are not completely known or evolving. The proposal was implemented and evaluated using historical weather and air pollution data, and two control cases that were defined based on a set of interviews. Finally, the benefits and challenges of the proposal are presented and analysed based on the results of the evaluation.

Keywords: Context-awareness · Case-based reasoning · Asthma · Personalisation

1 Introduction

Asthma is a heterogeneous respiratory condition characterised by an airway inflammation causing expiratory airflow limitation and respiratory symptoms that vary over time and intensity [21]. There is no cure for it, and its treatment is based on a self-management approach, whose aim is achieving control of the condition through pharmacological and non-pharmacological plans [20,21]. The personalisation of these plans is important and challenging because of the high heterogeneity of asthma, which applies to the triggers provoking exacerbations and the symptoms shown when an exacerbation occurs [19]. This means that people with asthma may be susceptible to several triggers, but a specific trigger does not affect all people with asthma [20,21]. Besides, people's triggers can change over the years, and their symptoms may even vary from nigth to day [23].

© Springer Nature Switzerland AG 2019
L. Rutkowski et al. (Eds.): ICAISC 2019, LNAI 11509, pp. 260–270, 2019.
https://doi.org/10.1007/978-3-030-20915-5_24

Context-aware solutions are promising tools to address the required personalisation of asthma treatments as, by definition, they are capable of adapting their features to the specific characteristics of each patient's asthma [2,13,19]. Unlike Dey's definition of context which goes from the system to the user, our person-centric approach goes from the user to the system, and the user defines what are the relevant *contexts*, that is "the information which is directly relevant to characterise a situation of interest to the stakeholders of a system". *Context-awareness* is then defined as "the ability of a system to use contextual information in order to tailor its services so that they are more useful to the stakeholders because they directly relate to their preferences and needs". Hence, personalised context-aware solutions can provide meaningful data to be used as input for more complex decision-making processes in asthma management [19].

Case-Based Reasoning (CBR) can be used together with Context-Aware Reasoning (C-AR) in order to build synergies in specific problem-solving situations involving multidimensional context-related data [14]. CBR is a type of Artificial Intelligence approach [1] that simulates the *"use of old experiences to understand and solve new problems"* [15]. It has been applied in several domains of the health sciences [8,10], and one of the main directions is using CBR to adapt medical knowledge and reasoning strategies for personalising contextual information [16].

This research work studies the application of CBR together with C-AR for aiding the personalisation of solutions supporting asthma management. The benefit of this is related to the relevance of personalising asthma management plans. Recently diagnosed people are likely to know little about the triggers provoking their exacerbations, and they go through a trial and error process until finding out what sets off their symptoms [21]. In this scenario, although C-AR can help to monitor indicators associated with the triggers of a person with asthma (like temperature or pollen level), it cannot discover their triggers by itself. CBR can be used at this point with the aim of creating cases that will be used as a base in order to aid discovering the triggers affecting the person with asthma.

The paper is divided as follows. Section 2 summarises the state-of-the-art on the subject. Section 3 explains the methodology that led the research and the results of a questionnaire that was applied in partnership with Asthma UK. Section 4 describes the proposal, its implementation and evaluation. Sections 5 and 6 present the discussion and the conclusions of the research work, respectively.

2   State-of-the-Art

The miniaturisation of electrical devices and the spread of wireless networks have allowed the creation of sensors that collect large amounts of data [3]. C-AR is crucial to interpret and understand this collected data as it aids in gathering meaningful information for specific purposes [18]. C-AR as part of Intelligent Environments has been applied to several areas [7], and the health care domain is a promising area in which C-AR can be used to enhance the quality of life [3].

A survey on C-AR in asthma shows a lack of solutions allowing personalised asthma management [19]. This means that users cannot choose the indicators to track nor the features to use according to the characteristics of someone's asthma. A more comprehensive way of framing the context of a person with asthma was proposed to address this personalisation issue [19]. It is suggested to use three types of indicators (Patient Indicators or PI, Indoor Environmental Indicators or IEI, and Outdoor Environmental Indicators or OEI) in order to allow personalisation and enhance decision-making of C-AR solutions supporting asthma management. This provides a basis for complex decision-making processes, and it can be used to apply CBR for asthma management personalisation.

CBR allows reusing information and knowledge from previous situations that are similar to the new problem to solve [1]. CBR problem-solving paradigm has found in the health science a promising application domain [10] because it can handle some issues better than other methods and techniques [11]. It has been used in the health sciences in tasks like diagnosis, classification, tutoring, treatment planning, and knowledge acquisition/management [8]. One future direction of CBR in the health sciences is adapting procedures and reasoning strategies to personal constraints described by the contextual information itself [16]. Asthma management fits under this category as recently diagnosed people need to discover their triggers and symptoms for adapting their plans to their personal constraints. This personalisation process can benefit from using CBR.

C-AR can be used together with CBR to solve problems that are not completely understood, like dealing with evolving context adaptation [14]. Asthma management corresponds to this issue as the condition evolves over time, which means that people with asthma are updating their triggers and symptoms while their condition develops. This evolution makes it challenging to create C-AR solutions supporting the personalisation of asthma management because they need to adapt considering that the indicators to monitor change over time.

CBR has been used to analyse symptoms of people with asthma in order to know their status and suitable care plans [22]. However, it has not been used to develop proactive solutions analysing triggers-related indicators for personalising preventive treatments and predicting risky situations. This paper reports on using CBR as a component of C-AR solutions supporting personalised asthma management. CBR is used to aid the discovery and adaptation of the indicators to monitor for a person with asthma, considering their triggers and symptoms.

3   Methodology

The research has been led by the User-Centred Intelligent Environments Development Process (U-C IEDP), whose basis is considering users as the heart of the development process in order to meet customers expectations as regards the required services [6]. The methodology is divided into 4 stages. The first one is a literature review that shows a lack of C-AR solutions supporting the personalisation of asthma management [19]. In the second stage four people with asthma, two health carers of people with asthma, and a physician expert in respiratory conditions were interviewed. Among other outcomes, this stage re-confirmed the necessity of solutions supporting the personalisation of asthma management [19].

A partnership with Asthma UK, a membership-based charity with a current membership of approx. 5,200 [5], was formed in the third stage. They distributed a questionnaire that was built based on the outcomes of the previous stages among their network of approx. 200 patients and carers representatives volunteers. A response rate of approx. 21% was accomplished (42 responses). Figure 1 shows the results for the questions asking participants to rate from 0 (non-important) to 5 (most important) the following features of a solution supporting asthma management: alerting as regards triggers, alerting as regards symptoms, and reporting about the development of triggers and symptoms (T&S). Most of them (71%, 79% and 79%, respectively) rated these features with 4 and 5, what evidences a high concern for the triggers and symptoms of people with asthma.

The fourth stage focused on designing, implementing and evaluating the algorithm for the CBR. More details about this stage are shown in Sect. 4.

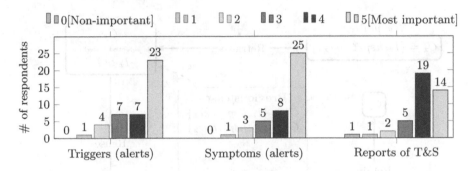

Fig. 1. Assessment of 3 features of solutions supporting asthma management

4 CBR for C-AR Solutions Supporting Personalised Asthma Management

CBR can aid the process of discovering the triggers of a person with asthma as it involves the use of multidimensional context-related data. A list of more than 25 potential triggers can be made using data provided by specialised organisations doing research on asthma [4,5,20,21]. A person with asthma has to narrow down this list until finding out what specific triggers affect them. CBR can also aid the context adaptation process. E.g. it can aid when someone's triggers change, or when they move to a new place with different environmental conditions.

A case for a CBR supporting asthma management (C_x) is made of a set of pairs indicator-value representing the context of a person with asthma (I_x), their predicted asthma health status (hsp_x) associated with I_x, and their real asthma health status (hsr_x) associated with I_x. The monitoring indicators can be PI (like heart rate or breathing rate), IEI (like temperature or humidity) or OEI (like temperature or pollen level). Equations 1 and 2 describe a case by a notation.

This feature vector representation will ease the explanation of the similarity measurement process that is part of the CBR cycle explained below [9].

$$C_x = \{I_x, hsp_x, hsr_x\} \tag{1}$$

$$I_x = \{(i_1, v_{1x}), (i_2, v_{2x}), ...(i_m, v_{mx})\} \tag{2}$$

Figure 2 presents how to use CBR for personalised asthma management. It has been adapted from the CBR cycle proposed by Aamodt and Plaza [1]. The *new problem* is a case (C_x) without its predicted health status (hsp_x) nor its real health status (hsr_x). The CBR then *retrieves* (from the database of *previous cases*) the case (C_s) that is most similar to C_x. If I_i and I_x are compared using the K-Nearest Neighbour (KNN) algorithm for a $k = 1$, the similarity between a case from the database (C_i) and C_x is $S_{ix} = \sqrt{\sum_{j=1}^{m}(v_{ij} - v_{xj})^2}$; and equation $S_{sx} = \min(S_{1x}, S_{2x}, ...S_{nx})$ defines the index (s) of the case to retrieve (C_s).

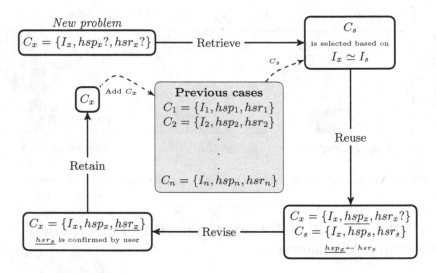

Fig. 2. CBR cycle adapted for personalised asthma management

Once C_s is selected, the CBR *reuses* its real solution (hsr_s) in order to attempt predicting the health status associated with C_x (hsp_x). The predicted solution is the predicted health status (hsp_x) of the person with asthma for the context to which s/he is exposed (I_x). Hence, hsp_x will get the value of the real health status associated with C_s (hsr_s). After this, the user determines their real health status (hsr_x) through the *revision* phase, and C_x is completely defined. Finally, C_x is *retained* by being stored in the database of previous cases.

4.1 Implementation and Evaluation: A Case Study

The CBR was implemented and evaluated using two control cases that were defined based on the interviews held [19]: *Person A* (PA) whose trigger is low temperature, and *Person B* (PB) whose triggers are low temperature and pollen. Hourly data about weather and air pollution at Postcode NW10 0TH (London, UK) was gathered using World Weather Online[1] and London Air[2] APIs. The time frame of the data is from 01/01/2018 00:00:00 to 31/10/2018 23:00:00.

A case to be analysed by the CBR (C_x) partially represents the weather and air pollution scenarios for a specific day $(day\ x)$. Hence, I_x is made of the minimum temperature $(minT)$, the maximum temperature $(maxT)$, the average feels like temperature (fl), the average temperature (t), the average humidity level (h), the average wind gust (wg) and the average values for ozone level (O_3), Particulate Matter 2.5 $(pm2.5)$ and 10 $(pm10)$ for $day\ x$.

The real health status for $day\ x$ (hsr_x) is defined for *Person A* using Eq. 3, and for *Person B* using Eq. 4. The limit value for $maxT$ is based on the recommendations from Asthma UK [5], and the limit value for $pm10$ is taken from the guideline provided by the Committee on the Medical Effects of Air Pollutants (COMEAP) [12]. The case represented by *Person B* considers $pm10$ for defining hsr_x as it is the indicator mostly used to monitor pollen level.

$$f(maxT) = \begin{cases} 0 & \text{for } maxT \geq 10 \\ 1 & \text{else} \end{cases} \qquad (3)$$

$$f(maxT, pm10) = \begin{cases} 0 & \text{for } maxT \geq 10 \wedge pm10 \leq 51 \\ 1 & \text{else} \end{cases} \qquad (4)$$

The raw values of the indicators defining I_x have different scales. E.g. humidity values vary from 0% to 100%, and $pm10$ values vary from 0 ug/m^3 to more than 400 ug/m^3. This assigns different weights to the indicators as the differentials (for each indicator) to use to compare the cases will have different scales. Hence, the values of the indicators should be normalised to achieve a weightless comparison. It is important not to use weights in the *retrieval* as the aim is to aid people when they do not know their triggers yet. Thus, they must be equally aware of the potential triggers-related indicators that may affect them.

The normalisation for this case study is based on indicator $pm10$, whose values are transformed to a scale that goes from 1 to 10. This scale is proposed by COMEAP to simplify the explanation of the effects that $pm10$ has on people's health [12]. Hence, all the indicators were normalised to use a scale that goes from 1 to 10, and Eqs. 3 and 4 were also adapted considering this normalisation.

The KNN algorithm was chosen to assess the similarity in the *retrieval* process as it is used to solve data classification problems [17]. Its simplicity and popularity [17] also aid the purpose of illustrating the application of the proposal. Thus, 304 cases (one for each day) were used for each control case and evaluated using the KNN algorithm for $k = 1$ and $k = 3$. The results are summarised in Figs. 3, 4, 5 and 6, where the accuracy (%) of the CBR is shown.

---

[1] https://www.worldweatheronline.com/developer/api/.
[2] https://www.londonair.org.uk/Londonair/API/.

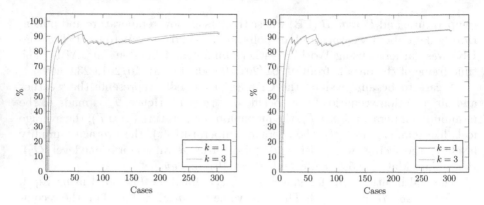

Fig. 3. PA: Cumulative accuracy   **Fig. 4.** PB: Cumulative accuracy

The final cumulative accuracies for $k = 1$ and $k = 3$ are similar (Figs. 3 and 4). The cumulative accuracy increases faster for $k = 1$, however using a $k = 3$ provides more stability when the CBR is fed with cases that are different from those that are stored. This is seen between cases 50 and 130 (approx.), and it is better illustrated in Figs. 5 and 6 that present the accuracy for the previous 20 cases that have been evaluated. These figures show the average accuracy for cases $C_{x-19}, C_{x-18}, ..., C_x$. Hence, a $k = 3$ makes the CBR has fewer low accuracy points when only the previous 20 cases are considered in the calculation.

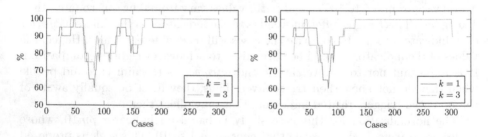

Fig. 5. PA: Previous 20 cases accuracy   **Fig. 6.** PB: Previous 20 cases accuracy

Table 1 shows how the CBR behaves considering previous short-term cases for a $k = 3$. It is read by choosing an accuracy threshold (e.g. >70%) and a column (e.g. *Person A - Previous 10*). That number (98, 2%) represents the times that the CBR was at least 70% accurate considering the previous 10 cases in the calculation of its accuracy for *Person A*. In other words, it can be said for this example that the 98, 2% of the times the CBR was accurate in at least 7 out of the previous 10 cases. This is important because knowing the short-term accuracy of the CBR would allow defining a confidence level of the system at a specific moment. Thus, the system could tell users about its confidence level when it suggests an outcome, it could ask the user to confirm their real health status more often as it predictions may be less accurate, or it could prevent overloading users with false positive until its confidence level increases.

Table 1. CBR accuracy (%) distribution considering previous cases for $k = 3$

Accuracy	Person A			Person B		
	Previous 5	Previous 10	Previous 20	Previous 5	Previous 10	Previous 20
>10%	100%	100%	100%	100%	100%	100%
>20%	99.3%	100%	100%	100%	100%	100%
>30%	99.3%	100%	100%	100%	100%	100%
>40%	98.3%	100%	100%	98.3%	100%	100%
>50%	98.3%	99.7%	100%	98.3%	100%	100%
>60%	91.3%	96.9%	100%	93.9%	99.7%	100%
>70%	91.3%	92.8%	99.7%	93.9%	93.8%	100%
>80%	77.8%	81.5%	85.1%	82.8%	87.7%	92.6%
>90%	77.8%	66.1%	67.4%	82.8%	73.0%	75.2%
=100%	77.8%	66.1%	54.6%	82.8%	73.0%	62.0%

5   Discussion

The results of the experiment show that CBR can make reasonably accurate predictions when there is no explicit information to define control limits. It also shows that the CBR is more accurate and stable for *Person B* who has a set of two triggers instead of only one. Although this cannot be concluded as experiments with more complex cases should be made, it is expected CBR to have a good performance solving multidimensional problems, what is interpreted as dealing with more complex sets of triggers. This suggests that CBR can aid C-AR supporting personalised asthma management when there is not enough evidence to define the indicators to monitor or to set their control limits.

The proposal aids personalised asthma management in several ways. The interaction between CBR and C-AR helps when the triggers are not known or partially known. In the first case, the C-AR component gathers data about the potential triggers-related indicators and the CBR component analyses it considering previous situations. If the triggers are partially known, users define the indicators and its control limits (C-AR) according to what they know about their triggers, and the CBR analyses more data in order to find risky situations that users do not perceive yet. Further, this interaction can help people with asthma when their triggers change, and when they move to a different location with weather and pollution characteristics to which they were not exposed before.

Several challenges arise from the proposal. First, defining the frequency of bringing a *new case/problem* to be assessed by the CBR is relevant as it must consider technical and cognitive issues. For instance, if the CBR is implemented in a mobile application, concerns about processing/storage capacity, battery duration, and not overloading users with non-relevant tasks and information should be addressed. Another issue is about what to do if there is not enough data to complete the case to assess. This might happen because it is expected to gather data from different sources, what is always challenging [7,18]. Some possible solutions are (i) not assessing the incomplete case, (ii) assessing the incomplete case as any other case, or (iii) assessing the case telling the user it is not complete.

The algorithm to *retrieve* the most similar case influences in the time needed to improve and stabilise the accuracy of the CBR. This is particularly challenging in the asthma context because the algorithms may have different behaviours depending on several factors like the number of monitored indicators and the characteristics of someone's triggers. Finally, determining the real health status (hsr_x) for a specific I_x is crucial to complete the *revision* stage. This is an issue as there are no commercial sensors able to monitor the asthma health status of a person constantly. Thus, a human-in-the-loop approach is needed to determine hsr_x. This step is important because the hsr_x sets the ground truth to attempt the prediction of future cases, and confirms the accuracy of the predictions.

The team is currently working on implementing the proposal in a C-AR mobile application (prototype) aiding personalised asthma management. The prototype will be validated in partnership with Asthma UK that will facilitate the interaction with people with asthma and carers. Efforts are also being focused on studying the Human-Computer Interaction factor, testing other classification algorithms and using data from multiple locations to assess effectiveness.

6   Conclusions

C-AR can aid personalised asthma management. However, it cannot cope with situations in which the context of a person with asthma is not completely known or changing. This research work proposes to use CBR to support C-AR when there is not enough explicit information to recognise risky situations for people with asthma. CBR infers possible outcomes from similar contexts to which the person has been exposed. A CBR supporting personalised asthma management was implemented and evaluated, showing positive results. It is shown that the proposal can aid people with asthma with few or no knowledge about their triggers in recognising potentially risky situations, discovering their triggers and adapting their asthma management plans to their personal constraints.

Acknowledgement. We thank Asthma UK for spreading the questionnaire (Sect. 3), among their representative network of people with asthma and carers. The link to the questionnaire is https://figshare.com/s/9f6b5e8a677ebd223f4a. The Context and Context-awareness definitions in Sect. 1 were provided by J.C. Augusto.

References

1. Aamodt, A., Plaza, E.: Case-based reasoning: foundational issues, methodological variations, and system approaches'. AI Commun. **7**(1), 39–59 (1994). https://doi.org/10.3233/AIC-1994-7104
2. Abowd, G.D., Dey, A.K., Brown, P.J., Davies, N., Smith, M., Steggles, P.: Towards a better understanding of context and context-awareness. In: Gellersen, H.-W. (ed.) HUC 1999. LNCS, vol. 1707, pp. 304–307. Springer, Heidelberg (1999). https://doi.org/10.1007/3-540-48157-5_29

3. Acampora, G., Cook, D.J., Rashidi, P., Vasilakos, A.V.: A survey on ambient intelligence in healthcare. Proc. IEEE **101**(12), 2470–2494 (2013). https://doi.org/10.1109/JPROC.2013.2262913
4. Asthma Australia: An asthma Australia site (2016). www.asthmaaustralia.org.au
5. Asthma UK: Asthma UK (2016). www.asthma.org.uk
6. Augusto, J., Kramer, D., Alegre, U., Covaci, A., Santokhee, A.: Theuser-centred intelligent environments development process as a guide to co-create smart technology for people with special needs. Univ. Access Inf. Soc. **17**(1), 115–130 (2018). https://doi.org/10.1007/s10209-016-0514-8
7. Augusto, J.C., Callaghan, V., Cook, D., Kameas, A., Satoh, I.: Intelligent environments: a manifesto. Hum.-Centric Comput. Inf. Sci. **3**(1), 12 (2013). https://doi.org/10.1186/2192-1962-3-12
8. Begum, S., Ahmed, M.U., Funk, P., Xiong, N., Folke, M.: Case-based reasoning systems in the health sciences: a survey of recent trends and developments. IEEE Trans. Syst. Man Cybern. Part C (Appl. Rev.) **41**(4), 421–434 (2011). https://doi.org/10.1109/TSMCC.2010.2071862
9. Bergmann, R., Kolodner, J., Plaza, E.: Representation in case-based reasoning. Knowl. Eng. Rev. **20**(3), 209–213 (2005). https://doi.org/10.1017/S0269888906000555
10. Bichindaritz, I.: Case-based reasoning in the health sciences: why it matters for the health sciences and for CBR. In: Althoff, K.-D., Bergmann, R., Minor, M., Hanft, A. (eds.) ECCBR 2008. LNCS (LNAI), vol. 5239, pp. 1–17. Springer, Heidelberg (2008). https://doi.org/10.1007/978-3-540-85502-6_1
11. Bichindaritz, I., Montani, S.: Advances in case-based reasoning in the health sciences. Artif. Intell. Med. **51**(2), 75–79 (2011)
12. COMEAP: Review of the UK air quality index (2011). www.gov.uk/government/publications/comeap-review-of-the-uk-air-quality-index
13. Dey, A.K.: Understanding and using context. Pers. Ubiquit. Comput. **5**(1), 4–7 (2001). https://doi.org/10.1007/s007790170019
14. Khan, N., Alegre, U., Kramer, D., Augusto, J.C.: Is 'context-aware reasoning = case-based reasoning'? In: Brézillon, P., Turner, R., Penco, C. (eds.) CONTEXT 2017. LNCS (LNAI), vol. 10257, pp. 418–431. Springer, Cham (2017). https://doi.org/10.1007/978-3-319-57837-8_35
15. Kolodner, J.L.: An introduction to case-based reasoning. Artif. Intell. Rev. **6**(1), 3–34 (1992). https://doi.org/10.1007/BF00155578
16. Montani, S.: How to use contextual knowledge in medical case-based reasoning systems: a survey on very recent trends. Artif. Intell. Med. **51**(2), 125–131 (2011). https://doi.org/10.1016/j.artmed.2010.09.004
17. Okfalisa, Gazalba, I., Mustakim, Reza, N.G.I.: Comparative analysis of k-nearest neighbor and modified k-nearest neighbor algorithm for data classification. In: 2017 2nd International conferences on Information Technology, Information Systems and Electrical Engineering (ICITISEE), pp. 294–298 (2017). https://doi.org/10.1109/ICITISEE.2017.8285514
18. Perera, C., Zaslavsky, A., Christen, P., Georgakopoulos, D.: Context aware computing for the internet of things: a survey. IEEE Commun. Surv. Tutor. **16**(1), 414–454 (2014). https://doi.org/10.1109/SURV.2013.042313.00197
19. Quinde, M., Khan, N., Augusto, J.C.: Personalisation of context-aware solutions supporting asthma management. In: Miesenberger, K., Kouroupetroglou, G. (eds.) ICCHP 2018. LNCS, vol. 10897, pp. 510–519. Springer, Cham (2018). https://doi.org/10.1007/978-3-319-94274-2_75

20. The British Thoracic Society: British guideline on the management of asthma: A national clinical guideline. Technical report (2016). www.brit-thoracic.org.uk
21. The Global Initiative for Asthma: Global strategy for asthma management and prevention. Technical report (2018). www.ginasthma.org
22. Tyagi, A., Singh, P.: ACS: asthma care services with the help of case base reasoning technique. Procedia Comput. Sci. **48**, 561–567 (2015). https://doi.org/10.1016/j.procs.2015.04.136
23. Waldron, J.: Asthma Care in the Community. Wiley, Hoboken (2007)

Deep Learning for Detection and Localization of Thoracic Diseases Using Chest X-Ray Imagery

Somnath Rakshit[1,2], Indrajit Saha[1]([✉]), Michal Wlasnowolski[2,3],
Ujjwal Maulik[4], and Dariusz Plewczynski[2,3]

[1] Department of Computer Science and Engineering,
National Institute of Technical Teachers' Training and Research, Kolkata, India
indrajit@nitttrkol.ac.in
[2] Centre of New Technologies, University of Warsaw, Warsaw, Poland
[3] Faculty of Mathematics and Information Science,
Warsaw University of Technology, Warsaw, Poland
[4] Department of Computer Science and Engineering,
Jadavpur University, Kolkata, India

Abstract. Classification of diseases from biomedical images is a fast growing emerging field of research. In this regard, chest X-Rays (CXR) are one of the most widely used medical images to diagnose common heart and lung diseases where previous works have explored the usage of various pre-trained deep learning models to perform the classification. However, these models are very deep, thus use large number of parameters. Moreover, it is still not possible to find readily available access to a practicing radiologist for proper diagnosis from an X-Ray image of chest. Hence, this fact motivated us to conduct this research with the aim to classify CXR images in an automated manner with smaller number of parameters during training for 14 different categories of thoracic diseases and produce heatmap for the corresponding image in order to show the location of abnormality. For the purpose of classification, transfer learning is used with the pre-trained network of Resnet18, while the heatmaps are generated using pooling along the channel dimension and then computing the average of class-wise features. The proposed model contains less parameters to train and provides better performance than the other models present in the literature. The trained model is then validated both quantitatively and visually by producing localized images in the form of heatmaps of the CXR images. Moreover, the dataset and code of this work are provided online (http://www.nitttrkol.ac.in/indrajit/projects/deeplearning-chestxray/).

Keywords: Deep learning · Chest X-Ray · Transfer learning · Class activation map

© Springer Nature Switzerland AG 2019
L. Rutkowski et al. (Eds.): ICAISC 2019, LNAI 11509, pp. 271–282, 2019.
https://doi.org/10.1007/978-3-030-20915-5_25

1   Introduction

Chest X-Ray (CXR) is one of the most widely accessible radiology examinations. They are generally the first choice of radiologists because of their non-invasiveness, ability to reveal information which may often go unnoticed, such as pathological alterations, low cost and low dose of radiation. They are widely used as a preliminary diagnosis tool. With the increase in the number of patients, the radiologists have been facing increasing workload. This makes it essential to develop an automated and computerized way of understanding the contents of the CXR images.

Recently, deep learning has revolutionized the field of computer vision. Deep learning has been widely used to solve image classification tasks. This has naturally led to the application of deep learning to biomedical images. However, deep learning needs large datasets in order to be successful. The absence of this type of large datasets previously made it tough to use deep learning to solve various problems. The recent advancements in biomedical research leads to many large datasets being released by various organizations. Thus, the availability of high volume datasets make it possible to apply deep learning in order to solve various computational intelligence tasks using biomedical images. Recently, large datasets like CXR dataset, which are generated by using ionized radiation in the form of X-ray images, from Open-i[1], ChestX-ray8 by Wang et al. [24] and ChestX-ray14 [24] by National Institute of Health (NIH) make it possible to apply deep learning effectively for computer aided diagnosis of heart and lung diseases. However, recent research shows that the methods that have been used to perform CXR image classification are successful, while these models are very deep and use large number of parameters to train the models. Apart from this, it is still not possible to get readily available access to a practising radiologist to diagnose diseases from CXR images.

To address the above facts, in this paper, transfer learning is used to classify CXR images effectively by means of easily available models that have been pre-trained on the ImageNet dataset. In this regard, a pre-trained ResNet18 [8] model is used to perform such classification using transfer learning on the Chest X Ray14 database. This database contains 112,117 frontal-view CXR images of 32,717 unique patients. They are classified into 14 types of diseases viz. Atelectasis, Cardiomegaly, Effusion, Infiltration, Mass, Nodule, Pneumonia, Pneumothorax, Consolidation, Edema, Emphysema, Fibrosis, Pleural Thickening and Hernia. The CXR images are preprocessed, augmented and then passed on to the ResNet18 model for encoding of features using deep learning and finally, classification using a fully connected network. Here ten-crops technique is then used during testing in order to increase the accuracy. The results of ResNet18 model is compared with the existing works such as Yao et al. [27], Li et al. [11], Wang et al. [24], DNetLoc [7] and Rajpurkar et al. [17] where DenseNet121, DenseNet169 [9] and deeper architectures are used respectively. This is to be noted that the advancement of deep neural networks motivates the researcher

---

[1] https://openi.nlm.nih.gov/.

to apply DenseNet in most of the cases while the shallow model like ResNet18 has not yet been evaluated for similar task to the best of our knowledge. The performance of the trained model is demonstrated quantitatively by means of Area Under Curve (AUC) of Receiver Operating Characteristic (ROC) curve and visually by generating heatmaps of CXR images pointing out the locations containing abnormalities. This model can be of great help to a radiologist in order to prioritize the severely abnormal cases first and to increase the confidence of the radiologist.

2   Background

This section contains a brief background of various diseases viz. Atelectasis, Cardiomegaly, Effusion, Infiltration, Mass, Nodule, Pneumonia, Pneumothorax, Consolidation, Edema, Emphysema, Fibrosis, Pleural Thickening and Hernia which are classified from the CXR images in this paper along with the various deep learning models used for classification and localization.

2.1   Brief Description of the Thoracic Diseases

Atelectasis is a disease in which closure of a lung occurs. It is a condition where the alveoli get deflated to reduced or even zero volume. On the other hand, Cardiomegaly [23] is caused by the enlargement of the heart. It is generally congenital in nature and may also be caused by heart valve diseases, thyroid disorders, pregnancy, kidney related diseases, diabetes and HIV infection among others. While effusion [12], or in this case, pleural effusion, is the condition in which excess fluid gets accumulated in the pleural cavity. This can hamper breathing since the expansion of the lung is limited by the presence of this unwanted liquid.

On the other hand, infiltration (more specifically, pulmonary infiltration) [18] is the presence of foreign objects, which accumulate gradually and can even fill the entire lung, causing life-threatening situation. While pulmonary mass is any opaque area of more than 30 mm size in the CXR image. If the opaque area measures less than 30 mm, it is known as lung nodule. Pulmonary nodules [14] itself do not show any symptoms. However, if the lung nodule was formed due to cancer, then certain symptoms like shortness of breath, pain in chest area, coughing up blood and weight loss may take place. While pneumonia [6] is a disease that is caused by the inflammation in lungs. The primarily affected parts are the alveoli. Apart from the earlier seven thoracic diseases, Pneumothorax is the presence of abnormal air space in the pleural space between the lung and the chest wall. While consolidation, or in this case, pulmonary consolidation [22], is a region of lung tissue that contains liquid instead of air. This disease is associated with the swelling and hardening of normally soft tissue of a normal lung. On the other hand, pulmonary edema [19] is a disease in which excess fluids accumulate in the lungs making breathing difficult. This may occur due to a congestive heart failure or acute lung injury. Emphysema [5] is a disease which results in shortness of breath. Rupturing of alveoli is one of the causes of this disease. In this condition, a large air space gets created inside the lungs instead of many small sized air spaces. While pulmonary fibrosis [3] is a lung disease in which the tissues present around and between the alveoli get hardened, thus making it difficult for the lung to function properly. Pleural thickening [26] is a condition in which the surrounding tissues of the lungs get scarred and start getting hardened. It is similar to pulmonary fibrosis in the sense that its symptoms cannot be felt early and is felt only when more and more scar tissues grow around the lungs. Lung Hernia [25] occurs when a portion of the lung extends outside the thoracic wall. In most cases, its symptoms are not felt. However, in advanced cases, the patient feels pain while inhaling and swelling in a particular area over the chest and fever is observed.

2.2   Brief Description of Deep Learning Models

ResNet is an image classification model that uses deep learning techniques. It was developed by He et al. [8] and was ranked first in the ImageNet Large Scale Visual Recognition Competition 2015 [4]. The ResNet model solves one of the most notorious problems in the field of machine learning, i.e. the vanishing gradient problem. In this problem, as the model gets deeper, its accuracy becomes saturated and rapidly starts decreasing. To overcome this problem, ResNet introduced the concept of identity shortcut. By reusing the activations of one of the previous layers, this model ensures that the layer next to the current one learns its weights properly. Here, an additive merge operation is performed, thus, forcing the network to learn residual errors. Densenet model was later developed by Huang et al. [9] in which instead of addition, concatenation of the output of previous layers to the output of the current layer was proposed. While the traditional convolutional neural networks have L connections (between each layer and its next one), the Densenet model has $L * (L + 1)/2$ connections. Here, for each layer, the feature maps of all previous layers are used as its inputs while the feature map of this layer is also used in the input of all subsequent layers. Densenet model overcomes the vanishing gradient problem in this fashion and is able to achieve feature reuse. Thus, counter to intuition, it is able to reduce the number of training parameters in spite of having a large network. Here, since each layer has direct access to the original input, better supervision is achieved while training.

Apart from these models, many other models such as Inception [21] and VGG [20] are also present to tackle the problem of efficient image classification using convolutional neural networks.

3   Method

This section describes the deep learning model/architecture used for classification of CXR images and generation of class activation maps (CAM) or heatmaps so as to obtain the localized CXR image. Apart from this, it is also described how

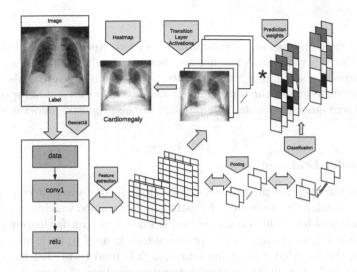

Fig. 1. Pipeline of the proposed model

transfer learning, preprocessing, data augmentation and localization of abnormalities are performed.

3.1 Architecture

The method used in this work can be divided into two stages. First, a pre-trained Resnet18 model is used for fine-tuning and training. It is a convolutional neural network that extracts the features present in the dataset of CXR images. Each of the feature vectors is a list of numbers that can be used by the dense layer in the next step for classification. It is a common practice to use a pre-trained network and fine-tune it for classification of images whose nature is different from the images that were used for training it during the ImageNet challenge. The dense layer thus takes the feature vectors from the Resnet18 model as input and generates a vector whose size is equal to the number of classes (14) as output. Further, a softmax layer is present that adds a non linearity and makes each of the 14 values to fall between 0 and 1. Now, each element of the vector contains a probability between 0 and 1. These are the probabilities of an image to fall in each of the 14 classes. This model is seen to contain 11,183,694 trainable parameters. Here, the objective is to use images and their corresponding diseases as input and generate classification for thoracic diseases for new CXR images. Later on, the CAM of the new images are also generated. Second, using the weights of the trained model, CAM is plotted for new CXR images. While training the model, the class averaged binary cross entropy loss is used. The loss function is described through Eqs. 1 to 3.

$$L = \{l_1, \ldots, l_N\}^\top \tag{1}$$

$$l_n = -w_n \left[y_n \cdot \log x_n + (1 - y_n) \cdot \log(1 - x_n) \right] \tag{2}$$

$$\ell(x, y) = mean(L) \tag{3}$$

In order to train the model, an optimizer is needed. Here, the Adam optimizer [10] is used for this purpose. Adam has low memory requirements and is invariant to the diagonal rescaling of the gradients. The Adam optimizer also has an efficient regret bound on the convergence rate. It is also well suited for problems involving large amount of data. The pipeline of the proposed model is shown in Fig. 1.

3.2   Transfer Learning

Training of the deep learning model can be done in two ways. It can either be done from scratch or it can be done by using the pre-trained weights in a different classification problem. The second method is known as transfer learning. In this method, knowledge obtained from a previous task is used to perform a different task. Thus, the knowledge from the source task is used to predict the outcome of the target task. Training from scratch requires significantly large datasets and hardware resources. However, a smaller dataset can be used in case of transfer learning.

In the present work, transfer learning is adopted. A Resnet18 model and its pre-trained weights based on the ImageNet challenge are used here as a feature extractor. Only the last layer of the classifier is modified. Instead of 1000 neurons in the case of ImageNet challenge, here 14 neurons have been used where each neuron correspond to each of the classes.

3.3   Preprocessing and Data Augmentation

In this work, the images present in the dataset are preprocessed and subjected to data augmentation. In the preprocessing step, the images are normalized after subtracting the mean of all pixels in the dataset from each pixel and then dividing the result by the standard deviation of the dataset. Data augmentation is the process of synthetically increasing the size of the training dataset. It is needed to decrease the chances of overfitting. In data augmentation, new images are synthetically generated from the images that are already present. Here, 2 ways are used to generate images synthetically. Firstly, images are randomly cropped and then resized using bilinear interpolation to form 224 * 224 images. Secondly, new images are generated by randomly flipping them horizontally. Horizontal flipping is performed to augment the training set so as to simulate images where the abnormality may be present in any of the lung, since lung diseases may take place in either lung. This step is important as it makes the model robust to abnormalities in CXR images.

3.4   Localization of Abnormalities

After obtaining a trained model, heatmaps are generated on test images that point out the exact location of the abnormality. This helps to visualize the most indicative areas used by the model during classification. The heatmaps are generated by using pooling along the channel dimension and then computing the average of class-wise features. The heatmaps show that the network that is trained on this architecture generalizes well and demonstrates good interpretation ability in localizing the areas of interest.

4   Experimental Results

This section describes the dataset, testbed and results.

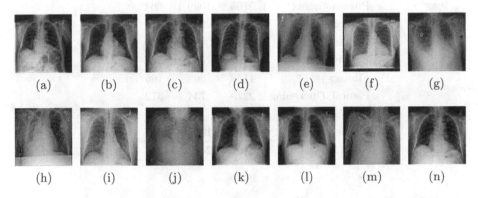

Fig. 2. Examples of the images present in the dataset. All 14 classes are represented here. (a) Atelectasis (b) Cardiomegaly (c) Effusion (d) Infiltration (e) Mass (f) Nodule (g) Pneumonia (h) Pneumothorax (i) Consolidation (j) Edema (k) Emphysema (l) Fibrosis (m) Pleural Thickening (n) Hernia

4.1   Dataset

To perform this experiment, the ChestX-ray14 dataset from National Institute of Health (NIH) has been used. This dataset contains 112,117 frontal images from 32,717 unique patients. The detailed breakdown of the dataset is provided in Table 1. All of the images have a resolution of 1024 * 1024 with 8 bits of gray scale. The dataset has been divided in 3 parts namely train, test and validation consisting of 70%, 20% and 10% of the total dataset respectively. Each image may have one or more labels viz. Atelectasis, Cardiomegaly, Effusion, Infiltration, Mass, Nodule, Pneumonia, Pneumothorax, Consolidation, Edema, Emphysema, Fibrosis, Pleural Thickening and Hernia. These labels were not created manually. Rather, they have been generated by analyzing medical records of patients using optical character recognition. The authors of the dataset have ensured that there is no patient overlap in the test and train data. CXR images from each class of data has been shown in Fig. 2.

Table 1. Table showing the class-wise number of images

Disease	Train	Test	Validation
Atelectasis	7996	2420	1119
Cardiomegaly	1950	582	240
Effusion	9261	2754	1292
Infiltration	13914	3938	2018
Mass	3988	1133	625
Nodule	4375	1335	613
Pneumonia	978	242	133
Pneumothorax	3705	1089	504
Consolidation	3263	957	447
Edema	1690	413	200
Emphysema	1799	509	208
Fibrosis	1158	362	166
Pleural Thickening	2279	734	372
Hernia	144	42	41
No disease	42404	11927	6078
No of images	78467	22432	11218

4.2 Testbed

The entire work has been implemented using PyTorch [15] and executed on a machine having 256 GB RAM and Intel Xeon CPU E5-2680 v4 processor with 28 cores. It has a NVIDIA GeForce GTX 1070 GPU. The Resnet18 model was chosen experimentally after trying out different other models like VGG19, VGG11 and DenseNet121. The training for the Resnet18 model took around 5 days in this configuration. The images have been generated using OpenCV [2] in Python. Also, scikit-learn [16] and numpy [13] libraries have been used for evaluation of the model. The model is trained on a batch size of 16 for 1000 epochs. In the Adam optimizer, the values of the learning rate is set as 0.0001 whereas the range of beta values are set in between 0.9 to 0.999. A weight decay of 10^{-5} and epsilon value of 10^{-8} have been used also.

4.3 Results

In this work, the performance of the model has been tested by means of Area Under Curve (AUC) metric. To test the model, the TenCrop technique [1] has been utilised. This helped in increasing the accuracy of the model slightly. The value of AUC of the model is compared with other models as shown in Table 2 and Fig. 3. It is observed that the Resnet18 model performs better than the other models that have been presented previously in literature. In 8 out of the 14 classes viz. Atelectasis, Effusion, Nodule, Pneumonia, Consolidation, Edema, Fibrosis

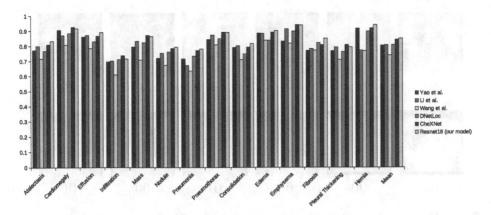

Fig. 3. Bar plot comparing the AUC scores of each of the models for each of the 14 classes along with the mean score

Table 2. Comparison of the proposed model with other models present in literature. The best score for each disease is formatted in bold.

Pathology	Yao et al. [27]	Li et al. [11]	Wang et al. [24]	DNetLoc [7]	CheXNet [17]	Resnet18 (our model)
Atelectasis	0.7720	0.8000	0.7160	0.7670	0.8094	**0.8318**
Cardiomegaly	0.9040	0.8700	0.8070	0.8830	**0.9248**	0.9151
Effusion	0.8590	0.8700	0.7840	0.8280	0.8638	**0.8890**
Infiltration	0.6950	0.7000	0.6090	0.7090	**0.7345**	0.7136
Mass	0.7920	0.8300	0.7060	0.8210	**0.8676**	0.8608
Nodule	0.7170	0.7500	0.6710	0.7580	0.7802	**0.7904**
Pneumonia	0.7130	0.6700	0.6330	0.7310	0.7680	**0.7788**
Pneumothorax	0.8410	0.8700	0.8060	0.8460	**0.8887**	0.8872
Consolidation	0.7880	0.8000	0.7080	0.7450	0.7901	**0.8138**
Edema	0.8820	0.8800	0.8350	0.8350	0.8878	**0.8985**
Emphysema	0.8290	0.9100	0.8150	0.8950	**0.9371**	0.9351
Fibrosis	0.7670	0.7800	0.7690	0.8180	0.8047	**0.8481**
Pleural Thickening	0.7650	0.7900	0.7080	0.7610	**0.8062**	0.7907
Hernia	0.9140	0.7700	0.7670	0.8960	0.9164	**0.9394**
Mean	0.8027	0.8064	0.7381	0.8066	0.8414	**0.8494**

and Hernia, the Resnet18 model shows superiority over other models. In terms of the mean AUC, it is seen that the Resnet18 model obtains the highest score of 0.8494. Also, the images obtained after localization are presented in Fig. 4. It is confirmed visually that the Resnet18 model is able to identify the areas of interest well and thus, can be of assistance to practicing radiologists. Hence, it is possible to detect thoracic diseases from CXR images with less expensive hardware.

In clinical procedures, automated detection and correct spatial localization of thoracic diseases will be of big help to radiologists and will assist them in decision-making as well as prioritization of cases. This work presents a model

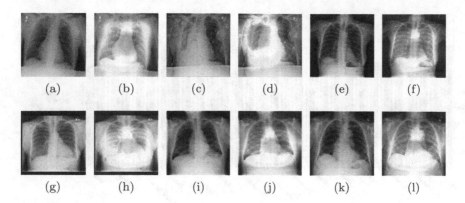

(a)   (b)   (c)   (d)   (e)   (f)

(g)   (h)   (i)   (j)   (k)   (l)

Fig. 4. Heatmaps generated using the trained model. The heatmaps of the following classes are shown: (a) and (b) Mass, (c) and (d) Pneumothorax (e) and (f) Infiltration (g) and (h) Nodule (i) and (j) Emphysema (k) and (l) Effusion

that is both efficient with respect to training time as well as produces better performance than the present state-of-the-art models. It only trains on labeled images and is able to classify as well as localize the areas of interest.

5   Conclusion

The emergence of large biomedical datasets have made it possible to apply deep learning models to perform various computational intelligence tasks. Detection of thoracic diseases from Chest X-Ray images is a challenging task since the machine does not have access to the patient's past medical history. Also, since the number of categories of disease is relatively high, it becomes difficult and tedious for a radiologist to correctly diagnose all diseases from Chest X-Ray images. Some prior works have attempted to solve this problem by using various deep learning models. However, comparatively shallow architectures like Resnet18 model has not been investigated previously. In this regard, it is shown that through transfer learning, Resnet18 model performs better on the ChestX-ray 14 dataset than all other deeper architectures used previously. The performance of this work has been evaluated quantitatively by means of AUC of ROC curve and visually by generating heatmaps. These heatmaps can help in detecting the areas of abnormality so that radiologist can prioritize the severe cases. Finally, we hope that this work will promote future work in the domain of detection of diseases using biomedical images.

Acknowledgment. This work has been co-supported by the Polish National Science Centre (2014/15/ B/ST6/05082), Foundation for Polish Science (TEAM to DP) and by the grant from the Department of Science and Technology, India under Indo-Polish/Polish-Indo project No.: DST/INT/POL/P-36/2016. The work was co-supported by grant 1U54DK107967-01 Nucleome Positioning System for Spatiotemporal Genome Organization and Regulation within 4DNucleome NIH program.

References

1. Krizhevsky, A., Sutskever, I., Hinton, G.: Imagenet classification with deep convolutional neural networks. In: Proceedings of the Advances in Neural Information Processing Systems, pp. 1097–1105 (2012)
2. Bradski, G.: The OpenCV Library. Dr. Dobb's J. Softw. Tools 25, 120–125 (2000)
3. Collard, H., et al.: Acute exacerbations of idiopathic pulmonary fibrosis. Am. J. Respir. Crit. Care Med. 176(7), 636–643 (2007)
4. Deng, J., Dong, W., Socher, R., Li, L., Li, K., Li, F.: Imagenet: a large-scale hierarchical image database, pp. 248–255 (2009)
5. Eriksson, S.: Pulmonary emphysema and alpha1-antitrypsin deficiency. Acta Med. Scand. 175(2), 197–205 (1964)
6. Fine, M., et al.: A prediction rule to identify low-risk patients with community-acquired pneumonia. N. Engl. J. Med. 336(4), 243–250 (1997)
7. Guendel, S., et al.: Learning to recognize abnormalities in chest x-rays with location-aware dense networks. arXiv preprint arXiv:1803.04565 (2018)
8. He, K., Zhang, X., Ren, S., Sun, J.: Deep residual learning for image recognition, pp. 770–778 (2016)
9. Huang, G., Liu, Z., Maaten, L.V.D., Weinberger, K.: Densely connected convolutional networks, pp. 2261–2269 (2017)
10. Kinga, D., Adam, J.: A method for stochastic optimization (2015)
11. Li, Z., et al.: Thoracic disease identification and localization with limited supervision. arXiv preprint arXiv:1711.06373 (2017)
12. Light, R., Macgregor, M.I., Luchsinger, P., Ball, W.: Pleural effusions: the diagnostic separation of transudates and exudates. Ann. Internal Med. 77(4), 507–513 (1972)
13. Oliphant, T.: Python for scientific computing. Comput. Sci. Eng. 9(3), 10–20 (2007)
14. Ost, D., Fein, A.M., Feinsilver, S.: The solitary pulmonary nodule. N. Engl. J. Med. 348(25), 2535–2542 (2003)
15. Paszke, A., et al.: Automatic differentiation in pytorch. In: NIPS-W (2017)
16. Pedregosa, F., et al.: Scikit-learn: machine learning in python. J. Mach. Learn. Res. 12(Oct), 2825–2830 (2011)
17. Rajpurkar, P., et al.: Chexnet: radiologist-level pneumonia detection on chest x-rays with deep learning. arXiv preprint arXiv:1711.05225 (2017)
18. Reeder, W., Goodrich, B.: Pulmonary infiltration with eosinophilia (PIE syndrome). Ann. Internal Med. 36(5), 1217–1240 (1952)
19. Robin, E., Cross, C., Zelis, R.: Pulmonary edema. N. Engl. J. Med. 288(6), 292–304 (1973)
20. Simonyan, K., Zisserman, A.: Very deep convolutional networks for large-scale image recognition. arXiv preprint arXiv:1409.1556 (2014)
21. Szegedy, C., Vanhoucke, V., Ioffe, S., Shlens, J., Wojna, Z.: Rethinking the inception architecture for computer vision, pp. 2818–2826 (2016)
22. Targhetta, R., Chavagneux, R., Bourgeois, J., Dauzat, M., Balmes, P., Pourcelot, L.: Sonographic approach to diagnosing pulmonary consolidation. J. Ultrasound Med. 11(12), 667–672 (1992)
23. Tavora, F., et al.: Cardiomegaly is a common arrhythmogenic substrate in adult sudden cardiac deaths, and is associated with obesity. Pathology 44(3), 187–191 (2012)

24. Wang, X., Peng, Y., Lu, L., Lu, Z., Bagheri, M., Summer, R.: Chestx-ray8: hospital-scale chest x-ray database and benchmarks on weakly-supervised classification and localization of common thorax diseases, pp. 3462–3471 (2017)
25. Weissberg, D., Refaely, Y.: Hernia of the lung. Ann. Thoracic Surg. **74**(6), 1963–1966 (2002)
26. Wu, R., Yang, P., Kuo, S., Luh, K.: "Fluid color" sign: a useful indicator for discrimination between pleural thickening and pleural effusion. J. Ultrasound Med. **14**(10), 767–769 (1995)
27. Yao, L., Poblenz, E., Dagunts, D., Covington, B., Bernard, D., Lyman, K.: Learning to diagnose from scratch by exploiting dependencies among labels. arXiv preprint arXiv:1710.10501 (2017)

A Multi-filtering Algorithm for Applying ICA in a Low-Channel EEG

Izabela Rejer[(✉)] [iD] and Paweł Górski[iD]

Faculty of Computer Science and Information Technology,
West Pomeranian University of Technology, Szczecin, Szczecin, Poland
irejer@wi.zut.edu.pl

Abstract. The paper presents an algorithm that enables the application of Independent Component Analysis (ICA) for a low-channel EEG. The idea behind the algorithm is to extend the original low-dimensional matrix of EEG signals by applying a set of zero phase moving average filters on each of the recorded signals. The paper first provides the details of the algorithm and discusses its parameters via a pure mathematical example and then presents its application for an offline classification of data gathered during the session with a Motor Imagery Brain-Computer Interface (MI-BCI). As it is shown in the paper, the average classification accuracy obtained after applying the proposed algorithm (73.17%) for a single-channel EEG recording was 12.18% higher than that obtained for raw EEG data (65.33%).

Keywords: Independent Component Analysis · ICA · EEG · Brain-Computer Interface · BCI

1 Introduction

The major drawback of an Independent Component Analysis (ICA), limiting its use for low-sensor EEG recordings, is that the number of components returned by ICA algorithms is the same as the number of sensors. This ICA feature stems from the linear algebra - ICA is just a linear filter that transforms the data set acquired by the matrix of sensors to another orthogonal base by rotating and scaling operations. Hence, if we use a 64-channel setup we can retrieve up to 64 components but if we use a three-channel setup, ICA will return at most the three components. In the extreme case when only one sensor is available, classic ICA is not able to perform any linear transformation on this signal and hence it is not able to recover any of the underlying sources.

So far only a few approaches to solve the underdetermined ICA model (it is a model where the number of output components should be greater than the number of sensors) have been proposed. For example, in [1,2] the authors proposed the DE (Dynamical Embedding) method which represents a single channel recording by a dynamical embedding matrix composed of a series of delay vectors taken from this recording. In [3] a method was proposed for estimating a

© Springer Nature Switzerland AG 2019
L. Rutkowski et al. (Eds.): ICAISC 2019, LNAI 11509, pp. 283–293, 2019.
https://doi.org/10.1007/978-3-030-20915-5_26

mixing matrix and inferring the most probable sources based on the expectation-maximization algorithm. In [4], the same problem was tackled by employing a sparse prior probability (in Laplacian form) on the basis coefficients to remove the redundancy inherent in an overcomplete representation. Other studies that have worked with the undetermined ICA model include [5–7].

The algorithm introduced in this paper is motivated by the DE method, however, it takes another approach to enlarge the dimension of the ICA input matrix. The algorithm transforms a low-channel recording to a multi-channel representation by applying a set of zero phase moving average filters. Next, one of the classic ICA algorithms is applied to the data set composed of the original channels and their filtered versions. The main difference between our approach and DE is that while the DE method completely cuts out some parts of the original signals before the ICA transformation, our multi-filtering algorithm introduces very subtle modifications along the entire signal, without changing the time association of each sample. Due to this feature, the algorithm can be easily applied for enhancing the SNR (signal to noise ratio) of even very short EEG signals recorded during successive trials of a BCI session. We propose the following scheme to deal with this task: the low-dimensional signal from the successive trials is folded together, introduced to the multi-filtering algorithm, linearly transformed by ICA, and then once again (after removing the artifact components) unfolded into the original low-dimensional trials of the same time association.

The aim of this paper is to: (1) present the details of the multi-filtering algorithm; (2) show that it is robust in regard to its parameters; (3) demonstrate that it can be successfully applied to enhance the SNR of EEG data recorded only from one channel. To deal with the second task, we will use the artificial mathematical system composed of two mixtures of 10 sinusoids of different frequencies. To deal with the third task, we will use the real EEG data recorded from channel Cz during the MI-BCI sessions with five subjects.

The rest of the paper is structured as follows. The next section discusses the proposed algorithm and describes in details the experimental procedure. Section 3 provides the results and their discussion. Finally, Sect. 4 concludes the paper.

2 Methods

2.1 Multi-filtering Algorithm

The filtering procedure performed by the multi-filtering algorithm proposed in this paper can be described as follows. Let's assume that x is a random column vector containing observations recorded from ch channels; $x = [x_1, x_2, \ldots x_c h]$. To create additional input dimensions each x_i $(i = 1, 2, \ldots, ch)$ is filtered k times with a zero phase moving average filter of different size of the averaging window (N). The output from the filtering operation (vector g) contains both, the ch original signals from vector x and k filtered versions of each signal. The pseudocode, given in Fig. 1, describes the filtering operation in details. Vector

g obtained after filtering procedure is the multi-dimensional representation of a low-channel recording. This vector can be later directly introduced as an input vector to one of the classic ICA algorithms.

```
s=0
for i=1 to ch
  s++
  g[s]= x_i
  for j=1 to k
    x_new=use filter h of averaging window size L[j] on x_i
    s++
    g[s]= x_new
  end
end
```

Fig. 1. The pseudocode for multi-filtering operation; g is the vector composed of s signals, where $s = ch(1 + k)$.

The size of the averaging window and the number of succeeding filters can be more or less arbitrarily chosen but the three following rules have to be maintained:

1. The similarity between each two input components from the vector g cannot be equal to 100%. This rule stems from the fact that to solve the ICA model, the mixing matrix must be invertible and hence it must be a full rank matrix. If two of the ICA input signals (two components from the vector g) are too highly correlated, this condition is violated since two columns of mixing matrix are linearly dependent.
2. The similarity between each new input vector, created in the filtering process, and the corresponding original signal from the vector x should be as high as possible but it cannot reach 100% (once again 100% similarity between two components introduced to ICA algorithm would violate the full rank matrix rule).
3. The similarity between the output ICA components cannot be too high. The high similarity between the components violates the components independence rule imposed by ICA itself.

All three rules can be addressed with a Pearson's correlation coefficient. Hence the values of the three parameters have to be chosen before running the multi-filtering algorithm:

- *MinOriginal* – the minimal acceptable correlation between the original signal x_i and its filtered versions;
- *MaxOriginal* – the maximal acceptable correlation between the original signal x_i and its filtered versions;

– *MaxOutputs* – the maximal acceptable correlation between each two output components.

The default values of these parameters (*MinOriginal* – 0.6, *MaxOriginal* – 0.98, and *MaxOutputs* – 0.4) were chosen during a set of tests. While the value of the second parameter is rather fixed (it stems from the second of the three rules mentioned above), the two other parameters have quite a big error margin. As will be shown later in the paper even if they are changed significantly, the algorithm still works correctly. In fact, the only difference that can be observed when these two parameters are changed is a different number of ICA components.

2.2   Procedure for Experiment 1 – Changes in Algorithm Parameters

For the first experiment, an artificial system composed of 10 sinusoid waveforms $y_1, \ldots, y_{10}$ of the same length (1000 samples) but different fundamental frequency was created. The frequencies of the succeeding waveforms were as follows: y_1 – 160 Hz, y_2 – 100 Hz, y_3 – 4.5 Hz, y_4 – 50 Hz, y_5 – 200 Hz, y_6 – 1 Hz, y_7 – 60 Hz, y_8 – 150 Hz, y_9 – 175 Hz, $y_1 0$ – 30 Hz. All ten sinusoids were mixed to form two linear compositions. The first composition contained the five first sinusoids with the weight 1 and the five last sinusoids with the weight 0.1, the second composition contained the five first sinusoids with the weight 0.1 and the five last sinusoids with the weight 1:

$$M1 = y_1 + y_2 + y_3 + y_4 + y_5 + 0.1(y_6 + y_7 + y_8 + y_9 + y_{10})$$
$$M2 = 0.1(y_1 + y_2 + y_3 + y_4 + y_5) + y_6 + y_7 + y_8 + y_9 + y_{10} \tag{1}$$

Next, the compositions $M1$ and $M2$ were submitted to the multi-filtering algorithm described in the previous section and then to ICA. Three different experiments with different sets of parameters were performed on this $M1 - M2$ system. In the first experiment, the parameters were set at the default levels proposed in Fig. 2 (*MinOriginal*: 0.6, *MaxOriginal*: 0.98, and *MaxOutputs*: 0.4). In the second experiment, we decreased *MinOriginal* and increased *MaxOutputs* to obtain fewer output components than original sinusoids sources (*MinOriginal*: 0.5, *MaxOutputs*: 0.5). Finally, in the last experiment, we increased *MinOriginal* and decreased *MaxOutputs* (*MinOriginal*: 0.7, *MaxOutputs*: 0.3).

2.3   Procedure for Experiment 2 – Denoising the EEG Data

To verify whether the proposed algorithm can enhance the classification accuracy when only single-channel recording is available we applied it to the data gathered during an MI-BCI session. The experiment was performed with five subjects according to the following scheme. The subject was placed in a comfortable chair and EEG electrodes were applied on his head. A short sound signal announced the start of the experiment. The main part of the experiment was divided into 120 trials. During each trial, an arrow pointing at left or right was presented to the subject. The subject task was to imagine the wrist rotation with a hand pointed by the arrow. The arrow directions for the succeeding trials were chosen randomly. The trial length was fixed and was equal to 10 s.

EEG data were recorded from one channel (Cz) at a sampling frequency of 256 Hz. The reference and ground electrodes were located at Fpz and the right mastoid, respectively. The impedance of the electrodes was kept below 5 kΩ. The EEG signal was acquired with Discovery 20 amplifier (BrainMaster). The EEG data were preliminarily filtered in the 1–30 Hz band with the Butterworth filter of the 4th order.

To perform the denoising operation EEG signals from all trials were concatenated together and submitted to the multi-filtering algorithm. Next, FastICA [8] was applied to the multi-component representation provided by the multi-filtering algorithm and a set of output components was obtained. Usually, at this moment of the procedure, the set of components is carefully scanned to find and remove the artifact components. We did not have to follow this track because of a very low probability that the artifact components were correlated with the randomly changing imagery of left-right hand movement. Regarding this fact, we assumed that the artifact components would be automatically discarded during the classifier training.

To prepare the data for the classification process the entire multi-components set was unfolded to the original trials. Each trial contained 2560 samples (10s x 256 Hz) and the number of signals equal to the number of components returned by ICA. Next, the band power features were extracted from each second and each channel of each trial. Since we applied four classic EEG frequency bands in our analysis: an alpha band (8–13 Hz) and three beta subbands: 13–18 Hz, 18–24 Hz, and 24–30 Hz, the number of features for a single trial was equal to 40 x number of components (number of components was different for different subjects). The feature set together with a set containing an appropriate class label for each trial (-1 for the left-hand trials and $+1$ for the right-hand trials) were submitted to the classification algorithm.

The 6-fold cross-validation scheme was applied in the classification step. Since the feature set contained from 40 (raw signal) to 1200 features (30-components set), the feature selection procedure was incorporated into the classification process. The validation scheme was as follows. First, the whole data set was divided into 6 testing subsets of 20 trials each. Next, at each cross-validation step, another subset was used to test the model trained on the remaining 100 trials. The training data was first submitted to the Lasso algorithm [9] which returned 6 features of the highest discrimination capabilities. Next, these 6 features were submitted to the SVM classifier of a linear kernel. After the training, the classifier performance was evaluated on the remaining 20 trials. The whole procedure was repeated 6 times, separately for each testing subset. The final classifier performance metric was the accuracy averaged over 6 testing subsets. For the comparison purpose, the same feature selection and classification scheme were used for the raw Cz signal.

3   Results and Discussion

3.1   Changes in Algorithm Parameters

Figure 2 presents two linear combinations obtained after mixing 10 source sinusoids described in Sect. 2.2 according to Eq. (1). The task of the multi-filtering algorithm was to take these two combinations as inputs and produce the multi-component representation that was next introduced to ICA. The output components returned by ICA were then compared with the true sources, it is the original sinusoids.

At first, the algorithm was run with the default set of parameters (*MinOriginal* – 0.6, *MaxOriginal* – 0.98, and *MaxOutputs* – 0.4). The components returned by ICA are presented in Fig. 3. As it can be noticed in the figure, the algorithm not only recovered the correct number of sources but also returned components of the same frequency as the source sinusoids. To calculate the similarity index, the Pearson correlation was computed per each combination of ICA components and original sinusoids. Table 1 presents 10 combinations (one combination per each source sinusoid) of the highest similarity index. As it can be noticed, the correlation between all source sinusoids and the ICA components was very high (0.99–1).

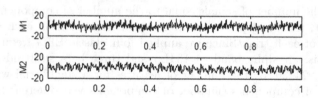

Fig. 2. The linear combinations of source sinusoids, mixed in proportions defined in Eq. (1).

Table 1. The correlation between ICA components and source sinusoids (default set of parameters).

Source signal	y_1	y_2	y_3	y_4	y_5	y_6	y_7	y_8	y_9	y_{10}
ICA component	IC5	IC9	IC2	IC8	IC10	IC1	IC6	IC7	IC4	IC3
Similarity index	0.99	0.99	0.99	0.99	1	1	1	1	1	0.99

Figure 4 and Tables 2 and 3 present the components returned by ICA run for mixtures from Fig. 2 with different values of parameters *MinOriginal* and *MaxOutputs*. In the first case (Fig. 4a), the parameters were set to: *MinOriginal* – 0.5; *MaxOutputs* – 0.5. Since that relaxed the stop conditions for defining new

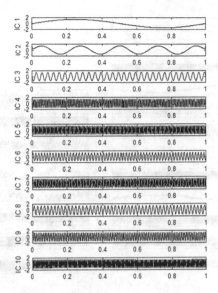

Fig. 3. The set of components returned by ICA ($IC1, IC2, \ldots, IC10$) for the default parameters of the multi-filtering algorithm: *MinOriginal* – 0.6, *MaxOriginal* – 0.98, and *MaxOutputs* – 0.4.

filters, more components (12) than sources (10) were returned. However, as it can be noticed in Table 2, presenting the correlation between the matching source-component pairs all the source signals were recovered with very high accuracy. In fact, the only difference between these two ICA runs was the appearance of the two additional components: one of them (IC9) was just a reversed version of another component (IC4) and the other (IC1) was a kind of mixture of other components.

The second case (Fig. 4b, Table 3), with more restrictive stop conditions (*MinOriginal* – 0.7; *MaxOutputs* – 0.3) was much more difficult to resolve. Since there were not enough components (8) to present all the original sources (10), ICA returned only four components highly correlated with the source signals (IC8 – y_1, IC7 – y_5, IC2 – y_8, and IC6 – y_9) and 4 components that were mixtures of the other sources (IC1, IC3, IC4, and IC5). However, as it can be noticed in the table, the correlations between each of these mixtures and the source sinusoids were also quite high (0.84–0.94).

Table 2. The correlation between the ICA components and source sinusoids (the case of more components than sources).

Source signal	y_1	y_2	y_3	y_4	y_5	y_6	y_7	y_8	y_9	y_{10}
ICA component	IC11	IC10	IC2	IC6	IC8	IC4; IC9	IC5	IC3	IC12	IC7
Similarity index	1	1	1	0.99	1	0.97; 0.95	1	1	1	1

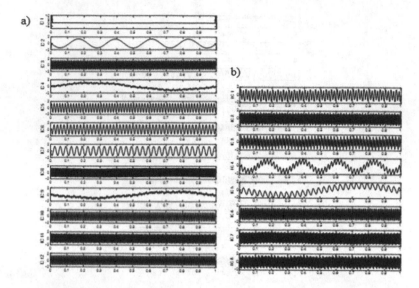

Fig. 4. The set of components returned by ICA run with the parameters: (a) *MinO-riginal* – 0.5, *MaxOriginal* – 0.98, and *MaxOutputs* – 0.5; (b) *MinOriginal* – 0.7, *MaxOriginal* – 0.98, and *MaxOutputs* – 0.3.

3.2 Denoising the EEG Data

Table 4 presents the classification accuracy of the classifier run over the multi-components' dataset obtained after applying the proposed multi-filtering algorithm on the raw single-channel EEG data. The table is composed of two main parts. The first part shows the results obtained after applying the multi-filtering algorithm to transform single-channel data into a multi-channel representation and the second part – the results obtained for raw EEG signal. In both parts, the classification accuracy calculated over the training and testing sets is presented. Two additional columns attached to the table (the first and last column) denote the subject number (the first column) and the increase in the testing classification accuracy obtained after applying the proposed algorithm (the last column). To facilitate the visual comparison, the final classification accuracy (it is the accuracy calculated over the testing sets) of both classifiers is additionally presented in Fig. 5.

Table 3. The correlation between the ICA components and source sinusoids (the case of fewer components than sources).

Source signal	y_1	y_2	y_3	y_4	y_5	y_6	y_7	y_8	y_9	y_{10}
ICA component	IC8	IC3	IC4	-	IC7	IC5	IC1	IC2	IC6	-
Similarity index	0.98	0.89	0.88	-	0.99	0.84	0.94	0.99	1	-

Table 4. Classification accuracy obtained for raw EEG signals and a multi-component' representation.

Subject	After multi-filtering + ICA			Raw signal		Testing accuracy increase [%]
	No. of components	Training accuracy [%]	Testing accuracy [%]	Training accuracy [%]	Testing accuracy [%]	
1	22	74.54	73.33	71.20	63.33	15.79
2	16	76.94	77.50	72.04	67.50	14.81
3	22	72.22	70.00	68.61	66.67	4.99
4	18	74.07	72.50	66.39	60.83	19.18
5	7	74.54	72.50	73.98	68.33	6.10

As it can be noticed in Table 4 the classification accuracy calculated per each subject was significantly higher when the raw EEG signal was preprocessed with multi-filtering algorithm and ICA. It should be underlined here that this increase in the classification accuracy cannot be attributed to the increase in the number of input signals. Since the classifier was trained always on the data set composed of 6 features, this increase in the classification accuracy means that after applying the proposed algorithm features of higher discrimination capabilities were extracted. The most probable explanation of this phenomena is that ICA separated at least some of the true brain sources from the artifact components.

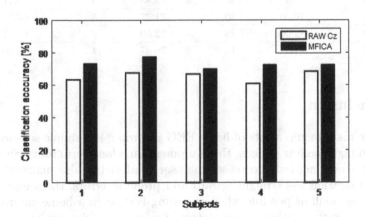

Fig. 5. The comparison of the classification accuracy calculated over the testing set obtained with and without application of the proposed multi-filtering algorithm.

In the sinus example, we showed that the multi-filtering algorithm performs well even when its default parameters are changed significantly. To find out whether the algorithm is also robust to the changes in parameters in a real case scenario, we set these parameters to the levels used in the sinus example and ran the algorithm for each of the two sets of parameters. Table 5 presents the number of components returned by ICA run over the input matrix created by the multi-filtering algorithm of different values of correlation parameters and the classification accuracy (calculated over the testing sets) obtained for all these sets of components. The results presented in the table are similar to those gathered in Tables 1, 2 and 3 more restrictive parameters resulted in fewer components, more relaxed parameters resulted in more components. In terms of classification accuracy, we can notice that when the parameters allowed for more components, the accuracy was usually the same or slightly higher than that obtained with the default parameters (apart from subject 2). For more restrictive parameters the classification accuracy for most subjects was smaller than that obtained with the default parameters, however, for all subjects, it was still higher than that calculated over the raw Cz signal.

Table 5. Classification accuracy obtained for three different sets of correlation parameters of the multi-filtering algorithm.

Subject	MinOriginal – 0.6 MaxOutputs – 0.4		MinOriginal – 0.5 MaxOutputs – 0.5		MinOriginal – 0.7 MaxOutputs – 0.3	
	No. of components	Testing accuracy [%]	No. of components	Testing accuracy [%]	No. of components	Testing accuracy [%]
1	22	73.33	29	74.17	4	66.67
2	16	77.50	22	75.83	4	74.17
3	22	70.00	30	71.67	5	67.50
4	18	72.50	28	72.50	4	66.67
5	7	72.50	12	76.67	4	72.50

4   Conclusion

One of the main requirements of home EEG recording is a simple sensors application and high comfort of using the equipment on a long-term basis. Since each additional sensor not only decreases the user comfort but also makes the EEG sensors application less straightforward and prone to errors, the sensor matrix should be as small as possible when recording is done in a home environment. The problem is that with a sensor matrix of a low-dimension we have no direct means to enhance the signal quality (which is usually very low outside a scientific laboratory). The algorithm, that we described in this paper, aims to solve this problem by creating artificial signals extending the true sensors matrix and hence enabling to apply spatial filtering techniques which usually significantly enhance the signal quality.

The paper shows that the proposed approach enables the representation of a low-dimensional signal by a high-dimensional set of components. The system of sinusoids presented in the paper shows that regardless of the algorithm parameters there is a high probability that at least some of the components are equivalent to the true sources of the signal recorded from the sensors. This thesis is also supported by the MI-BCI data, where after the application of the proposed algorithm the classification accuracy averaged over 5 subjects raised from 65.33% to 73.17%. Moreover, even the significant changes in the algorithm default parameters did not induce the drop of the classification accuracy to the level obtained with the raw EEG signal.

References

1. James, C.J., Gibson, O.J.: Temporally constrained ICA: an application to artifact rejection in electromagnetic brain signal analysis. IEEE Trans. Biomed. Eng. **50**(9), 1108–1116 (2003)
2. James, C.J., Gibson, O., Davies, M.E.: On the analysis of single versus multiple channels of electromagnetic brain signals. Artif. Intell. Med. **37**(2), 131–143 (2006)
3. Girolami, M.: A variational method for learning sparse and overcomplete representations. Neural Comput. **13**(11), 2517–2532 (2001)
4. Lewicki, M.S., Sejnowski, T.J.: Learning overcomplete representations. Neural Comput. **12**(2), 337–365 (2000)
5. Davies, M.E., James, C.J.: Source separation using single channel ICA. Sig. Process. **87**, 1819–1832 (2007)
6. Warner, E.S., Proudler, I.K.: Single-channel blind signal separation of filtered MPSK signals. IEEE Proc.-Radar Sonar Navig. **150**(6), 396–402 (2003)
7. Jung, T.P., et al.: Extended ICA removes artifacts from electroencephalographic recordings. In: Advances in Neural Information Processing Systems, pp. 894–900 (1998)
8. Tichavský, P., Koldovský, Z., Oja, E.: Performance analysis of the FastICA algorithm and Cramér-Rao bounds for linear independent component analysis. IEEE Trans. Sig. Process. **54**(4), 1189–1203 (2006)
9. Tibshirani, R.: Regression shrinkage and selection via the lasso. J. R. Stat. Soc. Ser. B **58**(1), 267–288 (1996)

Naive Bayes Learning of Dermoscopy Images

Grzegorz Surówka$^{(\boxtimes)}$ (ID) and Maciej Ogorzałek (ID)

Faculty of Physics, Astronomy and Applied Computer Science,
Jagiellonian University, 30-151 Kraków, Poland
grzegorz.surowka@uj.edu.pl

Abstract. We show naive Bayes models of the melanoma skin cancer represented by dermoscopy images from two different repositories. The dermoscopy images of each data set are recursively analyzed by the Mallat wavelet tree transform to extract a set of spatio-frequency filters, which are used to build energy based (rotation invariant) features. Such classifiers are built in different wavelet bases and (for one data set) in three image resolutions. Those simple models show varying classification performance, but some wavelet bases are preferable to differentiate between malicious (melanoma) and benign (displastic nevus) lesions and keep it in reduced image resolutions. The presented research contributes to the feature extraction (wrapper) methods.

Keywords: Feature extraction · Naive Bayes classification ·
Wavelets · CAD · Melanoma

1 Introduction

Wavelet transforms are widely used both in image pre/processing and machine learning [1]. The image pre/processing techniques involve noise removal, edge (object) detection, or image filtering, to mention the most important branches. There is a big variety of detection, or classification problems which are based on the wavelet features. This is because wavelets allow for a multi-scale and multi-resolution analysis. Implementation of Discrete Wavelet Transform (DWT) into an image produces wavelet coefficients that can show the frequency sub-bands of the signal in certain locations in the image. This can be interpreted in terms of signal models based on the field knowledge.

Wavelet feature extraction methods are important factors to gain high classification efficiency and appropriate interpretation of the problem [2]. In this work we want to contribute to the feature extraction methods by taking advantage of the Naive Bayes wrapper. The Naive Bayes approach is based on the assumption that the features are independent of one another within each class. This simplifies the training step since one can estimate the one-dimensional class-conditional density for each predictor individually. Thus less training data compared to other classifiers is required, which lowers the computational cost. This is particularly

© Springer Nature Switzerland AG 2019
L. Rutkowski et al. (Eds.): ICAISC 2019, LNAI 11509, pp. 294–304, 2019.
https://doi.org/10.1007/978-3-030-20915-5_27

effective for data sets containing many predictors. The class-conditional independence between predictors is generally not valid, but it works better than expected in practice. The Naive Bayes learning consists of the two steps: (1) From the training data, the algorithm estimates the parameters of a probability distribution, assuming predictors are conditionally independent given the class. (2) For any unseen data, the algorithm computes its posterior probability in each class. This class wins, that gains the largest posterior probability.

In this work we want to extract wavelet features appropriate for classification of dermoscopy images into two classes:

class 1: the pigment skin cancer (melanoma),
class 0: the displastic (atypical but benign) skin lesion.

This is a pronounced and medically sound problem that has been studied extensively for the last twenty years [3]. Below we briefly describe the medical background and show our interest in the melanoma research.

Melanoma is the neoplasm of the pigment cells (melanocytes) in the skin [4]. Before it gets mature and life-threatening, the skin undergoes certain changes. A red, brown, or even black spot increases its diameter, and its border may become unsharp. The mole gets simultaneously more colors (various shades of red, brown, or black) and at the end greyish, or white veil. This is the advanced stage of tumor when metastases take place. From the histopathological point of view, this evolution goes through the bundling of the melanocytes at the border between the skin (derma) and the epidermis (those stages are called 'nevi': junctional nevus, compound nevus), through deformations of the melanocyte nuclus (dysplastic nevus), and finally metastases to the lymph nodes. Usually well trained skin doctors can correctly assess the borderline between the benign (displastic nevus) and malicious (melanoma) skin moles. The latter cases should be extracted as soon, as they get examined. Such a diagnostic path seems to be straightforward, assumed long term practice and professional experience of the medical doctors. Unfortunately this is not always the case plus the evolution of melanoma may also take two other paths. First, 'ad-hoc' melanomas without the origin of the displastic nevus can grow up, without the alerting changes to come up and with very short time for a diagnosis. Second, the so called 'featureless' (tiny) melanomas can develop with no apparent melanoma features.

Our interest in the melanoma research is motivated by computer aided diagnosis (CAD) methods and tools [5–7]. To help the clinical diagnosis of melanoma, classifiers of dermoscopic images are being developed to go beyond the classical, visual tumor features (e.g. ABCD [8]). Especially wavelet features are suitable to scan the lesion texture despite of existing artifacts in the image and lack of typical melanoma indications. Fast and reliable CAD in this case may be a life-saving factor, and also become a mass screening system.

In this work for feature extraction the wrapper method will be used with the Naive Bayes wrapper [9]. We want to use data from two separate databases, and examine how the wavelet features perform under different image resolutions. Finally we will compare the results with the existing melanoma wavelet feature extraction experiments, performed with some other wrappers.

The naive Bayes approach to the discrimination of the melanoma cancer by the wavelet features is, according to literature in the field, studied for the first time.

2 Machine Learning Procedures

2.1 Data Sets

Experiments performed in this study include two data sets of anonymous dermoscopy images representing malignant (melanoma) and benign lesions

Data Set I (185 images)
It consists of 102 malignant melanoma (M) and 83 dysplastic nevus (D) images. The class labels are based on a hist-pat examination. This set was collected in 2012–2013 in a private clinic in south Poland (private communication). The examinations were performed under these conditions: a digital camera 2272×1704 with an extra dermoscopy extension and immersion liquid to remove light reflections were used. No magnification information was available, however most of the lesions were centered in the image with the lesion diameter being 1/3-1/2 of the image height. No pre-processing tasks were done to the dermoscopy images, because no rough artifacts/distortions were present (hairs, liquid light reflections etc.).

For the sake of experiments with downgraded image resolutions the original set of 2272×1704 pixels were averaged (twice) in a block of adjacent 2×2 elements to produce a set of 1136×852 and 568×426 images

Data Set II (117 images)
ADDI (Automatic computer-based Diagnosis system for Dermoscopy Images [10]) was collected in a Portuguese hospital and contains 200 dermoscopy images (80 common nevi, 80 atypical nevi, 40 melanomas) examined by a hist-pat procedure. This set also contains binary masks of the lesions and some image annotations (e.g. dermoscopic criteria), which is, however, not used in our research. In order to equalize this set with the data set I, we selected only 40 melanoma and 77 displastic lesion images. For the wavelet transform all the images were unified in size to 760×552 pixels.

Both data sets were JPEG-compressed 24-bit RGB images. To support wavelet transformations the dermoscopy images of the two sets were transformed to indexed images.

In the clinic the melanoma class is the minority class and is under-represented (approx. 5%) compared to the benign class. The comparable number of benign and malicious images in the data set I is the result of a selection of the displastic lesion cases from a pool of about 2000 displastic lesions. This process is however beyond our control (is done by dermatology specialists) and the data set I is accepted 'as is'. For the machine learning experiments data set I is balanced.

Inbalance [11] in data set II is not that dramatic (77:40) and in [20] we investigated such cases by experimenting with different sub-sampling ratios of the majority class. It turned out that no considerable bias to the classification results were introduced.

Our learning procedure is summarized by the following steps (the number in the parenthesis denotes the number of iterations):

{loop over set I and II (2) {loop over kernel functions (4) {loop over wavelet bases (53) {loop for 10-fold CV (9/10-learning, 1/10-testing)}}}}.

2.2 Wavelet Features

The discrete wavelet transform (DWT) is a signal decomposition with a set of orthonormal functions obtained through translation and dilation of a kernel function (the so called mother wavelet) [12]. It is not necessary to perform the dilation and translation with an arbitrarily small step, because in such a case the DWT algorithm would be too redundant. For that reason the Discrete Dyadic Wavelet Transform (DDWT) is defined. In DDWT transformations are performed at the pace of the powers of two and the signal is represented as:

$$s(n) = \sum_r c_{0,r}\phi_{0,r} + \sum_{p=0}^{u}\sum_r d_{p,r}\psi_{p,r}(n)$$

where $p, r, n \in \mathcal{Z}$ and:

$$c_{p,r} = \sum_n s(n)\phi^*(n2^{-p} - r)$$

$$d_{p,r} = \sum_n s(n)\psi^*(n2^{-p} - r)$$

The mother wavelet ψ fulfils the 'two-scale' difference equation and the scaling function ϕ is subject to some special relations with the kernel function.
Mallat [13] demonstrated that for the coefficients it holds true:

$$c_{p-1,r} = \sum_n L(n)c_p(n - r)$$

$$d_{p-1,r} = \sum_n H(n)c_p(n - r)$$

i.e. one iteration of the transform filters out the input sequence with the low-pass $L(n)$ and high-pass filter $H(n)$ and decimates the output signals by two.

The derived filters should provide certain properties such as: transformation reversibility, orthogonality of the scaling function to its wavelet (and its translations) and finite response.

The Mallat approach is easily interpreted in decomposing images. After a single DDWT transformation of the image four sub-images are produced (due to independent transforms of the columns and rows). They are: one average (coars) sub-image (LL), one sub-image of details in the rows (LH), one sub-image of details in the columns (HL), and a sub-image of details in both directions (HH). If this operation is done recursively to all the channels, this is called the Wavelet Packet Transform (WPT). Products of the transform are downsampled (decimated) by two at each level, thus the linear dimension of each sub-image is only a half the linear dimension of its parent.

WPT is a substantial expansion of DDWT in the number of the transformation branches, because in DDWT only the LL sub-band is recursively exploited. This makes the time (space) vs. frequency analysis in WPT much finer than in DDWT, which provides more precise information than in any other signal analysis techniques.

For the sake of these machine learning experiments we take advantage of three iterations of WPT. Since in one iteration four filters are produced, so in the three turns $b = 1 + 4 + 16 = 21$ different transformation branches are used.

As features, $c = 12$ measures based on the energy content of the sub-images are produced [14]. They are: energies (e_i), maximum energy ratios (e_i/e_{max}), and fractional energy ratios ($e_i/\Sigma e_k, k \neq i$). Energy e_i ($i = 1, 2, 3, 4$) is defined as a sum of the absolute values of the pixels. This definition makes our features (almost) rotation invariant. Since in each branch twelve features are produced, altogether $b * c = 21 * 12 = 252$ components of the feature vector are derived.

The feature extraction process is carried out in different wavelet bases: orthogonal wavelets (Haar, Daubechies, Symlets, Coiflets), bi-orthogonal wavelets, and reverse bi-orthogonal wavelets. Our goal is to make it optimal for the melanoma vs. dysplastic nevus classification. In the feature extraction wrapper methods, classification paradigms are used to extract optimal features. In this article the Naive Bayes paradigm is used.

2.3   The Paradigm of Naive Bayes Classification

Classification means assigning proper class labels to given data objects. Bayesian approach to classification assumes maximizing the probability of finding the best model given the data [15, 16].

From the Bayes rule, the Bayes Optimal Classifier (BOC) determines the most probable class for a new data point x as:

$$BOC(x) = \text{argmax}_k P(Y = k|x) = \text{argmax}_k \frac{P(x|Y = k)P(Y = k)}{P(x)}$$

$$= \text{argmax}_k \frac{P(x|Y = k)P(Y = k)}{\sum_{k=1}^{K} P(x|Y = k)P(Y = k)} \tag{1}$$

where data vectors are $x = (X_1, \cdots, X_M)$, and the model (hypothesis) is denoted as $Y = k$.

The achievement of this approach is the maximum a posteriori decision rule that substitutes the posterior probability $P(Y = k|x)$ by the prior probability $P(Y = k)$.

From statistics we know that such an approach is the optimal choice and the Bayes error is the smallest possible one. If all the (candidate) models or the probabilities involved are not known, simplifications are used.

The most popular approximation is called Naive Bayes Classifier (NBC) and is taken under following assumptions:

– the predictors are conditionally independent, given the class

$$P(x|Y = k) = \prod_{i=1}^{M} P(X_i|Y = k) \qquad (2)$$

– probability $P(x)$ is assumed to be constant under varying model,
$P(x) = \sum_{k=1}^{K} P(Y = k) \prod_{i=1}^{M} P(X_i|Y = k) = const.$
– prior probability that a class index is k, $P(Y = k)$, is known.

Finally NBC models posterior probabilities for all $k = 1, \ldots, K$ according to the rule:

$$NBC(x) = \operatorname{argmax}_k P(Y = k|x)$$
$$= \operatorname{argmax}_k \frac{P(Y = k) \prod_{i=1}^{M} P(X_i|Y = k)}{\sum_{k=1}^{K} P(Y = k) \prod_{i=1}^{M} P(X_i|Y = k)}$$
$$= \operatorname{argmax}_k P(Y = k) \prod_{i=1}^{M} P(X_i|Y = k) \qquad (3)$$

where Y is the random variable corresponding to the class index of an observation and $X_1, \ldots, X_M$ are the random predictors of an observation.

Although NBC loses the BOC optimality, it yields posterior distributions that are pretty robust to the biased class density estimates and poor conditional independence of the real predictors.

The training step in the NB classification is based on estimating the probability density of predictors X given class Y, which can only be estimated on the basis of training data. In the case of discrete features the probabilities $P(X_i|Y = k)$ can be evaluated as the frequencies of observing X_i values among the vectors of class $Y = k$. Continuous predictors are estimated a distribution of the a priori class probabilities, which is usually modeled by a Gaussian (normal) distribution $P(x_i|y) \propto N(\mu_i^y, \sigma_i^y)$, where μ_i^y and σ_i^y are respectively the mean value and the standard deviation of the i-th feature values observed among the training data vectors belonging to class $Y = k$. To estimate those parameters, separate values of the mean and standard deviation for each predictor in each single class are calculated based on the training data, assumed the training data set is large enough to model real distributions.

In a general case of continuous distributions one should not require that the assumption of normal distribution is valid. Instead, distribution of a predictor may be skewed, or have multiple peaks/modes, which requires appropriate kernel density estimation (smoothing) techniques. The kernel plays a role of a density estimator (weighting function), which has a certain number of derivatives and vanishing moments.

Let $I(x)$ denote the membership function for a variable x. We tested the following kernels:

- Uniform (box) kernel: $f(x) = \frac{1}{2}I(|x| \leq 1)$,
- Epanechnikov kernel: $f(x) = \frac{3}{4}(1 - x^2)I(|x| \leq 1)$,
- Gaussian kernel: $f(x) = \frac{1}{\sqrt{2\pi}}\exp(-\frac{x^2}{2})$,
- Triangular kernel: $f(x) = (1 - |x|)I(|x| \leq 1)$.

Using the estimated distributions, in the prediction step the algorithm calculates for any unseen test data the posterior probability of that sample belonging to each class. The method then assigns the test data to the class yielding the highest posterior probability.

3 Results and Discussion

Naive Bayes learning of the two data sets was performed in Matlab [17]. To produce AUC charts we averaged results from 10-fold cross-validation. At the cost of (potential) over-training we left all the features in the analysis to remove possible bias coming from feature selection methods [18]. As a result, we can compare (later on in this section) both the extracted best wavelet bases and the Naive Bayes classification efficiency, with the previous attempts with other wrappers.

In Figs. 1 and 2 the abscissa shows the wavelet numbers: 1 = Haar, 2–11 = Daubechies (db1–db10), 12–18 = symlets (sym2–sym8), 19–23 = coiflets (coif1–coif5), 24–38 = bi-orthogonal wavelets (Bior1.1, 1.3, 1.5, 2.2, 2.4, 2.6, 2.8, 3.1, 3.3, 3.5, 3.7, 3.9, 4.4, 5.5, 6.8), and 39–53 = reverse bi-orthogonal wavelets (RBio1.1, 1.3, 1.5, 2.2, 2.4, 2.6, 2.8, 3.1, 3.3, 3.5, 3.7, 3.9, 4.4, 5.5, 6.8).

In both figures we can clearly see the impact of the kernel function that estimates the densities of the predictors within each class. In this work we do not analyze the computational performance of the kernels (learning time, memory requirements), but their classification performance. The highest overall performance is reached for the normal kernel, the worst for the box. The gap in performance can reach 15% points. The normal kernel is least variable from all the kernels, but they all follow similar trends.

For the best (normal) kernel we can choose in Fig. 1 wavelet bases that outperform the other:

- 2272×1704: 50, 49, 31, 47, 5, 19, 35 (4xRBio, 1xBior, 1xCoif, 1xDaubechies),
- 1136×852: 46, 26, 25, 42, 39, 2, 1 (3xRbio, 2xBior, 1xDaubechies, 1xHaar),
- 568×426: 46, 42, 26, 39, 24, 2, 1 (3xRBio, 2xBior, 1xDaubechies, 1xHaar).

As far as the overall AUC level is concerned, the average AUC level is the highest at the nominal resolution 2272×1704, decreases at 1136×852, and slightly increases at 568×426. This means that not necessary the highest resolutions suit the best with the classifier.

Data Set 2 (ADDI, Fig. 2) shows a comparable result, i.e. the normal kernel outperforms all the other, but the gap between the best and the worst (box) kernel is now up to 20% points, and the results are more dispersed between the neighboring wavelet bases. Variability in the classification performance comes

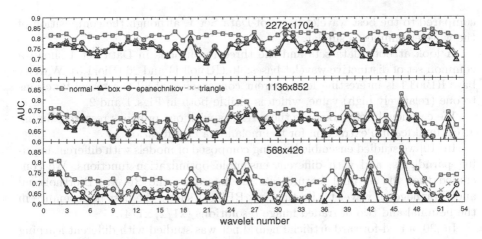

Fig. 1. Naive Bayes Classifier (NBC) performance (AUC) as a function of the wavelet number (see text) for Data Set 1 (2272 × 1704, top) and its resolution-reduced subsets: (1136 × 852, middle) and (568 × 426, bottom). NBC uses kernel estimation with: normal (square), box (triangle), Epanechnikov (circle), and triangle (x) function.

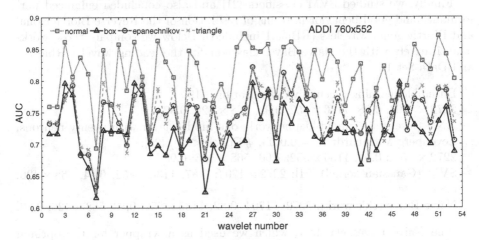

Fig. 2. NBC performance (AUC) as a function of the wavelet number for Data Set 2 (760 × 552). NBC uses kernel estimation with: normal (square), box (triangle), Epanechnikov (circle), and triangle (x) function.

both from the wavelet family (type of the scaling function and mother wavelet), and also individual wavelet properties. Enhanced dispersion (in the opposite direction) between close neighbors in Fig. 2 indicates that Data Set 2 may be subject to pre-processing steps, which are however unknown in kind and in number. There are no details about the original resolution and compression of Data Set 2. For these reasons the best AUC values calculated for the normal kernel: 26, 51, 3, 15, 35, 12, 48 (2xRBio, 2xBior, 2xSym, 1xDaubechies), cannot be directly compared to the best wavelet bases of Data Set 1, although the composition of the wavelet families is similar.

A look at both data sets and the three resolutions in Data Set 1 shows a common set of distinctive wavelet bases: 46 (RBio3.1) and 26 (Bior1.5). Wavelet base RBio3.1 is interesting for apparent convergence of all the kernel functions to one (relatively high) value, which is visible both in Figs. 1 and 2.

We can now briefly compare these results with our previous research aiming at optimal feature extraction for the melanoma classification.

In [19] we studied ensemble learning composed of models with different learning paradigms, and with different ensemble optimization functions. We concluded that the optimal feature sets are based on the Reverse Biorthogonal and Biorthogonal wavelets. Particularly RBio3.1 shows the best performance in the nominal and two degraded image resolutions (x1/2, x1/4).

In [20] a feed-forward artificial neural net was studied with different learning methods (from pure gradient descent to some conjugate adaptive systems), two activation functions, a number of pre-set topologies, and two performance functions. Due to big variety of setups we examined only the RBio3.1 wavelet base and found out the optimal operating points.

Finally, we studied SVM classifiers [21] and also concluded enhanced performance and good behavior in terms of resolution of the Reverse Biorthogonal and Biorthogonal wavelets (RBio3.1 included). Below we compare those works quantitatively with the Naive Bayes classifier for the leading wavelet Rbio 3.1 and Data Set 1.

- Ensemble learning (accuracy optimization) [19]:
  2272×1704: 0.98, 1136×852: 0.92, 568×426: 0.87.
- ANN (mse, full sigmoid-like network, one hidden layer with twenty neurons, Levenberg-Marquardt ($\mu = 0.001$), #Epoch < 20) [20]:
  2272×1704: 0.94, 1136×852: 1.00, 568×426: 0.98.
- SVM (Gaussian kernel) [21]: 2272×1704: 0.87, 1136×852: 0.84, 568×426: 0.86.
- Naive Bayes (this work): 2272×1704: 0.82, 1136×852: 0.83, 568×426: 0.86.

The Naive Bayes classifier, which we used as a wrapper for the optimal wavelet feature extraction, presents lower absolute AUC values than the above compared wrappers, but makes the selected wavelet features, as the other methods, durable for resolution degradation.

Features extraction is an important efficiency factor in any classification problem. The same is in force in the melanoma CAD. Optimal wavelet features secure not only the high classification performance and good convergence of the results, but also suitable behavior when the data vectors get worse in quality, like in case of image resolution degradation.

In this work we searched for optimal features with help of the Naive Bayes wrapper. Our results confirm high efficiency of the RBio and Bior wavelet families, particularly (RBio3.1 and Bior1.5), and support results from other wrappers (ensemble learning, ANN, SVM).

References

1. Tang, Y.Y., Yang, L.H., Liu, J., Ma, H.: Wavelet Theory and Its Application to Pattern Recognition, 2nd edn. World Scientific, Singapore (2009)
2. Tang, J., Alelyani, S., Liu, H.: Feature Selection for Classification: A Review, Data Classification: Algorithms and Applications, p. 37. CRC Press, Boca Raton (2014)
3. Skvara, H., Teban, L., Fiebiger, M., Binder, M., Kittler, H.: Limitations of dermoscopy in the recognition of melanoma. Arch Dermatol. **141**, 155–160 (2005)
4. Goodson, A.G., Grossman, D.: Strategies for early melanoma detection: approaches to the patient with nevi. J. Am. Acad. Dermatol. **60**(5), 719–735 (2009)
5. Oliveira, R.B., Papa, J.P., Pereira, A.S., Tavares, J.M.R.S: Computational methods for pigmented skin lesion classification in images: review and future trends, neural computing and applications (2016)
6. Korotkov, K., Garcia, R.: Computerized analysis of pigmented skin lesions: a review. Artif. Intell. Med. **56**(2), 69–90 (2012)
7. Masood, A., Al-Jumaily, A.: Computer aided diagnostic support system for skin cancer: a review of techniques and algorithms. Int. J. Biomed. Imaging **2013**(7), 323268 (2013)
8. Kittler, H., Pehamberger, H., Wolff, K., Binder, M.: Follow-up of melanocytic skin lesions with digital epiluminescence microscopy: patterns of modifications observed in early melanoma, atypical nevi, and common nevi. J. Am. Acad. Dermatol. **43**(3), 467–476 (2000)
9. Guyon, I., Gunn, S., Nikravesh, M., Zadeh, L.A. (eds.): Feature extractions: Foundations and Applications. Springer, Heidelberg (2006). https://doi.org/10.1007/978-3-540-35488-8
10. Mendonca, T., Ferreira, P.M., Marques, J.S., Marcal, A.R., Rozeira, J.: PH2-A dermoscopic image database for research and benchmarking. In: 35th International Conference on IEEE Engineering in Medicine and Biology Society, pp. 5437–5440 (2013)
11. Rastgoo, M., et al.: Tackling the problem of data imbalancing for melanoma classification. In: BIOSTEC - 3rd International Conference on BIOIMAGING (2016)
12. Daubechies, I.: Ten Lectures on Wavelets. In: CBMS, vol. 61. SIAM (1994)
13. Mallat, S.G.: A theory for multiresolution signal decomposition: the wavelet representation. IEEE Trans. Pattern Anal. Mach. Intell. **11**(7), 674–693 (1989)
14. Surówka, G., Merkwirth, C., Żabińska-Płazak, E., Graca, A.: Wavelet based classification of skin lesion images. Bio Alg. Med Syst. **2**(4), 43–49 (2006)
15. Hastie, T., Tibshirani, R., Friedman, J.: The Elements of Statistical Learning, 2nd edn. Springer, Heidelberg (2008). https://doi.org/10.1007/978-0-387-84858-7
16. Manning, C.D., Raghavan, P., Schütze, M.: Introduction to Information Retrieval. Cambridge University Press, Cambridge (2008)
17. MATLAB: The MathWorks Inc., USA, release: 2018B (1994–2018)
18. Maglogiannis, I., Doukas, C.N.: Overview of advanced computer vision systems for skin lesions characterization. IEEE Trans. Inf. Tech. Biomed. **13**(5), 721–733 (2009)
19. Surówka, G., Ogorzałek, M.: On optimal wavelet bases for classification of melanoma images through ensemble learning. In: Rutkowski, L., Korytkowski, M., Scherer, R., Tadeusiewicz, R., Zadeh, L.A., Zurada, J.M. (eds.) ICAISC 2016. LNCS (LNAI), vol. 9692, pp. 655–666. Springer, Cham (2016). https://doi.org/10.1007/978-3-319-39378-0_56

20. Surówka, G.: Search for resolution invariant wavelet features of melanoma learned by a limited ANN classifier. Schedae Informaticae **25**, 189–207 (2016)
21. Surówka, G., Ogorzałek, M.: Resolution invariant wavelet features of melanoma studied by SVM classifiers. PLOS One (2019). https://doi.org/10.1371/journal.pone.0211318

Multi-class Classification of EEG Spectral Data for Artifact Detection

Mikhail Tokovarov[(✉)], Małgorzata Plechawska-Wójcik,
and Monika Kaczorowska

Institute of Computer Science, Lublin University of Technology,
Nadbystrzycka 36B, 20-618 Lublin, Poland
{m.tokovarov, m.plechawska, m.kaczorowska}@pollub.pl

Abstract. Electroencephalographic signals are known to be highly sensitive to various types of noise originating from external and internal sources. External sources are usually related to experiment conditions whereas internal artifacts are usually generated by the persons examined. Internal artifacts, in contrast to external ones, are characterised by non-stationarity, which results in higher detection complexity. Typical internal artifacts are related to eye blinking, eye movement and muscle activity.

The paper presents the comparison results of various approaches to classification of EEG-related features. Another aspect reviewed in the paper is comparing normalisation methods of dealing with inter-subject variability.

The analysis process covered several parts. Preprocessing included signal filtering and bad-channel removal. Signal epoching with 50% overlap was applied in order to achieve better time resolution. Feature extraction was based on frequency analysis performed with the Welch method. Due to the high number of obtained features, the feature selection procedure was the essential part of the processing. Selected features were used to train and validate supervised classifiers. The accuracy was the main measure used in classifier performance assessment.

Keywords: EEG · Artifact detection · Classification · Normalisation

1 Introduction

Electroencephalography (EEG) is a technique of measuring bioelectrical brain activity. This non-invasive method of brain function is widely applied in medicine and rehabilitation, but also in examining cognitive processes, psychological research, performance monitoring, or in brain-computer interfaces [1–7]. Good temporal resolution and relatively low cost of examination [8] are undeniable advantages of this method.

Development of EEG technology covered not only computer-based quantitative EEG, but also discovering a mobile EEG acquisition system as well as introducing dry electrodes instead of traditional, gel-based ones. None of these improvements, however, solves the problem of low signal-to-noise (SNR) ratio of EEG recordings. What is more, the high-impedance of dry electrodes and the possibility to record EEG signal during movement with a mobile electroencephalograph equipment cause even higher

© Springer Nature Switzerland AG 2019
L. Rutkowski et al. (Eds.): ICAISC 2019, LNAI 11509, pp. 305–316, 2019.
https://doi.org/10.1007/978-3-030-20915-5_28

signal noise due to sensitivity to lower skin-electrode contact quality, the presence of movement effect as well as electrical interference [9].

Due to the specificity of the recording procedure it is impossible to avoid artifacts in EEG signal. Artifacts lower the quality of the signal, increase the level of noise and hinder the analysis process. In general, two types of artifacts might be distinguished: those originated from biological activity (such as eye blinks, eye movements, muscle or myogenic activity) and those with non-biological origin (related to, for example, interference of electronic devices or electrode displacements). Some non-biological artifacts, such as network interference, might be corrected with a properly performed filtration. Biological-based artifacts, however, need to be detected and corrected with dedicated methods. The amplitude of artifactual signal is higher than the amplitude of typical neural-activity related signal, so the problem of artifact detection and removal is crucial for the quality of the analysis [10].

The disturbances usually affect several, or even all electrodes depending on artifact origin. Their presence is usually local [11]. Some artifacts, such as eye blinks, are revealed as a short-range peak with high amplitude, whereas others, such as eye movements, have rectangular-shaped signal and last longer. Muscle artifact, such as the clenching of jaw muscles, are usually seen as high-frequency short duration potential.

There are several approaches to artifact detection and correction. Some non-biologically originated artifacts characterised with specific frequency bands might be successfully removed by signal filtering [12]. One of the most popular methods of artifact reduction are based on blind source separation (BSS) methods like independent component analysis (ICA) [13, 14] or principal component analysis (PCA) [15], where original EEG data are decomposed into a new set of source signals in a way to maximise their statistical independence. ICA components were also treated as a feature in the process of artifact classification. Tamburrro et al. [16] proposed an ICA-based fingerprint method of SVM-based classification and removal of biologically originated artifacts. Support Vector Machines (SVM) were applied for the artifactual component classification in electro-oculogram (EOG) and electromyogram (EMG) recordings [17]. SVMs and autoregressive models were also applied in [18]. Other approaches cover artifact detection based on signal-to-noise ratio and clutter-to-signal ratio (CSR) [19]. In [16], ICA and higher-order statistics, such as linear trends and data improbability, were applied. ICA and regression analysis was also applied to automatic artifact detection [20]. Other works [21] are based on statistical measures such as correlation with other channels, channel variance, mean of the channel correlation coefficients with the other channels or so-called Hurst exponent).

In the literature there are also extensive examples of EEG data classification performed in order to find patterns to tackle different problems. Beyond classification of artifacts, supervised learning was applied to classify cognitive workload [22], diagnosing such diseases as seizure, Alzheimer, or schizophrenia [23] or brain-computer interfaces [24]. Among the most popular classifiers the literature indicates SVM [22], linear regression [25, 26] and different versions of nearest neighbour algorithms [23].

The aim of the paper is to perform classification of biologically originated artifacts of EEG data based on a twelve-participant dataset. The analysis covered three types of artifacts (eye blinks, eye movement and muscle activity) and clean signal. Several types of classification methods were compared. What is more, the analysis was performed with distinguishing six methods of data normalisation and four types of feature selection and extraction methods. Two classification approaches were also compared. The first one was a two-stage classification consisting in distinguishing clean and artifactual signal (first step) and in three-class classification of artifacts (second step). The second approach was based on a four-class classification of data including clean signal and three types of artifacts. The features applied in the classification were extracted from EEG power spectra.

The novelty of the presented paper is in development of subject-independent method of various biological artifact detection applying extensive comparison of different normalization methods. Another novel aspect of the work is in development of two-stage ensemble classifier using different dimensionality reduction techniques applied on different stages of the procedure.

The rest of the paper is structured as follows. The second section covers description of the methods applied, the third one describes the dataset and the analysis procedure. The results obtained are presented in the fourth section, whereas discussion is contained in the last, fifth section.

2 Methods Applied

The experiment study covered several methods of classification and feature extraction. Among feature selection methods Principal Component Analysis (PCA) as well as ranking-based methods such as the Fisher scoring method [27, 28] and Eigenvector Centrality for Feature Selection (ECFS) [29, 30] method and normalised mutual information feature selection (NMIFS) [31, 32] were applied.

Several types of classifiers were applied in the study. The main focus was put on the family of Support Vector Machines (SVM) methods [33] – supervised learning models based on determination of the hyperplane in the transformed feature space. It might be linear or non-linear, with such kernels as polynomial (quadratic or cubic), Gaussian or hyperbolic.

3 Data Analysis

3.1 The Dataset

The dataset used in the study was taken from [16], who shared their data. The dataset contains EEG recordings with artifacts cued externally. Among available datasets we have chosen a dataset recorded with a conventional wet electrode cap containing 128 Ag/AgCl electrodes. Unipolar biosignal amplifier (RefaExt; Advanced Neuro Technologies B.V.) with a common average reference and a frequency of 1,024 Hz.

The dataset contains three types of cued artifacts: eye blinks, eye movements and muscle activity artifacts. Acquisition of eye blinks covered 50 eye blinks in 5-second intervals cued with a beep tone. In a single recording 250 s of eye blink duration was registered. Twelve male participants took part in this study, aged 28.5 ± 1.2 years. Horizontal eye movements were cued from ten participants (aged: 28.8 ± 1.9 years) seated in controlled environment (50 cm screen-eye distance was kept, visual field of the screen was also fixed). Eye movements were cued in such a way that volunteers were asked to follow the marker appearing in the centre screen and moving subsequently in a repeated deterministic sequence around the screen. Individual movement is considered as seven complete sequences, with inter-sequence intervals of 8 s. Single movement is determined as position change of approximately 16° within the visual field. Muscle activity artifacts is evoked by jaw movement. 10 participants (aged 26.7 ± 1.2 years) were asked to maximally contract jaw muscles throughout: 2 s inter-tone intervals for 11 contractions (average total duration: 44 s) or 3 s inter-tone intervals for 7 contractions (average total duration: 42 s).

3.2 Preprocessing

The preprocessing can be divided into three steps. The signal was band pass filtered in the frequency range between 0.3 Hz and 70 Hz to remove the most noised parts of the signal containing a low level of information. Notch filter with the notch frequency of 50 Hz was applied to remove the artifacts originating from electric power network interfering with the signal as well. After that, the channels containing high levels of technical artifacts originating from high impedance were removed by using kurtosis and the removed channels were replaced by interpolating the channels which were not removed.

3.3 Feature Extraction

The following steps were performed to extract the features:

- The data obtained from the preprocessing were divided into parts with one-second-long window and 50% overlapping.
- The one-second time segments were manually labelled. There were five types of labels: 1 – eye movements, 2 – eye blinking, 3 – muscle movement, 0 – clean and 4 – other. The intervals which were labelled as other included the artifacts which were not mentioned earlier and they were excluded from further analysis. As a result, the four labelled datasets obtained (0–3) were combined into one dataset.
- The following six types of normalisation were calculated:
  - Min-max normalisation;
  - Z-score normalisation based on mean/standard deviation
  - Robust Z-score normalization based on median/median standard deviation
- All three normalisation techniques were applied in two ways:

3.4 Feature Selection

As has been mentioned above, the dimensionality of the data was quite high: the total number of the electrodes was equal to 128, which, being multiplied by 70 (first 70 frequency bins were taken per each electrode) gave us a problematic feature number as high as 8960. In order to deal with the "dimensionality curse" several dimensionality reduction techniques were taken into account.

First and foremost, data aggregation, described in detail in Sect. 4, was applied: it led to a significant dimension reduction down to 768 features.

The following two approaches were applied for further dimensionality reduction:

– PCA, i.e. Principal Component;
– Rank based feature selection methods.

As for PCA, the value of explained variance was chosen to be the metric defining the number of the features in the final dataset. Along with the variance explained, however, the maximum feature number was set. The said values were used in the following way: firstly, the number of principal components corresponding to the value of explained variance was found. Afterwards, in the case the number of the principal components was greater than the PC number threshold, the number of the principal components was further lowered to the preset maximum number of PC. The value of the variance explained was eventually set to 99%, while the maximum principal component number was 100. The PCA was performed every time before training a classifier in order to gain the representation of the training data in the space of the principal components as well as to obtain the matrix transforming the test dataset to the PC space. It was very important not to use the observations belonging to testing set for PCA.

The rank based feature selection methods provided the result in a different manner. First of all, the distinctive feature of all the FS methods used in the present research is the fact that they should be applied to a two-class dataset. Hence for a n-class dataset the result would be the set of n feature rankings, each k-th consisting of the numbers of the features arranged in decreasing order in terms of the impact on the predictive capability of a two-class classifier having to distinguish between k-th class and the rest. Having to perform multiclass classification on the basis of the set of feature rankings obtained, one has to define the approach the rankings are treated in accordance with.

First, the feature selection method should be used for every class of the dataset in order to obtain feature ranking. This stage was repeated multiple times as it was noticed that the feature selection methods provide the results that slightly differ from trial to trial. The resulting ranking was built on the basis of the rankings obtained in the individual feature selection trials. Similarly to PCA, only test dataset observations were used for feature selection.

The main goal of the second stage of feature selection was to form feature sets for use in training/testing a classifier. The authors of the Feature Selection Toolbox for Matlab suggest to use the following strategy [34]: in the case it is decided to use p first features for classification, the resulting set R^p of features would be the intersection of n sets, R_k^p each containing first p elements of corresponding k-th ranking, in other words:

$$R^p = \bigcap_{k=1}^{n} R_k^p$$

where:

n –   number of classes;
k –   order number of ranking set;

p –   number of first features taken;

R_k –   feature ranking arranged in descending order in terms of predictive capability in 1-vs-rest classification of k-th class;

R_k^p –   subset of R_k containing first p features;

R^p –   the set being the intersection of R_k^p for $k = 1, 2…, n$

The other strategy employed the following approach: instead of intersecting R_k^p, i.e. first p features of every R_k, they were used in order to train a separate binary classifier dealing with k-th class in 1-vs-rest manner. The result, being the ensemble of classifiers each employing its own feature set, is presented in detail in Sect. 4.

3.5 Classification

The problem considered in the present research belongs to the field of multiclass classification as the analysed dataset containing the observations of the following classes: 0 – uncontaminated signal, 1 – signal with eye-blink artifacts, 2 – signal with eye-movement artifacts, 3 – signal with jaw muscle artifacts.

Depending on specific parameters, the classification techniques used in the present research can be divided into several groups:

In terms of the classification model organisation:

- 1-stage 4-class classification;
- 2-stage classification, where the first stage classifier was to distinguish between artifactual and uncontaminated signal and the second stage classifier was to recognize the exact type of the artifact detected by the first stage classifier

In terms of the dimensionality reduction technique used:

- PCA only;
- feature selection only;
- combined use of PCA and feature selection techniques.

In the last approach the initial classification was performed by binary one-vs-all classifiers, each applying its own set of features. The aim of the second stage was to resolve controversial situations, appearing in two cases: when two or more first stage classifiers provided a positive answer, or when neither of the classifiers provided a positive answer. The second stage was implemented in the form of a 4-class classifier, employing PCA as the dimensionality reduction technique.

In order to ensure statistical significance of the experiment, the training/testing cycles were repeated multiple times for every classification approach. The mean accuracy together with standard deviation was used for comparison of the tested classification approaches.

The research procedure composed of the steps discussed above is presented in Fig. 1.

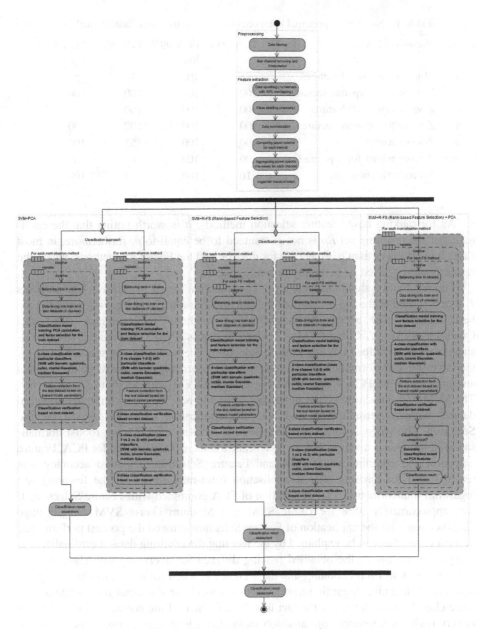

Fig. 1. The data processing procedure

4   Results

It was noticed that the method of normalisation and application/absence of the log transform had a strong influence on the number of principal components selected (Table 1).

Table 1. Number of principal components for various normalisation methods

No.	Normalization	PCA 99%	PCA 99% log	PCA 95%	PCA 95% log
1	Min-max across all features	98	100	16	55
2	Min-max for separate features	100	100	100	100
3	Z-score across all features	100	100	100	100
4	Z-score for separate features	100	100	100	100
5	Z-score robust	100	100	53	100
6	Z-score robust for separate features	100	100	64	100
7	No normalisation	16	100	9	100

As for ranking-based feature selection methods, it is worth noting that the cardinality of the resulting set Rp is not guaranteed to be equal to p, furthermore, in most cases it is far lower than p, especially for mRMR and the Fisher FS methods, where the resulting set occurred to be empty in many cases.

Figures 1 and 2 show the accuracy of classification for all 14 datasets. The numbers *1, 2* or *3* placed at the top of each bar indicate the classifier model having provided the best accuracy for a specific normalisation method. The numbers stand for: Quadratic SVM – *1*, Cubic SVM – *2*, Medium Gauss SVM – *3*. Figure 2 shows a 3-stage classification for PCA and Feature Selection. The best accuracy was achieved for the logarithm transformation dataset after min-max normalisation across all the features and application of PCA – approximately 93% for SVM with Medium Gauss kernel. The SVM with quadratic kernel turned out to be the best for logarithm transformation dataset without normalisation and with the application of ranking-based Feature Selection. The worst accuracy was reached for datasets after ZScore robust normalisation in individual features. Figure 3 presents a 1-stage classification for PCA, Feature Selection and combination of PCA and Feature Selection. The best accuracy was reached also for datasets after normalisation (min-max across all the features) and logarithm transformation after application of PCA combined with Feature Selection. It was approximately 95% for Cubic SVM and Medium Gauss SVM. Single stage classification with the application of Feature Selection showed the poorest performance in most cases, this can be explained by the fact that the resulting dataset cardinality was comparatively low as the obtained ranking differed for every separate class in most instances. It is worth mentioning that the accuracy reached for the dataset including not normalised data after logarithm transformation was above the mean for 2-stage and 1-stage classification. It reveals the fact that the influence of the normalisation technique is very high: an improper normalisation method can lead to even poorer performance compared to non-normalised data.

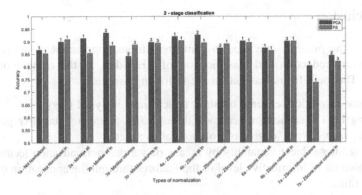

Fig. 2. 2-stage classification

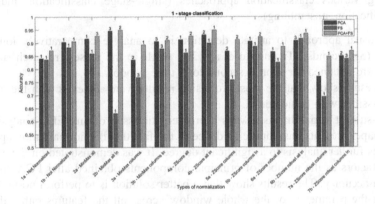

Fig. 3. 1-stage classification

Table 2 contains the best results achieved for every classification approach for the specific solutions, such as: classifier type, the best mean accuracy, standard deviation, normalisation, kernel type, feature number, feature selection method.

Table 2. Summary of separate classification approaches.

Class. approach	Mean	Std	Normalisation	Log	Kernel	Feature number	FS
FS + PCA ensemble	0.95	0.005	Min-max all feat	Yes	Cubic	8	mRMR
PCA 1-stage	0.946	0.015	Min-max all feat	Yes	Med. Gauss	N/A	N/A
PCA 2-stage	0.935	0.008	Min-max all feat	Yes	Med. gauss	N/A	N/A
FS 2-stage	0.915	0.005	ZScore robust all feat	Yes	Quadratic	4	ECFS
FS 1-stage	0.909	0.01	Not normalised	Yes	Cubic	3	ECFS

5 Conclusion

The aim of the present study was to compare various approaches of normalisation, dimensionality reduction and classification of EEG data in the context of artifact detection. The main focus was put on the following aspects:

- high time resolution, ensured by short epoch time analysed (1 s),
- ensuring high classification accuracy through fine-tuning of classifier parameters (various kernel types, degree of polynomial used, etc.)
- handling inter-subject variability by means of various normalisation techniques
- maximisation of informative level of the features through the application of the log transformation
- handling "the curse of dimensionality" problem through the use of dedicated methods of feature selection and their combination,
- testing various classification approaches (single-stage classification, multistage classification, ensembling)

The usual approach to artifact detection is to analyse comparatively long time intervals (3+ seconds); Tamburrro et al. [29], while in the present research sufficient results were obtained for short 1-second-long time window.

The results show that the most promising results were achieved with the use of a SVM classifier with cubic kernel.

Inter-subject variability is always a problematic issue of any EEG analysis. The current paper presents the empiric evidence of the fact that the normalisation approach influences further analysis to a significant degree. It was demonstrated on the example of such factors as the number of principal components obtained after PCA and classification accuracy. The results show that a better solution is to perform normalisation based on the parameters of the whole window across all the features rather than for each separate feature. As for the specific normalisation method, the min-max normalisation proved to be the most efficient.

The scientific literature shows positive influence of the log transform on the dataset normality which often results in better overall performance of the classifier applied. The present study reports that in a vast majority of cases the classification accuracy rises noticeably after application of log transformation (see Figs. 2 and 3).

The overall comparison of dimensionality reduction methods has indicated that PCA occurred to be more efficient in terms of classification accuracy, both in one-stage and in two-stage classification compared to ranking-based feature selection methods. Furthermore, the highest result was obtained for the ensemble classifier combining both PCA and ranking-based FS methods; however, the difference was minor. Besides accuracy, time complexity was taken into account. In terms of this measure PCA proved to be faster than ranking-based methods.

Testing various classifier approaches indicated that both one- and two-stage classification provided similar results, although the maximum accuracy values for models employing PCA and ranking-based methods was achieved for one-stage approach for both dimensionality reduction techniques. The highest classification accuracy among all approaches was provided by the ensemble classifier, combining PCA and ranking-based FS methods.

To summarise, the best result was obtained by the application of the following methods: min-max normalization across all channels, log transform, SVM with cubic kernel, ensemble approach combining Joint Mutual Information Maximisation and PCA.

References

1. Askamp, J., Putten, M.: Mobile EEG in epilepsy. Int. J. Psychophysiol. **91**(1), 30–35 (2013)
2. De Vos, M., Kroesen, M., Emkes, R., Debener, S.: P300 speller BCI with a mobile EEG system: comparison to a traditional amplifier. J. Neural Eng. **11**(3), 036008 (2014)
3. Michel, C.M., et al.: Microstates in resting-state EEG: current status and future directions. Neurosci. Biobehav. Rev. **49**, 105–113 (2014)
4. Lance, B.J., Kerick, S.E., Ries, A.J., Oie, K.S., McDowell, K.: Brain-computer interface technologies in the coming decades. Proc. IEEE **100**, 1585–1599 (2012)
5. Comani, S., et al.: Monitoring neuro-motor recovery from stroke with high-resolution EEG, robotics and virtual reality: a proof of concept. IEEE Trans. Neural Syst. Rehabil. Eng. **23**(6), 1106–1116 (2015)
6. Bissoli, A.L.C., Sime, M.M., Bastos-Filho, F.B.: Using sEMG, EOG and VOG to control an intelligent environment. IFAC-PapersOnLine **49**(30), 210–215 (2016)
7. Di Fronso, S., et al.: Neural markers of performance states in an olympic athlete: an EEG case study in air-pistol shooting. J. Sport. Sci. Med. **15**(15), 214–222 (2016)
8. Niedermeyer, E., Da Silva, F.: Electroencephalography, Basic Principals, Clinical Applications, and Related Fields. Lippincott Williams & Wilkins, Philadelphia (2005)
9. Lopez-Gordo, M.A., Sanchez-Morillo, D., Pelayo Valle, F.: Dry EEG electrodes. Sensors **14**, 12847–12870 (2014)
10. Urigüen, J.A., Garcia-Zapirain, B.: EEG artifact removal—state-of-the-art and guidelines. J. Neural Eng. **12**(3), 031001 (2015)
11. Li, Y., Ma, Z., Lu, W., Li, Y.: Automatic removal of the eye blink artifact from EEG using an ICA-based template matching approach. Physiol. Meas. **27**(4), 425–436 (2006)
12. Goncharova, I., Vaughanet, M.T., Mcfarland, D., Wolpaw, J.: EMG contamination of EEG: spectral and topographical characteristics. Clin. Neurophysiol. **114**(9), 1580–1593 (2003)
13. Delorme, A., Sejnowski, T., Makeig, S.: Enhanced detection of artifacts in EEG data using higher-order statistics and independent component analysis. NeuroImage **34**(4), 1443–1449 (2007)
14. Jung, T., et al.: Removing electroencephalographic artifacts by blind source separation. Psychophysiology **37**(2), 163–168 (2000)
15. Lins, O.G., Picton, T.W., Berg, P., Scherg, M.: Ocular artifacts in recording EEG and event-related potentials. II: source dipoles and source components. Brain Topogr. **6**(1), 65–78 (1993)
16. Tamburro, G., Fiedler, P., Stone, D., Haueisen, J., Comani, S.: A new ICA-based fingerprint method for the automatic removal of physiological artifacts from EEG recordings. PeerJ **6**, e4380 (2018)
17. Halder, S. et al.: Online artifact removal for brain-computer interfaces using support vector machines and blind source separation. Comput. Intell. Neurosci. **1**, 10–16 (2007)
18. Lawhern, V., et al.: Detection and classification of subject-generated artifacts in EEG signals using autoregressive models. J. Neurosci. Methods **2**, 181–189 (2012)

19. Goh, S.K., et al.: Automatic EEG artifact removal techniques by detecting influential independent components. IEEE Trans. Emerg. Top. Comput. Intell. **1**, 270–279 (2017)
20. Wang, D., Miao, D., Blohm, G.: Multi-class motor imagery EEG decoding for brain-computer interfaces. Front. Neurosci. **6**, 151 (2012)
21. Nolan, H., Whelan, R., Reilly, R.B.: FASTER: fully automated statistical thresholding for EEG artifact rejection. J. Neurosci. Methods **192**(1), 152–162 (2010)
22. Plechawska-Wójcik, M., et al.: Classifying cognitive workload based on brain waves signal in the arithmetic tasks' study. In: 2018 11th International Conference on Human System Interaction (HSI), pp. 277–283. IEEE (2018)
23. Parvinnia, E., Sabeti, M., Zolghadri Jahromi, M., Boostani, R.: Classification of EEG signals using adaptive weighted distance nearest neighbor algorithm. J. King Saud Univ. – Comput. Inf. Sci. **26**(1), 1–6 (2014)
24. Lee, K., et al.: A brain-controlled exoskeleton with cascaded event-related desynchronization classifiers. Robot. Auton. Syst. **90**(c), 15–23 (2017)
25. Liang, N., Bougrain, L.: Decoding finger flexion from band-specific ECoG signals in humans. Front. Neurosci. **6**, 6–91 (2012)
26. Lotte, F., et al.: A review of classification algorithms for EEG-based brain-computer interfaces: a 10-year update. J. Neural Eng. **15**(3), 031005 (2018)
27. Gu, Q., Li, Z., Han, J.: Generalized fisher score for feature selection. In: Proceeding UAI 2011 Proceedings of the Twenty-Seventh Conference on Uncertainty in Artificial Intelligence, pp. 266–273 (2011)
28. Dat T. H., Guan, C.: Feature selection based on fisher ratio and mutual information analyses for robust brain computer interface. In: 2007 IEEE International Conference on Acoustics, Speech and Signal Processing – ICASSP 2007. IEEE (2007)
29. Roffo, G., Melzi, S.: Ranking to learn: feature ranking & selection via eigenvector centrality. In: Appice, A., Ceci, M., Loglisci, C., Masciari, E., Raś, Z. (eds.) New Frontiers in Mining Complex Patterns, pp. 1–15. Springer, Heidelberg (2017). https://doi.org/10.1007/978-3-319-61461-8_2
30. Henni, K., Mezghani, N., Gouin-Vallerand, C.: Unsupervised graph-based feature selection via subspace and pagerank centrality. Expert Syst. Appl. **114**, 46–53 (2018)
31. Estévez, P.A., Tesmer, M., Perez, A., Zurada, J.M.: Normalized mutual information feature selection. IEEE Trans. Neural Netw. **20**(2), 189–201 (2009)
32. Bennasar, M., Hicks, Y., Setchi, R.: Feature selection using joint mutual information maximisation. Expert Syst. Appl. **42**(22), 8520–8532 (2015)
33. Cortes, C., Vapnik, V.: Support-vector networks. Mach. Learn. **20**(3), 273–297 (1995)
34. https://www.mathworks.com/matlabcentral/fileexchange/56937-feature-selection-library. Accessed 18 Dec 2018

Data Mining

Experimental Study of Totally Optimal Decision Rules

Mohammad Azad[iD] and Mikhail Moshkov[(✉)][iD]

Computer, Electrical and Mathematical Sciences and Engineering Division,
King Abdullah University of Science and Technology (KAUST),
Thuwal 23955-6900, Saudi Arabia
{mohammad.azad,mikhail.moshkov}@kaust.edu.sa

Abstract. In this paper, we experimentally study the existence of
totally optimal decision rules which are optimal relative to the length and
coverage simultaneously for nine decision tables from the UCI Machine
Learning Repository. Totally optimal rules can be useful when we consider decision rules as a way for knowledge representation. We study
not only exact but also approximate decision rules based on the three
uncertainty measures: entropy, Gini index, and misclassification error. To
investigate the existence of totally optimal rules, we use an extension of
dynamic programming that allows us to make multi-stage optimization
of decision rules relative to the length and coverage. Experimental results
show that totally optimal decision rules exist in many cases. However,
the behavior of graphs describing how the number of rows of decision
tables with totally optimal decision rules depends on the accuracy of
rules is irregular.

Keywords: Decision rule · Uncertainty measure · Length · Coverage ·
Totally optimal rule · Multi-stage optimization

1 Introduction

Decision rules are widely used to solve the problems of prediction and knowledge representation [8,9,13,14]. When decision rules are considered as a way for
knowledge representation, we would like to minimize their length (to make the
rules more understandable) and to maximize their coverage (to make the rules
more general).

In this paper, we experimentally investigate the existence of totally optimal decision rules that have the minimum length and the maximum coverage
simultaneously.

We can use two tools for the study of totally optimal decision rules that
are based on extensions of dynamic programming. These are (i) multi-stage
optimization of decision rules relative to two criteria, and (ii) construction of
the set of Pareto optimal points for bi-criteria optimization problem (totally
optimal decision rule exists if and only if there is exactly one Pareto optimal

© Springer Nature Switzerland AG 2019
L. Rutkowski et al. (Eds.): ICAISC 2019, LNAI 11509, pp. 319–326, 2019.
https://doi.org/10.1007/978-3-030-20915-5_29

point) [1]. In this paper, we use the first tool which is less time consuming. For experimenting, we use Dagger system created in KAUST to implement various extensions of dynamic programming [2,3].

One of the main goals of this paper is to experimentally study how the existence of totally optimal decision rules depends on the accuracy of such rules. We work with nine decision tables from the UCI Machine Learning Repository [12]. We study not only exact but also approximate decision rules defined based on the three uncertainty measures: entropy *ent*, Gini index *gini*, and misclassification error *me*. We consider 101 values of the threshold α from 0.00 to 1.00 with the step 0.01. This threshold describes the accuracy of decision rules: $\alpha = 0.00$ means 100 % accuracy (exact decision rules), and $\alpha = 1.00$ means 0 % accuracy.

Experimental results show that totally optimal decision rules exist in many cases. The behavior of graphs describing how the number of rows of decision tables with totally optimal decision rules depends on decision rule accuracy is irregular.

One of the main areas of applications of the obtained results (existence of totally optimal decision rules in many cases) is the rough set theory [10,15–17] in which decision rules are widely used. Another area of applications is the logical analysis of data (LAD) in which decision rules are known as patterns [5–7,11].

Note that exact totally optimal decision rules were studied in [1,4] both from theoretical and experimental points of view.

This paper consists of four sections. In Sect. 2, we consider main notions and tools. Section 3 is devoted to the consideration of experimental results. Section 4 contains short conclusions.

2   Main Notions and Tools

In this section, we discuss the notions of decision table, uncertainty measure, decision rule, cost function, and totally optimal decision rule. We consider also a way to prove the existence of totally optimal decision rules.

2.1   Decision Tables and Uncertainty Measures

A *decision table* is a rectangular table T with $n \geq 1$ columns filled with numbers from the set $\omega = \{0, 1, 2, \ldots\}$ of nonnegative integers. Columns of the table are labeled with *conditional* attributes $f_1, \ldots, f_n$. Rows of the table are pairwise different, and each row is labeled with a number from ω which is interpreted as a decision (a value of the *decision* attribute d). Rows of the table are interpreted as tuples of values of conditional attributes. We denote by $\mathcal{T}$ the set of all decision tables.

A decision table is called *empty* if it has no rows. The table T is called *degenerate* if it is empty or all rows of T are labeled with the same decision. Let $D(T)$ be the set of decisions attached to rows of T. We denote by $N(T)$ the number of rows in the table T and, for any $t \in \omega$, we denote by $N_t(T)$ the number of rows of T labeled with the decision t. By $mcd(T)$ we denote the *most common decision* for T which is the minimum decision t_0 from $D(T)$ such that $N_{t_0}(T) = \max\{N_t(T) : t \in D(T)\}$. If T is empty then $mcd(T) = 0$.

For any conditional attribute $f_i \in \{f_1, \ldots, f_n\}$, we denote by $E(T, f_i)$ the set of values of the attribute f_i in the table T. We denote by $E(T)$ the set of conditional attributes for which $|E(T, f_i)| \geq 2$.

Let T be a nonempty decision table. A *subtable* of T is a table obtained from T by removal of some rows. Let $f_{i_1}, \ldots, f_{i_m} \in \{f_1, \ldots, f_n\}$ and $a_1, \ldots, a_m \in \omega$. We denote by $T(f_{i_1}, a_1) \ldots (f_{i_m}, a_m)$ the subtable of the table T containing the rows from T which at the intersection with the columns $f_{i_1}, \ldots, f_{i_m}$ have numbers $a_1, \ldots, a_m$, respectively.

Let $\mathbb{R}$ be the set of real numbers. An *uncertainty measure* is a function $U : \mathcal{T} \to \mathbb{R}$ such that $U(T) \geq 0$ for any $T \in \mathcal{T}$, and $U(T) = 0$ if and only if T is a degenerate table. The following functions (we assume that, for any empty table, the value of each of the considered functions is equal to 0) are uncertainty measures:

- Entropy $ent(T) = -\sum_{t \in D(T)} (N_t(T)/N(T)) \log_2(N_t(T)/N(T))$.
- Gini index $gini(T) = 1 - \sum_{t \in D(T)} (N_t(T)/N(T))^2$.
- Misclassification error $me(T) = N(T) - N_{mcd(T)}(T)$.

2.2   Decision Rules and Cost Functions

Let T be a decision table with n conditional attributes $f_1, \ldots, f_n$ and $r = (b_1, \ldots, b_n)$ be a row of T. A *decision rule over* T is an expression of the kind

$$(f_{i_1} = a_1) \wedge \ldots \wedge (f_{i_m} = a_m) \to t \tag{1}$$

where $f_{i_1}, \ldots, f_{i_m} \in \{f_1, \ldots, f_n\}$, and $a_1, \ldots, a_m, t$ are numbers from ω. It is possible that $m = 0$. For the considered rule, we denote $T^0 = T$, and if $m > 0$ we denote $T^j = T(f_{i_1}, a_1) \ldots (f_{i_j}, a_j)$ for $j = 1, \ldots, m$. We will say that the decision rule (1) *covers* the row r if r belongs to T^m, i.e., $b_{i_1} = a_1, \ldots, b_{i_m} = a_m$.

A decision rule (1) over T is called a *decision rule for* T if $t = mcd(T^m)$, and either $m = 0$, or $m > 0$ and, for $j = 1, \ldots, m$, T^{j-1} is not degenerate, and $f_{i_j} \in E(T^{j-1})$. A decision rule (1) for T is called a *decision rule for* T *and* r if it covers r.

Let U be an uncertainty measure and α be a real number such that $0 \leq \alpha \leq 1$. A decision rule (1) for T is called a (U, α)-*decision rule for* T if $U(T^m) \leq \alpha U(T)$ and, if $m > 0$, then $U(T^j) > \alpha U(T)$ for $j = 0, \ldots, m - 1$. A (U, α)-decision rule (1) for T is called a (U, α)-*decision rule for* T *and* r if it covers r.

We now consider a notion of *cost function for decision rules*. This is a function $\psi(T, \rho)$ which is defined on pairs T, ρ, where T is a nonempty decision table and ρ is a decision rule for T, and has values from the set $\mathbb{R}$ of real numbers.

We will work with the following two cost functions for decision rules:

- The *length* $l(T, \rho) = l(\rho)$. The length of the rule (1) is equal to m.
- The *coverage* $c(T, \rho)$. The coverage of the rule (1) for table T is equal to $N_{mcd(T^m)}(T^m)$.

2.3 Totally Optimal Decision Rules

Let T be a decision table, r be a row of T, U be an uncertainty measure, and α be a real number such that $0 \le \alpha \le 1$.

We denote by $l^{U,\alpha}(T,r)$ the minimum length of a (U,α)-decision rule for T and r. By $c^{U,\alpha}(T,r)$ we denote the maximum coverage of a (U,α)-decision rule for T and r. A (U,α)-decision rule ρ for T and r is called a *totally optimal (U,α)-decision rule for T and r relative to the length and coverage* if $l(\rho) = l^{U,\alpha}(T,r)$ and $c(T,\rho) = c^{U,\alpha}(T,r)$, i.e., ρ is optimal relative to c and l simultaneously.

We now describe how to recognize the existence of a (U,α)-decision rule for T and r which is a totally optimal (U,α)-decision rule for T and r relative to the length and coverage.

First, we apply to T and r the procedure of optimization relative to c [1]. As a result, we obtain the number $c^{U,\alpha}(T,r)$. Next, we sequentially apply to T the procedures of optimization relative to the length l and coverage c [1]. As a result, we obtain the number $c_l^{U,\alpha}(T,r)$ which is the maximum coverage among all (U,α)-decision rules for T and r which have the minimum length (see [1]). One can show that a totally optimal (U,α)-decision rule for T and r relative to the length and coverage exists if and only if $c_l^{U,\alpha}(T,r) = c^{U,\alpha}(T,r)$.

3 Experimental Results

In this section, we consider results of computer experiments with nine decision tables from [12]. Before the experimental work, some preprocessing procedures are performed. A conditional attribute is removed if it has unique value for each row. The missing value for an attribute is filled up with the most common value for this attribute. In some tables, there are equal rows with, possibly, different decisions. In this case, each group of equal rows is replaced with a single row from the group with the most common decision for this group. As a result, we obtain consistent decision tables without missing values (a decision table is called consistent if it has no equal rows with different decisions).

Table 1. Decision tables used in experiments.

Decision table	Rows	Attributes
BALANCE-SCALE	625	5
BREAST-CANCER	266	10
CARS	1728	7
HAYES-ROTH-DATA	69	5
HOUSE-VOTES-84	279	17
LYMPHOGRAPHY	148	19
SOYBEAN-SMALL	47	36
TIC-TAC-TOE	958	10
ZOO-DATA	59	17

The nine decision tables from [12] used in experiments are described in Table 1. The first column 'Decision table' refers to the name of the decision table from [12], the second column 'Rows' refers to the number of rows, and the last column 'Attributes' refers to the number of conditional attributes.

For each decision table T, each row r of T, each uncertainty measure $U \in \{ent, gini, me\}$, and each $\alpha \in \{0.00, 0.01, 0.02, \ldots, 1.00\}$, we check if there exists a totally optimal (U, α)-decision rule for T and r relative to the length and coverage. We denote $Tot_U(T, \alpha)$ the number of rows r in the decision table T for each of which there exists a totally optimal (U, α)-decision rule for T and r relative to the length and coverage. By $Tot_U(\alpha)$ we denote the sum of numbers $Tot_U(T, \alpha)$ for all nine considered decision tables T.

The results of experiments can be found in Figs. 1, 2, and 3 for uncertainty measures ent, $gini$, and me, respectively. In each figure, the graph of the function $Tot_U(\alpha)$ is depicted for the uncertainty measure U considered in this figure.

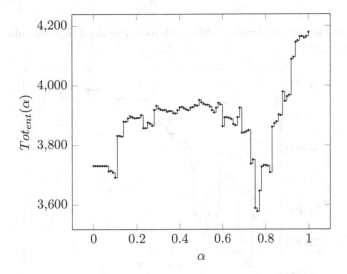

Fig. 1. Number of rows of decision tables with totally optimal decision rules for uncertainty measure ent.

The total number of rows in the considered decision tables is equal to 4179. The minimum values of the functions $Tot_{ent}(\alpha)$, $Tot_{gini}(\alpha)$, and $Tot_{me}(\alpha)$ are equal to 3578, 3571, and 3060, respectively. It means that, for each of the considered value of α, more than 85% of rows have totally optimal decision rules for the uncertainty measures ent and $gini$, and more than 73% of rows have totally optimal decision rules for the uncertainty measure me. The obtained results show that totally optimal decision rules exist in many cases. However, the behavior of graphs in Figs. 1, 2 and 3 describing how the number of rows with totally optimal decision rules depends on the accuracy of rules is irregular.

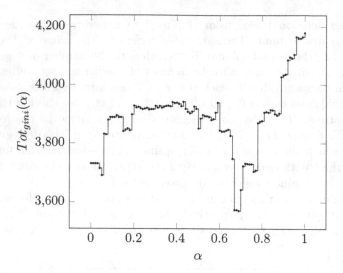

Fig. 2. Number of rows of decision tables with totally optimal decision rules for uncertainty measure *gini*.

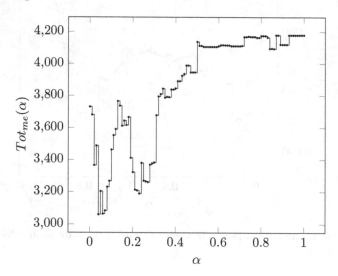

Fig. 3. Number of rows of decision tables with totally optimal decision rules for uncertainty measure *me*.

4   Conclusions

In this paper, we experimentally studied the existence of totally optimal decision rules (exact and approximate) for nine decision tables from the UCI Machine Learning Repository [12]. We showed that the totally optimal decision rules exist in many cases. In the future, we are planning to continue the study of totally optimal rules since they can be useful in applications related to knowledge representation. In particular, we are planning to use in the experiments not only whole datasets but also their samples to understand the stability of the obtained results.

Acknowledgments. Research reported in this publication was supported by King Abdullah University of Science and Technology (KAUST).

The authors are greatly indebted to the anonymous reviewer for useful comments.

References

1. AbouEisha, H., Amin, T., Chikalov, I., Hussain, S., Moshkov, M.: Extensions of Dynamic Programming for Combinatorial Optimization and Data Mining. ISRL, vol. 146. Springer, Cham (2019). https://doi.org/10.1007/978-3-319-91839-6
2. Alkhalid, A., Amin, T., Chikalov, I., Hussain, S., Moshkov, M., Zielosko, B.: Dagger: a tool for analysis and optimization of decision trees and rules. In: Ficarra, F.V.C., Kratky, A., Veltman, K.H., Ficarra, M.C., Nicol, E., Brie, M. (eds.) Computational Informatics, Social Factors and New Information Technologies: Hypermedia Perspectives and Avant-Garde Experiencies in the Era of Communicability Expansion, pp. 29–39. Blue Herons (2011)
3. Alkhalid, A., Amin, T., Chikalov, I., Hussain, S., Moshkov, M., Zielosko, B.: Optimization and analysis of decision trees and rules: dynamic programming approach. Int. J. Gen. Syst. **42**(6), 614–634 (2013)
4. Amin, T., Moshkov, M.: Totally optimal decision rules. Discrete Appl. Math. **236**, 453–458 (2018)
5. Bonates, T.O., Hammer, P.L., Kogan, A.: Maximum patterns in datasets. Discrete Appl. Math. **156**(6), 846–861 (2008)
6. Boros, E., Hammer, P.L., Ibaraki, T., Kogan, A.: Logical analysis of numerical data. Math. Program. **79**, 163–190 (1997)
7. Boros, E., Hammer, P.L., Ibaraki, T., Kogan, A., Mayoraz, E., Muchnik, I.: An implementation of logical analysis of data. IEEE Trans. Knowl. Data Eng. **12**, 292–306 (2000)
8. Fürnkranz, J.: Separate-and-conquer rule learning. Artif. Intell. Rev. **13**(1), 3–54 (1999)
9. Fürnkranz, J., Gamberger, D., Lavrac, N.: Foundations of Rule Learning. Cognitive Technologies. Springer, Heidelberg (2012). https://doi.org/10.1007/978-3-540-75197-7
10. Góra, G., Wojna, A.: RIONA: a new classification system combining rule induction and instance-based learning. Fundam. Inform. **51**(4), 369–390 (2002)
11. Hammer, P.L., Kogan, A., Simeone, B., Szedmák, S.: Pareto-optimal patterns in logical analysis of data. Discrete Appl. Math. **144**(1–2), 79–102 (2004)
12. Lichman, M.: UCI Machine Learning Repository. University of California, Irvine, School of Information and Computer Sciences (2013). http://archive.ics.uci.edu/ml
13. Michalski, R.S., Pietrzykowski, J.: iAQ: a program that discovers rules. In: 22nd AAAI Conference on Artificial Intelligence, AI Video Competition (2007)
14. Mingers, J.: Expert systems - rule induction with statistical data. J. Oper. Res. Soc. **38**, 39–47 (1987)

15. Pawlak, Z.: Rough Sets - Theoretical Aspect of Reasoning About Data. Kluwer Academic Publishers, Dordrecht (1991)
16. Pawlak, Z., Skowron, A.: Rudiments of rough sets. Inf. Sci. **177**(1), 3–27 (2007)
17. Sikora, M.: Decision rule-based data models using TRS and NetTRS – methods and algorithms. In: Peters, J.F., Skowron, A. (eds.) Transactions on Rough Sets XI. LNCS, vol. 5946, pp. 130–160. Springer, Heidelberg (2010). https://doi.org/10.1007/978-3-642-11479-3_8

Activity Learning from Lifelogging Images

Kader Belli[1]([⊠])(iD), Emre Akbaş[1](iD), and Adnan Yazici[2](iD)

[1] Department of Computer Engineering, Middle East Technical University,
06800 Ankara, Turkey
{kader.belli,emre}@ceng.metu.edu.tr
[2] Department of Computer Science, School of Science and Technology,
Nazarbayev University, 010000 Astana, Kazakhstan
adnan.yazici@nu.edu.kz

Abstract. The analytics of lifelogging has generated great interest for data scientists because big and multi-dimensional data are generated as a result of lifelogging activities. In this paper, the NTCIR Lifelog dataset is used to learn activities from an image point of view. Minute definitions are classified into activity classes using images and annotations, which serve as a basis for various classification techniques, namely SVMs and convolutional neural network structures (CNN), for learning activities. The performance of the classification methods used in this study is evaluated and compared.

Keywords: Lifelogging · Image classification · Text classification · SVM · CNN · ResNet-50 · Machine learning · Deep learning

1 Introduction

Advances in computer miniaturization and the investigation of wearable devices have led to the rise of the concept of lifelogging, which has been an active topic of research in various fields since the 1970s. Lifelogging enables people to create digital archives of their daily lives, which can include, among other things, body measurements, first-person imagery, location tracking, and activities, listening, reading, watching and browsing history. Research has been conducted on the design of user-friendly hardware and software components for life loggers. In addition, the concept of lifelogging is of great interest to data scientists because large-scale and multi-dimensional data is generated as a result of lifelogging activities [2,10].

One of the main tasks in lifelogging research is the classification of archived data using different features of the lifelogging data. Since lifelogging data have various dimensions, it is possible to approach the classification problem from different perspectives. In this paper, the NTCIR Lifelog dataset, which is described in detail in Sect. 2, is analyzed and processed. Among many different features of the lifelogging data, images taken from the first-person perspective are used to classify minute definitions into activity classes. Thus, the lifelogging data analytics are done using machine learning approaches, specifically Support Vector

© Springer Nature Switzerland AG 2019
L. Rutkowski et al. (Eds.): ICAISC 2019, LNAI 11509, pp. 327–337, 2019.
https://doi.org/10.1007/978-3-030-20915-5_30

Machines (SVM) and deep neural networks (CNN). In order to classify minutes into activity classes, images are used in two different ways:

1. With image annotations, referring to the text classification method
2. Plain original images, using image classification methods.

The main objective of our study is to apply text classification and image classification algorithms to lifelogging data and make a comparison between performances of the two approaches to reveal which approach would perform better in estimating the users' activity at the time when the image was generated.

This paper is organized as follows. The following section (Sect. 2) presents the NTCIR Lifelog dataset that we used in this study. Next, we discuss some of the recent related studies on learning from lifelogging data sets in Sect. 3. In Sect. 4, we present our approach to learning activities from lifelogging datasets, especially lifelogging images. In this section, we discuss different classification algorithms trained on the dataset. In Sect. 5, we test the performance of activity-based learning approaches; in particular, the performance of classification approaches, and compare their performance. Finally, in the last section (Sect. 6), we draw the conclusion and discuss some future research issues.

2   Dataset Description

The NTCIR Lifelog dataset was published for the first time by Gurrin et al. in [5]. The first collection of tests consists of lifelogging data of three users, including images taken from a wearable camera, location, and activity definition, which are recorded on a minute-by-minute basis. The data are presented as an XML document, which is also designed in a minute-based structure, and a folder containing image files, referenced by their relative file paths in the XML document [5].

The version analyzed in this paper is called the NTCIR-13 Full Phase-2 Lifelog-2 dataset. This version contains 90 days of lifelogging data, generated by the activities of two users. In addition to the features available in the first collection of tests, the Lifelog-2 Full Phase-2 dataset contains biometric data, generated by a minute-by-minute smartwatch by lifeloggers. This version also includes daily health logs (blood pressure, cholesterol, weight, etc.), food and beverage logs, as well as users' listening history for a few minutes [6].

Attached to the XML document, annotations of visual concepts for images are provided as pairs [image ID, concept] in a CSV file. An example image of the dataset, with visual annotations and a lifelogging record, is available in Figs. 1 and 2.

3   Related Studies

As noted in the previous section, the NTCIR Lifelog dataset was first published at the 12th NTCIR conference in 2016, and the extended Phase-2 Lifelog-2 dataset is introduced at the 13th NTCIR conference in 2017 [5,6]. The

```
<minute id="441">
  <location>
    <name>"Place in Northside, Dublin"</name>
    <latitude>53.350982</latitude>
    <longitude>-6.1623426</longitude>
  </location>
  <activity>walking</activity>
  <bodymetrics>
    <calories>3.1</calories>
    <heart-rate>101</heart-rate>
    <skin-temp>81.5</skin-temp>
    <steps>97</steps>
  </bodymetrics>
  <images>
    <image>
      <image-id>u1_2016-08-16_062145_1</image-id>
      <image-path>u1/2016-08-16/20160816_062145_000.jpg</image-path>
    </image>
  </images>
  <music>
    <song>Runaway Train</song>
    <song-mbid>bb7df441-35b2-4c0d-99b5-6560a5bbbc51</song-mbid>
    <artist>Soul Asylum</artist>
    <artist-mbid>b10db9ad-b4c3-47f3-a7a4-37864b134f65</artist-mbid>
    <album>Black Gold: The Best Of Soul Asylum</album>
    <album-mbid>4f2ff67a-d196-48a6-ba0a-bff6724b94ac</album-mbid>
  </music>
</minute>
```

Fig. 1. A sample image and corresponding annotations from NTCIR Lifelog dataset

Fig. 2. Minute definition for image in Fig. 1

researchers focused on 4 main tasks, which are described with the overview of the dataset:

– Lifelog Semantic Access Task (LSAT): Retrieve specific moments from life loggers archive according to given query sentences.

Example 1. Find the moment(s) when the user was watching television.

– Lifelog Event Segmentation Task (LEST): Develop approaches to event segmentation from continuous activities.

Example 2. Moments when user was preparing meals at any location are segmented into the "cooking" event.

– Lifelog Annotation Task (LAT): Develop approaches to annotate activity and visual environment of the user at any moment.

Example 3. At minute id 441, the user was walking, and the context of the image taken at that minute contained ocean, shore, sky and water.

– Lifelog Insight Task (LIT): Generate effective visualizations and insights from the life loggers' everyday life.

Example 4. Provide insights on how diet affects life loggers' blood sugar level [6].

Although the work we present in this paper is not designed to provide a complete solution to the issues listed above, our approach can be viewed as an initial perspective for LSAT and LAT tasks.

Among the tasks listed above, several researches have been conducted on the LSAT. In 2016, Xia et al. published their research on the integration of location information into images to improve the accuracy of segmentation [14].

Safadi et al. offers a framework that uses CNNs to index images, and then MSVMs (Multiple-SVMs) pre-trained to assign classes to images [12]. In 2017, Lin et al. re-design a framework using CNNs to query images and minutes of life loggers [9]. Lin et al. propose a method that uses a deep learning toolkit that allows them to apply several modern deep learning algorithms to the dataset and calculate the correlation between images and classes [8]. Recently, Yamamoto et al. introduce a common approach to solving the three tasks of LTC's LTC data group: LAT, LSAT and LEST. They analyze both images and locations using visual indexing and location indexing methods. They describe their approach in their paper to use the method commonly for the three tasks [15].

The related studies listed above are the main studies and have already been published for NTCIR Lifelog tasks. In addition to these, Molino et al. design a clustering algorithm for the ImageCLEF Lifelog task to summarize lifelog data [11]. Similarly, Amlinger published his study in which he compares the performance of different clustering algorithms on small and large size lifelog datasets [1]. Bolanos et al. provide an overview of the leading edge research published for the task of story-telling from lifelogging data [3]. In 2018, Truong et al. propose semantic concepts fusion approach to retrieve meaningful information from lifelogging data [13]. Recently, Dimicolli et al. publish their study in which they summarize state of the art methods together with their limitations, and future challenges in the subject of activity recognition from visual lifelogs [4].

In this paper, we propose an approach for the classification of data, using support vector machines and deep neural networks on lifelogging images.

4   Approach

Before discussing methods for classifying learning activities from lifelogging images, we first present the environment used for this study.

4.1   Development Environment

Platforms, software and libraries used for the development of our approach are listed below:

- Programming languages: Java programming language (JDK 1.8) is preferred in data preprocessing phase because of file I/O and database facilities, and object-oriented nature. In the learning phase, Python language is used because it provides a variety of library support for image processing and machine learning studies.
- Database management systems: The data are stored in MySQL relational database and MongoDB NoSQL database with the purposes of doing better data analytics on the lifelog dataset.
- Computer vision libraries: OpenCV is used for importing and reshaping images in the Python environment.

- Neural network libraries: Keras with Tensorflow support is used as the platform to design, train and test deep neural networks for classification.
- Data analysis and machine learning libraries: Scikit-learn library is used to preprocess data and apply machine learning algorithms.

4.2 Data Analysis and Preprocessing

In the NTCIR Lifelog dataset, the main component is the user. Each user is defined by a list of days, each of which is also defined by a list of minutes, in addition to several daily measurements. Each minute is defined by images taken at that minute, together with additional minute-based measurements and details which can be seen in Fig. 2. From this point of view, the Lifelog NTCIR dataset can be considered as an object-oriented model. Our first effort is therefore to analyze the XML document in an object-oriented model, whose structure is illustrated in Fig. 3. Next, this model is saved to MySQL and MongoDB databases with the purposes of improving data analytics and summarization.

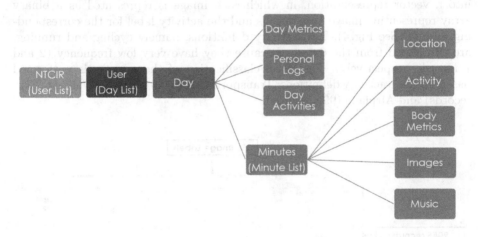

Fig. 3. The object oriented model

During our efforts to understand the dataset, we realize that the dataset had a lot of missing values, so it is necessary to analyze and preprocess the data to extract significant features. A summary of the numerical analysis of the dataset is given in Table 1.

These figures and the results of our preliminary research on recent studies have led us to use images to classify minutes into activity classes. In this task, two approaches are possible:

1. Text classification, i.e., using image annotations with activity definitions to classify the images
2. Image classification, i.e., using original images with activity definitions for classification

Table 1. Numerical analysis of the NTCIR Lifelog dataset

Feature	Value
Number of users	2
Number of days	90
Number of minutes (per day)	1440
Number of minutes (total)	129 600
Minutes with location information	104 118
Minutes with activity definition	11 041
Minutes with body measurements	90 000 (Approx.)
Minutes with images	70 000 (Approx.)
Minutes with music information	763
Number of activity definitions	5
Number of image labels (annotations)	356
Frequency of image labels	Ranges from 2 to 4000
Number of minutes having both activity definition and image annotations	9058

For the text classification approach, the dataset is processed and transformed into a vector representation, in which each image is represented as a binary array representing image annotations and the activity label for the corresponding minute (See Fig. 4). Two activity definitions, namely cycling and running, are eliminated from the dataset because they have very low frequency (2 and 1 records, respectively). Therefore, classification of the minutes is performed based on three activity definitions: Transportation (5743 records), Walking (2318 records) and Airplane (994 records).

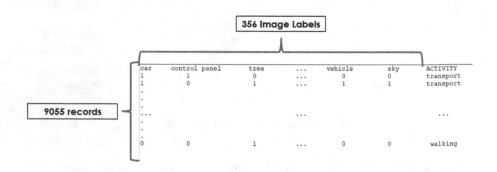

Fig. 4. Image annotation vector

To ensure consistency between different classification approaches, the same set of images and the same class definitions are used when classifying images.

In the following sections, the two classification approaches are described. The classification performance of the algorithms is then included comparatively in the Results section.

4.3   Text Classification

Text classification is performed by giving image annotations as input in the form of a binary vector, and the activity class as the output to classification tools.

Classification with Support Vector Machine (SVM). NTCIR Lifelog Dataset, which has been transformed into the vector representation in Fig. 4, is split into train and test sets, test set being 20% of the whole data. SVM definition from the Scikit-learn library is trained using different kernel functions (namely linear function, polynomial function and radial basis function (RBF)), different model parameters and decision functions. Model performances are compared with respect to their accuracy while classifying the minutes into activity classes. For each kernel type, best performance achieved is recorded.

Classification with Multilayer Perceptron (MLP). NTCIR Lifelog Dataset, which has been transformed into the vector representation in Fig. 4, is split into train and test sets, the test set being 20% of the whole data. Using Keras library in Python, MLP models are designed containing 1 and 2 hidden layers, dropout layers, ReLU and Softmax as activation functions.

The best performance is obtained in a two-layer model, using ReLU as an activation function between the hidden layers and Softmax in the output layer. The use of dropout layers with a loss rate of 0.5 makes it possible to avoid model overfits; resulting in high classification accuracy on the test data. The best-performing MLP model is shown in Fig. 5.

4.4   Image Classification

Image classification is performed using the same set of images, whose annotations are used as input to SVM classifiers and MLP models, in Grayscale and RGB color modes. Image files are imported using the OpenCV Python library. They are resized due to limited resources and built into CNN models using Keras.

Classification Using Grayscale Images. Input images are converted into grayscale images for faster training and with the purpose of understanding the effect of color dimension in image classification. Converted images are then fed into the CNN structure. Model parameters and number of hidden layers are tuned after several experimentation and model performance are evaluated with respect to classification accuracy.

Classification Using RGB Images. Input images are fed into the CNN structure without being converted to grayscale images. The CNN model is designed, and model parameters are set after several experimentation.

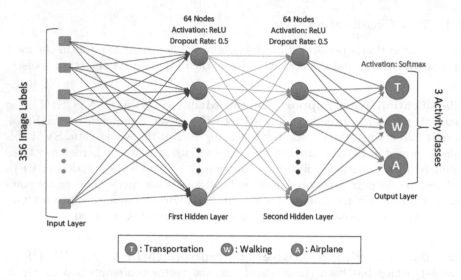

Fig. 5. The MLP model

The CNN structure consists of 3 convolutional layers, 2 of which are followed by a max-pooling layer. After the second max-pooling layer, image matrices are flattened into simple vectors. Following the flatten layer, 2 dense layers are added to increase the model depth. ReLU is the activation function which is used in each layer of the model, except for the output layer. In the output layer, Softmax is used as the activation function. In addition, 3 dropout layers are inserted into the model with the purpose of avoiding overfitting.

The model summary, generated by Keras library, is available in Fig. 6. CNN model is trained using RGB images as input and activity classes as output. Performance of the model is recorded.

Classification Using ResNet-50 Architecture. As a more competitive classification approach, input images are fed into a sample of ResNet-50 architecture, which is a deep residual learning network of up to 152 layers, pretrained on ImageNet dataset and known to perform well on visual recognition tasks [7].

The training time for the ResNet-50 architecture was longer than regular CNN architecture, as a result of the depth of the network. Correspondingly, ResNet-50 architecture appeared to perform better classification than regular CNN architectures, which will be shown in the following section (Sect. 5).

Layer (type)	Output Shape	Param #
conv2d_1 (Conv2D)	(None, 128, 128, 32)	896
activation_1 (Activation)	(None, 128, 128, 32)	0
conv2d_2 (Conv2D)	(None, 126, 126, 32)	9248
activation_2 (Activation)	(None, 126, 126, 32)	0
max_pooling2d_1 (MaxPooling2	(None, 63, 63, 32)	0
dropout_1 (Dropout)	(None, 63, 63, 32)	0
conv2d_3 (Conv2D)	(None, 61, 61, 64)	18496
activation_3 (Activation)	(None, 61, 61, 64)	0
max_pooling2d_2 (MaxPooling2	(None, 30, 30, 64)	0
dropout_2 (Dropout)	(None, 30, 30, 64)	0
flatten_1 (Flatten)	(None, 57600)	0
dense_1 (Dense)	(None, 64)	3686464
activation_4 (Activation)	(None, 64)	0
dropout_3 (Dropout)	(None, 64)	0
dense_2 (Dense)	(None, 3)	195
activation_5 (Activation)	(None, 3)	0

Total params: 3,715,299
Trainable params: 3,715,299
Non-trainable params: 0

Fig. 6. Keras summary of the CNN structure

5 Performance Results

Table 2 summarizes the performance of different classification methods on the NTCIR Lifelog data set. Because image annotations are synthetic data, it is expected that classification using original images rather than annotations can improve performance. In addition, we can deduce from the results that deep neural networks, CNNs, are powerful tools for image classification. These results also reveal that ResNet-50 architecture shows high performance in classifying lifelogging images into activity classes.

Table 2. Performances of classification algorithms

Resource	Algorithm	Accuracy
Image annotations	Linear SVM	0.831
	Nonlinear SVM (Sigmoid Kernel)	0.834
	Nonlinear SVM (RBF Kernel)	0.839
	Nonlinear SVM (Polynomial Kernel)	0.849
	MLP	0.850
Grayscale images	CNN	0.873
Color images	CNN	0.895
	ResNet-50	0.933

6 Conclusion

In this paper, the NTCIR Lifelog dataset is analyzed from the perspective of relationships between image and activity definitions. In order to classify the minutes into activity classes, the images are used with image annotations, with reference to the text classification method, and with original images, using the image classification method. Different classification and learning algorithms are formed for these input images. Performance results show that using original images results in better performance than using annotations for the classification problem. In other words, having color images and image annotations available on hand, better classification of images is obtained by using color images itself on the NTCIR Lifelog dataset.

As a future study, we plan to generate a fusion of the results of text classification and image classification models to obtain a single classifier, which uses the images together with their annotations. Then, in a subsequent step, different dimensions of the NTCIR Lifelog dataset, such as location and body measurements, can also be included in the classification model. In addition, we have plans to search for methods to generalize the classification over the whole dataset with increased number of activity classes so that every moment of lifeloggers' life could be assigned to an activity class.

Acknowledgement. This study is supported in part by NU Faculty - development competitive research grants program, Nazarbayev University, Grant Number - 110119FD4543.

References

1. Amlinger, A.: An evaluation of clustering and classification algorithms in lifelogging devices. Ph.D. thesis (2015). http://urn.kb.se/resolve?urn=urn:nbn:se:liu:diva-121630
2. Belimpasakis, P., Roimela, K., You, Y.: Experience explorer: a life-logging platform based on mobile context collection. In: 2009 Third International Conference on Next Generation Mobile Applications, Services and Technologies (2009). https://doi.org/10.1109/ngmast.2009.49

3. Bolaños, M., Dimiccoli, M., Radeva, P.: Towards storytelling from visual lifelogging: an overview. CoRR abs/1507.06120 (2015). http://arxiv.org/abs/1507.06120
4. Dimiccoli, M., Cartas, A., Radeva, P.: Activity recognition from visual lifelogs: state of the art and future challenges. In: Multimodal Behavior Analysis in the Wild, pp. 121–134 (2019). https://doi.org/10.1016/b978-0-12-814601-9.00017-1
5. Gurrin, C., Joho, H., Hopfgartner, F., Zhou, L., Albatal, R.: Overview of NTCIR-12 lifelog task. In: Kando, N., Kishida, K., Kato, M.P., Yamamoto, S. (eds.) Proceedings of the 12th NTCIR Conference on Evaluation of Information Access Technologies, pp. 354–360 (2016). http://eprints.gla.ac.uk/131460/
6. Gurrin, C., et al.: Overview of NTCIR-13 lifelog-2 task. In: Proceedings of the 13th NTCIR Conference on Evaluation of Information Access Technologies (2017). http://research.nii.ac.jp/ntcir/workshop/OnlineProceedings13/pdf/ntcir/01-NTCIR13-OV-LIFELOG-GurrinC.pdf
7. He, K., Zhang, X., Ren, S., Sun, J.: Deep residual learning for image recognition. CoRR abs/1512.03385 (2015). http://arxiv.org/abs/1512.03385
8. Lin, H.L., Chiang, T.C., Chen, L.P., Yang, P.C.: Image searching by events with deep learning for NTCIR-12 lifelog. In: Proceedings of the 12th NTCIR Conference on Evaluation of Information Access Technologies (2016)
9. Lin, J., Lim, J.H.: VCI2R at the NTCIR-13 lifelog-2 lifelog semantic access task (2017)
10. Mann, S.: Wearable computing: a first step toward personal imaging. Computer 30(2), 25–32 (1997). https://doi.org/10.1109/2.566147
11. del Molino, A.G., Mandal, B., Lin, J., Lim, J.H., Subbaraju, V., Chandrasekhar, V.: VC-I2R@ImageCLEF2017: ensemble of deep learned features for lifelog video summarization. In: CLEF (2017)
12. Safadi, B., Mulhem, P., Quénot, G., Chevallet, J.P.: LIG-MRIM at NTCIR-12 lifelog semantic access task. In: NTCIR (2016)
13. Truong, T.D., Dinh-Duy, T., Nguyen, V.T., Tran, M.T.: Lifelogging retrieval based on semantic concepts fusion. In: Proceedings of the 2018 ACM Workshop on the Lifelog Search Challenge - LSC 2018 (2018). https://doi.org/10.1145/3210539.3210545
14. Xia, L., Ma, Y., Fan, W.: VTIR at the NTCIR-12 2016 lifelog semantic access task. In: NTCIR (2016)
15. Yamamoto, S., Nishimura, T., Takimoto, Y., Inoue, T., Toda, H.: PBG at the NTCIR-13 lifelog-2 LAT, LSAT, and LEST tasks (2017)

Where's @Waldo?: Finding Users on Twitter

Kyle Clarkson[1], Gautam Srivastava[2,5]($\boxtimes$), Fatma Meawad[4],
and Ashutosh Dhar Dwivedi[2,3]

[1] Department of Computer Science, University of British Columbia,
Vancouver, Canada
clarkson@cs.ubc.ca

[2] Department of Mathematics and Computer Science, Brandon University,
Brandon, Canada
srivastavag@brandonu.ca

[3] Institute of Computer Science, Polish Academy of Sciences, Warsaw, Poland

[4] Information and Communication Technology,
Singapore Institute of Technology, Singapore, Singapore
fatma.meawad@singaporetech.edu.sg

[5] Research Center for Interneural Computing, China Medical University,
Taichung, Taiwan, Republic of China

Abstract. In today's social media world we are provided with an impressive amount of data about users and their societal interactions. This offers computer scientists among others many new opportunities for research exploration. Arguably, one of the most interesting areas of work is that of predicting events and developments based on social media data and trends. We have recently seen this happen in many areas including politics, finance, entertainment, market demands, health, and many others. Furthermore, there has been a lot of attention garnered on being able to predict a user's location based on their online activity taking into account that large amount of social interaction online is done behind usernames and anonymous titles. This area of research is well-known as **geolocation inference**. In this paper, we propose a novel model for geolocation inference of social media users using the aid of a discrete event: the Solar Eclipse of 2017. Being able to use the path pf the eclipse and timing of its path of travel to infer a user's location is a unique model seen only in this paper. We apply this unique model to Twitter data gathered from users during the Solar Eclipse of 2017 and attempt to determine if certain features of the data itself are indicative of users viewing the eclipse or of similar events. Taking advantage of Stanford's natural language processing software, we also consider the proportions and existences of many words, part-of-speech tags, and relations between users both found in our sample data, in an attempt to find key features of users who are viewing the eclipse. We discuss our results using our unique model and conclude by discussing the strengths and weaknesses of the model with the resulting potential future work.

© Springer Nature Switzerland AG 2019
L. Rutkowski et al. (Eds.): ICAISC 2019, LNAI 11509, pp. 338–349, 2019.
https://doi.org/10.1007/978-3-030-20915-5_31

Keywords: Data mining · Geolocation inference ·
Natural language processing · Twitter · Eclipse ·
Statistical probability

1 Introduction

With the ever growing popularity of social media, massive volumes of user generated data are produced everyday. This data provides many new opportunities and challenges for natural language processing (NLP). One such challenge is geolocation inference: predicting the geolocation of a message or user based on their social media posts and interactions. In this paper, we focus on user level geolocation inference based on the aggregated body of tweets from a user and estimate the user's geolocation based on their interaction with the Solar Eclipse. We gathered most of the data used in this paper in earlier work in [26,28], where we focused on sentiment analysis of the data alongside some STEM (Science, Technology, Engineering and Mathematics) analysis as well [15].

As is well established in previous work [6,8,13,24], it is reasonable to assume that user posts in social media reflect their geospatial locum, because lexical priors differ from region to region. In other words, a user in London is much more likely to talk about "Piccadilly" and "Britain" than a user in New York or Beijing. That is not to say that those terms are uniquely associated with London. Of course, the term "Britain" could be used by a user outside of the UK to discuss something relating to the UK. However, the use of a range of such terms with highly relative frequency is strongly indicative of the fact that a user is located in London. However, what do we do if users are all from the same area? For example, if we are looking at a data set of tweets with a predominant set of users from the United States of America? This situation leads to a different approach to geolocation inference which we explore in depth here.

As is given in [27], Twitter users have the option to enable location services on their account. This feature is off by default and requires users to opt-in to this service due to privacy issues. However, once it is enabled users can geotag their tweets with precise location data in the form of latitude and longitude [29]. Previous studies demonstrate that approximately 1.0% of tweets are geotagged, meaning that the exact position of where the tweeter was when the tweet was posted is recorded using longitude and latitude measurements [8]. In this paper, we use the geotagged tweets collected to help verify our model for geolocation inference.

We recognize the dangers of user location privacy. Users' location traces can leak a lot of information about the individuals' habits, interests, activities, and relationships as pointed out in [7]. Moreover, loss of location privacy can expose users to unwanted advertisements and location-based spam and scams, cause social reputation or economic damage, and ideal blackmail candidates. In this paper, we describe a location prediction technique based on a discrete event, which uses a sample of geotagged posts for verification. We build on previous work in [12] to focus here not on Twitter geolocation and network friendship data as was done previously, but on the proximity of users tweets to a discrete event. Namely, the Solar Eclipse of 2017. This work can be transferable to be used with any type of discrete event that has a geolocation fence around it. For example, analysis of the social media posts around a concert or live Television event, could verify which users are actually live at the event or just viewing it on TV. To our knowledge this is a novel and unique work in the area of geolocation inference to use a discrete event in this manner to help aid the prediction. In the next few sections we present this paper by applying the notions of geolocation inference to tweets gathered during the solar eclipse of 2017, we consider various features (hashtags #) and grammatical relationships found within the sample of tweets gathered and preform hypothesis testing to the proportion of tweets with specific features.

2   Related Work

Being able to geolocate users on social media has been a well studied topic to date. The main idea of social network based geolocation inference is built upon the notion of finding relationships on social media lending strongly to spatial proximity. We have seen many works is this field.

Backstrom et al. proposed one of the first geolocation inference methods using the social network Facebook [4]. McGee et al. extended the methods of [4] using Twitter instead of Facebook [20]. They mention clearly the challenges involving Twitter due to the limitations in precise data due to character counts. On Twitter, the character count per tweet was 140 character but has since increased to 280. At the time of data collection for this paper the character count was set to 140. Kong et al. propose several extensions to [4] based on strategies for weighting which of a user's friends are likely to be most predictive of their location [14].

We have also seen in works such as [16] an approach using combinations taking into account the influence of both users and of locations, and capturing the intuition that some users are more informative for predicting the locations of their neighbours. Furthermore, in [17], the authors add on the fact that users may often post from a few locations, therefore this must be taken into account when positively inferring geolocation.

A United Kingdom (UK) based approach was taken in [25] to assign a user to one of 4,295 cities in the UK using a follower based classification system. We have also seen very simple approaches such as in [10], where the authors just take the most common location among a user's social network to justify location.

In our extensive research of related work, we find our work here to be novel in approach, where an event with a distinct path as the Solar Eclipse given in Fig. 1 could be used to infer geolocation. We see extensions of the work here possible to similar astronomic occurrences and also to events that have distinct geolocation boundaries as mentioned earlier.

3   The Model

In this section we begin by describing the formulation of the model used. Consider a discrete event occurring during a specific time interval in one or multiple geographical locations specified by some respective boundary. From a sample of posts, which were posted within the time interval, we classify each post as either inside or outside of a set boundary as determined above. Now, from these two collections, inferences about features found within each collection are made. For example, the ratio of certain hashtags, the existence or absence of keywords, the contents of images attached to posts, and significant other features are noted about the collection of tweets. Furthermore, fair judging is made to determine whether these significant features are indicative of a user interacting with the event directly, or not. In other words, did the user actually observe the event they are describing or are they just a avid information spreader. Finally, the features indicative of interacting with the event are then applied to the population of total tweets within the time interval. From this, we infer whether the tweet originated within the bounded area or not. If the tweet was deemed to be within the bounded area, we can infer the geolocation of the tweet based on the path of the Eclipse at that time as this is a known parameter. We then verify the results using the geotagged tweets within the collection.

3.1   Model in Action: Solar Eclipse

The solar eclipse occurred on the 21st of August, 2017 and is the first to traverse over the continental United States of America (USA) during the era of social media and smartphones. Large areas of the country were able to view the partial eclipse, while the total eclipse was viewable from more than ten states from Oregon to South Carolina. However, as the eclipse traversed eastward, an area with a width of approximately 110 km formed in which only totality (100% coverage of the sun) was viewable as seen in Fig. 1.

Since the area in which the total eclipse is viewable is restricted to this bounded strip, we utilize the event of viewing the total eclipse as an indicator of geolocation for our model.

We begin by dividing this bounded region into fifteen smaller, disjoint regions based on where the eclipse was viewable at a given time. Beginning at 17:00 UTC the eclipse was over the Pacific Ocean. Every ten minutes, as the eclipse moved eastward, we defined the ending boundaries of the current class and the starting boundaries of the new class, creating the west/east boundaries of the class respectively. To define the north/south boundaries of a class, we considered the geographical coordinates of the optimum viewing location for the west and east boundary points (see the dark black line in Fig. 1). As the eclipse had a south-east trajectory, the western latitude was used to create the northern boundary and the eastern latitude to create the southern boundary. Finally, to ensure that the boundaries covered where the total eclipse was viewable, we increased/decreased these latitude coordinates by 0.5° respectively. For instance, the fourth class was dictated by the times 17:30 UTC (inclusive) and 17:40 UTC

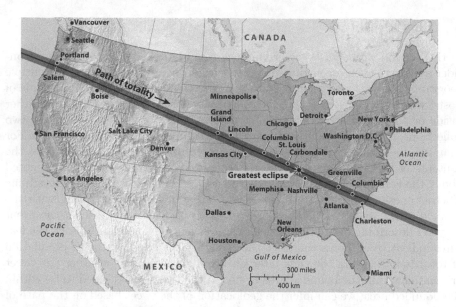

Fig. 1. Path of the Solar Eclipse [21]

(exclusive). At the former time, the optimum viewing location was (44.1°N, 114.5°W), and for the latter time (43.2°N,108.4°W). So, the coordinates 44.6°N, 108.4°W, 42.7°N, 114.5°W define the boundaries of the fourth class.

3.2   Gathering Data

To gather as much relevant data as possible at low cost, tweets were gathered in real time from Twitter's Public Streaming API [18], as laid out in our previous work [26,28]. Python 3.4 [22] and the Tweepy library [23] were used to access this API, which required a small portion of simple code and provided adequate reliability. Tweepy is open-sourced, hosted on GitHub and enables Python to communicate with the Twitter platform and use its API. There may be slight biases in how the Streaming API functions, although this seems minimal and not relevant to the analysis which was proved in [5]. The following Twitter accounts and keywords were tracked during the experiments:

Followed Users: *@NASA, @NASAedu, @NASASun, @Exploratorium*
Keywords: *NASA, Exploratorium, eclipse, umbra, totality, astronomy*

If a keyword was only part of a word in a tweet, it was still captured. For example, searching for *umbra* also provided tweets that contain only *penumbra* or *#umbra*. Along with the listed keywords, we also tracked some possible misspellings. For example, misspellings like *eclispe* were tracked and treated as its correct intention of *eclipse*.

Although all listeners were usually operational at the same time, it was not uncommon for one to receive tweets that the others had missed out on. This may be due to either too simple network issues or from some nuances of the Twitter's Streaming API. This difference seemed to crop up in each of the listeners and was usually well below 1%. However, sometimes this became 10% or greater for extended periods of time, particularly during high traffic periods.

We say that a geotagged tweet with some timestamp belongs to a class if the timestamp lies within the time interval that defines the class. Each tweet is geotagged via a Twitter's Place object, which describes various features of the location. One of these features is a collection of four geographical coordinates which creates a bounded area in a similar fashion as above. For some geotagged tweets belonging to a class, we say that the tweet is inside of the boundaries defined by the class if the intersection region of both boundaries is non-empty. Otherwise, we say the tweet is outside of the boundaries defined by the class.

4 Results

We now consider various features found among the two collections of tweets during the eclipse, namely inside bounds (inside one of the fifteen bounded boxes) or outside bounds. To begin, we consider the number of hashtags per tweet. Hashtags, denoted by a pound sign (#), have long been used in various information technology systems to denote significant meaning to specific terms [3]. In 2009, Twitter began supporting the use of hashtags, allowing users to index certain terms, which could then search for and viewed by other Twitter users.

Table 1. Hashtags per Tweet

Inside bounds		Outside bounds	
Hashtag count	Tweets	Hashtag count	Tweets
0	911	0	5348
1	511	1	2863
2	187	2	941
3	79	3	478
4	49	4	246
5	17	5	125
6	10	6	78
7	3	7	28
8	3	8	18
		9	8
		10	2
		11	1
Total tweets	1770	Total tweets	10136

Using the bounding boxes, we create the results in Table 1. We first notice for users outside of the boundaries, as the number of hashtags used per tweet increases, the number of tweets decrease. In particular, the number of tweets which feature zero to five hashtags halves as an additional hashtag is present. This was as expected as the use of hashtags for quick messages like tweets would decrease in proportion to hashtag count.

We further notice that the proportion of tweets inside of the boundaries which contain one or two hashtags is larger than its counterpart proportion outside of the boundaries. To explore this observation, we performed a hypothesis test to determine if the proportion of tweets inside the boundaries which contain one or two hashtags is larger than the same proportion outside of the boundaries. By using a 2×2 contingency test [9], we find a test statistic $\chi^2 = 5.9341$, which at a 5% level of significance, indicates there is sufficient evidence that the proportion of tweets with one or two hashtags inside of the boundaries is greater than the same proportion outside of the boundaries. Continuing with tweets that have either one or two hashtags, we consider the number of tweets which contain hashtags which may be indicative of a user viewing the total eclipse. We examine hashtags which contain the terms "eclipse", "nasa", or "total". Note: As various hashtags may pertain to the same topic (e.g., #eclipse2017, #solareclipse, #solareclipse17), we normalize these hashtags; only concerning ourselves if the above substrings are found.

Table 2. Tweets that contain Key Hashtags

Inside bounds		Outside bounds	
Hashtag	Tweets	Hashtag	Tweets
total	20	total	147
nasa	0	nasa	16
eclipse	183	eclipse	3760
eclipse/total	13	eclipse/total	188
$\sum$ Hashtags	255	$\sum$ Hashtags	5375
$\sum$ Tweets	199	$\sum$ Tweets	4303

It is interesting to observe that a large proportion of tweets outside of the boundaries have a hashtag which contains "eclipse". As a partial eclipse was viewable from a large area outside of the boundaries, one would not expect its presence to be an indicator of viewing the total eclipse (i.e., being inside of the boundaries) and thus be limited to a small proportion outside of the boundaries. Indeed, we may test the hypothesis that the proportion of tweets, with one or two hashtags, that contain a hashtag with "eclipse" inside of the boundaries is greater than the same proportion outside of the boundaries. Using the same testing method, we find a test statistic of $\chi^2 = 1.9149$, which is insufficient to suggest that our hypothesis is true at a 5% level of significance.

One may, however, expect that the proportion of hashtags which contain both "eclipse" and "total" (i.e., #totaleclipse) would be greater inside of the boundaries than outside of the boundaries. To test this claim, we ran our hypothesis test and arrive at a test statistic of $\chi^2 = 4.1792$, which at a 5% level of significance, indicates there is evidence that the proportion of tweets, with one or two hashtags, that contain both "eclipse" and "total" inside of the boundaries is larger than the same proportion outside of the boundaries.

Furthermore, we test that the proportion of tweets with one or two hashtags that contain a hashtag with "total" inside of the boundaries is greater than the same proportion outside of the boundaries. Again, at a 5% level of significance, the calculated test statistic $\chi^2 = 4.8411$ suggests there is evidence that the proportion of tweets, with one or two hashtags, of which one contains "total" is greater inside of the boundaries than outside.

Finally, we return to tweets with any number of hashtags and consider tweets with hashtags that contain both "eclipse" and "total", and tweets with hashtags which contain just "total". Performing hypotheses testing on both, splitting samples by being inside and outside of the boundaries, we find a test statistic of $\chi^2 = 4.5751$ with the former and a test statistic of $\chi^2 = 6.0371$ with the latter. Both of which indicate that the proportion of tweets with hashtags that contain "eclipse" and "total" and just "total" respectively, is greater inside of the boundaries than outside of the boundaries.

4.1 Geolocation Inference

From Table 2, we are able to with high statistical probability conclude that 199 unique user tweets occurred inside the bounding boxes during the Solar Eclipse of 2017. Using this data, we found that overall, roughly 3% of the tweets in our data set were geotagged overall ($11,710$ of $369,810$ usable tweets). Using these geotagged tweets as our markers, we observed a 90% accuracy rate, namely 179 of the 199 geotagged tweeters, falling within the desired fifteen bounding boxes. In other words, of the 199 tweeters that could be with high probability inferred to be inside the set of bounded boxes, we were correct in 179 of those inferences. This gave us a success rate overall of 90%.

5   Grammatical Dependencies

We conclude our examination of the tweets by considering the existence of various grammatical relationships within the language of the tweets using libraries from the Stanford Natural Language Processing Group [19]. We parse the contents of each tweet into a collection of dependencies, originating from a governor token and acting on a dependent token. In the context of a tree, a governor token is the parent node, while the dependent token plays the role of a child node. Furthermore, each token contains a part of speech tag (POS tag) which is used to indicate the token's tense and cardinality [2]. We direct interested readers to the following [1,11] for more information on various grammatical relations and POS tags respectively.

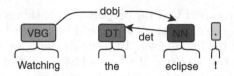

Fig. 2. Semantic Graph 1

We first consider the existence of a governor token with a VBG POS tag acting on a dependent token which contains the text "eclipse". The VBG tag refers to a present tense verb which ends with "-ing". (e.g., "seeing", "viewing"), as shown in Fig. 2. Secondly, we consider the same dependencies, but with the relationship "dobj"– which requires the dependency to be a noun. Third, we again consider a governor token with a VBG tag with a "dobj" relation on a dependent token containing "eclipse", yet we also require the VBG tagged token does not contain a "nmod:tmod" relation on any dependent token as shown in Fig. 3. The nmod:tmod relation, a subtype of the nmod relation, where the modifier is specifying a time. Our fourth and final test is the same as the third, yet where the second constraint is that the VBG tagged token does not contain an "nmod:tmod" relation on any dependent token which has an NN, singular noun, POS tag.

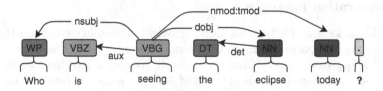

Fig. 3. Semantic Graph 2

We summarize our four tests as follows:

1. $VBG \rightarrow$ "eclipse"
2. $VBG - dobj >$ "eclipse"
3. $VBG - dobj >$ "eclipse" & $NOT\left[VBG - nmod : tmod > \underline{\hspace{2cm}}\right]$
4. $VBG - dobj >$ "eclipse" & $NOT\left[VBG - nmod : tmod > \underline{\hspace{2cm}}\right]$

We perform our hypothesis test to determine if the proportion of tweets which pass the above specifications is greater inside of the boundaries than those outside of the boundaries. For the four tests mentioned above, we calculate the respective test statistics $\chi^2 = \{1.7327, 1.7556, 1.9665, 1.9226\}$, none of which indicate there is sufficient evidence that the proportion of tweets, which satisfy the respective tests, is greater inside of the boundaries than outside of the boundaries. Indeed, dialog used in tweets is often quite informal and lacks

Table 3. Box bounds dependancy test

	Inside bounds		Outside bounds	
	Pass	Fail	Pass	Fail
Test 1	37	343	849	10677
Test 2	21	359	441	11085
Test 3	21	359	415	11111
Test 4	21	359	419	11107
$\sum$ Tweets		380	$\sum$ Tweets	11526

proper grammatical structuring, and one would not expect a reliable occurrence of certain grammatical structures to be present. It is still unclear to us if the new Twitter regulations of longer tweet size (140 characters expanded to 280 characters) will make a difference for future experiments (Table 3).

6   Future Work

Many tweets consisted of hyperlinks which directed to images on Twitter and other image sharing sites such as Instagram, Facebook, Pinterest to name a few. While this paper was concerned with textual features of tweets, one could use these linked images as features which may be indicative for geolocation inference. For instance, one could determine if the image is that of the eclipse and further determine the percentage of coverage of the sun/moon, which could then be referenced to where that percentage was viewable during the eclipse. Also, as we tested if the proportion of tweets which contained certain features was greater inside of the boundaries than those outside bounds, one could also test the strength of this proportion to determine if the existence of these features strongly indicates that a tweet originated within the boundaries.

7   Conclusion

We partitioned a dataset of tweets, and created a subset of geotagged tweets, classifying each tweet as either being inside or outside of a boundary in which the eclipse was viewable relative to the tweet's timestamp. We used hypothesis testing at a 5% level of significance to determine if the proportion of certain features within tweets inside of the boundaries is greater than the same proportion outside of the boundaries.

We found that the proportion of tweets which contained one or two hashtags was greater inside of the boundaries than those outside of the boundaries. Furthermore, from these tweets, the proportion of hashtags which contained the substrings of both "eclipse" and "total", as well as "total", within the boundaries was greater than the same proportion outside of the boundaries. We also found

for tweets of any number of hashtags that the proportion of tweets with hashtags that contain both "eclipse" and "total" and just "total" is greater inside of
the boundaries than the same proportion outside of the boundaries. Using this
information, we were able to infer geolocation with a 90% success rate which is
the strongest result of our unique model. The model created here can easily be
adapted to other events that have well established geolocation boundaries.

We also considered the presence of certain grammatical structures using
libraries created by the Stanford Natural Language Processing Group. We found
insufficient evidence that the proportion of tweets with these structures inside
of the boundaries is greater than the same proportion outside of the boundaries.
It is clear that trying to show grammatical structures within tweets continues
to be an open problem due to the character limitations imposed on tweets thus
not allowing them to be fully descriptive .

References

1. Alphabetical list of part-of-speech tags used in the Penn Treebank project. https://
   www.ling.upenn.edu/courses/Fall_2003/ling001/penn_treebank_pos.html
2. POS tags. https://www.sketchengine.eu/pos-tags/
3. The PDP-11 Assembly Language, August 2011. https://programmer209.
   wordpress.com/2011/08/03/the-pdp-11-assembly-language/
4. Backstrom, L., Sun, E., Marlow, C.: Find me if you can: improving geographical
   prediction with social and spatial proximity. In: Proceedings of the 19th International Conference on World Wide Web, pp. 61–70. ACM (2010)
5. Bifet, A., Frank, E.: Sentiment knowledge discovery in Twitter streaming data. In:
   Pfahringer, B., Holmes, G., Hoffmann, A. (eds.) DS 2010. LNCS (LNAI), vol. 6332,
   pp. 1–15. Springer, Heidelberg (2010). https://doi.org/10.1007/978-3-642-16184-
   1_1
6. Caverlee, J., Cheng, Z., Sui, D.Z., Kamath, K.Y.: Towards geo-social intelligence:
   mining, analyzing, and leveraging geospatial footprints in social media. IEEE Data
   Eng. Bull. **36**(3), 33–41 (2013)
7. Cheng, R., Zhang, Y., Bertino, E., Prabhakar, S.: Preserving user location privacy
   in mobile data management infrastructures. In: Danezis, G., Golle, P. (eds.) PET
   2006. LNCS, vol. 4258, pp. 393–412. Springer, Heidelberg (2006). https://doi.org/
   10.1007/11957454_23
8. Cheng, Z., Caverlee, J., Lee, K.: You are where you tweet: a content-based approach to geo-locating Twitter users. In: Proceedings of the 19th ACM International
   Conference on Information and Knowledge Management, pp. 759–768. ACM (2010)
9. Conover, W.: Practical Nonparametric Statistics. Wiley Series in Probability and
   Statistics. Wiley, New York, 3 edn. (1999). [u.a.]. http://gso.gbv.de/DB=2.1/
   CMD?ACT=SRCHA&SRT=YOP&IKT=1016&TRM=ppn+24551600X&sourceid
   =fbw_bibsonomy
10. Davis Jr., C.A., Pappa, G.L., de Oliveira, D.R.R., de Arcanjo, F.L.: Inferring the
    location of Twitter messages based on user relationships. Trans. GIS **15**(6), 735–
    751 (2011)
11. De Marneffe, M.C., Manning, C.D.: Stanford typed dependencies manual. Techni-
    cal report, Stanford University, Technical report (2008)

12. Jurgens, D., Finethy, T., McCorriston, J., Xu, Y.T., Ruths, D.: Geolocation prediction in twitter using social networks: a critical analysis and review of current practice. ICWSM **15**, 188–197 (2015)
13. Kinsella, S., Murdock, V., O'Hare, N.: I'm eating a sandwich in Glasgow: modeling locations with tweets. In: Proceedings of the 3rd International Workshop on Search and Mining User-generated Contents, pp. 61–68. ACM (2011)
14. Kong, L., Liu, Z., Huang, Y.: SPOT: locating social media users based on social network context. VLDB Endow. **7**(13), 1681–1684 (2014)
15. Kuenzi, J.J.: Science, Technology, Engineering, and Mathematics (STEM) Education: Background, Policy, and Legislative Action (2008)
16. Li, R., Wang, S., Chang, K.C.C.: Multiple location profiling for users and relationships from social network and content. VLDB Endow. **5**(11), 1603–1614 (2012)
17. Li, R., Wang, S., Deng, H., Wang, R., Chang, K.C.C.: Towards social user profiling: unified and discriminative influence model for inferring home locations. In: 18th ACM SIGKDD, pp. 1023–1031. ACM (2012)
18. Makice, K.: Twitter API: Up and Running Learn How to Build Applications with the Twitter API, 1st edn. O'Reilly Media Inc., Newton (2009)
19. Manning, C., Surdeanu, M., Bauer, J., Finkel, J., Bethard, S., McClosky, D.: The Stanford CoreNLP natural language processing toolkit. In: Proceedings of 52nd Annual Meeting of the Association for Computational Linguistics: System Demonstrations, pp. 55–60 (2014)
20. McGee, J., Caverlee, J.A., Cheng, Z.: A geographic study of tie strength in social media. In: Proceedings of the 20th ACM international conference on Information and knowledge management. pp. 2333–2336. ACM (2011)
21. Panther, J.: Please explain why the total solar eclipse in August 2017 starts on the west coast and progresses eastward. http://www.astronomy.com/magazine/ask-astro/2016/01/2017-solar-eclipse-path 5 (2017)
22. Python, J.: Python Programming Language. In: USENIX Annual Technical Conference (2007)
23. Roesslein, J.: Tweepy Documentation (2009). http://tweepy.readthedocs.io/en/v3.5
24. Roller, S., Speriosu, M., Rallapalli, S., Wing, B., Baldridge, J.: Supervised text-based geolocation using language models on an adaptive grid. In: Proceedings of the 2012 JCEMNLP, pp. 1500–1510. Association for Computational Linguistics (2012)
25. Rout, D., Bontcheva, K., Preoţiuc-Pietro, D., Cohn, T.: Where's@ wally?: a classification approach to geolocating users based on their social ties. In: 24th ACM HSM, pp. 11–20. ACM (2013)
26. Shumay, M., Spencer, D., Srivastava, G., Pickering, D.: Repeatable measurement of Twitter user impact nasa and the great American eclipse of 2017. FILOMAT **32**(5), 12 (2018)
27. Sloan, L., Morgan, J.: Who tweets with their location? Understanding the relationship between demographic characteristics and the use of geoservices and geotagging on twitter. PloS one **10**(11), e0142209 (2015)
28. Srivastava, G.: Gauging ecliptic sentiment. In: 2018 41st International Conference on Telecommunications and Signal Processing (TSP), pp. 1–5. IEEE (2018)
29. Wang, Y., Liu, J., Qu, J., Huang, Y., Chen, J., Feng, X.: Hashtag graph based topic model for tweet mining. In: 2014 IEEE International Conference on Data Mining (ICDM), pp. 1025–1030. IEEE (2014)

The Dynamically Modified BoW Algorithm Used in Assessing Clicks in Online Ads

Marcin Gabryel[1(✉)] and Krzysztof Przybyszewski[2,3]

[1] Institute of Computational Intelligence,
Czestochowa University of Technology,
Al. Armii Krajowej 36, 42-200 Częstochowa, Poland
marcin.gabryel@iisi.pcz.pl
[2] Information Technology Institute, University of Social Sciences,
90-113 Łodz, Poland
[3] Clark University, Worcester, MA 01610, USA

Abstract. In this paper we present an algorithm that identifies fraud in online advertising systems such as CPC (Cost Per Click also called PPC Pay-Per-Click). This model used in online advertising is particularly sensitive because it can be exploited by making invalid clicks on an advertisement. This results in additional costs for the advertiser, reduced possibility of reaching the most interested viewers and fraudulent results of an advertising campaign. The dynamically modified BoW (Bag-Of-Words) algorithm presented in the article allows us to identify repetitive clicks made by dishonest publishers or by automatic software, i.e. bots. The algorithm uses data obtained directly on an advertiser's website. The paper also presents the results of an experimental research confirming effectiveness of the proposed methods.

Keywords: Click fraud · Ad fraud detection · Bag-Of-Words algorithm

1 Introduction

There are three main parties that make up an online advertising campaign, including (1) publishers who provide resources for advertising traffic, (2) advertisers who purchase traffic in order to deliver their advertisements to the public, and (3) affiliate networks, which act as an intermediary between publishers and advertisers. Publishers provide network services to users, i.e. they generate advertising traffic when the user visits their websites. In other words, a user's visit to a publisher's website enables one or more advertisements to be displayed to that user. Thus, the publisher may sell this possibility to those advertisers who are interested in displaying their ads. Most often this is done through an intermediary in the form of an affiliate network.

A high return on investment is the ultimate goal for advertisers, affiliate networks and publishers alike. Unfortunately, in order to increase revenue, all parties involved in a digital advertising system can engage in unethical and unfair activities to achieve their goals. For example, some advertisers may exhaust their competitors' marketing budgets through a carefully conducted abuse. Similarly, some publishers generate various traps which are meant to lure users to browse or click ads about products that

L. Rutkowski et al. (Eds.): ICAISC 2019, LNAI 11509, pp. 350–360, 2019.
https://doi.org/10.1007/978-3-030-20915-5_32

users are not actually interested in. Affiliate networks, on the other hand, do not react to irregular clicking behaviour hoping to earn commissions. In some circumstances, malicious advertisers as well as publishers become fraudsters. In the commonly used different pricing models, i.e. CPM (Cost Per Mile), CPC (Cost Per Click) and CPA (Cost Per Action), despite different security measures, fraudsters are constantly trying to introduce new types of fraud using display, click or action-based scams.

An example of the CPC model is Google's AdWords service, where the CPC model used brings mutual benefits to advertisers and publishers alike. Advertisers are able to distribute their budget between the chosen keywords and to continuously control and change them. They can adjust expenses at any time. Other methods, such as fixed advertising in the form of banners, usually require advertisers to commit to at least a full month or minimum expenses that do not provide such flexibility. Publishers, on the other hand, benefit from AdWords services by being able to continuously modify the demand for keywords and the rates charged for them.

Despite such a well thought-out solution, the problems of abuse and fraud prove to be present here. It is becoming increasingly popular to "click" on competitors' advertisements. Using appropriate automatic software (bots, robots) or even manually, companies can click on each other's ads. Fraudulent clicking results primarily in additional costs for advertisers. Their advertisements may fail to appear on the sites found interesting to customers because they will disappear once their display limit has been reached. In such situation a competitor-fraudster increases its chances to have its advertisement shown in the subsequent visits to that particular page. Publishers can also make additional clicks in order to earn more and faster on the advertisement placed on their website. It is estimated that only in 2017 every fifth click was fraudulent, and this number is increasing all the time [3].

For some time now, Google has been trying to fight against "ads clicking" by detecting invalid clicks, i.e. accidental clicks and clicks coming from malware i.e. malicious software [2]. Appropriate algorithms capture some of the clicks that hold no value to the advertiser, for example:

- an accidental double click on an advertisement at the same time by the same user,
- an increased traffic coming from one IP address or the same location,
- clicks made by automatic tools, robots or other less complex software.

However, despite these counter measures, Google reimburses advertisers for some of the losses incurred due to bots generating fake ad traffic [5]. More complex bots or the use of affiliate networks that do not have the mechanisms offered by Google may make it necessary to use additional algorithms such as the one presented in this paper. Collecting additional information from the advertiser's website will later make it possible to lodge appropriate complaints regarding billing for invalid clicks.

Fraudulent clicks are performed by autonomous software (bots, robots, web bots), whose behavior on the website usually does not differ from that of a human using the browser. Detection of bots, or rather of their behavior during contact made with the web server in order to simulate a human behaviour pattern usually takes place through an analysis of the web server access log file. The data contained therein include information about the access request to each of the resources on the web server. They contain information about access time, http client's business card (User-Agent header),

URL address and IP number from which the request was made. Such data are sufficient to allow for accurate traffic analysis, identifying all kinds of scrapers and bots indexing web content, but most unfortunately not all advertisers are able to provide their web server access log files for real time analysis. In addition, there is no information about what happens to the website which has been downloaded, i.e. whether it is rendered at all and whether there has been any interaction with its user. For this reason, the simplest method may involve placing a JavaScript on the website, which will enable downloading the relevant data and transferring them to a database for analysis. The presented algorithm is based on such solution. It works successfully on the website of a large online shop and analyses data on individual visits to its website pages within a few minutes.

Computational intelligence problems may significantly help when searching for bot activity in an online advertising system. Artificial neural networks learned by learning algorithms [6] or popular deep learning methods [10] might become excellent classifiers which allow to distinguish abuse from valid clicks. Clustering algorithms, on the other hand, will make it possible to compare similar features of user behavior on a website and distinguish them from bot behaviour. Then there are evolutionary algorithms [8] and their modifications [7, 24], which can ensure a better adjustment of parameters selected for proper operation of the algorithm. Fuzzy systems [11, 21], for example, can be perfect for generating rules that will allow the creation of interpretable rules. The use of these algorithms requires, however, quick access to a huge amount of data and appropriate data preprocessing.

In the literature the subject of click fraud is mentioned quite rarely. One of the few books on this subject is [10], where most of the available information about abuse occurring in online advertising, including the mechanisms of fraud in the CPC model discussed herein, has been collected. A study analysing the behaviour of bots clicking on advertisements on the Internet can be found in [9]. The bots' behavior in the case of four different advertising systems offered by Google, Facebook, LinkedIn and Yahoo was examined therein. Many works, e.g. [11, 12] use server logs obtained directly from web servers and analyze them looking for botnets or bot farms. However, it is difficult to identify real algorithms that could help with bot-human behaviour classification.

The presented algorithm is an extension of the [1] algorithm, in which expert knowledge and TF-IDF, k-NN and Differential Evolution algorithms were used for the classification of valid clicks and clicks made by bots. This algorithm was based on expert knowledge, which is based on a laborious analysis of a great number of data collected when clicks were being made, searching for irregularities and inconsistencies between the values of different parameters of the browser and the device. The expert's task was therefore to discern and mark human clicks and automated clicks. This algorithm has been extended to include the possibility of checking click repeatability in a certain time window.

The article is divided into the following sections where Sect. 2 describes the basic version of the BoW algorithm that allows the classification of data. Its modified version customized to detect the repeatability of clicks is described in detail in Sect. 3. The next section presents the results of the algorithm's performance. The paper ends with conclusions.

2 Bag-of-Words Algorithm for Classification

The classical Bag-of-Words algorithm is based on the concept of text search methods within collections of documents. Terms are stored in dictionaries with an emphasis on words appearing in various documents. Each term is used as an attribute of the data set represented in the attribute-value form. A term can be represented by simple words (1-gram) or compound words (2, 3,..., n-gram) that occur in the document. Each of n documents consists of m terms and can be understood as a histogram $d_i = [a_{i1}, a_{i2}, \ldots, a_{im}]$. Value a_{ij} refers to the value of the jth term of the ith document. In the presented Bag-of-Words algorithm a_{ij} is a count of the number of occurrences of term t_j in document d_i. Documents are compared by comparing the distances between two histograms d_{i1} and d_{i2}, which can be measured with different distance metrics.

The BoW algorithm can be successfully used in the data classification process. [1]. Let us consider herein a set of given data $\mathbf{X} = \{\mathbf{x}_1, \ldots, \mathbf{x}_N\}$, where N – a number of all data, $\mathbf{x}_i = [x_{i,1}, \ldots, x_{i,n}]$ is a vector of values of features, $i = 1, \ldots N$, $x_{i,j}$ is a value of single feature j of lead i, $j = 1, \ldots n$ and n is the number of all types of features. Each vector data $\mathbf{x}_i$ has class $c(\mathbf{x}_i)$, where $c(\mathbf{x}_i) \in \Omega$, $\Omega = \{\omega_1, \ldots, \omega_C\}$ is a set of all classes and C is the number of all classes.

The next steps of the algorithm are as follows:

1. Creating a dictionary:
   a. On the basis of $\mathbf{X}$ for each class c and for each type of feature i create dictionaries $D_i^c = \{d_{i1}^c, \ldots, d_{iN_i^c}^c\}$, where each one comprises N_i^c of unique words d_{ij}^c, $j = 1, \ldots, N_i^c$, $i = 1, \ldots, n$, N_i^c – the number of unique words of feature i in class c.
   b. Calculate the number of occurrences designated as $h_i^c(d_{ij}^c)$ of each of words d_{ij}^c for each class c and each type i, according to the following formula:

$$h_i^c\left(d_{ij}^c\right) = \sum_{k=1}^{N} \delta_{ij}^c(k), \tag{1}$$

where

$$\delta_{ij}^c(k) = \begin{cases} 1 & \text{if } d_{ij}^c = x_{k,i} \text{ and } c(\mathbf{x}_i) = \omega_c \\ 0 & \text{otherwise} \end{cases} \tag{2}$$

and $j = 1, \ldots, N_c$, $k = 1, \ldots, N$.

2. Classification process:
   a. There are given data of the query of vector data $\mathbf{x}_q = [x_1^q, \ldots, x_n^q]$.
   b. Searching the dictionary for words – for each class c and each feature type i find those values d_{iq}^c which have the same values as features x_i^q

$$\bigwedge_{c \in \{1,\ldots,C\}} \bigvee_{p \in \{1,\ldots,N_c\}} x_i^q = d_{ip}^c, \tag{3}$$

where $i = 1, \ldots, n$.

c. Calculate the number of occurrences of d_{ip}^c counted for each one from class c. Having the maximum value, class c_{win} is the class to which query vector data $\mathbf{x}_q$ belongs:

$$c(\mathbf{x}_q) = \omega_{c_{win}} \Leftrightarrow \sum_{i=1}^{n} \left(\frac{h_i^{c_{win}} \left(d_{ip}^{c_{win}} \right)}{N_i^{c_{win}}} \right) = \max_{c=1,\dots,c} \sum_{i=1}^{n} \left(\frac{h_i^c \left(d_{ip}^c \right)}{N_i^c} \right) \quad (4)$$

The algorithm is straightforward enough to be implemented directly in a database. Similar solutions are presented in papers [15, 16] and [22].

3 Proposed Algorithm

The algorithm presented in this paper is based on the algorithm described in [1]. The algorithm discussed therein recognizes clicks that come from a bot, however, its capabilities are limited as it classifies each click on the basis of similarities to the clicks that have been previously assessed by an expert. There are no mechanisms for analysing the repeatability of such clicks. It may happen that clicks are treated as valid, but their repeatability clearly indicates abuse. The previously presented algorithm has been extended to include the analysis of the repeatability of clicks on the examined website.

The discussed method is based on the BoW algorithm. However, it has been modified and adapted to meet the specifics of the problem. The algorithm primarily uses data in a time window, which requires its dictionary to be continuously modified. Another modification is the interpretation of the dictionary contents and the analysis of word frequency occurrence. Appropriate combinations of the values of the analyzed results determine the assessment of what is and what is not abuse.

The specifics of the protection against invalid ad clicking consist in classifying at the right moment the bot program or person performing automatic clicks and blocking the ad display for viewing and clicking. Since the data from clients' websites are collected online, it is necessary in the analysis to determine a period of time during which the data will be collected and analysed. The analysis of the data which have been collected so far in one of the large Polish online shops shows that the sale takes place after an average of two clicks on an advertising banner within a time period of one week. Therefore, this implies that multiple clicks on ads can be treated as abuse, and the advertiser actually refuse to be billed for such clicks.

The BoW algorithm modified for the analysis of the occurrence of repetitive clicks works for predefined time window t. Similar to the algorithm discussed in Sect. 2, let us consider herein a set of given data $\mathbf{X} = \{\mathbf{x}_1, \dots, \mathbf{x}_N\}$ defined in time window t, where N – a number of all data, $\mathbf{x}_i = [x_{i,1}, \dots, x_{i,n}]$ is a vector of values of features, $i = 1, \dots N$, $x_{i,j}$ is a value of single feature j of data i, $j = 1, \dots n$ and n is the number of all types of features. The first step is to create a dictionary of unique words

$$D_i = \left\{ d_{i1}, \dots, d_{ik}, \dots, d_{iN_i} \right\}, \quad k = 1, \dots, N_i, \quad N_i - \text{ the number of features for}$$

document i. Other features collected from the investigated website used in the said algorithm have the following values k:

1. identifier of the source of access to the website,
2. soft device fingerprint,
3. hard device fingerprint,
4. client's IP number,
5. identifier of the ISP,
6. identifier of the Autonomous System (AS).

Other features i are generated when creating the dictionary:

7. the total number of visits in time window t for the pair of soft and hard device fingerprint,
8. the total number of visits in time window t for the pair of soft and hard device fingerprint hard from a given IP number,
9. the total number of visits in time window t for the pair of soft and hard device fingerprint from a given ISP,
10. the total number of visits in time window t for the pair of soft and hard device fingerprint from a given AS.

Fingerprint of the device used for testing the website is generated on the basis of various parameters obtained from the browser [4]. Two types of device fingerprint are generated: soft and hard. The soft fingerprint is created from the parameters whose values it is difficult to change or such process would require an extensive labour input. The hard fingerprint, on the other hand, is created using all available parameters, including those that can be changed by bots to deceive analytical algorithms (e.g. the HTTP User-Agent header value).

On the basis of the data collected in the dictionary, further visits to the website are examined. After its evaluation an entry is automatically included in the data of current time window X, and at the same time the previous data which no longer fit in the time window are deleted. The algorithm must therefore dynamically analyze subsequent data appearing in the database by entering new data into the dictionary and at the same time deleting those that no longer fit the time window. In addition to the evaluation carried out by the algorithm discussed in [1], there are 6 abovementioned features (identifier of the source from which the site was accessed, both fingerprints, IP number, ISP identifier, and AS identifier) which are analyzed. The next 4 features are the numerators which increase when the database is provided with similar data. The algorithm generating the BoW dictionary for data X from given time window t is therefore as follows:

1. For all data $X = \{x_1, \ldots, x_N\}$, where $x_j = [x_{j,1}, \ldots, x_{j,n}]$ from time window t, $n = 6$, carry out points 2–5.
2. Find in dictionary $D_i = \{d_{i1}, \ldots, d_{iN_d}\}$ such data i which have the same feature values $x_{j1} = d_{i1}$ (source identifier), $x_{j2} = d_{i2}$ (soft device fingerprint), $x_{j3} = d_{i3}$ (hard device fingerprint), that $i = 1, \ldots, N_D$, N_D – the number of all the documents in the dictionary, $N_d = 10$ – the number of features in the dictionary.

3. When item i is found, then the numerator of the total number of entries d_{j7} is increased. Additionally, in the case of other identical feature values, the numerators are also increased:

   a. if $d_{i4} = x_{j4}$, then $d_{i8} = d_{i8} + 1$ (for the same value of the IP number),
   b. if $d_{i5} = x_{j5}$ then $d_{i9} = d_{i9} + 1$ (for the same value of the ISP identifier),
   c. if $d_{i6} = x_{j6}$ then $d_{i10} = d_{i10} + 1$ (for the same value of the AS identifier).

4. When item i is not found, then add to the dictionary a new document with the value of $D_{N_D+1} = \{x_{j1}, x_{j2}, x_{j3}, x_{j4}, x_{j5}, x_{j6}, 1, 1, 1, 1\}$, $N_D = N_D + 1$.

5. Delete from the dictionary those values which do not fit in the time window. To do it, it is necessary to decrease the numerators, depending on the similarities of the subsequent features as shown in point 3. Update N_D.

Having created a dictionary in this particular way, it is now possible to assess repeatability of the last click performed – $\mathbf{x}_p$ and assess whether any kind of abuse has taken place or not. Similar to point 2 of the above-presented algorithm, in the dictionary is found document i having the same values $k = 1, 2$ and 3. Next, the following conditions are examined so as to assess whether a fraud has been committed:

- if $d_{i8} > d_{i7}/5$ then a fraud has been committed,
- if $d_{i9} > d_{i7}/10$ then a fraud has been committed,
- if $d_{i10} > d_{i7}/15$ then a fraud has been committed.

If any of the above conditions are met, the examined data $\mathbf{x}_j$ are treated as an invalid click. The above assessment has been determined on an experimental basis and results from the frequency of clicking coming from the same device, from the same source at the same time with:

- entering the site five times from the same IP,
- entering the site 10 times from the same ISP,
- entering the site 15 times from the same AS.

These conditions allow for an immediate evaluation of the site being entered from the same IP number and evaluation of the frequently used technique of changing IP numbers.

4 Experimental Results

The research was carried out with the use of authentic data collected in 2018 when the website of a large online store was being visited. This shop is visited several thousand times a day. The clicks came from different sources (different affiliate networks, Google Adwords, mailing, price comparison engines and others). The number of data flowing into the databases was therefore enormous. In order to collect, catalogue and classify the data, a multi-layered system of data collection and analysis was introduced. The system consists of several databases that store data at different stages of processing:

- raw data,
- catalogued data (all links between incoming data are analyzed, the data is arranged and compared with existing data and supplemented by information provided by third parties),
- classified data ready to be presented.

Raw data is collected directly from the website using JavaScript software. The data are collected from the moment the script is activated. They are mainly public data, which are provided by an internet browser. The most important collected data include the following:

- the class of the IP address,
- the fingerprint - an identifier based on various parameters available from the JavaScript language in the browser [4],
- the source of the visit,
- the features of the visit:
  - the number of pages visited,
  - number of pages in the browsing history,
  - number of visits,
  - the header of the http User-agent,
  - the heading of the http Referrer
- the parameters of the browser or of the computer equipment:
  - screen resolution,
  - screen orientation (vertical, horizontal),
  - information on the language,
- traps to detect anomalies in the browser or in the equipment,
- user behavior:
  - mouse movements monitoring data,
  - monitoring page scrolling,
- keystroke data.

This data is then classified by the algorithm described in [1]. Classification is undertaken on the basis of comparison of new data with archive data, where the class (legitimate click/fraud) has been determined by an expert.

A module detecting repeatable clicks described in Sect. 3 can be added to the algorithm described above. After obtaining a positive evaluation generated by the algorithm [1], it is verified by testing the repeatability of the click. If on the second evaluation the click proves to be a repeatable click, the click is then treated as a fraudulent one. The influence of this solution on click evaluation is presented in Table 1. For the tests 10 sources which provided most clicks were selected. The second column of Table 1 shows the number of all the clicks tested for each of the sources. The following two columns give the number of valid clicks and the number of those classified as a fraud performed by the algorithm [1]. An assessment is then made by the algorithm presented in this paper. The last columns present an evaluation taking into account repetitive clicks. In Fig. 1 there are a percentage chart of difference between fraud clicks classified by the algorithm [1] (marked as Algorithm 1), fraud clicks classified by proposed algorithms (Algorithm 2) and fraud clicks classified by both of them (Algorithm 3). There it is shown that different sources provide different quality of clicks. In some of them, for example in S8 or S9, the repeatability of clicks hardly occurs at all. In some others (S1, S2, S4, S5, S7) it proves to be rather significant. The high value of the fraud clicks returned by the proposed algorithm most likely means that most of those clicks come from click farms and require a better matching of the bots detection algorithm described in [1].

Table 1. Results achieved by presented algorithms showing the division into different sources of clicks.

Source	Total number of clicks	Classifying algorithm (Algorithm 1)		Algorithm identifying repeatable clicks (Algorithm 2)		Classifying algorithm with repeatable clicks detection module (Algorithm 3)	
		Valid clicks	Fraud	Valid clicks	Fraud	Valid clicks	Fraud
S1	456818	413094	37596	315488	141330	296122	160692
S2	344069	305565	34957	255434	88635	232856	111037
S3	263545	239660	21702	246826	16719	225373	36677
S4	239255	218969	17424	160705	78550	153625	85626
S5	212410	186998	22420	137299	75111	127434	84975
S6 .	202391	179253	21202	179581	22810	160747	40299
S7	152987	135594	15810	97807	55180	91374	61612
S8	151102	135145	13744	150559	543	134640	14249
S9	125836	109829	12044	125750	86	109772	12101
S10	114572	95885	15967	112329	2243	95315	16579

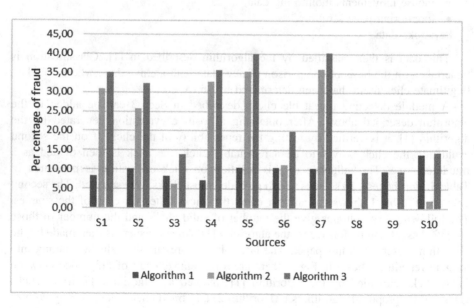

Fig. 1. Percentage of fraud clicks for individual algorithms.

5   Conclusions

The article presents the algorithm that allows to detect the repeatability of clicks in the model of CPC billing in online advertising. Publishers and affiliate networks try to derive maximum benefits from online advertising, often ignoring obvious click fraud, leaving the advertiser unable to verify or react to this kind of Internet fraud. Therefore, the presented algorithm provides an opportunity to generate one's own assessment of the effectiveness of CPC advertising and the evaluation of publishers publishing online advertisements. As presented in Sect. 4, different sources generate different quality of clicks.

The algorithm can also be implemented using other mechanisms of computational intelligence: fuzzy systems [18, 20], artificial neural networks, parallel computing mechanisms [23] clustering algorithms [17] and others [19]. However, the presented method is simple and effective enough that it can be successfully implemented directly in a database.

References

1. Gabryel, M.: Data analysis algorithm for click fraud recognition. In: Damaševičius, R., Vasiljevienė, G. (eds.) ICIST 2018. CCIS, vol. 920, pp. 437–446. Springer, Cham (2018). https://doi.org/10.1007/978-3-319-99972-2_36
2. https://www.google.com/ads/adtrafficquality/index.html. 23.12.2018
3. http://blog.pixalate.com/desktop-ad-click-fraud-rising-stats-data-2017. Accessed 23 Dec 2018
4. https://github.com/Valve/fingerprintjs2. Accessed 23 Dec 2018
5. https://support.google.com/adwords/answer/42995?hl=en. Accessed 23 Dec 2018
6. Bilski, J., Kowalczyk, B., Żurada, J.M.: Application of the givens rotations in the neural network learning algorithm. In: Rutkowski, L., et al. (eds.) ICAISC 2016. LNCS (LNAI), vol. 9692, pp. 46–56. Springer, Cham (2016). https://doi.org/10.1007/978-3-319-39378-0_5
7. Deepak, D., Simone, A.L.: Effect of strategy adaptation on differential evolution in presence and absence of parameter adaptation: an investigation. J. Artif. Intell. Soft Comput. Res. 8(3), 211–235 (2018). https://doi.org/10.1515/jaiscr-2018-014
8. Tambouratzis, G.: Using particle swarm optimization to accurately identify syntactic phrases in free text. J. Artif. Intell. Soft Comput. Res. 8(1), 63–67 (2018). https://doi.org/10.1515/jaiscr-2018-0004
9. Neal, A., Kouwenhoven, S, SA., O.: Quantifying online advertising fraud: Ad-click bots vs humans. Technical. report, Oxford Bio Chronometrics, 2015
10. Chang, O., Constante, P., Gordon, A., Singana, M.: A novel deep neural network that uses space-time features for tracking and recognizing a moving object. J. Artif. Intell. Soft Comput. Res. 7(2), 125–136 (2017). https://doi.org/10.1515/jaiscr-2017-0009
11. Riid, A., Preden, J.-S.: Design of fuzzy rule-based classifiers through granulation and consolidation. J. Artif. Intell. Soft Comput. Res. 7(2), 137–147 (2017). https://doi.org/10.1515/jaiscr-2017-0010
12. Zhu, X., et al.: Fraud Prevention in Online Digital Advertising. Springer, Heidelberg (2017). https://doi.org/10.1007/978-3-319-56793-8
13. Seyyar, M.B., Çatak, F.Ö., Gül, E.: Detection of attack-targeted scans from the Apache HTTP Server access logs. Appl. Comput. Inf. 14(1), 28–36 (2018)

14. AsSadhan, B., Moura, J., Lapsley, D., Jones, C., Strayer, W.: Detecting botnets using command and control traffic. In: Eighth IEEE International Symposium on Network Computing and Applications, 2009. NCA, pp. 156–162 (2009)
15. Korytkowski, M.: Novel visual information indexing in relational databases. Integr. Comput.-Aided Eng. **24**(2), 119–128 (2017)
16. Gabryel, M.: A bag-of-features algorithm for applications using a NoSQL database. In: Dregvaite, G., Damasevicius, R. (eds.) ICIST 2016. CCIS, vol. 639, pp. 332–343. Springer, Cham (2016). https://doi.org/10.1007/978-3-319-46254-7_26
17. Starczewski, A.: A new validity index for crisp clusters. Pattern Anal. Appl. **20**(3), 687–700 (2017)
18. Łapa, K., Cpałka, K., Wang, L.: New method for design of fuzzy systems for nonlinear modelling using different criteria of interpretability. In: Rutkowski, L., Korytkowski, M., Scherer, R., Tadeusiewicz, R., Zadeh, L.A., Zurada, J.M. (eds.) ICAISC 2014. LNCS (LNAI), vol. 8467, pp. 217–232. Springer, Cham (2014). https://doi.org/10.1007/978-3-319-07173-2_20
19. Zalasiński, M., Cpałka, K.: Novel algorithm for the on-line signature verification using selected discretization points groups. In: Rutkowski, L., Korytkowski, M., Scherer, R., Tadeusiewicz, R., Zadeh, L.A., Zurada, J.M. (eds.) ICAISC 2013. LNCS (LNAI), vol. 7894, pp. 493–502. Springer, Heidelberg (2013). https://doi.org/10.1007/978-3-642-38658-9_44
20. Nowicki, R.K., Starczewski, J.T.: A new method for classification of imprecise data using fuzzy rough fuzzification. Inf. Sci. **414**, 33–52 (2017)
21. Starczewski, J.T.: Centroid of triangular and Gaussian type-2 fuzzy sets. Inf. Sci. **280**, 289–306 (2014)
22. Korytkowski, M., Scherer, R., Staszewski, P., Woldan, P.: Bag-of-features image indexing and classification. In: Microsoft SQL Server Relational Database, pp. 478–482 (2015). https://doi.org/10.1109/cybconf.2015.7175981
23. Bilski, J., Wilamowski, B.M.: Parallel Levenberg-Marquardt algorithm without error backpropagation. In: Rutkowski, L., Korytkowski, M., Scherer, R., Tadeusiewicz, R., Zadeh, L.A., Zurada, J.M. (eds.) ICAISC 2017. LNCS (LNAI), vol. 10245, pp. 25–39. Springer, Cham (2017). https://doi.org/10.1007/978-3-319-59063-9_3
24. Dziwiński, P., Bartczuk, Ł., Przybyszewski, K.: A population based algorithm and fuzzy decision trees for nonlinear modeling. In: Rutkowski, L., et al. (eds.) ICAISC 2018. LNCS (LNAI), vol. 10842, pp. 516–531. Springer, Cham (2018). https://doi.org/10.1007/978-3-319-91262-2_46

A New Concept of Nonparametric Kernel Approach for Edge Detection

Tomasz Gałkowski[1]([⊠]) and Krzysztof Przybyszewski[2,3]

[1] Institute of Computational Intelligence,
Czestochowa University of Technology, Czestochowa, Poland
tomasz.galkowski@iisi.pcz.pl
[2] Information Technology Institute,
University of Social Sciences, 90-113 Lodz, Poland
kprzybyszewski@san.edu.pl
[3] Clark University, Worcester, MA 01610, USA

Abstract. An important thing is to have a piece of information if the collected data are genuine, reliable the originals, i.e. the information sources did not change their characteristics. However, all of data types can be changed in many ways. If this occurs the next question is: what is the essence of this change and where or when they have arise. This is a challenge to detect the change and qualify it accordingly.

In this paper, there is proposed a new solution for abrupt changes detection, based on the Parzen kernel method of estimation of the derivatives of the regression functions in the presence of probabilistic noise. The extension to the multidimensional case is also formulated.

Keywords: Edge detection · Regression · Nonparametric estimation

1 On the Importance of Change Detection

In nowadays the unprecedented amounts of heterogeneous collections of information are stored, processed and transmitted by the internet. There is a variety of types: texts, images, audio or video files or streams, metadata descriptions, thereby ordinary numbers. The important thing is to have a piece of information if these collected data are genuine, reliable the originals, i.e. the information sources did not change their characteristics. Otherwise, the next question is: what is the essence of this change and where or when it occurred? It is a challenge to detect the change and properly qualify it.

There are several methods and algorithms useful to detect abnormalities or deviations in the data. Usually, the research is based on the probabilistic approach and statistical tests or model building. Such strategy follows from the impossibility of precise and complete mathematical description of the process generating the observed data, even if we apply the known physics, biology or medicine principles and equations. One can mention the following general types of changes (see e.g. [1]).

© Springer Nature Switzerland AG 2019
L. Rutkowski et al. (Eds.): ICAISC 2019, LNAI 11509, pp. 361–370, 2019.
https://doi.org/10.1007/978-3-030-20915-5_33

- glitches or anomalies: accidental, fortuitous, often single, less important aberration or simply error in observations. It seems to be purposeful to remove them from the data by appropriate filtering,
- abrupt or jumping changes: significant deviation from the standard or model observed yet. They are important for the observer. It may indicate the case which needs the proper reaction. The abrupt changes in the stock market, abnormalities in physiological parameters of hospital patients, tomography, geological processes, especially in seismology, cartography, and in several industrial processes. In the internet data, e.g. an increase of network traffic including web clickstreams, sensor data, phone calls quantities can stand for the hacker attack and general lack of information security and the network and system threats.
- gradual changes, trends or drifts: subtle shifts that cannot be easily detected manually. They proceed slowly, seen scarcely in the long period, more difficult to detect and classify as important. For instance, the changes in the global temperature of the earth's surface, the amount of underground water resources in certain areas, the gradual general degradation of air quality, changes in the magnetic field, all of them threaten the human civilization and even life on earth, in the long perspective.

This article is in a wide range of the classification tasks, diagnostics, computer vision, etc. (see e.g. [17–19, 23–25]). The approach basing on regression analysis is developed as an attractive tool also in classification and modelling of objects (e.g. [21, 22]), forecasting of phenomena (e.g. [16, 20]), and entire methodology of machine learning like neural networks, fuzzy sets, genetic algorithms (e.g. [26–28]).

The main goal of this paper is to formulate the new proposition of simpler method of edge detection derived from the nonparametric approach based on Parzen kernel algorithms of the estimation of unknown functions and its derivatives from the set of noisy measurements.

2 A Short Survey on the Methodology of Edge Detection

The survey on edge detectors techniques concerning edge detection in $2d$-image processing one may found in e.g. [2, 3]. The authors present some solutions of edge detection problem via classical gradient-based methods derived from the first derivatives operators like Sobel, Prewitt, Robert's [5] and Canny [6] at which the distribution of intensity values in the neighborhood of given pixels determines the probable edges. However, the analysis of the second derivative by applying the Laplacian and Gaussian filtering and detecting of zeros techniques leads to identify edges in images [4].

In the present, the typical approach methodology is to analyze the phenomena as a realization of statistical processes modelled by multidimensional probability density functions in continuous d-dimensional spaces, and distributions in the case of discrete series of random numbers representing statistical processes, also multidimensional.

The natural approach (often applied in change detection methods) is to model the data via distributions or densities [1]. The significant features could be compared using different sample sets. This comparison may result in the detection of a change of some parameters. When a parameter of the process is estimated the so-called parametric approach is applied.

Contrary, the nonparametric methods are used when no distributional assumptions on the data have been made. Many statistical tests have been used - like the Kolmogorov-Smirnov test or Wilcoxon test, for instance (see [8]). The aim is to compute a scalar function of the data (so-called test statistics) and compare the values to determine whether the defined before the significant change has occurred. One of the most general measure of representing the distance between two distributions is the relative entropy known as the Kullback-Leibler distance [7].

The above methods are effective when the amount of the data is not very large, and usable off-line. So, for streaming data, they are not applicable directly. One may find the interesting article series on various regression models for stream data mining in [32–37].

In general the phenomena can be mathematically described as a function $R(.)$ of the d-dimensional vector variable $\mathbf{x}$. Then the methods based on regression function analyzing can be applied. An abrupt change in the course of the function $R(.)$ in a point p may be recognized as a jump discontinuity of the function. In the unidimensional case ($d = 1$) it may be the much more steep chart. The main problem is to find the point p at which this occurs. In the case $d > 1$ the place of change (the edge) take the form of a curve in d-dimensional space (across which R is discontinuous) and its calculation is more difficult and needs much more computational costs. It can be proposed to compare likelihood between the subsequent examples using adjacent sliding time-windows. The point p could be estimated when we observe a decreasing likelihood.

An interesting alternative solution in the literature applies the Kulback-Leibler divergence e.g. in [9]. The data in succeeding time-windows are clustered using k-means into K clusters respectively. The discrete distribution is calculated where each cluster has a probability proportional to the number of examples it contains. When two distributions are identical the Kulback-Leibler divergence is close to 0; when they are very different the Kulback-Leibler divergence is close to 1.

The combined method (the semi-parametric log-likelihood detector) is a compromise between Hoteling (parametric detector) and non-parametric Kulback-Leibler divergence. It was recently studied in [9] using among others the Mahalanobis distance, and Gaussian mixture of distributions.

Another interesting approach is based on radial basis functions (RBF). The described in [10] method uses the scalable radial kernels in the form $K(\mathbf{x}, \mathbf{y}) := \Phi(\mathbf{x} - \mathbf{y})$ where Φ is a radial function, defined on R^d. It can be rewritten in the form $\Phi(r)$ where $r = \|.\|$ denotes the distance norm and $\Phi : [0, \infty) \to \Re$ -

a function of a single non-negative real variable. The authors have chosen the Wendland kernels - the polynomial of minimal degree for given dimension d and have even order of smoothness. Kernels on R^d can be scaled by the positive factor delta in the following way: $K(\mathbf{x}, \mathbf{y}, \delta) := K\left(\frac{\mathbf{x}}{\delta}, \frac{\mathbf{y}}{\delta}\right), \forall \mathbf{x}, \mathbf{y} \in R^d$.

The main idea is to interpolate the data with the radial kernel functions, next calculate the set of the coefficients of this interpolation in some cardinal function. The main result is basing on the known Gibbs phenomenon: when the approximated function has the discontinuity at the point p in the Fourier series near this point the high-frequency components arise, so the corresponding Fourier coefficients take larger absolute values in this region. A suitable thresholding strategy could be used to detect the point p.

In this paper, we have focused attention on the challenge of abrupt change detection, also named as the edge detection problem, by presenting the new original approach.

3   A New Concept of the Algorithm of the Edge Detection

The described above method basing on RBFs is of a general type of the kernel methods.

We consider the model of the object in the form:

$$y_i = R(\mathbf{x}_i) + \varepsilon_i, i = 1, ..., n \tag{1}$$

where $\mathbf{x_i}$ is assumed to be the d-dimensional vectors of deterministic inputs, $\mathbf{x}_i \in R^d$, y_i is the set of probabilistic outputs, and ϵ_i is a measurement noise with zero mean and bounded variance. $R(.)$ is a completely unknown function. The initial problem is to find the estimator $\hat{R}_n(\mathbf{x})$ of function $R(.)$ at the point $\mathbf{x}$ basing on the set of measurements y_i, $i = 1, ..., n$.

We use the integral type of the Parzen kernel based estimator:

$$\hat{R}(\mathbf{x}) = h_n^{-d} \sum_{i=1}^{n} y_i \int_{D_i} \mathbf{K}(\frac{\|\mathbf{x} - \mathbf{u}\|}{h_n}) d\mathbf{u} \tag{2}$$

where $\|\mathbf{x} - \mathbf{u}\|$ denotes a norm or the distance function defined for the points $\mathbf{x}$ and $\mathbf{u}$ in d-dimensional space.

Factor h_n is called the smoothing factor depending on number of observations n.

Let us mention that we have not any assumptions neither on the shape of unknown function (like e.g. in the spline methods or linear regression) nor on a mathematical formula with a certain set of parameters to be found.

The domain area D (the space where the function R is defined) has been partitioned into n disjunctive sub-spaces D_i and the measurement points $\mathbf{x}_i$ are chosen from D_i, i.e.: $\mathbf{x}_i \in D_i$. For instance, in unidimensional case let the $D = [0,1]$, then $\cup D_i = [0, 1]$, $D_i \cap D_j = \emptyset$ for $i \neq j$, the points x_i are chosen from D_i, i.e.: $x_i \in D_i$.

The set of input values $\mathbf{x}_i$ (independent variable in the model (1) are chosen in the process of collecting data, e.g. sampled equally distributed values of ECG signal in time domain, or stock exchange information, or internet activity on specified TCP/IP port of the web or ftp server logs recorded in time, for instance. This data points should provide a balanced representation of function R in the domain D. The standard assumption in theorems on convergence is that the $max\,|D_i|$ (maximum size in some measure of D_i) tends to zero if n tends to infinity (see e.g. [11–13]). We may suppose that in the set of pairs $(\mathbf{x}_i, \mathbf{y}_i)$ there is present the information on essential properties of function R, like its smoothness.

The nonparametric approach to application of estimation of unknown functions and their derivatives was previously proposed and studied in the univariate case in e.g. [14,15], and recently in [29–31]. In the next subsection, we present a detailed study of the unidimensional problem of the estimation of functions and their derivatives by the kernel method.

3.1 The Unidimensional Case of the Algorithm

The kernel function $\mathbf{K}$ in unidimensional case $K(.)$ is defined as follows:

$$K(t) = \begin{cases} K(t) = 0 & \text{for } t \in (-\tau, \tau), \tau > 0 \\ \int_{-\tau}^{\tau} K(t)dt = 1 \\ |K(t)| < \infty \end{cases} \qquad (3)$$

In our proposition we will use the kernel based on the trigonometric cosine function in the form:

$$K(t) = \begin{cases} \frac{\pi}{4}\cos\left(\frac{\pi}{2}t\right) & \text{for } t \in (-1, 1) \\ 0 & \text{otherwise} \end{cases} \qquad (4)$$

In the sequel we propose the algorithm for the estimation of the derivatives of order k in the unidimensional case:

$$\hat{R}^{(k)}(x) = h_n^{-1} \sum_{i=1}^{n} y_i \int_{D_i} K^{(k)}\left(\frac{x-u}{h_n}\right) du \qquad (5)$$

Of course, the kernel $K(.)$ must be the k-th order differentiable function, the trigonometric kernel is fulfilling this condition.

To assess the dynamics of changes in any function, the course of its first derivative is tested. The more rapid the change occurs - the higher the first derivative. The steeper the slope - the larger the tangent to the horizon surface at a given point. As a conclusion from these facts let us propose as a detector of abrupt changes to use the nonparametric estimator of the derivatives described previously. The integral version of nonparametric kernel estimation algorithms (2), using the Parzen kernel (3), enables not only estimation of the value of the desired regression function, but also the estimation of the value of its first derivative and higher order derivatives in the presence of the probabilistic noise, too.

The appropriate strategy using the estimates of the first and the second derivatives of R for edge detection is proposed as follows. From the first derivative the thresholding strategy detects jumps in function R, however, applying the second derivative and finding the zero values leads to detecting edges directly.

There are performed a series of simulations showing how this method works. In our simulations we used the testing functions similar to those proposed by Romani et al. in [10] (slightly modified) in the form:

$$f(x) = \begin{cases} (1+x)^6 - 2 & for\ 0 \leq x < 0.16 \\ (1-x)^4 + 1 & for\ 0.16 \leq x < 0.33 \\ (2+x)^3 + 12.5 & for\ 0.33 \leq x < 0.5 \\ \sin(30x - 2) & for\ 0.5 \leq x < 0.66 \\ -x + 0.5 & for\ 0.66 \leq x < 0.83 \\ x^2 & for\ 0.83 \leq x \leq 1 \end{cases} \tag{6}$$

Exemplary results are presented in Fig. 1. in two columns: the left concerning the case with no additive noise and the right, the case with additive noise. Diagrams show the original function (6) (the black solid line) and its nonparametric estimates (blue points and line). Red pluses on each diagram represent the noised measurements (at the left noise is zero). In the second row, there are shown the estimates of the first derivatives in both cases (no noise and noised). The maxima of the first derivatives mean the points of possible jumps or abrupt changes. In the third row, we have the second derivatives. By observing the zeros of this function in relation to the maxima of the first derivative we may figure out at which points the jumps have occurred.

Let us note that the nonparametric algorithm of the Parzen kernel type presented here has the smoothing properties depending on the parameter h_n. The choice of its value plays an important role in the interpretation of results. The bigger the h_n the bigger the level of smoothness, then detection at which point the jump occurred is more difficult. Otherwise, a too small value of h_n causes higher oscillations of the estimates of the derivatives and, simultaneously, the presence of more sharp peaks of the first derivative.

3.2   The Multidimensional Development of the Algorithm

In this subsection, we propose a draft of the multidimensional extension of the nonparametric method of edge detection.

In the multidimensional case there are two commonly used approaches:

– the radial kernel (using e.g. the norm in Euclidean sense) given by:

$$\mathbf{K}(\mathbf{u}) = c \cdot \sqrt{\mathbf{u}^T \mathbf{u}} \tag{7}$$

– the product kernel given by:

$$\mathbf{K}(\mathbf{x}, \mathbf{u}, h_n) = \prod_{p=1}^{d} K\left(\frac{x_p - u_p}{h_n}\right) \tag{8}$$

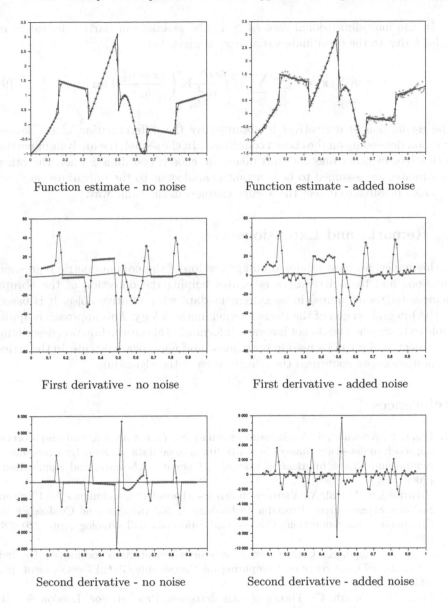

Fig. 1. Simulation example - function defined by (6)

The computationally more efficient is the radial kernel, but the simplicity and ease of application of product kernels make them more preferred in practice, particularly when differentiation is needed. We use the product kernel in this paper.

In the multidimensional case ($d > 1$) the estimate of partial derivative of order k due to the coordinate variable x_j is given by:

$$\hat{R}_{x_j}^{(k)}(\mathbf{x}) = h_n^{-d} \sum_{i=1}^{n} y_i \int_{D_i} \frac{\partial^k}{\partial x_j^k} \mathbf{K} \left(\frac{\|\mathbf{x} - \mathbf{u}\|}{h_n} \right) d\mathbf{u} \tag{9}$$

The estimation of derivatives is obtained by the differentiation of the kernel function depending on the chosen coordinate. In the sequel, the analysis of partial derivatives of order one and two taken for chosen coordinate when the other coordinates are assumed to be constant is analogous to the univariate case and it is also possible to detect the abrupt changes in the same way.

4   Remarks and Extensions

In this paper, we have proposed an application of the nonparametric regression functions and their derivatives estimates helping the detection of the abrupt changes (edges or jumps) in measurement data with additive noise. It is based on the integral version of the Parzen kernel methodology. This approach is applicable to tasks when we do not have any information about the function describing the object, and it can be used in both linear and non-linear systems. In the series of simulations we confirmed the effectiveness of the algorithm.

References

1. Dasu, T., Krishnan, S., Venkatasubramanian, S., Yi, K.: An information-theoretic approach to detecting changes in multi-dimensional data streams. In: Proceedings Symposium on the Interface of Statistics, Computing Science, and Applications (2006)
2. Bhardwaj, S., Mittal, A.: A survey on various edge detector techniques. In: Elseiver, SciVerse ScienceDirect, Procedia Technology 4, 2nd International Conference on Computer, Communication, Control and Information Technology, pp. 220–226 (2012)
3. Singh, S., Singh, R.: Comparison of various edge detection techniques. In: 2nd International Conference on Computing for Sustainable Global Development, pp. 393–396 (2015)
4. Marr, D., Hildreth, C.: Theory of edge detection. Proc. R. Soc. London Ser. B. **207**, 187–217 (1980)
5. Pratt, W.K.: Digital Image Processing, 4th edn. John Wiley Inc., Hoboken (2007)
6. Canny, J.F.: A computational approach to edge detection. IEEE Trans. PAMI. **8**(6), 679–698 (1986)
7. Kullback, S., Leibler, R.A.: On information and sufficiency. Ann. Math. Stat. **22**(1), 79–86 (1951)
8. Corder, G.W., Foreman, D.I.: Nonparametric Statistics: A Step-by-Step Approach. Wiley, Hoboken (2014)
9. Faithfull, W.J., Rodríguez, J.J., Kuncheva, L.I.: Combining univariate approaches for ensemble change detection in multivariate data. Inf. Fusion **45**, 202–214 (2019)

10. Romani, L., Rossini, M., Schenone, D.: Edge detection methods based on RBF interpolation. J. Comput. Appl. Math. **349**(15), 532–547 (2019)
11. Gasser, T., Müller, H.-G.: Kernel estimation of regression functions. In: Gasser, T., Rosenblatt, M. (eds.) Smoothing Techniques for Curve Estimation. LNM, vol. 757, pp. 23–68. Springer, Heidelberg (1979). https://doi.org/10.1007/BFb0098489
12. Gałkowski, T., Rutkowski, L.: Nonparametric recovery of multivariate functions with applications to system identification. In: Proceedings of the IEEE, Vol. 73, pp. 942–943, New York (1985)
13. Gałkowski, T., Rutkowski, L.: Nonparametric fitting of multivariable functions. IEEE Trans. Autom. Control **AC–31**, 785–787 (1986)
14. Gałkowski, T.: On nonparametric fitting of higher order functions derivatives by the kernel method - a simulation study. In: Proceedings of the 5-th International Symposium on Applied Stochastic Models and data Analysis, Granada, Spain, pp. 230–242 (1991)
15. Gasser, T., Muller, H.-G.: Estimating regression functions and their derivatives by the kernel method. Scand. J. Stat. **11**(3), 171–185 (1984)
16. Lam, M.W.Y.: One-match-ahead forecasting in two-team sports with stacked Bayesian regressions. J. Artif. Intell. Soft Comput. Res. **8**(3), 159–171 (2018). https://doi.org/10.1515/jaiscr-2018-0011
17. Davis, J.J., Lin, C.-T., Gillett, G., Kozma, R.: An integrative approach to analyze EEG signals and human brain dynamics in different cognitive states. J. Artif. Intell. Soft Comput. Res. **7**(4), 287–299 (2017). https://doi.org/10.1515/jaiscr-2017-0020
18. Tezuka, T., Claramunt, C.: Kernel analysis for estimating the connectivity of a network with event sequences. J. Artif. Intell. Soft Comput. Res. **7**(1), 17–31 (2017). https://doi.org/10.1515/jaiscr-2017-0002
19. Devi, V.S., Meena, L.: Parallel MCNN (PMCNN) with application to prototype selection on large and streaming data. J. Artif. Intell. Soft Comput. Res. **7**(3), 155–169 (2017). https://doi.org/10.1515/jaiscr-2017-0011
20. Rivero, C.R., Pucheta, J., Laboret, S., Sauchelli, V., Patiño, D.: Energy associated tuning method for short-term series forecasting by complete and incomplete datasets. J. Artif. Intell. Soft Comput. Res. **7**(1), 5–16 (2017). https://doi.org/10.1515/jaiscr-2017-0001
21. Łapa, K., Cpałka, K., Przybył, A., Grzanek, K.: Negative space-based population initialization algorithm (NSPIA). In: Rutkowski, L., Scherer, R., Korytkowski, M., Pedrycz, W., Tadeusiewicz, R., Zurada, J.M. (eds.) ICAISC 2018. LNCS (LNAI), vol. 10841, pp. 449–461. Springer, Cham (2018). https://doi.org/10.1007/978-3-319-91253-0_42
22. Łapa, K., Cpałka, K., Przybył, A.: Genetic programming algorithm for designing of control systems. Inf. Technol. Control **47**(5), 668–683 (2018)
23. Grycuk, R., Scherer, R., Gabryel, M.: New image descriptor from edge detector and blob extractor. J. Appl. Math. Comput. Mech. **14**(4), 31–39 (2015)
24. Grycuk, R., Knop, M., Mandal, S.: Video key frame detection based on surf algorithm. In: Rutkowski, L., Korytkowski, M., Scherer, R., Tadeusiewicz, R., Zadeh, L.A., Zurada, J.M. (eds.) ICAISC 2015. LNCS (LNAI), vol. 9119, pp. 566–576. Springer, Cham (2015). https://doi.org/10.1007/978-3-319-19324-3_50
25. Grycuk, R., Gabryel, M., Scherer, M., Voloshynovskiy, S.: Image descriptor based on edge detection and crawler algorithm. In: Rutkowski, L., Korytkowski, M., Scherer, R., Tadeusiewicz, R., Zadeh, L.A., Zurada, J.M. (eds.) ICAISC 2016. LNCS (LNAI), vol. 9693, pp. 647–659. Springer, Cham (2016). https://doi.org/10.1007/978-3-319-39384-1_57

26. Cpałka, K., Rutkowski, L.: Evolutionary learning of flexible neuro-fuzzy systems. In: Proceedings of the 2008 IEEE International Conference on Fuzzy Systems (IEEE World Congress on Computational Intelligence, WCCI 2008), Hong Kong, CD, 1–6 June, pp. 969–975 (2008)

27. Rutkowski, T., Romanowski, J., Woldan, P., Staszewski, P., Nielek, R., Rutkowski, L.: A content-based recommendation system using neuro-fuzzy approach. In: 2018 FUZZ-IEEE, pp. 1–8 (2018)

28. Rutkowski, T., Romanowski, J., Woldan, P., Staszewski, P., Nielek, R.: Towards interpretability of the movie recommender based on a neuro-fuzzy approach. In: Rutkowski, L., Scherer, R., Korytkowski, M., Pedrycz, W., Tadeusiewicz, R., Zurada, J.M. (eds.) ICAISC 2018. LNCS (LNAI), vol. 10842, pp. 752–762. Springer, Cham (2018). https://doi.org/10.1007/978-3-319-91262-2_66

29. Duda, P., Jaworski, M., Rutkowski, L.: Convergent time-varying regression models for data streams: tracking concept drift by the recursive parzen-based generalized regression neural networks. Int. J. Neural Syst. **28**(2), 1750048 (2018)

30. Duda, P., Jaworski, M., Rutkowski, L.: Knowledge discovery in data streams with the orthogonal series-based generalized regression neural networks. Inf. Sci. **460–461**, 497–518 (2018)

31. Duda, P., Rutkowski, L., Jaworski, M., Rutkowska, D.: On the Parzen kernel-based probability density function learning procedures over time-varying streaming data with applications to pattern classification. IEEE Trans. Cybern. 1–14 (2018). https://doi.org/10.1109/TCYB.2018.2877611

32. Jaworski, M., Duda, P., Rutkowski, L.: New splitting criteria for decision trees in stationary data streams. IEEE Trans. Neural Netw. Learn. Syst. **29**(6), 2516–2529 (2018)

33. Pietruczuk, L., Rutkowski, L., Jaworski, M., Duda, P.: How to adjust an ensemble size in stream data mining? Inf. Sci. **381**(C), 46–54 (2017)

34. Rutkowski, L., Pietruczuk, L., Duda, P., Jaworski, M.: Decision trees for mining data streams based on the McDiarmid's bound. IEEE Trans. Knowl. Data Eng. **25**(6), 1272–1279 (2013)

35. Rutkowski, L., Jaworski, M., Pietruczuk, L., Duda, P.: Decision trees for mining data streams based on the gaussian approximation. IEEE Trans. Knowl. Data Eng. **26**(1), 108–119 (2014)

36. Rutkowski, L., Jaworski, M., Pietruczuk, L., Duda, P.: The CART decision tree for mining data streams. Inf. Sci. **266**, 1–15 (2014)

37. Rutkowski, L., Jaworski, M., Pietruczuk, L., Duda, P.: A new method for data stream mining based on the misclassification error. IEEE Trans. Neural Netw. Learn. Syst. **26**(5), 1048–1059 (2015)

38. Rutkowski, L., Jaworski, M., Duda, P.: Stream Data Mining: Algorithms and Their Probabilistic Properties. Springer, Heidelberg (2019). https://doi.org/10.1007/978-3-030-13962-9

Associative Pattern Matching and Inference Using Associative Graph Data Structures

Adrian Horzyk[1]([⊠]) [iD] and Agata Czajkowska[2]

[1] AGH University of Science and Technology,
Mickiewicza Av. 30, 30-059 Krakow, Poland
horzyk@agh.edu.pl
[2] Warsaw University of Technology, Koszykowa 75, 00-662 Warsaw, Poland
acczajkowska@gmail.com

Abstract. Inference on the still growing amount of data is a challenging problem that must be solved to operate efficiently and mine Big Data sources successfully and in a sensible time. This paper introduces a new inference method based on associative recalling of data and their relationships stored in associative graph data structures (AGDS) used for pattern matching for given criteria. These structures represent a richer set of relationships than popular tabular structures do because of their natural limitations. They recall relationships and related data faster than the time-consuming search algorithms based on many loops and conditions on tabular structures. It explains why brain processes trigger information so quickly, outperforming solution based on the Turing Machine and contemporary fast processors. The presented associative inference can work in constant time thanks to the specific data organization, access and direct representation of more relationships in AGDS structures than in the commonly used tabular structures.

Keywords: Associative pattern matching · Associative inference ·
Data access · Associative graph data structures · AVB+trees · Big Data ·
Neural networks

1 Introduction

Fast inference about collected data is crucial for making right decisions. The more data we have, the bigger problems come up with data mining and decision making because we need to analyze data to choose the right things or decide about a matter that is considered [4]. We need to find out important relationships that control processes or influence their maintenance. Therefore, the data and relations must be stored in such a form that is easy and fast to be searched through, and retrieve the demanded information.

For many years, we focused on data: data collecting, data storing, data sorting, data search algorithms, databases, database management systems, data mining, etc., but the real goal was to find out valuable relationships between data. The focus on data instead of their relationships limits the computational abilities and efficiency of many contemporary solutions, methods, and approaches. To get demanded goals faster, we

© Springer Nature Switzerland AG 2019
L. Rutkowski et al. (Eds.): ICAISC 2019, LNAI 11509, pp. 371–383, 2019.
https://doi.org/10.1007/978-3-030-20915-5_34

should collect, store and mine relationships with the same attention as data or even more because pure data without relationships are worthless. Hence, we should focus much more on efficient relation storing, relation mining, and relation discovery as important goals of future research in artificial intelligence and knowledge engineering.

Our brains are daily fed up with a huge amount of information and remember the most relevant objects, their classes, and relationships that go along with our needs. They also automatically find various relationships and implement them to similar objects. This process expands our intelligence and knowledge about the world. We can ask, how it is possible that so slowly working biological neurons can find out various relationships or conclude so quickly? Our brains cannot look through a huge amount of data in the manner our computers do and cannot store the big sets of precise values that define objects like data tables. The clue to answering this question must be hidden in the neuronal structure of our brains, and the specific way real neurons work.

This work presents an associative inference algorithm for pattern matching that can be implemented in the brain-inspired associative graph data structures (AGDS) [7–9]. These structures allow storing many relationships between data and objects using direct or indirect connections between nodes. In consequence, we do not need to search for the demanded relationships in many loops as contemporary algorithms on data tables do, but we can find them out quickly. Therefore, we use the AGDS as a data-relation structure, focusing on the relationships rather than on the stored data. The data are also important, but the data storage mechanism of AGDS structures is determined by the relationships that link data appropriately. New relationships between the stored data or objects (coming out from the data analyses and processing) can be easily stored in the AGDS structure to expand the further inference processes. This mechanism is inspired by the associative processes that take place in brains. Whereas other approaches to the construction of associative memories try to associate objects in schema one-to-one, one-to-many or many-to-many [12], the AGDS graphs associate various kinds of objects and their features context-sensitively and with the adaptable strength taking into accounts various kinds of associations [7–9]. This paper presents the use of AGDS structures for associative inferences which resemble the data processing made by neural networks. It will be presented together with some examples and comparisons to similar inferences made by k nearest neighbors [2, 9, 13, 14].

2 Associative Graph Data Structures

Associative Graph Data Structures (AGDS) first introduced in [7] were developed to reproduce the natural abilities of real brains to store various relationships between data and objects represented by neurons. The brain structure is a complex graph of neurons connected to other neurons, various receptors, and actuators. Each neuron can represent a group of time-spread combinations of input stimuli which activate it or make it spiking [10, 11]. Thus, the related input data (supplied by the receptors or neurons) or already represented objects (by other neurons) can stimulate connected neurons and make them active (spiking) if only the stimulations are frequent, strong enough, and consolidated in time to achieve their activation thresholds. We do not expect that all connected neurons will be activated by the input stimuli but only those neurons which are mostly related to the input stimuli. When real neurons spike in close time successions, associations (represented by the connections) between data and objects (represented by the activated neurons) are established or reinforced [11, 15]. These associations can represent various relationships such as similarity, sequence, chronology, defining of more complex objects etc. This simple mechanism available in real neurons allows modeling the world and the creatures equipped with networks of such neurons behaving intelligently. The AGDS structures do not model real neurons but only their structure which consists of nodes representing input data or objects defined on their basis and connections representing relationships between them. This associative representation of data and objects aggregates and counts up all duplicates of values and objects in a simplistic form. The AGDS also connects values according to their similarity and order or relationships to objects which are defined by these values. It allows for a fast finding of relationships between objects or values, data mining, and various inferences.

AGDS structures weigh the stored relationships, and the weights define the strengths of associations between the objects represented by the connected nodes. These weights are used in the inference process to appropriately stimulate other nodes and express the associative strength between input data defining search conditions (source) and the output data representing results (goals). We define results in terms of the confidence of the compliance of the results with the assumptions and input conditions. For example, we can find the best candidates for the presented job offer or the best job offer for the candidate taking into account various criteria with different strengths.

AGDS structures can be enriched by the self-sorting, self-aggregative, and self-balancing AVB+trees which accelerate data access. The AVB+trees [8] aggregate and count up all duplicated values of each input attribute separately, automatically sort and connect nodes representing the unique values of each attribute, and provide access to all stored data in logarithmic time of the number of unique values. This time is always smaller or equal the number of logarithmic time of the number of all objects of the (training) dataset. Hence, for real datasets, we usually get access in constant time as described in [9, 11]. The aggregative mechanism of AVB+trees perfectly matches the aggregative mechanism of AGDS structures. Thus, AVB+trees have been combined with AGDS structures to accelerate associative inferences presented in this paper.

3 Associative Inference

Inferences are typically defined as some steps in reasoning – moving from premises to logical consequences [3]. An inference process is usually defined on the basis of some logical approaches like deduction, induction, or abduction. In computer science, inference and reasoning systems are software systems that generate conclusions from available knowledge using logical techniques or computational intelligence methods. In this paper, inferences will be defined on the basis of the associative mechanisms inspired by the way biological neurons develop their structures and work in the network.

The inference steps are many times determined by the appropriate matching mechanisms which allow selecting the most suitable objects for further inferences and reasoning steps. For the given search criteria, we have to find objects that meet those criteria and sort them according to the degree of their matches. We can use a modified k nearest neighbors (kNN) method [2, 9, 14] to find the objects that are closest in space to the given criteria, find the most frequently matching patterns using an Apriori method [1, 13], or use various neural networks or fuzzy systems [6, 14]. Many of these methods are computationally inefficient especially when the matching criteria are wide, and those methods must be run many times for the same data to get results. We also need to define a numerical measure for all non-numerical attributes if we want to use other similar values which do not exactly match the input criteria. Our brains use the gained knowledge (based on associations which define correlations) to automatically use similar features or objects in the inference steps and reasoning.

In this work, the matching process searches for the strongest associated objects with input criteria. We start the matching process from the data or objects that meet the input criteria and go along the defined relationships, computing the associative strengths of other data or objects represented by the connected nodes until we compute association strength of the objects representing the answer of the network. First, we need to define input data and the goals that should be achieved during the inference process. The input data will be represented by the source nodes and the goals by the destination nodes in the associative structure. The input data initially set up the associative reasoning system and start computing associative strengths of connected nodes. The goal is achieved when the destination nodes representing these goals are activated.

Each AGDS node can be in an open, active, or closed state for the performed inference operation. In the beginning, all nodes are open and can be closed only once per a single inference operation. To perform associative inference operation, each AGDS node n consists of two extra parameters: a charging level x_n and a number θ_n of incoming charging stimuli which the node must receive to switch its state. For the nodes storing simple values such as a boolean, number, or string, this threshold level (θ_n) is always 1, i.e. a single stimulus is enough to activate this node. In the open state, the node can be stimulated and charged until the number s_n of stimuli achieves its threshold level θ_n. Then, the node becomes active and immediately forward its charging level x to all connected nodes which are still in the open state. After the stimuli are sent, the node switches to the closed state and becomes insensitive for any next stimuli until the end of the currently running inference process. The closed state reproduces absolute refraction of real neurons and allows to control the inference process in the graph structure to avoid looping of the stimuli. It resembles the behavior of real neurons [11, 14], but real neurons do not define a number of input stimuli to become active. Instead of this, they use activation thresholds that react to the charging levels of neurons.

The associative inference process is an inference process that uses associations between values or objects stored in an associative structure like AGDS. This process can be very quick because the related values and objects are directly or close indirectly connected in this structure, so we do not waste time searching for the related data. AGDS nodes can be charged different numbers of times and with a different strength. In this process, we move from node to node along the connections, charging connected nodes in a similar way as in artificial neural networks of the first and second generations, but this process takes place in a graph of nodes, not in a one-way neural network. The input stimuli can come in different time, and their strengths are added during a single inference process. Each input stimulus can have different strength x_k and is weighted by the connection weight w_k. The charging level x of the internally stimulated node n is defined as a weighted sum:

$$x_n = \sum_{k=1}^{s_n} x_k \cdot w_k \tag{1}$$

where x_k is an internal stimulus of another node that is equal to its charging level, and s_n is a number of input stimuli during the running inference process. When the number s_n of input stimuli achieves its threshold level θ_n, the node becomes active and the computed charging level x_n is forwarded to the connected nodes in the open state.

An edge between two nodes can be either reciprocal or directed. Reciprocal edges are created between value nodes $V_i^{a^k}$ and $V_j^{a^k}$ representing similar values $v_i^{a^k}$ and $v_j^{a^k}$ of the same attribute a^k and forward stimuli in both directions with the same weight:

$$w_{v_i^{a^k}, v_j^{a^k}} = 1 - \frac{\left| v_i^{a^k} - v_j^{a^k} \right|}{r^{a^k}} \tag{2}$$

where $v_i^{a^k}, v_j^{a^k}$ are neighbor values in the range of adjacent value nodes of the attribute a^k, $r^{a^k} = v_{max}^{a^k} - v_{min}^{a^k}$ is a variation range of values of the attribute a^k. Values of each attribute are represented by an AVB+tree [8] to provide high search efficiency.

Directed edges connect value nodes and object nodes or object nodes between each other. They forward the stimuli in one way only. The weight of the edge for the signal passing from the value node $V_i^{a^k}$ to the object node O_n can be calculated after:

$$w_{v_i^{a^k}, O_n} = \frac{1}{\theta_n} \tag{3}$$

where θ_n is the number of values and objects that define the object nodes O_n and activate this node. The weight of the edge for the signal passing from the defining object node O_m to the object node O_n can be calculated after:

$$w_{O_m, O_n} = \frac{1}{\theta_n} \tag{4}$$

The stimuli passing through the edge in the opposite direction (from the object node to the defining value node or object node) are weighted by 1:

$$w_{O_n, v_i^{a^k}} = 1, \; w_{O_n, O_m} = 1 \tag{5}$$

The associative inference on the AGDS structure performs a multithread operation on multiple parameters. The order of the operations is determined by a BFS tree [5] spanned over the nodes in the open state. The BFS search algorithm does not go through all AGDS nodes, but it gradually stretches the BFS tree over the mostly associated nodes starting from the node defining input criteria and finishing in the nodes representing results. Each inference operation has the pessimistic time complexity $O(|V| + |E|)$, where $|V|$ is the number of vertexes in a graph and $|E|$ is the number of edges, when computations are performed sequentially. It is usually computed in constant time when computed in parallel because all connected nodes in the open state can be updated simultaneously.

The first step of the associative inference operation starts in a single question node. Next, the destination nodes are marked for sending their association strengths out of the network as an answer to the given question. The question node is a node which represents the question that the inference operation should answer. The question node is directly connected to source nodes, which define the matching criteria that should be satisfied by the searched solution, i.e. the nodes representing the answer. The connection strength of the edges between the question node and the source nodes reproduce the importance of the matching criteria. The set of the destination nodes defines an answer to the question, i.e. the goal of the inference.

The associative inference process in AGDS graph networks starts from the question node that is stimulated by one, immediately changing its state to active and stimulating the connected source nodes. The input criteria can be defined with different priorities. The more important the criteria are, the higher their strengths are. The strengths of desired criteria should be positive, conversely to undesirable ones which the solution should not be related to. These strengths define the weights between the question node and the source nodes. In effect, the source nodes are charged to the levels equal to these strengths. Then all source nodes become active. They stimulate connected open nodes and switch to the closed state. The source nodes are connected to various nodes defining other similar values and associated objects, so the inference process can start to propagate stimuli over the AGDS graph in the BFS order until all or a demanded number of the destination nodes become active. The BFS algorithm [5] conducts stimulations of other open nodes in the right order, starting from the directly connected nodes to the source nodes, and moving away to more distant open nodes, until the destination nodes are achieved. Each activated destination node sends its charging level (association strength) out of the graph as its matching level to the input criteria. On the basis of the matching levels sent by the activated destination nodes, the given question could be answered, and the mostly matching patterns are used in the final answer.

4   Examples of Associative Inference and Experiments

4.1   A Sample of Searching for the Best Candidates

Assume that a software company wants to extend its development team by hiring a new .net developer. The set of requirements (input criteria) consists of technical, personal, and language skills that the ideal candidate should have. There is given the minimum experience time, minimum education level, timework type, salary, etc. which can be required or provided for a demanded new employee. For the stated fields of interest and the skills within those fields, their importance has been described by the connection weights (Table 1) coming from the question node JobOffer to the source nodes representing demanded skills of the ideal candidate. An ideal candidate is an imaginary person who entirely fulfills all requirements. The more important the skill is, the higher the connection weight on the scale of one to ten is. In Table 1, five candidates with various skills had applied for the offered job represented by the set of requirements determined by the recruitment team.

To solve this problem using associative inference, an AGDS graph was constructed for the data presented in Table 1. Using the associative inference process, we find a candidate who resembles the ideal candidate the most, i.e. who is the strongest associated with the referenced requirements. The set of the destination nodes consists of all nodes representing candidates in the created AGDS graph.

Table 1. Set of requirements for .net developer job and profiles of applying candidates.

| | Technical Skills | | | PersonalSkills | | | LanguageSkills | | | Education | Sallary | Time Work | Field |
	Name	Years	Weight	Name	Level	Weight	Name	Level	Weight	Level		Type	Importance
Job Offer	C# Entity Framwork T-SQL Cloud dev	≥3 ≥3 ≥2 ≥1	(10/10) (9/10) (8/10) (6/10)	Communication skills Ability to work under pressure Decision making	60%-80% 80%-100% 60%-80%	(8/10) (10/10) (7/10)	English Polish	≥C1 ≥Native	(8/10) (7/10)	Bachelor	7500	FullTime	TechnicalSkills (9/10) PersonalSkills (8/10) LanguageSkills (5/10) Education (10/10) Sallary(10/10) TimeWorkType (10/10)
Candidate 1	C# T-SQL Cloud dev	2 3 2	X	Ability to work under pressure Communication skills	70% 80%	X	Polish	Native	X	Bachelor	7000	HalfTime	X
Candidate 2	Entity Framwork C# T-SQL	3 1 1	X	Communication skills Decision making Ability to work under pressure	70% 90% 90%	X	English	B2	X	Master	6500	FullTime	X
Candidate 3	Cloud dev C#	2 2	X	Communication skills Decision making	80% 90%	X	Polish English	Native C1	X	Master	6500	HalfTime	X
Candidate 4	Entity Framework C# T-SQL Cloud dev	1 1 2 2	X	Ability to work under pressure Decision making	70% 50%	X	English	Native	X	Bachelor	8000	FullTime	X
Candidate 5	Cloud dev Entity Framework T-SQL	1 2 3	X	Communication skills Ability to work under pressure Decision making	70% 80% 90%	X	Polish	C1	X	Bachelor	7000	HalfTime	X

In the first step of associative inference, the question node JobOffer switches its state to active, propagates the signal to the connected source nodes, and finally becomes closed. The strength of the signal propagated from the question node equals to one. The connections from the question node to the source nodes are weighted due to the priorities of skills (attributes) that should have an ideal candidate. The nodes representing skills store single-value information and have their $\theta_n = 1$. Therefore, at the moment, they receive the input stimulus, they become immediately active and start forwarding their charging levels x_n through the AGDS network stimulating connected open nodes.

Weights of the edges connecting the question node with the source nodes representing skills are equal to the importance of skill in the requirements set. For example, the weight of an edge connecting the question node JobOffer and node 3 of the attribute TechnicalSkill_EF is a product of the importance of technical skills field and Entity Framework skill ($x_3 = 0.8 \cdot 0.9 = 0.81$). Figure 1 shows the AGDS graph after the first step of the associative inference operation where the question node JobOffer stimulated source nodes defining the criteria of the ideal candidate. The nodes storing values of attributes are represented by AVB+trees and are located in the blue round boxes. The nodes representing objects are grey. The activated nodes are colored in red.

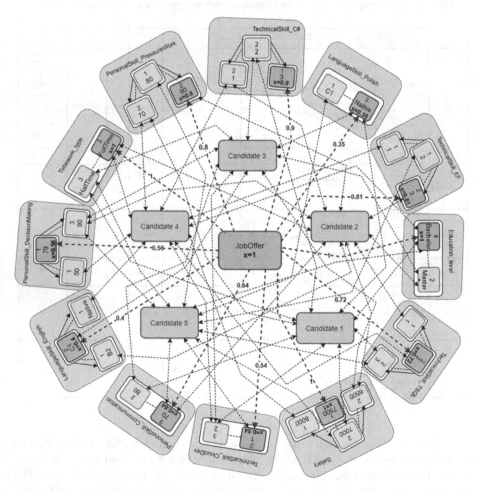

Fig. 1. State of the AGDS graph after the first step of the associative inference. (Color figure online)

In each of the following steps, the activated nodes in the previous step propagate the stimuli to the connected open nodes. The weight of an edge between two nodes reflects the associative strength between values or objects represented by these nodes. For example, if a bachelor has a satisfactory level of education for the future employee, a candidate who is a master entirely also fulfills this requirement because each master is also a bachelor. Therefore, the weight of the edge from the bachelor node to the master node equals to 1.0. Against, the weight in the opposite direction is 0.7 because averagely it takes 3.5 years to become a bachelor and 5 years to graduate from the university (3.5/5 = 0.7). The weight of the edge connecting an object node with a node representing a single value of any attribute defining this object equals to 1.0. While in the opposite direction it depends on the number of the defining values as defined in (3).

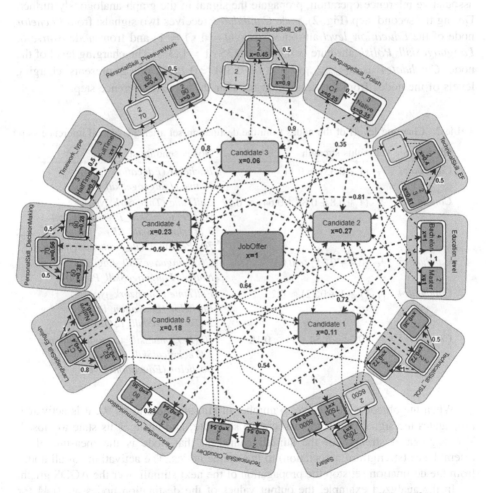

Fig. 2. The state of the AGDS graph after the second step of the associative inference.

Figure 2 shows the next inference step where the node representing value *3* of attribute *TechnicalSkill_C#* passes the stimulus to the connected node representing value 2. Because $\theta_2 = 1$ its state is changed to active, it sends its charging level x_2 further, and its state is closed. The strength of the received stimulus is $x_2 = 0.5 \cdot 0.9 = 0.45$. The node *Native* of the attribute *LanguageSkill_Polish* sends three stimuli: to the node *C1* of the same attribute, to the object node *Candidate3* and to the object node *Candidate1*. The node *C1* stores a single value ($\theta_{C1} = 1$), so after single stimulation, it is activated and closed after forwarding the stimulation. The objects *Candidate1* and *Candidate3* are defined by nine attributes each. Therefore, they need to receive nine stimuli ($\theta_{Candidate1} = 9$, $\theta_{Candidate2} = 9$) to be activated and closed. Till then object nodes sum the weighted stimuli and count a number of stimulations ($s_{Candidate1}$, $s_{Candidate2}$).

The ideal candidate is described here by 12 attributes, so the balancing aggregation factor of object nodes equals $1/12$. Other nodes, closed in the first step of the running associative inference operation, propagate the signal in the graph analogously further. During the second step (Fig. 2), node *Candidate1* receives two signals: from *Bachelor* node of the *Education_level* attribute (*strenght* $= 1 \cdot 1 = 1$) and from node *Native* of *LanguageSkill_Polish* attribute (*strenght* $= 0.35 \cdot 1 = 0.35$). The charging level of the node *Candidate1* is $x_{Candidate1} = \frac{1}{12} \cdot (1 + 0.35) \approx 0.11$. Table 2 presents charging levels of the nodes from the destination set after the second inference step.

Table 2. Charging levels of the nodes from the destination set after the second inference step.

Object node	Stimulus strength	Nodes sending signal
Candidate1	$\frac{1}{12} \cdot (1 + 0.35) \approx 0.11$	*Bachelor (Education_level)* *Native (LanguageSkill_Polish)*
Candidate2	$\frac{1}{12} \cdot (1 + 0.8 + 0.81 + 0.64) \approx 0.27$	*FullTime (Timework_type)* *90 (PersonalSkill_PressureWork)* *3 (TechnicalSkill_EF)* *70 (PersonalSkill_Communication)*
Candidate3	$\frac{1}{12} \cdot (0.4 + 0.35) \approx 0.06$	*C1 (LanguageSkill_English)* *Native (LanguageSkill_Polish)*
Candidate4	$\frac{1}{12} \cdot (1 + 1 + 0.72) \approx 0.23$	*FullTime (Timework_type)* *Bachelor (Education_level)* *2 (TechnicalSkill_TSQL)*
Candidate5	$\frac{1}{12} \cdot (0.64 + 0.54 + 1) \approx 0.18$	*70 (PersonalSkill_Communication)* *1 (TechnicalSkill_CloudDev)* *Bachelor (Education_level)*

When the object node receives a number of stimuli equal to its θ_n, it is activated, propagates the signal out of the associative structure, and changes its state to closed. The aggregated strength of the stimuli gained in that node is the measure of its resemblance (strength of association) to the source nodes. The activations of all nodes from the destination set stop the propagation of the next stimuli over the AGDS graph.

In the analyzed example, the output values of the destination nodes are 0.44 for Candidate1, 0.53 for Candidate2, 0.42 for Candidate3, 0.46 for Candidate4, and 0.48 for Candidate5. Therefore, according to performed associative inference operation, the suggested candidate for this position would be Candidate2.

4.2 Experiments on Bigger Datasets

We performed associative inference operations on bigger datasets (ranging from 10 objects and 5 attributes to 1000 objects and 20 attributes. We chose a set of three parameters: a number of candidates, minimum and maximum numbers of skills describing each candidate applying for a job offer. The analyzed values of these attributes were:

- candidatesCount ∈ {10, 50, 100, 200, 500, 1000},
- minimumSkillsPerCandidate ∈ {1, 5, 10, 15},
- maximumSkillsPerCandidate ∈ {5, 10, 15, 20}.

For the stated parameters sets, data of each candidate profile was generated by choosing a random subset of the features describing an ideal candidate. The size of subset skills is an arbitrarily chosen number in the range within stated minimum and maximum. Next, the selected size was randomly divided between language, personal, and technical skills count. Levels of language skills, percent of personal skills, and years of experience for technical ones were selected randomly for each ability. Each candidate was described by availability date, education level, and expected salary.

For the kNN method [2, 9, 13], all previously randomly selected values were normalized. In the next step, there were calculated distances between the candidates and the object describing the ideal candidate for each candidate. The distances were calculated using the Euclidean distance. Finally, to get the best matching candidates, the results were sorted by their distances. Figure 3 shows the average time spent on an associative inference operation after 50 random attempts for the given parameters sets.

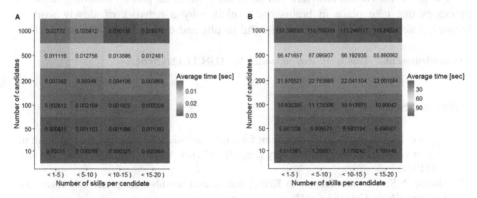

Fig. 3. Averaged time spent (in seconds) for 50 attempts for each parameter set on: (A) the associative inference operations using the AGDS, (B) the inference operations using the kNN.

In Fig. 3, the average time spent on operation is presented in two ways by the number on each tile and its color. The more blueish the color is, the more time the operation has taken. For example, calculations for 1000 candidates and 10–15 skills per candidate took 0.03 s. The layout of the results on the heatmaps means that a number of candidates is the feature diverging the results. For the group of the same count but a different number of skills describing a single candidate, the time needed for completing association operation is almost the same. The same inferences made by the KNN algorithm took a few hundred times longer time than the associative inferences made using associative graph data structures and the presented algorithm.

5 Conclusions

This paper proposed a new associative inference method for pattern matching using an associative graph data structure (AGDS) for storing data and weighted relationships. The richer set of stored relationships in comparison to classic tabular approaches allowed to quickly find associated data and express their strengths of associations to the source conditions. The presented approach used the BFS algorithm adapted to AGDS graphs to control the stimulation processes during associative inferences.

The presented approach allowed finding associated objects very fast because we only needed to go along the connections representing relationships associated with the matching conditions, compute associative strengths and search for destination objects. The other nodes in the AGDS graphs were neglected. Hence, this process is very quick especially for Big Data collections where AGDS structures consist of many nodes, but only a small part of the associated nodes are used to produce the answer. During this associative process, we do not need to loop many times along the data or evaluate many conditions like using other classic methods. Presented experiments have shown that brain-inspired associative structures storing a richer set of relations are beneficial for the presented inferences as well as can be useful in other inference tasks.

The presented AGDS structure and inference process for pattern matching resemble processes that take place in brains and explain why a network of slowly working biological neurons can produce meaningful results and draw conclusions so quickly.

Acknowledgments. This work was supported by AGH 11.11.120.612.

References

1. Agrawal, R., Srikant, R.: Fast algorithms for mining association rules. In: Proceedings of the 20th International Conference on Very Large Data Bases, VLDB, Santiago, Chile, pp. 487–499 (1994)
2. Altman, N.S.: An introduction to Kernel and nearest-neighbor nonparametric regression. Am. Stat. **46**(3), 175–185 (1992)
3. Barwise, J., Etchemendy, J.: Language, Proof and Logic. CSLI Publications, Stanford (2008)
4. Berry, M.J.A., Linoff, G.S.: Data Mining Techniques, 2nd edn. Wiley Publishing Inc., Hoboken (2004)
5. Cormen, T., Leiserson, Ch., Rivest, R., Stein, C.: Introduction to Algorithms, 3rd edn, pp. 484–504. MIT Press, Cambridge and McGraw-Hill, New York (2009)
6. Goodfellow, I., Bengio, Y., Courville, A.: Deep Learning. MIT Press, Cambridge (2016)
7. Horzyk, A.: Artificial Associative Systems and Associative Artificial Intelligence, pp. 108–111. Academic Publishing House EXIT, Warsaw (2013)

8. Horzyk, A.: Associative graph data structures with an efficient access via AVB+trees. In: 2018 11th International Conference on Human System Interaction (HSI), pp. 169–175. IEEE Xplore (2018)
9. Horzyk, A., Gołdon, K.: Associative graph data structures used for acceleration of k nearest neighbor classifiers. In: Kůrková, V., Manolopoulos, Y., Hammer, B., Iliadis, L., Maglogiannis, I. (eds.) ICANN 2018. LNCS, vol. 11139, pp. 648–658. Springer, Cham (2018). https://doi.org/10.1007/978-3-030-01418-6_64
10. Horzyk, A.: Neurons can sort data efficiently. In: Rutkowski, L., Korytkowski, M., Scherer, R., Tadeusiewicz, R., Zadeh, L., Zurada, J. (eds.) ICAISC 2017. LNCS (LNAI), vol. 10245, pp. 64–74. Springer, Cham (2017). https://doi.org/10.1007/978-3-319-59063-9_6
11. Kalat, J.W.: Biological Grounds of Psychology, 10th edn. Wadsworth Publishing, Belmont (2008)
12. Kohonen, T.: Self-Organization and Associative Memory, vol. 8. Springer, Heidelberg (2012). https://doi.org/10.1007/978-3-642-88163-3
13. Larose, D.T.: Discovering knowledge from data. In: Introduction to Data Mining. PWN, Warsaw (2006)
14. Rutkowski, L.: Techniques and Methods of Artificial Intelligence. PWN, Warsaw (2012)
15. Tadeusiewicz, R., Korbicz, J., Rutkowski, L., Duch, W. (eds.): Biomedical Engineering. Basics and Applications. Neural Networks in Biomedical Engineering, vol. 9. EXIT, Warsaw (2013)

Resource-Aware Data Stream Mining Using the Restricted Boltzmann Machine

Maciej Jaworski[1]([✉])[iD], Leszek Rutkowski[1,2][iD], Piotr Duda[1][iD], and Andrzej Cader[2,3]

[1] Institute of Computational Intelligence, Czestochowa University of Technology, Czestochowa, Poland
{maciej.jaworski,leszek.rutkowski,piotr.duda}@iisi.pcz.pl
[2] Information Technology Institute, University of Social Sciences, Łódź, Poland
acader@san.edu.pl
[3] Clark University, Worcester, MA, USA

Abstract. In this paper, we consider the problem of data stream mining with an application of the Restricted Boltzmann Machine (RBM). If the data incoming rate is very fast, an appropriate algorithm should be resource-aware and work as fast as possible. Two RBM learning algorithms are investigated, i.e. the Contrastive Divergence and the Persistent Contrastive Divergence. We test three strategies for dealing with a buffer overflow in the case of high-speed data streams: load shedding, minibatch resizing, and controlling the number of Gibbs steps in the learning algorithm. Considered approaches are verified on the real MNIST dataset which is treated as a part of a data stream.

Keywords: Restricted Boltzmann Machine · Data stream mining · Resource-awareness

1 Introduction

Due to a significant increase of digital data production in various areas of human activity, data stream mining became recently a very interesting field of research [1,2,7,16,25,36,39,41]. By data stream, we understand a possibly infinite sequence of independent data elements. The data often arrive at the system with very high speeds, therefore the parallel and distributed approaches to learning algorithms are often applied [9,10,13,50]. The subsequent data are not assumed to be identically distributed, however, there may exist some periods of time during which the data probability distribution is stationary. The changes in data distribution are known in the literature under the name 'concept drift' [51]. These changes may have different nature, e.g. sudden, incremental, gradual or recurring. A good data stream mining algorithm should be able to react to any type of changes [15,17,19,28]. In the literature the majority of data stream mining algorithms are devoted for supervised learning tasks, among which the most common seem to be decision trees [8,14,29,42–45] or ensemble methods

© Springer Nature Switzerland AG 2019
L. Rutkowski et al. (Eds.): ICAISC 2019, LNAI 11509, pp. 384–396, 2019.
https://doi.org/10.1007/978-3-030-20915-5_35

[6,32,38]. In this paper, we consider the task of unsupervised learning on data streams using Restricted Boltzmann Machines (RBM) [46], which is able to learn the probability distribution of data [21]. It was proved that given enough hidden units, the RBM can learn any probability distribution [40]. Hence, properly trained RBM can be used to detect potential concept drifts. This idea was first proposed in [26], where the RBM was applied as a tool for data distribution monitoring. The variant of this method able to deal with labeled data was presented in [27]. It is also worth mentioning that the RBM can be applied to imprecise or incomplete data, which is an issue often considered in the literature [31,37].

In this paper by data stream we understand a possibly infinite and ordered sequence of data elements $S = (X_1, X_2, \dots)$. Each data element is a D-dimensional vector

$$X_n = [X_n^1, \dots, X_n^D] \in [0; 1]^D. \tag{1}$$

We investigate the issue of learning the RBM in data stream scenario, regarding the available computational power. The RBM (as well as other neural networks) are often trained data by data using the Stochastic Gradient Descent (SGD) or using minibatches of data. These approaches are particularly suitable for the task of data stream mining. In this paper, we apply the former. The stream S is partitioned into minibatches of size B, e.g. $B \approx 20$. The t-th minibatch is defined as follows

$$S_t = (X_{Bt+1}, \dots, X_{Bt+B}) \in S. \tag{2}$$

The data streams often have very high speeds and this feature should be taken into account while designing an appropriate algorithm. An applied method has to be resource-aware [18,30,33], then it can guarantee the best trade-off between the processing time and accuracy. In this paper, we take into account two commonly used algorithms for training the RBM: the Contrastive Divergence (CD) and the Persistent Contrastive Divergence (PCD). We propose three strategies for dealing with high-speed data streams to ensure the resource-awareness of the considered learning methods: load shedding (LS), minibatch resizing (MBR) and Gibbs steps number controlling (GSNC) in the CD and the PCD algorithms.

The rest of the paper is organized as follows. In Sect. 2 the RBM is briefly recalled. The learning algorithms for RBM are discussed and analyzed from the perspective of data stream mining scenario. In Sect. 3 the three strategies for dealing with high-speed data streams are proposed. Section 4 demonstrates the results obtained in experimental simulations. Section 5 concludes the paper and discusses possibilities for future work.

2   Restricted Boltzmann Machines (RBM)

The RBM is a special case of the Boltzmann Machine [24], which is an energy-based model [35]. The RBM consists of two layers: the first one consisting of D visible neurons $\mathbf{v} = [v_1, \dots, v_D]$ and the second one with H hidden neurons $\mathbf{h} = [h_1, \dots, h_H]$. The neurons from the same layer are not connected. The hidden units are random variables from binomial distributions. The standard RMB requires visible units to be binary assuming that they are sampled from the binomial distribution as well. However, it is a common practice to allow the visible units to take continuous values from interval $[0; 1]$. This value is interpreted as the probability of turning the considered visible unit on. Nonetheless, it should be noted that the methods discussed in this paper can be naturally extended to other distributions from the exponential family [49], e.g. the Gaussian or the Poison's one. Let w_{ij} denote the weight of connection between units v_i and h_j. Let a_i and b_j be the biases of neurons v_i and h_j, respectively. Then the following energy function can be defined for the RBM

$$E(\mathbf{v}, \mathbf{h}) = -\sum_{i=1}^{D} v_i a_i - \sum_{j=1}^{H} h_j b_j - \sum_{i=1}^{D}\sum_{j=1}^{H} v_i h_j w_{ij}. \tag{3}$$

The energy function defines the probability that the RBM is in state $(\mathbf{v}, \mathbf{h})$ (this is called the Boltzmann distribution)

$$P(\mathbf{v}, \mathbf{h}) = \frac{\exp\left(-E(\mathbf{v}, \mathbf{h})\right)}{Z}, \tag{4}$$

where Z is a normalization constant also known as the 'partition function'. The aim of learning the RBM is to minimize the negative loglikelihood of data elements using a gradient descent method [23]. In data stream scenario the most suitable is the Stochastic Gradient Descent (SGD) method, which updates the weights incrementally after processing each data element. In practice, learning on minibatches of data provides more accurate results [20]. If the size of minibatches is small enough, e.g. $B \approx 20$, the procedure can still meet the rigorous time complexity requirements of data stream processing. Obviously, the RBM can be learned using any gradient-based method related to SGD, e.g. AdaGrad, Adam, SGD with momentum, etc.

A simple but tedious calculus leads to the following gradient of negative loglikelihood with respect to the weight w_{ij} (see e.g. [4])

$$\frac{\partial(-\log P(\mathbf{v}))}{\partial w_{ij}} = \sum_{\mathbf{v},\mathbf{h}} P(\mathbf{v},\mathbf{h}) v_i h_j - \sum_{\mathbf{h}} P(\mathbf{h}|\mathbf{v}) v_i h_j. \tag{5}$$

For minibatch of data (defined by (2)) we take the arithmetic average over data elements

$$\frac{\partial(-\log P(S_t))}{\partial w_{ij}} = \sum_{\mathbf{v},\mathbf{h}} P(\mathbf{v},\mathbf{h}) v_i h_j - \frac{1}{B}\sum_{n=1}^{B}\sum_{\mathbf{h}} P(\mathbf{h}|\mathbf{v} = X_{Bt+n}) v_i h_j. \tag{6}$$

The second term on the right-hand side of Eq. (6) is called the 'positive phase' and it is easy to compute. Regarding the first term, called the 'negative phase', it is even very hard to be approximated, since it requires sampling from the current model. The most popular way of obtaining an approximate data sample is to use the Markov chain Monte Carlo (MCMC) family of methods. The structure of the RBM allows computing the conditional probabilities $P(\mathbf{v}|\mathbf{h})$ (and $P(\mathbf{h}|\mathbf{v})$) relatively easy and, in consequence, sample from it. In the MCMC methods the two layers, i.e. the visible and hidden, ale alternately sampled, using the mentioned conditional probabilities. The single procedure of subsequent updating the layers is called the Gibbs step. After K steps we hope that the RBM reaches its thermal equilibrium and we obtain one set of $\mathbf{v}$ and $\mathbf{h}$ values used to estimate the 'negative phase' of gradient (6). The get a statistically significant set of samples to estimate the 'negative phase' the whole procedure have to be repeated several times. The common practice is to obtain number of samples equal to the size of the minibatch.

In this paper, we consider two algorithms for learning the RBM. Below, we briefly describe them and analyze from the data stream mining point of view. The methods of 'negative phase' estimation differ in a way of starting the MCMC.

- The Contrastive Divergence (CD) [11,22] - the MCMC starts by clamping a data element to visible layer. The experiments demonstrate that even $k = 1$ provides satisfactory results for static data [5]. The method is quite fast which makes it applicable for data streams. However, the CD can keep high values of the probability density for regions which are far away from data.
- The Persistent Contrastive Divergence (PCD) [48] - after finishing an MCMC running procedure, the values of neurons are stored in memory (they are called 'fantasy particles') and they are reused in subsequent chains as starting points. Usually, the number of particles stored in the memory is equal to the size of minibatch. The method assumes that the current model does not change much after each update of the RBM parameters.

Obviously, the highest number of Gibbs steps K results in longer processing times of data minibatches. Hence, this parameter is crucial in data stream scenario. For other methods of learning the RBM and estimating the 'negative phase' the reader is referred to [20]. In this paper, we refer to the CD and the PCD algorithms with K Gibbs steps in negative phase estimation as CDK and $PCDK$, respectively.

3   Resource-Awareness in the RBM Learning

In this section, we describe three strategies used to deal with the high-speed data stream in the CDK and PCDK algorithms for learning the RBM. We assume that the stream data arrive at the system with constant speed v, measured in data elements per some time unit tu. The processing time of the t-th minibatch of size B_t takes some time T_t. During this time, the number of data elements which should be collected in the buffer and awaiting to be processed in the next step is given by

$$N_t = vT_t. \tag{7}$$

Obviously, the number of data N_t usually does not fit to the current size of the minibatch. The most problematic is the case in which the buffer is overflow. We propose to use three strategies to solve this problem:

- load shedding (LS) - in this strategy the data which do not fit to the buffer size are simply neglected [3, 12, 47]. The minibatch size is kept equal ($B_t = B$) and the number of refused data is $\max\{N_t - B, 0\}$;
- minibatch resizing (MBR) - in this strategy the minibatch is resized to take into account all the awaiting data, i.e. $B_{t+1} = N_t$. However, we put the constraints on the minibatch size to be from the interval $[B_{min}; B_{max}]$. Hence, if N_t is lower than B_{min}, then $B_{t+1} = B_{min}$. If $N_t > B_{max}$, then $B_{t+1} = B_{max}$ and the load shedding is performed on the overflowing data;
- Gibbs steps number controlling (GSNC) - this strategy is similar to the MBR one, but additionally, the number of Gibbs steps in the estimation of negative phase is modified during learning. It is obvious that higher values of K lead to longer processing times. In the GSNC strategy, if N_t is greater than the current minibatch size B_t, then the number of Gibbs steps is reduced by one, $K_{t+1} = K_t - 1$, if $K_t > 1$. Otherwise, if $N_t < B_t$, then the number of Gibbs steps is incremented, $K_{t+1} = K_t + 1$.

4   Experimental Results

The algorithms and strategies discussed in previous sections were verified experimentally on the MNIST handwritten digit database [34]. This dataset consists of 60000 gray-scale image data of size $28 \times 28 = 784$. Although this dataset is designed for static algorithms, we treat it as a stream - the dataset it processed data by data in an incremental manner. The aim of the simulations is to investigate the trade-off between the accuracy and processing time of the considered methods and strategies.

4.1   Parameters Setting

The size of the visible layer is equal to $D = 784$, which is enforced by the dimensionality of data. There is a large set of other hyperparameters which affect the performance of the RBM, however, there is not enough space to analyze the influence of all of them. Therefore, we decided to choose their values based on some preliminary experiments. Finally, we set the hidden layer size to $H = 100$ and the learning rate to $\eta = 0.1$. We used the gradient descent learning on minibatches with momentum, where the friction parameter was set to $\gamma = 0.7$. For the MBR strategy we set $[B_{min}; B_{max}] = [20; 50]$. The starting minibatch size was set to $B_1 = 20$. We considered the CD and PCD algorithms with $K = 1$ and $K = 3$, denoted by $CD1$, $CD3$, $PCD1$, and $PCD3$, respectively. To measure the performance of algorithms, we used the reconstruction error and we applied the prequential evaluation.

4.2   Comparison of Different Strategies for Dealing with High-Speed Data Stream

First, we compare the performance of different strategies. We considered three algorithms, i.e. CD1 and PCD1, and three different speeds of data stream, i.e.

$20/tu$, $60/tu$ and $100/tu$. The results for the CD1 and the PCD1 algorithms are presented in Figs. 1 and 2, respectively.

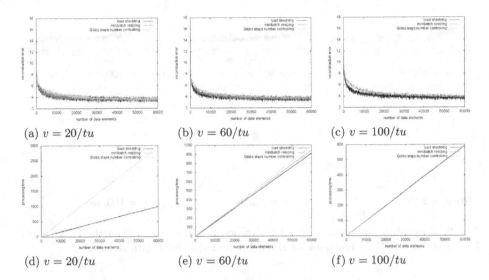

(a) $v = 20/tu$ (b) $v = 60/tu$ (c) $v = 100/tu$

(d) $v = 20/tu$ (e) $v = 60/tu$ (f) $v = 100/tu$

Fig. 1. Reconstruction error (a, b, c) and processing time (d, e, f) of the CD1 algorithm with LS, MBR, and GSNC strategies for three different speeds of data stream.

From the figures, one can conclude that the performance of all three the considered strategies in terms of reconstruction error is comparable (for high speed of data stream the GSNC strategy seems to be slightly worse at the beginning stages of data stream processing). However, the processing time for the GSNC is much longer in the case of lower speeds, which is a big disadvantage of this strategy. The LS strategy is slightly faster than the MBR one.

4.3   Comparison of Different RBM Learning Algorithms

In the next experiment, the performance of different algorithms was compared. We considered three different speeds of the data stream, i.e. $20/tu$, $60/tu$ and $100/tu$. For the LS and the MBR strategies we have taken into account the CD1, CD3, PCD1, and PCD3 algorithms. Since in the GSNC strategy the parameter K is modified during learning, the CD1 and CD3 (PCD1 and PCD3) algorithms are equivalent after several minibatches. Therefore, we consider only two algorithms named CD and PCD in this case. The results obtained for the LS, MBR, and GSNC strategies are presented in Figs. 3, 4, and 5, respectively. For the GSNC strategy, the processing times for the CD and the PCD algorithms are hardly distinguishable, we decided to not show the corresponding graph to reduce the space of the paper.

As can be seen, the performance of the algorithms from the CD family (CD1, CD3, and CD in the case of the GSNC strategy) is significantly better than for

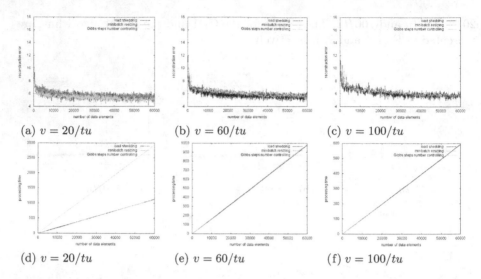

(a) $v = 20/tu$ (b) $v = 60/tu$ (c) $v = 100/tu$

(d) $v = 20/tu$ (e) $v = 60/tu$ (f) $v = 100/tu$

Fig. 2. Reconstruction error (a, b, c) and processing time (d, e, f) of the PCD1 with LS, MBR, and GSNC strategies for three different speeds of data stream.

the PCD algorithms. The reason might be that the CD learning algorithm is more suitable for reconstruction of the data using the RBM. It is probable that if the loglikelihood was used as a performance measure then the PCD algorithms would provide better results. Unfortunately, the calculations of the loglikelihood in the case of the RBM is intractable. The plots of processing time also confirm the obvious fact that the algorithms with lower K work faster. Therefore, it seems that the CD1 algorithm is the best choice if the minimalization of the reconstruction error is the aim.

4.4 Comparison of Various Algorithms and Strategies Performance for Different Data Stream Speeds

In the last experiment, we investigated how the performance of considered algorithms and strategies depend on the speed of the data stream. We analyzed the CD1 and the PCD1 algorithms with combined with all three strategies considered in this paper (as previously, for the GSNC strategy the CD1 and PCD1 become the CD and the PCD, respectively). Obtained results are shown in Fig. 6. As was expected, the reconstruction error increases with the increasing speed of the data stream. However, it seems that the LS strategy (in combination with both the CD1 and the CD3 algorithms) is the least sensitive to the changes in the data stream speed among all three considered strategies.

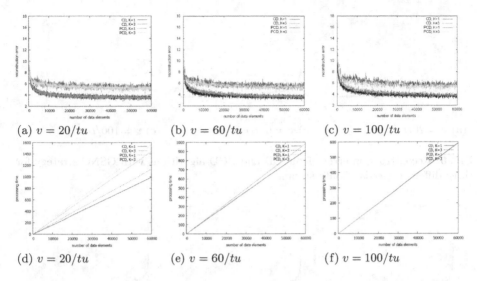

(a) $v = 20/tu$ (b) $v = 60/tu$ (c) $v = 100/tu$

(d) $v = 20/tu$ (e) $v = 60/tu$ (f) $v = 100/tu$

Fig. 3. Reconstruction error (a, b, c) and processing time (d, e, f) of the CD1, CD3, PCD1, and PCD3 algorithms with LS strategy for three different speeds of data stream.

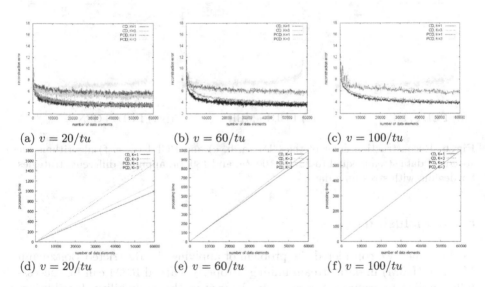

(a) $v = 20/tu$ (b) $v = 60/tu$ (c) $v = 100/tu$

(d) $v = 20/tu$ (e) $v = 60/tu$ (f) $v = 100/tu$

Fig. 4. Reconstruction error (a, b, c) and processing time (d, e, f) of the CD1, CD3, PCD1, and PCD3 algorithms with MBR strategy for three different speeds of data stream.

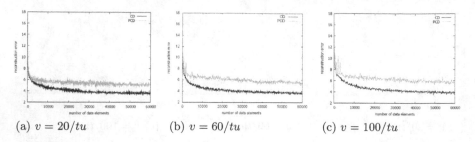

(a) $v = 20/tu$ (b) $v = 60/tu$ (c) $v = 100/tu$

Fig. 5. Reconstruction error of the CD and PCD algorithms with GSNC strategy for three different speeds of data stream.

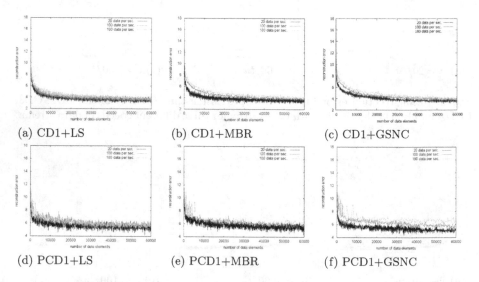

(a) CD1+LS   (b) CD1+MBR   (c) CD1+GSNC

(d) PCD1+LS   (e) PCD1+MBR   (f) PCD1+GSNC

Fig. 6. Reconstruction error of the CD1 (a, b, c) and PCD1 (d, e, f) algorithms for speeds of data stream equal to $20/tu$, $100/tu$, and $180/tu$, applying different strategies for dealing with streaming data.

5 Conclusions

In this paper, we considered the problem of applying the Restricted Boltzmann Machine (RBM) in data stream mining. Properly learned RBM can be successfully applied to monitor the possible changes in the probability distribution. However, the data stream elements are fed into the system with very high rates and this feature should be definitely taken into account while designing a proper method. An algorithm must be resource-aware to guarantee the best trade-off between accuracy and time complexity. Therefore, in this paper we proposed three strategies to modify the commonly known RBM learning methods, i.e. the Contrastive Divergence (CD) and the Persistent Contrastive Divergence (PCD), to ensure their resource-awareness. The first strategy is the load shedding - data elements which cannot be stored in the buffer are simply rejected. The second strategy is to resize the minibatch to fit the number of data currently stored in the buffer. However, the constraints on minimum and maximum values of minibatch size were put. The third strategy aims at controlling the number of Gibbs sampling steps performed in both the CD and the PCD algorithms. The strategies were verified experimentally. The numerical experiments performed on the MNIST dataset demonstrated that all strategies ensure the comparable performance of algorithms measured by the reconstruction error. However, the strategy of Gibbs steps number controlling is the most inefficient in terms of the processing time. The most effective seems to be the load shedding strategy.

Acknowledgments. This work was supported by the Polish National Science Centre under grant no. 2017/27/B/ST6/02852.

References

1. Akdeniz, E., Egrioglu, E., Bas, E., Yolcu, U.: An ARMA type Pi-Sigma artificial neural network for nonlinear time series forecasting. J. Artif. Intell. Soft Comput. Res. **8**(2), 121–132 (2018)
2. Dias de Assunçao, M., da Silva Veith, A., Buyya, R.: Distributed data stream processing and edge computing: a survey on resource elasticity and future directions. J. Netw. Comput. Appl. **103**, 1–17 (2018)
3. Babcock, B., Datar, M., Motwani, R.: Load shedding techniques for data stream systems. In: Proceedings of the 2003 Workshop on Management and Processing of Data Streams (2003)
4. Bengio, Y.: Learning deep architectures for AI. Found. Trends Mach. Learn. **2**(1), 1–127 (2009)
5. Bengio, Y., Delalleau, O.: Justifying and generalizing contrastive divergence. Neural Comput. **21**(6), 1601–1621 (2009)
6. Bertini Junior, J.R., do Carmo Nicoletti, M.: An iterative boosting-based ensemble for streaming data classification. Inf. Fusion **45**, 66–78 (2019)
7. Bifet, A.: Adaptive Stream Mining: Pattern Learning and Mining from Evolving Data Streams. Frontiers in Artificial Intelligence and Applications. IOS Press, Amsterdam, Berlin (2010)
8. Bifet, A., et al.: Extremely fast decision tree mining for evolving data streams. In: Proceedings of the 23rd ACM SIGKDD International Conference on Knowledge Discovery and Data Mining, pp. 1733–1742. ACM, New York (2017)
9. Bilski, J., Kowalczyk, B., Grzanek, K.: The parallel modification to the Levenberg-Marquardt algorithm. In: Rutkowski, L., Scherer, R., Korytkowski, M., Pedrycz, W., Tadeusiewicz, R., Zurada, J.M. (eds.) ICAISC 2018. LNCS (LNAI), vol. 10841, pp. 15–24. Springer, Cham (2018). https://doi.org/10.1007/978-3-319-91253-0_2
10. Bilski, J., Wilamowski, B.M.: Parallel learning of feedforward neural networks without error backpropagation. In: Rutkowski, L., Korytkowski, M., Scherer, R., Tadeusiewicz, R., Zadeh, L.A., Zurada, J.M. (eds.) ICAISC 2016. LNCS (LNAI), vol. 9692, pp. 57–69. Springer, Cham (2016). https://doi.org/10.1007/978-3-319-39378-0_6
11. Carreira-Perpinan, M.A., Hinton, G.E.: On contrastive divergence learning (2005)

12. Chi, Y., Wang, H., Yu, P.S.: Loadstar: load shedding in data stream mining. In: Proceedings of the International Conference on Very Large Data Bases, pp. 1302–1305 (2005)
13. Devi, V.S., Meena, L.: Parallel MCNN (PMCNN) with application to prototype selection on large and streaming data. J. Artif. Intell. Soft Comput. Res. **7**(3), 155–169 (2017)
14. Domingos, P., Hulten, G.: Mining high-speed data streams. In: Proceedings of the 6th ACM SIGKDD International Conference on Knowledge Discovery and Data Mining, pp. 71–80 (2000)
15. Duda, P., Rutkowski, L., Jaworski, M., Rutkowska, D.: On the parzen kernel-based probability density function learning procedures over time-varying streaming data with applications to pattern classification. IEEE Trans. Cybern. 1–14 (2018). https://ieeexplore.ieee.org/document/8536871
16. Duda, P., Jaworski, M., Rutkowski, L.: Convergent time-varying regression models for data streams: tracking concept drift by the recursive parzen-based generalized regression neural networks. Int. J. Neural Syst. **28**(02), 1750048 (2018)
17. Duda, P., Jaworski, M., Rutkowski, L.: Knowledge discovery in data streams with the orthogonal series-based generalized regression neural networks. Inf. Sci. **460–461**, 497–518 (2018)
18. Gaber, M.M., Krishnaswamy, S., Zaslavsky, A.B.: Resource-aware mining of data streams. J. Univ. Comput. Sci. **11**, 1440–1453 (2005)
19. Gomes, J., Gaber, M., Sousa, P., Menasalvas, E.: Mining recurring concepts in a dynamic feature space. IEEE Trans. Neural Netw. Learn. Syst. **25**(1), 95–110 (2014)
20. Goodfellow, I., Bengio, Y., Courville, A.: Deep Learning. MIT Press (2016). http://www.deeplearningbook.org
21. Hinton, G.E.: To recognize shapes, first learn to generate images. Prog. Brain Res. **165**, 535–547 (2007)
22. Hinton, G.E.: Training products of experts by minimizing contrastive divergence. Neural Comput. **14**(8), 1771–1800 (2002)
23. Hinton, G.E.: A practical guide to training restricted Boltzmann machines. In: Montavon, G., Orr, G.B., Müller, K.-R. (eds.) Neural Networks: Tricks of the Trade. LNCS, vol. 7700, pp. 599–619. Springer, Heidelberg (2012). https://doi.org/10.1007/978-3-642-35289-8_32
24. Hinton, G.E., Sejnowski, T.J., Ackley, D.H.: Boltzmann machines: constraint satisfaction networks that learn. Technical report, CMU-CS-84-119, Computer Science Department, Carnegie Mellon University, Pittsburgh, PA (1984)
25. Isokawa, T., Yamamoto, H., Nishimura, H., Yumoto, T., Kamiura, N., Matsui, N.: Complex-valued associative memories with projection and iterative learning rules. J. Artif. Intell. Soft Comput. Res. **8**(3), 237–249 (2018)
26. Jaworski, M., Duda, P., Rutkowski, L.: On applying the restricted Boltzmann machine to active concept drift detection. In: Proceedings of the 2017 IEEE Symposium Series on Computational Intelligence, Honolulu, USA, pp. 3512–3519 (2017)
27. Jaworski, M., Duda, P., Rutkowski, L.: Concept drift detection in streams of labelled data using the restricted Boltzmann machine. In: 2018 International Joint Conference on Neural Networks (IJCNN), pp. 1–7 (2018)
28. Jaworski, M.: Regression function and noise variance tracking methods for data streams with concept drift. Int. J. Appl. Math. Comput. Sci. **28**(3), 559–567 (2018)
29. Jaworski, M., Duda, P., Rutkowski, L.: New splitting criteria for decision trees in stationary data streams. IEEE Trans. Neural Netw. Learn. Syst. **29**(6), 2516–2529 (2018)

30. Jaworski, M., Pietruczuk, L., Duda, P.: On resources optimization in fuzzy clustering of data streams. In: Rutkowski, L., Korytkowski, M., Scherer, R., Tadeusiewicz, R., Zadeh, L.A., Zurada, J.M. (eds.) ICAISC 2012. LNCS (LNAI), vol. 7268, pp. 92–99. Springer, Heidelberg (2012). https://doi.org/10.1007/978-3-642-29350-4_11

31. Jordanov, I., Petrov, N., Petrozziello, A.: Classifiers accuracy improvement based on missing data imputation. J. Artif. Intell. Soft Comput. Res. **8**(1), 31–48 (2018)

32. Krawczyk, B., Cano, A.: Online ensemble learning with abstaining classifiers for drifting and noisy data streams. Appl. Soft Comput. **68**, 677–692 (2018)

33. Kumar, T., Rohil, H.: Quality assured resource aware data stream mining. Int. J. Appl. Eng. Res. **6**, 2563–2567 (2011)

34. LeCun, Y., Cortes, C.: MNIST handwritten digit database (2010). http://yann.lecun.com/exdb/mnist/

35. LeCun, Y., Huang, F.: Loss functions for discriminative training of energy-based models. In: AISTATS 2005 - Proceedings of the 10th International Workshop on Artificial Intelligence and Statistics, pp. 206–213 (2005)

36. Lemaire, V., Salperwyck, C., Bondu, A.: A survey on supervised classification on data streams. In: Zimányi, E., Kutsche, R.-D. (eds.) eBISS 2014. LNBIP, vol. 205, pp. 88–125. Springer, Cham (2015). https://doi.org/10.1007/978-3-319-17551-5_4

37. Nowicki, R.K., Starczewski, J.T.: A new method for classification of imprecise data using fuzzy rough fuzzification. Inf. Sci. **414**, 33–52 (2017)

38. Pietruczuk, L., Rutkowski, L., Jaworski, M., Duda, P.: How to adjust an ensemble size in stream data mining? Inf. Sci. **381**(C), 46–54 (2017)

39. Ramirez-Gallego, S., Krawczyk, B., García, S., Woźniak, M., Herrera, F.: A survey on data preprocessing for data stream mining: current status and future directions. Neurocomputing **239**, 39–57 (2017)

40. Roux, N.L., Bengio, Y.: Representational power of restricted Boltzmann machines and deep belief networks. Neural Comput. **20**(6), 1631–1649 (2008)

41. Rutkowski, L., Jaworski, M., Duda, P.: Stream Data Mining: Algorithms and Their Probabilistic Properties. Springer, Cham (2019). https://doi.org/10.1007/978-3-030-13962-9

42. Rutkowski, L., Jaworski, M., Pietruczuk, L., Duda, P.: The CART decision tree for mining data streams. Inf. Sci. **266**, 1–15 (2014)

43. Rutkowski, L., Jaworski, M., Pietruczuk, L., Duda, P.: Decision trees for mining data streams based on the Gaussian approximation. IEEE Trans. Knowl. Data Eng. **26**(1), 108–119 (2014)

44. Rutkowski, L., Jaworski, M., Pietruczuk, L., Duda, P.: A new method for data stream mining based on the misclassification error. IEEE Trans. Neural Netw. Learn. Syst. **26**(5), 1048–1059 (2015)

45. Rutkowski, L., Pietruczuk, L., Duda, P., Jaworski, M.: Decision trees for mining data streams based on the McDiarmid's bound. IEEE Trans. Knowl. Data Eng. **25**(6), 1272–1279 (2013)

46. Smolensky, P.: Information processing in dynamical systems: foundations of harmony theory. In: Parallel Distributed Processing: Explorations in the Microstructure of Cognition, vol. 1, pp. 194–281. MIT Press, Cambridge (1986)

47. Tatbul, N., Çetintemel, U., Zdonik, S., Cherniack, M., Stonebraker, M.: Load shedding in a data stream manager. In: Proceedings of the 29th International Conference on Very Large Data Bases, VLDB 2003, vol. 29, pp. 309–320. VLDB Endowment (2003)

48. Tieleman, T.: Training restricted Boltzmann machines using approximations to the likelihood gradient. In: Proceedings of the 25th International Conference on Machine Learning, ICML 2008, pp. 1064–1071. ACM, New York (2008)

49. Welling, M., Rosen-Zvi, M., Hinton, G.: Exponential family harmoniums with an application to information retrieval. In: Proceedings of the 17th International Conference on Neural Information Processing Systems, NIPS 2004, pp. 1481–1488. MIT Press, Cambridge (2004)
50. Zhao, Y., Liu, Q.: A continuous-time distributed algorithm for solving a class of decomposable nonconvex quadratic programming. J. Artif. Intell. Soft Comput. Res. 8(4), 283–291 (2018)
51. Zliobaite, I., Bifet, A., Pfahringer, B., Holmes, G.: Active learning with drifting streaming data. IEEE Trans. Neural Netw. Learn. Syst. 25(1), 27–39 (2014)

Fuzzy Approach for Detection
of Anomalies in Time Series

Adam Kiersztyn and Paweł Karczmarek[✉]

Institute of Computer Science, Lublin University of Technology,
ul. Nadbystrzycka 36B, 20-618 Lublin, Poland
adam.kiersztyn.pl@gmail.com, pawel.karczmarek@gmail.com

Abstract. Detecting and removing anomalies in the time series describing physical phenomena is a big challenge faced by scientists from many fields. The aim of the article is to present the assumptions of a tool for the detection of anomalies related to any issue. The proposed universal solution based on fuzzy logic and multicriteria can be applied to any time series. Through the use of aggregation of various approaches, a universal tool based on expert knowledge was obtained. The framework was tested on the energy consumption logs received from a telecommunications company and historical data from the records from the parish registers.

Keywords: Anomaly detection · Energy consumption ·
Particle swarm optimization method · Decision supporting system ·
Data aggregation

1 Introduction

The analysis of time series has been a very complex problem [4,5,15,21,26] studied for a very long time [12,23]. The analysis of time series is made on many fields of science. The study of time series deals with economists [9,10], in particular, financiers [7,16,22,25], also psychologists [6,11,18], as well as engineers [1], or sociologists [2,20]. One of the main problems in the time series is detecting anomalies. It is a very wide and complex issue [3,14,19,24], which depends on a large extent of the type of analyzed time series. The key issue is to develop a set of methods independent on the type of time series. Much attention is devoted to the detection of anomalies in the course of electricity consumption in telecommunications equipment [8,13,17,28,29]. The main goal of this study is to present fuzzy methods of detecting anomalies and to indicate potential ways of aggregating results from various independently considered approaches. We propose the use of many known methods of detecting anomalies in time series based on statistical analysis. The novelty of the method involves the use of fuzzy equivalents of classical methods and the aggregation of fuzzy results. The remainder of this research is organized as follows. Section 2 presents the description of proposed method, broken down into approaches using only the analyzed object

© Springer Nature Switzerland AG 2019
L. Rutkowski et al. (Eds.): ICAISC 2019, LNAI 11509, pp. 397–406, 2019.
https://doi.org/10.1007/978-3-030-20915-5_36

(Subsect. 2.1) and other objects similar to it (Subsect. 2.2). Selected examples of applications of the proposed model are presented in Sect. 3. The last section contains the summary and future research directions.

2   Model Description

The proposed model assumes the use of a wide spectrum of independent methods for detecting anomalies in time series. This approach works on abstract objects and can equally be used on a variety of data types. Let us assume that we have a group of objects, say $X_1, X_2, \ldots, X_n$, which can be divided according to different categories into classes. In addition, a time series $Y_{X_i, t}, t \geq 0$ is available for each object describing the course of the analyzed phenomenon. We will limit our considerations to time series with discrete time. We assume that all analyzed objects are characterized by a certain repeatability in time, which can be identified with seasonality or diurnal cycle. Let us introduce the notion used in the further part of the study. Let $y_{X_i,n}^k$ for $k = 0, 1, 2, \ldots, K; n = 1, 2, \ldots$, means the value of the analyzed series of object X_i in the $k - th$ phase of the cycle, which was read n cycles from the analyzed moment. For example, if the object is characterized by daily cycles, then $y_{X_i,5}^3$ means the reading made at three o'clock, 5 days before the analyzed moment.

2.1   Consistency at the Level of One Object

In many cases, the typical course of the time series for a single object is characterized by a certain repetition, which we will call a cycle. At the same time, several types of cycles can be defined (see Fig. 1). For simplicity, we will refer the shortest cycle of the basic cycle (daily), and subsequent cycles of complex successive levels. For the data from Fig. 1 we distinguish the basic cycle, the composite cycle of the first type (weekly cycle), and the composite cycle of the second type (annual cycle).

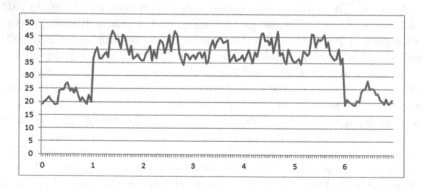

Fig. 1. Sample data with visible cycles

Consistency of Information at the Level of the Basic Cycle (Daily).
In order to analyze the data consistency of one object, it is proposed to use
methods based on moving average, median and confidence intervals. Each of the
proposed methods should be applied independently of the others, and then the
results should be aggregated. In order to increase the transparency of the record,
if it will not lead to a misunderstanding description $y^3_{X_{i,5}}$ will be replaced by y^3_5.

The most intuitive way to detect anomalies in the course of a time series is
to use the moving average and a typical area of variation based on this average.
Let

$$\overline{y}^k_N = \frac{1}{N} \sum_{n=1}^{N} y^k_n \tag{1}$$

be the average calculated from the value of the time series in the $k-th$ phase
of the cycle. Then the standard deviation is given by

$$s^k_N = \sqrt{\frac{1}{N} \sum_{n=1}^{N} \left(y^k_n - \overline{y}^k_N\right)^2} \tag{2}$$

We will say that the value of the time series is in a typical range of variation,
if

$$y^k_0 \in \left(\overline{y}^k_N - s^k_N; \overline{y}^k_N + s^k_N\right). \tag{3}$$

In the further part of the work, the markings $LN = \overline{y}^k_N - s^k_N$, $UN = \overline{y}^k_N + s^k_N$
were used to increase the clarity of the charts. In the formula 3 it is reasonable to
introduce modifications consisting in adding a weight with which the standard
deviation will be taken into account. Namely, if

$$y^k_0 \in \left(\overline{y}^k_N - \alpha s^k_N; \overline{y}^k_N + \alpha s^k_N\right), \; for \; \alpha \geq 1, \tag{4}$$

then we will say that the reading at the level of $1 - \alpha/2$ belongs to a typical area
of variation. It is advisable to perform tests for different values of the parameter
N. In addition, the arithmetic mean can be replaced by the median of N values.
Based on this type of compartment, a simple anomaly detection system is built.
The system returns the degree of membership to a set stating the detection of
anomalies. The degree of membership is determined by the formula $(\alpha - 1)/2$.
Systems based on the arithmetic average and the median for different values of
the parameter N operate independently of each other.

**Consistency of Information at Higher Levels of Granulation (Weekly,
Monthly, Yearly Cycle).** One of the ways to include typical values for weekly,
monthly or annual cycles in a typical daily course is to use the average given by
the formula

$$\overline{y}^k_0 = \frac{a \cdot \sum_{n=1}^{4} y^k_{7n} + b \cdot \sum_{n=1}^{3} y^k_{30n} + c \cdot \sum_{n=1}^{2} y^k_{365n}}{4a + 3b + 2c} \tag{5}$$

where parameters $a, b, c > 0$ minimize the value

$$s_0^k = \sqrt{\frac{\sum_{n=1}^4 \left(y_{7n}^k - \overline{y}_0^k\right)^2 + \sum_{n=1}^3 \left(y_{30n}^k - \overline{y}_0^k\right)^2 + \sum_{n=1}^2 \left(y_{365n}^k - \overline{y}_0^k\right)^2}{9}} \tag{6}$$

The factor y_{7n}^k is responsible for the day of the week, the y_{30n}^k coefficient corresponds to the day of the month, and the coefficient y_{365n}^k for the day of the year. The parameter values $a, b, c > 0$ can be obtained via the PSO method. Similarly to the previous one (see 3), a typical variability interval is created and it is checked whether the analyzed value belongs to this area. As before, the typical area of variability is considered and the weighted-average system returns the level of belonging to the range.

2.2   Consistency at the Level of Object Classes

In the case when at the same time a significant number of time series describing analogous phenomena in various objects is analyzed, it is reasonable to define classes of objects having certain common features, i.e., to enter information granules, the most reasonable and intuitive is to use fuzzy sets for class representation. Having the division of all analyzed objects into classes, one is able to analyze the coherence of the time series within individual classes.

The correlation coefficient is a typical measure of the compliance of the time series. This coefficient can be determined directly for the time series values, but also for the time series value increments. Interesting results are brought by the application of a similarity measure based on the degree of belonging of objects to particular classes [27]. In addition, in the case of very few classes of objects, it is advisable to use data aggregation before determining the correlation coefficient. One of the most intuitive methods of aggregation is the use of decile values for a given time series in a given period of time. In this case, the aggregation function takes the form

$$f\left(y_{X_i,n}^k\right) = \begin{cases} 0, & \text{if } y_{X_i,n}^k \leq d_1, \\ l, & \text{if } d_l < y_{X_i,n}^k \leq d_{l+1}, \quad l = 1, \ldots, 8, \\ 9, & \text{if } d_9 < y_{X_i,n}^k. \end{cases}$$

where $d_i, i = 1, 2, \ldots, 9$ represents successive deciles.

Having the values of correlation coefficients and other measures determining the similarity of two objects, it is possible to verify whether the course of the time series of the given object X_i in the $n - th$ primary cycle does not deviate from the norm. Within each class of objects to which the analyzed object X_i belongs, objects strongly correlated with it are determined. The set of all objects strongly correlated with object X_i are denote by $R(X_i)$. We will say that the object is coherent at the level of object if the time series value is consistent with the strongly correlated objects behavior, i.e., the value of the function

$$F(X_i) = \sum_{X_j \in R(X_i)} \rho_{i,j} \cdot sign\left(\Delta X_i, \Delta X_j\right) \tag{7}$$

is positive. The function analyzes the increments $\Delta X_i, \Delta X_j$ of time series and associates them with the correlation $\rho_{i,j}$ of historical runs of the analyzed time series. Systems using correlation coefficients calculated for raw or transformed data as a result return the value determined from the formula

$$S\left(X_i\right) = \begin{cases} 0, & if F\left(X_i\right) \geq 0, \\ \frac{|F(X_i)|}{R(X_i)} & if F\left(X_i\right) < 0 \end{cases} \tag{8}$$

which for the positive values of the function F returns zero, and for negative values the average of the values of correlation coefficients of objects behaving differently from the analyzed one.

2.3   Data Aggregation

A very important element of the proposed system is proper aggregation of results from many independent anomaly detection systems. Each system independently examines the occurrence of anomalies in the analyzed time series. As a result, a positive value indicating the significance of the detected anomaly is returned. As already mentioned, larger values of particular parameters suggest a more significant anomaly. Many functions can be used as the aggregation function. One of the most intuitive approaches is the use of sum or weighted average, where the weights of individual subsystems are determined based on expert knowledge. Aggregated value from individual subsystems should suggest the system user the appropriate response. Let us consider three approaches:

1. rigorous signals aggregation (R)
2. balanced signals aggregation (B)
3. liberal signals aggregation (L).

Again, based on expert knowledge, a different response to individual values should be suggested. The proposed rules are presented in the Table 1.

Table 1. Rules proposed for signals aggregation

Approach	Rule
R	If the aggregated signal value exceeds the value α_2, immediate intervention is recommended
R	If the aggregated signal value exceeds the value α_1, intervention is indicated
R	If the aggregated signal value does not exceed the value α_1, the object should be observed
B	If the aggregated signal value exceeds the value β_2, immediate intervention is recommended
B	If the aggregated signal value exceeds the value β_1, intervention is indicated
B	If the aggregated signal value does not exceed the value β_1, the object should be observed
L	If the aggregated signal value exceeds the value γ_2, immediate intervention is recommended
L	If the aggregated signal value exceeds the value γ_1, intervention is indicated
L	If the aggregated signal value does not exceed the value γ_1, the object should be observed

where $\alpha_2 < \alpha_1 \leq \beta_2 < \beta_1 \leq \gamma_2 < \gamma_1$ are determined on the basis of expert knowledge.

3   Examples of Applications

The general model of anomaly detection proposed in the time series literature is universal and can be used to analyze data describing various natural, economic or social phenomena. We will present a potential application in the analysis of energy consumption in telecommunications facilities and the analysis of the birth number in historical demography.

3.1   Analysis of Energy Consumption

Rapid detection of disturbances in energy consumption values is of great importance in many areas of the economy. In the case of telecommunications facilities, an anomaly in the course of a time series describing the amount of energy consumed by a single object is most often related to the improper operation of devices, which may cause failure and disruption in network operation. Therefore, telecommunications companies try to analyze the value of energy consumption in individual facilities and respond immediately to detected anomalies. In the case of the largest companies, it is typical to install smart meters in telecommunications facilities recording energy consumption at intervals of 15 min or one hour. The readout values from the example telecommunications object are shown in Fig. 2.

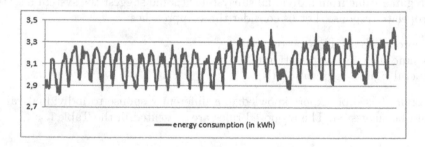

Fig. 2. Monthly energy consumption values

In the course of the analyzed time series, it is easy to distinguish between basic cycles, which in this case are daily readings of energy consumption values. For such data, one can analyze the consistency at the level of one object. The key aspect here is the availability of source data. A comparison of the value of energy consumed with typical compartments is shown in Fig. 3.

Figure 3 presents a comparison of the real level of electricity consumption with the forecasted volatility channels obtained by means of formula 3. In the case of consistency analysis at the level of object classes, one should have values of energy readings from many objects with similar technical features. Correlation values between increments of energy consumption in the analyzed object X_0 and other objects from the same class are presented in the Table 2.

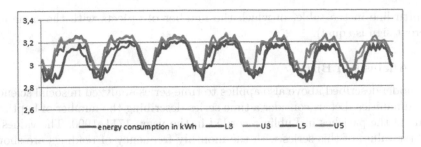

Fig. 3. Weekly energy consumption readings with typical variability ranges, for N = 3 (L3, U3) and N = 5 (L5, U5)

Table 2. Correlations between energy consumptions

Object	X_1	X_2	X_3	X_4	X_5	X_6
Correlation	0.95	0.96	0.99	0.97	0.98	0.96

The value of increments in electricity consumption (based on meter readings) in the analyzed facilities in the following hours and values of the read consistency function are presented in the Table 3.

Table 3. Increments and values of function F

X_0	X_1	X_2	X_3	X_4	X_5	X_6	$F(X_0)$
0.0013	0.0395	0.1024	−0.0817	0.0207	−0.0014	0.0388	1.87
−0.07	−0.1167	0.0056	−0.0802	−0.0057	−0.0309	−0.0684	3.89
−0.0713	0.044	−0.0653	0.0027	−0.0701	−0.0668	−0.0042	1.93
−0.0617	−0.0005	−0.0811	−0.0727	−0.0616	−0.0756	−0.0939	5.81
0.0796	0.0648	−0.0197	0.0729	−0.0376	−0.055	0.1186	−0.01
−0.0069	0.0461	−0.0743	−0.0596	0.0809	0.0973	−0.0432	0.01
0.0108	0.0038	0.0041	−0.0224	0.0231	−0.0015	0.0707	1.87
0.0073	−0.0072	−0.009	−0.0122	0.0112	0.0044	−0.0624	−1.91
−0.01	−0.0461	−0.0062	−0.0097	−0.0096	0.0094	0.0024	1.93

Table 3 shows an example of the effect of using the F function. In the case when the increase of energy consumption in the analyzed object has the same sign as in objects strongly correlated with it, the function returns a positive value, which signals lack of anomalies. In the case when the increase of energy consumption has a different character than most strongly correlated objects, then the negative value of the F function signals an anomaly. The value of the correlation coefficient, which determines the final results, is important here (see

the fifth line in the table, in which the number of objects with the same and
different sign is equal).

3.2   Analysis of Birth

The model described above also applies to time series analyzed in social sciences
and humanities. Let us consider a time series describing the number of baptisms
in one of the parishes in Lublin recorded in the years 1711–1900. The values of
the first values of this series with the monthly frequency of readings are shown
in Fig. 4.

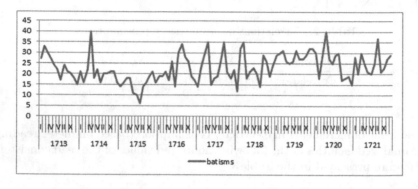

Fig. 4. Baptisms 1713–1721

For this time series, the most intuitive basic cycle is the annual period. When
analyzing the consistency at the level of one parish using a typical variation
interval (see Fig. 5), We can see that the proposed method well estimates the
values and allows the detection of unusual values.

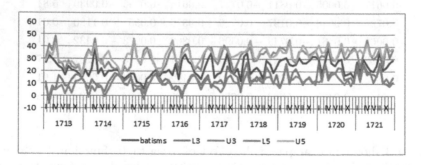

Fig. 5. Comparison of baptisms and typical variation interval

Figure 5 presents a comparison of the real baptism level with the predicted
values obtained by formula 3. We can see that the use of such a simple model
allows for a relatively good forecast.

4 Summary and Future Work

The proposed method uses several independent approaches to detect anomalies in time series. The analysis of the value of a single series by means of typical intervals of variation within a given value in neighboring cycles allows the detection of anomalies at the lowest level. The use of the weighted average method allows detection of anomalies at the level of different cycles. The use of basic cycle descriptors enables to easily analyze large time intervals by reducing dimensions. The analysis of the similarity between objects belonging to one class of objects brings very interesting results. It is advisable to continue research on the description of cycles in the time series and visualization of the data so obtained. In addition, work is being carried out to automate the process of detecting anomalies based on a series of independent approaches.

References

1. Asafu-Adjaye, J.: The relationship between energy consumption, energy prices and economic growth: time series evidence from Asian developing countries. Energy Econ. **22**(6), 615–625 (2000)
2. Beck, N., Katz, J.N.: Modeling dynamics in time-series–cross-section political economy data. Annu. Rev. Polit. Sci. **14**, 331–352 (2011)
3. Bianco, A.M., Ben, M.G., Martinez, E.J., Yohai, V.J.: Outlier detection in regression models with arima errors using robust estimates. J. Forecast. **20**(8), 565–579 (2001)
4. Box, G.E., Jenkins, G.M., Reinsel, G.C., Ljung, G.M.: Time Series Analysis: Forecasting and Control. Wiley, Hoboken (2015)
5. Brockwell, P.J., Davis, R.A.: Time Series: Theory and Methods. Springer, New York (2013)
6. Cohen, M.X.: Analyzing Neural Time Series Data: Theory and Practice. MIT Press, Cambridge (2014)
7. DeFusco, R.A., McLeavey, D.W., Pinto, J.E., Anson, M.J., Runkle, D.E.: Quantitative Investment Analysis. Wiley, Hoboken (2015)
8. Fontugne, R., Ortiz, J., et al.: Strip, bind, and search: a method for identifying abnormal energy consumption in buildings. In: 2013 ACM/IEEE International Conference on Information Processing in Sensor Networks (IPSN), pp. 129–140 (2013)
9. Granger, C.W.J., Newbold, P.: Forecasting Economic Time Series. Academic Press, Cambridge (2014)
10. Granger, C.W.J., Hatanaka, M.: Spectral Analysis of Economic Time Series. (PSME-1). Princeton University Press, Princeton (2015)
11. Gregson, R.A.M.: Time Series in Psychology. Psychology Press, Abingdon (2014)
12. Hamilton, J.D.: Time Series Analysis. Princeton, Princeton University Press (1994)
13. Kim, H., Shin, K.G.: System and method for detecting energy consumption anomalies and mobile malware variants. U.S. Patent 8,332,945 (2012)
14. Liu, J.P., Weng, C.S.: Detection of outlying data in bioavailability/bioequivalence studies. Stat. Med. **10**(9), 1375–1389 (1991)
15. Lätkepohl, H.: New Introduction to Multiple Time Series Analysis. Springer, Heidelberg (2005). https://doi.org/10.1007/978-3-540-27752-1

16. Papana, A., Kyrtsou, C., Kugiumtzis, D., Diks, C.: Detecting causality in non-stationary time series using partial symbolic transfer entropy: evidence in financial data. Comput. Econ. **47**(3), 341–365 (2016)
17. Rajasegarar, S., Leckie, C., Palaniswami, M.: Anomaly detection in wireless sensor networks. IEEE Wirel. Commun. **15**(4), 34–40 (2008)
18. Richman, J.S., Moorman, J.R.: Physiological time-series analysis using approximate entropy and sample entropy. Am. J. Physiol.-Heart Circ. Physiol. **278**(6), 2039–2049 (2000)
19. Rousseeuw, P.J., Leroy, A.M.: Robust Regression and Outlier Detection. Wiley, New York (1987)
20. Stowell, J.I., Messner, S.F., McGeever, K.F., Raffalovich, L.E.: Immigration and the recent violent crime drop in the United States: a pooled, cross-sectional time-series analysis of metropolitan areas. Criminology **47**(3), 889–928 (2009)
21. Strogatz, S.H.: Nonlinear Dynamics and Chaos: with Applications to Physics, Biology, Chemistry, and Engineering. CRC Press, Boca Raton (2018)
22. Taylor, S.J.: Modelling Financial Time Series. World Scientific, Singapore (2008)
23. Tong, H.: Non-linear Time Series: A Dynamical System Approach. Oxford University Press, Oxford (1990)
24. Tsay, R.S., Pea, D., Pankratz, A.E.: Outliers in multivariate time series. Biometrika **87**(4), 789–804 (2000)
25. Tsay, R.S.: Analysis of Financial Time Series, vol. 543. Wiley, Hoboken (2005)
26. Wei, W.W.: Time series analysis. In: The Oxford Handbook of Quantitative Methods in Psychology, vol. 2 (2006)
27. Wiechetek, Ł., Banaś, J., Kiersztyn, A., Mędrek, M., Tatarczak, A.: Multi-criteria decision-making system for detecting anomalies in the electrical energy consumption of telecommunication facilities. In: IX International Conference "Optimization and Applications", OPTIMA 2018 (2018)
28. Windmann, S., Jiao, S., Niggemann, O., Borcherding, H.: A stochastic method for the detection of anomalous energy consumption in hybrid industrial systems. In: 11th IEEE International Conference on Industrial Informatics (INDIN), pp. 194–199 (2013)
29. Zhang, Y., Chen, W., Black, J.: Anomaly detection in premise energy consumption data. In: Power and Energy Society General Meeting, pp. 1–8 (2011)

A Scalable Segmented Dynamic Time Warping for Time Series Classification

Ruizhe Ma[(✉)], Azim Ahmadzadeh, Soukaïna Filali Boubrahimi,
and Rafal A. Angryk

Georgia State University, Atlanta, GA 30302, USA
{rma1,aahmadzadeh1,sfilaliboubrahimi1}@student.gsu.edu
angryk@cs.gsu.edu

Abstract. The Dynamic Time Warping (DTW) algorithm is an elastic distance measure that has demonstrated good performance with
sequence-based data, and in particular, time series data. Two major
drawbacks of DTW are the possibility of pathological warping paths and
the high computational cost. Improvement techniques such as pruning off
impossible mappings or lowering data dimensions have been proposed to
counter these issues. The existing DTW improvement techniques, however, are either limited in effect or use accuracy as a trade-off. In this
paper, we introduce segmented-DTW (segDTW). A novel and scalable
approach that would speed up the DTW algorithm, especially for longer
sequences. Our heuristic approaches the time series mapping problem
by identifying global similarity before local similarity. This global to
local process initiates with easily identified global peaks. Based on these
peaks, time series sequences are segmented to sub-sequences, and DTW
is applied in a divide-and-compute fashion. By doing so, the computation naturally expands to the parallel case. Due to the paired peaks, our
method can avoid some pathological warpings and is highly scalable. We
tested our method on a variety of datasets and obtained a gradient of
speedup relative to the time series sequence length while maintaining
comparable classification accuracy.

Keywords: Sequence alignment · Time series · Classification ·
Dynamic Time Warping

1 Introduction

Time series data is commonly applied in a variety of domains, from voice recognition, the stock market, to solar activities, medical research, and many other
scientific and engineering fields where measurements in the temporal sense are
important. Distance measures can be categorized as lock-step and elastic. Lock-
step measures generally refer to L_p norms, where the i-th element in one sequence
is always mapped to the i-th element in another sequence, while elastic measures
allow for one-to-many, or even one-to-none mappings [1]. With the commonly

© Springer Nature Switzerland AG 2019
L. Rutkowski et al. (Eds.): ICAISC 2019, LNAI 11509, pp. 407–419, 2019.
https://doi.org/10.1007/978-3-030-20915-5_37

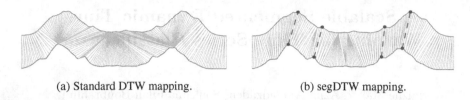

(a) Standard DTW mapping.   (b) segDTW mapping.

Fig. 1. A comparison of segDTW with standard DTW, (a) shows the mapping from standard DTW, with some unintuitive warpings, and (b) shows the mapping results for segDTW, which can be processed in parallel.

seen temporal discrepancies in time series, traditional lock-step distance measures are not as effective as elastic measures when identifying similarities [2].

One of the most widely used elastic measures is the Dynamic Time Warping (DTW) algorithm [3]. The global optimum mapping between two time series sequences is determined based on the computation and comparisons of several options at each step; this choice is referred to as "step pattern". While the choice at each step contributes to the high performance of DTW with sequential data, the amount of computations required makes the algorithm very expensive to compute. Also, the problem with the way in which DTW is computed is that although it achieves global optimal warping path, the path is never readjusted, which means highly similar patterns are not guaranteed to be linked. The best example of overlooked similarity patterns is when the warping path does not match the intuitive mapping. When the warping path is never readjusted, and a feature point is mapped to an incorrect point, the optimal match would never be found. We go from global similarity to local similarity by adding a layer of peak identification before mapping the points and computing the similarity; in doing so, we hope to mimic how humans perceive sequential similarity.

The main feature of our segDTW heuristic is shown in Fig. 1. We start by identifying the peak features of each time series sequence. Then we match the peaks and carry out DTW on each sub-sequence, shown in Fig. 1(b). Because global peaks are already paired, the mapping of segDTW is more intuitive than the standard DTW, shown in Fig. 1(a). Conceptually, any feature extracted from the data that could meaningfully segment time series can be used. In this work, we use peaks because they are easy to recognize and utilize; valleys should perform the same way. With the goal of speeding up the DTW algorithm, we propose a simple, yet effective version of DTW: segmented-DTW (segDTW). Our contribution comes in two folds: first, segDTW provides a more intuitive mapping; second, this approach makes it possible and easy to parallelize DTW computation within a pair of time series comparison. As a result, our method is scalable and thus set apart from previous DTW improvement methods.

The rest of this paper is organized as follows: Sect. 2 gives the background on DTW improvement techniques, Sect. 3 formally introduces our heuristic: segDTW, Sect. 4 shows the effectiveness of segDTW when compared to the standard DTW algorithm and Derivative DTW in terms of accuracy and efficiency, and finally, Sect. 5 concludes this paper.

2 Background

2.1 Dynamic Time Warping

DTW is an algorithm that measures the similarity between two ordered sequences which may vary in time or speed. By allowing one-to-many mappings, DTW has more flexibility than lock-step measures when computing distances and this allow computers to find an optimal mapping between sequences. Originally, DTW was used in speech recognition [4], later it was adapted to various real-world data mining problems. Given two time series sequences $Q = \{q_1, q_2, \ldots, q_i, \ldots, q_n\}$, and $C = \{c_1, c_2, \ldots, c_j, \ldots, c_m\}$, Eqs. 1 and 2 show the computation for Euclidean and DTW distances respectively. Euclidean distance is only valid for equal length sequences $(n = m)$, while DTW is valid for both equal and unequal length sequences.

$$dist_{Euclidean}(Q, C) = \sqrt{\sum_{i=1}^{n}(q_i - c_i)^2} \qquad (1)$$

$$D(i,j) = dist(q_i, c_j) + min \begin{cases} D(i, j-1) \\ D(i-1, j-1) \\ D(i-1, j) \end{cases} \qquad (2)$$

When computing the DTW distance, an n-by-m distance matrix is first constructed containing the pairwise distance information between all the elements from the two sequences. The distance between two data points q_i and c_j from time series Q and C for DTW is computed as the Euclidean distance between them. The warping path denoted as $W = \{w_1, w_2, \ldots, w_k, \ldots, w_K\}$ is identified within the distance matrix. While there are exponentially many warping paths, only the minimized path is of interest [5].

The basic requirements of DTW include the boundary condition, monotonicity, and continuity [6]. The boundary condition means that every element has to have a mapping component, and the first and last components from two compared sequences are always mapped respectively. Monotonicity refers to the single direction of time, and a warping path cannot go back in time. The continuity constraint, also known as the step pattern constraint, it is where the warping path can only follow the allowed steps. In other words, for each step, i and j can only increase by 1. segDTW inherits the same conditions from the original DTW algorithm.

Many studies have been dedicated to the comparison between Euclidean and DTW performance [4,7–9]. Therefore we will not further add to the proof that DTW is more effective than Euclidean when computing time series similarities. Instead, we will solely discuss the variations of the DTW algorithm.

2.2 Existing DTW Improvement Methods

In order to provide a more natural alignment between time series, DTW avoids the naïve injective mapping. Despite its general success, the algorithm often attempts to compensate the variability on the y-axis by extensive warping on the x-axis. This undesirable phenomenon is referred to as a "singularity", and could lead to pathological warping [5]. With the goal of avoiding pathological warpings, as well as to speed up the alignment procedure, many approaches have been proposed over the years.

Windowing has been used by different researchers for a long time, and was formally summarized by Berndt and Clifford [8]. It effectively prunes the corners of the matrix so that any potential warping path is bounded within a fixed margin. This method can mitigate the singularity problem to some extent, but cannot prevent it [10]. Some well-known global windowing constraints include the *Sakoe-Chiba Band* [4], which is a slanted diagonal window, and the *Itakura parallelogram* [11].

Slope weighting encourages the warping path to remain close to the diagonal. Depending on the specific weighting factor, it reduces the frequency of singularities [12].

Step pattern is another approach which encourages changes to the warping path to avoid pathological paths, some widely used step patterns are shown in Fig. 2. Based on symmetry and slope bounds, Sakoe and Chiba proposed *symmetric1*, *symmetric2* [4], and *asymmetric* [13] approaches, shown in Fig. 2(a), (b) and (c) respectively. The first is a basic step pattern. The second favors the diagonal warping path similar to slope weighting, and the third limits time expansion to a factor of two. Rabiner and Juang introduced *rabinerJuangStepPattern*, shown in Fig. 2(d) [14], it is based on the continuity constraint, slope weighting, and the state of being smooth or Boolean. We use the *symmetric1* step pattern for segDTW and all the experiments in this paper.

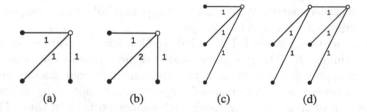

(a)   (b)   (c)   (d)

Fig. 2. Step patterns: (a) *symmetric1* is the basic step pattern, (b) *symmetric2* favors the diagonal warping path, (c) *asymmetric* limits time expansion to a factor of two, and (d) *rabinerJuangStepPattern* has attributes local continuity constraint type, slope weighting, and the state of smoothed or not.

Another avenue for improving the DTW algorithm is by defining tight and fast lower bounding functions to prune sequences that cannot provide a better match in the process of finding the warping path. The idea is to favor the execution time needed for calculating the similarity matrices on large datasets using indexing. While Yi et al. [15] gave an approximation for indexing, the lower bounding function introduced in LB_Kim [16] was the first to define an exact indexing. Compared to the earlier works, LB_Keogh [17] had an overall greater pruning power, could give tighter bounding measures, and act as a proxy to DTW.

Additionally, Piecewise DTW (PDTW) [18], Derivative DTW (DDTW) [5], and shapeDTW [19] are some of the other methods which attempt to manipulate the input time series to either guide the warping path or improve the processing time. The primary achievement of PDTW is to increase the speed factor by one to two orders of magnitude on average while maintaining the accuracy of DTW. Instead of using raw data, a piece-wise aggregated representation of time series is processed. Similarly, DDTW utilizes an approximated derivative of the time series to work on a higher level of similarity between two time series. A similar approach is shapeDTW. Zhao et al. represented each temporal point q_i of a time series Q by a shape descriptor d_i which encodes the structural information of a fixed-width neighborhood of q_i. The choice of the descriptor depends on the general structure of the time series and the users' requirements. Some of the widely used descriptors are namely the slope, piece-wise aggregate approximation (PAA), discrete wavelet transform (DWT), and the histogram of oriented gradient for 1D time series (HOG1D).

The goal of methods such as windowing, slope weighting, and step pattern is to avoid pathological warpings by trying to encourage the warping path to stay close to the diagonal rather than to stray excessively vertical or horizontal. DTW global constraints, along with lower bounding can also speed up the computation process by eliminating certain calculations. Other methods utilize approximated values or dimensionality reduction to speed up computation. Hence, to the best of our knowledge, all the existing DTW improvement methods compare time series sequences linearly. Meaning the computation time would be proportional to the length of the given time series.

3   Methodology

Despite the execution of the algorithm, each pair of time series sequences in all the previously mentioned DTW improvement methods compare time series from beginning to end. In our earlier work [20], we discussed the effect of segmentation on the DTW algorithm. Here we improve upon the simple segmentation and introduce automatic pairing of time series peak features. We refer to the DTW improvement heuristic with segmentation as *segDTW*; it differs from previous works in the sense that it is designed to parallelize the computation of DTW on segments of time series. A layer of global approximation is added as a prior step to DTW similarity computation by detecting significant time series sequence peaks, followed by pairing peaks and segmenting accordingly. Since segmentation can avoid some pathological warpings as well as providing more intuitive results, we should expect improvement of computation efficiency.

3.1   Time Series Segmentation

The global optimal solution of DTW can often overlook highly similar features in time series sequences. segDTW can divide the problem of finding the global optimal mapping into smaller, more manageable pieces. As a result of the boundary condition, peaks are specifically mapped during computation; this can minimize mismatches and avoid pathological warping paths. The pairing of corresponding peaks is used for segmentation, then the optimal DTW mapping for each sub-sequence is found, and the distances of all the sub-sequences are aggregated to obtain the overall distance between two time series sequences.

We reiterate the applied segmentation for segDTW in Algorithm 1. The definition of a peak is formulated as follows. Point c_i with temporal index i is considered a *candidate peak* when $c_i > c_{i-1}$ and $c_i > c_{i+1}$. This simple definition of a *candidate peak* equipped with the parameters t, d, and n forms a peak detection method that provides the criteria necessary to distinguish a set of selected peaks we refer to as *significant peaks*. t is the peak magnitude threshold; any candidate peak below t will be ignored. d is the minimum peak radius distance. For any identified peak, any adjacent peak within a radius of d will be considered as either noise or insignificant. And n is the maximum number of peaks to be taken into account. Since the peak values will be sorted before being analyzed, only the top n peaks that have met the other criteria will be considered.

Algorithm 1. Time Series Peak Selection

Input: $C = \{c_1, \cdots, c_m\}$ time series data,
d: minimum radius from a selected peak,
t: minimum peak value threshold,
n: maximum number of peaks to be detected.
Output: list of peaks with both their indices and values,
$peaks = \{p_1, ..., p_n\}$.

```
 1: procedure FIND PEAKS
 2:     peaks, candidates ← list()
 3:     for all c_i ∈ C do
 4:         if ((c_i > c_{i+1}) & (c_i > c_{i−1})) then
 5:             candidates.add((i, c_i))
 6:         end if
 7:     end for
 8:     peaks ← sortByValue(candidates)
 9:     for all (i, c_i) ∈ peaks do
10:         if c_i < t then
11:             peaks.remove((i, c_i))
12:         end if
13:     end for
14:     indices ← peaks.getIndices()
15:     for all i ∈ indices do
16:         for all j ∈ {i − d, · · · , i + d} \ i do
17:             if peaks.hasIndex(j) then
18:                 peaks.remove((j, c_j))
19:             end if
20:         end for
21:     end for
22:     peaks ← peaks.getNFirstElements(n)
23:     return peaks;
24: end procedure
```

Initially, all candidate peaks are found and sorted based on their values (Algorithm 1 lines 3–7). Then, the magnitude threshold t is applied, and all the candidate peaks below the threshold will be removed from the list (lines 8–13). For each of the remaining peaks, their neighboring peaks within the radius of d will be removed as well (lines 15–21). The algorithm processes the peaks based on its values in descending order; this is to guarantee that the presence of a smaller peak never justifies the removal of a larger peak. Finally, among the peaks left in the list, only the top n peaks will survive.

In the worst case, the time complexity of the peak identification process for an unordered sequence, if implemented naïvely, is $max\{O((p \cdot (p+1))/2), s)\}$ where p is the number of candidate peaks and s is the time bound of the utilized sorting algorithm. The worst case refers to the situation where $d = 0$, $n = \infty$, and $t = min(C)$, and all points in the time series are considered significant peaks. However, by taking the order of the indices into account, in addition to the order of the values, the time complexity would only be determined by the sorting step. Therefore, the worst case running time would decrease to $O(n \cdot \log(n))$ which reflects the lowest possible complexity of a sort algorithm such as merge sort or heap sort.

3.2   Pairing of Identified Peaks

Once the peaks are identified, we need to pair the peaks detected in each of the time series Q and C. The mapping method in such a situation plays a crucial role in achieving sensible results. A prerequisite condition for segDTW is that it has to satisfy all the basic requirements of DTW. This can be extended to the condition that no set of peak pairs in segDTW could cross another pair of peaks, as this would be a violation of the monotonicity requirement of DTW. Since segDTW inherits the properties of the standard DTW, and when boundary and continuity requirements are satisfied for each time series segment, they are automatically satisfied as a whole. The task of pairing and mapping of peaks, in many situations, is a subjective task and it is not always possible to agree on any ground truth even when visually analyzing the time series. Therefore, we set our goal to minimize the total distances of the pairs. To this end, we employ the Hungarian algorithm [21] to achieve a global optimum peak pairing.

The Hungarian algorithm is a well-known assignment problem which is regarded as a relative of the traveling salesman problem. The assignment problem can be defined as follows: given an n-by-n matrix $R = (r_{ij})$ of positive integers, the objective is to find the permutation $\{j_1, j_2, \cdots, j_n\}$ of the integers $\{1, 2, \cdots, n\}$ such that it maximizes the sum $\{r_{ij_1} + r_{ij_2} + \cdots + r_{ij_n}\}$. The Hungarian method utilizes linear programming to tackle this problem. Although the assignment problem can always be reduced to the case where R takes only ones and zeros, representing paired and non-paired integers, it is not limited to this binary case. In addition, the problem can be easily extended to the non-square matrices. Thus, this approach is well suited for our peak pairing problem. The sequence of the integers is the indices of the peaks in the time series Q and C, and the permutation of interest is the mapping between the peaks of one time series with the other. The entries of the assignment matrix (i.e., R) for our problem can be defined as follows:

$$r_{ij} = \text{temporal distance between } \hat{q}_i \text{ and } \hat{c}_j$$

where $\hat{q}_i$ and $\hat{c}_j$ are the i-th and j-th peaks in the time series Q and C, respectively. The objective here is to find a permutation that minimizes the total temporal distance of the paired peaks. When the number of significant peaks is different in the two time series, only those contributing to the global optimum are selected.

4   Experiments

In this section, we show the performance of segDTW compared to the standard DTW, and DDTW in terms of computation efficiency and classification accuracy. Our goal is to demonstrate the efficiency and scalability of segDTW, while at the same time maintaining comparable accuracy. Classification time efficiency is evaluated through the use of k-nearest neighbor classifier and accuracy will be discussed for completeness.

4.1   Datasets

We demonstrate our findings using the UCR time series dataset archive [22]. UCR contains both synthetic data and real-world data from various domains, of different class numbers, training and testing ratio, as well as sequence duration. We follow the original train-test-split from the UCR archive and perform 1NN classification on the testing dataset. 1NN is the k-nearest neighbors algorithm with $k = 1$. We compared the computation time demonstrated by the standard DTW, DDTW, and segDTW, as well as the classification accuracy. In order to keep the comparison simple and fair, we did not apply windows or any improvement methods in conjunction with DTW, DDTW, or segDTW. In other words, the original time series data is used without additional pruning or indexing heuristics; therefore, the computation time may be slower than some reported results from the state-of-the-art methods. While the time series length within each UCR dataset is uniform, segDTW can be applied toward time series of different length just as DTW can.

4.2   Parameter Settings

We first explore the effect of different peak identification parameters on 20 datasets from the UCR repository. The minimum peak identification radius d is given values: $\frac{1}{2}, \frac{1}{4}, \frac{1}{8}, \frac{1}{16}, \frac{1}{32}, \frac{1}{64}$, and $\frac{1}{128}$ of the sequence length L. The threshold for peak identification t is given values of first quantile (Q1), median (M), and the third quantile (Q3) of time series magnitude values. No maximum peak number n is enforced. Effect of different combinations of the two peak identification parameters is shown in Fig. 3, where segDTW accuracy is compared among different peak selection parameter combinations. The accuracy is generally better with peak selection radius $d = \frac{1}{32}$. Among the three peak threshold values, $t =$ Q3 has overall better performance and is more selective.

Typically, when the peak selection radius d is large or when the peak threshold t is large, fewer peaks are identified and fewer sub-sequences created. In the extreme case, when no peaks are detected, and no segmentation is imposed, segDTW degenerates to the standard DTW. In contrast, when the peak detection radius is small or when the peak threshold is low, there are generally more peaks and sub-sequences, which leads to more segments and potentially shorter processing time. However, more segments in time series sequences introduce risks of identifying false peaks, which could potentially lead to lower accuracy and performance. In addition, the overhead of peak detection needs to be taken into account when sequences are not long enough in proportion to the number of peaks.

When applying segDTW in time series classification, we choose the more selective third quantile (Q3) as the threshold t, and minimum peak radius $d = \frac{1}{32}L$, with no maximum number of peaks n enforced. This is by no means a set of optimal parameters for peak selection, rather a more general case. Given the high variability and individual differences of time series data, it is up to the user's domain knowledge to determine the optimal set of parameters for the task and dataset on hand.

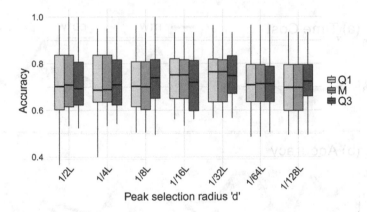

Fig. 3. Peak identification parameters effect on accuracy, shown with combinations of peak selection radii $d = \frac{1}{2}, \frac{1}{4}, \frac{1}{8}, \frac{1}{16}, \frac{1}{32}, \frac{1}{64}$ and $\frac{1}{128}$ of data length L, with peak value thresholds $t = $ Q1, M, and Q3.

For fair comparisons, there is no parallelization on the time series event level. The computation between training and testing events can always be distributed to different threads. Because this event-level parallel computing can be done for any DTW based method, we take away the common factor and utilize multiple processor cores for computation only when time series are segmented. In short, parallelization occurs within time series sequences, not between independent event sequences; this means our experiments are overall intentionally slowed down to a controlled state of having a single variable.

While the computation between training and testing events could always be performed on multiple cores, there is a limit on the number of cores the standard DTW could utilize. Since all sub-sequences in segDTW could be computed simultaneously, it can take better advantage of a parallel environment. Essentially, segDTW can raise the limit of simultaneous computation. Of course, the number of cores segDTW can utilize depends on the number of peaks and sub-sequences, but in most cases, this limit is higher than the standard DTW. In the worst case, when no peaks are identified in the time series data, segDTW would become the standard DTW. Since the segmentation takes time, the effects of segDTW should only become apparent when the overhead cost of segmentation and pairing become less relevant. Therefore, in a limitless processor core environment, given the same number of events data, segDTW should have higher efficiency than the standard DTW and DDTW.

4.3   Result Analysis

The performance of segDTW is evaluated using time series classification. Figure 4(a) shows the computation time for standard DTW, DDTW, and segDTW on the logarithmic scale, with the datasets ordered by sequence length in ascending order. Generally, DDTW is more efficient than standard DTW and

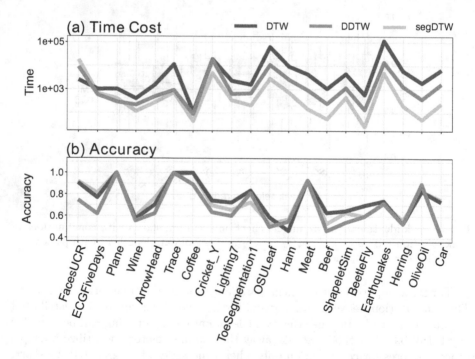

Fig. 4. Datasets are in ascending order of time series length, (a) shows the processing time for standard DTW, DDTW, and segDTW on the logarithmic scale, with segDTW speedup becoming more apparent as time series lengths increase; (b) shows the corresponding accuracy performance.

segDTW is more efficient than DDTW. Out of the 20 datasets, there is only 1 case where segDTW did not outperform standard DTW, and 3 cases where segDTW did not outperform DDTW, all of which occurred for the 3 datasets with the shortest data length. There are also 10 cases where compared to the standard DTW, segDTW had over $10x$ increase in processing time. Since the scalability of segDTW is segment dependent, it makes sense for this advantage to be more apparent for datasets with longer time series sequences; when the overhead of the time spent on segment computation becomes less relevant compared to the linear calculation time spent on an entire sequence pair. Almost all the significant speed increases occurred for the longer sequences.

In an optimal situation, segDTW should improve accuracy and execute faster than DTW and DDTW. However, we are using the same general set of peak detection parameters for every dataset, disregarding the vast difference between datasets. Therefore we argue that for segDTW to be a valid and workable heuristic in the general case, it should maintain comparable accuracy despite the improvement in computation efficiency. Figure 4(b) shows the accuracy of the standard DTW, DDTW, and segDTW to be equally matched. While certain method demonstrated higher accuracy for some datasets, there is no definitive pattern. For certain datasets, the accuracy performance remains the same regardless of the method used. From the general performance of segDTW and DTW, we did not see a clear correlation between class number, train-test ratio or accuracy. The accuracy performance is very much domain (data) dependent. Again, this means that the peak identification parameters are by no means universal, and should be fine-tuned when applied to specific datasets.

5   Conclusion

In this paper, we proposed and tested a novel DTW improvement heuristic: segDTW. Unlike its predecessors, it is scalable and easy to parallelize. This merit is especially apparent for time series datasets with longer sequences. Under general peak detection parameters, we achieved an overall speedup, while maintaining comparable accuracy.

We would like to add that segDTW is not an optimum choice under all conditions. When time series sequences are very short, or if there are a very limited number of processor cores, segDTW would be more costly than the standard DTW. However, when we are dealing with very long time series sequences, and have multiple processor cores at our disposal, using segDTW can definitely speedup computation. While all DTW computation can be parallelized, segDTW expands the limit of utilized processor cores. This paper is a proof of concept that by using peak selection to segment time series sequences and to perform parallel elastic measure calculation, we can obtain scalability on the otherwise linear DTW sequence computation. In the future, we are interested in additional significant feature definitions and identifications, the application of segDTW combined with other DTW improvement heuristics, as well as its operations in clustering.

Acknowledgment. This project has been supported in part by funding from the Division of Advanced Cyber infrastructure within the Directorate for Computer and Information Science and Engineering, the Division of Astronomical Sciences within the Directorate for Mathematical and Physical Sciences, and the Division of Atmospheric and Geospace Sciences within the Directorate for Geosciences, under NSF award #1443061. It was also supported in part by funding from the Heliophysics Living With a Star Science Program, under NASA award #NNX15AF39G.

References

1. Wang, X., Mueen, A., Ding, H., Trajcevski, G., Scheuermann, P., Keogh, E.: Experimental comparison of representation methods and distance measures for time series data. Data Min. Knowl. Discov. **26**(2), 275–309 (2013)
2. Ranacher, P., Tzavella, K.: How to compare movement? A review of physical movement similarity measures in geographic information science and beyond. Cartography Geogr. Inf. Sci. **41**(3), 286–307 (2014)
3. Serra, J., Arcos, J.L.: An empirical evaluation of similarity measures for time series classification. Knowl.-Based Syst. **67**, 305–314 (2014)
4. Sakoe, H., Chiba, S.: Dynamic programming algorithm optimization for spoken word recognition. IEEE Trans. Acoust. Speech Signal Process. **26**(1), 43–49 (1978)
5. Keogh, E.J., Pazzani, M.J.: Derivative dynamic time warping. In: Proceedings of the 2001 SIAM International Conference on Data Mining, pp. 1–11. SIAM (2001)
6. Müller, M.: Information Retrieval for Music and Motion, vol. 2. Springer, Heidelberg (2007). https://doi.org/10.1007/978-3-540-74048-3
7. Myers, C., Rabiner, L.: A level building dynamic time warping algorithm for connected word recognition. IEEE Trans. Acoust. Speech Signal Process. **29**(2), 284–297 (1981)
8. Berndt, D.J., Clifford, J.: Using dynamic time warping to find patterns in time series. In: KDD Workshop, Seattle, WA, vol. 10, pp. 359–370 (1994)
9. Rakthanmanon, T., et al.: Searching and mining trillions of time series subsequences under dynamic time warping. In: Proceedings of the 18th ACM SIGKDD International Conference on Knowledge Discovery and Data Mining, pp. 262–270. ACM (2012)
10. Biba, M., Xhafa, F.: Learning Structure and Schemas from Documents, vol. 375. Springer, Heidelberg (2011). https://doi.org/10.1007/978-3-642-22913-8
11. Itakura, F.: Minimum prediction residual principle applied to speech recognition. IEEE Trans. Acoust. Speech Signal Process. **23**(1), 67–72 (1975)
12. Kruskall, J., Liberman, M.: The symmetric time warping algorithm: from continuous to discrete. Time warps, string edits and macromolecules (1983)
13. Sakoe, H., Chiba, S.: Comparative study of DP-pattern matching techniques for speech recognition. In: 1973 Technical Group Meeting Speech Acoustical Society of Japan (1973)
14. Rabiner, L.R., Juang, B.-H., Rutledge, J.C.: Fundamentals of Speech Recognition, vol. 14. PTR Prentice Hall, Englewood Cliffs (1993)
15. Yi, B.-K., Jagadish, H., Faloutsos, C.: Efficient retrieval of similar time sequences under time warping. In: Proceedings of the 14th International Conference on Data Engineering, pp. 201–208. IEEE (1998)
16. Kim, S.-W., Park, S., Chu, W.W.: An index-based approach for similarity search supporting time warping in large sequence databases. In: Proceedings of the 17th International Conference on Data Engineering, pp. 607–614. IEEE (2001)

17. Keogh, E., Ratanamahatana, C.A.: Exact indexing of dynamic time warping. Knowl. Inf. Syst. **7**(3), 358–386 (2005)
18. Keogh, E.J., Pazzani, M.J.: Scaling up dynamic time warping for datamining applications. In: Proceedings of the Sixth ACM SIGKDD International Conference on Knowledge Discovery and Data Mining, pp. 285–289. ACM (2000)
19. Zhao, J., Itti, L.: shapeDTW: shape dynamic time warping. arXiv preprint arXiv:1606.01601 (2016)
20. Ma, R., Ahmadzadeh, A., Boubrahimi, S.F., Angryk, R.A.: Segmentation of time series in improving dynamic time warping. In: 2018 IEEE International Conference on Big Data (Big Data), pp. 3756–3761. IEEE (2018)
21. Kuhn, H.W.: The Hungarian method for the assignment problem. Naval Res. Logist. (NRL) **2**(1–2), 83–97 (1955)
22. Chen, Y., et al.: The UCR time series classification archive, July 2015. www.cs. ucr.edu/~eamonn/time_series_data/

Determining the Eps Parameter
of the DBSCAN Algorithm

Artur Starczewski[1]([⊠]) and Andrzej Cader[2,3]

[1] Institute of Computational Intelligence, Częstochowa University of Technology,
Al. Armii Krajowej 36, 42-200 Częstochowa, Poland
artur.starczewski@iisi.pcz.pl
[2] Information Technology Institute, University of Social Sciences,
90-113 Łódź, Poland
acader@san.edu.pl
[3] Clark University, Worcester, MA 01610, USA

Abstract. Clustering is an attractive technique used in many fields and
lots of clustering algorithms have been proposed so far. The Density-
Based Spatial Clustering of Applications with Noise (DBSCAN) is one
of the most popular algorithms, which has been widely applied in many
different applications. This algorithm can discover clusters of arbitrary
shapes in large datasets. However, the fundamental issue is the right
choice of two input parameters, i.e. radius *eps* and density threshold
MinPts. In this paper, a new method is proposed to determine the value
of *eps*. The suggested approach is based on an analysis of the sorted
values of the distance function. The performance of the new approach
has been demonstrated for several different datasets.

Keywords: Clustering algorithms · DBSCAN · Data mining

1 Introduction

Data clustering is one of the most important approaches used to discover
naturally occurring structures in a dataset. Clustering is a process, which refers
to grouping objects into meaningful clusters so that the elements of a cluster are
similar, whereas they are dissimilar in different clusters. Nowadays, a variety of
large collections of data are created. This brings a great challenge for clustering
algorithms, so new different clustering algorithms and their configurations are
being intensively developed, e.g. [12–15,26]. Data clustering is applied in many
areas, such as biology, spatial data analysis, business, and others. It should be
noted that there is no a clustering algorithm, which creates the right data partition for all datasets. Moreover, the same algorithm can also produce different
results depending on the input parameters applied. Therefore, cluster validation should be also used to assess results of data clustering. So far, a number
of authors have proposed different cluster validity indices or modifications of
existing ones, e.g., [11,25,29–31].

© Springer Nature Switzerland AG 2019
L. Rutkowski et al. (Eds.): ICAISC 2019, LNAI 11509, pp. 420–430, 2019.
https://doi.org/10.1007/978-3-030-20915-5_38

Among clustering algorithms four categories can be distinguished: partitioning, hierarchical, grid-based and density-based clustering. For example, the well-known partitioning algorithms are, e.g. *K-means*, *Partitioning Around Medoids* (*PAM*) [6,34] and *Expectation Maximization* (*EM*) [19], whereas the hierarchical clustering includes agglomerative and divisive approaches, e.g. the *Single-linkage*, *Complete-linkage* or *Average-linkage* or *DIvisive ANAlysis Clustering* (*DIANA*) [20,24]. Then, the grid-based approach includes methods such as e.g. the *Statistical Information Grid-based* (*STING*) or *Wavelet-based Clustering* (*WaveCluster*) [21,28,32]. The next category of clustering algorithms is the density-based approach. The *Density Based Spatial Clustering of Application with Noise* (*DBSCAN*) is the most famous density-based algorithm [10]. It can discover clusters of an arbitrary shape and size, but is rarely used to cluster multidimensional data due to so-called *"curse of dimensionality"*. Consequently, it has many extensions, e.g. [5,7,8,18,27,33]. However, the *DBSCAN* also requires two input parameters, i.e. radius *eps* and density threshold *MinPts*. Determination of these parameters is crucial to the right performance of this clustering method. Especially the *eps* radius is very difficult to be determined correctly. Recently, new concepts have been proposed for the determining of these input parameters [16]. It is important to note that clustering methods can be used during a process of designing various neural networks [1–3], fuzzy and rule systems [4,9,17,22,23].

In this paper, a new approach to determining the *eps* radius is proposed. It is based on an analysis of a *knee*, which appears in the sorted values of the distance function used in the dataset. This paper is organized as follows: Sect. 2 presents a detailed description of the *DBSCAN* clustering algorithm. In Sect. 3 the new method to determine the *eps* radius is outlined while Sect. 4 illustrates experimental results on datasets. Finally, Sect. 5 presents conclusions.

2   The Concept of the DBSCAN Clustering Algorithm

In this section the basic concept of the *DBSCAN* algorithm is described. As mentioned above, it is a very popular algorithm because it can find clusters of arbitrary shapes and requires only two input parameters, i.e. the *eps* radius and the density threshold *MinPts*. To understand the basic concept of the algorithm several terms should be explained. Let us denote the *eps* radius by ε and a dataset by X, where a point $p \in X$. The ε is usually determined by the user and the right choice of this parameter is a key issue for this algorithm. The *MinPts* is the minimal number of neighboring points belonging to a so-called *core point*.

Definition 1: The ε-*neighborhood* of point $p \in X$ is called $N_\varepsilon(p)$ and is defined as follows: $N_\varepsilon(p) = \{q \in X | dist(p,q) \leq \varepsilon\}$, where $dist(p,q)$ is a distance function between p and q.

When a number of points belonging to the ε-*neighborhood* of p is greater or equal to the *MinPts*, p is called the *core point*.

Definition 2: A point p is *directly density-reachable* from a point q with respect to ε and the $MinPts$ when q is a *core point* and p belongs to the ε-*neighborhood* of q.

When a point p is *directly density-reachable* from a point q and a number of points belonging to the ε-*neighborhood* of p is smaller than the $MinPts$, p is called a *border point*.

Definition 3: A point p is a *noise* if it is neither a *core point* nor a *border point*.

Definition 4: A point p is *density-reachable* from a point q with respect to the ε and the $MinPts$ when there is a chain of points $p_1, p_2, \ldots, p_n, p_1 = q, p_n = p$ so that p_{i+1} is *directly density-reachable* from p_i.

Definition 5: A point p is *density-connected* to a point q with respect to the ε and the $MinPts$ when there is a point o such that p and q are *density-reachable* from the point o.

Definition 6: A cluster C with respect to the ε and the $MinPts$ is a non-empty subset of X, where the following conditions are satisfied:

1. $\forall p, q$: if $p \in C$ and q is *density-reachable* from p with respect to the ε and the $MinPts$, then $q \in C$.
2. $\forall p, q \in C$: p is *density-connected* to q with respect to the ε and the $MinPts$.

The DBSCAN algorithm creates clusters according to Definition 6. At first, a point p is selected randomly and if $|N_\varepsilon(p)| \geq MinPts$ than the point p will be the *core point* and will be marked as a new cluster. Next, the new cluster is expanded by the points which are *density-reachable* from p. This process is repeated until no cluster found. On the other hand, if $|N_\varepsilon(p)| < MinPts$, then the point p will be considered as a new *noise*. However, this point can be included in another cluster if it is *density-reachable* from some *core point*.

3   Explanation of the New Approach to Determine the Eps Parameter

As mentioned above the right choice of the *eps* (ε) parameter is a fundamental issue for a high performance of the DBSCAN. However, it is a very difficult

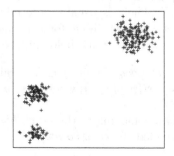

Fig. 1. An example of 2-dimensional dataset consisting of three clusters.

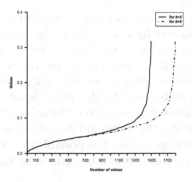

Fig. 2. Sorted values of the k_{dist} function with respect to $k = 5$ and $k = 6$ for the dataset.

task. One of the most popular ideas bases on a distance function which computes a distance between each point $p \in X$ and its k-th nearest neighbor. This function can be denoted by k_{dist}. It requires an input parameter k, which is the number of the nearest neighbors of the point p. For instance, Fig. 1 shows an example of a 2-dimensional dataset consisting of three clusters. The clusters contain 150, 100 and 50 elements, respectively. The k_{dist} function can be used in the dataset, and then the results are sorted in an ascending order. Figure 2 presents the sorted results for two values of the k parameter, i.e. $k = 5$ and $k = 6$. It can be observed that the plots include a *"knee"*, where the distances change significantly. Moreover, the number of calculated distances for $k=6$ is greater than for $k = 5$, because additional distances have to be calculated. The fundamental issue is the appropriate determining of a *threshold point*, which defines the maximal k_{dist} value in the clusters of a dataset. All the points with k_{dist} values higher than the maximal k_{dist} value are considered to be a noise. It can be noted that the *threshold point* refers to the *"knee"* but it is very difficult to determine this point correctly. To solve this problem, a new method, which

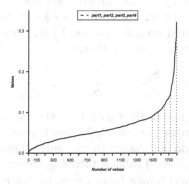

Fig. 3. Partition of the *range* for four equal parts: *part1*, *part2*, *part3* and *part4*.

consists of a few steps, is proposed. Let us denote a set of all the sorted values of k_{dist} function for the X dataset by V_{sdist}. The ε (*eps*), mentioned above, depends on the *threshold point* occurring in the dataset for the given k number of the nearest neighbors of the point. It should be noted that in Fig. 2 the values of the k_{dist} function increase abruptly when they are to the right of the "*knee*". This means that there are points beyond the *threshold point* of the dataset and they can be interpreted as a noise. Moreover, the "*knee*" usually appears at the end of the sorted values of the k_{dist} function and its size depends on the properties of the dataset. Among the sorted values, it is possible to determine a *range*, which indicates the *knee* more precisely. It can be defined by v_{start} and v_{stop} points as follows:

$$v_{start} = |V_{sdist}| - |X|$$
$$v_{stop} = |V_{sdist}|$$

(1)

where $|V_{sdist}|$ is the number of the elements of the V_{sdist} and $|X|$ is the number of the elements of the X. Furthermore, the *range* is divided into four equal parts, i.e. *part1*, *part2*, *part3* and *part4*. The size of such part is equal to $|X|/4$. For example, Fig. 3 shows the partition of the *range* for four equal parts. Next, for each of the parts the average values are calculated as follows:

$$S_{v1} = \frac{1}{n} \sum_{i=v1}^{n} k_{dist}(i)$$

$$S_{v2} = \frac{1}{n} \sum_{i=v2}^{n} k_{dist}(i)$$

$$S_{v3} = \frac{1}{n} \sum_{i=v3}^{n} k_{dist}(i)$$

$$S_{v4} = \frac{1}{n} \sum_{i=v4}^{n} k_{dist}(i)$$

(2)

where n is the number of the k_{dist} values occurring in each part and v_j is the start point of the jth part, $j = 1..4$. These start points are defined as follows: $v1 = v_{start}$, $v2 = v1 + n$, $v3 = v2 + n$ and $v4 = v3 + n$. Next, the "*knee*" can be analyzed by these calculated averages values. First, three factors a, b and c are computed. They can be expressed as follows:

$$a = \frac{S_{v2}}{S_{v1}} \quad b = \frac{S_{v3}}{S_{v2}} \quad c = \frac{S_{v4}}{S_{v3}}$$

(3)

These factors play a key role in the analysis of the "*knee*". For instance, when the values of the k_{dist} increase very slowly in *part1*, *part2* and *part3*, the average values S_{v1}, S_{v2}, S_{v3} also do not change significantly. Thus, the values of a and b are almost equal. Furthermore, if values of the k_{dist} function increase abruptly in *part4*, then parameter c will have a large value. In this case, the ε should equal S_{v4} because there is a high probability that the S_{v4} refers to the *threshold point* occurring in this dataset so it can be expressed as:

$$if(a \approx b) \wedge (c \geq T) \quad then$$
$$\varepsilon = S_{v4} \tag{4}$$

where T is a *constant value* and is determined experimentally ($T = 1.4$). On the other hand, when $c < T$, the values of the k_{dist} increase slowly in *part4* and the *"knee"* can be quite wide, so smaller values of the k_{dist} function refer to the *threshold point*. In this case, the ε should be calculated with respect to *part2*, *part3* and *part4* so it is defined as follows:

$$if(a \approx b) \wedge (c < T) \quad then$$
$$\varepsilon = \frac{S_{v2} + S_{v3} + S_{v4}}{3} \tag{5}$$

Next, when the values of the k_{dist} increase significantly in *part1*, *part2* and *part3*, the values of a and b are different, i.e. the b is much bigger than the a factor. It means that the *threshold point* refers to the values from *part3* and *part4*. Thus, the ε can be defined as follows:

$$if(a \neq b) \quad then$$
$$\varepsilon = \frac{S_{v3} + S_{v4}}{2} \tag{6}$$

In the next section, the results of the experimental studies are presented to confirm the effectiveness of this new approach.

4 Experimental Results

In this section, several experiments have been conducted on 2-dimensional artificial datasets using the original *DBSCAN* algorithm. This algorithm is one of most popular clustering methods, because it can recognize clusters with arbitrary shapes. Artificial datasets include clusters of various sizes and shapes. The first

Table 1. A detailed description of the artificial datasets

Datasets	No. of elements	Clusters
Data 1	75	4
Data 2	500	4
Data 3	700	6
Data 4	700	3
Data 5	900	4
Data 6	500	4
Data 7	700	2
Data 8	2300	7
Data 9	3000	3

parameter k ($MinPts$) equaled 6 in all the experiments. Such value of the k guarantees that the algorithm does not create clusters of too low a density threshold. To automatically determine the radius ε, the new approach described above is used. Moreover, the evaluation of the accuracy the DBSCAN algorithm is conducted by visual inspection. It can be noted that this algorithm is rarely used to cluster multidimensional data due to the so-called *"curse of dimensionality"*. Recently, however, a modification of this algorithm has been proposed to solve this problem [7].

4.1   Datasets

In the conducted experiments nine 2-dimensional datasets are used. Most of them come from the R package. The artificial data are called *Data* 1, *Data* 2, *Data* 3, *Data* 4, *Data* 5, *Data* 6, *Data* 7, *Data* 8 and *Data* 9, respectively.

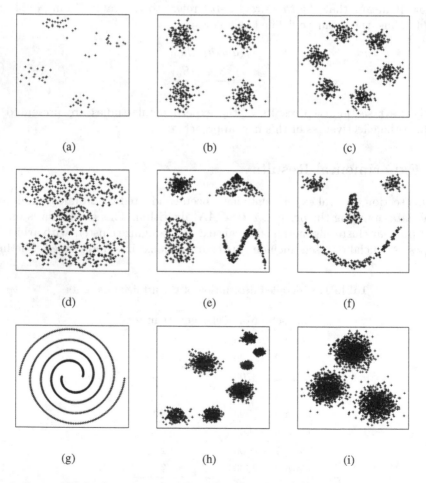

(a)   (b)   (c)

(d)   (e)   (f)

(g)   (h)   (i)

Fig. 4. Examples of 2-dimensional artificial datasets: (a) *Data* 1, (b) *Data* 2, (c) *Data* 3, (d) *Data* 4, (e) *Data* 5, (f) *Data* 6, (g) *Data* 7, (h) *Data* 8 and (i) *Data* 9.

They consist of various number of clusters, i.e. 2, 3, 4, 6, and 7 clusters. The scatter plot of these data is presented in Fig. 4. As it can be observed on the plot, the distances between the clusters are very different and some clusters are quite close. Generally, the clusters are located in different areas and some of the clusters are very close and others quite far. For instance, in *Data* 5 the elements create Gaussian, square, triangle and wave shapes, *Data* 6 consists of 2 Gaussian eyes, a trapezoid nose and a parabola mouth (with a vertical Gaussian one) and *Data* 7 is so-called the spirals problem, where points are on two entangled spirals. Moreover, the sizes of the clusters are different and they contain a various number of elements. Table 1 shows a detailed description of these datasets used in the experiments.

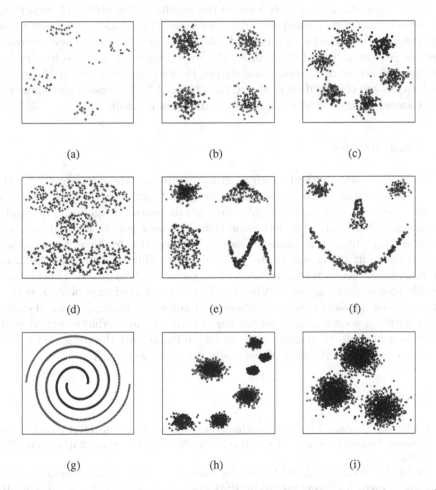

(a)   (b)   (c)

(d)   (e)   (f)

(g)   (h)   (i)

Fig. 5. Results of the *DBSCAN* clustering algorithm for 2-dimensional datasets: (a) *Data* 1, (b) *Data* 2, (c) *Data* 3, (d) *Data* 4, (e) *Data* 5, (f) *Data* 6, (g) *Data* 7, (h) *Data* 8 and (i) *Data* 9

4.2   Experiments

The experimental analysis is designed to evaluate the performance of the new method to automatically specify the ε parameter. As mentioned above, this parameter is very important for the $DBSCAN$ algorithm to work correctly and it is usually determined by visual inspection of the sorted values of the k_{dist} function. On the other hand, the new approach described in Sect. 3 allows us to determine this parameter in an automatic way. In these experiments the nine 2-dimensional datasets used are called $Data$ 1, $Data$ 2, $Data$ 3, $Data$ 4, $Data$ 5, $Data$ 6, $Data$ 7, $Data$ 8 and $Data$ 9 datasets. It needs to be noted that the value of the k ($MinPts$) parameter equals 6 in all the experiments. Then, when the ε parameter is specified by the new method, the $DBSCAN$ algorithm can be used to cluster these datasets. Figure 5 shows the results of the $DBSCAN$ algorithm, where each cluster is marked with different signs. The data elements classified as the *noise* are marked with a circle. It should be noted that the new approach provides correct values of the ε in all the experiments. Thus, despite the fact that the differences of distances and shapes between clusters are significant, all the datasets are clustered correctly by the $DBSCAN$. Moreover, the number of data elements classified as noise in all the datasets is small.

5   Conclusions

In this paper a new method is proposed for computing the ε parameter for the DBSCAN algorithm. This method uses the k_{dist} function, which computes the distance between each point $p \in X$ and its kth nearest neighbor. The fundamental issue is to correctly determine the *threshold point*, which defines the maximal k_{dist} value in the dataset clusters. To solve this problem, first, the new method finds out the *region* of the k_{dist} values creating the *knee* and divides it into four parts. Next, average values of these parts are determined. This makes it possible to calculate the right value of ε. In the conducted experiments, several 2-dimensional datasets were used, where the number of clusters, sizes and shapes varied within a wide range. From the perspective of the conducted experiments this automatic way to compute ε is useful and easy. All the presented results confirm a very high efficiency of the newly proposed approach.

References

1. Bilski, J., Smoląg, J.: Parallel architectures for learning the RTRN and Elman dynamic neural networks. IEEE Trans. Parallel Distrib. Syst. **26**(9), 2561–2570 (2015)
2. Bilski, J., Wilamowski, B.M.: Parallel learning of feedforward neural networks without error backpropagation. In: Rutkowski, L., Korytkowski, M., Scherer, R., Tadeusiewicz, R., Zadeh, L.A., Zurada, J.M. (eds.) ICAISC 2016. LNAI, vol. 9692, pp. 57–69. Springer, Cham (2016). https://doi.org/10.1007/978-3-319-39378-0_6

3. Bilski, J., Kowalczyk, B., Grzanek, K.: The parallel modification to the Levenberg-Marquardt algorithm. In: Rutkowski, L., Scherer, R., Korytkowski, M., Pedrycz, W., Tadeusiewicz, R., Zurada, J.M. (eds.) ICAISC 2018. LNCS, vol. 10841, pp. 15–24. Springer, Cham (2018). https://doi.org/10.1007/978-3-319-91253-0_2

4. Bologna, G., Hayashi, Y.: Characterization of symbolic rules embedded in deep DIMLP networks: a challenge to transparency of deep learning. J. Artif. Intell. Soft Comput. Res. **7**(4), 265–286 (2017)

5. Boonchoo, T., Ao, X., Liu, Y., Zhao, W., He, Q.: Grid-based DBSCAN: indexing and inference. Pattern Recogn. **90**, 271–284 (2019)

6. Bradley, P., Fayyad, U.: Refining initial points for K-Means clustering. In Proceedings of the Fifteenth International Conference on Knowledge Discovery and Data Mining, pp. 9–15. AAAI Press, New York (1998)

7. Chen, Y., Tang, S., Bouguila, N., Wanga, C., Du, J., Li, H.: A fast clustering algorithm based on pruning unnecessary distance computations in DBSCAN for high-dimensional data. Pattern Recogn. **83**, 375–387 (2018)

8. Darong, H., Peng, W.: Grid-based DBSCAN algorithm with referential parameters. Phys. Proc. **24**(Part B), 1166–1170 (2012)

9. D'Aniello, G., Gaeta, M., Loia, F., Reformat, M., Toti, D.: An environment for collective perception based on fuzzy and semantic approaches. J. Artif. Intell. Soft Comput. Res. **8**(3), 191–210 (2018)

10. Ester, M., Kriegel, H.P., Sander, J., Xu, X.: A density-based algorithm for discovering clusters in large spatial databases with noise. In: Proceeding of 2nd International Conference on Knowledge Discovery and Data Mining, pp. 226–231 (1996)

11. Fränti, P., Rezaei, M., Zhao, Q.: Centroid index: cluster level similarity measure. Pattern Recogn. **47**(9), 3034–3045 (2014)

12. Gabryel, M.: The bag-of-words method with different types of image features and dictionary analysis. J. Univ. Comput. Sci. **24**(4), 357–371 (2018)

13. Gabryel, M.: Data analysis algorithm for click fraud recognition. In: Damaševičius, R., Vasiljevienė, G. (eds.) ICIST 2018. CCIS, vol. 920, pp. 437–446. Springer, Cham (2018). https://doi.org/10.1007/978-3-319-99972-2_36

14. Gabryel, M., Damaševičius, R., Przybyszewski, K.: Application of the bag-of-words algorithm in classification the quality of sales leads. In: Rutkowski, L., Scherer, R., Korytkowski, M., Pedrycz, W., Tadeusiewicz, R., Zurada, J.M. (eds.) ICAISC 2018. LNCS, vol. 10841, pp. 615–622. Springer, Cham (2018). https://doi.org/10.1007/978-3-319-91253-0_57

15. Hruschka, E.R., de Castro, L.N., Campello, R.J.: Evolutionary algorithms for clustering gene-expression data. In: Fourth IEEE International Conference on Data Mining, ICDM 2004, pp. 403–406. IEEE (2004)

16. Karami, A., Johansson, R.: Choosing DBSCAN parameters automatically using differential evolution. Int. J. Comput. Appl. **91**, 1–11 (2014)

17. Liu, H., Gegov, A., Cocea, M.: Rule based networks: an efficient and interpretable representation of computational models. J. Artif. Intell. Soft Comput. Res. **7**(2), 111–123 (2017)

18. Luchi, D., Rodrigues, A.L., Varejao, F.M.: Sampling approaches for applying DBSCAN to large datasets. Pattern Recogn. Lett. **117**, 90–96 (2019)

19. Meng, X., van Dyk, D.: The EM algorithm - an old folk-song sung to a fast new tune. J. Roy. Stat. Soc. Ser. B (Methodol.) **59**(3), 511–567 (1997)

20. Murtagh, F.: A survey of recent advances in hierarchical clustering algorithms. Comput. J. **26**(4), 354–359 (1983)

21. Patrikainen, A., Meila, M.: Comparing subspace clusterings. IEEE Trans. Knowl. Data Eng. **18**(7), 902–916 (2006)

22. Prasad, M., Liu, Y.-T., Li, D.-L., Lin, C.-T., Shah, R.R., Kaiwartya, O.P.: A new mechanism for data visualization with TSK-type preprocessed collaborative fuzzy rule based system. J. Artif. Intell. Soft Comput. Res. **7**(1), 33–46 (2017)
23. Riid, A., Preden, J.-S.: Design of fuzzy rule-based classifiers through granulation and consolidation. J. Artif. Intell. Soft Comput. Res. **7**(2), 137–147 (2017)
24. Rohlf, F.: Single-link clustering algorithms. In: Krishnaiah, P.R., Kanal, L.N. (eds.) Handbook of Statistics, vol. 2, pp. 267–284 (1982)
25. Sameh, A.S., Asoke, K.N.: Development of assessment criteria for clustering algorithms. Pattern Anal. Appl. **12**(1), 79–98 (2009)
26. Serdah, A.M., Ashour, W.M.: Clustering large-scale data based on modified affinity propagation algorithm. J. Artif. Intell. Soft Comput. Res. **6**(1), 23–33 (2016). https://doi.org/10.1515/jaiscr-2016-0003
27. Shah, G.H.: An improved DBSCAN, a density based clustering algorithm with parameter selection for high dimensional data sets. In: Nirma University International Engineering, NUiCONE, pp. 1–6 (2012)
28. Sheikholeslam, G., Chatterjee, S., Zhang, A.: WaveCluster: a wavelet-based clustering approach for spatial data in very large databases. Int. J. Very Large Data Bases **8**(3–4), 289–304 (2000)
29. Shieh, H.-L.: Robust validity index for a modified subtractive clustering algorithm. Appl. Soft Comput. **22**, 47–59 (2014)
30. Starczewski, A.: A new validity index for crisp clusters. Pattern Anal. Appl. **20**(3), 687–700 (2017)
31. Starczewski, A., Krzyżak, A.: A modification of the Silhouette index for the improvement of cluster validity assessment. In: Rutkowski, L., Korytkowski, M., Scherer, R., Tadeusiewicz, R., Zadeh, L.A., Zurada, J.M. (eds.) ICAISC 2016. LNCS, vol. 9693, pp. 114–124. Springer, Cham (2016). https://doi.org/10.1007/978-3-319-39384-1_10
32. Wang, W., Yang, J., Muntz, R.: STING: a statistical information grid approach to spatial data mining. In: Proceedings of the 23rd International Conference on Very Large Data Bases, VLDB 1997, pp. 186–195 (1997)
33. Viswanath, P., Suresh Babu, V.S.: Rough-DBSCAN: a fast hybrid density based clustering method for large data sets. Pattern Recogn. Lett. **30**(16), 1477–1488 (2009)
34. Zalik, K.R.: An efficient K-Means clustering algorithm. Pattern Recogn. Lett. **29**(9), 1385–1391 (2008)

Speed Limits Can Be Determined from Geospatial Data with Machine Learning Methods

Piotr Szwed[✉]

AGH University of Science and Technology, Kraków, Poland
pszwed@agh.edu.pl

Abstract. Various country-wide guidelines for speed limits setting make use of diverse parameters specifying properties of roads, their environment, as well as traffic intensity, statistical distribution of measured vehicle speeds and history of crash accidents. We argue, that although such extensive data are not present in public geospatial datasets, they can be inferred as latent features in machine learning models trained to predict speed limits. To verify this hypothesis we performed an experiment, in which we extracted tag-based and geometrical features from Open Street Map for Poland and applied various classification methods to predict class labels corresponding to speed limits. In spite of the fact that the datasets were imbalanced (with majority classes corresponding to default speed limits) we obtained F1 scores ranging from 0.72 to 0.91 for lower speed roads. The neural network classifier implemented with Tensorflow framework turned out to be the most efficient.

Keywords: Speed limits determination · Geospatial data ·
Machine learning · Neural networks

1 Introduction

Speed limits within a road network are important factors of traffic organization, as they affect safety, mobility, throughput and air pollution. Multiple country-wide guidelines for speed limits setting are used over the world [1,5,6,10,13]. They take a form of rule systems, algorithms or decision tables and often use detailed information on road properties, distance to specific objects like schools or hospitals, they also rely on measured local variables like traffic density, statistical distribution of drivers speed and history of traffic accidents.

Examining free, publicly available geospatial datasets, as for example Open Street Map [14], it can be observed that they become more and more rich, detailed and reliable. They comprise a vast amount of information related to the transport network, as well as various objects: buildings, schools, parking lots and public amenities.

The fact that this information partially overlap with input data used in various speed limits setting standards, suggests a hypothesis that speed limits

© Springer Nature Switzerland AG 2019
L. Rutkowski et al. (Eds.): ICAISC 2019, LNAI 11509, pp. 431–442, 2019.
https://doi.org/10.1007/978-3-030-20915-5_39

can be determined from pure geospatial data. Apparently, when comparing the map data with the variables appearing in guidelines, it can be stated that a lot of information is missing. Guidelines often use more detailed road design parameters, map dataset like OSM neither refer to the traffic volumes, nor actual drivers speed, nor traffic accidents. However, it can be expected that various dependencies exist between such factors as traffic intensity, number of accidents, population density, road geometry and concentration of specific objects.

To verify our hypothesis we built a workflow shown in Fig. 1. It comprised two basic steps: *Feature extraction* and *Prediction*. As the source OSM map data for Poland was used. We extracted two kinds of features: based on *tags* attributed in OSM to geometric primitives and features related to *road geometry*.

The *Prediction* step can be implemented either as classification or a regression task. In the first case classifier is trained to predict discrete labels. In the second case continuous output of regression function can be rounded to the closest speed limit step. In this paper we focused on the approach based on classification and tested a number of classification algorithms on roads of various classes.

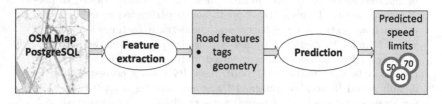

Fig. 1. Basic steps of a system for speed limit prediction from geospatial data

A system that internally uses machine learning methods to predict speed limits can be used to perform exhaustive verification of posted speeds within the whole road network, discover anomalies and indicate discrepancies, either local or between regions. An advantage of the discussed approach is that an estimator, once learned, can process massive amounts of data in a short time, whereas using traditional approach speed limits are established for individual cases, by examining the detailed design documentation and collecting data during costly surveys. Another imaginable use case is to employ it within an expert system, which would aid a human user to make the final decision.

The paper is organized as follows: next Sect. 2 provides a short review of authorship attribution problems. It is followed by Sect. 3, which discusses the types of features extracted from map data. Section 4 presents datasets used and reports results of conducted experiments. Section 5 provides concluding remarks.

2   Related Works

Spatial data mining aims at discovering interesting, non-trivial patterns in spatial data, the patterns that are useful, general enough to be applied to new data, and, preferably, interpretable by humans [11]. Most common patterns fall into four categories [16]: outliers (spatial locations with atypical features), co-locations (subsets of features appearing often together), location predictions for a particular concept or event type and hotspots (spatial grouping of events). The specificity of geospatial datasets is pointed out in [12]: although they use very simple representations of geographic objects (like points, polylines, polygons), spatial relations tend to be more complex than relations in other sources. They are based on such concepts as distance, area, length, overlapping, connectivity and intersection.

In [15] a number of common data mining tasks is discussed: classification, clustering, anomaly detection, association rule mining and trend detection in spatio-temporal data. Domains of application include: transport, tourism, ecology and land use management.

Geospatial data mining in transport engineering is used for analysis of vehicle flows, preparation of navigation data, road pavement evaluation and accident analysis [2]. Probably the most abundant literature concerns the last topic: geolocated accident data are mined either in order to predict accidents severity [3,18] or their probable locations [8].

To our knowledge, using machine learning methods to determine speed limits based on geospatial data has not ever been performed before.

As this work is related to methods for speed limits setting, we provide their brief characteristic. Report [6] reviews various approaches for setting speed limits over world. *Operating speed* method, used in various U.S. states, is based on V85 parameter defined as 85 percentile of measured vehicle speed. Such approach follows the observed regularity that 85% of drivers correctly perceive safe speed (usually V85 is a little above the actual speed limit). *Road risk*, which is applied in Canada [10] and New Zealand [13], is based on such factors as road properties, adjacent land use, traffic and accidents history. *Expert system* supported by software is employed in the United States and Australia [5]. A prototype expert system has been also developed recently in Poland [4]. *Optimal speed* methods attempt to balance risk, costs of crashes and medical care with impact on mobility and environmental. Methods aiming at *injury minimization* are employed in Sweden and Netherlands. It is pointed out in [6] that the cost of data collection depends on the method, in particular the cost is significant for the optimal speed approach, where multiple parameters extracted from a large number of locally collected data are fed into model equations.

Regardless of the primary factors used for speed limit determination, all guidelines include into analysis additional properties of road segments, such as density of access roads, visibility, road class, number of lanes, road width and geometry. They also adjust speed limits in the vicinity of schools or hospitals.

Considering the datasets used in this work, guidelines for Poland [7] are of particular interest. Following the road risk approach, in the first place they refer to geospatial properties: density of access roads, presence of traffic lights or pedestrian crossing, type of road intersections, road geometry and specific areas like school zones. The second group of important factors are: traffic intensity and history of accidents. The V85 (85 percentile) criterion is not employed.

Due to limited space we do not discuss machine learning concepts, such as classification methods, metrics, neural networks architectures and learning frameworks. Their details can be found in comprehensive `scikit-learn` and TensorFlow documentation available online [9,17].

3   Feature Extraction from GIS Data

3.1   Open Street Map Data Model

Open Street Map (OSM) [14] is a community project aiming at creation of a free world map. The map data is collected using free sources, mainly GPS devices and aerial images. Details are gathered during local surveys. The project attracted over 4 millions active users and map data was delivered by 1 million contributors.

OSM comprises information on speed limits that, according to information found on various web fora, is very reliable for the map of Poland. Starting from 2015 OSM is the source of map data used by Yanosik, a popular service used in Poland for navigation and speed control warning. This issue is of great importance, as it justifies using speed limits extracted from OSM as a ground truth.

OSM data model defines a map as a collection of primitives of three basic types: nodes (points with longitude and latitude attributes), ways (node sequences forming polylines or polygons) and relations (sets of other vectors assigned with roles). OSM uses tags, i.e. (*key, value*) pairs that can be assigned vectors and relations in order to define their semantics. This allows to interpret them as map objects of a specific type.

Example of OSM data is shown in Fig. 2a. Polylines (OSM ways) are marked with tags indicating that they constitute roads (primary or residential). Polygon is assigned with typical tags used to describe building. When a high-level object, e.g. a road, comprises multiple parts with different properties, usually each part is represented by a separate graphical primitive with different sets of tags. Hence, the segment BC, which is marked with a tag indicating bridge, is internally modeled as a separate OSM way.

3.2   Features

Primary objects of interest for speed limits determinations are directed road segments, therefore feature extraction process is divided into two basic steps: extracting road segments and collecting their features from GIS data.

We assumed that the segments end at intersections with public roads, what conforms the general rule that in such situation posted speed limits are reset to default values. In consequence, roads are split at intersection points and two segments pointing at opposite directions are generated for two-way roads. Road segments ends are also consistent with underlying OSM ways (polylines).

Figure 2b shows an example of splitting the road ABCDE into segments. As the segment BC is additionally tagged as a bridge, its set of features will be also different.

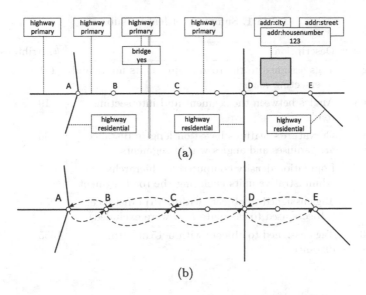

Fig. 2. (a) OSM model (b) the directed road segments

Procedure. OSM map data for Poland was downloaded from the `geofabrik` repository[1] and imported into PostgreSQL database with `osm2pgsql` tool. Segmentation of all roads yielded nearly 2000000 segments, among them 150000 road segments assigned with route symbol, i.e. belonging to national and voivodeship roads. In further experiments we used route segments only.

Features for route segments were extracted and cached in the database. Apart from a very few numeric features, as `maxspeed` (class label), number of lanes or `maxaxleload`, that could be read directly from OSM data, the majority of values result from computations, e.g. counting occurrences of tags within a certain distance, calculating angles, radiuses, etc. Therefore the extraction procedures were written in PLpgSQL (a procedural language for PostgreSQL) using PostGIS functions to accelerate geospatial queries. Finally, in experiments we used exported datasets comprising a selection of route segments made according to a specific road class or region.

Features assigned to route segments are logically divided into six subsets being summarized in Table 1, which gives their code names, short description and number of attributes. More details are developed in subsequent paragraphs.

Subset tags. The subset contains features extracted form three groups of tags:

1. assigned to road segments (e.g indicating surface type, number of lanes, incline),
2. their nodes (street lights, lighting, pedestrian crossing, maximum axle load, speed camera),

---

[1] https://download.geofabrik.de/europe/poland.html.

Table 1. Summary of feature subsets

Subset	Description	#attributes
tags	Tags assigned to the road segment, its nodes and intersecting roads	121
conn	Angles between the segment and intersecting roads	19
curv	Curvature - features based on length, distance, arc radiuses and angles within segments	36
admin	Population density computed for hierarchy of administrative units enclosing the road segment	5
n15	Tags assigned to objects within 15 m distance (objects used to calculate *tags* were excluded)	951
n50	Tags assigned to objects within 15 m–50 m distance	1555

3. intersecting OSM ways (other roads and their types including pedestrian or bicycle roads, but also ditches, barriers).

The features from this group describe road properties, convey information on infrastructure objects as well as on the direct neighborhood, e.g. density of intersecting access ways.

Subset conn. Features belonging to this subset describe geometry of road connections. They include: angles between the segment and the next segment in the route, as well as inflows and outflows on the left and right.

For the situation depicted in Fig. 3a extracted angle values are the following: α is the angle between route segments AB and AC. Angles between AB segment and the inflow (outflow) on the left are equal 90°. For inflows on the right two distinct values would be extracted: $\alpha_{min} = 45°$ and $\alpha_{max} = 90°$.

Subset curv. The subset contains features characterizing road curvature. They include the distance between road segment ends, its length, angles between component segments and radiuses computed as distance to intersection of perpendicular bisectors of two consecutive component segments (see Fig. 3b). As multiple values are computed, their statistical properties (minimal, maximal, mean values and standard deviation) are included. It can be observed that speed limits are usually set at a certain distance between sharp turns, therefore curvature features were also extracted from nodes in a distance windows (d_b, d_f), where d_b and d_f are distances in backward and forward directions. Two windows: $(100\,m, 700\,m)$ and $(300\,m, 1200\,m)$ were used.

Both *conn* and *curv* are geometric features. We supposed that they could be relevant for lower class routes, which often conserve historical layout, especially, while traversing urban areas. Probably, they have lower influence on high speed roads that were designed from scratch or remodeled with heavy terrain forming to apply design rules specific for a road class.

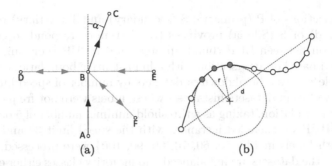

Fig. 3. Geometric features (a) road connections (b) curvature

Subset admin. Features from *admin* subset specify population densities for five levels of administration units appearing in the OSM map. Some of values were estimated (inherited after higher level unit) in the cases, where the population was not defined. It was assumed that the population density has influence on traffic intensity and in consequence on accidents and fatalities, what usually triggers initiatives to lower speed limits.

Subset n15 and n50. Both subsets were extracted with the same procedure that collects tags assigned to objects laying in the neighborhood within a distance interval (d_{min}, d_{max}). The intervals were set to $(0\,m, 15\,m)$ for *n15* and $(15\,m, 50\,m)$ for *n50*. As multiple $(key, value)$ pairs appear in the neighborhood, the features are built upon counting their occurrences. It was supposed that these features would encode information on such objects as buildings, places of worship, schools, shops or sport facilities, which periodically cause increased local traffic and risky inhabitants behavior.

Ranges selection may be considered a bit arbitrary. Actually, the 15 m distance addressed an old definition of built up area in Poland, which based it on a presence of at least three buildings within 15 m distance. This specification was given up a few dozens years ago, implicit speed limits were replaced by posted built up area signs. However, we assumed that many contemporary speed limits might be inherited from this epoch.

Features from *n15* and *n50* subsets have typical bag-of-words characteristic, i.e. they form sparse vectors of numeric values with prevailing zeros. This suggested applying Naïve Bayes classifier, which, as it can be seen in the next section, turned out to be ineffective.

4   Experiments

4.1   Datasets

We performed experiments on 12 datasets obtained by selecting road segments according to road class and region. Their details are given in Table 2. Segments in Mw-A and Tr-A datasets comprise all motorways and trunks in Poland. The others are selections of P (primary), S (secondary) and T (tertiary) routes in K (Lesser Poland) or S (Silesia) provinces (the letters correspond to car plates). The distinction between BUP (build up area) and NBUP (non build up area) was estimated based on intersection with administrative boundaries of cities and villages. Table 2 gives a breakdown of datasets by number of speed limits labels.

We removed from datasets instances, whose labels were not frequent enough to apply cross-validation, taking as a threshold minimal number of 5 occurrences, e.g. for P-S-BUP we excluded instances with the speed limit 30 and only road segments with labels in {40, 50, 60, 70, 80, 90, 100} were processed. It can be observed that the datasets are imbalanced and majority classes either correspond to default speed limits for particular road types (140 for motorways and 120 for trunks) or they are grouped around 50 (default for build up area) and 90 (default for non build up area) for other types of roads.

For Mw-A and Tr-A datasets n15 and n50 subsets were not used, as it was assumed that high-class roads are physically separated from enclosing land and the neighborhood has very little influence on speed limits. For PST*, P* and S* datasets all subsets of features were extracted.

Table 2. Datasets used in experiments. Naming convention: Mw: *motorways*, Tr: *trunks*, P: *prmiary*, S: *secondary*, T: *tertiary* roads, A: *all* regions, K: *Lesser Poland province*, S: *Silesia province*, BUP: *build up area*, NBUP: (*non build up*) area. Columns give numbers of instances assigned with a particular speed limit value, #ints: total number of instances, #att: number of attributes.

Dataset	20	30	40	50	60	70	80	90	100	110	120	140	#inst	#att
Mw-A	2	0	70	44	16	33	57	17	126	397	95	3741	4598	181
Tr-A	15	1	24	48	82	208	60	291	915	37	3286	1	4968	181
PST-K-BUP	0	22	323	5572	361	1161	13	1438	156	0	0	0	9046	2687
PST-K-NBUP	0	2	130	1072	77	208	0	318	32	0	0	0	1839	2687
P-K-BUP	0	6	44	2970	297	860	13	1002	156	0	0	0	5348	2687
P-K-NBUP	0	0	14	350	8	132	0	155	32	0	0	0	691	2687
S-K-BUP	0	16	279	2601	64	301	0	436	0	0	0	0	3697	2687
S-K-NBUP	0	2	116	722	69	76	0	163	0	0	0	0	1148	2687
P-S-BUP	0	3	65	2048	77	810	100	300	785	0	0	0	4188	2687
P-S-NBUP	0	0	39	668	13	198	3	247	224	0	0	0	1392	2687
S-S-BUP	0	23	153	3330	6	222	3	415	6	0	0	0	4158	2687
S-S-NBUP	0	8	118	1236	2	64	0	394	2	0	0	0	1824	2687

4.2   Classification

This section summarizes results of experiments whose goal was to confirm the supposition that map data and extracted features would allow to predict existing speed limits. We performed initial tests, during which several classifiers from `scikit-learn` [9] Python library were used. They included: Naïve Bayes, k-Nearest Neighbors, Logistic Regression (run in two modes: binary *one versus rest* and *multinomial*), Support Vector Machines with RBF kernel and Random Forest. Results for these classifiers are given in Tables 3 and 4.

Table 3. Accuracy scores for tested classifiers: *nb*: Naïve Bayes, *knn3*: k-Nearest Neighbors (k = 3), *logreg*: Logistic Regression, *logregmn*: Multinomial Logistic Regression, *svmrbf*: Support Vector Machines with RBF kernel, *rforest*: Random Forest, *ann* - Artificial Neural Network (architecture is given in *ann model* column). Mean values from 5-fold cross validation are reported.

Dataset	nb	knn3	logreg	logregmn	svmrbf	rforest	ann	ann model
Mw-A	0.0655	0.8838	0.8464	0.8486	0.8410	**0.9217**	0.8860	p66r_p33r
Tr-A	0.0576	0.8017	0.7688	0.7729	0.7580	**0.8641**	0.8174	p66r_p33r
PST-K-BUP	0.2594	0.6945	0.7504	0.7628	0.6160	0.8519	**0.8637**	p50r
PST-K-NBUP	0.4860	0.7060	0.7746	0.7937	0.5836	0.8743	**0.9200**	p50r
P-K-BUP	0.3313	0.6726	0.7509	0.7637	0.5563	0.8572	**0.8594**	p66r_p33r
P-K-NBUP	0.7147	0.6831	0.8177	0.8393	0.5066	0.8962	**0.9073**	p66r_p33r
S-K-BUP	0.3982	0.7328	0.7893	0.8006	0.7035	0.8596	**0.8969**	p66r_p33r
S-K-NBUP	0.5855	0.7130	0.7967	0.8229	0.6300	0.8840	**0.8962**	p66r_p33r
P-S-BUP	0.4017	0.7589	0.7907	0.7998	0.6358	0.8337	**0.8387**	p66r_p33r
P-S-NBUP	0.5306	0.6954	0.7971	0.8122	0.6184	**0.8618**	0.8473	p66r_p33r
S-S-BUP	0.5076	0.8130	0.8698	0.8777	0.8014	0.9134	**0.9261**	p66r_p33r
S-S-NBUP	0.5165	0.7478	0.8308	0.8484	0.6791	0.8918	**0.9259**	p66r_p33r

Table 4. F1 macro scores for tested classifiers obtained during 5-fold cross validation.

Dataset	nb	knn3	logreg	logregmn	svmrbf	rforest	ann	ann model
Mw-A	0.0780	0.5258	0.2259	0.2662	0.1541	**0.6038**	0.5379	p66r_p33r
Tr-A	0.0754	0.4734	0.2413	0.2775	0.1509	**0.5452**	0.4865	p66r_p33r
PST-K-BUP	0.2962	0.4933	0.4744	0.5113	0.0953	0.6379	**0.7399**	p50r
PST-K-NBUP	0.4854	0.5995	0.6584	0.6977	0.1228	0.8057	**0.8608**	p50r
P-K-BUP	0.3221	0.5608	0.5042	0.5193	0.0906	0.6252	**0.7713**	p66r_p33r
P-K-NBUP	0.7324	0.5139	0.6479	0.7070	0.1121	0.7849	**0.8553**	p66r_p33r
S-K-BUP	0.3131	0.4047	0.3985	0.4384	0.1377	0.6035	**0.8144**	p66r_p33r
S-K-NBUP	0.5347	0.5421	0.6609	0.7167	0.1546	0.8270	**0.8439**	p66r_p33r
P-S-BUP	0.3397	0.6013	0.5919	0.6144	0.2571	0.6807	**0.7296**	p66r_p33r
P-S-NBUP	0.4961	0.6153	0.6691	0.6970	0.2480	0.7702	**0.7999**	p66r_p33r
S-S-BUP	0.3217	0.4619	0.3665	0.4718	0.1271	0.5748	**0.7228**	p66r_p33r
S-S-NBUP	0.4011	0.4855	0.5774	0.6244	0.1618	0.6856	**0.9085**	p66r_p33r

As the obtained scores were not quite satisfactory, we decided to employ classifiers based on artificial neural networks (ANN). They were implemented using Keras deep learning framework with Tensorflow [17] backend supporting GPU acceleration. A few network architectures were tested and the best performing were included into the final comparison.

In Tables 3 and 4 accuracy and F1 (macro averaged) metrics computed during 5-fold cross validation are given. Best values are marked with boldfont. Two best performing classifiers can be pointed out: the first is the classifier based on neural network model, which occurred superior in the cases of PST*, P* and S* datasets and the second is Random Forest, which yielded the best scores for Mw-A and Tr-A and was the second for the other datasets.

As the neural network classifier occurred the most efficient, we provide some technical details. Columns *ann model* in Tables 3 and 4 specify network architectures. The entry p66r_p33r corresponds to a network with two hidden layers: having $0.66 \cdot n$ and $0.33 \cdot n$ neurons, where n is the input size. For p50r the network comprised one hidden layer of $0.5 \cdot n$ neurons. *ReLU* was used as the activation function, what is indicated by r letter. We also tested models with *sigmoid* activation function, but they were harder to train. Sizes of output layers were always equal to the number of expected class labels. For the last layer the activation function was *softmax* and *softmax cross-entropy* was used as the loss. Number of training epochs varied depending on the dataset: for Mw-A, Tr-A and PST* datasets it was set to 500, for the other 100 or 150 epochs were applied. In all cases Adam optimizer was used.

4.3   Discussion

As can be observed from Table 2, the datasets submitted to classification are imbalanced, e.g. for Mw-A the speed limit 140 is present in 81% cases, whereas for S-K-BUP 70% instances are labeled with 50. In general, class imbalance skews such metrics as accuracy or micro averaged F1. This explains the observed high accuracy values in Table 3, in particular for Mw-A dataset. The macro averaged F1 scores reported in Table 4 seem much more trustworthy in this case.

For high speed roads (motorways and trunks) Random Forest outperformed other classifiers. However, resulting F1 scores are lower than for other road types.

All classifiers, and in particular ANN, performed much better on datasets containing segments belonging to low speed roads. Obtained best F1 scores range from 0.72 up to 0.91. This can be attributed to extended sets of features based on tags assigned to objects in the road neighborhood (subsets *n15* and *n50*). In consequence, for Mw-A and Tr-A datasets only 181 attributes were used, whereas for the other datasets their number was equal to 2687.

Nevertheless, it is hard to find a rationale for using neighborhood information in the case of high speed (highways and trunks) roads, as they are physically separated from their environment. In some cases they are, actually, connected with a small number of infrastructure objects, e.g. entrances and exits from rest areas and gas stations. Presence of such objects may surely influence the speed limits, but for a moment the implemented feature extraction algorithms are not capable or separating them from objects behind the barriers.

Another problem that can be identified is the use of appropriate metric for evaluation. We applied typical classification scores for nominal class labels, whereas speed limits are at least ordinal. This is clearly visible for confusion matrices shown in Fig. 4. An algorithm that groups values close to the matrix diagonal should be probably considered better than the one that produces scattered values. To tackle this problem scores should be weighted, i.e. positions far from the diagonal should have higher error weight.

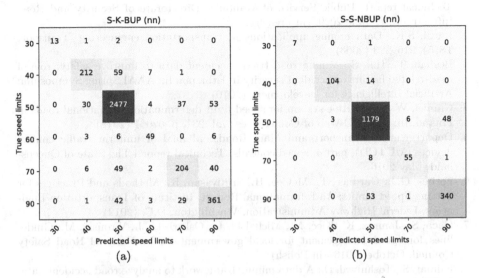

Fig. 4. Confusion matrices for the neural network classifier applied to S-K-BUP (secondary roads, Lesser Poland province, build up area) and S-S-NBUP (secondary roads, Silesia province, non-build up area)

5   Conclusions

In this paper we report results of experiment aiming at answering to the question, whether speed limits can be determined from geospatial data in public datasets with machine learning methods. We find that in the case of lower class roads, where features based on neighborhood were used, prediction are consistent with real speed limits. In spite of the fact that the datasets were imbalanced (with majority classes corresponding to default speed limits) we obtained F1 scores ranging from 0.72 to 0.91 for lower speed roads.

From various checked classification methods, prediction models based on artificial neural networks turned out to be the most efficient and we plan to focus on them in the future. We believe that obtained results can be further improved by feature engineering and by developing more sophisticated classification model, e.g. using stacked classifiers. Another promising approach, that was not tested, is to apply regression.

References

1. Antoine, D., Henin, A.: Guide of speed limits determination for the road network. Technical report, Public Service of Wallonia, Directorate of Security and Road Infrastructure, June 2009. (in French)
2. Barai, S.K.: Data mining applications in transportation engineering. Transport **18**(5), 216–223 (2003)
3. Beshah, T., Hill, S.: Mining road traffic accident data to improve safety: role of road-related factors on accident severity in Ethiopia. In: AAAI Spring Symposium: Artificial Intelligence for Development (2010)
4. Chmiel, W., et al.: Rule system for speed limit determination on national roads in Poland. In: MATEC Web of Conferences, vol. 231, p. 02001 (2018)
5. Department of Transport and Main Roads: Manual of uniform traffic control devices (MUTCD), part 4: speed controls. Technical report, The State of Queensland, May 2016
6. Forbes, G.J., Gardner, T., McGee, H., Srinivasan, R.: Methods and Practices for Setting Speed Limits: An Informational Report. Institute of Transportation Engineers, Federal Highway Administration, Washington, D.C. (2012)
7. Gaca, S., Jamroz, K., Kieć, M., Michalski, L., Oskarbski, J., Wroński, M.: Guidelines for speed management for local government roads. National Road Safety Council, October 2016. (in Polish)
8. Kumar, S., Toshniwal, D.: A data mining framework to analyze road accident data. J. Big Data **2**(1), 26 (2015)
9. scikit learn: Machine Learning in Python (2019). https://scikit-learn.org/stable/. Accessed 10 Jan 2019
10. Lemay, G., et al.: Guide of speed limits determination for the road of urban network. Technical report, Directorate of Communication, Ministry of Transport of Québec (2002). (in French)
11. Miller, H.J., Han, J.: Geographic Data Mining and Knowledge Discovery. CRC Press, Boca Raton (2009)
12. National Research Council: IT Roadmap to a Geospatial Future. The National Academies Press, Washington, DC (2003)
13. NZ Transport Agency, Ministry of Transport: Land Transport Rule, Setting of Speed Limits 2017, Rule 54001/2017. Wickliffe NZ Ltd., August 2017
14. OpenStreetMap: OpenStreetMap Wiki (2019). https://wiki.openstreetmap.org/wiki/Main_Page. Accessed 10 Jan 2019
15. Perumal, M., Velumani, B., Sadhasivam, A., Ramaswamy, K.: Spatial data mining approaches for GIS - a brief review. In: Satapathy, S., Govardhan, A., Raju, K., Mandal, J. (eds.) Emerging ICT for Bridging the Future - Proceedings of the 49th Annual Convention of the Computer Society of India CSI Volume 2. AISC, vol. 338, pp. 579–592. Springer, Cham (2015). https://doi.org/10.1007/978-3-319-13731-5_63
16. Shekhar, S., Kang, J.M., Gandhi, V.: Spatial data mining. In: Liu, L., Özsu, M.T. (eds.) Encyclopedia of Database Systems, pp. 2695–2698. Springer, Boston (2009). https://doi.org/10.1007/978-0-387-39940-9
17. TensorFlow: an open source machine learning framework for everyone (2019). https://www.tensorflow.org. Accessed 10 Jan 2019
18. Tesema, T.B., Abraham, A., Grosan, C.: Rule mining and classification of road traffic accidents using adaptive regression trees. Int. J. Simul. **6**(10–11), 80–94 (2005)

Appropriate Data Density Models in Probabilistic Machine Learning Approaches for Data Analysis

Thomas Villmann[1(✉)], Marika Kaden[1], Mehrdad Mohannazadeh Bakhtiari[1], and Andrea Villmann[1,2]

[1] Saxony Institute for Computational Intelligence and Machine Learning, University of Applied Sciences Mittweida, Mittweida, Germany
thomas.villmann@hs-mittweida.de

[2] Berufliches Schulzentrum Döbeln-Mittweida, Mittweida, Germany

Abstract. This paper investigates the mathematically appropriate treatment of data density estimators in machine learning approaches, if these estimators rely on data dissimilarity density models. We show exemplarily for two well-known machine learning approaches for classification and data visualization that this dependence is apparently analyzing the respective mathematical models. We show by numerical experiments that data sets generate different data dissimilarity densities depending on the dissimilarity measure in use. Thus an appropriate choice in machine learning models is mandatory to process the data consistently.

1 Introduction

Many machine learning models in modern data analysis are based on probabilistic models. Further, it is widely assumed for those methods that the underlying probability densities in the data space are modeled by probability densities regarding the data dissimilarities. Frequently, mixtures of Gaussians based on the squared Euclidean distance are in use due to its computational simplicity. The Gaussian's are centered at $\mathbf{w}_k \in \mathbb{R}^n$ such that the squared Euclidean distances $d_E^2(\mathbf{x}, \mathbf{w}_k)$ between the data $\mathbf{x} \in X \subseteq \mathbb{R}^n$ and center $\mathbf{w}_k$ is applied. However, this choice is not consistent in general: If the data are distributed according to a multi-dimensional Gaussian distribution the squared Euclidean distances between the data would be distributed according to the χ^2-density [1].

Generally, Gaussian approaches are widely used in classification and clustering as well as regression problems [2–4]. For example, robust soft learning vector quantization (RSLVQ [5]) strongly rely on mixture of Gaussians as well as many approaches in information theoretic learning for classification and clustering [6–9]. The stochastic neighbor embedding (SNE [10]) method for data visualization uses Gaussians to model data dissimilarity distributions as well as for the distances in the visualization space. In [11] VAN DER MAATEN and HINTON presented a technique called t-SNE, which is a variation of SNE considering

© Springer Nature Switzerland AG 2019
L. Rutkowski et al. (Eds.): ICAISC 2019, LNAI 11509, pp. 443–454, 2019.
https://doi.org/10.1007/978-3-030-20915-5_40

a student-t-distribution in the visualization space, to cope with 'crowding' problems. The resulting visualizations are often more likely and represent intrinsic data structures more accurate, which is dedicated to the heavy-tailed-property of the student-t-distribution [12]. The tt-SNE supposes the Student-t distribution also for the data space distance density [13].

However, many of the approaches have in common that the data density is modeled based on the assumption that it relies only on the data dissimilarity. In this case estimation of the data distribution in a potentially high-dimensional data space $X \subseteq \mathbb{R}^n$ is reduced to a one-dimensional density determination in the data dissimilarity space $\mathcal{D}$. Further, if stochastic gradient descent learning (SGDL) or variants thereof are used for model optimization, the involved gradients depend also on the derivatives of the data dissimilarity density estimator in use. Hence, an appropriate choice of the dissimilarity density is an inevitable requirement for consistent data modeling. Unfortunately, this key ingredient of probabilistic machine learning is frequently neglected.

In this paper, we draw the attention particular to this problem. For this purpose, we exemplarily reconsider probabilistic prototype-based classification approaches known as robust and interpretable classifiers as well as stochastic neighbor embedding to show explicitly their dependencies on the underlying data density usually estimated *implicitly* via the data dissimilarity densities. Thereafter, we investigate well-known standard datasets regarding their dissimilarity density depending on the applied dissimilarity measure. For this purpose, the empirical data dissimilarity density is compared with standard analytical one-dimensional densities including heavy-tailed densities. The comparison is performed using divergence measures. Here we apply the standard Kullback-Leibler-divergence as well as the more robust Rényi-divergence. We will show that for different dissimilarity measures for the same dataset the data dissimilarity density may change remarkable.

2   Preliminaries Regarding Data Densities and Analytical Density Functions

In the following we assume data $\mathbf{x}_i \in X \subseteq \mathbb{R}^n$ with the usually unknown data density $P(\mathbf{x}_i)$. Further, we assume an arbitrary non-negative dissimilarity measure $D(\mathbf{x}_i, \mathbf{x}_j)$ according to [14] such that $D : \mathbb{R}^n \times \mathbb{R}^n \longrightarrow \mathcal{D} \subseteq \mathbb{R}_+$, where $\mathcal{D}$ is the *data dissimilarity space*. Let the conditional probability

$$P(\mathbf{x}_i|\mathbf{x}_j) = P_{\mathcal{D}}(D(\mathbf{x}_i, \mathbf{x}_j)) \tag{1}$$

be only depending on the measure $D(\mathbf{x}_i, \mathbf{x}_j)$. Hence, $P_{\mathcal{D}}(D(\mathbf{x}_i, \mathbf{x}_j))$ is a density of one-dimensional quantities, i.e. is assumed to rely on a *dissimilarity density model*. For prototype based data modeling, like supervised and unsupervised vector quantization [15], the parameter set $W = \{\mathbf{w}_1, \ldots, \mathbf{w}_N\}$ is assumed with $P(\mathbf{x}_i|\mathbf{w}_k) = P_{\mathcal{D}}(D(\mathbf{x}_i, \mathbf{w}_k))$, i.e. the elements $\mathbf{w}_k \in W$ are supposed as prototypes in the data space. Thus we have

$$\frac{\partial P\left(\mathbf{x}_i|\mathbf{w}_k\right)}{\partial \mathbf{w}_k} = \frac{\partial P_{\mathscr{D}}\left(D\left(\mathbf{x}_i,\mathbf{w}_k\right)\right)}{\partial D\left(\mathbf{x}_i,\mathbf{w}_k\right)} \cdot \frac{\partial D\left(\mathbf{x}_i,\mathbf{w}_k\right)}{\partial \mathbf{w}_k} \tag{2}$$

as the gradient used for prototype adaptation in SGDL.

As mentioned above, many machine learning approaches estimate data densities by their data dissimilarity densities. We suggest to estimate first the empirical data dissimilarity density and compare it with analytical one-dimensional standard densities. Several probability density functions are depicted in Table 1 including heavy-tailed distributions. Probability densities are usually compared in terms of divergences. There exist a large variety of different divergences, which can be collected into several classes according to their mathematical properties and structural behavior for machine learning tasks [16,17]. The most prominent are the *Kullback-Leibler-divergence (KLD)*

$$D_{KL}\left(p||q\right) = \int p\left(x\right) \cdot \log\left(\frac{p\left(x\right)}{q\left(x\right)}\right) dx \tag{3}$$

based on the *Shannon-entropy* $H\left(p\right) = -\int p\left(x\right) \cdot \log\left(p\left(x\right)\right) dx$ [18,19] and the *Rényi-α-divergence*

$$D_\alpha\left(p||q\right) = \frac{1}{\alpha - 1} \log\left(\int \left(p\left(x\right)\right)^\alpha \cdot \left(q\left(x\right)\right)^{1-\alpha} dx\right) \tag{4}$$

introduced in [20]. We have $D_{KL}\left(p||q\right) = \lim_{\alpha \to 1} D_\alpha\left(p||q\right)$ is valid [21].

In the following we demonstrate for well-known machine learning approaches for classification and data visualization their dependencies on the data density estimator based on data dissimilarities.

3   Probabilistic Learning Vector Quantization Based on Data Dissimilarity Densities

Learning vector quantization (LVQ) as introduced by KOHONEN in [22] assumes a set $W = \{\mathbf{w}_1, \dots, \mathbf{w}_N\}$ of prototypes $\mathbf{w}_k \in \mathbb{R}^n$ to represent and to classify data $\mathbf{x} \in \mathbb{R}^n$. For this purpose, each prototype is assigned to be responsible for a certain class by the class label $c\left(\mathbf{w}_k\right) \in \mathscr{C} = \{1, \dots, C\}$. Each class is represented by at least one prototype. Further, a dissimilarity $D\left(\mathbf{x}, \mathbf{w}_j\right)$ is assumed.

For classification learning, we suppose training data $(\mathbf{X}, \mathbf{T}) = \{\mathbf{x}_i, \mathbf{t}_i\}_{i=1}^{N_D}$ where $\mathbf{t}_i \in [0,1]^C$ provides the probabilistic *target* class information for $\mathbf{x}_i$ with $t_{ij} \in [0,1]$ and $\sum_j t_{ij} = 1$. For unique mutually exclusive classification training data $t_{ij} \in \{0,1\}$ is required yielding a crisp class information. For this latter case the respective target class assignment is denoted by $\tau\left(\mathbf{x}\right)$. In the following we briefly explain two probabilistic variants.

In the following we explain two probabilistic LVQ classifiers, which finally are based on densities $p\left(\mathbf{x}|\mathbf{w}_j\right)$ estimated as functions $p\left(D\left(\mathbf{x}, \mathbf{w}_j\right)\right)$ of the given dissimilarity measure. Obviously, $p\left(D\left(\mathbf{x}_k, \mathbf{w}_j\right)\right)$ is a one-dimensional probability function (density) and should be taken consistently to the empirical data dissimilarity density $P_e\left(D_{ik}\right)$ which is an estimator for $P_{\mathscr{D}}\left(D_{ik}\right)$.

Table 1. Probability density functions together with their derivatives. The type indicates heavy-tailed densities (ht).

Type	Distribution	Density	Derivative
	Gaussian	$G(x,\mu,\sigma) = \frac{1}{\sqrt{2\pi}\sigma}\exp\left(-\frac{(x-\mu)^2}{2\sigma^2}\right)$	$\frac{\partial G(x,\mu,\sigma)}{\partial x} = \frac{(\mu-x)}{\sqrt{2\pi}\sigma^3}\exp\left(-\frac{(x-\mu)^2}{2\sigma^2}\right)$
	Weibull	$W(x,\beta,\sigma,\mu) = \frac{\beta}{\sigma}\cdot\left(\frac{x-\mu}{\sigma}\right)^{\beta-1}\cdot\exp\left(-\left(\frac{x-\mu}{\sigma}\right)^\beta\right)$	$\frac{\partial W(x,\beta,\sigma,\mu)}{\partial x} = -\exp\left(-\left(\frac{x-\mu}{\sigma}\right)^\beta\right)\cdot\left(\frac{x-\mu}{\sigma}\right)^{\beta-2}\cdot\frac{\beta\cdot\left(\beta\left(\frac{x-\mu}{\sigma}\right)^\beta-\beta+1\right)}{\sigma^2}$
	χ^2	$\chi^2(x,n) = \frac{x^{\frac{n}{2}-1}\cdot\exp(-\frac{x}{2})}{2^{\frac{n}{2}}\cdot\Gamma(\frac{n}{2})}$	$\frac{\partial\chi^2(x,n)}{\partial x} = -\frac{x^{\frac{n}{2}-1}\cdot\exp(-\frac{x}{2})}{2^{\frac{n+2}{2}}\cdot\Gamma(\frac{n}{2})}\cdot(2x^2-n+2)$
	γ-distribution	$\gamma(x,\beta,\sigma) = \frac{x^{\beta-1}}{\sigma^\beta\cdot\Gamma(\beta)}\cdot\exp\left(-\frac{x}{\sigma}\right)$	$\frac{\partial\tau_n(x)}{\partial x} = -\frac{x^{\beta-2}}{\sigma^{\beta+1}\cdot\Gamma(\beta)}\cdot\exp\left(-\frac{x}{\sigma}\right)\cdot(x-\sigma\cdot(\beta-1))$
	logistic	$L(x,\mu,\sigma) = \frac{\exp\left(-\frac{x-\mu}{\sigma}\right)}{\sigma\cdot(1+\exp\left(-\frac{x-\mu}{\sigma}\right))}$	$\frac{\partial L(x,\mu,\sigma)}{\partial x} = -\frac{\exp\left(-\frac{x-\mu}{\sigma}\right)}{\sigma^2\cdot(1+\exp\left(-\frac{x-\mu}{\sigma}\right))}$
ht	Student-t	$\tau_n(x) = \frac{\Gamma\left(\frac{n+1}{2}\right)}{\sqrt{n\pi}\Gamma\left(\frac{n}{2}\right)}\cdot\left(1+\frac{x^2}{n}\right)^{-\frac{n+1}{2}}$	$\frac{\partial\tau_n(x)}{\partial x} = -\frac{\Gamma\left(\frac{n+1}{2}\right)}{\sqrt{n\pi}\Gamma\left(\frac{n}{2}\right)}\cdot\left(1+\frac{x^2}{n}\right)^{-\frac{n+3}{2}}\cdot\frac{n+1}{n}\cdot x$
ht	Lévy density	$\lambda(x,\mu,\sigma) = \sqrt{\frac{\sigma}{2\pi}}\cdot\frac{1}{(x-\mu)^{\frac{3}{2}}}\cdot\exp\left(-\frac{\sigma}{2(x-\mu)}\right)$	$\frac{\partial\lambda(x,\mu,\sigma)}{\partial x} = \sqrt{\frac{\sigma}{2\pi}}\cdot\frac{\exp\left(-\frac{\sigma}{2(x-\mu)}\right)}{2(x-\mu)^{\frac{7}{2}}}\cdot(\sigma-3(x-\mu))$
ht	Cauchy-Lorenz	$\zeta(x,\mu,\sigma) = \frac{1}{\pi}\cdot\frac{\sigma}{\sigma^2+(x-\mu)^2}$	$\frac{\partial\lambda(x,\mu,\sigma)}{\partial x} = \frac{\sigma}{\pi}\cdot\frac{2(\mu-x)}{(\sigma^2+(x-\mu)^2)^2}$
ht	log-γ-distribution	$\log\gamma(x,\beta,\sigma) = \frac{x^{-\left(\frac{1}{\sigma}+1\right)}}{\sigma^\beta\cdot\Gamma(\beta)}\cdot(\log(x))^{\beta-1}$	$\frac{\partial\log\gamma(x,\beta,\sigma)}{\partial x} = \frac{(\log(x))^{\beta-2}}{x^{\frac{1}{\sigma}+2}\cdot\sigma^{\beta+1}\cdot\Gamma(\beta)}\cdot((1+\sigma)\log(x)+\sigma(1-\beta))$
ht	log-logistic	$\log L(x,\mu,\sigma) = \frac{1}{\alpha\sigma}\cdot\frac{\left(\frac{x}{\alpha}\right)^{\frac{1}{\sigma}-1}}{\left(1+\left(\frac{x}{\alpha}\right)^{\frac{1}{\sigma}}\right)^2}$ for $\alpha=\exp(\mu)$	$\frac{\partial\log L(x,\mu,\sigma)}{\partial x} = -\frac{\beta\cdot\left(\frac{x}{\alpha}\right)^\beta}{x^2\cdot\left(1+\left(\frac{x}{\alpha}\right)^\beta\right)^3}\cdot\left(\left(\frac{x}{\alpha}\right)^\beta(1+\beta)+1-\beta\right)$

3.1   Robust Soft Learning Vector Quantization

Robust Soft learning vector quantization (RSLVQ) was established in [5]. It estimates the posterior probabilities $p\left(c|\mathbf{x}\right)$ for a given class $c \in \mathscr{C}$ for unique classification training data. RSLVQ considers

$$P_W\left(\mathbf{x}\right) = \sum_{j=1}^{N} p\left(\mathbf{x}|\mathbf{w}_j\right) p\left(\mathbf{w}_j\right) \tag{5}$$

as the probability density for $\mathbf{x}$ generated by the model with the prototypes $W = \{\mathbf{w}_1, \ldots, \mathbf{w}_N\}$ taken as model parameters and $p\left(\mathbf{x}|\mathbf{w}_j\right)$ is the probability that $\mathbf{x}$ is generated by the jth model component $\mathbf{w}_j$. The probabilities $p\left(\mathbf{w}_j\right)$ are the priors for the model components.

The model based estimator of the joint probability for $\mathbf{x}$ and an arbitrarily given but fixed class $c \in \mathscr{C}$ is

$$P_W\left(\mathbf{x}, c\right) = \sum_{j:c(\mathbf{w}_j)=c} p\left(\mathbf{x}|\mathbf{w}_j\right) p\left(\mathbf{w}_j\right) \tag{6}$$

and, analogously, we have

$$P_W\left(\mathbf{x}, \neg c\right) = \sum_{j:c(\mathbf{w}_j)\neq c} p\left(\mathbf{x}|\mathbf{w}_j\right) p\left(\mathbf{w}_j\right) \tag{7}$$

as model based probability of the complement. Further, the probabilities

$$p_c\left(\mathbf{w}_j|\mathbf{x}\right) = \frac{p\left(\mathbf{x}|\mathbf{w}_j\right) p\left(\mathbf{w}_j\right)}{P_W\left(\mathbf{x}, c\right)} \text{ and } p_{\neg c}\left(\mathbf{w}_j|\mathbf{x}\right) = \frac{p\left(\mathbf{x}|\mathbf{w}_j\right) p\left(\mathbf{w}_j\right)}{P_W\left(\mathbf{x}, \neg c\right)} \tag{8}$$

are the (posterior) probabilities that a data point $\mathbf{x}$ is assigned to the prototype $\mathbf{w}_j$ given that this data point was generated by class c, and under the opposite assumption that this data point was not generated any other class than c, respectively. The class prediction probability $p_W\left(c|\mathbf{x}\right)$ of RSLVQ for each class $c \in \mathscr{C}$ is obtained as

$$p_W\left(c|\mathbf{x}\right) = \frac{P_W\left(\mathbf{x}, c\right)}{P_W\left(\mathbf{x}\right)} = \frac{\sum_{j:c(\mathbf{w}_j)=c} p\left(\mathbf{x}|\mathbf{w}_j\right) p\left(\mathbf{w}_j\right)}{\sum_{k=1}^{N} p\left(\mathbf{x}|\mathbf{w}_k\right) p\left(\mathbf{w}_k\right)} \tag{9}$$

such that $\sum_{c=1}^{C} p\left(c|\mathbf{x}\right) = 1$ is valid.

RSLVQ uses the negative log-likelihood ratio

$$l_{RSLVQ}\left(\mathbf{x}_k, W\right) = -\ln\left(\frac{P_W\left(\mathbf{x}_k, \tau_k\right)}{P_W\left(\mathbf{x}_k\right)}\right) \tag{10}$$

as *local cost* for given training data $(\mathbf{x}_k, \tau\left(\mathbf{x}_k\right))$, such that the cost function becomes

$$L_{RSLVQ}\left(X, W\right) = -\sum_{k} \ln\left(\frac{P_W\left(\mathbf{x}_k, \tau_k\right)}{P_W\left(\mathbf{x}_k\right)}\right) \tag{11}$$

using the abbreviation $\tau_k = \tau(\mathbf{x}_k)$ for the target class. SGDL for prototype learning regarding the cost function $L_{RSLVQ}(X, W)$ takes place as

$$\Delta \mathbf{w}_j \propto -\varepsilon(t) \cdot \frac{\partial l_{RSLVQ}(\mathbf{x}_k, W)}{\partial \mathbf{w}_j} \tag{12}$$

with the local gradients

$$\frac{\partial l_{RSLVQ}(\mathbf{x}_k, W)}{\partial \mathbf{w}_j} = p(\mathbf{w}_j) \cdot \left(\frac{\delta(c(\mathbf{w}_j), \tau_k)}{P_W(\mathbf{x}_k, \tau_k)} - \frac{1}{P_W(\mathbf{x}_k)} \right) \cdot \frac{\partial p(\mathbf{x}_k|\mathbf{w}_j)}{\partial \mathbf{w}_j} \tag{13}$$

according to [5]. $\delta(c, \tau)$ is the Kronecker symbol with $\delta(c, \tau) = 1$ iff $c = \tau$ and zero elsewhere.

The learning rate $\varepsilon(t) > 0$ has to fulfill the usual conditions $\sum_t \varepsilon(t) = \infty$ and $\sum_t (\varepsilon(t))^2 < \infty$ [23]. The priors frequently are chosen to be $p(\mathbf{w}_j) = \frac{1}{N}$ giving no bias to any prototype.

SEO&Obermayer specified in [5] the probabilities $p(\mathbf{x}|\mathbf{w}_j)$ as Gaussian's (exponential density)

$$p(\mathbf{x}|\mathbf{w}_j) = \exp\left(\frac{-D_E^2(\mathbf{x}_k, \mathbf{w}_j)}{2\sigma^2} \right)$$

where $D_E^2(\mathbf{x}_k, \mathbf{w}_j)$ is the squared Euclidean metric. Here we make the more general ansatz

$$p(\mathbf{x}_k|\mathbf{w}_j) = P_{\mathscr{D}}(D(\mathbf{x}_k, \mathbf{w}_j)). \tag{14}$$

Thus $p(\mathbf{x}_k|\mathbf{w}_j)$ is assumed to be modeled as a dissimilarity density in $\mathscr{D}$. For the gradient (13) this leads to

$$\frac{\partial l_{RSLVQ}(\mathbf{x}_k, W)}{\partial \mathbf{w}_j} = \frac{1}{N} \left(\frac{\delta(c(\mathbf{w}_j), \tau_k)}{P_W(\mathbf{x}_k, \tau_k)} - \frac{1}{P_W(\mathbf{x}_k)} \right) \cdot \frac{\partial P_{\mathscr{D}}(D(\mathbf{x}_k, \mathbf{w}_j))}{\partial D(\mathbf{x}_k, \mathbf{w}_j)} \cdot \frac{\partial D(\mathbf{x}_k, \mathbf{w}_j)}{\partial \mathbf{w}_j} \tag{15}$$

using the chain rule for the derivative.

Obviously, due to the assumption (14), $P_{\mathscr{D}}(D(\mathbf{x}_k, \mathbf{w}_j))$ is computable if a respective differentiable probability density function is available. In [24] $P_{\mathscr{D}}(D(\mathbf{x}_k, \mathbf{w}_j))$ is considered to be a Student-t probability density. Yet, we can switch to an arbitrary differentiable density like given in Table 1. For this purpose, we have to compare these density functions with the empirical data dissimilarity density $P_e(d_{ij})$ and to select the best fitting.

3.2 Probabilistic LVQ

Probabilistic LVQ (PLVQ [25]) uses information theoretic concepts to estimate the model probabilities $p_W(c|\mathbf{x})$. Let $\mathbf{p}(\mathbf{x}) = (p_1(\mathbf{x}), \ldots, p_C(\mathbf{x}))$ be the class probability vector for sample $\mathbf{x}$ and $\mathbf{p}_W(\mathbf{x}) = (p_W(1|\mathbf{x}), \ldots, p_W(C|\mathbf{x}))$ the respective predicted class probability vector provided by a probabilistic classifier model depending on the parameter set $W = \{\mathbf{w}_1, \ldots, \mathbf{w}_N\}$ as before. Again, the vectors $\mathbf{w}_k$ are interpreted as prototypes. The mutual information between them is maximized if the corresponding KLD $D_{KL}\left(\mathbf{p}\left(\mathbf{x}\right)\|\mathbf{p}_W\left(\mathbf{x}\right)\right)$ is minimized, which is equivalent to maximize the cross-entropy

$$Cr\left(\mathbf{t}\left(\mathbf{x}\right)\|\mathbf{p}_W\left(\mathbf{x}\right)\right) = \sum_c p_c\left(\mathbf{x}\right)\cdot\log\left(p_W\left(c|\mathbf{x}\right)\right) \tag{16}$$

as shown in [7, p. 221ff]. For PLVQ the cross-entropy $Cr\left(\mathbf{t}\left(\mathbf{x}\right)\|\mathbf{p}_W\left(\mathbf{x}\right)\right)$ plays the role of a local cost such that

$$L_{PLVQ}\left(X,W\right) = -\sum_k Cr\left(\mathbf{t}\left(\mathbf{x}_k\right)\|\mathbf{p}_W\left(\mathbf{x}_k\right)\right) \tag{17}$$

has to be minimized [25]. Alternatively,

$$L_{PLVQ}^{\alpha}\left(X,W\right) = \frac{1}{1-\alpha}\sum_k\log\left(\sum_c\left(\mathbf{t}\left(\mathbf{x}_k\right)\right)^{\alpha}\cdot\left(p_W\left(c|\mathbf{x}_k\right)\right)^{1-\alpha}\right) \tag{18}$$

based on the Rényi divergence D_{α} from (4) could be taken as cost function. Again $p_W\left(c|\mathbf{x}_k\right)$ depends on $p\left(\mathbf{x}|\mathbf{w}_j\right)$ via (9) and the gradients can be found in [17]. Hence, assuming (14) is valid, an arbitrary differentiable density function can be used.

4   Stochastic Neighbor Embedding

Stochastic Neighbor Embedding (SNE) realizes a non-linear data projection $\pi\left(\mathbf{x}_j\right) = \mathbf{y}_j : \mathbb{R}^{n_d} \rightarrow \mathbb{R}^{n_p}$ into the projection space $\mathbb{R}^{n_p}$ with $n_p \ll n_d$ frequently chosen to be $n_p = 2$ for visualization [10]. More precisely, SNE seeks for projection space coordinate vectors $\mathbf{y}_j$ such that the intrinsic data structure is preserved as best as possible. The respective cost function to be minimized by SNE is the KLD $D_{KL}\left(P_{\mathscr{D}}\|Q\right)$ where $P_{\mathscr{D}}\left(d_{ij}\right)$ and $Q\left(\varDelta_{ij}\right)$ are the probability densities of the data distances $d_{ij} = D\left(\mathbf{x}_i,\mathbf{x}_j\right)$ in the data and $\varDelta_{ij} = \varDelta\left(\mathbf{y}_i,\mathbf{y}_j\right)$ in the projection space, respectively. Alternative divergences to the KLD, including Rényi-divergences $D_{\alpha}\left(P_{\mathscr{D}}\|Q\right)$, are considered in [26].

In SNE, both probabilities $P_{\mathscr{D}}\left(d_{ij}\right)$ and $Q\left(\varDelta_{ij}\right)$ depend explicitly only on the dissimilarities d_{ij} and $\varDelta_{ij}$, respectively. The probabilities are assumed to be Gaussian (exponential) distributions whereas t-SNE assumes a Student-t distribution for $Q\left(\varDelta_{ij}\right)$ with freedom degree $\eta = 1$ [11]. A t-SNE with free learnable freedom parameter is proposed in [27], requiring an estimation of the Hausdorff-dimension (intrinsic data dimensionality).[1] The tt-SNE takes Student-t distribution for both $Q\left(\varDelta_{ij}\right)$ and $P_{\mathscr{D}}\left(d_{ij}\right)$ [13].

---

[1] A respective approach is the Grassberger-Procaccia-method estimating the so-called correlation dimension as an approximation for the Hausdorff-dimension [28–30].

Assuming a differentiable dissimilarity measure Δ_{ij} in the projection space, optimization in SNE can be realized by SGDL for a given divergence with respect to the projection space coordinates $\mathbf{y}_j$. In case of the KLD we write

$$D_{KL}\left(P_{\mathscr{D}}\|Q\right) = \sum_i \sum_j f\left(P_{\mathscr{D}}\left(d_{ij}\right), Q\left(\Delta_{ij}\right)\right) \tag{19}$$

with $f\left(P_{\mathscr{D}}, Q\right) = P_{\mathscr{D}} \cdot \log P_{\mathscr{D}} - P_{\mathscr{D}} \cdot \log Q$. Then, the stochastic gradient is

$$\frac{\partial_S D_{KL}\left(P_{\mathscr{D}}\|Q\right)}{\partial \mathbf{y}_k} = \sum_i \frac{\delta f\left(P_{\mathscr{D}}\left(d_{ik}\right), Q\left(\Delta_{ik}\right)\right)}{\delta Q\left(\Delta_{ik}\right)} \cdot \frac{\partial Q\left(\Delta_{ik}\right)}{\partial \Delta_{ik}} \cdot \frac{\partial \Delta_{ik}}{\partial \mathbf{y}_k}$$

$$+ \sum_j \frac{\delta f\left(P_{\mathscr{D}}\left(d_{kj}\right), Q\left(\Delta_{kj}\right)\right)}{\delta Q\left(\Delta_{kj}\right)} \cdot \frac{\partial Q\left(\Delta_{kj}\right)}{\partial \Delta_{kj}} \cdot \frac{\partial \Delta_{kj}}{\partial \mathbf{y}_k}$$

which becomes for symmetric quantities d_{ij} and Δ_{ij} simply

$$\frac{\partial_S D_{KL}\left(P_{\mathscr{D}}\|Q\right)}{\partial \mathbf{y}_k} = 2 \sum_i -\frac{P_{\mathscr{D}}\left(d_{kj}\right)}{Q\left(\Delta_{kj}\right)} \cdot \frac{\partial Q\left(\Delta_{ik}\right)}{\partial \Delta_{ik}} \cdot \frac{\partial \Delta_{ik}}{\partial \mathbf{y}_k} \tag{20}$$

using the Fréchet-derivative $\frac{\delta f_{KL}(P_{\mathscr{D}}, Q)}{\delta Q} = -\frac{P_{\mathscr{D}}}{Q}$ [17]. For the Rényi divergence we analogously consider

$$D_\alpha\left(P_{\mathscr{D}}\|Q\right) = \frac{1}{\alpha - 1} \cdot \log\left(\sum_i \sum_j \left(P_{\mathscr{D}}\left(d_{ij}\right)\right)^\alpha \cdot \left(Q\left(\Delta_{ij}\right)\right)^{1-\alpha}\right) \tag{21}$$

and obtain

$$\frac{\partial_S D_\alpha\left(P_{\mathscr{D}}\|Q\right)}{\partial \mathbf{y}_k} = \frac{1}{\alpha - 1} \cdot \frac{\sum_l \left(\frac{P_{\mathscr{D}}\left(d_{lk}\right)}{Q\left(\Delta_{lk}\right)}\right)^\alpha \cdot \frac{\partial Q\left(\Delta_{lk}\right)}{\partial \Delta_{lk}} \cdot \frac{\partial \Delta_{lk}}{\partial \mathbf{y}_k}}{\sum_i \sum_j \left(P_{\mathscr{D}}\left(d_{ij}\right)\right)^\alpha \cdot \left(Q\left(\Delta_{ij}\right)\right)^{1-\alpha}}$$

$$+ \frac{1}{\alpha - 1} \cdot \frac{\sum_m \left(\frac{P_{\mathscr{D}}\left(d_{km}\right)}{Q\left(\Delta_{km}\right)}\right)^\alpha \cdot \frac{\partial Q\left(\Delta_{km}\right)}{\partial \Delta_{km}} \cdot \frac{\partial \Delta_{km}}{\partial \mathbf{y}_k}}{\sum_i \sum_j \left(P_{\mathscr{D}}\left(d_{ij}\right)\right)^\alpha \cdot \left(Q\left(\Delta_{ij}\right)\right)^{1-\alpha}}$$

which reduces to

$$\frac{\partial_S D_\alpha\left(P_{\mathscr{D}}\|Q\right)}{\partial \mathbf{y}_k} = \frac{\frac{2}{\alpha-1} \cdot \sum_l \left(\frac{P_{\mathscr{D}}\left(d_{lk}\right)}{Q\left(\Delta_{lk}\right)}\right)^\alpha}{\sum_i \sum_j \left(P_{\mathscr{D}}\left(d_{ij}\right)\right)^\alpha \cdot \left(Q\left(\Delta_{ij}\right)\right)^{1-\alpha}} \cdot \frac{\partial Q\left(\Delta_{km}\right)}{\partial \Delta_{km}} \cdot \frac{\partial \Delta_{km}}{\partial \mathbf{y}_k} \tag{22}$$

for the symmetric quantities d_{ij} and Δ_{ij}. The most prominent case $\alpha = 2$ leads to

$$\frac{\partial_S D_{\alpha=2}\left(P_{\mathscr{D}}\|Q\right)}{\partial \mathbf{y}_k} = \frac{\sum_l \left(\frac{P_{\mathscr{D}}\left(d_{lk}\right)}{Q\left(\Delta_{lk}\right)}\right)^2}{\sum_i \sum_j \frac{\left(P_{\mathscr{D}}\left(d_{ij}\right)\right)^2}{Q\left(\Delta_{ij}\right)}} \cdot \frac{\partial Q\left(\Delta_{km}\right)}{\partial \Delta_{km}} \cdot \frac{\partial \Delta_{km}}{\partial \mathbf{y}_k} \tag{23}$$

Obviously, both gradients $\frac{\partial_S D_{KL}(P_\mathscr{D}\|Q)}{\partial \mathbf{y}_k}$ and $\frac{\partial_S D_\alpha(P_\mathscr{D}\|Q)}{\partial \mathbf{y}_k}$ depend explicitly on the derivative $\frac{\partial Q(\Delta_{km})}{\partial \Delta_{km}}$ of the density $Q(\Delta_{km})$. If a data dissimilarity appropriate choice is done for $P_\mathscr{D}(d_{lk})$ based on the empirical data dissimilarity $P_e(d_{lk})$, the respective $Q(\Delta_{lk})$ density should be selected consistently. For example, if the data has the intrinsic dimension n_d and the data dissimilarity density is $\chi^2(d_{lk}, n_d)$, then the projection space data dissimilarity density has to be selected as $\chi^2(\Delta_{lk}, n_p)$ accordingly. In this way we obtain a consistent SNE approach for the data.

5   Best Fitting Analytical Density Function for the Empirical Data Dissimilarity Density $P_e(d_{ij})$ – Results and Discussion

In this section we investigate for several well-known standard example machine learning data sets equipped with different data dissimilarities, which density function reflects the empirical data dissimilarity density $P_e(d_{ij})$ best. For this purpose, we consider the densities depicted in Table 1. We measure the similarity between the densities by the Kullback-Leibler-Divergence (3) as well as by the Rény-divergence (4) with $\alpha = 2$.

The data sets considered in this investigation are:

1. **Illustrative Gaussian**: two-dimensional Gaussian distributed data set (with zero mean and unit variance), i.e. $n = 2$; number of data 500
2. **TECATOR**: spectral data set of meat probes, data dimension $n = 100$, spectral range 850 - 1050 nm, number of data: 215, source and detailed description: $StaLib^2$
3. **PIMA**: Indian diabetes data set, data dimension $n = 8$, number of data: 768, and detailed description: UCI repository[3]

For Tecator and PIMA the intrinsic data dimensions were estimated by the Grassberger-Procaccia-approach [28], which yields $\eta_{Tec} \approx 2.36$ and $\eta_{PIMA} \approx 5.35$, respectively. These values have to be taken into account if density function require the degree of freedom as parameter.

We determined for each data set and l_p-distances the best matching densities with respective parameter settings obtained by a grid search. All results are collected in Table 2.

As expected, in case of the illustrative $2d$-Gaussian with the squared Euclidean distance, the best matching density is the χ^2-density. Yet, if any l_p-distance is chosen, different density deliver better fitting models. Moreover, for the real world data sets we observe that heavy-tailed densities frequently approximate the empirical densities best. This observation is in agreement with the successful experiences of t-SNE for data visualization. Hence, respective machine learning algorithm like the explained SNE or probabilistic LVQ variants, should take these densities instead of the standard exponential density.

---

[2] The Tecator data set is available at http://lib.stat.cmu.edu/datasets/tecator.

[3] The PIMA data set is available at http://www.ics.edu/mlearn/MLRepository.html.

Table 2. The first three best matching density distributions with the according parameters and the value of the Kullback-Leibler-divergence (D_{KL}) and quadratic Rényi-divergence (D_2) for the different l_p-distances together with the squared Euclidean distance E^2 (* marks heavy-tailed distributions).

		$l_{0.5}$	l_1	l_2	l_3	E^2
2D Gaussian						
1		$\gamma(x, 0.8, 2.5)$	$\gamma(x, 0.41, 3)$	$G(x, 0.89, 0.51)$	$N(x, 0.84, 0.51)$	$\chi^2(x, 2)$
	D_{KL}	0.022	0.022	0.022	0.026	0.0005
		$\gamma(x, 1.19, 2.0)$	$\gamma(x, 0.41, 3)$	$G(x, 0.89, 0.51)$	$N(x, 0.84, 0.51)$	$\chi^2(x, 2)$
	D_2	0.066	0.042	0.043	0.028	0.0007
2		$G(x, 2.1, 1.9)$	$N(x, 1.13, 0.71)$	$\gamma(x, 0.31, 3)$	$\gamma(x, 0.3, 2.5)$	$L(x, 0, 2.0)$
	D_{KL}	0.085	0.027	0.0022	0.034	0.021
		$G(x, 2.08, 1.19)$	$N(x, 1.13, 0.71)$	$\gamma(x, 0.41, 2.5)$	$\gamma(x, 0.3, 2.5)$	$L(x, 0, 2.0)$
	D_2	0.121	0.049	0.076	0.068	0.041
3		$\zeta^*(x, 2.08, 1.19)$	$logL^*(x, 0, 0.41)$	$\zeta^*(x, 0.89, 0.41)$	$\zeta^*(x, 0.84, 0.41)$	$logL^*(x, 0, 0.81)$
	D_{KL}	0.092	0.057	0.076	0.081	0.071
		$\zeta^*(x, 2.08, 1.19)$	$logL^*(x, 0, 0.41)$	$\zeta^*(x, 0.89, 0.46)$	$\zeta^*(x, 0.84, 0.41)$	$\zeta^*(x, 0, 2.0)$
	D_2	0.153	0.084	0.122	0.130	0.106
TECATOR (intrinsic dimensionality: 2.36)						
1		$\gamma(x, 74, 1.5)$	$\gamma(x, 0.71, 1.5)$	$\gamma(x, 0.09, 1.5)$	$\gamma(x, 0.04, 1)$	$\zeta^*(x, 0, 0.81)$
	D_{KL}	0.048	0.046	0.059	0.054	0.117
		$L(x, 109, 73)$	$L(x, 1.10, 0.81)$	$L(x, 0.11, 0.09)$	$L(x, 0.05, 0.04)$	$\zeta^*(x, 0, 0.81)$
	D_2	0.094	0.097	0.118	0.120	0.237
2		$L(x, 109, 73)$	$L(x, 1.10, 0.71)$	$L(x, 0.11, 0.09)$	$L(x, 0.05, 0.04)$	$\tau^*(x, 1)$
	D_{KL}	0.057	0.062	0.086	0.082	0.126
		$\zeta^*(x, 0, 88)$	$\tau^*(x, 2)$	$\gamma(x, 0.11, 1)$	$\zeta^*(x, 0, 0.04)$	$\tau^*(x, 2)$
	D_2	0.148	0.118	0.155	0.186	0.263
3		$\zeta^*(x, 0, 88)$	$logL^*(x, 0, 0.61)$	$\zeta^*(x, 0, 0.11)$	$\zeta^*(x, 0, 0.04)$	$\chi^2(x, 2)$
	D_{KL}	0.098	0.068	0.112	0.129	0.220
		$\gamma(x, 89, 1)$	$\zeta^*(x, 0, 0.91)$	$\zeta^*(x, 0, 0.11)$	$\gamma(x, 0.04, 1)$	$\gamma(x, 3, 1)$
	D_2	0.190	0.150	0.155	0.247	0.664
PIMA (intrinsic dimensionality: 5.35)						
1		$\gamma(x, 0.91, 7.5)$	$logL^*(x, 0, 0.21)$	$G(x, 0.47, 0.17)$	$G(x, 0.38, 0.14)$	$\gamma(x, 0.91, 2)$
	D_{KL}	0.033	0.028	0.040	0.048	0.024
		$\zeta^*(x, 6.87, 3)$	$G(x, 1.05, 0.51)$	$G(x, 0.47, 0.17)$	$\zeta^*(x, 0.38, 0.11)$	$L(x, 2, 1.5)$
	D_2	0.153	0.115	0.106	0.138	0.135
2		$N(x, 6.87, 3)$	$\gamma(x, 0.21, 5)$	$\gamma(x, 0.11, 4.5)$	$\zeta^*(x, 0.38, 0.11)$	$L(x, 2, 1.5)$
	D_{KL}	0.040	0.029	0.058	0.087	0.096
		$L(x, 6.87, 3)$	$\zeta^*(x, 1.1, 0.31)$	$\zeta^*(x, 0.47, 0.17)$	$G(x, 0.38, 0.21)$	$\chi^2(x, 2)$
	D_2	0.421	0.173	0.150	0.179	0.188
3		$\zeta^*(x, 0.47, 0.11)$	$G(x, 1.1, 0.39)$	$\zeta^*(x, 0.47, 0.11)$	$\gamma(x, 0.11, 4)$	$\chi^2(x, 2)$
	D_{KL}	0.098	0.036	0.098	0.091	0.132
		$\gamma(x, 3, 1)$	$L(x, 1.05, 0.51)$	$L(x, 0.47, 0.21)$	$L(x, 0.38, 0.21)$	$\gamma(x, 2, 1)$
	D_2	1.19	0.53	0.549	0.539	0.188

6   Conclusion

In this paper we studied the (empirical) data dissimilarity densities in comparison to analytically given standard probability densities including heavy-tailed distributions. We show that different dissimilarities may lead to different optimal densities. Hence, these densities should be applied in machine learning approaches which rely on dissimilarity density models for data density estimators. Two real world examples of those machine learning approaches in the context of classification and data visualization are explicitly considered in this context. It is explained analytically, how these methods depend on an appropriate choice. Future research should include the numerical behavior of these algorithms in dependence of the density functions in use.

References

1. Sachs, L.: Angewandte Statistik, 7th edn. Springer, Heidelberg (1992). https://doi. org/10.1007/978-3-540-32161-3
2. Bishop, C.M.: Pattern Recognition and Machine Learning. Springer, Heidelberg (2006)
3. Duda, R.O., Hart, P.E.: Pattern Classification and Scene Analysis. Wiley, New York (1973)
4. Haykin, S.: Neural Networks. A Comprehensive Foundation. Macmillan, New York (1994)
5. Seo, S., Obermayer, K.: Soft learning vector quantization. Neural Comput. **15**, 1589–1604 (2003)
6. Torkkola, K.: Feature extraction by non-parametric mutual information maximization. J. Mach. Learn. Res. **3**, 1415–1438 (2003)
7. Principe, J.C.: Information Theoretic Learning. Springer, Heidelberg (2010). https://doi.org/10.1007/978-1-4419-1570-2
8. Bishop, C.M., Svensén, M., Williams, C.K.I.: GTM: the generative topographic mapping. Neural Comput. **10**, 215–234 (1998)
9. Lazebnik, S., Raginsky, M.: Supervised learning of quantizer codebooks by information loss minimization. IEEE Trans. Pattern Anal. Mach. Intell. **31**(7), 1294–1309 (2009)
10. Hinton, G.E., Roweis, S.T.: Stochastic neighbor embedding. In: Advances in Neural Information Processing Systems, vol. 15, pp. 833–840. The MIT Press, Cambridge (2002)
11. van der Maaten, L., Hinten, G.: Visualizing data using t-SNE. J. Mach. Learn. Res. **9**, 2579–2605 (2008)
12. Bryson, M.C.: Heavy-tailed distributions: properties and tests. Technometrics **16**(1), 61–68 (1974)
13. de Bodt, C., Mulders, D., Verleysen, M., Lee, J.A.: Perplexity-free t-SNE and twice Student tt-SNE. In: Verleysen, M. (ed.) Proceedings of the 26th European Symposium on Artificial Neural Networks, Computational Intelligence and Machine Learning (ESANN 2018), Bruges (Belgium), Louvain-La-Neuve, Belgium, pp. 123–128 (2018). i6doc.com
14. Nebel, D., Kaden, M., Villmann, A., Villmann, T.: Types of (dis−)similarities and adaptive mixtures thereof for improved classification learning. Neurocomputing **268**, 42–54 (2017)

15. Biehl, M., Hammer, B., Villmann, T.: Prototype-based models in machine learning. Wiley Interdisciplinary Rev.: Cogn. Sci. **7**(2), 92–111 (2016)
16. Cichocki, A., Amari, S.-I.: Families of alpha- beta- and gamma- divergences: flexible and robust measures of similarities. Entropy **12**, 1532–1568 (2010)
17. Villmann, T., Haase, S.: Divergence based vector quantization. Neural Comput. **23**(5), 1343–1392 (2011)
18. Kullback, S., Leibler, R.A.: On information and sufficiency. Ann. Math. Stat. **22**, 79–86 (1951)
19. Shannon, C.E.: A mathematical theory of communication. Bell Syst. Tech. J. **27**, 379–432 (1948)
20. Rényi, A.: On measures of entropy and information. In: Proceedings of the Fourth Berkeley Symposium on Mathematical Statistics and Probability, Berkeley. University of California Press (1961)
21. Rényi, A.: Probability Theory. North-Holland Publishing Company, Amsterdam (1970)
22. Kohonen, T.: Learning vector quantization. Neural Netw. **1**(Suppl. 1), 303 (1988)
23. Robbins, H., Monro, S.: A stochastic approximation method. Ann. Math. Stat. **22**, 400–407 (1951)
24. Emerencia, A.: Student's t-distribution in learning vector quantization. Master's thesis, Institute for Mathematics and Computing Science, University of Groningen (2009)
25. Villmann, A., Kaden, M., Saralajew, S., Villmann, T.: Probabilistic learning vector quantization with cross-entropy for probabilistic class assignments in classification learning. In: Rutkowski, L., Scherer, R., Korytkowski, M., Pedrycz, W., Tadeusiewicz, R., Zurada, J.M. (eds.) ICAISC 2018. LNCS (LNAI), vol. 10841, pp. 724–735. Springer, Cham (2018). https://doi.org/10.1007/978-3-319-91253-0_67
26. Bunte, K., Haase, S., Biehl, M., Villmann, T.: Stochastic neighbor embedding (SNE) for dimension reduction and visualization using arbitrary divergences. Neurocomputing **90**(9), 23–45 (2012)
27. van der Maaten, L.: Learning a parametric embedding by preserving local structure. In: Proceedings of the 12th AISTATS, Clearwater Beach, Fl, pp. 384–391 (2009)
28. Grassberger, P., Procaccia, I.: Measuring the strangeness of strange attractors. Physica **9D**, 189–208 (1983)
29. Takens, F.: On the numerical determination of the dimension of an attractor. In: Braaksma, B.L.J., Broer, H.W., Takens, F. (eds.) Dynamical Systems and Bifurcations. LNM, vol. 1125, pp. 99–106. Springer, Heidelberg (1985). https://doi.org/10.1007/BFb0075637
30. Theiler, J.: Satistical precision of dimension estimators. Phys. Rev. A **41**, 3038–3051 (1990)

Open Set Subject Classification of Text Documents in Polish by Doc-to-Vec and Local Outlier Factor

Tomasz Walkowiak[(✉)] [iD], Szymon Datko [iD], and Henryk Maciejewski [iD]

Faculty of Electronics, Wrocław University of Science and Technology,
Wrocław, Poland
{tomasz.walkowiak,szymon.datko,henryk.maciejewski}@pwr.edu.pl

Abstract. In this work, we expand the emerging fastText method capabilities to open set classification. It is done by utilization of the Local Outlier Factor (LOF) algorithm. It allows extending the closed set classifier with an additional class that identifies outliers. The analyzed text documents are represented by averaged word embeddings calculated using the fastText method on training data. We evaluate these approach in the task of categorization of Polish language Wikipedia articles with 34 subject areas. Conducting the experiment with two different outlier corpora we show how the LOF parameter (contamination) and the dimension of the feature space (vector representation of documents) influence the open set classification results. The results show that the proposed extension of fastText is capable to work effectively for the open set classification task. Moreover, experiments for different dimensions of word embedding show that even the dimension as low as 5 is sufficient to achieve good results.

Keywords: Text mining · Open-set classification ·
Subject classification · Word embedding · fastText ·
Local Outlier Factor

1 Introduction - Problem Formulation

Automatic classification of text documents in terms of the subject areas is one of the important tasks of text mining. Promising applications of this technology range from the classification of articles in the Internet or newspaper repositories to categorization of scientific papers or tech-support requests.

In this work, we use the emerging methodology based on word-embedding techniques [9], which idea is to represent words in continuous vector spaces and build document representation as an average of word embedding [8]. Such document to vector representation can be used as a base for text classification [14]. An efficient algorithm called *fastText* for learning such representations using a corpus of text documents was proposed in [7]. Experiments described in [14,15] suggest that fastText, a data-driven, NLP-free method, outperforms the commonly used

© Springer Nature Switzerland AG 2019
L. Rutkowski et al. (Eds.): ICAISC 2019, LNAI 11509, pp. 455–463, 2019.
https://doi.org/10.1007/978-3-030-20915-5_41

BoW [6] approach in terms of classification accuracy. These results seem appealing as it entirely leaves out the laborious NLP step, commonly regarded as a mandatory in languages with rich inflection, such as Polish.

One of the limitations of fastText and other approaches is the fact that standard classifiers (as well as a linear soft-max classifier used in fastText) effectively split the feature space into areas related to the trained classes. Hence, they associate a new document with one of the trained classes, even if the document is actually not related to any of the classes (subject categories) known to the classifier. In this work, we propose a method which attempts to avoid this problem and extends fastText to open-set classification. The algorithm labels new documents which are not similar enough to one of the trained classes as 'outlier' class. We propose to use the Local Outlier Factor [1], a distance-based measure, to discover abnormal data, i.e. outliers.

Recent approaches to open-set classification of text documents involve the utilization of statistical-based concepts, like inter-quartile range-based criteria, [13], or similarity estimation with simple threshold-based decision mechanism applied for the aposteriori probability [2,4]. More sophisticated approaches are based on the usage of convolutional neural networks [12].

The paper is organized as follows. Section 2 describes the doc-to-vec representation of a document by the fastText method, the Local Outlier Factor and developed by us approach to the open set classification. In Sect. 3 we present the used corpus results of performed experiments. Finally, we discuss the benefits of the proposed approaches in Sect. 4.

2   Open Set Classification

2.1   Doc-to-Vec

To classify and represent a document in a feature space we have used a recent deep learning method – fastText [7]. It is based on a representation of documents as an average of word embeddings and uses a linear soft-max classifier [5] to assign doc-to-vec representation to one of the known classes. This hidden representation is used by the linear classifier for all classes, allowing information about word embedding learned for one class to be used by others. FastText by default ignores word order, much like the classical BoW method. The main idea behind fastText is to perform word embedding and classifier learning in parallel. Since fastText forms the linear model, it is very effective to train and achieves several orders of magnitude faster solution than other competing methods [7]. During classification, words that do not exist in the embedding model (due to not existing in training corpora) are omitted from the averaging.

2.2   Local Outlier Factor

To discover outliers, we propose to use the Local Outlier Factor (LOF) [1], a distance-based measure based on the weighted Euclidean metric. The LOF aims to find outliers by comparing to their local neighborhoods, instead of the global data distribution. For a given object (represented by a multidimensional feature vector), it works by calculating *local reachability distance*, defined as an average distance between given point, its neighbors and their neighbors to determine the local density of points. The relative density of an object against its neighbors is used as an indicator of the degree of the object being an outlier. The Local outlier factor is formally defined as the average of the ratio of local reachability of an object and of its k-nearest neighbors. If the LOF value for a given object is larger then a given threshold it is assumed as being an outlier.

Practical application of the LOF requires a set of training points and the threshold value. Both of them form the LOF model. The threshold could be calculated based on LOFs of all training points and assumption that the training data set includes a given proportion of outliers (objects with the largest values of LOF). This proportion is called contamination. Its influence on open set classification results is analyzed within this paper. In performed experiments, we used the implementation for Python programming language, available as part of the open scikit-learn[1] library.

2.3 Open Set Classification

The proposed approach to the open-set classification, similarly to closed set ones, consists of two stages: learning and classification. During learning, based on training data the models are built and then used for testing. Similarly to closed-set classification, the models are built only based on closed-set data. The used model consists of four elements:

1. word embedding,
2. linear classifier weights,
3. standardization parameters,
4. LOF model for each class.

The first two elements of the classification model are calculated using standard fastText procedure [7]. Next, the feature vectors (averaged word embeddings) are calculated for each document in a training set. The vectors are standardized using its mean and standard deviation - to match the requirement of normal data distribution. Mean and standard deviation are stored to be used during classification and form the third element of the open set classification model. For each class, the LOF model is built on the standardized doc-to-vecs. The set of LOF models (one for each class) forms the fourth element of the classification model.

The classification process consists of two steps:

1. closed set classification with fastText algorithm,
2. detection of an outlier against the winning class by LOF.

---

[1] https://scikit-learn.org/0.19/modules/generated/sklearn.neighbors.LocalOutlierFac tor.html.

During the first step (standard procedure of fastText) the doc-to-vec representation of an unknown document is calculated and it is assigned to one of known classes (*winning class*). Next, we quantify dissimilarity between the standardized representation of unknown document and the winning class. It is done by calculation of Local Outlier Factor on the winning class LOF model. If the LOF is above the threshold (see Sect. 3) we reject the decision made by the fastText classifier and we assign the unknown model to the 'outlier' class.

3 Evaluation

3.1 Data Sets

To evaluate the proposed method, closed set data and outlier ones are needed. For closed set data we have used the Polish language Wikipedia articles, coming from 34 subject areas and used as closed set class labels: *Airplanes, German military, Football, Diseases, Karkonosze mountains, Comic books, Catholicism, Political propaganda, Culture of China, Plants ecology, Optics, Strength sports, Branches of law, Chess, Skiing, Animated films, Albani, Egypt, Cars, Jews, Arabs* and *Cats*.

The training partition [11] includes 6885 articles which translates into ca. 200 articles per class (with the class *Arabs* slightly underrepresented). Performance of closed set classifier was evaluated based on the test partition [10] of 2,952 articles. Then, during experiments, we have used two different outlier sets. The first one (novels) consisted of 2,952 texts (chunks of size around 20,000 bytes) randomly selected from the corpus of the late 19th- and early 20th-century Polish novels written by various authors [3]. The size of texts was set to be similar to the average size of documents in the closed set.

The second outlier set (Press) consists of randomly selected articles from Polish press news [16]. The texts were assigned by press agency to 5 subject categories: *diplomacy, sport, disasters and accidents, business and finances* and *transportation*. We assumed that the number of outliers is equal to the number of articles in test partition for both outlier sets. The first outlier set represents texts that are far away from wikipedia articles, represents different subject areas, the second one (Press) partially overlaps with closed set data.

3.2 Experiment Overview

The proposed method was tested on the data set described in the previous section. The experiment was conducted as follows. First, the fastText model (Sect. 2.1) was trained on Wikipedia training set. Next, the LOF models for each class was built (Sect. 2.2). Then, a constructed model was examined on both testing sets, labeling all documents to trained categories (closed set classification). Later the Local Outlier Factor measure was used to verify if the assignment to categories was correct and catch incorrect labels, marking mismatched data as outliers (open set classification) for both outlier data sets (Novels and Press).

Finally, knowing all true labels from the original dataset, the evaluation of classification was performed. We measured the number of correct decisions from all assignments made to a specific class (precision) and the number of correct decisions from all assignments expected to specific class (recall). And finally a harmonic mean of these values, called **f1-score** is calculated.

3.3   Results

In Table 1 we report the f1-score calculated for the closed and open set tasks for 100-dimensional word embeddings and contamination parameter equal to 0.15. In closed set task (second column) only the closed set test data were used, while for the open set task the closed set test data and outliers are used. It could be noticed (second and third column of Table 1) that introducing outlier data (50% of all documents) to original fastText method results in 50% degradation of f1-score. The proposed method is capable to improve the outcome and achieve almost 72% or 53% of f1-score, depending on the outlier data set. The results for Press outliers are worse then for Novel data set due to the fact that Press data set partly overlapped with Wikipedia one in subject areas.

Table 1. Classification results (dimension: 100, contamination: 0.15)

Datatset	Closed-set data	Open-set data		
		Novels	Novels	Press
Method	fastText		fastText+LOF	
f1-score	0.8333	0.4166	0.7181	0.5337

Figure 1 presents the relation between contamination parameter of Local Outlier Factor and f1-score for Novels outlier data set. For reference, which could be interpreted as the bottom and top limit, we also present f1-score for pure fastText method (it does not depend on the contamination value). When values of contamination are rising, the accuracy, according to f1-measure, is improving. Achieving its maximum, around 72%, at contamination value equal to 0.2 and 0.25. After that, there is a small decrease. For a better understanding of this behavior, we have presented precision, recall and f1-score on Fig. 2 only for outlier class (for Novels as outliers).

As visible recall is strongly rising in a function of contamination, achieving 1 for value 0.4. This is a result of the detection of more outliers by LOF algorithm due to larger values of contamination (objects with smaller LOFs are assumed to be outliers). On the other hand, more and more objects from closed set classes are assumed to be outliers resulting in dropping the value of precision.

Figure 3 shows the obtained f1-score in a function of word embedding size. As visible, within most of the measured range (5 – 1000 elements), the impact

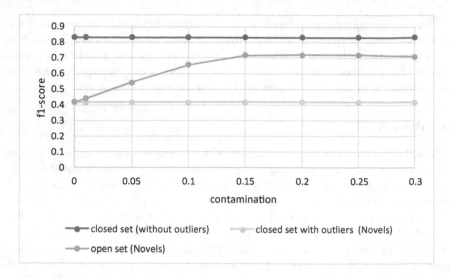

Fig. 1. f1-score in a function of contamination for open set and closed set classifier in closed and open set task

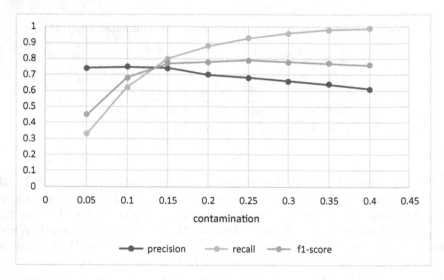

Fig. 2. Precision, accuracy and f1-score for open set classifier for outlier class.

of doc-to-vec dimension on overall performance is not very significant. This may suggest that fastText algorithm is so effective in finding well-distinguishing features that after some specific dimension there is only insignificant redundancy introduced. The computational complexity of all the methods used here depends on the feature vector dimension, so acceptable results for dimension 5 give a high speed up. Moreover, the results for open set classification for 3 dimensions are

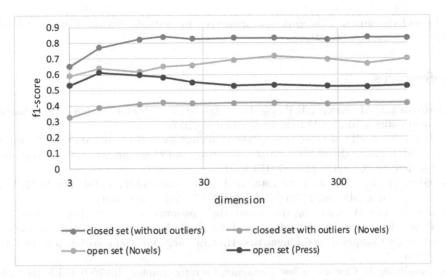

Fig. 3. f1-score in a function of feature vector dimension for open set classifier (for Novels and Press outliers) and closed set classifier in closed and open set tasks.

very interesting since they do not differ a lot from the best one and such small dimension allows to use the techniques for data visualization.

4 Conclusion

In this work, we showed how to extend the emerging fastText algorithm for the open set classification. It is done by utilizing the Local Outlier Factor on document embedding generated and internally used by fastText. In the experiment, we evaluated the proposed method on Wikipedia articles in Polish (34 subject areas) and used Polish Novels and Press news to mimic outliers. The results show that the proposed extension of fastText is capable to work effectively in an open set environment.

We studied how Local Outlier Factor can be involved in the process of detecting outliers. However, the reduction of incorrect assignments comes with a risk of rejecting also correct labels. This is visible in the relation between the two common measures of classifier performance: precision and recall. With awareness of that phenomena, a correct threshold for decision function can be selected (defined by contamination parameter), optimizing the f1-score.

Moreover, we performed an analysis of the impact of the feature vectors dimensions on the performance of the classification algorithm. This shows that fastText algorithm is a useful tool for finding good discriminatory features in text corpora, effective for subject classification of texts. Selected size of feature vectors turned to have a minor impact on achieved classification results.

Acknowledgments. This work was sponsored by National Science Centre, Poland (grant 2016/21/B/ST6/02159).

References

1. Breunig, M.M., Kriegel, H.P., Ng, R.T., Sander, J.: LOF: identifying density-based local outliers. SIGMOD Rec. **29**(2), 93–104 (2000)
2. Doan, T., Kalita, J.: Overcoming the challenge for text classification in the open world. In: 2017 IEEE 7th Annual Computing and Communication Workshop and Conference (CCWC), pp. 1–7. IEEE (2017)
3. Eder, M., Rybicki, J.: Late 19th- and early 20th-century polish novels (2015). http://hdl.handle.net/11321/57. CLARIN-PL digital repository
4. Fei, G., Liu, B.: Breaking the closed world assumption in text classification. In: Proceedings of the 2016 Conference of the North American Chapter of the Association for Computational Linguistics: Human Language Technologies, pp. 506–514 (2016)
5. Goodman, J.: Classes for fast maximum entropy training. In: 2001 IEEE International Conference on Acoustics, Speech, and Signal Processing. Proceedings (Cat. No.01CH37221), vol. 1, pp. 561–564 (2001)
6. Harris, Z.: Distributional structure. Word **10**(2–3), 146–162 (1954)
7. Joulin, A., Grave, E., Bojanowski, P., Mikolov, T.: Bag of tricks for efficient text classification. In: Proceedings of the 15th Conference of the European Chapter of the Association for Computational Linguistics: Volume 2, Short Papers, pp. 427–431. Association for Computational Linguistics (2017)
8. Mikolov, T., Chen, K., Corrado, G., Dean, J.: Efficient estimation of word representations in vector space. CoRR abs/1301.3781 (2013). http://arxiv.org/abs/1301.3781
9. Mikolov, T., Yih, W.T., Zweig, G.: Linguistic regularities in continuous space word representations. In: Proceedings of the 2013 Conference of the North American Chapter of the Association for Computational Linguistics: Human Language Technologies, pp. 746–751. Association for Computational Linguistics, Atlanta (2013)
10. Młynarczyk, K., Piasecki, M.: Wiki test - 34 categories (2015). CLARIN-PL digital repository. http://hdl.handle.net/11321/217
11. Młynarczyk, K., Piasecki, M.: Wiki train - 34 categories (2015). CLARIN-PL digital repository. http://hdl.handle.net/11321/222
12. Prakhya, S., Venkataram, V., Kalita, J.: Open set text classification using convolutional neural networks. In: Proceedings of the 14th International Conference on Natural Language Processing, pp. 466–475. NLP Association of India, Kolkata (2017)
13. Walkowiak, T., Datko, S., Maciejewski, H.: Algorithm based on modified angle-based outlier factor for open-set classification of text documents. Appl. Stoch. Models Bus. Ind. **34**(5), 718–729 (2018)
14. Walkowiak, T., Datko, S., Maciejewski, H.: Feature extraction in subject classification of text documents in polish. In: Rutkowski, L., Scherer, R., Korytkowski, M., Pedrycz, W., Tadeusiewicz, R., Zurada, J.M. (eds.) ICAISC 2018. LNCS (LNAI), vol. 10842, pp. 445–452. Springer, Cham (2018). https://doi.org/10.1007/978-3-319-91262-2_40

15. Walkowiak, T., Datko, S., Maciejewski, H.: Bag-of-words, bag-of-topics and Word-to-Vec based subject classification of text documents in polish - a comparative study. In: Zamojski, W., Mazurkiewicz, J., Sugier, J., Walkowiak, T., Kacprzyk, J. (eds.) DepCoS-RELCOMEX 2018. AISC, vol. 761, pp. 526–535. Springer, Cham (2019). https://doi.org/10.1007/978-3-319-91446-6_49
16. Walkowiak, T., Malak, P.: Polish texts topic classification evaluation. In: Proceedings of the 10th International Conference on Agents and Artificial Intelligence - Volume 2: ICAART, pp. 515–522. INSTICC, SciTePress (2018)

A Greedy Algorithm for Extraction of Handwritten Strokes

Michał Wróbel[1]([✉])(iD), Janusz T. Starczewski[1](iD), Katarzyna Nieszporek[1],
Piotr Opiełka[1], and Andrzej Kaźmierczak[2,3]

[1] Institute of Computational Intelligence,
Czestochowa University of Technology,
Czestochowa, Poland
michal.wrobel@iisi.pcz.pl
[2] Information Technology Institute,
University of Social Sciences, Lodz, Poland
[3] Clark University, Worcester, MA 01610, USA

Abstract. This paper presents an algorithm for the extraction of handwritten strokes from a binary image. Each stroke is represented by a family of discs covering the area of the handwritten word. These discs are selected and connected to each other using heuristic (especially greedy) techniques.

1 Introduction

Handwriting recognition is a wide area in the field of artificial intelligence applications. Some history of a research in this area is described in [11]. One of the approaches for handwritten text recognition is to extract single moves of a hand, called strokes. This issue is still under development (e.g. [5,10]).

A goal of the stroke extraction is to transform a digital image (a matrix of pixels) into a set of objects. Each stroke may have its own vector of features, and according to it, the stroke can be classified. Some issues connected with the feature extraction and object classification are considered in [3,12]. An idea of representing stroke by the vector of features is presented in [13]. In that paper, a stroke is approximated by a couple of polynomials and the vector of features is created by the polynomials' coefficients.

This paper presents an algorithm for handwritting stroke extraction. This algorithm uses some ideas from [9] (definition of a stoke as a family of discs, approximation of stroke by polynomials) but uses them in a quite different way. A set of selected discs in a word is treated as a weighted graph while strokes are created by a greedy algorithm for selecting edges in this graph.

2 Preprocessing

The algorithm works on the binary image. If letters in the image are very thin (1–2 pixels width), it may be made bold by morphological dilatation with a small structuring element.

L. Rutkowski et al. (Eds.): ICAISC 2019, LNAI 11509, pp. 464–473, 2019.
https://doi.org/10.1007/978-3-030-20915-5_42

Sets of interior and border pixels must be created. Let $\mathbf{I}$ be the set of all interior pixels. The set of boundary pixels $\mathbf{B}$ may be defined as $\mathbf{B} = \mathbf{I_d} - \mathbf{I}$ where $\mathbf{I_d}$ is a result of morphological dilation of $\mathbf{I}$ by 3×3 cross ($\mathbf{B}$ contains all background pixels having an interior pixel in 4-neighborhood). To make the algorithm faster, the image should be segmented. Each area of pixels can be analyzed separately.

3 Extraction of Discs

3.1 Definitions

In [9] a stroke is defined as a family of discs. A disc contains its center and two points tangent to the boundaries. Each of these points is defined in $\mathbf{R}^2$. In this paper, the center is denoted by C and tangent points are denoted by P_1, P_2.

With these three points, it is possible to designate vectors $r_1 = \overrightarrow{CP_1}$ and $r_2 = \overrightarrow{CP_2}$. The radius of the disc (denoted by r) is an average length of r_1 and r_2. An angle between r_1 and r_2 is denoted by α An example of the disc is presented in Fig. 1.

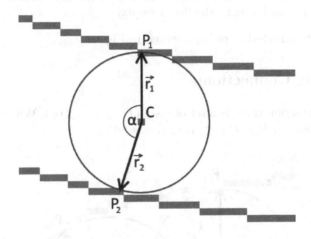

Fig. 1. One disc

A correct disc should fulfill two conditions: $|r_{i,1}| \approx |r_{i,2}|$ and $\alpha_i \approx \pi$. These conditions may be formally defined as:

$$||r_2| - |r_2|| < \delta_{max},\tag{1}$$

$$\alpha > \alpha_{min}.\tag{2}$$

3.2   The Algorithm

To find all correct discs following algorithm may be used. For each pixel $C \in \mathbf{I}$:

1. find a pixel $P_1 \in \mathbf{B}$ for which the distance $|CP_1|$ is the lowest,
2. create a subset $\mathbf{B_t}$ containing pixels from $\mathbf{B}$ fulfilling conditions (1) and (2),
3. if $\mathbf{B_t} \neq \emptyset$ find a pixel $P_2 \in \mathbf{B_t}$ for which the distance $|CP_2|$ is the lowest, then save a disc (C, P_1, P_2).

Because of $\alpha \in [0, \pi]$ and since the cosine is descending in $[0, \pi]$, the condition 2 may be also defined as $\cos(\alpha) < cos(\alpha_{min})$. The cosine of α may be easily calculated by

$$\cos(\alpha) = \frac{\boldsymbol{r_1} \circ \boldsymbol{r_1}}{|\boldsymbol{r_1}| \cdot |\boldsymbol{r_2}|}. \tag{3}$$

A set of disc created during execution of this algorithm is too large – there is one disc for each pixel in the skeleton. Reduction of the number of discs may be realized by a greedy algorithm:

1. put all discs into a list sorted descending by $q = r \cdot \cos(\pi - \alpha)$,
2. pop and save the first disc from the list, get C and r of this disc,
3. remove from the list all discs which center is closer to C than r,
4. repeat steps 2. and 3. until the list is empty.

An example of extracted discs is presented in Fig. 4a.

4   Creating Connections

After discs extraction there is a set of discs $(D_1, D_2, ..., D_N)$. With each disc D_i there are related C_i, $P_{1,i}$, $P_{2,i}$, $\boldsymbol{r_{1,i}}$, $\boldsymbol{r_{2,i}}$, α_i and r_i.

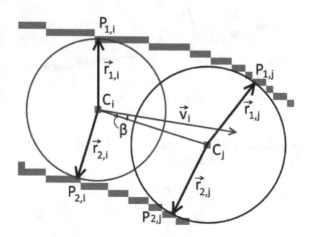

Fig. 2. Connection between discs D_i and D_j

An example of two discs is shown in Fig. 2. This figure also presents the vector v_i which shows the direction where the neighbor of D_i in the stroke is expected. It may be any vector perpendicular to a line connecting tangent points $(v_i \perp \overrightarrow{P_{1,i}P_{2,i}})$. A simple way to get v_i is just a rotation $\overrightarrow{P_{1,i}P_{2,i}}$ by $\frac{\pi}{2}$.

A proper neighbor of D_i (denoted as D_j) should fulfill following conditions:

- the distance between centers of both discs $|C_iC_j|$ should not be very large,
- areas of both discs should be similar,
- an angle β between a line connecting centers and a vector v (or $-v$) should be small.

To imagine this, Fig. 3 may be helpful. These three conditions could be expressed by a quality index defined by the formula

$$q_{i,j} = \frac{|C_iC_j|}{r_i}\left(\frac{min(r_i, r_j)}{max(r_i, r_j)}\right)^2 \cos^2(\beta), i \neq j.$$

$\cos(\beta)$ may be calculated similarly to (3).

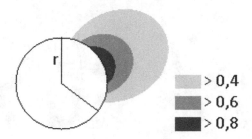

$> 0{,}4$

$> 0{,}6$

$> 0{,}8$

Fig. 3. Illustration of $\frac{|C_iC_j|}{r_i} \cos^2(\beta)$ depended on C_j location

This way there is created the matrix Q. This is an adjacency matrix of a directed weighted graph. In order to improve the method, very poor connections from the graph (set $q_{i,j} = 0$ if $q_{i,j} < q_{min}$) can be removed.

This matrix could be modified to an adjacency matrix of undirected graph Q' by a T-norm, for instance, the minimum

$$q'_{i,j} = q'_{j,i} = min(q_{i,j}, q_{j,i}).$$

Due to the fact that $\cos^2(\beta) = \cos^2(\pi - \beta)$, the value $q_{i,j}$ is the same for vectors v_i and $-v_i$. To distinguish if $\beta < \frac{\pi}{2}$ the following formula may be used:

$$m_{i,j} = sgn(\cos\beta).$$

A set of all possible connections includes each pair (D_i, D_j) for which $q'_{i,j} > 0$ (see Fig. 4b). Now, there is a need to choose the best subset of this set where each disc has at most one neighbor on each side. This problem may be solved by a greedy algorithm (quite similar to Kruskal's MST Algorithm or a greedy algorithm used in TSP). We propose such formulation of the algorithm:

1. put into a list $\mathbf{C_1}$ all connections (D_i, D_j), where $i < j \wedge q'_{i,j} > 0$,
2. sort the list $\mathbf{C_1}$ in descending order by $q'_{i,j}$,
3. pop and save in a set $\mathbf{C_2}$ first connection (D_i, D_j) from the list $\mathbf{C_1}$,
4. remove from the list $\mathbf{C_1}$ all connections, where $m_{i,a} = m_{i,j} \vee m_{j,a} = m_{j,i}$,
5. repeat steps 3. and 4. until the list $\mathbf{C_1}$ is empty.

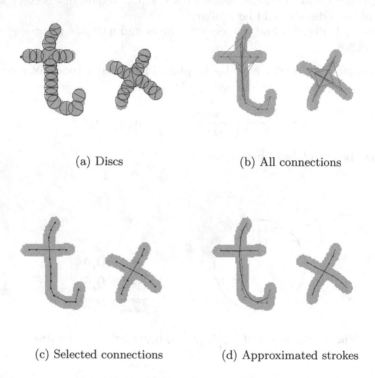

(a) Discs   (b) All connections

(c) Selected connections   (d) Approximated strokes

Fig. 4. Example of execution of algorithm

5   Generating Strokes

After creating connections, the list $\mathbf{C_2}$ should be transformed into a set of strokes. The algorithm guarantees that each node belongs to at most two connections. Due to this fact, the set of strokes $\mathbf{S}$ may be created the following way. At the beginning, $\mathbf{S} = \emptyset$. Next, for each connection (C_i, C_j) in $\mathbf{C_2}$:

1. find in $\mathbf{S}$ a stroke $S_1 = (S_{1,1}, S_{1,2}, ..., S_{1,L_1})$ containing a point C_i or set $S_1 = \emptyset$ if no such stroke exists,
2. find in $\mathbf{S}$ a stroke $S_2 = (S_{2,1}, S_{2,2}, ..., S_{2,L_2})$ containing a point C_j or set $S_2 = \emptyset$ if no such stroke exists,
3. if $S_1 = \emptyset \wedge S_2 = \emptyset$, create the stroke (C_i, C_j) and add it to $\mathbf{S}$,

4. if $S_1 \neq \emptyset \wedge S_2 = \emptyset$:
   (a) create the stroke $S_3 = (C_j, S_{1,1}, ..., S_{1,L_1})$ if $S_{1,1} = C_i$ or $S = (S_{1,1}, ..., S_{1,L_1}, C_j)$ otherwise,
   (b) replace the stroke S_1 by S_3 in **S**,
5. if $S_1 = \emptyset \wedge S_2 \neq \emptyset$:
   (a) create the stroke $S_3 = (C_i, S_{2,1}, ..., S_{2,L_1})$ if $S_{2,1} = C_j$ or $S = (S_{2,1}, ..., S_{2,L_1}, C_i)$ otherwise,
   (b) replace the stroke S_2 by S_3 in **S**,
6. if $S_1 \neq \emptyset \wedge S_2 \neq \emptyset \wedge S_1 \neq S_2$:
   (a) remove S_1 and S_2 from **S**,
   (b) create the stroke S_3:
      i. $S_3 = (S_{1,1}, ..., S_{1,L_1}, S_{2,1}, ..., S_{2,L_2})$ if $S_{1,L_1} = C_i \wedge S_{2,1} = C_j$,
      ii. $S_3 = (S_{1,1}, ..., S_{1,L_1}, S_{2,L_2}, ..., S_{2,1})$ if $S_{1,L_1} = C_i \wedge S_{2,L_2} = C_j$,
      iii. $S_3 = (S_{1,L_1}, ..., S_{1,1}, S_{2,L_2}, ..., S_{2,1})$ if $S_{1,1} = C_i \wedge S_{2,L_2} = C_j$,
      iv. $S_3 = (S_{1,L_1}, ..., S_{1,1}, S_{2,1}, ..., S_{2,L_2})$ if $S_{1,1} = C_i \wedge S_{2,1} = C_j$,
   (c) add S_3 to **S**.

Strokes containing less than three points should be removed from **S**, since they are apparently noise.

5.1 Approximation

In [13], a handwritten stroke $\mathbf{S} = (C_1, C_2, ..., C_L)$ is approximated by two third degree polynomials (see Fig. 4d):

$$f_x(t) = a_3 t^3 + a_2 t^2 + a_1 t + a_0,$$
$$f_y(t) = b_3 t^3 + b_2 t^2 + b_1 t + b_0, t \in [0, 1].$$

A parameter t is a distance from the beginning of the stroke. In case of a point C_i, it equals to

$$t_i = \frac{d_i}{d_L}$$

where

$$d_i = \sum_{j=1}^{i-1} |C_j C_{j+1}|$$

5.2 Cutting Strokes with a High Degree of Curvature

After approximation of a stroke S, it is possible to calculate an error ϵ_S defined as

$$\epsilon_S = \frac{\sum_{i=1}^{L} |C_i \hat{C}_i|}{L \cdot d_L}, \hat{C}_i = (f_x(t_i), f_y(t_i)) \tag{4}$$

If the error is not small enough ($\epsilon_S > \epsilon_{max}$), the stroke S cannot be represented properly by polynomials (5.1), because it is very crooked. In this case, the stroke S probably should not be treated as a single stroke (see Fig. 5a), hence there is a need to cut it into parts $S_1 = (C_1, ..., C_a)$ and $S_2 = (C_a, ..., C_L)$. To determine the index a of the cutting point there is a need to find the center of mass of the region under the error function

$$e(x) = |C_x \hat{C}_x|$$

where

$$\hat{C}_i = (f_x(t_i), f_y(t_i)).$$

An example of such function is presented in Fig. 5b. This imples that the argument a for which the function

$$m(a) = |\sum_{i=1}^{a-1} e(i) - \sum_{i=a}^{L} e(i)|$$

attains its global minimum must be found. On the graph presented in Fig. 5b, a is shown by the dotted line.

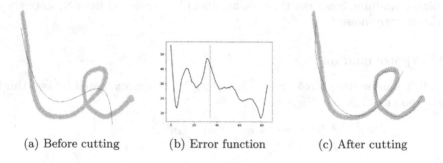

(a) Before cutting   (b) Error function   (c) After cutting

Fig. 5. Example of stroke cutting

After cutting, strokes S_1 and S_2 should be recursively approximated and possibly cut. Before each approximation, less than three-point strokes should be always removed. A comprehensive example of stroke cutting is presented in Fig. 5.

6   Results

An example of extraction is presented in Fig. 6. The constants in the algorithm were experimentally determined as follows:

$$\delta_{max} = 1.0$$
$$\alpha_{min} = 0.8\pi$$
$$q_{min} = 0.1$$
$$\epsilon_{max} = 0.04$$

Fig. 6. Example of extraction

6.1 Comparative Research

The well-extracted stroke should be smooth, as the angle between adjacent segments of the stroke should not change rapidly. Let $f(i)$ ($i \in [1, L-1]$, L is a number of points in the stroke S) be a signed angle between vectors $\overrightarrow{C_{i-1}C_i}$ and $\overrightarrow{C_iC_{i+1}}$. For a smooth stroke, a derivative $f'(i)$ should be close to zero, hence smoothness of the stroke can be measured by the formula

$$\epsilon_{2,S} = \frac{1}{L-3} \sum_{i=1}^{L-2} [f(i+1) - f(i)]. \tag{5}$$

The algorithm was compared with the method presented in [10] (with small modification of a line-fitting algorithm – termination condition was here defined as $d_{max} \leq s \vee N \leq 3$). Results obtained by this algorithm is presented in Fig. 7.

The error function for the obtained set of strokes was defined as an average stroke error; however, the stroke error was defined by (5) or (4). Results of both algorithms are compared in Tables 1 and 2.

Table 1. Quality of strokes obtained by the algorithm proposed in this paper

Picture	Number of strokes	Average (5)	Average (4)
Figure 4c	4	2.679	0.007
Figure 5c	2	3.051	0.019
Figure 4	10	3.298	0.022

Table 2. Quality of strokes obtained by algorithm described in [10]

Picture	Number of strokes	Average (5)	Average (4)
Figure 4c	4	5.481	0.012
Figure 5c	4	1.200	0.013
Figure 4	13	4.942	0.027

(a) See Fig. 4c   (b) See Fig. 5c   (c) See Fig. 4

Fig. 7. Strokes obtained by the comparative algorithm

7 Conclusion

The algorithm presented in this paper gives encouraging results. Obtained strokes are generally smoother than strokes received by the algorithm being compared. In figures, it can be observed that the number of unwanted strokes has decreased. Future works may concern the acceleration of the algorithm operation as well as its use in natural language processing [6,8] compared to neural networks (eg. [1,2]) and their deep convolutional architectures (eg. [4,7]).

References

1. Bartczuk, Ł., Dziwiński, P., Red'ko, V.G.: The concept on nonlinear modelling of dynamic objects based on state transition algorithm and genetic programming. In: Rutkowski, L., Korytkowski, M., Scherer, R., Tadeusiewicz, R., Zadeh, L.A., Zurada, J.M. (eds.) ICAISC 2017. LNCS (LNAI), vol. 10246, pp. 209–220. Springer, Cham (2017). https://doi.org/10.1007/978-3-319-59060-8_20
2. Bilski, J., Smoląg, J., Żurada, J.M.: Parallel approach to the levenberg-marquardt learning algorithm for feedforward neural networks. In: Rutkowski, L., Korytkowski, M., Scherer, R., Tadeusiewicz, R., Zadeh, L.A., Zurada, J.M. (eds.) ICAISC 2015. LNCS (LNAI), vol. 9119, pp. 3–14. Springer, Cham (2015). https://doi.org/10.1007/978-3-319-19324-3_1
3. Bustamam, A., Sarwinda, D., Ardenaswari, G.: Texture and gene expression analysis of the MRI brain in detection of alzheimer's disease. J. Artif. Intell. Soft Comput. Res. **8**(2), 111–120 (2018)
4. de Souza, G.B., da Silva Santos, D.F., Pires, R.G., Marananil, A.N., Papa, J.P.: Deep features extraction for robust fingerprint spoofing attack detection. J. Artif. Intell. Soft Comput. Res. **9**(1), 41–49 (2019)
5. Dinh, M., Yang, H.-J., Lee, G.-S., Kim, S.-H., Do, L.-N.: Recovery of drawing order from multi-stroke english handwritten images based on graph models and ambiguous zone analysis. Expert Syst. Appl. **64**, 352–364 (2016)
6. Gabryel, M.: The bag-of-words method with different types of image features and dictionary analysis. J. Univ. Comput. Sci. **24**(4), 357–371 (2018)
7. Hou, Y., Holder, L.B.: On graph mining with deep learning: introducing model R for link weight prediction. J. Artif. Intell. Soft Comput. Res. **9**(1), 21–40 (2019)
8. Ke, Y., Hagiwara, M.: An english neural network that learns texts, finds hidden knowledge, and answers questions. J. Artif. Intell. Soft Comput. Res. **7**(4), 229–242 (2017)

9. L'Homer, E.: Extraction of strokes in handwritten characters. Pattern Recogn. **33**, 1147–1160 (2000)
10. Phan, D., Na, I.-S., Kim, S.-H., Lee, G.-S., Yang, H.-J.: Triangulation based skeletonization and trajectory recovery for handwritten character patterns. KSII Trans. Internet Inf. Syst. **9**, 358–377 (2015)
11. Plamondon, R., Srihari, S.N.: Online and off-line handwriting recognition: a comprehensive survey. IEEE Trans. Pattern Anal. Mach. Intell. **22**(1), 63–84 (2000)
12. Riid, A., Preden, J.-S.: Design of fuzzy rule-based classifiers through granulation and consolidation. J. Artif. Intell. Soft Comput. Res. **7**(2), 137–147 (2017)
13. Wróbel, M., Nieszporek, K., Starczewski, J.T., Cader, A.: A fuzzy measure for recognition of handwritten letter strokes. In: Rutkowski, L., Scherer, R., Korytkowski, M., Pedrycz, W., Tadeusiewicz, R., Zurada, J.M. (eds.) ICAISC 2018. LNCS (LNAI), vol. 10841, pp. 761–770. Springer, Cham (2018). https://doi.org/10.1007/978-3-319-91253-0_70

The Method for Improving the Quality of Information Retrieval Based on Linguistic Analysis of Search Query

Nadezhda Yarushkina(iD), Aleksey Filippov(iD), Maria Grigoricheva(iD),
and Vadim Moshkin(✉)(iD)

Ulyanovsk State Technical University, Street Severny Venets 32,
432027 Ulyanovsk, Russian Federation
{jng,al.filippov}@ulstu.ru, gms4295@mail.ru, postforvadim@ya.ru,
http://www.ulstu.ru/

Abstract. The paper describes the process of research and development of methods for linguistic analysis of search queries. Linguistic analysis of search query is used to improve the quality of information retrieval. Original search query translated to a search query in a new format after syntactic analysis. Using the features of query language allow improving the quality of information retrieval. Also, the paper describes the results of experiments that confirm the correctness of the method.

Keywords: Information retrieval · Syntactic analysis ·
Search queries

1 Introduction

The growth of data volume and the need to reduce search time led to the need to improve the information retrieving methods. The first information retrieval systems worked primarily with factual information. The factual information can include, for example, the characteristics of objects and their relationships. Currently, information retrieval systems can process text documents in natural language and other data presentation formats [1,2].

Currently, a large amount of data is presented in an unstructured form. This fact proves the relevance of research in the field of information retrieval and text mining. The count of full-text databases still increases. Full-text databases are electronic analogs of printed publications and documents. Unstructured presentation of information is one of the factors strongly affecting information retrieval systems [1,2].

The quality of search in information retrieval systems is usually characterized by two criteria: recall and precision. The recall is determined by the ratio between the total count of found relevant documents and the total count of all relevant documents. The precision is determined by the ratio between the found relevant documents and the total count of found documents [2].

L. Rutkowski et al. (Eds.): ICAISC 2019, LNAI 11509, pp. 474–485, 2019.
https://doi.org/10.1007/978-3-030-20915-5_43

The characteristics of the information retrieval system itself and the quality of the search query affects the quality of the search. An ideal search query can be formed by a user who knows well the domain area. Also, to form an ideal query, a user needs to know the features of current information retrieval system and their information retrieval query language. Otherwise, a search result will have low precision or low recall values [2].

2 Main Problem

Information retrieval is the process of searching in an extensive collection of data some semi-structured (unstructured) material (document) that satisfies the information needs of a user.

Semi-structured data is data that does not have a clear, semantically visible and easily distinguishable structure. Semi-structured data is the opposite of structured data. The canonical example of structured data is relational databases. Relational databases are typically used by enterprises to store product registers, employee personal data, etc. [2].

To information retrieval, a user formulates a search query. A search query is the formalized way of expressing the information needs of information retrieval system users. Information retrieval query language is used for the expression of information needs. The syntax of information retrieval query language varies from system to system. Modern information retrieval systems allow entering a query in natural language in addition to the information retrieval query language [1]. Information retrieval system finds documents containing the specified keywords or words that are in any way related to the keywords based on the user search query. The result of an information retrieval system is a list of documents, sorted by relevance [2].

In this paper, will consider the work of the proposed method on the example of the existing information retrieval subsystem of the system for opinion mining in social media (SOM). Understanding the meaning of publications in social media is the most critical and complex element of automated text processing [3, 4].

The SOM consists of the following subsystems (Fig. 1):

1. Subsystem for importing data from external sources. This subsystem works with popular in Russia social network VKontakte [5] through the public application programming interface (VK API). Massmedia loader retrieves data from HTML pages of mass media sites based on rules. The creation of own rules for each mass media is needed. The rule should contain a set of CSS-selectors. Ontology loader allows loading ontologies in OWL or RDF format into the data storage subsystem. Ontology is used for a description of the features of the problem area [6].
2. Data storage subsystem provides the representation of information extracted from social and mass media in a unified structure that is convenient for further processing. The data is stored in the context of users, collections, data sources, versions, etc. As database management systems are used:

- Elasticsearch for indexing and retrieving data [7];
- MongoDB for storing data in JSON format [8];
- Neo4j for storing graphs of social interaction (social graph) and ontology [9].
3. Data converter converts the data imported from social and mass media into an internal SOM unified structures.
4. Social graph builder constructs a social graph. The social graph based on the relationships of users and communities of the social network.
5. The OWL/RDF-ontology translator translates ontology into the graph representation [10].
6. Semantic analysis subsystem performs preprocessing of text resources. Also, this subsystem performs statistical and linguistic analysis of text resources.
7. Information retrieval subsystem finds objects related to a specific search query. In this case, the search query can be semantically extended using an ontology.

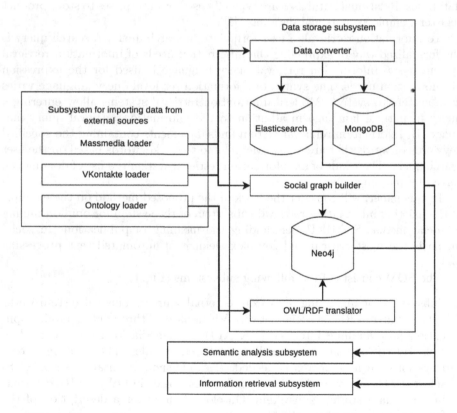

Fig. 1. The architecture of the system for opinion mining in social media.

Elasticsearch provides a full Query DSL [11]. Think of the Query DSL as an AST of queries, consisting of two types of clauses:

1. Leaf query clauses look for a particular value in a specific field, such as the match, term or range queries. These queries can be used by themselves.
2. Compound query clauses wrap other leaf or compound queries and are used to combine multiple queries logically, or to alter their behavior.

The query string is parsed into a series of terms and operators. A term can be a single word – *quick* or *brown* – or a phrase, surrounded by double quotes – *"quick brown"* – which searches for all the words in the phrase, in the same order.

Users allow to customize the search:

1. By default, all terms are optional, as long as one term matches. A search for *foo bar baz* will find any document that contains one or more of *foo* or *bar* or *baz.*
   The preferred operators are + (this term must be present) and - (this term must not be present). All other terms are optional. For example, this query: *quick brown +fox -news*
   states that:
   - *fox* must be present;
   - *news* must not be present;
   - *quick* and *brown* are optional – their presence increases the relevance.
2. Multiple terms or clauses can be grouped with parentheses, to form sub-queries:
   (quick OR brown) AND fox.

Therefore, the SOM search algorithm, based on Elasticsearch Query DSL, has several disadvantages:

1. A user may not know the features of Elasticsearch Query DSL.
2. Words joined by the *OR* operator is using by default in information retrieval. The using of the *OR* operator unnecessarily increases the recall of information retrieval and reduces its precision.

It is necessary to develop the method of linguistic analysis and translation of a search query into a search query in the format of Elasticsearch Query DSL. The new form of search query allows to take into account the features of Elasticsearch Query DSL and improve the quality indicators (precision and recall) of information retrieval.

3   The Model of the Neo4j Repository

Neo4j was chosen to store the description of the problem area (PrA) in the applied ontology form since the ontology is actually a graph. In this case, it is only necessary to limit the set of nodes and graph relations into which ontologies on RDF and OWL will be translated.

The context of an ontology is some state of ontology obtained during versioning. Context can also be a subject area.

Formally the ontology is:

$$O = \langle T, C^{T_i}, I^{T_i}, P^{T_i}, S^{T_i}, F^{T_i}, R^{T_i} \rangle, i = \overline{1, t}, \tag{1}$$

where t is a number of the ontology contexts;
$T = \{T_1, T_2, \ldots, T_n\}$ is a set of ontology contexts;
$C^{T_i} = \{C_1^{T_i}, C_2^{T_i}, \ldots, C_n^{T_i}\}$ is a set of ontology classes within the i-th context;
$I^{T_i} = \{I_1^{T_i}, I_2^{T_i}, \ldots, I_n^{T_i}\}$ is a set of ontology objects within the i-th context;
$P^{T_i} = \{P_1^{T_i}, P_2^{T_i}, \ldots, P_n^{T_i}\}$ is a set of ontology classes properties within the i-th context;
$S^{T_i} = \{S_1^{T_i}, S_2^{T_i}, \ldots, S_n^{T_i}\}$ is a set of ontology objects states within the i-th context;
$F^{T_i} = \{F_1^{T_i}, F_2^{T_i}, \ldots, F_n^{T_i}\}$ is a set of the logical rules fixed in the ontology within the i-th context;
R^{T_i} is a set of ontology relations within the i-th context defined as:

$$R^{T_i} = \{R_C^{T_i}, R_I^{T_i}, R_P^{T_i}, R_S^{T_i}, R_F^{T_i}\},$$

where $R_C^{T_i}$ is a set of relations defining hierarchy of ontology classes within the i-th context;
$R_I^{T_i}$ is a set of relations defining the 'class-object' ontology tie within the i-th context;
$R_P^{T_i}$ is a set of relations defining the 'class-class property' ontology tie within the i-th context;
$R_S^{T_i}$ is a set of relations defining the 'object-object state' ontology tie within the i-th context;
$R_F^{T_i}$ is a set of relations generated on the basis of logical ontology rules in the context of i-th context.

The relations $R_C^{T_i}$ and $R_I^{T_i}$ (Eq. 1) may be functional relations. Functional relations are characteristic of the OWL language.

It is necessary to select structural elements of TBox (structure, scheme) and ABox (content) of graph (knowledge base) KB respectively for successful translation of RDF or OWL ontology to graph KB objects.

Formally the functions of translating an RDF/OWL ontology to a graph KB are:

$$f_O^{RDF} : RDF \to O,$$
$$f_O^{OWL} : OWL \to O,$$

where $RDF = \{C^{RDF}, I^{RDF}, P^{RDF}, S^{RDF}, R^{RDF}\}$ – set of entities of RDF ontology,
$OWL = \{C^{OWL}, I^{OWL}, P^{OWL}, S^{OWL}, R^{OWL}\}$ – set of entities of OWL ontology,
O – set of ontology entities of the graph KB (Eq. 1).

Table 1 shows the correspondence of the RDF/OWL-ontology entities to the graph KB entities.

The main entities of RDF and OWL ontologies correspond to the ontology of the graph KB. The graph KB entities unify different formats of ontologies and form a data model.

Table 1. Correspondence of RDF/OWL-ontology entities to the graph KB entities

RDF	OWL	Graph KB
TBox		
rdfs:Resource	owl:Thing	$C_i^{T_i} \in C^{T_i}$
rdfs:Class	owl:Class	$C_i^{T_i} \in C^{T_i}$
rdfs:subClassOf	owl:SubclassOf	$R_{Ci}^{T_i} \in R_C^{T_i}$
rdf:Property	owl:ObjectProperty owl:DataProperty	$P_i^{T_i} \in P^{T_i}$
rdfs:domain	owl:ObjectPropertyDomain owl:DataPropertyDomain	$R_{Pi}^{T_i} \in R_P^{T_i}$
rdfs:range	owl:ObjectPropertyRange owl:DataPropertyRange	$R_{Pi}^{T_i} \in R_P^{T_i}$
ABox		
rdf:type	owl:NamedIndividual	$I_i^{T_i} \in I^{T_i}$
rdf:ID	owl:ClassAssertion	$R_{Ii}^{T_i} \in R_I^{T_i}$
rdf:resource rdf:ID	owl:ObjectPropertyAssertion owl:DataPropertyAssertion	$S_i^{T_i} \in S^{T_i}$ $R_{Si}^{T_i} \in R_S^{T_i}$

4 The Method of Linguistic Analysis of Search Query for Improving Quality of Information Retrieval

The primary goal of the developed method of linguistic analysis and translation of a search query into a search query in the format of Elasticsearch Query DSL is the improvement of information retrieval quality. The main task is to select in a search query the groups of terms, united by some semantics.

4.1 The Method of Linguistic Analysis and Translation of a Search Query

The scheme of linguistic analysis of texts does not depend on the natural language itself. Regardless of the language of a source text, its analysis goes through the same stages [12,13]:

1. Splitting the text into separate sentences.
2. Splitting the text into separate words.
3. Morphological analysis.
4. Syntactic analysis.
5. Semantic analysis.

The first two stages are the same for most natural languages. Language-specific differences usually appear in the processing of word abbreviations, and in the processing of punctuation marks to determine the end of a sentence.

The results of the syntactic analysis are used to select in a search query the groups of terms, united by some semantics. To identify a noun phrase from a query is the identification of meaningful query terms is necessary. It is also necessary to define the relationship between the terms of a query. A noun phrase or nominal phrase is a phrase that has a noun (or indefinite proper noun) as its head or performs the same grammatical function as such a phrase. Noun phrases are ubiquitous cross-linguistically, and they may be the most frequently occurring phrase type.

SyntaxNet as an implementation of the syntactic analysis process is used. SyntaxNet is the TensorFlow-based syntax definition framework that uses a neural network. Currently, 40 languages including Russian are supported. The source code of the already-trained Parsey McParseface neural network model that is suitable for parsing text is published for TensorFlow. The main task of SyntaxNet is to make computer systems able to read and understand human language. The precision of the model trained in the SinTagRus case is estimated at 87.44% for the LAS metric (Label Attachment Score), 91.68% for the UAS metric (Unlabeled Attachment Score) and determines the part of speech and the grammatical characteristics of words with an accuracy of 98.27% [14].

It is necessary to parse a search query to obtain the parse tree on the first step of the algorithm. To collect data about the search query structure, dependencies between words and the types of these dependencies the resulting parse tree will be used.

The parse tree can be represented as the following set:

$$T = \{t_1, t_2, \ldots, t_k\}, \tag{2}$$

where k is a count of nodes in the parse tree;
t_i is a node of the parse tree can be described as:

$$t_i = (i, w_i, m_j, c), i = \overline{1, k},$$

where i is an index of the word in the search query;
$w_i \in W, W = \{w_1, w_2, \ldots, w_k\}$, W is set of words of the search query;
$m_j \in M, M = \{Noun, Pronoun, Verb, Adverb, Adjective, Conjunction, Preposition, Interjection\}$ is a set of parts of speech for natural language;
c is an index of the word in the search query, that depends on the i-th word.

Thus, the search query is converted into a parse tree on the first step of the algorithm. For each word in the search query the part of speech, index of this word in the search query, and relations with other words of the search query are set.

The description of the parse tree in the form of a structure containing information about two or more related words with the indication of their parts of speech and location in the original request is used on the second step of the algorithm.

In the process of analysis of the input parse tree, the nodes that reflect the semantics of this query are selected. Search and translation of selected nodes into Elasticsearch Query DSL is executed using a set of rules. The translation process uses a set of rules. Rules are used to add special characters from the Elasticsearch Query DSL to the words of the search query. Also, stop words are deleted from search query during the translation. The result of the algorithm is a new search query that takes into account the semantics of information needs and features of the Elasticsearch Query DSL.

This algorithm can be represented as the following equation:

$$F^{Query} : (T, R) \rightarrow Q^*,$$

The input parameters of the function F^{Query} are the parse tree of search query T (Eq. 2) and the set of rules R, and the result is a translated query Q^*.

$R = \{R_1, R_2, \ldots, R_n\}$ is the set of rules for searching elements in parse tree and their translation in Elasticsearch Query DSL.

Each rule can be represented as the following expression:

$$R_i(p, t_1, t_2, \ldots, t_m) = Q_j^*,$$

where p is rule priority;

t_k is k-th element of a rule that allows selecting the node (nodes) of the parse tree to processing;

m is a count of elements in the rule;

$Q_j^* \in Q^* = \{Q_1^*, Q_2^*, \ldots, Q_q^*\}$ is element of translated query. Each element of a translated query contains the word or words of the original search query escaped by a symbol from the set of Elasticsearch Query DSL operators.

4.2 Examples of Rules for Linguistic Analysis and Translation of a Search Query

The formal description of the rule to search the noun phrase in the search query can be represented as follows:

$$R_{noun\_phrase} = (4, \langle i, w_i, Noun, c \rangle, \langle i+1, w_{i+1}, Adjective, i \rangle,$$
$$\langle i+2, w_{i+2}, Adjective, i \rangle, \ldots, \langle i+d, w_{i+d}, Adjective, i \rangle)$$
$$= +'' w_{i+1} w_{i+2} \ldots w_{i+d} w_i'',$$

where d is a count of adjectives in the noun phrase.

Extraction of noun phrase from the parse tree of the search query finds one or more adjective that subordinates to the current noun tree node. The result of this rule is a noun phrase, escaped with ' +" ' at the beginning and ' " ' at the end.

The formal description of the rule to search the related nouns in the search query can be represented as follows:

$$R_{noun\_noun} = (3, \langle i, w_i, Noun, c \rangle, \langle i+1, w_{i+1}, Noun, i \rangle,$$
$$\langle i+2, w_{i+2}, Noun, i \rangle, \ldots, \langle i+d, w_{i+d}, Noun, i \rangle)$$
$$= +'' w_{i+1} w_{i+2} \ldots w_{i+d} w_i'',$$

where d is a count of nouns that related to i-th noun.

Extraction of related nouns from the parse tree of the search query finds one or more noun that subordinates to the current noun tree node. The result of this rule is a set of nouns, escaped with ' +" ' at the beginning and ' " ' at the end.

The formal description of the rule to search the proper noun in the search query can be represented as follows:

$$R_{proper\_noun} = (1, \langle i, w_i, Pronoun, c \rangle, \langle i+1, w_{i+1}, Pronoun, i \rangle,$$
$$\langle i+2, w_{i+2}, Pronoun, i \rangle, \ldots, \langle i+d, w_{i+d}, Pronoun, i \rangle)$$
$$= +'' w_{i+1} w_{i+2} \ldots w_{i+d} w_i'',$$

where d is a count of proper nouns that related to i-th proper noun.

Extraction of proper nouns from the parse tree of the search query finds one or more proper noun that subordinates to the current proper noun tree node. The result of this rule is a set of nouns, escaped with ' +" ' at the beginning and ' " ' at the end.

5 Experiments

To test the method of linguistic analysis of search query proposed in this study a number of experiments were conducted.

Figure 2 shows the parse tree for search query: "Amount of fare in public transport in Ulyanovsk". Ulyanovsk is a city in Russia [15]. The nodes of the parse tree are the words of the search query. Each node is assigned a part of speech.

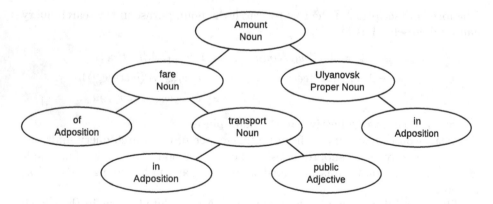

Fig. 2. The parse tree for search query "Amount of fare in public transport in Ulyanovsk"

After work of the algorithm, the significant elements were found in the parse tree (Fig. 3). In the resulting tree (Fig. 3), the nodes labeled as a rule with which they were found.

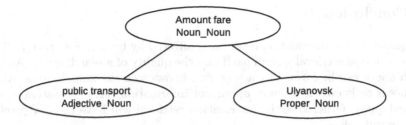

Fig. 3. The result tree for search query "Amount of fare in public transport in Ulyanovsk"

Thus, after linguistic analysis and translation the resulting search query for search query "Amount of fare in public transport in Ulyanovsk" is '+" Amount fare" +" public transport" + Ulyanovsk'.

To assess the quality of the proposed method, the precision indicator of information retrieval is used. The precision value is calculated using the following expression:

$$P = \frac{a}{b}, \tag{3}$$

where a is the count of relevant documents in the search result;
b is a total count of documents in the search result.

The recall value is not used because the data storage subsystem of SOM contains the large count of documents.

For search query Q^O "Amount of fare in public transport in Ulyanovsk" the count of relevant documents in the search result of the information retrieval is 8. The total count of documents is 44857. Thus, the precision $P(Q^O)$ of the information retrieval for search query "Amount of fare in public transport in Ulyanovsk" is (Eq. 3):

$$P(Q^O) = \frac{8}{44857} = 0.00018.$$

For search query Q^T '+" Amount fare" +" public transport" +Ulyanovsk' translated from search query "Amount of fare in public transport in Ulyanovsk" using the proposed method the count of relevant documents in the search result of the information retrieval is 8. The total count of documents is 8. Thus, the precision $P(Q^T)$ of the information retrieval for search query '+" Amount fare" +" public transport" +Ulyanovsk' is (Eq. 3):

$$P(Q^T) = \frac{8}{8} = 1.$$

Thus, the using of proposed method improve the precision of information retrieval by reason of reducing the count of documents in the search result.

484 N. Yarushkina et al.

6 Conclusion

The quality of the information retrieval is affected by both the characteristics of the information retrieval system itself and the quality of a search query. An ideal search query can be formed by a user who knows well the domain area. Also, a user needs to know the features of current information retrieval system to form an ideal query. Otherwise, the information retrieval will have the low precision or low recall values.

In this paper, the work of the proposed method was considered on the example of the existing information retrieval subsystem of SOM.

Information retrieval subsystem of SOM based on Elasticsearch. Elasticsearch provides a full Query DSL. Elasticsearch Query DSL has several disadvantages:

1. The user may not know the features of Elasticsearch Query DSL.
2. Words joined by the OR operator is using by default in information retrieval. The using of the OR operator unnecessarily increases the recall and reduces the precision of information retrieval.

A method of linguistic analysis and translating of a search query in Elasticsearch Query DSL allows improving the precision of information retrieval.

A search query is converted into a parse tree on the first step of the algorithm. For each word in a search query a part of speech, index of this word in a search query, and relations with other words of a search query are set.

The description of a parse tree in the form of a structure containing information about two or more related words with the indication of their parts of speech and location in the original request is used on the second step of the algorithm.

In the process of analysis of an input parse tree, the nodes that reflect the semantics of the search query are selected. Search and translation of selected nodes into Elasticsearch Query DSL is executed using a set of rules. The translation process uses a set of rules. Rules are used to add special characters from the Elasticsearch Query DSL to the words of a search query. Also, stop words are deleted from search query during the translation. The result of the algorithm is a new search query that takes into account the semantics of information needs and features of the Elasticsearch Query DSL.

According to the results of 20 computational experiments can conclude: the use of the proposed method allows to increase the precision of information retrieval by an average of 18 times.

Acknowledgments. The study was supported by:

– the Ministry of Education and Science of the Russian Federation in the framework of the project No. 2.1182.2017/4.6. Development of methods and means for automation of production and technological preparation of aggregate-assembly aircraft production in the conditions of a multi-product production program;

– the Russian Foundation for Basic Research (Grants No. 18-47-732007 and 18-47-730019).

References

1. Voorhees, E.M.: Natural language processing and information retrieval. In: Pazienza, M.T. (ed.) Information Extraction. LNCS (LNAI), vol. 1714, pp. 32–48. Springer, Heidelberg (1999). https://doi.org/10.1007/3-540-48089-7_3
2. Manning, C., Raghavan, P., Schütze, H.: Introduction to Information Retrieval. Cambridge University Press, Cambridge (2008)
3. Crammer, K., Dekel, O., Keshet, J., Shalev-Shwartz, S., Singer, Y.: Online passive-aggressive algorithms. JMLR **7**(Mar), 551–585 (2006)
4. Turney P.: Thumbs up or thumbs down? Semantic orientation applied to unsupervised classification of reviews. In: Proceedings of the Association for Computational Linguistics, pp. 417–424 (2002)
5. VKontakte. https://vk.com/. Accessed 20 Oct 2018
6. Gruber, T.: Ontology. http://tomgruber.org/writing/ontology-in-encyclopedia-of-dbs.pdf. Accessed 20 Oct 2018
7. Elasticsearch. https://www.elastic.co/. Accessed 20 Oct 2018
8. MongoDB. https://www.mongodb.com/. Accessed 20 Oct 2018
9. Neo4j. https://neo4j.com/. Accessed 20 Oct 2018
10. Yarushkina, N., Filippov, A., Moshkin, V.: Development of the unified technological plat-form for constructing the domain knowledge base through the context analysis. In: Kravets, A., Shcherbakov, M., Kultsova, M., Groumpos, P. (eds.) CIT&DS 2017. CCIS, vol. 754, pp. 62–72. Springer, Cham (2017). https://doi.org/10.1007/978-3-319-65551-2_5
11. Elasticsearch Query DSL. https://www.elastic.co/guide/en/elasticsearch/reference/2.3/query-dsl-query-string-query.html. Accessed 20 Oct 2018
12. SRILM - The SRI Language Modeling Toolkit. http://www.speech.sri.com/projects/srilm. Accessed 20 Oct 2018
13. Manning, C., Schutze, H.: Foundations of Statistical Language processing. The MIT Press, Cambridge (1999)
14. Sboev, A.G., Gudovskikh, D.V., Ivanov, I., Moloshnikov, I.A., Rybka, R.B., Voronina, I.: Research of a deep learning neural network effectiveness for a morphological parser of Russian language (2017). http://www.dialog-21.ru/media/3944/sboevagetal.pdf. Accessed 20 Oct 2018
15. Ulyanovsk. https://en.wikipedia.org/wiki/Ulyanovsk. Accessed 20 Oct 2018

Various Problems of Artificial Intelligence

AQuA: Automatic Quality Analysis
of Conversational Scripts in Real-time

Kumar Abhinav[1](✉), Alpana Dubey[1], Sakshi Jain[1], Veenu Arora[1],
Asha Puttaveerana[1], and Susan Miller[2]

[1] Accenture Labs, Bangalore, India
{k.a.abhinav,alpana.a.dubey,sakshi.c.jain,veenu.arora,
asha.puttaveerana}@accenture.com
[2] Accenture Federal, Arlington, USA
susan.miller@accenture.com

Abstract. Call center is a point of contact between customers and the organization. A service agent represents the organization in one way and act as the face of the organization. The quality of service provided to a customer by a service agent strongly determines the reputation of an organization. Hence, good quality service is of utmost importance for an organization's continual growth in the present dynamic market situation. In order to streamline the process of providing exceptional service, organizations have placed human experts to evaluate the quality of calls. However, evaluation through human experts is labour-intensive, limited to few random calls and expensive. In this paper, we propose a Quality AI Assistant which actively monitors all agents' interactions and provides feedback to improve call quality in real-time. We also propose a model to predict the customer satisfaction. We apply Deep Learning based approach to evaluate the quality of calls on different organizational compliance aspects and predict the customer satisfaction. We evaluated the performance of our system on an in-house contact centre dataset of finance domain. The experiment results demonstrate the effectiveness of the approach which is quite promising.

Keywords: Contact center · Call quality · Customer experience ·
Interaction mining

1 Introduction

The success of a call center is determined by good customer experience. Good customer experience promises a high rate of customer loyalty and yields considerable benefits to the organization. The inclusion of Artificial Intelligence (AI) technology in call centers is changing the way it has been functioning. The deployment of AI in call centers has shown to yield noteworthy results and substantial benefits [17]. AI is in a position to analyze customer needs, provide virtual assistance, automate various processes and improve the overall customer

© Springer Nature Switzerland AG 2019
L. Rutkowski et al. (Eds.): ICAISC 2019, LNAI 11509, pp. 489–500, 2019.
https://doi.org/10.1007/978-3-030-20915-5_44

experience. Various AI based technologies such as machine learning, natural language processing, and even sentiment analysis, are being deployed strategically in order to bring high quality customer experience at low cost [17]. AI augments the human operators to perform their tasks efficiently. Human operators are now in a position to handle more calls with the help of AI technology. According to the latest statistics by Oracle, eight out of ten businesses have already implemented or are planning to adopt AI as a customer service solution by 2020 [19]. This will result into substantial amount of financial benefits to the organization.

Customer experience is a major focus in any call center. The level of customer experience is measured typically by two ways - (1) analyzing the customer's feedback post call, which is captured to determine customers' level of satisfaction by the service that was provided to them, and (2) monitoring the quality of calls between customers and the service agents. Currently, human experts evaluate the quality of calls. They monitor the conversations and score each of them on various aspects based on certain criteria. For instance, one of the aspects of evaluation could be if the service agent apologized customers for any issue or inconvenience being faced by them. After the evaluation of call on both the aspects, a report, that describes the overall quality of the monitored calls is generated. This report is then presented to the supervisors who analyze the overall level of call quality. This process is expensive and labour-intensive. Moreover, manual call quality evaluation has several drawbacks. Firstly, the quality of conversations is determined by monitoring only few random sample calls as it is highly expensive to get all the calls evaluated by humans. This may result into missing the problematic or crucial calls that could be important to determine the level of customer experience being provided. Secondly, as the service agents are not evaluated immediately after their conversation, they continue to violate some of the important call quality aspects till they receive their evaluation report. Typically, this process takes weeks which is really a long time for correcting the service agents.

To address these challenges, we propose a Quality AI Assistant which actively monitors all agents' interactions and provides feedback to improve call quality in real-time. Due to real-time feedback, with a good traceability between evaluation and the call, the service agent can relate well the improvements suggested by quality assistant. We apply Deep Learning based approach to evaluate the conversation in real-time and provide feedback to the agent on different organizational compliance aspects. We leverage the state-of-the-art Natural Language Processing (NLP) techniques to analyze the conversation. The system analyzes conversation between service agents and customers and reports any violation of call quality aspects. This report can be used by the supervisor to recommend relevant trainings to the service agent. We also proposed a model to predict the Customer Satisfaction. We evaluated the performance of our system on an in-house contact centre dataset of finance domain. Earlier approaches either assess calls over customer satisfaction or on high level aspects. These high level aspects are not concrete enough to guide service agent to improve the call handling. With a finer level evaluation, our approach can give more concrete suggestions to service agent and their supervisors for improving their call handling abilities. For instance, instead of suggesting a service engineer that (s)he was not courteous in the call, suggesting him/her to use greeting words is more helpful. Assessment of any verbal communication has two parts - sentences uttered and the tone in which the sentences were uttered. In this paper, we focus on the assessment of sentences used by the service engineer to provide concrete suggestion. The present system brings four main advantages: (a) Reduce call quality evaluation cost for the organization, (b) Better customer experience as operators can correct themselves for the call based on real-time support, (c) Provide easier access of call assessment information to agents and their supervisor, and (d) Better training of call center agents.

The remainder of this paper is structured as follows: Sect. 2 discusses the related work on call conversation analysis. In subsequent Sect. 3, we describe the proposed approach for real-time call quality monitoring analysis and present the model architecture. We describe our evaluation methodology and discuss results in Sect. 4. Section 5 discusses the integration of system to contact centre dashboard. Finally, Sect. 6 concludes with summary of our findings.

2   Related Work

Several studies have been conducted in monitoring and analyzing the interaction between customer and human agent within contact center to provide assistance to the human agents and supervisors. Kummamuru et al. [1] proposed an unsupervised approach to automatically identify the segments from the conversational script and detect the compliance deviation from the defined call flow. Roy et al. [2] proposed an approach to measure the customer satisfaction and call quality assurance using statistical and rule-based NLP techniques. They focused on identifying emotions (such as sad, apologetic or angry) of customers from their utterances using Conditional Random Field algorithm and obtain sentiment categories (such as positive, negative) as a by-product. They also proposed an approach to summarize the conversation so that supervisors can quickly gather context. Further, they [18] improved the emotion categorization task using neural network method that eliminates the feature engineering. Negi et al. [4] proposed an unsupervised method of finding sub-tasks and pre-conditions from the conversation interaction. Park et al. [3] presented an approach for automatic call quality monitoring that classifies the conversation as good or bad. Park et al. [5] have also proposed a machine learning approach to automatically measure customer satisfaction by analyzing call transcripts. Llimona et al. [12] studied the effect of gender and call duration on customer satisfaction in call center. Godbole et al. [13] developed an approach for predicting customer satisfaction. Our approach can be differentiated with the state-of-the-art techniques along three dimensions. Firstly, previous work relies solely either on rule-based methodology or pattern matching techniques and classifies conversation as good or bad calls. However, our work leverages the Deep Learning approach to provide a detailed quality report of service agents on different aspects. Secondly, the quality assistant would provide a real-time feedback to the service agents that allows them to improve during the conversation based on the feedback. Finally, unlike earlier machine learning approaches which classify calls on a very few high level dimensions, such as good, bad, emotion and sentiment, our approach classifies calls over 10 finer level aspects (Table 1). These aspects are more concrete and informative to help service agent's future call performance.

3   Call Quality Assistant

In this section, we describe the technical details of the proposed call quality assistant. The Quality AI assistant operates in the following two modes:

1. On-call assistance: The assistant analyzes the ongoing conversation between agent and customer and then provides a proactive support to handle the conversation properly. For instance, if the agent has not greeted the customer, the assistant recommends to do that.
2. Post-call assistance: The assistant provides a comprehensive quality evaluation after the call is over. The call is rated over quality metrics typically used in contact center. The results are reviewed by operator and also shared with the supervisor. The supervisor recommends the relevant training to the agent based on the call quality report.

Table 1. Organizational compliance

Call quality aspects
The agent thanked the customer for calling (A1)
The agent asked for the caller's name (A2)
The agent apologized for the issue, inconvenience or cost associated with the problem (A3)
The agent asked the customer if they have any additional questions or issues before ending the call (A4)
The agent was courteous, friendly, polite and professional (A5)
The agent adequately resolved the customer's issue, or provided a timeframe for resolution (A6)
The agent received the customer's permission to place them on hold before doing so (A7)
The agent asked the customer if the service they were provided was within their standards (A8)
The agent maintained confidentiality (A9)
The agent adhered to the call closure script (A10)

It has been observed that the calls received at contact centre mostly follow well-defined patterns [1,2]. There has been many work to identify these patterns in an unsupervised way by segmenting the conversation. Most commonly observed pattern sequence is Greetings and introduction ⇒ Problem description ⇒ Problem resolution ⇒ Closure [2]. Detecting deviations from this prescribed order and identifying missing states are important aspects of manual QA process. Some of the call quality aspects are valid only to a particular state (for instance, the Agent thanked the customer for calling is only applicable to "Greeting" state) and some of them will be valid throughout the conversation i.e. across all the states (for instance, the agent was courteous, friendly, polite and professional). We describe the aspects in Table 1, that we considered for call quality evaluation.

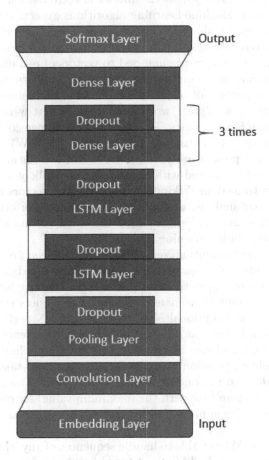

Fig. 1. Model architecture

We apply Deep Learning based approach to evaluate the conversation in real-time and provide feedback to the agent on different organizational compliance aspects. The architecture of Deep Learning model consists of Embedding layer, 1 Convolution layer (CNN), 2 Long Short Term Memory (LSTM) layers and 5 dense layers. CNN is able to learn local response from temporal or spatial data to extract features and LSTM is specialized for sequential modeling. The architecture utilizes CNN to extract a sequence of higher-level phrase representations, and are fed into LSTM to obtain the feature representation. The CNN is constructed on top of the pre-trained word vectors from conversational data to learn feature representation. Then, to learn sequential correlations from higher-level sequence representations, the feature maps of CNN are organized as sequential window features to serve as the input of LSTM. The structure is able to capture both local features of phrases as well as global and temporal sentence semantics.

1. Embedding Layer: The input to the model is conversation between service agent and customer. Machine Learning algorithms expects the textual inputs to be encoded as real numbers. We apply word embedding technique for learning word vector representations through neural language models i.e. words or phrases from the vocabulary are mapped to vectors of real number. We could not train embedding model on our dataset as the data size was less considering embedding requires a lot of data to understand the semantic relationship. We use the publicly available "word2vec" vectors that were trained on 100 billion words from Google News. The vectors have dimensionality of 300 and were trained using the continuous bag-of-words (CBOW) architecture [6]. Words that are not present in the set of pre-trained words are initialized randomly. We also experimented with another set of publicly available "GloVe" [7] word vectors trained on Wikipedia. The "GloVe" vectors have dimensionality of 300. In our analysis, we found "Glove" model performance better as compared to "word2vec". We fine-tuned the word vectors along with other model parameters during training.

2. Convolution layer: Convolution Neural Networks (CNNs) are good at extracting and representing the features for both unstructured text and images. CNN models have subsequently been shown to be effective for NLP and have achieved excellent results in semantic parsing, search query retrieval, sentence modeling, and other traditional NLP tasks [14]. CNN perform very well in extracting n-gram features at different positions of a sentence through filters, and can learn short and long-range relations through pooling operations. We apply Max Pooling operation over the feature map and take the maximum value as the feature corresponding to a particular filter. This is to capture the most important feature (one with the maximum value) for each feature map. The model uses multiple filters (with varying filter sizes) to obtain multiple feature maps.

3. LSTM Layers: LSTM layer able to handle sequences of any length and capture long-term dependencies. LSTM propagates historical information via a chain-like neural network architecture. While processing sequential data, it looks at the current input as well as the previous output of hidden state at each time step.

4. Fully Connected Layer: These features from LSTM layer are passed to a fully connected network (dense layers). The final layer is the Softmax layer which predicts the probability distribution over multiple classes.

The model architecture is shown in Fig. 1. We leveraged the same architecture for predicting the Customer Satisfaction model except for the number of classes in Softmax layer and loss function. The architecture utilizes a backpropagation technique to optimize the weights so that the neural network can learn to map arbitrary inputs to outputs during training [8]. The predicted output of the network is compared to the expected output and an error is calculated. The error is then back propagated through the network, one layer at a time, and the weights are updated according to the amount contributed to the error. We use "Dropout" Regularization technique to prevent neural networks from overfitting [9]. This is a technique where randomly selected neurons within the network are ignored while training the model. The dropout is applied after LSTM and each hidden layers. The "Relu" activation function is applied to all the hidden layers. Activation functions convert an input signal of node to an output signal and introduce non-linear properties to neural network.

The system utilizes the call conversations and the evaluation score provided by human experts on different aspects. The call conversations are passed to Feature Pre-processing unit where we apply basic NLP techniques (such as tokenization, stemming etc.) to the conversation. Then, Deep Learning model is trained for predicting the call quality. The call quality report can be used for recommending the training content.

Table 2. Call quality prediction analysis

Aspects	F-measure
A1	0.952
A2	0.92
A3	0.94
A4	0.87
A5	0.81
A6	0.85
A7	0.89
A8	0.91
A9	0.74
A10	0.94

4   Dataset and Evaluation

In order to evaluate our approach, we collected conversation dataset from in-house contact centre. The dataset is of financial domain which consists of conversation between service agent and customer, date, service agent name, customer identifier and feedback provided by the customer post call. Out of 9,104 instances, we have only 300 conversations for which the human experts have manually evaluated based on 10 call quality aspects. We trained separate models for each call quality aspects. Each model predicts the probability that whether the corresponding aspect (aspect for which evaluation is being made) is satisfied or not. The architecture of the Deep learning model is discussed in Sect. 3. We used F-measure as metric for evaluating the performance of the model. The F-measure for different aspects is captured in Table 2. We observe that for most of the aspects model was better in prediction except aspect "A9". This may be due to there was not enough instances that capture the confidentiality was maintained or not. Roy et al. [2] reported an accuracy of 79.8% for categorizing emotions.

Next, we measure the customer satisfaction from the conversation. There were 1,500 conversations for which the customer feedback was available. These feedbacks were collected from the customer post call. This captures mainly whether the customers were satisfied with the call or not. The customer rated their call experience on a scale of 1–5. For predicting the overall Customer Satisfaction, we converted the feedback into three categories: Good (feedback ≥ 3.5), Average ($2.5 \leq$ feedback < 3.5) and Poor ($1 \leq$ feedback < 2.5). We pose it as a multi-class classification problem. The trained model predicts the class among these three categories. The F-measure of the trained model was 0.92. The selection of the range values might impact the F-measure score. Roy et al. [2] reported an accuracy of 82% for categorizing sentiments (good and bad). As the dataset used by existing approaches was publicly not available and the categories in which existing approaches classify a service engineers dialogue were not exactly the same what our approach does, our approach cannot be compared with them. Finally, we also tried to capture the correlation between call quality aspect score and the feedback provided by the customer. We applied chi-squared test to measure the association between these two. We did not find any correlation between these two. This shows that the call quality score is independent of customer satisfaction. This may be due to customer feedback being more dependent on whether the problem was resolved or not and might not be dependent on how the call was handled. Even though customers seem to give high rating if their issue is being resolved, the second level of experience which is largely driven by how politely and emphatically the call was handled is an important factor and potentially leaves a lasting impact on customer experience. Therefore, we need to capture both the metrics (call quality and customer satisfaction) separately.

We split our dataset into train set (80%) and validation set (20%). The reported F-measures are on validation set. The training process was run for a fixed number of iterations through the training dataset called epochs. We used 15 as epoch size. We specified batch size as 10. Batch size is the number of instances that are evaluated in the training set before the weights are updated in the neural network. We applied efficient Gradient Descent algorithm "Adam" [10], an optimizer used to search through different possible weights for the network that minimize loss. Deep learning model requires tuning a number of hyperparameters such as the number of hidden layers, number of neurons in each hidden layer, batch size, epochs, optimizer, activation function etc. We used GridSearch [16] techniques to find the best parameters for a prediction algorithm. It performs exhaustive search over specified parameters for any estimator object. The parameters of the estimator object are optimized by grid-search. We use "GridSearch" library in scikit-learn [16]. We also use trial and experimentation approach to arrive at the optimal number of neurons at each hidden layer and units at LSTM layer. For word embedding (word2vec and GloVe), we used "Gensim" [15] module from Python. For fine tuning the model, we used an early stopping criterion to identify the number of epochs after which validation loss is not improving. The loss function is "binary_crossentropy" for call quality model and "categorical_crossentropy" for customer satisfaction prediction model. All the experiments presented in this paper have been performed using "Keras" Deep learning framework [11] and scikit-learn [16]. Keras provides several neural network architectures as well as different learning procedures for the desired network configuration and tools for creating new custom layer.

Fig. 2. Real time suggestion to improve ongoing call

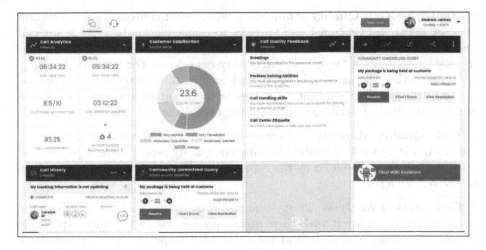

Fig. 3. Call quality report post call

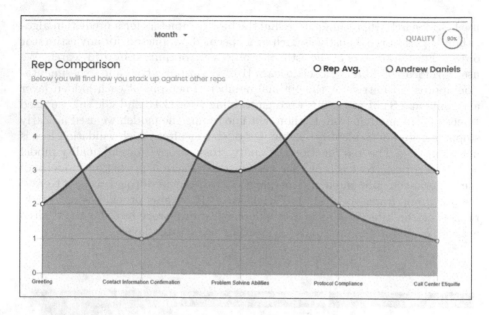

Fig. 4. Call quality comparison

5   System Implementation

The proposed approach is integrated with our Contact Center dashboard system. The system consists of the following three major components:

1. **Real-time Call Quality Analysis:** The system monitors the conversation between agent and Customer and provides recommendation to agent if any call quality criteria did not meet. The agents can proactively act upon the recommendation to improve the overall call quality experience. For instance, in Fig. 2, we observe that the agent missed to apologize to the customer for the inconvenience caused. The assistant recommends the agent to apologize. Thus, the real-time feedback to the agent helps in improving the call experience.

2. **Call Quality Report:** The supervisors can view the call quality report (shown in Fig. 3) weekly/monthly for different quality aspects. The report on call quality analysis can be used by the supervisor to recommend relevant trainings to the service agent.

3. **Comparison Analysis:** The system also provides an option to compare the performance of an agent with their peers over various call quality aspects. It also compares the performance of the agent with respect to the organization's standard score and highlights the deviation with respect to quality aspect (shown in Fig. 4).

6   Conclusion

In this work, we proposed a Quality AI Assistant which actively monitors all agents' interactions and provides feedback to improve call quality in real-time. We leverage Deep Learning based approach to evaluate the quality of calls on different organizational compliance aspects. We also proposed a predictive model to predict the customer satisfaction level. We observed that models performed quite well in identifying the deviation of call quality aspects and predicting the customer satisfaction.

References

1. Kummamuru, K., Roy, S., Venkata Subramaniam, L.: Unsupervised segmentation of conversational transcripts. In: Proceedings of the 2008 SIAM International Conference on Data Mining. Society for Industrial and Applied Mathematics (2008)
2. Roy, S., et al.: QART: a system for real-time holistic quality assurance for contact center dialogues. In: AAAI (2016)
3. Park, Y.: Your call may be recorded for automatic quality-control. IBM Research Report RC24574 (W0806–018), 5 June 2008
4. Negi, S., et al.: Automatically extracting dialog models from conversation transcripts. In: Ninth IEEE International Conference on Data Mining, ICDM 2009. IEEE (2009)
5. Park, Y., Gates, S.C.: Towards real-time measurement of customer satisfaction using automatically generated call transcripts. In: Proceedings of the 18th ACM conference on Information and knowledge management. ACM (2009)
6. Mikolov, T., et al.: Distributed representations of words and phrases and their compositionality. In: Advances in Neural Information Processing Systems (2013)
7. Pennington, J., Socher, R., Manning, C.: Glove: global vectors for word representation. In: Proceedings of the 2014 Conference on Empirical Methods in Natural Language Processing (EMNLP) (2014)
8. Hecht-Nielsen, R.: Theory of the backpropagation neural network. In: Neural Networks for Perception, pp. 65–93 (1992)
9. Srivastava, N., et al.: Dropout: a simple way to prevent neural networks from overfitting. J. Mach. Learn. Res. **15**(1), 1929–1958 (2014)
10. Kingma, D.P., Ba, J.: Adam: a method for stochastic optimization. arXiv preprint arXiv:1412.6980 (2014)
11. Chollet, F.: Keras (2015)
12. Llimona, Q., et al.: Effect of gender and call duration on customer satisfaction in call center big data. In: Sixteenth Annual Conference of the International Speech Communication Association (2015)
13. Godbole, S., Roy, S.: Text to intelligence: building and deploying a text mining solution in the services industry for customer satisfaction analysis. In: IEEE International Conference on Services Computing, SCC 2008, vol. 2. IEEE (2008)
14. Zhou, C., et al.: A C-LSTM neural network for text classification. arXiv preprint arXiv:1511.08630 (2015)
15. Rehurek, R., Sojka, P.: Software framework for topic modelling with large corpora. In: Proceedings of the LREC 2010 Workshop on New Challenges for NLP Frameworks (2010)

16. Pedregosa, F., et al.: Scikit-learn: machine learning in Python. J. Mach. Learn. Res. **12**, 2825–2830 (2011)
17. Kirkpatrick, K.: AI in contact centers. Commun. ACM **60**(8), 18–19 (2017)
18. Mundra, S., Sen, A., Sinha, M., Mannarswamy, S., Dandapat, S., Roy, S.: Fine-grained emotion detection in contact center chat utterances. In: Kim, J., Shim, K., Cao, L., Lee, J.-G., Lin, X., Moon, Y.-S. (eds.) PAKDD 2017. LNCS (LNAI), vol. 10235, pp. 337–349. Springer, Cham (2017). https://doi.org/10.1007/978-3-319-57529-2_27
19. Can Virtual Experiences Replace Reality? https://www.oracle.com/webfolder/s/delivery_production/docs/FY16h1/doc35/CXResearchVirtualExperiences.pdf. Accessed 15 Dec 2018

A Conceptual Model to Improve Understanding of Distance Related Uncertain Information

H. M. Ravindu T. Bandara[(⊠)], H. P. Chapa Sirithunge,
A. G. Buddhika P. Jayasekara, and D. P. Chandima

University of Moratuwa, Moratuwa 10400, Sri Lanka
ravitharaka11@gmail.com, {ra-chapa,buddhika,chandima}@uom.lk

Abstract. Assistive robots should be friendly, reliable, active, and comprehensible in order to be a friendly companion for humans. Humans tend to include uncertain terms related to direction and distance to describe or express ideas. Therefore assistive robot should be capable of analyzing and understanding the numerical meaning of the uncertain term for the purpose of creating a conceptual map for effective navigation in three-dimensional space. Therefore this paper proposes a method to understand spatial information in uncertain terms considering the three-dimensional data and a conceptual model to interpret uncertainties of the uncertain terms using conceptual factors. Experiments have been carried out to analyse the impact of conceptual factors on uncertain information interpretation. The proposed method has been implemented on MIRob platform. The experiments have been carried out in an artificially created domestic environment and the results have been analyzed to identify the behaviours of the proposed concept.

Keywords: Social robotics · Conceptual dimension · Certainty level

1 Introduction

Human robot interaction techniques for assistive robots are being enhanced every day. Researchers are making more progress on implementing artificial intelligence much more similar to the human brain [11]. Robots are expected to work in both industrial and domestic environments. In order to work in different environments and to adapt for different tasks a robotic system needs a knowledge base similar to a human. Learning approaching methods are very important to assistive robots since it incrementally makes human robot interaction friendlier over time [7,10,12]. With recent developments in robotics human-like robot systems are getting more attention in technology. The one of the ultimate goal of artificial intelligence and robotic science is to create human like robots. In that case understanding the vocal instructions or description is an essential factor to replicate human likeness.

© Springer Nature Switzerland AG 2019
L. Rutkowski et al. (Eds.): ICAISC 2019, LNAI 11509, pp. 501–511, 2019.
https://doi.org/10.1007/978-3-030-20915-5_45

Vocal instructions or description used in object manipulation vary based on the type of task, environment and state of perspective view [5]. It is well known that humans elicit various conscious and subconscious responses. Such that most of the times human instructions may include uncertain terms to describe a direction, distance or quantity such as "near to the table", "left of the TV" or "little amount of sugar". Also when humans observe objects, various modules are activated in human brains in order to read sensory inputs. An important point here is that the reactions coming from these modules are associated with the focal conscious and nonconscious processing which is different from person to person [3]. As a result of that the definition of uncertain term in numerical domain may also vary from person to person. As an example if a person asked to "come near to the table" and another person was asked to do the same. The second person may understand numerical value expressed by uncertain term "near" differently than the first person. Also the same term can be expressed in a different meaning based on the task. "Near to the chair" and "near to kitchen" can be considered as an example with the same uncertain term implying different numerical value ranges.

In navigation task it is important that the robot understands the meaning of uncertain terms such as "far", "near", "middle", "left", "right","behind", "in front of" and "close to". Since it is not possible to assign constant or predefined values to those terms a robot should have a capable system to understand uncertainty of such terms by processing information real time. When processing information it is essential to consider the parameters such as object dimensions, environment, previous experience and point of view. As an example, an object such as television has a well defined front side. Therefore if the description says "in front of the tv" the direction is obvious. However human are confused in giving a reaction to a description like "in front of the table" since the object like a table does not contain a clearly defined front and they tend to choose front side based on their perspectives. In imagining or creating a conceptual virtual environment based on knowledge conveyed from another person using natural voice instruction without actually seeing the environment will reduce the complexity if robot has the same cognitive ability that a human possess [1,2]. Therefore to comprehend knowledge via natural language phrases with the uncertain terms robot should possess capability in interpreting uncertain terms.

A probabilistic framework that enables robots to follow commands given in a natural language, without any prior knowledge of the environment has been proposed [4]. The proposed method enables the robots to interpret and execute natural language commands that refer to unknown regions and objects in the robot's environment [6]. However the essential factors such as the object size or object orientation are not considered in the proposed system. A method to create the conceptual spatial representation of the indoor environments for mobile robots has been introduced [14]. The system is capable of linking the knowledge acquired through conversations with the maps created from a laser scanner and a vision sensor. A method to evaluate the uncertain information in user commands by replicating the natural tendencies of humans about the spatial arrangement of the environment and robot system that can acquire knowledge through interactive discussion with the user while handling the uncertain information in the user instructions are proposed in [8,9,13]. However, above proposed methods are lacking ability of interpreting uncertain information in language instructions related to the spatial descriptions. Moreover, the proposed systems are not effective when uncertain information is included. As an example, the methods are not capable of effectively extracting the language phrase such as, "table is far away from the refrigerator". Furthermore, the systems are not capable of evaluating the specific objects in environment in order to understand the uncertain terms more accurately. Also proposed systems are only processing 2 dimensional data to make decisions which can be more accurate in considering 3D space. Therefore, this paper proposes a novel method that can be utilized for a service robot to understand uncertain terms based on 3D space properties and create virtual maps about previously unknown environments based on the descriptive language instructions. These virtual maps will eventually contribute for efficient navigation of the robot.

2   Identification of Factors

2.1   Certainty Level - C

Certainty Level is the measurement which refers to a probability of an absolute awareness of a position in related to a congenitally enhanced inveterate cognitive frame.

2.2   Experiment I-Identification of the Impact of Object Size When Interpreting Uncertain Term "Near"

An experiment was carried out with 15 participants to identify the impact of object size in interpreting uncertain term "near". Experiment was carried out as follows. Every participant was asked to go "near" to a table with a height and width of 1 m in 15 times and the coordinates were marked according to the position of the table and the participant. Figure 1(a) shows the interpretation of the coordinates. After that participants were asked to keep a pen "near" to a book of 210 * 299 mm which was on the top of the table and the coordinations were taken according to the position of the book. Figure 1(b) shows the interpretation of the coordinates.

2.3   Experiment II-Identification of Certainty Levels Related with Uncertain Term "Near"

An experiment was carried out with 15 participants and asked them to assign a number from 1 to 10 which reflects the idea "near" with their views in accordance to the change of placement done when a person who is sitting on a chair near to the table is moving away a pen touched to the book by 3 cm in each consecutive

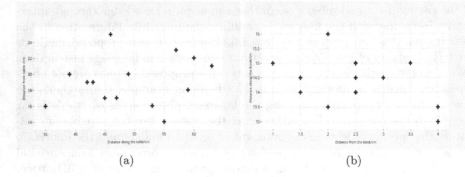

Fig. 1. Experiment I results. (a) Participants movements relative to table and (b) Participants movements with pen and book

turn. The main objective is to configure the distance assigned to the term "near" according to the point of view. After that participants were asked to assign from 1 to 10 which reflects the idea "near" with their views in accordance to the change in placement done by a person who is standing very close to the table is moving away by 10 cm in each consecutive turn. The main attempt is to configure the distance assigned related to the term "near" according to the point of view.

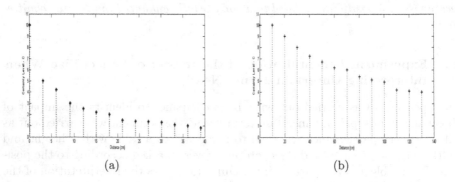

Fig. 2. Certainty levels for Experiment II. (a) Certainty levels calculated for chair and table movements. (b) Certainty levels calculated for book and pen movements

Certainty levels of experiment I was calculated using 1. Where i is response value and n is number of given responses and N is number of total responses.

$$C = \sum \frac{i \times n_i}{N} \tag{1}$$

As shown in Fig. 2(a) and (b) certainty level varies based on environment. In Experiment I, main difference between two scenarios was object size. In Fig. 2(a) certainty level is on it's maximum value for some distance range and after that it gradually decreases. However in Fig. 2(b) certainty level is decreasing from the beginning. It implies that object size has an impact on distance uncertainty.

3   Conceptual Dimensions

It can be seen that almost all the times uncertain terms such as "far", "near" were defined in physical dimensions. Furthermore uncertainty of distance was expressed by words like "far" and "near" were interpreted using a numerical frame. However in case of human brain uncertainty of distance measured using concepts. As an example in [9] "near" is expressed as a numerical value. Subsequently the final output remains predictable even though these systems use fuzzy systems to add fuzziness to output values. However in the real world "near" gives different interpretation based on several factors explained in Sect. 3.1 Such as "near to the fire place" and "near to the table" are two different ideas which should be considered defining numerical value range. Human will definitely define distance mean by "near" in "near to fireplace" more than "near" in "near to the table".

Artificial intelligence is an essential tool that enhances data processing, information processing in service robots. In the performance of the service tasks it is not an essential factor to be a human like robot. Nevertheless being a human like robot is vital if it is supposed to play the role of a companion through performing the tasks related to the human. Relevant to this scenario the robot should be capable to identify the uncertainty in the distance. Furthermore intellectual skills used by the human brain in the identification of the uncertainty in the distance may not be similar to the way of identifying the uncertainty in the distance by the human-like robots. Nevertheless respond given by both parties related to an action with the uncertainty in the distance should match with each other.

3.1   Conceptual Factors in Distance

Distance uncertainty depends on several conceptual factors such as size, color, temperature, taste/smell, sound level and weight.

4   Impact of Object Size in Certainty Level - C

Certainty level of "near" with respect to an object can be represented as in Eq. 2. Where S is conceptual factor and 'd' is distance from the object.

$$C \, \alpha \, \frac{1}{d^S} \tag{2}$$

value of the conceptual factor of size (S) is decide based on 3, 4 and 5. where
h = Effective height of object
h_i = Effective height of robot

d_0 = projectional diametre of the object on XY plane
d_p = projectional diametre of the robot on XY plane

$$h_c \leq h + h_i \;\; \delta\delta \;\; d < d_p \Rightarrow S = 0 \tag{3}$$

$$h_c = h + h_i \;\; \delta\delta \;\; d \geq d_p \Rightarrow S = 1 \tag{4}$$

$$h_c = (\, h + h_i \,) - (\, h \cap h_i \,) \tag{5}$$

Therefore certainty level can be given in 6 where K is non-dimensional constant.

$$C = K\, \frac{1}{d^S} \tag{6}$$

When conceptual factor does not have impact on certainty level C must be zero. Therefore By assigning initial values

$$When \; S = 0 \; \Rightarrow \; C = 0$$

So that

$$k = d_p$$

Distance from an object for required certainty level calculation is given in 7.

$$d = \log^{-1}\{\frac{\log d_p - \log C}{S}\} \tag{7}$$

Therefore volumetrical space for a uncertainty term "near" can be shown as 8.

$$V_{near} = \int\int\int \log^{-1}\{\frac{\log d_p - \log c}{S}\}\, d_x d_y d_z - V_0 \tag{8}$$

when choosing x, y, z for calculating V_{near} maximum certainty level should be choose.

5 Position Identification

Section 4 explained evaluation of certainty level based on conceptual factor size. Algorithm 1 has been developed to calculate position with required certainty level based on uncertain term and uncertainty term "middle" will be identified based on the reference positions as shown in Fig. 3(c).

6 Results and Discussion

6.1 Research Platform

The proposed concept has been implemented on MIRob [9] platform. The experiments have been carried out in an artificially created domestic environment inside the laboratory environment. REM model similar to [9] has been used to feed detailed map to system.

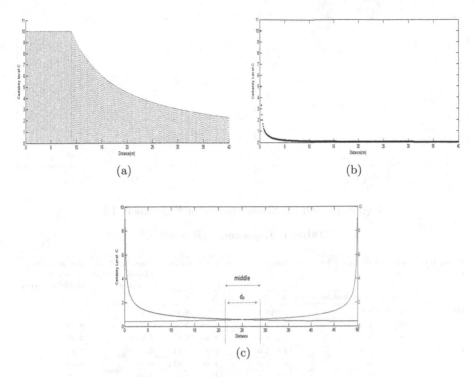

(a)   (b)

(c)

Fig. 3. (a) and (b) Certainty level calculated for Experiment I based on proposed method. (c) Middle range identification based on certainty level

6.2   Experimental Setup

Two experiments have been carried out to analyse robot certainty level evaluation capability and uncertain information evaluating capability with reference to a human.

Experiment III. The setup which is apposite to the experiment III has been arranged under the laboratory environment. In this scenario, the interpretation done by the robot relevant to the various initial points of an object (table) in accordance to the distance uncertainty has been analyzed. The results procured through the experiment III has been compared with the results of the human study which has been carried under the same laboratory circumstances. Furthermore robot has been assigned to create a decision relevant to the positions in the term of different uncertainties featuring to the initial positions as represented in the Fig. 4(a). Moreover the decided positions of the robot have been specified to 10 participants at a glance and instructed them to assign a numerical value in the range of 1–10 based on the uncertainty term. Additionally participants have been asked to represent the certainty behind those positions since the main endeavor is to recognize the certainty. Subsequently the same experiment has been carried out with an object (chair) with a different size as shown in Fig. 4(b). Experiment results are shown in Table 1.

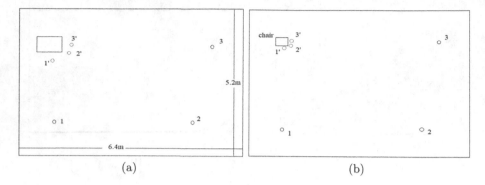

(a)   (b)

Fig. 4. (a) and (b) Shows results for Experiment III

Table 1. Experiment III result

Experiment no.	Selected certainty level - C		Initial position		Final position		Distance from object to final position	Distance from object to initial position
	System	From human study	X	Y	X	Y		
III	10	9.9	1.0	1.0	0.96	3.38	0.22	2.9
	10	10	5.0	1.0	1.38	3.59	0.1	4.98
	10	9.8	5.5	1.3	1.46	3.9	0.064	4.55
IV	10	9.9	1.0	1.0	0.977	3.81	0.09	2.9
	10	10	5.0	1.0	1.16	3.911	0.02	4.82
	10	10	5.5	1.15	1.2	4.05	0.05	4.35

Experiment IV. Experiment IV was carried in the same laboratory environment with more area and more objects as shown in the Fig. 5. In this structure robot has been commanded at 5 times using the system similar to [9] and the decided positions were taken under the consideration in advance. Respectively 10 participants have been selected and the same commands have been stated to them in different turns as the each participant is not aware of the destinations of others. The results of their positions have been included in the Table 2 and comparison between result derived from human study and system generated data are shown in Table 3.

In the consideration to the prominent factors of Tables 1 and 2, the derivation of the term of uncertainty which has been defined in relation to the distance has been varies with the size of the object. As an example, in accordance to the Table 1 the term of uncertainty 'near' corresponding to the table (Fig. 5) is 0.22 m and in comparison to the chair (Fig. 4(b)) is 0.1 m respectively. Further it substantiates the capability of the system to ascertain the term of uncertainty in comparison to the object size.

Moreover Table 2 reveals the capability of the system to define the term of uncertainty 'middle' in comparison to the other objects in the environment (Table 2 - row 3). In addition the system is proficient to identify the uncertainties in comparison to the robot itself (Table 2 - row 8).

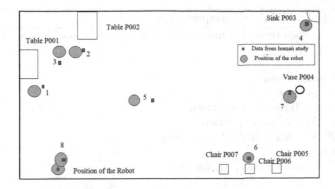

Fig. 5. Experiment IV setup

Table 2. Experiment IV result

No.	Uncertain term	Reference object	Object details			Position of robot		Distance (m)
			h(m)	d(m)	Area(m)	Initial X,Y	Final X,Y	
1	near	Table P001	0.84	0.514	0.54	1, 0.2	0.5, 2.7	0.20
2	near	Table P002	0.84	0.514	0.54	1, 0.2	1.5, 3.9	0.21
3	middle	Table P001, Table P002	0.84, 0.84	0.514, 0.514	0.54, 0.54	1, 0.2	1.25, 3.89	0.34, 0.40
4	near	Sink P003	1.04	0.32	0.070	1, 0.2	8.75, 4.7	0.1
5	far	Table P001	0.84	0.514	0.54	1, 0.2	3.6, 2.45	2.844
6	near	Chair P005, P006, P007	0.46, 0.46, 0.46	0.230, 0.230, 0.230	0.105	1, 0.2	7.0, 0.65	0.5, 0.1, 0.55
7	near	Vase	0.45	0.30	0.07	1, 0.2	8.25, 2.54	0.05
8	near	Initial position (robot)	1.43	0.45	0.2025	1, 0.2	1.3, 0.4	0.4

Table 3. Comparison between Experiment IV results

No.	Final position of robot		Data from human study		Diffference
	X, Y	Distance from reference object	Xmean, Ymean	Distance from reference object	
1	0.5, 2.7	0.20	0.7, 2.85	0.22	0.02
2	1.5, 3.9	0.21	1.9, 4.1	0.285	0.075
3	1.25, 3.89	0.34, 0.40	1.2, 3.7	0.35, 0.38	0.01, 0.02
4	8.75, 4.7	0.1	8.8, 4.8	0.11	0.01
5	3.6, 2.45	2.844	4.1, 2.4	3.42	0.576
6	7.0, 0.65	0.5, 0.1, 0.55	7.0, 0.61	0.45, 0.15, 0.57	0.05, 0.05, 0.02
7	8.25, 2.54	0.05	6.2, 2.65	0.08	0.03
8	1.3, 0.4	0.4	1.3, 0.55	0.46	0.06

Algorithm 1. Spatial data Interpretation

Require: : Uncertain term, Detailed map, reference, Initial position X_0, Y_0
Ensure: : X, Y

    if reference found **then**
        X_1, Y_1 = reference
        if Uncertain Term = "near" **then**
            if X_0, $Y_0 \in c_{near-max}$ **then**
                X, Y = 0.5 × highest c_{near} range
            end if
            X, Y = nearest $c_{near-max}$ position
        end if
        if Unvertain Term = "far" **then**
            X, Y = 0.25 of $c_{near-max}$ position
        end if
    else
        X_1, $Y_1 = X_0$, Y_0
        if Uncertain Term = "near" **then**
            if X_0, $Y_0 \in c_{near-max}$ **then**
                X, Y = 0.5 × highest c_{near} range
            end if
            X, Y = nearest $c_{near-max}$ position
        end if
        if Uncertain Term = "far" **then**
            X, Y = 0.25 of $c_{near-max}$ position
        end if
    end if

---

7 Conclusions

A method has been proposed to effectively understand uncertainties related to navigational commands. Proposed method has capability to understand uncertain information related to distance and direction in a way similar to the probabilistic behaviour shown by humans when they understanding uncertain information in navigation command.

A novel conceptual model with conceptual factors has been introduced to improve understanding of uncertain terms. Mathematical model has been developed for representing a conceptual dimension in physical measurement units. A method has been proposed to identify a position related to uncertain terms using certainty level rather than directly selecting a position which will be helpful to replicate the unpredictability in robot that human posses. Mathematical model for understanding certainty level has also been proposed.

The system is capable of understanding and interpreting uncertain information in physical quantities in a more similar manner to humans which makes robot more human friendly and effective in navigation task.

References

1. Bandara, H.M.R.T., Muthugala, M.V.J., Jayasekara, A.B.P., Chandima, D.: Cognitive spatial representative map for interactive conversational model of service robot. In: 2018 27th IEEE International Symposium on Robot and Human Interactive Communication (RO-MAN), pp. 686–691. IEEE (2018)
2. Bandara, H.M.R.T., Muthugala, M.V.J., Jayasekara, A.B.P., Chandima, D.: Grounding object attributes through interactive discussion for building cognitive maps in service robots. In: 2018 IEEE International Conference on Systems, Man, and Cybernetics (SMC), pp. 3775–3780. IEEE (2018)
3. Beran, M.J.: Foundations of Metacognition. Oxford University Press, Oxford (2012)
4. Duvallet, F., et al.: Inferring maps and behaviors from natural language instructions. In: Hsieh, M.A., Khatib, O., Kumar, V. (eds.) Experimental Robotics. STAR, vol. 109, pp. 373–388. Springer, Cham (2016). https://doi.org/10.1007/978-3-319-23778-7_25
5. Gärdenfors, P.: Conceptual Spaces: The Geometry of Thought (2004)
6. Hemachandra, S., Duvallet, F., Howard, T.M., Roy, N., Stentz, A., Walter, M.R.: Learning models for following natural language directions in unknown environments. In: 2015 IEEE International Conference on Robotics and Automation (ICRA), pp. 5608–5615. IEEE (2015)
7. Johnson, D.O., et al.: Socially assistive robots: a comprehensive approach to extending independent living. Int. J. Soc. Robot. 6(2), 195–211 (2014)
8. Muthugala, M.A.V.J., Jayasekara, A.G.B.P.: Interpreting uncertain information related to relative references for improved navigational command understanding of service robots. In: 2017 IEEE/RSJ International Conference on Intelligent Robots and Systems (IROS). Accepted for publication (2017)
9. Muthugala, M.V.J., Jayasekara, A.B.P.: Enhancing human-robot interaction by interpreting uncertain information in navigational commands based on experience and environment. In: 2016 IEEE International Conference on Robotics and Automation (ICRA), pp. 2915–2921. IEEE (2016)
10. Rabbitt, S.M., Kazdin, A.E., Scassellati, B.: Integrating socially assistive robotics into mental healthcare interventions: Applications and recommendations for expanded use. Clin. Psychol. Rev. 35, 35–46 (2015)
11. Sheridan, T.B.: Human-robot interaction: status and challenges. Hum. Factors 58(4), 525–532 (2016)
12. Siciliano, B., Khatib, O.: Springer Handbook of Robotics. Springer, Heidelberg (2016). https://doi.org/10.1007/978-3-319-32552-1
13. Talbot, B., Lam, O., Schulz, R., Dayoub, F., Upcroft, B., Wyeth, G.: Find my office: navigating real space from semantic descriptions. In: 2016 IEEE International Conference on Robotics and Automation (ICRA), pp. 5782–5787. IEEE (2016)
14. Zender, H., Mozos, O.M., Jensfelt, P., Kruijff, G.J., Burgard, W.: Conceptual spatial representations for indoor mobile robots. Robot. Auton. Syst. 56(6), 493–502 (2008)

Hybrid Genetic Algorithm for CSOP to Find the Lowest Hamiltonian Circuit in a Superimposed Graph

Khaoula Bouazzi[1]([✉]), Moez Hammami[2], and Sadok Bouamama[3]

[1] URMAN, Higher Institute of Applied Science and Technology
of KASSERINE (ISSAT), COSMOS,
National School of Computer Science (ENSI),
University of Manouba, Manouba, Tunisia
khaoula.bouazzi@ensi-uma.tn
[2] COSMOS, Higher Institute of Management of Tunis (ISG),
University of Tunis, Tunis, Tunisia
moezhammami@gmail.com
[3] Higher College of Technology, Dubai Men's College,
Dubai, United Arab Emirates
sbouamama@hct.ac.ae

Abstract. Many fields use the graphs as a tool of representation such as multimodal networks, computer networks, wireless sensor networks, energy distribution. But, beyond the representation of data, the graphs also serve to propose solutions to certain problems mentioning the well-known problem finding the shortest Hamiltonian circuit in a graph. The aim of this paper is to elucidate a mechanism to obtain the most efficient Hamiltonian circuit among specified nodes in a given superimposed graphs (SGs). The Hamiltonian circuit is a circuit that visits each node on the graph exactly once. The SG represents a scheme of multimodal transportation systems and takes into account distance among other variables. The Hamiltonian path may be constructed and adjusted according to specific constraints such as time limits. This paper introduces new constraint satisfaction optimization problem formalism (CSOP) for the problem of finding the lowest Hamiltonian circuit in superimposed graphs, and as a resolution method, we use the genetic algorithm. As a case study, we adopt the transportation data of Guangzhou, in China.

Keywords: Constraint satisfaction problems · Hamiltonian circuit problem · Superimposed graphs · Hybrid metaheuristics · Genetic algorithm

1 Introduction

A Hamiltonian circuit [1] in a graph is an ordering for a set of vertices that every two consecutive vertices are joined by an edge. The issue of finding the shortest Hamiltonian circuit in a graph is one of the most famous problems in graph theory. For arbitrary graphs, the Hamiltonian circuit problem (HCP) is outstanding known to be NP-complete. It is based on finding the shortest path. The most used algorithm for finding the shortest path is undoubtedly Dijkstra [1].

© Springer Nature Switzerland AG 2019
L. Rutkowski et al. (Eds.): ICAISC 2019, LNAI 11509, pp. 512–525, 2019.
https://doi.org/10.1007/978-3-030-20915-5_46

In the literature, special consideration has been given to problems using exact methods such as branch and bound [2], A* algorithm [3] and dynamic programming [4]. These techniques are effective for small size problems. For problems with more than two criteria or larger sizes there is no exact effective approach, given the concurrent difficulties of the NP-hard complexity, and the multi-criteria framework of the problems [5]. Metaheuristics are usually represented by local search methods such as simulated annealing, tabu research, and evolutionary algorithms, in particular genetic algorithms and evolution strategy algorithms [6]. Genetic algorithms are inspired by the mechanisms of evolution of living creatures and modern genetics, and are a powerful tool for optimization.

Many other problems were raised for finding the shortest Hamiltonian circuit; research has been carried out to solve it in recent years, citing:

The traveling salesman problem (TSP) [7] is a well known NP-complete problem. It is applicable to different branches of science and engineering. In the traveling salesman problem, a salesman person has to visit different cities for his business purposes. All the cities are connected together. The salesman can start his journey from any city visiting all the cities and returned back to the same city.

The vehicles routing problems (VRP) [8] are extensions of traveling salesmen problem. It gains its value from the growing importance of traveling and freight transportation nowadays. It consists of determining a circuit routed by a vehicle, so as to serve a set of clients in a network at minimal cost. The problem of vehicle routing was widely studied during the second half of the last century. The VRP principle is: given a depot D and a set of customers' orders C = (C1, C2, ... Cn), to build a package routing, for a finite number of vehicles, beginning and ending at a depot. In these routing, a customer must be served only once by a single vehicle and a vehicle capacity transport for a routing should not be exceeded.

Another extensive works have been done to solve problems which are based on finding the shortest Hamiltonian circuit such as the multi-objective multiple travelling salesmen, problem (MOmTSP). Bolaños et al. in [9] used a non–dominated sorting genetic algorithm (NSGA-II) to solve (MOmTSP). The main objective of algorithm NSGA-II is to find a set of solutions ordered by fronts under the concept of Pareto dominance.

Other metaheuristics used to solve the problem of the shortest Hamiltonian circuit in a multimodal transportation system. Minif and Bouamama in [10] used a multi-objective firework algorithms based on the Pareto-dominance method to find the shortest and efficient itinerary of satisfying a certain set of demands and operational constraints the multimodal transportation system.

No matter how the vertices are connected or characterized, the previous works just focus on finding the best solution trying to ameliorate the algorithms. Most of the researchers used the simple graphs to model the problem of finding the shortest Hamiltonian circuit. In our case we focus on finding a new framework that model this kind of problems, so we propose the superimposed graphs.

This paper proposes a new problem based on finding the lowest time Hamilton path in a superimposed graph (SG). In the second section, we introduce the overall context such as the superimposed graphs and constraint satisfaction problems (CSP). In the third section we describe the new problem then we model it using constraint satisfaction optimization problem (CSOP). We use an exact method branch and cut to validate the model using CPLEX. In the forth section, we introduce the resolution methods used to solve this problem. In the last part, we introduce a new hybrid genetic algorithm applied Dijkstra algorithm as a hybrid technique. Then we compare the results of the Hamiltonian circuit in superimposed graph with the results provided by a standard genetic algorithm. We used real data as a benchmark provided by the transportation system of Guangzhou city of China to evaluate our approach.

2 Over All Context

Graph theory is a wide field i.e. in constant evolution. Graphs are used to model many situations. Many graphs definitions are announced in literature. We will go along with the definition of J. A. Bondy and U. S. R. Murty mentioned in their book [13]. A graph G is a pair (V(G), E(G)) consisting of a nonempty set V(G) of vertices and a set E(G) of edges, joining the different elements of V(G).

In many cases, a simple graph cannot model some problems. Moreover, in some problems, vertices can exist in different categories, genres, and levels. However, simple graphs cannot guarantee this representation correctly, so we need a new model. Thus, we create a new graph called Superimposed graph (SG) published our previous works [12, 20].

2.1   The Superimposed Graphs

We suppose a set of non-oriented graphs $X1, X2, \ldots, Xn$ from different levels and different genres, with V a collection of sets of vertices $(V1, V2, \ldots, Vn)$ linked by E a collection of sets of edges $(E1, E2, \ldots, En)$ and n is the total number of graphs:

$$X1\left(V1, E_{in}^1\right), X2\left(V2, E_{in}^2\right), X3\left(V3, E_{in}^3\right) \ldots, Xn\left(Vn, E_{in}^n\right); \tag{1}$$

We suppose that the superimposition of the graphs is:

$$G(X, E) = \left(\{X1, \ X2, \ldots, \ Xn\}, \left\{E_{ex}^1, E_{ex}^2, \ldots, E_{ex}^m\right\}\right); \tag{2}$$

That means:

$$G(X, E) = \left(\left\{X1\left(V1, E_{in}^1\right), X2\left(V2, E_{in}^2\right), \ldots, Xn\left(Vn, E_{in}^n\right)\right\}, \left\{E_{ex}^1, E_{ex}^2, \ldots, E_{ex}^m\right\}\right); \tag{3}$$

- Each **vertex** X_Q of G(X, E) represents a graph; where $Q < n$.
- E_{in}^k: a set of **internal** edges connecting the vertices of each graph in X_Q.
- E_{ex}^k: a set of **external** edges, an edge $e_{ex} \in E_{ex}^k$, is connecting a vertex $v_i \in V_i$ and a vertex $v_i \in V_i$ such as $j \neq i$.
- The vertices V_k of the graph G(X, E) could be:

$$V_k = \begin{cases} - \mathbf{V_s}: \text{Significant vertices: must be visited in the tour;} \\ - \mathbf{V_{ns}}: \text{Significant vertices: must be visited in the tour.} \end{cases}$$

Graphs are used to illustrate problems. The purpose of a graph is to represent problems that are too numerous or complicated to be described adequately in a text. Moreover, graphs simplify the problem's resolution.

In optimization problems our main goals generally are to minimize the loss, maximize the gain and/or find the best solution. Therefore, to improve the problem's modeling; we should work on sets of networks (sub-graphs), avoiding consistently some vertices that make the problem more complicated or waste the time of execution. Simple graphs cannot provide that, all the vertices are similar with different links' weight.

In superimposed Graphs (SG) we don't have just similar vertices; we have two sets of vertices. The significant vertices V_s, the important ones, which must be visited and the non-significant vertices V_{ns} which could be visited if it upgrades the solution's research.

Moreover, in the SG case the edges also are divided into two sets, internal edges connecting the vertices of each network E_{in}^k and external edges E_{ex}^k which are connected vertices from different networks (sub-graphs). These partitions can decrease the flow's intricacy. As it was mentioned previously, superimposed graphs are very important to model problems and simplify the way to find solutions. It minimizes complexity and waste of time. SG can be considered as a very relevant addition in the graph theory.

2.2 Constraint Satisfaction Problem

Many real-world problems in artificial intelligence and in fields of computer science and engineering can be efficiently modeled as constraint satisfaction problems (CSPs) [14] and solved using constraint programming techniques, such as finding the shortest Hamiltonian circuit which is an NP-complete problem; it is an essential issue in many problems, in particular for transportation domains.

A CSP $p = (V, D, C)$ is a mathematical problem [14] defined as follows:

- A set of n variables $V = \{V_1, V_2 ..., V_n\}$
- A set of n domains: $D = \{D_1, D_2 ..., D_n\}$, D_i is the set of possible values that can take the variable V_i.
- A set of p constraints $C = \{C_1, C_2 ..., C_n\}$, on an arbitrary subset of variables in V.

The Constraint Satisfaction Optimization Problem (CSOP) [14] is defined as a CSP together with an optimization function f which maps every solution tuple to a numerical value. The task in a CSOP is to find the solution tuple with the optimal (minimal or maximal) f-value. The CSOP can be solved using two types of methods. First, the complete methods based on backtrack, such as Branch and Bound. They are able to find optimal solutions. Unluckily they have a big flaw which is the combinatorial explosion. The second is the incomplete methods, such as metaheuristics (genetic algorithms, ant colony, particle swarm optimization...) aim to avoid the trap of local optima.

3 Mathematical Formalism

Many of real life situations of communication or transportation networks can be well modeled into superimposed graphs (SG). The problem of finding the shortest Hamilton circuit in an agglomeration of superimposed graphs is a new problem based on some constraints, different from TSP, VRP and their extensions in a simple graph.

Due to the increasing interest in the management of transportation systems, there are needs to find minimum Hamilton paths in large graphs (e.g., a road network), where the weights associated with edges can be presented by time, distance and/or cost.

We adapt the problem of the lowest Hamiltonian circuit in the superimposed graph (SG) with a multimodal transportation system.

The constraint satisfaction optimization problem (CSOP) is an extension of CSP. It is the problem of finding different assignment to all variables that satisfies all constraints and at the same time optimizes an objective function.

Inspired of the CSOP formalism for the Travelling salesman problem (TSP) presented in [15], the problem of finding the lowest Hamiltonian circuit in superimposed graphs will be modeled with CSOP as follows:

Given a superimposed graph $G = (X, E)$, with n is the total number of the vertices and m is the total number of significant vertices.

A CSOP in superimposed graphs is defined by the 4-tuplet (X, D, C, F):

Variables: The variable X represents a set of m significant vertices and p non-significant vertices.

$$X = Xs \cup Xns = \{X_{S1}, X_{S2}, \ldots, X_{Sm}\} \cup \{X_{nS1}, X_{nS2}, \ldots, X_{Snp}\}; \tag{4}$$

Domain:

- The domain for the significant vertices is:

$$D(Xs_i) = \{1 \ldots 2m\}; \tag{5}$$

- The domain for the non-significant vertices is:

$$D(Xns_j) = \left\{w \in \{0, 1\}^{2m}\right\}; \tag{6}$$

Where:

- $2m$ is the maximum number of visited vertices (significant and non-significant).
- The vector $W_j[i]$ indicates if the vertex is visited or not, as follows:

$$W_j[i] = \begin{cases} -1 \text{ if the non - significant vertex } V_j \text{ is visited in the } i^{th} \text{ step.} \\ -0 \text{ otherwise.} \end{cases}$$

Constraints:

$$\sum_{j=1}^{m} W_i^j = 1; \quad \forall i = 1 \ldots m \tag{7}$$

$$\sum_{i=1}^{m} W_i^j = 1; \quad \forall j = 1 \ldots m \tag{8}$$

$$Min(\sum_{i=0}^{n-1} T_{i,i+1} + T_{n,1}) < Max\_waiting\_time; \tag{9}$$

$$\sum_{j=1}^{|Xns|} \sum_{i=1}^{2m} W_j[i] \leq m; \tag{10}$$

The constraints (7) and (8) guarantee the Hamiltonian circuit condition which is: visit each significant vertex exactly once.

The constraint (9) preserves the time window limits in the graph, the max_waiting_time is a fixed value (constant) for the maximum time of the tour and the $C_{i,i+1}$ is a function that gives the cost between the vertices V_i and V_{i+1}.

The constraint (10) ensures the number of visited non-significant vertices must be lower than the number of the significant vertices m.

Objective function:

$$Min(\sum_{i=0}^{m-1} C_{Vsi,Vsi+1} + C_{Vsm,1}); \tag{11}$$

Equation (11) minimizes the cost (Time or distance) the total cost of the path passing through the significant vertices: $C_{i,i+1}$ is a function that calculates the time between the vertices V_i and V_{i+1}.

4 Resolution Methods

4.1 Branch and Bound Method

We use an exact method to evaluate our approach including lower bound computation based on the branch and cut method. The branch-and cut [16] method is an exact algorithm method, it is consisting of a combination of a cutting plane method and a branch-and-bound algorithm.

It is a method of combinatorial optimization for solving integer linear programs (ILPs). Branch and cut involves running a branch and bound algorithm and using cutting planes to tighten the linear programming relaxations. Note that if cuts are only used to tighten the initial LP relaxation, the algorithm is called cut and branch.

4.2   Dijkstra Algorithm

Dijkstra algorithm [17] is an algorithm for finding the shortest paths between nodes in a graph, which may represent, e.g., road networks. It was conceived by computer scientist Edsger W. Dijkstra in 1956.

4.3   Standard Genetic Algorithm

Inspired by observation of natural processes in the real world, John Holland invented the first genetic algorithm in 1970. Genetic algorithms (GAs) [11] in their most general form are methods of moving from one generation of chromosomes to another. Each chromosome can be thought of as a bit of string, representing the encoding of one particular solution to a problem. These algorithms can be applied to machine learning, complex optimization problems or to simulations of real-life phenomena as has been done in this paper.

The basic structure of a standard genetic algorithm is given by the following five steps:

Step 1: Generate chromosome number of the population, and the initialization value of the genes chromosome with a random value;
Step 2: Evaluation of fitness value of chromosomes by calculating objective function;
Step 3: Process steps 4–7 until the number of generations is met;
Step 4: Chromosomes selection;
Step 5: Crossover;
Step 6: Mutation;
Step 7: Solution (Best Chromosomes).

5   Proposed Approach: Hybrid Genetic Algorithm

In recent years, hybrid metaheuristics have been used by many researchers in the field of optimization [18]. Hybrid algorithms showed superior performance in solving many practical or academic problems. In this approach, local search techniques were embedded into GA algorithm to control the search process.

Dijkstra has been developed to obtain optimal solutions for the expanded capacity of available paths in the superimposed graph.

Step 1: Initialize Population

The individuals of the population are randomly initialized. The size of the chromosome is equal to the size of the total number of the vertices. The initialization of one individual consists in randomly attributing values to its genes. It is worthy to note that, an individual is a complete instantiation of the problem's variables. Its gene is represented by (0 or 1); 0 for not visited vertices and 1 for visited significant vertices.

Hence every chromosome represents each possible solution of the problem, in our case the shortest Hamilton circuit in superimposed graph, respecting the constraints.

Step 2: Hybridization using Dijkstra

1:   **For each chromosome**
2:   **As input:** *we use only non-significant vertex to calculate the shortest path in the graph*
3:   **As output:**
4:   **If** *the non-significant vertex is visited it takes (-1) as a value in the chromosome*
5:   **Else** *it takes (0);*
6:   **End;**

Algorithm 1. GA hybridization using Dijkstra

Step 3: Fitness Evaluation
In this step, for each individual we calculate its Fitness value by calculating the total distance. That's mean the sum of distances spend from one vertex V_i to V_j during the Hamiltonian circuit.

The GA tends to minimize the distance of each chromosome in the population.
Let $C(X)$ be the objective function:

$F(X) = C_{max} - C(X)$

$F(X)$: Evaluation function, C_{max}: constant value, $C(X)$: the objective function

Step 4: Selection
In this phase of the algorithm, we use roulette wheel selection method. The selection of every chromosome is by a probability Pi.

$$Pi = f(\theta i) / \sum_i^n f(\theta i);   \tag{12}$$

With $f(\theta i)$ is the fitness function and n is the size of the initial population. The new survivors will be recombined and mutated to create another generation.

Step 5: Crossover
Many crossover techniques exist which use different data structures and different principles. In this case, we use a Two-point crossover. Two points are selected on two chromosomes which we considerate as parents. Everything between the two points is swapped between the parents, rendering two child organisms. The swapping between chromosomes is just for the non-significant vertex visited or not, that implies the genes which esteem "0" or "−1".

Step 6: Mutation
Mutation is applied to each child individually after crossover. It randomly alters each gene with a small probability (typically 0.001). Mutation only affects the genes that represent the non-significant vertices.

Step7: Best global solution update
The fitness of the best and the average individual in each generation increases towards a global optimum. This generational process is repeated until a termination condition has been reached.

6   Experimentations and Results

6.1   Data Set

For the testing phase we used the multimodal transportation system of Guangzhou china as a benchmark. The data were provided by a Laboratory of geographical information system GIS, in the School of Public Management, Guangdong University of Finance and Economics, Guangzhou China [19]. The transportation system of Guangzhou city of China [19] is the most suitable for our case, because of the heterogeneity of the transportation means. Furthermore, we tried the algorithm to find the lowest Hamiltonian circuit in the areas of Guangzhou china. In our example, we simulate with many means of transport. These modes are metro, bus, bicycle, and cars.

6.2   Comparison Using Exact Methods

In our previous works [20] we used IBM iLOG CPLEX 12.4 optimization studio to implement the CSOP model in superposed graphs. This choice of CPLEX is justified by its convivial aspect, its maintenance requirements, the availability restrictions, and the possibility of modeling constraint programming formalism as well as mathematical programming formalism. The goal of our experiments is to compare the CPU time spend amid the exploration for the shortest Hamiltonian circuit in both simple graph and superimposed graph. We use a real multimodal transportation network of Guangzhou China. For the implementation we use a cut and bound method as an exact method. The constraint satisfaction optimization problem model for finding the shortest Hamiltonian circuit in simple graphs is mentioned by the work of Aguayo in [21].

So for each problem size, we compare the two approaches to solve HCP and find the exact solution respecting the constraints mentioned previously. To evaluate our approach we care more about the CPU time needed to solve the problem because our main purpose is to show the efficiency of the superimposed graphs.

Table 1. CPLEX CPU time for HCP in simple graphs

Vertices size in simple graph	CPU time for simple graph (min)
10	0.09
15	0.11
20	0.23
30	0.8

The Table 1, shows in the first column the vertices size in simple graph, then the corresponded CPU runtime result using CPLEX to solve HCP.

Table 2. CPLEX CPU time for HCP in SG

Problem instance	CPU time for SG (min)
(10,15)	0.08
(10,99)	0.14
(15,30)	0.13
(15,99)	0.08
(20,30)	0.22
(20,50)	0.17
(30,40)	0.67
(30,99)	0.70

In Table 2 the first column represents the size of the significant and non-significant vertices by the couple (significant vertices, non-significant vertices). The second column represents the CPU runtime resulted in the case of the SG.

Figure 1 below shows by the dark blue bars the CPU time needed to solve the problem of the lowest Hamiltonian circuit in simple graphs, for each iteration the size of vertices takes the value: {10, 15, 20, 30}.

The light blue bars shows the CPU time needed to solve the problem of the lowest Hamiltonian circuit in superimposed graphs for different vertices couples {(10,15), (10,99),(15,30), (15,99), (20,30), (20,50), (30,40), (30,99).} Presented by the series {1, 2, 3, 4, 5, 6, 7, 8}.

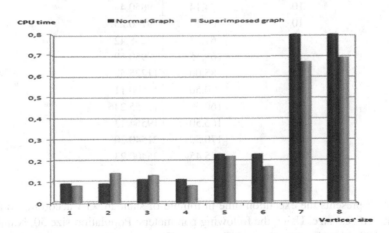

Fig. 1. The CPU time to solve HCP in normal graphs and superimposed graphs. (Color figure online)

Figure 1 compares the results occurred during the implementation of the CSOP formalism for finding the lowest Hamiltonian circuit in graphs and in the superimposed graphs obtained by the branch and cut technique using CPLEX. For different iterations, we compare the CPU time for the simple graph and the superimposed graph for a given significant vertex size value. The results in Fig. 1 show that our approach is more efficient with a large size of non-significant vertices. As we can see with series 1, 5, 4, 6, 7 and 8, where the non-significant vertices take the values 15, 30, 40, 50 and 99 and the significant vertices take the values 10, 15, 20 and 30, the CPU time needed to solve HCP in simple graphs is greater than the CPU time needed to solve HCP in SG, as we can see in Table 2.

Based on the above analysis, we can observe that introducing the novel model of graphs can induce a favorable CPU time for funding the lowest circuit in a superimposed graph. In the same way, we can notice that the version using the novel graph's model has a better behavior compared to another version, especially with bigger significant vertices.

6.3   Comparison Using Metaheuristics

After validating the CSOP model to find the lowest Hamiltonian circuit in superimposed graphs with the exact method cut and bound on smaller size problem. In this section, our proposed algorithm HGA and standard GA will be compared. The comparison is performed in terms of both execution time and objective function. We implement the genetic algorithm of the previous sections using JAVA.

Table 3. Time and function results to solve HCP in SG using standard GA

Visited vertices	Time (min)	Distance (m)
10	74.14	9850.4
10	66.12	9120.23
15	61.23	7258.42
15	68.15	9950.59
20	85.00	11225.52
20	90.50	12500.11
30	160.90	15755.246
30	166.50	19564.23
40	170.50	21540.20
40	175.45	25400.23

Table 3 presents the execution time in minute of standard GA according to the 10 different vertices' size. Using the following parameters: Population size 50, Number of iteration 100, Mutation rate 0.3 and Crossover Two-point crossover method.

Table 4. Results to solve HCP in SG using Hybrid GA

Problem instance	Time (min)	Distance (m)
(10;15)	50.23	5502.325
(10;99)	65.65	6710.23
(15;30)	49.03	5548.67
(15;99)	57.02	8430.239
(20;30)	64.50	8835.25
(20;50)	75.06	9732.025
(30;40)	120.35	13051.257
(30;90)	130.99	14090.80
(40;15)	136.40	15563.688
(40;99)	150.25	17580.25

The Table 4 represents in the second column the time in minutes spending during the visit of 10, 15, 20, 30 and 40 significant vertices. The column distance represents the distance in meters between all the significant vertices during the visit.

For both standard genetic algorithm (GA) and hybrid genetic algorithm (HGA) we used the same hardware and software, and the same parameters.

As we can see in the Fig. 2 below, HGA achieves better performance in terms of the tour time. The maximum spending time to find the shortest Hamiltonian circuit in superposed graph is 136.4 min contrariwise using standard genetic algorithm gives 175.45 min.

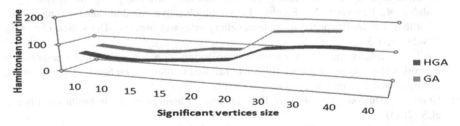

HGA and GA Hamiltonian Circuit time in Superiposed graph

Fig. 2. Comparative Hamiltonian tour time for HGA and GA Superimposed graph

7 Conclusions

Minimizing time by finding a shortest itinerary is the most challenging problem in transportation systems, especially in cities with a huge population. In this paper, we have presented a new solution to this problem which involved the determination of the most time efficient Hamilton circuit on a superimposed graph. We have created a new

Constraint satisfaction optimization problem (CSOP) framework to model the previously discussed circuit. We then developed a hybrid genetic algorithm using real data of a transportation system to evaluate our approach. The problem and the framework can be adapted and tested with any transportation system.

No doubt further refinement of this approach would allow its performance to be improved. Further work could be done in terms of improving the hybrid genetic algorithm to obtain better results and compare its performance with other metaheuristics. On the other hand, we can also test the CSOP framework on other in fields other than transportation.

References

1. LACOMME: Philippe, PRINS, Christian and SEVAUX, Marc.: Algorithmes de graphes. Eyrolles Paris (2003)
2. Wu, E.-F., Jin, Y., Bao, J.-S., Hu, X.-F.: A branch-and-bound algorithm for two-sided assembly line balancing. Int. J. Adv. Manuf. Technol. **39**(9–10), 1009–1015 (2008)
3. Zeng, W., Church, R.L.: Finding shortest paths on real road networks. Int. J. Geograph. Inf. Sci. **23**(4), 531–543 (2009)
4. Wang, F.-Y., Zhang, H., Liu, D.: Adaptive dynamic programming: an introduction. IEEE Comput. Intell. Mag. **4**(2), 41–43 (2009)
5. Nesmachnow, S.: An overview of metaheuristics: accurate and efficient methods for optimisation. Int. J. Metaheuristics **3**(4), 320–347 (2014)
6. Sörensen, K., Glover, F.W.: Metaheuristics. In: Gass, S.I., Fu, M.C. (eds.) Encyclopedia of Operations Research and Management Science, pp. 960–970. Springer, Boston (2013). https://doi.org/10.1007/978-1-4419-1153-7
7. Hoffman, K.L., Padberg, M., Rinaldi, G.: Traveling salesman problem. In: Gass, S.I., Fu, M. C. (eds.) Encyclopedia of Operations Research and Management Science, pp. 1573–1578. Springer, Boston (2013). https://doi.org/10.1007/978-1-4419-1153-7
8. Lalla-Ruiz, E., Expósito-Izquierdo, C., Taheripour, S., Vo, S.: An improved formulation for the multi-depot open vehicle routing problem. OR Spectrum **38**(1), 175–187 (2016)
9. Bolaños, R., Echeverry, M., Escobar, J.: A multiobjective non-dominated sorting genetic algorithm (NSGA-II) for the multiple travelling salesman problem. Decis. Sci. Lett. **4**(4), 559–568 (2015)
10. Mnif, M., Bouamama, S.: A multi-objective formulation for multimodal transportation network's planning problems. In: IEEE International Conference on Service Operations and Logistics, and Informatics, pp. 144–149 (2017)
11. Braun, U., Muldoon, S.F., Bassett, D.S.: On human brain networks in health and disease. eLS (2015)
12. Bouazzi, K., Hammami, M., Bouamama, S.: Modelling the shortest hamiltonian circuit problem in superimposed graphs with distributed constraint optimization problems. In: International Conference on Metaheuristics and Nature Inspired Computing, Marrakech in Morocco (2018)
13. Bondy, J.A., Murty, U.S.R.: Graph Theory. Graduate Texts in Mathematics, vol. 1, no. 244, p. 2 (2008)
14. Tsang, E.: Foundations of Constraint Satisfaction: The Classic Text. BoD–Books on Demand (2014)

15. Pesant, G., Gendreau, M., Potvin, J.-Y., Rousseau, J.-M.: An exact constraint logic programming algorithm for the traveling salesman problem with time windows. Transp. Sci. **32**(1), 12–29 (1998)
16. Padberg, M., Rinaldi, G.: A branch-and-cut algorithm for the resolution of large-scale symmetric traveling salesman problems. SIAM Rev. **33**(1), 60–100 (1991)
17. Deng, Y., Chen, Y., Zhang, Y., Mahadevan, S.: Fuzzy Dijkstra algorithm for shortest path problem under uncertain environment. Appl. Soft Comput. **12**(3), 1231–1237 (2012)
18. Talbi, E.-G.: Metaheuristics from Design to Implementation, vol. 74. Wiley, Hoboken (2009)
19. Chen, S., Claramunt, C., Ray, C.: A spatio-temporal modelling approach for the study of the connectivity and accessibility of the Guangzhou metropolitan network. J. Transp. Geogr. **36**, 12–23 (2014)
20. Bouazzi, K., Hammami, M., Bouamama, S.: CSOP framework for lowest hamiltonian circuit in superimposed graph. In: The International Society for Engineers and Researchers - International Conference on Science, Technology, Engineering and Management (ICSTEM), New York, USA (2018)
21. Aguayo, M.M., Sarin, S.C., Sherali, H.D.: Solving the single and multiple asymmetric Travelling Salesmen Problems by generating subtour elimination constraints from integer solutions. IISE Trans. **50**(1), 45–53 (2018)

Allowing Users to Create Similarity Relations for Their Flexible Searches over Databases

Mohammad Halim Deedar[✉] and Susana Muñoz-Hernández[iD]

Universidad Politécnica de Madrid, Escuela Técnica Superior de Ingenieros Informáticos, Campus de Montegancedo s/n,
28660 Boadilla del Monte, Madrid, Spain
halim.deedar@alumnos.upm.es, susana@fi.upm.es

Abstract. A bi-valued logic is not enough to make an intelligent search engine to give us the result for the queries like "I am looking for a cheap restaurant, Mediterranean food or similar type". With the integration of Fuzzy Logic and Logic Programming, we were able to model and pose flexible queries over databases. Therefore, we present a framework that allows users to pose their expressive queries based on defining similar relation criteria over various modern and conventional data formats such as JSON, SQL, CSV, XLS, and XLSX. The interest is in, for example, obtaining "drama movie" when asking for "romantic movie" (only if the similarity relation between drama and romantic movie is explicitly defined in the configuration file). The uses of similarity relation between values allow us to obtain more answers apart from the identical one. The searches that use two or more criteria are much more expressive and accurate. This framework provides the facility to define, modify and remove similarity relations from a user-friendly interface (without the need to be concern about the low-level syntax of the similarity criteria).

Keywords: Fuzzy logic · Similarity relation · Expressive searches · Search engine · Framework

1 Introduction

Assume a database storing information on films, containing entities such as film's name, genre, etc. A user wants to retrieve "a list of all the films existing in the film database which are very similar to a drama film". It is not functional to store fuzzy information with those fuzzy concepts (very similar, completely similar, cheap, far, etc.) in a database. However, it is not surprising that an end-user being a human to have that type of queries, as they always think and query in an expressive (fuzzy) way. Although searching in a fuzzy way not only gives us the exact information we are looking for, but it lets us to retrieve all the possible and available information close to the criteria which we have set for our query. For example, if we do a normal query (non-fuzzy) using any other

© Springer Nature Switzerland AG 2019
L. Rutkowski et al. (Eds.): ICAISC 2019, LNAI 11509, pp. 526–541, 2019.
https://doi.org/10.1007/978-3-030-20915-5_47

standard query languages such as SQL to retrieve a movie from a film database (having a crisp information) which is of genre romance, we get a list of all the existing romance movies from the database but we may miss the ones who are not explicitly defined as a romance movie but they are quite similar to romantic movie (because a drama movie sometime can be romantic too) and this could be the movie that the user is looking for. Therefore, we aim to provide a flexible database searching system that allows the user to pose their expressive queries over various data formats and get the best possible results.

A similarity is a relation between two real-world concepts. For a human being, it is not so difficult to decide how two things are similar or not to each other. In order to represent the real-world concepts as the human being understands, we need to introduce all the required information (or knowledge) explicitly. Therefore, for representing the real-world concept to the machines, we need a logic much more than a bi-valued logic (that defines if an individual belongs to a set or not by using only two value which is "true/false" or "yes/no").

Fuzzy logic [19,20] has substantiated its capability devoted to the management of vague information in a different number of applications (such as control systems, database or expert systems). The integration of Fuzzy Logic and pure logic programming [9] provides Fuzzy Logic Programming with the capability of dealing with ambiguity and approximate reasoning. This integration provided us the facility to program the machines in order to understand the fuzzy characteristics (it is cold), fuzzy rules (if it is cold, turn on the heater) and fuzzy actions (since it is not too cold, turn on the heater at medium degree). Therefore, in our approach the representation of similarity relation between two real-world concepts is provided using the integration of Prolog which is more declarative and a successful programming language for representing knowledge, and the Fuzzy Logic that defines not only if an individual belongs to a set or not, but it also provides us the degree of its belonging from that set. Supposing, a film database and the definition for the criteria "old" in (Fig. 1), and the question "is film X is old?" with fuzzy logic we can deduce that Casablanca is "very" old, The Godfather is "almost" old, Thor is "hardly" old, and Halloween is "not" old. We highlight the words "very", "almost", "hardly", and "not" because the usual answers for the query are "1", "0.9", "0.1" and "0" for the individuals Casablanca, The Godfather, Thor, and Halloween.

Many tools have been developed and implemented based on the fuzzy set theory introduced by Zadeh (as cited in [19]) to represent the fuzzy knowledge as Prolog-Elf system by Ishizuka and Kanai [7], the FRIL Prolog system by Baldwin et al. [1], the F-Prolog language by Li and Liu [8], the FuzzyDL reasoner by Bobillo and Straccia [2], the Fuzzy Logic Programming Environment for Research (FLOPER) by Morcillo and Moreno [12], the Fuzzy Prolog system by Guadarrama et al. [6], RFuzzy by Muñoz-Hernández et al. [13], and the theoretical frameworks as Vojtáš [17]. But we have used RFuzzy with priorities [14,15] in our approach to add a link between fuzzy and non-fuzzy concept because we need our approach to have the capability to decide the preferred results among

film_name	genre	release_year
Casablanca	Romance	1946
The Godfather	Drama	1972
Thor	Action	2013
Halloween	Horror	2018

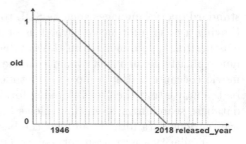

Fig. 1. Film database content and old fuzzification criterion.

the ones provided by different rules, it does not matter if the last rule provides a result with higher truth value.

We aim to present a framework intelligent and flexible enough that allows users to perform fuzzy (expressive) queries over databases (having crisp data) adding the similarity relation criteria. To our knowledge, the works similar to ours are [3–5,18]. The main distinctive characteristics of our approach in comparison to other ones are (1) that we do not force our relations to be equivalence (reflexive, symmetric, or transitive) for our similarity criteria. (2) We are not trying to evaluate the closeness (or similarity) between two fuzzy propositions. Our work is different: The item which is similar to the one we are looking for is returned as a result after computing its similarity value. (3) There is no limitation on posing the expressive query only over a single data format because our framework allows the users to pose their expressive query over conventional and modern data formats such as JSON, SQL, CSV, XLS, and XLSX. (4) We allow the end-users to define, modify and remove similarity relations between two concepts without knowing the low-level syntax of the function, which can reduce the gap between the database end-users and the logic programming users.

This paper is structured as follows: A brief details about the general RFuzzy rule syntax, the syntax for defining databases, and the introduction to the Similarity syntax and semantics are given in (Sect. 2). In (Sect. 3) we present the implementation of the framework (web application) including the details about the system architecture and the steps for defining, querying, and modification of Similarity relations, and the results of the query after posing it over the database. Finally, in (Sect. 4) we give our conclusions and the current work.

2   Syntax and Semantics of Similarity Relation

Before discussing the syntax and semantics of similarity relations of our approach, we include a brief detail about the general RFuzzy rule syntax (Sect. 2.1) and the syntax for database definition (Sect. 2.2) because by some means they are related to each other.

2.1 General RFuzzy Rule Syntax

The general structure that is used to define RFuzzy rules in according to a multi-adjoint logic semantics is shown in Eq. 1 [14]

$$P(argsP_j, V_j) \xleftarrow{(Pr_j, V_{cj})\&_i} @_j (Q_1 (argsQ_{1j}, V_{1j})),$$
$$\ldots (Q_n (argsQ_{nj}, V_{nj})). \tag{1}$$

Where P is the predicate, j is one of the definitions from a set of definitions $j \in [1, N]$ (where N is number of rules that we have to define for predicate P, and j identifies one of these rules). $argsP_j$ are the arguments of P in the rule j, in the same way $argsQ_i$ are the arguments of Q_i where $i \in [1, n]$ and n is the number of elements of the body of the clause. V_i is the truth value of the $Q_i(argsQ_i, V_i)$. $@_j$ is the aggregation operator of the rule j. V_{cj} is the credibility to calculate the truth value and Pr_j is the priority of j rule with respect to other rules of P definition.

The multi-adjoint algebra as presented in [10,11] is used to give semantics to our framework. The purpose of using this structure is that it provides credibility for the rules that we give in our program. We highlight this point, so the reader knows why our approach is based on this structure and not some other. Since comprehensive details about the semantics can be found in the papers cited.

2.2 Database Definition Syntax

The syntax which is responsible for outlining the contents of a database into concepts that we can use in our searches is shown in Eq. 2 Where P is the name of the database table, A is its arity, N is the name assigned to a column (field) of the database table where values are of type T, $i \in [1, A]$ identifies each field of the table. We give an example in Eq. 3, to elucidate, that the film table has four columns, the first one is for the name assigned to each film, the second is for the year in which the films have released, the third is for duration of the films in minutes, and the last one is for the genre of each film whose value belongs to an enumerate range (comedy, thriller, drama, romantic, adventures, etc.).

$$define\_database(P/A, [(N_i, T_i)]). \tag{2}$$

define_database (film/4,
[(film_name, string_type),
(release_year, integer_type),   (3)
(duration_in_minutes, integer_type),
(genre, enum_type)]).

The web interface and setters/getters obtain plenty of information from the database definition.

2.3 Similarity Definition Between Values

The syntactical construction which is used for modeling a similarity relation between the values of a field is shown in Eq. 4. Where P and N are the same as in Eq. 2, $V1$ and $V2$ are the possible values for the column N of table P, and TV is the truth value (a float number) that we assign to the similarity between $V1$ and $V2$. To clarify, we give an example in Eq. 5, saying that "romance films are 0.7 similar to drama films".

$$similarity\_between(P, N, [(V1), N(V2), TV]). \qquad (4)$$

$$similarity\_between(film, genre(romance), \atop genre(drama), 0.7). \qquad (5)$$

The semantic for defining conditioned similarity is shown in Eq. 6 where P, N, TV, $V1$, and $V2$ are the same as in Eq. 4. p is the priority, v is the credibility, $\&_i$ is the product, and $COND$ is a bi-valued condition. To clarify, we give an example in Eq. 7, saying that the *films* with the genre *drama* are "very similar" to the films with the genre "romance" by "0.9" degree and with the credibility of "1" if the films are directed by *Richard*. This means, with the help of this structure we can define the similarity relation between two values based on a condition with the credibility of "1". For example, after posing a query for searching the similarity degree between "drama" and "romance" films, we may obtain multiple films of type "drama" and "romance", but with the help of the syntax in (Eq. 7) with a condition and the credibility value a user can deduce that the films which are directed by "Richard" (a film director) their similarity relation of being "drama" and "romantic" are more credible in comparison to the rest of the films.

$$similarity(P(N(V1, V2))) \xleftarrow{(p,v)\&_i} TV \; if \; COND \qquad (6)$$

$$similarity(film(genre(drama, romance))) \atop \xleftarrow{(1,1),prod} 0.9 \; if \; director = ``Richard''. \qquad (7)$$

2.4 Synonyms Definition

The syntactical constructions for defining synonyms based on the similarity relations between fuzzy predicates is shown in Eq. 8, where *fPredName* is the name of the fuzzy predicate (expensive, cheap, etc.), P is the same as in Eq. 4, *credOp* is the operator (product by default), and *credVal* is the credibility (a type float number, which is 1 by default). To clarify, we give an example in Eq. 9, saying that "inexpensive is similar (or synonym) to cheap".

$$fPredName(P) :\sim$$
$$synonym\_of(fPredName2(P), \quad credOp, credVal). \tag{8}$$

$$inexpensive(restaurant) :\sim$$
$$synonym\_of(cheap(restaurant), prod, 1). \tag{9}$$

Attending to this definition, any query asking for inexpensive restaurants will return the cheap ones.

2.5 Similarity Relation Definition Between Concepts

With the syntax in Eq. 10, we can define a fuzzy predicate from another fuzzy predicate by defining the similarity relation between both fuzzy concepts when a condition is satisfied. We can define "inexpensive" from "cheap", "gorgeous" from "beautiful" etc. This will lead to getting a huge vocabulary for fuzzy searching without defining or storing a definition for all new words which does not exist in our vocabulary. In the syntax *fPredName* is the same as in Eq. 8, an individual is an element of the database for which we want to obtain the fuzzy value, and COND is the same as in Eq. 6. To clarify, we give an example in Eq. 11, where we can get the answer for the query "I am looking for an inexpensive car" for this query we will get the list of all the cars (stored in the database) which have been defined as a cheap. COND equal to true means that the similarity relation is always satisfied.

$$fPredName(individual) \xleftarrow{(p,v)\&_i} fPredName2(individual) \; if \; COND. \tag{10}$$

$$inexpensive(individual) \xleftarrow{(0,1),prod} cheap(individual) if true. \tag{11}$$

3 Implementation Details

Our proposed system is a combination of a web interface and a framework, developed mainly in Java, JavaScript, HTML, and AJAX. It uses RFuzzy package which is a Prolog library developed for Ciao Prolog [16]. The web interface is used to pose flexible queries over multiple conventional and modern data formats "JSON, SQL, CSV, XLS, and XLSX". The framework part of our system is used for defining the links between the crisp information stored in a database and the fuzzy concepts that we can use in a query. As for as we know, our system is novel in the idea of allowing the regular users (without having knowledge about database and programming) to create a link between the crisp information and the fuzzy concepts, and we allow them to define the similarity relation between concepts without knowing the low-level syntax of the criteria. Moreover, we provide them the facility to perform their flexible query over multiple data formats such as "JSON, SQL, CSV, XLS, and XLSX" (they do not need to have their database in a particular format such as "Prolog" which is not so familiar to the most regular users).

3.1 System Architecture

The system architecture, which is shown in Fig. 2, has five main parts: (i) Criteria Definition module: through which users can define, modify, personalize, and remove the similarity relations. (ii) Flexible Query Engine: is the main part, where users can pose their flexible queries devoted similarity relation. (iii) Flexible query process module that takes the flexible queries as an input from the users and provides the results as output after several computations of similarity relations. (iv) An engine (ciao prolog) that compiles our query for allowing the system to understand it and compute the corresponding similarity relations for it. (v) A database (configuration file) where data, similarity relations, quantifiers, modifiers, and negation operator are stored.

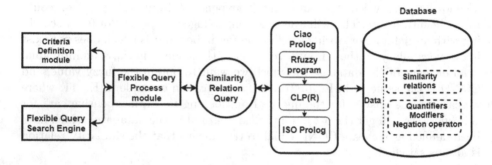

Fig. 2. System architecture

3.2 Data Files Uploading Interface

We present the uploading interface in Fig. 3, in which we can see a list of data-files of various formats. The framework allows users to define the types for the existing data in the data-file. To clarify, we provide an example in Fig. 4, where we assigned the data-types for each column of the film database. After assigning the data-types, the interface will prepare the configuration file (Prolog file) which stores the similarity relation for performing fuzzy and flexible searches. We present the structure of the configuration file in (Example 3.1).

Example 3.1. We take an example of a film database that by the way was in SQL format, which contains 6 columns and 16 records. After uploading it to the system (Fig. 3) and assigning the data-types (Fig. 4), the database gets converted into a configuration file (Prolog). The contents of the configuration file are as follows:

```
    % Configuration file (Prolog file):
:- module(car, _, [rfuzzy, clpr]).

% database definition define_database(film/6,
[(film_name, rfuzzy_string_type),
(release_year, rfuzzy_integer_type),
(duration_in_minutes,
```

rfuzzy_integer_type),
(genre, rfuzzy_enum_type),
(original_language, rfuzzy_enum_type),
(directed_by, rfuzzy_enum_type)]).
film('The Godfather', 1972, 207, drama, english, 'Francis Ford Coppola').
film('Casablanca', 1946, 172, romance, english, 'Michael Curtiz').
film('Cera una volta il West', 1968, 165, western, italian, 'Sergio Leone').
film('El laberinto del fauno', 2006, 107, drama, spanish, 'Guillermo del Toro').
film('Il buono, il brutto, il cattivo', 1967, 141, adventure, italian, 'Sergio Leone').
film('Finding Nemo', 2003, 112, comedy, english, 'Andrew Stanton and Lee Unkrich').
film('Thor - The dark world', 2013, 90, action, english, 'Alan Taylor').
film('Blue Jasmine', 2013, 98, action, english, 'Woody Allen').
film('The Collection', 2013, 82, thriller, english, 'Marcus Dun-stan').
film('Before Sunrise', 1995, 101, romantic_drama, english, 'Rich-ard Linklater').
film('Before Midnight', 2013, 109, romantic_drama, english, 'Richard Linklater').
film('Quien mato a Bambi?', 2013, 89, comedy, spanish, 'Santi Amodeo'). film('Not
Suitable for Children', 2012, 96, romantic_comedy, english, 'Peter Templeman').
film('Alien vs Predator', 2004, 115, science_fiction, english, 'Paul W.S. Anderson'.
film('Despicable Me', 2010, 95, comedy, english, 'Pierre Coffin and Chris Renaud').
film('Despicable Me 2', 2013, 98, comedy, english, 'Pierre Coffin and Chris Renaud').

As we can see, the configuration file is made up of four different parts: (1) the
header ":- module(film,_,[rfuzzy, clpr])." that includes the packages and libraries
of RFuzzy and CLPR (Constraint Logic Programming) which helps us to introduce the structure of fuzzy criteria to the search engine while posing an expressive query. (2) is the definition of the database that defines the columns and
their data-types, (3) is a table storing the crisp data. (4) Is the part where the
similarity relation defined by users get stored.

3.3   Defining Similarity Relation Interface

In order to perform a query based on the similarities, you need to have the criteria already defined inside the configuration file. Since the low-level syntax for
defining the similarity criteria (as defined in Sect. 2) is not so easy for a user
without having knowledge of database or programming, therefore, we present
a user-friendly interface in Fig. 5 that allows end-users to create the similarity
relation criteria (without being concerned about the low-level syntax of the criteria), and then they can apply that criteria over various types of modern and
conventional data formats such as (JSON, SQL, Prolog, CSV, XLS, and XLSX)
for performing flexible queries. Once the data file is uploaded to the system,
with the help of "Define new similarity relations" option the user can create
the criteria by assigning a degree of similarities between two values. We have
explained the steps for defining similarity relations in below.
The steps for creating a similarity relation are as follows:

- i. Selecting the database: As there can be more than one database in a configuration file such as (film, restaurant, etc.) therefore, the interface asks the

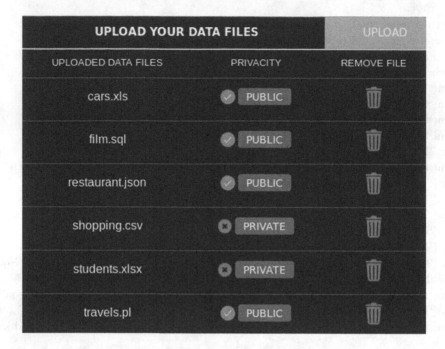

Fig. 3. Data files uploading interface

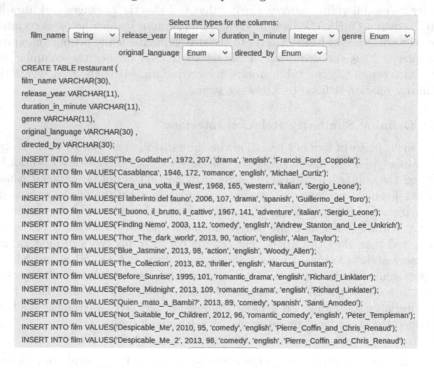

Fig. 4. Assigning data-types for the columns

user to select the one on which he/she wants to define the similarity relation criterion.

- ii. Selecting the column: In this step, the interface asks for the column on which the users want to define the similarity relations. Such as (genre, etc.).
- iii. Selecting the values: after selecting the column, the interface asks for two values/items such as (romance, drama, action, comedy, horror, etc.) on which the user want to assign the similarity degree.
- iv. Defining the similarity degree: Finally, the user has to a sign a similarity degree (a real number between 0 and 1) to define whether the items are (completely different, quite different, very different, similar, very similar, and completely similar). After clicking the save button, the criteria get created inside the configuration file.

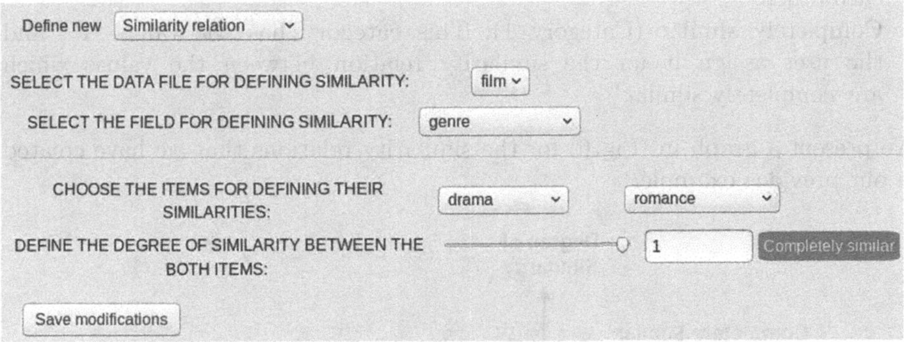

Fig. 5. Defining similarity relation interface

Example 3.1 (Continued). Once the configuration file is generated for the film database, now the user can create the similarity relations over the values of the film database. For example, the user wants to define the similarity relations between "drama" genre and other genres such as (romance, action, comedy, horror, and adventure). Thus, the similarity relations will get created as follows:

%Similarity relations defined over genres:
define_similarity_between(film, genre(drama), genre(adventure), 0.8).
define_similarity_between(film, genre(drama), genre(romance), 0.7).
define_similarity_between(film, genre(drama), genre(comedy), 0.5).
define_similarity_between(film, genre(drama), genre(horror), 0.3).
define_similarity_between(film, genre(drama), genre(action), 0).

We can see that the user has created five similarity relations between the genre "drama" and "romance, adventure, comedy, horror, and action", and the user has presented the similarity by assigning them different degree (between 0 and 1). We have considered six different categories for the similarity degrees created in our framework to make the end-users understand what we exactly mean by these real numbers (0 and 1) while defining the similarity relation. These categories are as follows:

- i. Completely different (Category 0): This category has the value "0", and the user is going to assign it for the similarity relation between the values, that he/she thinks they are "completely different".
- ii. Very different (Category 0.1 – 0.3): This category has the values between "0.1" and "0.3", the user will assign these degrees between the values that he/she thinks they are "very different".
- iii. Quite different (Category 0.3 – 0.5): This category has the values between 0.3 and 0.5, the user assigns these degrees between the values that he/she thinks they are "quite different".
- iv. Similar (Category 0.5): This category defines the relation between the values that the user thinks they are "similar" to each other.
- v. Very similar (Category 0.6 – 0.9): By assigning any degree of this category in a similarity relation, the user means the two values are "very similar" to each other.
- Completely similar (Category 1): This category has the value "1", and the user assign it for the similarity relation between the values which are "completely similar".

We present a graph in (Fig. 6) for the similarity relations that we have created in our previous example:

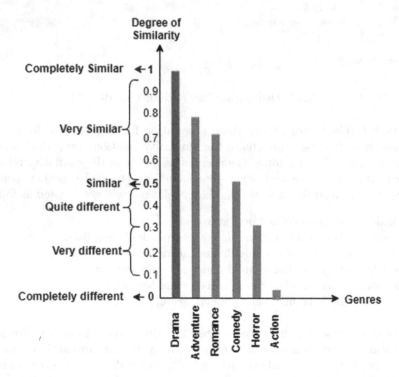

Fig. 6. Similarity relation between drama and other genres.

3.4   Query Interface

In order to perform a query over a database we need to follow the following steps:

- i. In querying interface, we select the database (such as film, restaurant, etc.) on which we want to pose the query as shown in Fig. 7.
- ii. After selecting the database, the framework will provide us a list of predicates such as (genre, film_name, release_year, original_language, etc.) and their values such as (drama, horror, action, romance, comedy, etc.) as shown in Fig. 8, we need to select the predicate with an enum_type and a corresponding value, and then we define the modifier similar $(= =)$ between them.
- iii. After defining all the criteria, we click the search button for executing our query.

Example 3.1 (Continued): After defining the similarity relations between "drama" and other genres (romance, action, comedy, horror, and adventure) of the film database, now the user wants to query: "I am looking for the film whose genre is similar to drama" Or, "I am looking for the film whose genre is similar to romance, etc." By posing these queries, our system will provide us a list of all the films from different categories devoted on the similarity degrees assigned for each relation (completely different, very different, quite different, similar, very similar, and completely similar).

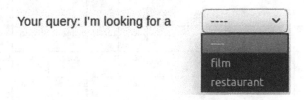

Fig. 7. Selecting the database.

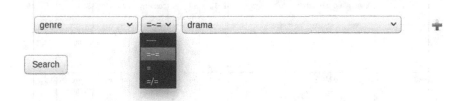

Fig. 8. Selecting the predicates and the modifiers.

3.5 Answering Interface

The answering interface provides different sets of in different tabs (10 best results, results in over 70%, results in over 50%, results in over 0 %, and all the results). These tabs provide different choices to the users to select the one which satisfies his/her needs.

- The tab with "10 best results" provides us the 10 best items (or less, it depends on the number of items existed in the database) which are similar to each other with a highest degree of similarity.
- The tab with the "results over 70%" provides us with a greater number of options with the similarity degrees between the range of (0.8 to 1). That means the user can get the items from the categories (very similar, and completely similar).
- The tab with the "results over 50%" provides us the items with the similarity degrees between the range of (0.6 to 1) that includes the items from the categories (similar, very similar, and completely similar).

10 best results	Results over 70%	Results over 50%	Results over 0%	All results

film	film name	release year	duration in minutes	genre	original language	directed by	Truth Value
n°.1	The Godfather	1972	207	drama	english	Francis Ford Coppola	1
n°.2	El laberinto del fauno	2006	107	drama	spanish	Guillermo del Toro	1
n°.3	Il buono, il brutto, il cattivo	1967	141	adventure	italian	Sergio Leone	0.8
n°.4	Casablanca	1946	172	romance	english	Michael Curtiz	0.7
n°.5	Finding Nemo	2003	112	comedy	english	Andrew Stanton and Lee Unkrich	0.5
n°.6	Quien mato a Bambi?	2013	89	comedy	spanish	Santi Amodeo	0.5
n°.7	Despicable Me	2010	95	comedy	english	Pierre Coffin and Chris Renaud	0.5
n°.8	Despicable Me 2	2013	98	comedy	english	Pierre Coffin and Chris Renaud	0.5

Fig. 9. The 10 best results tap.

– The tab with "the results over 0%" includes the items from the categories (quite different, very different, similar, very similar, and completely similar) with the similarity degree between the range of (0.1 to 1) excluding "0".
– And the tab with "all results" provide us the items from all the categories with a similarity degree from (0 to 1) including "0".

Ajax has been used for getting the result form each tab to avoid waste of computing time.

Example 3.1 (Continued): After posing the query, "I am looking for the film whose genre is similar to drama". The results provided by the system are as follows: The system provided us with the top 8 best results out of 10 (after selecting the tab with 10 best results) as there is only eight films which are having the highest similarity degree with drama films.).

We can see in the results (Fig. 9), it includes two films of genre "drama" with a degree "1", which indicates that all the films from the same genre (for example drama and drama) are "completely similar" to each other. The third best answer is the film with the genre "adventure" with a similarity degree "0.8", that indicates this film is "very similar" to the drama film based on the relation assigned between them. The fourth best answer is the "romance" film with a degree "0.7", and the rest four movies are with degree "0.5" which are "similar" to "drama" film. We can see that, with the help of the similarity degree assigned to each film a user can easily conclude which film is "similar, very similar, and completely similar" to "drama".

4   Conclusions

We have presented a framework which is a flexible and fuzzy search engine for querying over various data formats devoted on similarity relations. We provide details about the syntax and semantics of the constructions for representing the real-world similarity relations using fuzzy logic (Sect. 2). We have presented the details about the implementation and the architecture of our system (Sect. 3) with a comprehensive introduction about the steps for creating and modifying the criteria, and we have described the querying structure of our framework and the results to justify our work. The distinctive characteristics of our system in comparison to the existing ones are: (1) we do not force the similarity relation to be reflexive, symmetric and transitive, i.e., an equivalence relation. (2) the promising prototypes are devoted to minority data formats as Prolog, but our framework provides the possibilities to the user to pose their expressive (fuzzy) queries devoted to similarity relations over various conventional and modern data formats. (3) our user-friendly interface that reduces that gap between the database users and the logic programming users by allowing them to search their crisp data in conventional formats flexibly and expressively without knowing about the low-level syntax and semantics of the fuzzy relations. As a result, we obtain a fuzzy search engine for querying over modern and conventional data formats devoted to the similarity relations between the real-world concepts. We believe, our work contributes to the advancement of intelligent search engines. Our current research is on allowing users to personalize fuzzy criteria for their flexible searches over databases. so that every user of our system will be able to pose queries and get the result based on his/her personalized criteria.

References

1. Baldwin, J.F., Martin, T.P., Pilsworth, B.W.: Fril- Fuzzy and Evidential Reasoning in Artificial Intelligence. Wiley, New York (1995)
2. Bobillo, F., Straccia, U.: fuzzyDL: an expressive fuzzy description logic reasoner. In: International Conference on Fuzzy Systems (FUZZ-08), pp. 923–930. IEEE Computer Society (2008)
3. Dubois, D., Prade, H.: Comparison of two fuzzy set-based logics: similarity logic and possibilistic logic. In: Proceedings of 1995 IEEE International Fuzzy Systems, International Joint Conference of the Fourth IEEE International Conference on Fuzzy Systems and The Second International Fuzzy Engineering Symposium, vol. 3, pp. 1219–1226 (1995)
4. Esteva, F., Garcia, P., Godo, L., Ruspini, E.H., Valverde, L.: On similarity logic and the generalized modus ponens. In: Proceedings of the Third IEEE Conference on Computational Intelligence, Fuzzy Systems, IEEE World Congress on Computational Intelligence, vol.2, pp. 1423–1427 (1994)
5. Godo, L., Rodríguez, R.O.: A fuzzy modal logic for similarity reasoning. In: Cai, K.Y., Chen, G., Ying, M. (eds.) Fuzzy Logic And Soft Computing. Kluwer Academic (1999)
6. Guadarrama, S., Muñoz-Hernández, S., Vaucheret, C.: Fuzzy prolog: a new approach using soft constraints propagation. Fuzzy Set. Syst. **144**(1), 127–150 (2004)
7. Ishizuka, M., Kanai, N.: Prolog-ELF incorporating fuzzy logic. In: Proceedings of the 9th International Joint Conference on Artificial Intelligence, pp. 701–703. Morgan Kaufmann Publishers Inc, San Francisco (1985)
8. Li, D., Liu, D.: A Fuzzy Prolog Database System. Wiley, New York (1990)
9. Lloyd, J.W.: Foundations of Logic Programming, 2nd edn. Springer, Berlin (1987). https://doi.org/10.1007/978-3-642-83189-8
10. Medina, J., Ojeda-Aciego, M., Vojtás, P.: Similarity-based unification: a multi-adjoint approach. Fuzzy Set. Syst. **146**(1), 43–62 (2004)
11. Medina, J., Ojeda-Aciego, M., Vojtáš, P.: A multi-adjoint approach to similarity-based unification. Electr. Notes Theor. Comput. Sci. **66**, 70–85 (2002)
12. Morcillo, P., Moreno, G.: Floper, a fuzzy logic programming environment for research. In: Gij (ed.) Proceedings of VIII Jornadas sobre Programacion y Lenguajes (PROLE 2008), pp. 259–263 (10 2008)
13. Muñoz-Hernández, S., Pablos-Ceruelo, V., Strass, H.: RFuzzy: syntax, semantics and implementation details of a simple and expressive fuzzy tool over prolog. Inf. Sci. **181**(10), 1951–1970 (2011)
14. Pablos-Ceruelo, V., Muñoz-Hernández, S.: Introducing priorities in RFuzzy: syntax and semantics. In: CMMSE 2011: Proceedings of the 11th International Conference on Mathematical Methods in Science and Engineering, vol. 3, pp. 918–929. Benidorm (Alicante), Spain, June 2011
15. Pablos-Ceruelo, V., Muñoz-Hernández, S.: Getting answers to fuzzy and flexible searches by easy modeling of real-world knowledge. In: In IJCCI 2013 – Proceedings of the 5th International Joint Conference on Computational Intelligence (2013)

16. The CLIP lab: The Ciao Prolog Development System. http://www.clip.dia.fi.upm.
    es/Software/Ciao
17. Vojtáš, P.: Fuzzy logic programming. Fuzzy Set. Syst. **124**(3), 361–370 (2001)
18. Wang, J.B., Xu, Z.Q., Wang, N.C.: A fuzzy logic with similarity. In: Proceedings
    of the 2002 International Conference on Machine Learning and Cybernetics, vol.
    3, pp. 1178–1183 (2002)
19. Zadeh, L.A.: Fuzzy sets. Inf. Control **8**(3), 338–353 (1965)
20. Zadeh, L.A.: Calculus of fuzzy restrictions. In: Fuzzy Sets and Their Applications
    to Cognitive and Decision Processes, pp. 1–39 (1974)

Automatic Recognition of Melody Similarity

Tomasz Grębski[1] ⓘ, Krzysztof Pancerz[2](✉) ⓘ, and Piotr Kulicki[1] ⓘ

[1] Faculty of Philosophy, John Paul II Catholic University of Lublin,
Al. Racławickie 14, 20-950 Lublin, Poland
`tomasz@rey.edu.pl`, `kulicki@kul.pl`
[2] Faculty of Mathematics and Natural Sciences, University of Rzeszów,
Pigonia Street 1, 35-310 Rzeszów, Poland
`kpancerz@ur.edu.pl`

Abstract. The problem of the automatic recognition of a melody similarity is considered. A special data set with a number of different artificial modifications of original melodies was created to test several classification algorithms. The best algorithm (J48) was chosen to carry out a wider analysis. The results showed that the melody similarity can be described mathematically.

Keywords: Machine learning · Similarity recognition ·
Music perception · Classification

1 Introduction

In the paper we tackle several questions concerning the possibility of the formalization of human perception of melodies. Can human feelings about the similarity of melodies be described mathematically, and then, on this basis, can they be used to train the machine to recognize the similarity? What are the criteria that determine the similarity?

One of the definitions of *artificial intelligence* (by P. Stacewicz) states that AI is *a certain property of information systems, thanks to which they exhibit signs of human intelligence* [9]. The following problem will be analyzed: is it possible for a computer to recognize similarity of melodies like the humans do? The problem formulated is not about the recognition of a specific musical composition, but about the perception of the similarity between two melodies or between the original melody and its modification in general.

The aim of the paper is to present some results of recognizing the similarity of melodies by a computer which uses automatic learning tools. To analyze the automatic recognition of melody similarity, first, the term *similarity* must be clarified. This term means compatibility, commonality of certain features of two, or more, people, objects, etc. Whether a given object or a phenomenon is similar to another one is very subjective. We are able to say that something is more or

© Springer Nature Switzerland AG 2019
L. Rutkowski et al. (Eds.): ICAISC 2019, LNAI 11509, pp. 542–552, 2019.
https://doi.org/10.1007/978-3-030-20915-5_48

less similar to something else, but very often we do not know the criterion for making such a decision.

Why will the melody of a musical piece be analyzed? Each of us undoubtedly listens to some of our favorite music and often hums a song. What exactly are we humming? What is the most important feature of music we are humming? It is mainly thanks to melodies that we recognize songs. A melody is a sequence of successive sounds arranged in accordance with tonal, rhythmical and formal principles, forming a whole. A music track is obviously not just a melody. It also consists of the rhythm, meter, harmony, timbre, dynamics, agogics and it has a formal structure. Thus, a melody is only one of the features of a song, but it is the melody that determines the originality of a song. The rest of the features decide more about the nature of a song, its style or genre. A melody is usually associated with one particular tonality and uses sounds belonging to it. It can be recorded with the use of the so-called music notation. From the point of view of physics, each sound is a constant frequency, the unit of which is Hertz (Hz). The basic features of a sound are: height, volume, length, tone. Thus, we have several measurable quantities here, so the use of mathematics seems to be justified.

Computer based measuring of melody similarity has already been the subject of research, see e.g. [2, 4–7]. Our approach differs from the previous works in two main aspect. The first one is that instead of using existing melodies from some repository we automatically generate melodies to compare. That gives us immediately a wide range of examples that are relatively easy to analyze. The other one is that we use to predict human sense of similarity a very simple model. The model consists of a plain list of parameters measuring various aspects of the distance between two melodies.

2   Data

266 melody samples were prepared for the study. It started with recording of melodies with the use of a musical instrument *Kurzweil PC3x* and a music program *Cubase v.5.0*. The recordings and their implementation were made by one of the authors of this paper. Then, these melodies were introduced to a program designed for the purpose, called further *Generator*. The program modified the initially recorded melodies. There were created 266 melody samples and next Attribute-Relation File Format (ARFF) [10] files describing them. During the modification of the melodies, different models were adopted, for example: random change of every second note by at most 5 halftones, random change of every third note by at most 5 halftones, random change of every third note by at most 12 halftones, changing any note by at most 2 halftones, changing any note by at most 5 halftones, transposition of any "up" note by at most 9 semitones, random change of notes with the exception of ten consecutive selected notes, random change of notes with the exception of five consecutive selected notes, generating a melody from the end (the so-called cancer), inverting the melody in relation to the second Gis staff (the so-called inversion), combination of cancer with inversion, transposition by any (but constant) number of semitones of all sounds - changing the key in any way.

One of the goals of the study was to create mathematical attributes (parameters) that would allow automatic learning to recognize similarity as perceived by humans. The attributes are statistical quantities and their modifications. After modifying a melody in the *Generator* program, the data for further processing were created, i.e., the program performed calculations to create the attribute values which, after the test, were entered into *WEKA* (Waikato Environment for Knowledge Analysis) [10]. These attributes are numerical ones, according to which the data are classified and the final decision on similarity is made.

Let x_i be the i-th note of the original melody, y_i be the i-th note of the generated melody, n be the number of notes. The following condition attributes have been created.

- **AvgOfDiff** - an average of differences between the pitch of the generated melody and the original melody: $\bar{a} = \frac{1}{n} \sum_{i=1}^{n} (x_i - y_i)$.
- **MedOfDiff** - a median of differences between the pitch of the generated melody and the original melody. At the beginning, differences $(x_i - y_i)$, where $i = 1, \ldots, n$, are sorted. Next, a median Me is calculated: $Me = a_{\frac{n+1}{2}}$ (for n odd) or $Me = \frac{1}{2} \left(a_{\frac{n}{2}} + a_{\frac{n}{2}+1} \right)$ (for n even).
- **MedOfDiffMod** - a median of absolute values (modules) of differences between the pitch of the generated melody and the original melody. The method of calculating this median is analogous to *MedOfDiff*, only the absolute values of differences are used.
- **MinStdDevOfDiff** - a minimum standard deviation of differences chosen from all horizontal shifts of the generated melody. The purpose of this attribute is to determine the standard deviation, modified in order to obtain *insensitivity* to melody shifts. It is about avoiding the situation when we compare a melody with the same melody but moved left or right on the time line. The standard deviation would be different from zero, and yet the melody would be the same (the standard deviation of the melody itself is of course equal to 0). It is known that we still have the same melody, so it is advisable to consider such an attribute. To obtain insensitivity to the offset, the standard deviation for each offset is calculated separately, and then the smallest value is selected from the results obtained. In other words, a shift is searched for, for which the differences between the notes are the most concentrated around zero. The standard deviation for one set of melodies is calculated from the formula: $\sigma = \sqrt{\frac{(a_1-\bar{a})^2+(a_2-\bar{a})^2+\ldots(a_n-\bar{a})^2}{n}}$, where a_i is the value of the difference $(x_i - y_i)$, $\bar{a}$ is the average of differences (see *AvgOfDiff*), n is the number of elements. We calculate the discussed value as the square root of the arithmetic mean of the squares of differences between the value of the expression $(x_i - y_i)$ and its mean. By matching the pattern now we get $\sigma = \sqrt{\frac{(x_1-y_1-\bar{a})^2+(x_2-y_2-\bar{a})^2+\ldots(x_n-y_n-\bar{a})^2}{n}}$, where $\bar{a}$ is the average of differences (see *AvgOfDiff*). The next standard deviation is counted for the first melody shifted by one note to the left. Without losses on the quality of the calculation, we only move the first melody. That is what we do for all shifts. Then the smallest value is selected from the results.

Let $x = [x_1, x_2, x_3, x_4]$ and $y = [y_1, y_2, y_3, y_4]$. We create all possible shifts of the melody, i.e., $[x_1, x_2, x_3, x_4]$ and $[y_1, y_2, y_3, y_4]$, $[x_2, x_3, x_4, x_1]$ and $[y_1, y_2, y_3, y_4]$, $[x_3, x_4, x_1, x_2]$ and $[y_1, y_2, y_3, y_4]$, $[x_4, x_1, x_2, x_3]$ and $[y_1, y_2, y_3, y_4]$. Next, we calculate the differences between the relevant pairs of elements of the following sets. Set 1: $(x_1 - y_1)$, $(x_2 - y_2)$, $(x_3 - y_3)$, $(x_4 - y_4)$; Set 2: $(x_2 - y_1)$, $(x_3 - y_2)$, $(x_4 - y_3)$, $(x_1 - y_4)$; Set 3: $(x_3 - y_1)$, $(x_4 - y_2)$, $(x_1 - y_3)$, $(x_2 - y_4)$; Set 4: $(x_4 - y_1)$, $(x_1 - y_2)$, $(x_2 - y_3)$, $(x_3 - y_4)$. For each set, we calculate its average value, e.g. for Set 1 we have $\bar{a} = \frac{1}{4} \sum_{i=1}^{4} (x_i - y_i)$. For each set, we calculate its standard deviation, e.g. for Set 1 we have $\sigma = \sqrt{\frac{(x_1 - y_1 - \bar{a})^2 + (x_2 - y_2 - \bar{a})^2 + \ldots (x_4 - y_4 - \bar{a})^2}{4}}$. We choose the smallest value from the results.

- **SameNoteNumb** - a number of the same notes. This process is based on passing through all of the notes of the original melody one by one and comparing them with the value of the corresponding notes in the generated melody. In case of equal values, the element is counted.
- **SameNoteNumb%** - a percentage value of the number of the same notes. The counting method is similar to the previous one but it is expressed as percentage.
- **StdDevOfDiff** - a standard deviation of differences between the pitch of the generated melody and the original melody. In this case, we carry out similar calculations as for *MinStdDevOfDiff*, but we do not take into account the shifts of the melody.
- **SumOfDiffMod** - a sum of absolute values of differences between the pitch of the generated melody and the original melody, i.e., $\sum_{i=1}^{n} |x_i - y_i|$.

One decision attribute **AreTheSame** $\{YES, NO\}$ have been created.

3   Study

After the preparation of 266 melody samples in our *Generator* program, a test was carried out, which involved assessing the similarity of the samples to the original melody. The similarity was assessed by 9 people. Participants of the study, first, heard the original melody and then its modification. Then, they assessed the similarity, and entered their results in a suitably prepared table. People were divided into 3 groups, 3 people in each of them. The study was conducted in three rounds due to the long study time. Listening to all of 266 samples, original melodies and their modifications takes one person about 7 h. Due to the reduced ability to concentrate over time, the study was conducted in series of about 2 h. The collected data have been entered into an *Excel* spreadsheet and the *WEKA* software.

3.1   Tools

In order to be able to make automatic analysis, it was necessary to conduct a proper examination and prepare the appropriate data. The *Kurzweil PC3x* musical instrument and the following software were used to prepare and analyze the data: *Cubase v.5.0, Generator, Excel 2010* and *WEKA v.3.9.1*. Let us describe the *Generator* program as the original author program written in the *Java* environment. *Generator* was created in order to randomly generate new melodies from the master melody. It uses a mathematical library and generates melodies in a random way based on mathematical functions and activities. The important features of *Generator* are as follows: creating its own generators using mathematical functions and logical operators (the ability to generate sounds horizontally and vertically, i.e., the ability to change the place and pitch of the sound), graphic representation of sounds, playing the original and generated melody, import/export of melodies in MIDI (Musical Instrument Digital Interface) format, export data to an ARFF file (*WEKA* format), generating attributes and previewing them, generating any number of samples at one time, launching *WEKA*, edition of the ARFF files, possibility of manual assessment of similarity after listening.

3.2 Automatic Training

To automatically recognize the similarity of the melody, we used the *WEKA* software, version 3.9.1 [10] that is a set of machine learning tools written in *Java*. The software includes a rich set of data processing and visualization tools as well as algorithms for data analysis and predictive modeling, enriched with a graphical user interface, which facilitates access to various program functions. One of the most important methods of data mining is the classification method, the aim of which is to build a model called a classifier. In order to achieve the goal of our research, many trials were carried out with various classifiers implemented in *WEKA*, the results of which were compared. Table 1 presents five selected classifiers and the results obtained by means of them.

Table 1 shows that the best results were obtained using the classifier which is J48 (a version of the well-known C4.5 algorithm [8]). In practice, this is one of the most commonly used methods.

Let TP (true positive) be a number of cases from the class YES classified correctly, FP (false positive) be a number of cases from the class NOT classified incorrectly, FN (false negative) be a number of cases from the class YES classified incorrectly, and TN (true negative) be a number of cases from class NOT classified correctly. We obtain the following parametric measures of model (classifier) evaluation: *TP rate* or *Recall*: $TPrate = \frac{TP}{TP+FN}$, *FP rate*: $FPrate = \frac{FP}{FP+TN}$, *Precision*: $Precision = \frac{TP}{TP+FP}$, *F-Measure*: $FMeasure = \frac{2TP}{2TP+FP+FN}$, Accuracy or correctly classified cases: $Accuracy = \frac{TP+TN}{TP+FN+FP+TN}$. One of the parameters that combines all the results is the statistic (coefficient) Kappa (Kappa statistic) [1]. Let T be designation for the number of test cases, A_k be the accuracy of the classifier and A_1 be the accuracy of the random classifier. The Kappa coefficient is calculated from the formula $Kappa = \frac{A_k - A_l}{T - A_l}$. Let $p \in \{YES, NO\}$ be the predicted value, $k \in \{YES, NO\}$

Table 1. Results obtained in WEKA

Algorithm	J48	Decision table	Mutilayer perceptron	Naive bayes	SGD
Accuracy	95.86%	93.99%	89.85%	67.67%	79.70%
Tree size	17	n/a	n/a	n/a	n/a
Kappa coeff.	0.9128	0.8745	0.7873	0.3754	0.5804
MAE	0.0526	0.1216	0.1223	0.3143	0.2030
RMSE	0.2041	0.2244	0.2872	0.5296	0.4506
RAE	10.94%	25.28%	25.42%	65.34%	42.19%
RRSE	41.61%	45.75%	58.56%	107.99%	91.88%
TP rate for YES	0.907	0.916	0.850	0.832	0.766
FP rate for YES	0.006	0.044	0.069	0.428	0.182
Precision for YES	0.990	0.933	0.892	0.567	0.739
Recall for YES	0.907	0.916	0.850	0.832	0.799
F-Measure for YES	0.96	0.925	0.871	0.674	0.752
ROC area for YES	0.960	0.963	0.918	0.801	0.792
TP rate for NO	0.994	0.956	0.931	0.572	0.818
FP rate for NO	0.093	0.084	0.150	0.168	0.234
Precision for NO	0.940	0.944	0.902	0.835	0.839
Recall for NO	0.994	0.956	0.931	0.572	0.818
F-Measure for NO	0.966	0.950	0.916	0.679	0.828
ROC area for NO	0.960	0.963	0.918	0.801	0.792

be the current value, T be the number of test cases, and $\bar{k} = \sum_{i=1}^{T} k_i$. In WEKA, we can also use *Mean absolute error* $MAE = \frac{\sum_{i=1}^{T}|p_i - k_i|}{T}$, *Root mean squared error* $RMSE = \sqrt{\frac{\sum_{i=1}^{T}(p_i - k_i)^2}{T}}$, *Relative absolute error* $RAE = \frac{\sum_{i=1}^{T}|p_i - k_i|}{\sum_{i=1}^{T}|k_i - \bar{k}|}$ and *Root relative squared error* $RRSE = \sqrt{\frac{\sum_{i=1}^{T}(p_i - k_i)^2}{\sum_{i=1}^{T}(k_i - \bar{k})^2}}$. Another method used to determine classification abilities is the ROC (Receiver Operating Characteristics) curve analysis [3]. The area under the ROC curve, marked with the abbreviation AUC (Area Under ROC Curve), is in the interval $[0, 1]$. The ideal classifier gives a curve adjacent to the left and top edges of the graph.

4 Results

4.1 Study in Excel

The Excel spreadsheet compiled all data, and a manual comparison of the similarity between individuals was made. In total, 36 comparative couples were obtained. The term *Compatibility A with B* means the conformity of the similarity assessment between person A and person B expressed as a percentage. We have obtained the following results: *maximum compliance* is 89.10%, *minimum compliance* is 68.05%, and *average compliance* is 78.99%.

4.2   Study in WEKA

In *WEKA*, automatic training was carried out in the Training Set mode, and new cases were classified in the Test Set mode. The classification consisted in determining what category put a new case to. The training set was a set of records with the same structure that consists of attribute/value of an attribute. In addition, each record was assigned to the appropriate category. Based on these values, new data has been classified. The decision attribute has been manually entered based on the experiments with students. The attribute values in the ARFF files refer to the original melody. Therefore, these are not random values, but values related to the parameters of the original melody. The obtained results in Situation 1 have been presented in detail. For the remaining situations, the most important data is presented in the summary table (see Table 2). The number of situations is consistent with the number of persons whose data were the training data. The Similarity Score by Person 1 was used in the training stage. Then, the compatibility of people's results was compared with the compatibility of program results.

Table 2. Results for all situations obtained by means of Algorithm J48

J48	S1	S2	S3	S4	S5	S6	S7	S8	S9
#cases	266	266	266	266	266	266	266	266	266
- corr. class.	262	252	252	240	247	259	260	258	253
- incorr. class.	4	14	14	26	19	7	6	8	13
- unclass.	0	0	0	0	0	0	0	0	0
Accuracy	98.49%	94.74%	94.74%	90.23%	92.86%	97.37%	97.74%	96.99%	95.11%
Tree size	17	33	29	11	25	21	21	43	31
Kappa coeff.	0.9686	0.8934	0.8917	0.7969	0.8525	0.947	0.94	0.9336	0.9003
MAE	0.0254	0.0784	0.0828	0.168	0.103	0.0503	0.0405	0.0473	0.0665
RMSE	0.1127	0.198	0.2035	0.2898	0.2269	0.1586	0.1423	0.1438	0.1824
RAE	5.28 %	16.13%	16.84%	34.16%	20.98%	10.11%	10.32%	10.25%	13.46%
RRSE	22.98%	40.16%	41.04%	58.45%	45.81%	31.79%	32.16%	32.02%	36.68%

We have compared the percentage agreement of each pair of people. When comparing the decision of two people in Excel using $COMPARE(a, b)$, the order of a and b is irrelevant. Hence, 36 pairs were obtained. In case of automatic training in *WEKA*, the order of data is relevant, i.e., different results are obtained if the training set is A and the test set is B, than if the training set is B, and the test set is A. The differences in the study described are not too large, because they reach the size of several percentage points, and their standard deviation ranges from 0.5 to 1.7% points. The data entered into *WEKA* contained 266 cases and 9 attributes (8 conditional and one decision). Automatic training was considered for all 72 possible pairs, dividing them into 9 groups. The results of this comparison are presented in Table 3. $A{\rightarrow}B$ means: A is a person on whom *WEKA* was trained, B is a person whose grade has been tested by *WEKA*. On average, over 77% compliance was obtained. Summary of compliance using the COMPARE function in Excel: *maximum compliance* is 89.10%, *minimum compliance* is 68.05%, *average compliance* is 78.99%. Summary of compliance for *WEKA* ($A{\rightarrow}B$): *maximum compliance* is 85.71%, *minimum compliance* is 65.04%, *average compliance* is 77.47%. Summary of compliance for *WEKA* ($B{\rightarrow}A$): *maximum compliance* is 87.59%, *minimum compliance* is 63.53%, *average compliance* is 77.19%. Conditional attributes that are taken into account when creating decision trees depend on individual situations. The detailed use of attributes is presented in Table 4. It is easy to see that not all attributes were used when assessing similarity. The program automatically rejected the least significant attributes. *StdDevOfDiff* was never used. The following attributes were used each time, which, as should be inferred, proved to be the most significant: *MinStdDevOfDiff, SameNoteNumb%*.

The attributes can be selected in the manner proposed in *WEKA*. We can obtain the so-called attribute ranking. Below, there is an example of ranking for the first situation with the parameters (attribute evaluator: InfoGainAttributeEval, search method: Ranker): 0.6206 - *MinStdDevOfDiff*, 0.6206 - *StdDevOfDiff*, 0.5346 - *SameNoteNumb%*, 0.3926 - *SumOfDiffMod*, 0.1835 - *MedOfDiffMod*, 0.1788 - *SameNoteNumb*, 0.049 - *AvgOfDiff*, 0.0341 - *MedOfDiff*. According to the attribute rating, the least-significant attributes were subtracted from the analysis of results. As such, the efficiency of automatic training decreased. Of course, removing the attributes that WEKA automatically rejected (Table 4) did not affect the result.

The described analyzes concerned the situations tested on the same 266 samples, which were evaluated by 9 people. After this test, further data files containing a different number of samples were analyzed and evaluated by other people than in the previous study. Based on the analysis for automatic learning, it was found that the more samples the training file contained, the greater the efficiency of automatic learning. The situations described above concerned data with a high level of authenticity. *WEKA* was great at making decisions then. And what will happen if the data entered into *WEKA* are not perfect, i.e., noisy data? An analysis was carried out for this purpose for 400 cases, when 50% of the data were falsified. It turned out that the results from *WEKA* were correct at around 50%. *WEKA* created very complex decision trees, but the accuracy was not satisfactory. The value of Kappa coefficient significantly differs from the value of 1 and it is close to 0 or often 0. The value of all errors is very large. In addition, *WEKA* made a decision with a prediction of about 0.506. Therefore, these indicators can be used to assess not only the effectiveness of automatic training, but also the accuracy of the data (Table 5).

Table 3. Comparison of the similarity assessment

Weka		Excel
1→2: 81.95%	2→1: 84.96%	83.46%
1→3: 84.59%	3→1: 87.59%	85.34%
1→4: 88.35%	4→1: 91.35%	89.10%
1→5: 75.94%	5→1: 72.56%	75.97%
1→6: 82.33%	6→1: 81.20%	83.08%
1→7: 82.70%	7→1: 84.21%	82.71%
1→8: 73.31%	8→1: 75.56%	72.18%
1→9: 83.46%	9→1: 80.08%	85.34%
2→3: 82.33%	3→2: 77.07%	79.32%
2→4: 81.58%	4→2: 80.83%	79.32%
2→5: 68.05%	5→2: 73.68%	75.94%
2→6: 79.32%	6→2: 75.94%	77.07%
2→7: 72.18%	7→2: 71.43%	69.92%
2→8: 77.07%	8→2: 77.82%	77.44%
2→9: 76.70%	9→2: 71.80%	75.56%
3→4: 85.71%	4→3: 87.21%	88.72%
3→5: 76.32%	5→3: 73.68%	79.32%
3→6: 81.95%	6→3: 84.59%	86.47%
3→7: 83.08%	7→3: 77.82%	79.32%
3→8: 83.46%	8→3: 82.71%	83.08%
3→9: 78.57%	9→3: 79.70%	81.20%
4→5: 71.80%	5→4: 73.68%	71.80%
4→6: 77.44%	6→4: 80.08%	82.71%
4→7: 80.08%	7→4: 74.06%	75.56%
4→8: 76.70%	8→4: 75.19%	79.32%
4→9: 78.57%	9→4: 75.94%	81.20%
5→6: 82.71%	6→5: 85.71%	88.35%
5→7: 65.04%	7→5: 68.42%	69.92%
5→8: 68.42%	8→5: 74.06%	73.68%
5→9: 78.57%	9→5: 77.82%	79.32%
6→7: 71.43%	7→6: 71.80%	73.31%
6→8: 73.31%	8→6: 72.18%	73.31%
6→9: 84.96%	9→6: 85.71%	86.47%
7→8: 74.06%	8→7: 77.82%	73.68%
7→9: 69.92%	9→7: 63.53%	68.05%
8→9: 71.05%	9→8: 69.17%	71.80%
Avg: 77.47%	**Avg: 77.19%**	**Avg: 78.99%**

Table 4. Summary of the use and type of attributes in individual situation

Situation	Attributes used	Unused attributes
1	AvgOfDiff, MedOfDiffMod, MinStdDevOfDiff SameNoteNumb, SameNoteNumb%, SumOfDiffMod	MedOfDiff StdDevOfDiff
2	MedOfDiffMod, MinStdDevOfDiff, SameNoteNumb SameNoteNumb%, SumOfDiffMod, MedOfDiff	AvgOfDiff StdDevOfDiff
3	AvgOfDiff, MedOfDiffMod, MinStdDevOfDiff SameNoteNumb, SameNoteNumb%, MedOfDiff	SumOfDiffMod StdDevOfDiff
4	MinStdDevOfDiff, SameNoteNumb, SameNoteNumb% SumOfDiffMod	StdDevOfDiff AvgOfDiff MedOfDiffMod MedOfDiff
5	AvgOfDiff, MedOfDiffMod, MinStdDevOfDiff SameNoteNumb%, MedOfDiff	SumOfDiffMod StdDevOfDiff SameNoteNumb
6	MedOfDiffMod, MinStdDevOfDiff, SameNoteNumb% MedOfDiff, SumOfDiffMod, SameNoteNumb	StdDevOfDiff AvgOfDiff
7	MedOfDiffMod, MinStdDevOfDiff, SameNoteNumb% SumOfDiffMod, SameNoteNumb, AvgOfDiff	StdDevOfDiff MedOfDiff
8	MedOfDiffMod, MinStdDevOfDiff, SameNoteNumb% SumOfDiffMod, SameNoteNumb, AvgOfDiff MedOfDiff	StdDevOfDiff
9	MedOfDiffMod, MinStdDevOfDiff, SameNoteNumb% SumOfDiffMod, SameNoteNumb, MedOfDiff	StdDevOfDiff AvgOfDiff

Table 5. Results for noisy data

Algorithm	J48	Algorithm	J48
#cases	400	Kappa coefficient	0
#correctly classified cases	202	MAE	0,5
#incorrectly classified cases	198	RMSE	0,5
#unclassified cases	0	RAE	100%
Accuracy	50,5%	RRSE	100%

5   Conclusions

The aim of the research was to train the machine to recognize a melody similarity, just like a human. The goal has been achieved and its effectiveness is close to 80%. This result can be improved by throwing away some cases of contradictory responses of the persons examined. It can also be said that the way a person feels and assesses melody similarity can be transferred to mathematical indicators. This is an important achievement because human feelings are immeasurable and the results of the study indicate that the recognition of a melody similarity could be described mathematically. The quality of automatic training is affected by the reliability of the training set, but also by the reliability of the respondents' answers. The results achieved can contribute to the creation of an intelligent machine or artificial mind, which can be said to have similar feelings as humans.

Identifying melody similarity can also be used to determine the plagiarism of music. The automatic examination of the similarity between songs can significantly accelerate the procedure of plagiarism detection.

As for the future work we plan to go further beyond the simple recognition of melody similarity and try to extend the answers, so that they are not limited only to the YES/NO, but they contain the degree of similarity (slightly similar, very similar, etc.). This would allow to design more intelligent systems using the fuzzy set approach. Moreover, the research can be extended to the issue of similarity of objects of different types, e.g. images.

References

1. Cohen, J.: A coefficient of agreement for nominal scales. Educ. Psychol. Measure. **20**(1), 37–46 (1960)
2. Thomas, N.G., Pasquier, P., Eigenfeldt, A., Maxwell, J.B.: A methodology for the comparison of melodic generation models using Meta-Melo. In: Proceedings of the 14th International Society for Music Information Retrieval Conference (2013)
3. Hanley, J., McNeil, B.: The meaning and use of the area under a receiver operating characteristic (ROC) curve. Radiology **143**(1), 29–36 (1982)
4. Harrison, P.M., Musil, J.J., Müllensiefen, D.: Modelling melodic discrimination tests: descriptive and explanatory approaches. J. New Music Res. **45**(3), 265–280 (2016)
5. Hewlett, W.B., Selfridge-Field, E. (eds.): Melodic Comparison: Concepts, Procedures, and Applications, Computing in Musicology, no. 11 (1998)
6. Müllensiefen, D., Frieler, K.: Cognitive adequacy in the measurement of melodic similarity: algorithmic vs. human judgments. Comput. Musicol. **13**, 147–176 (2004)
7. Müllensiefen, D., Frieler, K.: Evaluating different approaches to measuring the similarity of melodies. In: Batagelj, V., Bock, H.H., Ferligoj, A., Žiberna, A. (eds.) Data Science and Classification, pp. 299–306. Springer, Berlin, Heidelberg (2006). https://doi.org/10.1007/3-540-34416-0_32
8. Quinlan, J.R.: C4.5: Programs for Machine Learning. Morgan Kaufmann, Burlington (1993)
9. Stacewicz, P.: The mind and the models of learning machines. Contemporary Computer Science Research from Philosophical Point of View (In Polish). AOW EXIT (2010)
10. Witten, I.H., Frank, E.: Data Mining: Practical Machine Learning Tools and Techniques. Morgan Kaufmann, Burlington (2005)

Prototypes of Arcade Games Enabling Affective Interaction

Paweł Jemioło[✉], Barbara Giżycka, and Grzegorz J. Nalepa

AGH University of Science and Technology,
al. Mickiewicza 30, 30-059 Krakow, Poland
{pjm,bgizycka,gjn}@agh.edu.pl

Abstract. The use of emotions in the process of creating video games is still a challenge for the developers from the fields of Human-Computer Interaction and Affective Computing. In our work, we aim at demonstrating architectures of two operating game prototypes, implemented with the use of affective design patterns. We ground our account in biological signals, i.e. heart rate, galvanic skin response and muscle electrical activity. Using these modalities and the game context, we reason about emotional states of the player. For this purpose, we focus on defining rules with linguistic terms. What is more, we address the need for explainability of biological mechanics and individual differences in terms of reactions to different stimuli. We provide a benchmark, in the form of a survey, to verify our approach.

1 Introduction

Due to a demand for ubiquitous technology, applications that use emotions for the purpose of Human-Computer Interaction (HCI) have been gaining a lot of attention lately [20]. Ideally, a system based on information from human body [2] and using current context [1] can modify its actions to adapt to current situation. Affective Computing paradigm (AfC) opens a way to develop devices and services sensitive to actual needs of a specific user [24].

In relation to convenience of defining precise context, video games have become a field of interest for affective computing developers and researchers [19]. Using emotions to interact with the computer could be a remedy for derivative productions in times of great competitiveness, being a consequence of rapid growth in the entertainment industry.

We aim to show that mechanics underlying the base of affective games [4] can be identified in early stage of the design phase and then implemented, using the Affective Loop as a core concept. The main contribution of this paper is an investigation into the process of creating affective game prototypes, ones which implement emotion detection and emotion inference. Our approach relies on rule-based system for developing affective inferences. In order to answer the

---

The paper is supported by the grant of AGH University of Science and Technology.

L. Rutkowski et al. (Eds.): ICAISC 2019, LNAI 11509, pp. 553–563, 2019.
https://doi.org/10.1007/978-3-030-20915-5_49

contemporary need for adaptive, personalized experiences, we propose a solution using physiological signals measured with a non-medical device. What is more, we pay attention to explainability of methods adapted in architectures of designed applications. Then, we demonstrate the experimental procedure prepared for testing of created prototypes. Our work follows our early ideas with affective design patterns discussed in [22] and in [11].

The rest of the paper is composed as follows. In Sect. 2 we present the AfC paradigm and its methods that can be implemented in games. Section 3 provides the reader with our objectives and current state-of-the-art. In Sect. 4 we discuss architecture of created prototypes. Then, in Sect. 5 we specify experimental procedure and results. Section 6 describes other related works. The paper ends with Sect. 7, where we summarize our work and outline our future plans.

2   From Affective Computing to Games

In 1997, Rosalind Picard proposed Affective Computing as a new paradigm for Human-Computer Interaction. It was the first time when the need to integrate emotional processes in contact with machines has been clearly marked [24].

The goal of AfC is to examine methods of collecting data about emotions, interpreting them, generating changes in the system according to them, and invoking affective responses in the end users [24]. The whole mechanism derives from the assumptions of automatics and robotics, as well as control theory, and is called the Affective Loop (Fig. 1).

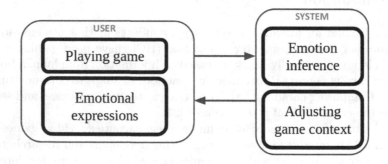

Fig. 1. Affective loop in video games

The key element of systems based on the paradigm of AfC seems to be the indication of the way of reading and inferring about the emotional states of an individual. Modern emotion theories very often indicate, among the components of emotions, changes to the bodily states [16], behavior [5] and human cognition [15] during affective reactions. The first two aspects are especially interesting from the perspective of creating systems for Human-Computer Interaction, with regard to ubiquitous wearable devices. These platforms enable measurement of modalities such as heart- and brain-work, galvanic skin response, as well as recording changes in facial expressions or postures.

As Prinz points out, in his Embodied Appraisal Theory [25], context is another important indicator when reading emotions, e.g. a quiet sound of creaking door in the attic. The ease of context generating, the potential to customize a number of parameters [34] and to produce different scenarios [12] are the reasons why computer games are so eagerly used in the AfC paradigm.

On this basis, as Hudlicka [14] suggested, the design of computer games is closely related to the emotional sphere, which manifests itself through modeling, recognition, and the need to evoke appropriate feelings in the user, already on the level of the design phase. Additionally, as Björk and Holopainen showed, the core elements of games can be decomposed into game design patterns [4], analogous to patterns in object-oriented programming [33]. They can be understood as solutions to frequently recurring issues regarding gameplay. What is more, as shown in [6,8,22], they can be cross-culturally associated with certain emotions, which is a development of Hudlicka's ideas about game design. For example, the player character's unexpected death will invariably be associated with negative emotions, and a sudden loud sound can, with high probability, elicit fear.

3 Affective Loop in Games

Initially, affective loop was intended as a design approach to systems that exploit user's affective interactions in order to make them gradually more involved with the system [13].

From the beginning of forming of this concept, strong impact was placed on the bodily aspect of interaction [13,28].

Embodiment [9] is a notion referring to human experience of the world, being constructed through components that are both cognitive and physical. In terms of interaction with technologies, this creates a specific perspective, where tools and interfaces are designed in a way that would respond to what is already familiar to the user. In everyday interactions, people often manifest their affective states by means of emotional gestures or facial expressions. A system developed with such an approach is able to react directly to naturally performed actions, without user consciously realizing what exactly those actions are.

Physical affective expressions can be observed both on behavioral level and on physiological level. Emotions are usually accompanied by various reactions of sympathetic and parasympathetic systems [18]. Some of such reactions include changes regarding heart rate or electrodermal activity.

The collected physiological data is interpreted within the affective loop, where details and precise algorithms of data handling are a vast research topic on itself [17]. Ultimately, the system has to generate an affective response, in order for the loop to close. Such a response can be brought by various modalities, including sounds, visuals, or even haptics.

Considering computer games, the response can be performed as a change of game world elements, character abilities, environment parameters, etc.

In consequence, new emotional behaviors and reactions may arise, thus pulling the player back into the loop.

To date, several attempts have been made to implement the affective loop into a computer game. The adaptive features included changing modes of control [3], player character skills [10], or other various elements contributing to game difficulty level [29].

The affective loop has to be simple enough that even an ordinary player, who did not know the concept of AfC, would be able to understand how the game works [14]. The loop consists of a few simple steps: (1) calibration, (2) detection, and (3) influence. The loop, constructed in this way, together with collecting information about, i.e., heart rate, can also be used in research on emotions.

4   Implementation of Game Prototypes with AfC Loop

We developed two prototype games implementing affective loop. The first one is a classic arcade space shooter, whereas the second extends a Survival shooter provided by Unity. They both use the measurement equipment described next.

4.1   Measurement

BITalino (r)evolution Kit. When designing affective games, we used BITalino (r)evolution kit platform, consisting of a plate and additional sensors that can be plugged into it. We focused on three modalities:

1. **ECG**—an electrocardiogram measuring the electrical activity of the heart. One (black) electrode was placed under the neck, at the beginning of the sternum, another (red) on the left side, so that the heart is between them. A reference electrode (white) was placed between the right side and the front, on the last rib.
2. **EMG**—an electromyogram measuring the tension of subcutaneous muscles, such as forearm or double-headed muscles. Depending on the game, two electrodes are placed either on the inside of the left forearm, or on the right biceps just next to each other but without contact, reference on the ulna bone.
3. **EDA**—electrodermal activity, also known as galvanic skin response. It is related to skin conductance and the amount of sweat produced by sweat glands. Depending on the game, two electrodes were placed either on two fingers of the right hand, or on the left wrist, so that the user has no problem with pressing the arrow keys on the keyboard.

Physiological Signals. The readings from the sensors described above were used to calculate four game modifying parameters:

1. Average heart rate—calculated on the basis of ECG readings. Raw reading from the sensor is filtered using a bandpass filter, and then pulse values are calculated based on local maximums representing QRS complex peaks.

2. Average electrodermal activity.
3. Measurement of muscle shrinkage—calculated as an average of EMG's filtered absolute values.
4. Emotional index—calculated on the basis of the excerpt of article by Vecchiato et al. [32]. The emotional index is defined by taking into the account the GSR and HR standard score values, which are updated as the game progresses. Negative and positive values of the emotional index are related to negative and positive emotions, respectively (Fig. 2).

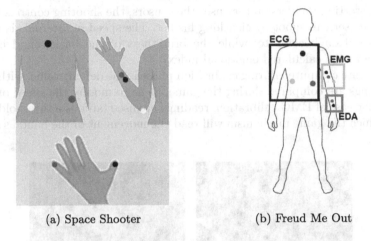

(a) Space Shooter   (b) Freud Me Out

Fig. 2. Placement of electrodes, separately for each sensor and game (Color figure online)

Calibration. After starting the game, a calibration is performed to adjust the default parameter settings and set reference points for later read values. It is preceded by a five-seconds (in case of Space Shooter) or thirty-seconds (in case of Freud Me Out) preparation, during which the user should relax. Then, baselines of heart rate, EDA and EMG signals are calculated.

4.2 Inference Methods

Created prototypes implement rule-based systems, which refer to the model of emotions proposed by Russell [26]. It consists of two dimensions called valence and arousal. The first one is related to the *tone* of emotion, and the second refers its intensity. For example, according to this model, excitement consists of high degree of both pleasure and stimulation.

Similarly to [6], we used linguistic terms and a set of predefined rules to determine emotional state. In our system, changes in heart rate and galvanic skin response are connected to arousal dimension, whereas valence corresponds to the context of game—its visual aspects and storyline.

4.3   Space Shooter

Space Shooter[1] is a modified version of the arcade style shooter, created on the basis of the Unity guide [30]. Main goal of the game is to steer a spaceship and destroy incoming asteroids. The player receives points for destroying an asteroid before it reaches the bottom of the screen.

As it is shown in the Fig. 3, after starting the game, a simple menu appears, where the player can choose whether he wants to use biosignal sensors in the game or not. This allows him to play the standard version first and get acquainted with the game, without using sensor-based mechanics.

After starting the version that uses the sensors, the shooting controls change a bit—the user can shoot by clenching his fist. The speed of asteroids is manipulated based on heart rate, while the brightness of the background changes according to the calculated emotional index.

Heart rate computed during calibration phase is the default value, with which the readings are compared during the game, so as to modify the speed of asteroids. In the case of EMG calibration, readings are used later as a threshold value, above which the game mechanism will read the movement of the hand as a shot.

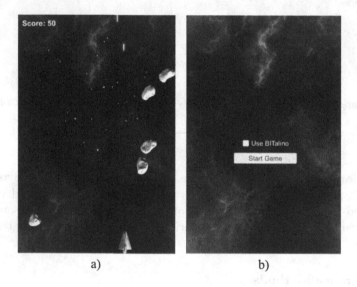

a)   b)

Fig. 3. (a) Main screen that user sees during gameplay (b) Menu of the game

Regarding the affective loop, user reacts to the game and at the same time tries to control it. Asteroids faster falling cause increase in stress levels. This and the changing background brightness show user that he must try to keep his heart rate at the right level. In the same way, he knows that he has to tighten his hand if he wants to shoot.

---

[1] Student's project created by Kamil Osuch.

4.4   Freud Me Out

Freud Me Out is our affective game prototype that extends the application based
on popular Unity tutorial called Survival Shooter [31]. The name of the game
is related to storyline elements that refer to the concept of Sigmund Freud's
psychoanalysis. The player is drawn into an unconventional therapy, in which
he must face opponents lurking inside his consciousness, preconsciousness and
unconsciousness. Throughout the entire game, the player is kept in contact with a
psychotherapist who helps him and clarifies how the system works. For example,
when the player is very frustrated or very angry, enemies adjust their speed to
those emotions and proper information is provided. The guidance is a key point
in explainability of affective loop implemented in our application, as well as in
keeping the player interested.

Similarly to the previous prototype, this one also allows for play with- and
without the affective loop. Physiological signals extend standard control using
the mouse and the keyboard. The player's task is to eliminate specified number
of enemies using a gun, or by the activation of the *SuperPower* that allows
to eliminate many opponents at once, by flexing the two-headed muscle of the
upper arm. The speed of opponents' movement is adjusted depending on the
heart rate. What is more, randomness of spawning points is modified based on
heart rate and electrodermal activity combination (Fig. 4).

Fig. 4. Freud Me Out game scene.

When the player gets nervous, enemies become slower and spawn more pre-
dictably. Following the affective loop concept, it influences the player who relaxes
and his heart rate and electrodermal activity eases down. Those current values
are compared to values calculated during calibration phase. If they drop below

the specified level, mechanics related to speed and randomness of the appearance of enemies are activated. If the situation in the game is critical, he can use the *SuperPower*. In case of this game, calibration stage was extended from five to thirty seconds due to accuracy issues.

5   Evaluation of Prototypes

Preliminary tests on Freud Me Out prototype were carried out, consisting of three main phases. During the first part, the subject of the experiment played a prepared computer game, a version implementing affective loop. The next variant was analogous, but without measuring devices. Then, a survey was filled.Nine people were examined, two female and seven male. Due to such a large disproportion, it was impossible to analyze the results in terms of gender differences. Participants in the experiment belong to a group of students and working young adults or high school students. The age of the subjects ranged from 16 to 24 years.

As Table 1 shows, the survey was divided into three dimensions. Firstly, we checked which kind of mechanics were preferred by players. Then, we assessed immersion generation and game level adjustment. As results suggest, affective loop version of the game was indicated as the one that enables users to more fully interact with the game world. It also turned out to be more adapting to current state of player. This could be an outcome of much more frequent choice of affective mechanics in terms of defining the favorite one. What is more, we believe that those evidences suggest that implementing affective loop in games may lead to more time spending on playing by end users.

Table 1. Survey answers according to separate dimensions.

	With AfC loop	Without AfC loop	No difference
Favourite mechanics	17	1	n/a
Immersion generation	18	0	18
Game level adjusting	15	2	19

What is more, based on the game logs, it was checked which of the two versions of mechanics were more willingly used. In case of *SuperPower* mechanic, affective mechanic was used 1.5 times more often that its non-affective equivalent, activated by pressing a keyboard button. It could be connected with choosing biosignals basing version of this mechanic in the survey as a favorite by most of examined participants.

It is worth mentioning that both Freud Me Out and modified version of Space Shooter were presented during Humanizing AI workshop at IJCAI 2018 as a proof-of-concept demonstration.

6   Related Works

There has been a lot of work related to affective games in recent years, some of them were connected with the idea of in-game patterns.

With Bersak et al.'s paper [3] establishing the affective gaming research field, many other studies inquired opportunities to entwine affective technologies into video games. Quite often researchers used games inspired by existing titles [21,29]. A considerable number of them is comprised of custom games and prototypes [7,23]. In this paper, we describe the games developed using Unity tutorials, although the narrative of Freud me Out is our original creation.

[22] discusses the role of selection of affective patterns in base stage of games creation. It follows the ideas of Björk and Holopainen [4] about universal mechanics, which can be identified in almost every game, and enriches them with emotional factor. It is a continuation of idea of Dormann, who identified patterns for learning purposes [8]. We propose a game created using predefined patterns, though we do not implement affective loop.

The paper [6] describes an investigation into the process of creating affective computer game based on collection of patterns connected with emotions. The application is created using Unity and uses biological signals to interact with game world. Data acquisition is performed with NeXus-10, a medical class device. Authors propose a set of direct and indirect mechanics [19]. A similar approach is taken by [27], who provides a platform game with several controllable features, such as the number and placement of enemies, which he recognizes as having a potential impact on player's affective state.

7   Conclusions and Future Work

We introduced prototypes of affective games based on the concept of the affective loop. The paper extends our previous idea on affective game design patterns. In this concept, each game consists of small elements that interact with each other, and their occurrence can elicit specific emotional states in the player.

Our contribution lies in presenting an architecture of working game prototypes using physiological signals such as electrodermal, cardiac and muscle activity, measured with a non-medical device, to influence the game state. We presented metrics and methods used in a practical example of AfC application. We proposed a calibration phase to eliminate individual differences and a tutorial phase to extend explainability of integrated methods.

The prototypes were created using Unity environment, but in the future we plan to address other platforms like Godot or UnrealEngine. We also intend to implement other modalities like face recognition, or use more promising indicators like heart rate variability. We want to extend our inference system and implement methods based on neural networks and evolutionary algorithms. Additionally, we want to focus more on indirect behavioral feedback and detecting affective scenarios in games. We want to integrate those future plans in series of experiments, as we are currently preparing procedures for new tests.

References

1. Abowd, D., Dey, A.K., Orr, R., Brotherton, J.: Context-awareness in wearable and ubiquitous computing. Virtual Reality **3**(3), 200–211 (1998)
2. Anttonen, J., Surakka, V.: Emotions and heart rate while sitting on a chair. In: Proceedings of the SIGCHI Conference on Human Factors in Computing Systems, pp. 491–499. ACM (2005)
3. Bersak, D., et al.: Intelligent biofeedback using an immersive competitive environment. Paper Presented at the Designing Ubiquitous Computing Games Workshop at UbiComp (2001)
4. Björk, S., Holopainen, J.: Patterns in Game Design. Charles River Media, Needham Heights (2005)
5. Bradley, M.M., Lang, P.J.: Measuring emotion: behavior, feeling, and physiology. Cogn. Neurosci. Emot. **25**, 49–59 (2000)
6. Caminha, D.C.C.: Development of emotional game mechanics through the use of biometric sensors. Master's thesis, Faculdade de Engenharia da Universidade do Porto (2017)
7. Dekker, A., Champion, E.: Please biofeed the zombies: enhancing the gameplay and display of a horror game using biofeedback. In: DiGRA Conference (2007)
8. Dormann, C., Whitson, J.R., Neuvians, M.: Once more with feeling: game design patterns for learning in the affective domain. Games Cult. **8**(4), 215–237 (2013)
9. Dourish, P.: Where the Action Is: The Foundations of Embodied Interaction. MIT Press, Cambridge (2004)
10. Drachen, A., Nacke, L.E., Yannakakis, G., Pedersen, A.L.: Correlation between heart rate, electrodermal activity and player experience in first-person shooter games. In: Proceedings of the 5th ACM SIGGRAPH Symposium on Video Games, pp. 49–54. ACM (2010)
11. Giżycka, B., Nalepa, G.J., Jemioło, P.: AIded with emotions - a new design approach towards affective computer systems. CoRR abs/1806.04236 (2018). http://arxiv.org/abs/1806.04236
12. Hastings, E.J., Guha, R.K., Stanley, K.O.: Automatic content generation in the galactic arms race video game. IEEE Trans. Comput. Intell. AI Games **1**(4), 245–263 (2009)
13. Höök, K.: Affective loop experiences – what are they? In: Oinas-Kukkonen, H., Hasle, P., Harjumaa, M., Segerståhl, K., Øhrstrøm, P. (eds.) PERSUASIVE 2008. LNCS, vol. 5033, pp. 1–12. Springer, Heidelberg (2008). https://doi.org/10.1007/978-3-540-68504-3_1
14. Hudlicka, E.: Affective computing for game design. In: Proceedings of the 4th International North American Conference on Intelligent Games and Simulation (GAMEON-NA) (2008)
15. Izard, C.E.: Basic emotions, relations among emotions, and emotion-cognition relations. Psychol. Rev. **99**(3), 561–565 (1992)
16. James, W.: What is an emotion? Mind **9**(34), 188–205 (1884)
17. Kowalczuk, Z., Czubenko, M.: Computational approaches to modeling artificial emotion-an overview of the proposed solutions. Front. Robot. AI **3**, 21 (2016)
18. Kreibig, S.D.: Autonomic nervous system activity in emotion: A review. Biol. Psychol. **84**(3), 394–421 (2010). http://www.sciencedirect.com/science/article/pii/S0301051110000827. The biopsychology of emotion: current theoretical and empirical perspectives

19. Lara-Cabrera, R., Camacho, D.: A taxonomy and state of the art revision on affective games. Future Gener. Comput. Syst. **92**, 516–525 (2019)

20. Lazar, J., Feng, J.H., Hochheiser, H.: Research Methods in Human-computer Interaction. Morgan Kaufmann, Burlington (2017)

21. Liu, C., Agrawal, P., Sarkar, N., Chen, S.: Dynamic difficulty adjustment in computer games through real-time anxiety-based affective feedback. Int. J. Hum.-Comput. Interact. **25**(6), 506–529 (2009)

22. Nalepa, G.J., Gizycka, B., Kutt, K., Argasinski, J.K.: Affective design patterns in computer games. Scrollrunner case study. In: Communication Papers of the 2017 Federated Conference on Computer Science and Information Systems, FedCSIS 2017, pp. 345–352 (2017). https://doi.org/10.15439/2017F192

23. Parnandi, A., Ahmed, B., Shipp, E., Gutierrez-Osuna, R.: Chill-out: relaxation training through respiratory biofeedback in a mobile casual game. In: Memmi, G., Blanke, U. (eds.) MobiCASE 2013. LNICST, vol. 130, pp. 252–260. Springer, Cham (2014). https://doi.org/10.1007/978-3-319-05452-0_18

24. Picard, R.W.: Affective Computing. MIT Press, Cambridge (1997)

25. Prinz, J.: Which emotions are basic? In: Evans, D., Cruse, P. (eds.) Emotion, Evolution, and Rationality, pp. 69–88. Oxford University Press, New York (2004)

26. Russell, J.A.: A circumplex model of affect. J. Pers. Soc. Psychol. **39**(6), 1161–1178 (1980)

27. Shaker, N., Asteriadis, S., Yannakakis, G.N., Karpouzis, K.: A game-based corpus for analysing the interplay between game context and player experience. In: D'Mello, S., Graesser, A., Schuller, B., Martin, J.-C. (eds.) ACII 2011. LNCS, vol. 6975, pp. 547–556. Springer, Heidelberg (2011). https://doi.org/10.1007/978-3-642-24571-8_68

28. Sundström, P., Ståhl, A., Höök, K.: A user-centered approach to affective interaction. In: Tao, J., Tan, T., Picard, R.W. (eds.) ACII 2005. LNCS, vol. 3784, pp. 931–938. Springer, Heidelberg (2005). https://doi.org/10.1007/11573548_119

29. Tijs, T., Brokken, D., IJsselsteijn, W.: Creating an emotionally adaptive game. In: Stevens, S.M., Saldamarco, S.J. (eds.) ICEC 2008. LNCS, vol. 5309, pp. 122–133. Springer, Heidelberg (2008). https://doi.org/10.1007/978-3-540-89222-9_14

30. Unity Technologies: Space Shooter tutorial (2018). https://unity3d.com/learn/tutorials/s/space-shooter-tutorial

31. Unity Technologies: Survival Shooter tutorial (2018). https://unity3d.com/learn/tutorials/s/survival-shooter-tutorial

32. Vecchiato, G., et al.: How to measure cerebral correlates of emotions in marketing relevant tasks. Cogn. Comput. **6**(4), 856–871 (2014). https://doi.org/10.1007/s12559-014-9304-x

33. Pree, W.: Design Patterns for Object-Oriented Software Development, vol. 15. Reading (1994)

34. Yamada, A., Shirai, Y., Miura, J.: Tracking players and a ball in video image sequence and estimating camera parameters for 3D interpretation of soccer games. In: Proceedings of the 16th International Conference on Pattern Recognition, vol. 1, pp. 303–306. IEEE (2002)

SMT-Based Encoding of Argumentation Dialogue Games

Magdalena Kacprzak[1], Anna Sawicka[2(✉)], and Andrzej Zbrzezny[3]

[1] Bialystok University of Technology, Bialystok, Poland
m.kacprzak@pb.edu.pl
[2] Polish-Japanese Academy of Information Technology, Warsaw, Poland
asawicka@pja.edu.pl
[3] Jan Długosz University in Częstochowa, Częstochowa, Poland
a.zbrzezny@ujd.edu.pl

Abstract. The aim of this work is to explore possibilities of performing semantic verification of dialogue game argumentation protocols. To this end, we analyse a chosen dialogue system which allows for the simulation of a parent-child discourse. The system under analysis is enriched by the addition of elements of emotional reasoning. In this paper, we show only the first stage of applying the verification technique. It consists of encoding a mathematical game model as an SMT formula. Then, we compute the satisfiability of the conjunction of this formula with another formula that encodes a feature of the model. This technique can be used to verify the correctness of the protocol in the sense of it satisfying the expected properties.

Keywords: Argumentation dialogue game · Dialogue protocol ·
Reachability analysis · Bounded model checking · SMT solver

1 Introduction

Modern systems equipped with artificial intelligence are doing better and better in solving assigned tasks. To achieve the goal they must interact. Therefore, there is a need to coordinate their activities, not only in the form of central control but also through communication. Designing a speaking program requires defining its architecture and characterising the rules that regulate the course of a conversation. To be sure whether the program will work in accordance with the assumptions adopted by the designer, it is necessary to verify them. More specifically, when having a dialogue protocol there is a need to check what properties does it meet. In this article, we focus on the first task, i.e. correctness verification. In other words, we test whether the dialogue system is designed in such a way that it can achieve the dialogue goal. To this end, we apply the model checking technique, commonly used to verify computational systems involving concurrency against some desirable properties like deadlock-freedom, safety or reachability. This method is applicable for finite state systems and operates on the formal semantic model rather than on the actual system. Firstly, in this method the system is

© Springer Nature Switzerland AG 2019
L. Rutkowski et al. (Eds.): ICAISC 2019, LNAI 11509, pp. 564–574, 2019.
https://doi.org/10.1007/978-3-030-20915-5_50

represented by a finite model M. Secondly, the property for verification is represented by a formula φ. Finally, the verification method calculates if φ is true in M.

In recent years, many algorithms have been proposed to verify multi-agent systems. Less attention has been paid to building communication protocols, and even less to their verification (see e.g. [1]). One of the most-used paradigms for formal modelling of communication between agents is a dialogue game. In such a game, agents play a move in turn by performing utterances in accordance with a pre-defined set of rules. The dialogue games are great for modelling different types of dialogues: inquiry, information seeking, deliberation, persuasion or negotiation. Much attention has been devoted to persuasion dialogues. Starting with semi-formal persuasive systems proposed by Walton and Krabbe [12], up to contemporary systems such as described by Prakken [10] or multi-party paraconsistent and paracomplete persuasion introduced by Dunin-Kęplicz and Strachocka [3]. The next step is to enrich dialogue games with elements of emotional inference [6,7,11].

The purpose of our research is to propose a model checking algorithm for verification of communication between autonomous agents interacting using dialogue games, which are governed by a set of logical rules. In the paper [5], the formal model for one of the most popular dialectical games was introduced. It applied the Nash-style game theory to Mackenzie's DC system and investigated two types of solutions determining the instructions for playing a given game: dominant strategies and Nash equilibrium [9]. This paper [5] was the inspiration for a dialogue game presented in [6] where a formal system serving as a base for human-machine tools for implementing persuasive dialogues was given. In addition, it was enriched with the ability to analyse the emotions of players so that they faithfully reflect the characteristics of human-to-human dialogue. In this paper, we are making the first step towards the verification of this system, namely we show the encoding of its model.

What distinguishes our approach from other described in the field (see e.g. [1]) is the fact that our dialogues simulate typical human-to-human dialogues, in which the content of the locution can be a natural language expression. In addition, to reflect all aspects of human-to-human argumentation, the game has been equipped with elements of affective reasoning. Moreover, the system constructed in this way and its formal mathematical model are going to be verified using the satisfiability modulo theories based (SMT-based) reachability analysis. Due to the complexity and multifaceted nature of such dialogue systems and their protocols, the application of model checking methods requires developing of new and adapting of existing verification techniques.

2   Dialogue Game Model

In this section, the general model of argumentative dialogue game with emotional reasoning is described. When defining this model we use the following standard notation. Given a set Σ, the set of all finite sequences over Σ is denoted by Σ^* and the set of all infinite sequence over Σ is denoted by Σ^ω. The empty sequence is denoted by ε and the operation of concatenation is denoted by $\cdot$. Given sets A, B, $C \subseteq A$, $D \subseteq B$, and a function $f : A \to B$, we use $\overrightarrow{f}(C)$, to denote the image of C, and $\overrightarrow{f}^{-1}(D)$ to denote the inverse image of D.

Let SAS be a non-empty and countable set called the *set of atomic statements*. The *set of statements*, $FORM$, is a minimal set such that: $SAS \subseteq FORM$, and if $\alpha \in FORM$, then $\neg\alpha \in FORM$. The *set of locutions*, L, is then defined as follows:

$L = \{\varepsilon\} \cup \{claim\ \alpha, concede\ \alpha, why\ \alpha, scold\ \alpha, nod\ \alpha, \alpha\ since\ \{\beta_1, \ldots, \beta_n\},$
$retract\ \alpha, question\ \alpha : \alpha, \beta_1, \ldots, \beta_n \in FORM\}$.

All the expressions from the set $FORM$, which have been spoken are treated as public declarations of players and are called *commitments*. The commitments of player i are stored in the *commitment set* C_i. This set changes during the course of the dialogue.

The key element of argumentative dialogues is influencing the emotions of the opponent. There are five emotions considered in this dialogue system: *fear, disgust, joy, sadness*, and *anger*. These emotions are recognised by Ekman [4] as emotions which are universal despite the cultural context. They are universal for all human beings and are experienced and recognised in the same way all around the world. Other emotions are mixed and built from those basic emotions.

The strength (intensity) of emotions is represented by natural numbers from the set $\{1, 2, \ldots, 10\}$. Thus, the emotion vector E_i is a 5-tuple consisting of five values which refer to *fear, disgust, joy, sadness*, and *anger*, respectively. The change in the intensity of the emotions is dependent on the type of the performed locution as well as on its content.

Given a set of atomic statements, SAS, the *argumentative dialogue game* is a tuple

$$\Gamma_{[SAS]} = \langle Pl, \pi, H, TH, (\precsim_i)_{i \in Pl}, (A_i)_{i \in Pl}, (AAF_i)_{i \in Pl}, (C_i)_{i \in Pl}, (E_i)_{i \in Pl}, (Init_i)_{i \in Pl} \rangle$$

where

- $Pl = \{W, B\}$ is the set of players.
- $H \subseteq L^* \cup L^\omega$ is the *set of histories*. A history is a (finite or infinite) sequence of locutions from L. The set of finite histories is denoted by $\bar{H}$.
- $\pi : \bar{H} \to Pl \cup \{\varnothing\}$ is the *player function* assigning to each finite history the player who moves after it, or $\varnothing$, if no player is to move. The set of histories at which player $i \in Pl$ is to move is $H_i = \overrightarrow{\pi}^{-1}(i)$.
- $TH = \overrightarrow{\pi}^{-1}(\varnothing) \cup (H \cap L^\omega)$ is the set of *terminal histories*. A terminal history is a history after which no player is to move, hence it consists of the set of finite histories mapped to $\varnothing$ by the player function and the set of all infinite histories.
- $\precsim_i \subseteq TH \times TH$ is the *preference relation* of player i defined on the set of terminal histories. The preference relation is a total preorder, i.e. it is total and transitive.
- $A_i = L$ is the *set of actions* of player $i \in Pl$.
- $AAF_i : H_i \to 2^{A_i}$ is the *admissible actions function* of player $i \in Pl$, determining the set of actions that i can choose from after history $h \in H_i$.
- $C_i : L^* \to 2^{FORM}$ is the *commitment set function* of player $i \in Pl$, designating the change of commitments.
- $E_i : L^* \to Emotion_i$ is the *emotion intensity function* of player $i \in Pl$, designating the change of emotions; $Emotion_i$ is the set of emotional states of i.
- $Init_i$ determines the initial attributes of player i and consists of the set of initial commitments IC_i and the initial state of emotions IE_i.

In this system, we assume that players perform their actions alternately: $\pi(h) \in \{B, \varnothing\}$ if $|h|$ is odd and $\pi(h) \in \{W, \varnothing\}$ if $|h|$ is even. Having defined the sets of actions for the players and the player function, we move on to define the admissible actions functions of the players. The functions are determined by the rules of dialogue which are defined using the notion of players' commitment sets and emotion levels.

The *commitment set function* of player i is a function $C_i : L^* \rightarrow 2^{FORM}$, assigning to each finite sequence of locutions $h \in L^*$ the *commitment set* $C_i(h)$ of i at h. The commitment set function of $i \in Pl$ is defined inductively in [6]. The *emotion intensity function* of player i is a function $E_i : L^* \rightarrow Emotion_i$, assigning to each finite sequence of locutions $h \in L^*$ the *emotion vector* $E_i(h)$ of i at h. The set $Emotion_i$ consists of all possible 5-tuples for levels of emotions, i.e., $Emotion_i = \{(n_1, \ldots, n_5) : n_k \in \{1, \ldots, 10\} \wedge k \in \{1, \ldots, 5\}\}$. The emotion intensity function of $i \in Pl$ determines the change of intensity of emotions and is defined inductively in [6]. In the same paper we define the *admissible actions function* AAF_i of player $i \in Pl$. For given $h \in H_i$, $AAF_i(h)$ is a maximal set of locutions available for the player i after the history h.

3 Sample Dialogue

Consider a dialogue between a parent (B) and his 10-year-old child (W). Dialogue is presented in 2 different versions. The rules of this dialogue game are quite strict. The beginning of these two dialogues is the same. At some point, the parent can choose one of the two strategies by responding in different ways. The result of these dialogues is of course different.

Dialogue - version 1

B: *You should make your bed.* (*claim* α_1)
W: *Make my bed? No, I don't think so.* (*claim* $\neg \alpha_1$)
B: *Why not?* (*why* $\neg \alpha_1$)
W: *What for? In the evening I will go to bed again.* ($\neg \alpha_1$ *since* $\{\alpha_2\}$)
B: *That's right, but you should still do it.* (*concede* α_2)
W: *Do you really think I'll make it?* (*question* α_3)
B: *Yes, I am sure you'll do that.* (*claim* α_3)
W: *Why would I?* (*why* α_3)
B: *Because you must clean up your room.* (α_3 *since* $\{\alpha_4\}$)
W: *But why?* (*why* α_4)
B: *Because I said so.* (α_4 *since* $\{\alpha_5\}$)
W: *Many times I had a mess in my room and nothing happened to me.* (*claim* α_6)
B: *That's not the way it works!* (*scold* $\neg \alpha_7$)
W: *This is my mess and my business.* (*claim* α_8)
B: *It's not just your thing, we live in this house together.* (*scold* $\neg \alpha_8$)
W: *You don't have to look at it!.* (*scold* α_8)
B: *Unfortunately, I have to ... .* (*scold* $\neg \alpha_8$)
W: *I'll make my bed if you let me play games.* (*claim* α_9)
B: *I don't agree.* (*claim* $\neg \alpha_9$)
W: *Why?* (*why* $\neg \alpha_9$)
B: *Because I'm the grown-up and I said so. You are such a muddler!* ($\neg \alpha_9$ *since* $\{\alpha_{10}\}$)
W: *Why are you yelling these things at me?* (*why* α_{11})
B: *I'm sorry, I didn't mean it.* (*retract* α_{11})

In this version, the child is trying not to clean the room. He asks a lot of questions, talks back and leads the parent to irritation and resignation. The parent feels a sense of guilt because of screaming at the child and decides to back down. The child wins the dialogue.

Dialogue - version 2

B: *You should make your bed.* (*claim* α_1)
W: *Make my bed? No, I don't think so.* (*claim* $\neg\alpha_1$)
B: *Why not?* (*why* $\neg\alpha_1$)
W: *What for? In the evening I will go to sleep again.* ($\neg\alpha_1$ *since* $\{\alpha_2\}$)
B: *You always have such a mess in your room!* (*scold* α_{14})
W: *Take a look at yourself and our living room!* (*scold* α_{15})
B: *You are never serious about your responsibilities!* (*scold* α_{16})
W: *I'll never clean up my room!* (*claim* α_{17})
B: *You are such a mess!* (*scold* α_{18})

In the second version of the dialogue, the parent often uses the action *scold*. The response of the child who feels cornered is screaming and wailing. As a result, no one wins. For both this situation is not favourable.

The above dialogues can be played in a single dialogue game. The players perform alternate actions, each action consists of locution and its contents. There are eight types of locution in this dialogue game: *claim*, *why*, *since*, *concede*, *question*, *scold*, *retract*, *nod*. There are 18 applied contents, $\alpha_1,...,\alpha_{18}$ of the form '*You should make your bed.*', '*What for? In the evening I will go to bed again.*', etc.

4   Encoding for Game Model Checking

We decided to use as our first approach to reachability analysis the method based on the translation to SMT. We choose SMT [13] as it provides a good compromise between expressiveness and efficiency. The translation of our model to SMT is less complex than to SAT and its formulae are more easy to interpret, in particular with such a high complexity of the model. The first step of this method is to encode actions and states (local and global) as vectors of individual variables, and hence to encode the transition relation by a quantifier-free first-order logic formula.

The aim of this work is to present the idea of encoding the transition relation of our model by encoding rules describing the specific dialogue game given in the GERDL language. In this section, we want to present an encoding for a dialogue game between a parent (B) and his child (W) presented in the previous section. We described details of our full model in [11]. Here, we demonstrate examples of encoding the transition relation, but the description of the entire model requires more analyses. The full encoding depends on the specific game and our work is heading towards automatic translation of rules defined in GERDL into formula encoding the whole model.

Since the set G of states of M is finite, each state g of M can be represented by a valuation of a vector w (called a symbolic global state) of individual variables. This vector can be perceived as divided into three sections - subvectors w_d, w_{l_W}, and w_{l_B}, which correspond to the components of the global state g. Thus, the vector w takes the form $w = (w_d, w_{l_W}, w_{l_B})$. The vector $w_m = (w_{d_m}, w_{l_{W_m}}, w_{l_{B_m}})$ corresponds to the g_m - the m-th global state in sequence π (if not crucial in the current context, we are omitting index m). The subvector w_d corresponds to $d(g)$ - a sequence of double-numbered global actions leading to the state g. Let us assume, that we have a limit m_d on the number of global actions in $d(g)$ (it can be defined by the dialogue game designer) since we do not allow for infinite dialogues and this assumption let us use bounded model checking.

A single action consists of one of m_l locutions and up to two arguments. The first one represents one content used with the locution (we allow also a negation of the content), the second one (in this specific dialogue game effectively used only with locution *since*) represents a subset of the set of available contents and their negations. We decided to limit the number of arguments, but the expressiveness of our approach is sufficient for the analysed dialogue game. Generally, to encode a subset of the set of t elements we need t individual Boolean variables $x_1, x_2, \ldots, x_t$; each of them encodes the membership of the specific element in the subset. Since the second argument is the union of the subset of the finite set of contents $FORM$ ($m_f = |FORM|$) and the subset of the set of their negations, we encode it as two subsets. Thus, we can encode specific i-th action in the dialogue using a vector of variables: $a_i = (p_i, r_i, l_i, c1_i, c21_i, c22_i, \ldots, c2_{m_{fi}}, nc21_i, nc22_i, \ldots, nc2_{m_{fi}})$, where $i \in \{1, \ldots, m_d\}$, $c1_i$ characterises first argument of the locution (single content) and $c2_{ti}$, $nc2_{ti}$ (where t is the number of the content, $t \in \{1, \ldots, m_f\}$) characterise respectively the membership of the content number t and the membership of its negation in the second argument.

Therefore, in this case to encode one double-numbered global action a_i we need one integer variable p_i which indicates player, one integer variable r_i which corresponds to double-numbered global action the considered i-th action refers to ($r_i \in \{0, .., m_d\}$), one integer variable l_i to encode a locution type ($l_i \in \{0, .., m_l\}$), one integer variable $c1_i$ to encode the content of the first argument (the negation of the content is represented by the additive inverse of the number corresponding to the content) and $2 * m_f$ Boolean variables $c2_{ti}$, $nc2_{ti}$ to encode two subsets. To encode a whole sequence of double-numbered global actions with respect to the order of moves and references between these moves, the vector w_d takes the form $(a_1, a_2, \ldots, a_{m_d})$, where m_d denotes the maximum number of actions in the dialogue. The order of the moves within the sequence is encoded by the positions of actions in the vector w_d. By definition, we do not allow repetitions of double-numbered global actions, so the set of possible sequences is finite.

Subvectors w_{l_W} and w_{l_B} correspond to local states of players $l_W(g)$ and $l_B(g)$. Each one of them describes the current player's sets of emotions and commitments. The set of emotion E_p is a 5-tuple with bounded integers values and it needs five integer variables to be encoded. Since the current set of player's commitments is a finite subset of the set of contents $FORM$, ($m_f = |FORM|$) unioned with a finite subset of the set of negations of contents, we can encode such a subset by the means of $2 * m_f$ Boolean variables.

Thus, the vector w_{l_W} (w_{l_B} is constructed analogously) takes the form:
$(e_{W_1}, e_{W_2}, \ldots, e_{W_5}, cs_{W_1}, cs_{W_2}, \ldots, cs_{W_{m_f}}, ncs_{W_1}, ncs_{W_2}, \ldots, ncs_{W_{m_f}})$ where each e_{W_q} ($q \in \{1, \ldots, 5\}$, $e_{W_q} \in \{1, \ldots, 10\}$) is the integer variable which corresponds to the specific player's emotion in state g, cs_{W_j} ($j \in \{1, \ldots, m_f\}$) is the Boolean variable encoding the membership of the content $f_j \in FORM$ in the player's set of commitments and ncs_{W_j} ($j \in \{1, \ldots, m_f\}$) is the Boolean variable encoding the membership of the negation of the content $f_j \in FORM$ in the player's set of commitments.

The initial states of vectors w_{l_W} and w_{l_B} are defined as follows. The vectors of emotions contain any values that meet the conditions $ew_q \in \{1, \ldots, 10\}$, $q \in \{1, \ldots, 5\}$ (the same applies to e_{B_q}). We can treat these values as parameters for the verification. At the beginning of the dialogue the commitments sets are empty (players commit neither to any content nor its negation). Therefore, cs_{W_t}, cs_{B_t}, ncs_{W_t}, ncs_{B_t} for $t \in \{1, \ldots, m_f\}$ are set to $false$. The vector w_d represents an empty dialogue, that contains only "inactive" actions (that is, those that have locution variable l set to 0).

As we mentioned, $(m+1)$-th global state g_{m+1} (generally denoted below as $g\prime$) is the result of applying the transition relation T to the global state g_m (denoted below as g), and the action a_m (denoted below as a). In our system, such a result is a direct consequence of the rules written in the input GERDL file (more details about GERDL was included in [11]), which we want to automatically incorporate into our formula.

For example, we have the Child's evolution rule of the following form:

$Child.X = true$ **if** $(Child.lastAction = claim.X$ or $Child.lastAction = scold.X)$

which means, that if the last action of the player Child was the locution $claim$ or $scold$ with some content X, then the content X becomes the commitment of the player $Child$.

To illustrate our method let us consider, that we have global state g and the encoded double-numbered global action a has a variable p set on the value corresponding to the player $Child$ (let us assume that this value is 1) and variable l set on the value corresponding to the locution $claim$ (let us assume it is 2) or to $scold$ (let us assume it is 5), and the same one of the content variables of this action $(c1_1, c1_2, \ldots c1_{m_f}, c2_1, c2_2, \ldots c2_{m_f})$ which was set to $true$ is also set to $true$ as a commitment in the vector w_{l_W} corresponding to the local state of the agent $White$ in the global state $g\prime$, then $(g, a, g\prime) \in T$. All components of the vector corresponding to $g\prime$ we denote with $\prime$. As we mentioned, we have 18 different contents in our dialogue game, $m_f = 18$ and locutions $claim$ and $scold$ are bound with one argument being a single content. So the formula corresponding to the above rule is a conjunction of the below formulae describing:

– the actual player of the action and the locution type (Subformula No. 1.1)

$$p = 1 \wedge (l = 2 \vee l = 5)$$

– the change of the specific Child's commitment used in the action as one and only content (Subformula No. 1.2):

$$((c1 = 1 \wedge cs'_{W_1} \wedge cs'_{W_2} = cs_{W_2} \wedge cs'_{W_3} = cs_{W_3} \wedge \ldots \wedge cs'_{W_{18}} = cs_{W_{18}} \wedge$$
$$ncs'_{W_1} = ncs_{W_1} \wedge ncs'_{W_2} = ncs_{W_2} \wedge ncs'_{W_3} = ncs_{W_3} \wedge \ldots \wedge ncs'_{W_{18}} = ncs_{W_{18}}) \vee$$

$$\ldots$$

$$(c1 = 18 \wedge cs'_{W_1} = cs_{W_1} \wedge cs'_{W_2} = cs_{W_2} \wedge cs'_{W_3} = cs_{W_3} \wedge \ldots \wedge cs'_{W_{18}} \wedge$$
$$ncs'_{W_1} = ncs_{W_1} \wedge ncs'_{W_2} = ncs_{W_2} \wedge ncs'_{W_3} = ncs_{W_3} \wedge \ldots \wedge ncs'_{W_{18}} = ncs_{W_{18}}) \vee$$
$$(c1 = -1 \wedge ncs'_{W_1} \wedge ncs'_{W_2} = ncs_{W_2} \wedge ncs'_{W_3} = ncs_{W_3} \wedge \ldots \wedge ncs'_{W_{18}} = ncs_{W_{18}} \wedge$$
$$cs'_{W_1} = cs_{W_1} \wedge cs'_{W_2} = cs_{W_2} \wedge cs'_{W_3} = cs_{W_3} \wedge \ldots \wedge cs'_{W_{18}} = cs_{W_{18}}) \vee$$

$$\ldots$$

$$(c1 = -18 \wedge ncs'_{W_1} = ncs_{W_1} \wedge ncs'_{W_2} = cs_{W_2} \wedge ncs'_{W_3} = ncs_{W_3} \wedge \ldots \wedge ncs'_{W_{18}} \wedge$$
$$cs'_{W_1} = cs_{W_1} \wedge cs'_{W_2} = cs_{W_2} \wedge cs'_{W_3} = cs_{W_3} \wedge \ldots \wedge cs'_{W_{18}} = cs_{W_{18}}))$$

- the lack of changes in Child's emotions (Subformula No. 1.3)

$$e'_{W_1} = e_{W_1} \land e'_{W_2} = e_{W_2} \land e'_{W_3} = e_{W_3} \land e'_{W_4} = e_{W_4} \land e'_{W_5} = e_{W_5}$$

- the lack of changes in Parent's emotions (Subformula No. 1.4)

$$e'_{B_1} = e_{B_1} \land e'_{B_2} = e_{B_2} \land e'_{B_3} = e_{B_3} \land e'_{B_4} = e_{B_4} \land e'_{B_5} = e_{B_5}$$

- the lack of changes in Parent's commitments (Subformula No. 1.5)

$$cs'_{B_1} = cs_{B_1} \land cs'_{B_2} = cs_{B_2} \land \ldots \land cs'_{B_{18}} = cs_{B_{18}} \land$$
$$ncs'_{B_1} = ncs_{B_1} \land ncs'_{B_2} = ncs_{B_2} \land \ldots \land ncs'_{B_{18}} = ncs_{B_{18}}$$

- the lack of the second argument in the action (Subformula No. 1.6):

$$\neg c2_1 \land \neg c2_2 \land \neg c2_3 \land \ldots \land \neg c2_{18} \land \neg nc2_1 \land \neg nc2_2 \land \neg nc2_3 \land \ldots \land \neg nc2_{18}$$

The second evolution rule also describes changes in the player's set of commitments, but the specified action is more complex because it uses locution which expects two arguments. The first argument is a single content, and the second one is a subset of the contents and its negations set:

Child.X = true and Child.Z1...ZN = true **if** *Child.lastAction = X.since.Z1...ZN*
The above rule means, that if the last action of the player Child was *since* with contents understood as the set of premises $Z1...ZN$ and the conclusion X, then all contents X, $Z1...ZN$ become the commitments of the player *Child*. Let us assume that the value for the variable l associated with the locution *since* is 4. The formula corresponding to such a rule is a conjunction of the below formulae, which describe:

- the actual player of the action and the locution type (Subformula No. 2.1)

$$p = 1 \land l = 4$$

- the change of Child's commitments $Z1...ZN$, which were used in the action as a set of premises in the second argument (Subformula No. 2.2)

$$(c2_1 \rightarrow cs'_{W_1}) \land (\neg c2_1 \rightarrow cs'_{W_1} = cs_{W_1}) \land (c2_2 \rightarrow cs'_{W_2}) \land (\neg c2_2 \rightarrow cs'_{W_2} = cs_{W_2}) \land$$
$$\ldots \land (c2_{18} \rightarrow cs'_{W_{18}}) \land (\neg c2_{18} \rightarrow cs'_{W_{18}} = cs_{W_{18}}) \land$$
$$(nc2_1 \rightarrow ncs'_{W_1}) \land (\neg nc2_1 \rightarrow ncs'_{W_1} = ncs_{W_1}) \land (nc2_2 \rightarrow ncs'_{W_2}) \land$$
$$(\neg nc2_2 \rightarrow ncs'_{W_2} = ncs_{W_2}) \land \ldots \land (nc2_{18} \rightarrow ncs'_{W_{18}}) \land (\neg nc2_{18} \rightarrow ncs'_{W_{18}} = ncs_{W_{18}})$$

- the change of the specific Child's commitment used in the action as single X content of the first argument (Subformula No. 2.3)

$$(c1 = 1 \rightarrow cs'_{W_1}) \land (\neg c1 = 1 \rightarrow cs'_{W_1} = cs_{W_1}) \land$$
$$(c1 = 2 \rightarrow cs'_{W_2}) \land (\neg c1 = 2 \rightarrow cs'_{W_2} = cs_{W_2}) \land \ldots \land$$
$$(c1 = 18 \rightarrow cs'_{W_{18}}) \land (\neg c1 = 18 \rightarrow cs'_{W_{18}} = cs_{W_{18}}) \land$$
$$(c1 = -1 \rightarrow ncs'_{W_1}) \land (\neg c1 = -1 \rightarrow ncs'_{W_1} = ncs_{W_1}) \land$$
$$(c1 = -2 \rightarrow ncs'_{W_2}) \land (\neg c1 = -2 \rightarrow ncs'_{W_2} = ncs_{W_2}) \land \ldots \land$$
$$(c1 = -18 \rightarrow ncs'_{W_{18}}) \land (\neg c1 = -18 \rightarrow ncs'_{W_{18}} = ncs_{W_{18}})$$

– the lack of changes in: Child's emotions (already defined as Subformula No. 1.3), Parent's emotions (Subformula No. 1.4), Parent's commitments (Subformula No. 1.5)

Depending on the structure and types (evolution, protocol) of given input rules, the formula encoding our model has many subformulae of various forms. Some of the rules of evolution functions represent properties of the dialogue game itself (e.g. changes in the sets of commitments) and the other ones can be rather understood as elements of player's emotional profile (e.g. changes in the levels of emotions). The protocol description (corresponding to the protocol function in our model) reflects the rules of the given type of dialogues. In order to verify some dialogue game properties (also emotion-based properties), the designer should define the specification according to some existing or created dialogue game and define a verified property. The possible found counterexamples are dialogues compliant with the dialogue game, but not having this property.

5   Reachability Analysis of the Dialogue Game Protocol

Given a dialogue system and a property, the reachability problem consists in establishing whether a state satisfying this property is reachable from a given initial state of the system. The verified properties of dialogue systems are expressed in language based on CTL logic introduced by Emerson and Clarke [2] enriched with commitment and emotion components [8]. Since we want to analyse dialogue games with respect to emotional states of the interlocutors, the property which reachability we want to verify can concern players' emotions (e.g. their state). To solve this problem we propose a Bounded Model Checking (BMC) method.

To check the reachability of a state satisfying a given property, we unfold iteratively the transition relation of a dialogue system in k steps. Then, the unfolding is encoded by a quantifier-free first order formula, that characterises the set of all the feasible paths through the transition relation with the length equal to k. Next, we translate the property to a quantifier-free first order formula. Finally, the conjunctions of the formula representing the "unfolded" transition relation and the translation of the property is tested for satisfiability using an SMT-solver. The unfolding of the transition relation can be terminated when either a state satisfying the property has been found or all the states of the system have been searched.

Our aim is to verify a reachability property represented by a given quantifier-free first order formula $\varphi(\mathbf{w}_0, \ldots, \mathbf{w}_k)$, where $\mathbf{w}_0, \ldots, \mathbf{w}_k$ are symbolic states. Let $I(\mathbf{w})$ be a quantifier-free first-order formula that encodes the set of initial states, and $T(\mathbf{w}, \mathbf{a}, \mathbf{w}')$, where $\mathbf{a}$ is a symbolic action, be a quantifier-free first order formula that encodes any possible transition. Now let us define the formula $[M]_k$ that represents the unfolding to the depth k of the transition relation of M:

$$[M]_k := \bigwedge_{i=0}^{k-1} T(\mathbf{w}_i, \mathbf{a}_i, \mathbf{w}_{i+1})$$

In order to check the reachability property represented by the formula φ one has to check the satisfiability of the following conjunction:

$$[M]_k^{\varphi} := I(\mathbf{w}_0) \wedge [M]_k \wedge \varphi(\mathbf{w}_0, \ldots, \mathbf{w}_k)$$

starting with $k = 0$. If for a given k the formula $[M]_k^\varphi$ is not satisfiable, then k is increased and the resulting formula is to be checked by an SMT-solver again.

Note that the algorithm in question also terminates when, for some k, the available resources (memory or time) are either insufficient to generate the formula $[M]_k^\varphi$ or are insufficient for the SMT-solver. In such a case, it means that due to limited resources available the algorithm is not able to check whether the property expressed by the formula $\varphi(\mathbf{w}_0, \ldots, \mathbf{w}_k)$ holds in the system M.

6 Conclusions

An essential element of a system of interacting artificial entities is the establishment of a mode of communication. A given protocol defines the rules by which a dialogue is conducted. Dialogues can be argumentative, persuasive, negotiating, etc. In this case, the protocol determines the correctness and the effectiveness of these processes. That is why it is so important to have the possibility of verifying the implemented systems. In this work, we show how a dialogue system with emotional reasoning can be encoded as an SMT formula. This system highlights an argumentation between a parent and a child. It is based on a formal logical model which characterises a certain class of argumentation. The key element of parent-child dialogues is an emotional exchange. This aspect is also included in the model. Given a dialogue game model we describe it in terms of an SMT formula. SMT is the problem of determining whether such a formula is satisfiable. The encoding is the basis for further verification of the properties of the given protocol, which must also be represented by appropriate SMT formulae. In this paper, we show only the encoding of the model, not properties. We will consider dialogue games properties in the context of their encoding and verification in our further works.

One of the main difficulties of this project is the encoding of the model, because the conditions determining the legality of the action, i.e., whether a given action can be performed, refer not only to the state of the current system but also to the history of the dialogue. Which in turn requires storing in memory and then encoding the whole history or at least the sets of actions. The difficulty is not in the structure of the set but in its size. An additional obstacle is the encoding of actions consisting of two parts: the name of the speech act and the content, which may also be a complex sentence. Also, since our main goal is to verify games, not to simulate them, one of the weaknesses of this approach is that it represents and encodes a narrower class of dialogue games than some existing tools, that only perform simulations.

Acknowledgment. The work of M. Kacprzak was supported by the Bialystok University of Technology, Poland, as part of the research grant of the Faculty of Computer Science and funded by the resources for research by Ministry of Science and Higher Education, Poland (research subsidy of the Faculty of Computer Science, Bialystok University of Technology).

References

1. Bentahar, J., Meyer, J.J.C., Wan, W.: Model checking agent communication. In: Dastani, M., Hindriks, K., Meyer, J.J. (eds.) Specification and Verification of Multi-agent Systems, pp. 67–102. Springer, Boston (2010). https://doi.org/10.1007/978-1-4419-6984-2_3
2. Clarke, E.M., Emerson, E.A., Sistla, A.P.: Automatic verification of finite state concurrent systems using temporal logic specifications: a practical approach. In: Wright, J.R., Landweber, L., Demers, A.J., Teitelbaum, T. (eds.) Conference Record of the Tenth Annual ACM Symposium on Principles of Programming Languages, Austin, Texas, USA, January 1983, pp. 117–126. ACM Press (1983)
3. Dunin-Kęplicz, B., Strachocka, A.: Paraconsistent multi-party persuasion in TalkLOG. In: Chen, Q., Torroni, P., Villata, S., Hsu, J., Omicini, A. (eds.) PRIMA 2015. LNCS (LNAI), vol. 9387, pp. 265–283. Springer, Cham (2015). https://doi.org/10.1007/978-3-319-25524-8_17
4. Ekman, P.: An argument for basic emotions. Cogn. Emot. **6**, 169–200 (1992)
5. Kacprzak, M., Dziubiński, M., Budzyńska, K.: Strategies in dialogues: a game-theoretic approach. In: Computational Models of Argument - Proceedings of COMMA 2014, pp. 333–344 (2014)
6. Kacprzak, M.: Persuasive strategies in dialogue games with emotional reasoning. In: Polkowski, L., et al. (eds.) IJCRS 2017. LNCS (LNAI), vol. 10314, pp. 435–453. Springer, Cham (2017). https://doi.org/10.1007/978-3-319-60840-2_32
7. Kacprzak, M., Sawicka, A., Zbrzezny, A.: Towards verification of dialogue protocols: a mathematical model. In: Rutkowski, L., Korytkowski, M., Scherer, R., Tadeusiewicz, R., Zadeh, L.A., Zurada, J.M. (eds.) ICAISC 2016. LNCS (LNAI), vol. 9693, pp. 329–339. Springer, Cham (2016). https://doi.org/10.1007/978-3-319-39384-1_28
8. Kacprzak, M., Sawicka, A., Zbrzezny, A., Rzeńca, K., Żukowska, K.: A formal model of an argumentative dialogue in the management of emotions. Logic Log. Philos. **27**(4), 471–490 (2017). http://apcz.umk.pl/czasopisma/index.php/LLP/article/view/LLP.2017.024
9. Mackenzie, J.D.: Question-begging in non-cumulative systems. J. of Philos. Logic **8**, 117–133 (1979)
10. Prakken, H.: Formal systems for persuasion dialogue. Knowl. Eng. Rev. **21**, 163–188 (2006)
11. Sawicka, A., Kacprzak, M., Zbrzezny, A.: A novel description language for two-agent dialogue games. In: Polkowski, L., et al. (eds.) IJCRS 2017. LNCS (LNAI), vol. 10314, pp. 466–486. Springer, Cham (2017). https://doi.org/10.1007/978-3-319-60840-2_34
12. Walton, D.N., Krabbe, E.C.W.: Commitment in Dialogue: Basic Concepts of Interpersonal Reasoning. State University of New York Press, New York (1995)
13. Zbrzezny, A.M., Zbrzezny, A., Raimondi, F.: Efficient model checking timed and weighted interpreted systems using SMT and SAT solvers. In: Jezic, G., Chen-Burger, Y.-H.J., Howlett, R.J., Jain, L.C. (eds.) Agent and Multi-Agent Systems: Technology and Applications. SIST, vol. 58, pp. 45–55. Springer, Cham (2016). https://doi.org/10.1007/978-3-319-39883-9_4

Affective Context-Aware Systems: Architecture of a Dynamic Framework

Mateusz Z. Łępicki and Szymon Bobek[✉]

AGH University of Science and Technology,
al. Mickiewicza 30, 30-059 Krakow, Poland
{mzl,sbobek}@agh.edu.pl
http://www.agh.edu.pl

Abstract. Affective computing gained a lot of attention from researchers and business over the last decade. However, most of the attempts for building systems that try to predict, or provoke affective state of users were done for specific and narrow domains. This complicates reusing such systems in other, even similar domains. In this paper we present such a solution, that aims at solving such problem by providing a general framework architecture for building affective-aware systems. It supports designing and development of affective-aware solutions, in a holistic and domain independent way.

Keywords: Affective computing · Context-awareness · Frameworks · Mobile

1 Introduction

Affective computing is an emerging research area that rapidly evolved over the last decade. This evolution might be connected with the fast development of mobile devices and artificial intelligence methods. The former one allows for seamless knowledge acquisition of many contextual information, including psychophysical information about user. The latter provides mechanisms for analyzing and understanding such data in a way that can be used for automated reasoning. Such a synergy of these two technological advancements allowed for development of affective computing systems that are aware of human emotions, can predict these emotions and provoke them in a controlled way.

Although the progress in this field of science has been noticeable in recent years, there is still a need for research in this area. Most of the emotion-aware systems that were developed are solutions dedicated to solve specific problems or tasks. They were crafted individually for that purposes and are hardly reusable.

In our work we focus on a development of a solution that will provide general architecture for affective-computing systems, making the process of development specific systems easier and more controllable allowing for re-usage of

© Springer Nature Switzerland AG 2019
L. Rutkowski et al. (Eds.): ICAISC 2019, LNAI 11509, pp. 575–584, 2019.
https://doi.org/10.1007/978-3-030-20915-5_51

some components in other systems. We argue that affective computing systems share common characteristics with context-aware systems [1]. This in particular includes the highly dynamic environment with huge amount of data streaming every second requiring at the same time from the system to work under soft real-time constraints. Furthermore such systems are user centric, in a sense that their user is not only the passive receiver of system's output but rather its conscious operator that can and want to have impact on how the system works and adapts.

Those similarities allowed us to extend our previous work in the field of context-aware, and transfer it to the field of affective computing. The original contribution of this paper include proposal of architecture for affective computing systems and prototype of toolkit that supports building such systems and integrate them seamlessly with context-aware systems. We argue that such a synergy will benefit in both areas.

The rest of the paper is organized as follows. In Sect. 2 the state of the art in the field of affective computing was presented and motivation for our work was stated. Section 3 is for Context and Emotion terms used in this paper. The affective context-aware platform design and detailed description of its main components was described in Sect. 4. Use case scenarios that aim at demonstrating possible usage of our platform in various fields of affective and context-aware systems is presented in Sect. 5. Finally, the summary and future work plans are presented in Sect. 6.

2   Related Works

Affective state information gains more and more attention of researches since Picard [2] described *Affective Computing*. Early works were focused on recognition based on face and speech [3], text [4] or body gestures [5]. Although those methods do not allow accurate emotion recognition, they are still under continuous investigation. Another approach is to use physiological signals. In a review paper of Kreibig [6] a total number of 134 papers with subject related to physiological signal emotion recognition were summarized. While this domain is under development for years, there is a relatively small advancement in usage of affective states in context-aware systems. As a consequence, there is a very limited amount of existing frameworks with those capabilities and lot of them are conceptual only.

Horace Ip and Belton Kwong describe in their work [7] a conceptual framework for interactive learning. They proposed a system providing a real-time feedback in learning to facilitate active participation. According to the authors, mentioned system should align dynamically to current affective state and progress of an individual student. The presented architecture consists of a multimodal sensing module for gathering signals like motion, a feature extraction and analysis module and an affect classification module.

Bahreini et al. [8] introduces a Framework for Improving Learning Through Webcams And Microphones (FILTWAM). Their approach combines face and speech emotion recognition to provide a feedback for enhancing communication skills of learners. This paper presents a high-level architecture of proposed framework and working proof of concept.

During our research we found out, there is no general context-aware solution that provides affective state for a wider purpose. Therefore our motivation was to create a mobile context-aware framework with affective state information, modularized architecture and dynamic configuration capabilities.

3   Context and Emotion

3.1   Context Awareness

In the computing, context is associated with the task and describes a minimal set of data which allows for interruption and then problem-less continuation of a given task. In this paper, context concept is a supplement to a context awareness idea. Similar to [1], the most fitting definition for this work is the one proposed by Dey [9], which describes context as *"any information that can be used to characterize the situation of an entity."* In this case entity means a user or a mobile device whereas information is any data obtained from mentioned user or device directly or indirectly by inference. In particular this set contains user's physiological data like heart rate or galvanic skin response, device data like GPS coordinates, inertial navigation system data and more.

3.2   Emotion Ontology

Emotion may be described as a *conscious experience* which is a organism's reaction for a given stimulus [10]. This response can be positive, negative or neutral but there is an ongoing discussion whether it is cross-culture or culture specific. There is also an ongoing discussion on theories of emotion and it is hard to point a leading one. However, we established our research on the more neurological approach, where we assume that change of a physiological state in human organism is a result of given affect. In conclusion, measurement of physiological signals and their changes across time may give a way to name affect state of the investigated person. During the research, we were not able to develop a simple model of emotion classification as a relation to signals and their changes. First experiments show the differences between each of participants. Creation of a general model and an adaptation mechanism is the next step in our research and it is connected to development of the whole architecture described further in this paper.

It is important to emphasize that the emotion ontology piece in this architecture might supply from simple rule-based system to complex machine learning algorithms and may vary on the implementation of those mechanisms. At this stage, it is a supplement for a rule-based system to a PAD model. In the future, along with development of next Context providers like visual or sound signals, it might be not enough.

Pleasure-Arousal-Dominance (PAD) emotional state model is a psychology model and was developed by Albert Mehrabian and James A. Russel in 1974. Emotions are represented in three dimensions, Pleasure, Arousal and Dominance. The relation of signals from different providers to dimensions will be a part of future research. Figure 1 shows average location of Fear/Anger based on our previous research. Figure 2 is an example of simple ontology used for the system.

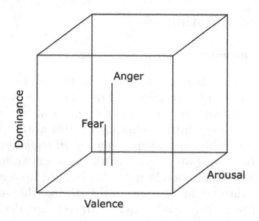

Fig. 1. PAD emotional state model and Fear/Anger location

Label: Anger

Class: Negative

Dimension:

    Valence: Medium, Medium-Low

    Arousal: Medium-High, High

    Dominance: High

Label: Fear

Class: Negative

Dimension:

    Valence: Medium-Low, Low

    Arousal: Medium-High, High

    Dominance: Medium-Low, Low

Fig. 2. Simple emotion ontology example

4 Affective Context-Aware Platform

The affective context-aware platform is a framework which integrates user affective state information, mediation logic and dynamic configuration capabilities with context-aware system. Its origin lays in a need inside our research group

IF   inputIsArray = TRUE AND InteractionLevel <> NOINTERACTION

THEN   useMediator = TRUE, passInput = TRUE

...

IF   hour >= 7 AND hour <=8 AND inMotion = TRUE

THEN   InteractionLevel = NOINTERACTION

Fig. 3. Knowledge base fragment from dynamic configuration rule-based system

for a tool which could allow us to test different research concepts around affective computing in mobile environments. To our best knowledge there is no solution on the market that would provide all required components. Therefore the primary goal of the work presented in this paper was to design and create proposed tool.

The architecture does not force solutions implementations. Those can be created as mobile applications, distributed systems or personal computing programs. However our research directions are focused on mobile personal devices, in particular smartphones and wristbands, therefore rest of the work aims at this environment. Colors used in Fig. 4 groups elements by current state in our work related to creation of mobile context-aware systems with mediation and dynamic configuration. States are as follow:

1. **Green** - already available solutions, only integration needs extra work.
2. **Orange** - elements under development, need work to be finished and integrated.
3. **Red** - components need to be created, integration layer do not exists.

We strongly believe, modularization of the whole framework will enable better management and integration for all key components. This will also allow to experiment with more than one paradigm of main concepts like Emotion recognition or Dynamic configuration. Moreover it will be easier to replace power draining elements with better optimized or less particular substitutes.

4.1   Context Instrumentation Framework

Context-aware system needs providers of data that define a context. Mentioned providers can exist as a part of a system implementation but they also can be kept outside. Embedded logic could be less time consuming in initial work and faster in communication with other built-in components. On the other hand, independent logic is potentially easier to maintain in the advanced phase of the product, more manageable in the configuration perspective and more replaceable. In the proposed architecture, the second option is assumed as a better approach, because of needs for dynamic configuration of the context. More-over effortless creation of extensions is crucial for further evaluation of future concepts.

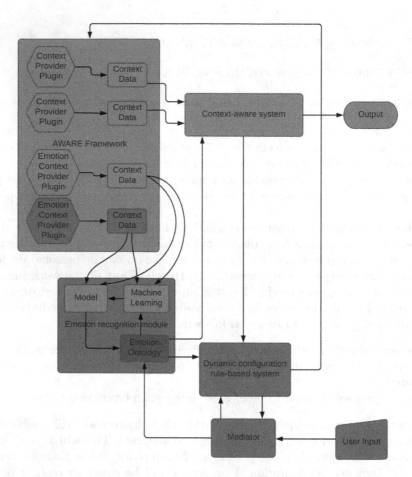

Fig. 4. Architecture of a dynamic framework for context-aware systems extended with the emotion recognition and mediation. (Color figure online)

For presented architecture, the component responsible for context should allow to: (a) gather data through *Context Provider Plugins*, (b) manage config-uration and disable single input/output modules, (c) manage transform mecha-nism in *Context Data* element, (d) send data further through *Context Data* ele-ment. Data from single sensor will be read by *Context Provider Plugin* and trans-formed in corresponding *Context Data* element. Next it will be sent to *Context-aware System* and *Emotion Recognition module* (described in more details in Sects. 4.2 and 4.3). Each *Context Data* output can be used as an input for both components simultaneously or separately for one of them. The main assumption for the whole system is its ability to be dynamically reconfigured and this will be partially done in this module through connected *Configuration Rule-based system* (described in Sect. 4.5).

We decided to use an existing context instrumentation framework from our previous works related to mobile context-aware systems. This decision was motivated by our awareness of the tool, well-documented process for creation of new providers, in this case named plugins and simple management system. AWARE, an open source context instrumentation framework, was created at University of Oulu in Finland (http://www.awareframework.com/). However, in the future, any tool capable of gathering, transforming and sending data, with configuration mechanism could be used in described system. Other research work conducted in our group focus in creation of new AWARE plugins for selected wearable devices with data available through them. Therefore we decided to set up our own AWARE infrastructure for deeper integration and better testing purposes.

4.2   Context-Aware System

The context-aware system module is a heart mechanism of described architecture. Main responsibility is to provide logic for any context awareness. We plan to extend existing architecture proposed in [1] by affective awareness. Extended system described in mentioned work will be a core for this module. Furthermore a more detailed description would not be provided this time.

This component will use data from *Context instrumentation framework* for its context awareness. Additional *Context Data* stream will be provided from *Emotion Recognition module* as a recognized emotion or probability of affect. The output from the module will be sent to *Configuration Rule-based system* (described in Sect. 4.5) as one of decisions variables and it will be a general output for the whole system, i.e. behavior of an application, a custom notification or a recommendation.

4.3   Emotion Recognition Module

The emotion recognition module is designed to provide information about recognized or highest ranked affection state. This can be done using lot of different approaches and implementations of distinct models. Module will get information from *Context instrumentation framework Context Data* stream and optionally from *Mediator*.

Despite of the fact that there is a lot of possibilities for emotion recognition, for testing purposes, first version of this module will be created with simple architecture of machine learning model connected with chosen Emotion Ontology component. Output from the module will be send to *Context-aware System* and *Configuration Rule-based System*.

4.4   Mediator

The mediator module is responsible for gathering additional information from the user. Dynamically collected data will be used for emotion recognition improvement and aligning rest of the system to its user. We decided to integrate and adjust an existing technology, the *semantic context mediation*, described in [1, p. 86]. It provides intelligibility for the user and similar abstracts in communication between user and the machine. We believe that this approach can be easily adjusted with affective reasoning mechanisms to provide valuable information straight from the user.

Aforementioned work describes also two main methods for semantic context mediation, implicit and explicit way of collecting feedback from user. Implicit method uses a knowledge component for questions generation, which are then used in communication with user for resolving ambiguity or creation of new knowledge. Explicit method provides the user a way to give a feedback by revealing the models and giving methods for their modification. Both mechanisms are important and both need some additional work for system described in this paper. In addition mediation mechanism will be managed by *Configuration Rule-based System* for better user experience.

4.5 Dynamic Configuration Rule-Based System

The configuration rule-based system module is the most important part in the presented architecture. Based on the input from the emotion recognition, context-aware and mediation modules, with use of the internal rules model, a dynamic of the whole system is provided. One of its responsibilities is AWARE framework plugins management. It will adjust data streams from providers by turning them on and off within current context. It is important to react quickly to changing conditions as some signals can potentially introduce unnecessary noise and others can be superfluous in different situations. The second role of this module is a supervision on the mediation mechanism. Not all interactions should be triggered immediately after detection of knowledge gap in the system. Not all of them can be triggered in some law-restricted situations. It is a gap in user experience that should be addressed. This module partially consists of rule-based system fundamentals and logic described more in the paper mentioned in Sect. 4.4. Figure 3 shows a fragment of the knowledge base for this module.

5 Use-Case Scenarios

The real world implementation consists of a wristband and a mobile phone. The wristband especially provides physiological signals like electrodermal activity and heart rate, whereas the mobile phone serves as a computing device for the system and a provider for other context data. Values described below are all artificial, but in a proper range for each type of information.

For this use case, let's assume that GSR and HR signals are streamed continuously from the wristband to the system. Both signals are sent with 100 Hz frequency and this can be changed by Dynamic configuration rule-based system through Mediator module by the user, for example by setting the power saving mode. Electrodermal activity can be additionally standardized by reducing it to a given scale. All of this is gathered by AWARE Framework and Emotion Context Provider Plugins and then exposed (after standardization) as a Context Data. In our use-case scenario, Heart Rate constantly increases from 85 bits per minute to 120 bits per minute and Galvanic Skin Response as a resistance signal decreases from $7\,k\Omega$ to $5\,k\Omega$.

Next processing units are also configured using Dynamic configuration rule-based system which can be set up directly by a configuration file. In this case, both signals are sent only to Emotion recognition module. Inside of it, the signal is used as an input to a Model, which is pre-trained. In this case, output from a model is high arousal as 0.7 and medium-low valence as 0.4 which flags state as 0.44 probability of fear and 0.46 probability of anger. As the emotion ontology is very basic, the emerging uncertainty is configured to send the output further to dynamic configuration rule-based system. This module decides, by rules and the rest of the context information, when and how the Mediator module should be used. If the user is in a motion between 7 AM and 8 AM, it is configured to not ask directly because of a high probability of an interruption during car drive. In this case, it is 9 AM and the Mediator module asks questions like: Was the event rapid? What do you feel right now, please point in the scale of 5 between fear and anger.

6   Summary and Future Work

In this paper we presented the architecture for affective-aware computing systems and a set of tools that supports its implementation in real environments. The architecture allows to build such systems in a more efficient way, allowing for combining several autonomous components into one system with usage of a rule-based configuration mechanism. The architecture was designed to best fit characteristics of an uncontrolled environment, where the system operates ultimately. This was achieved by including a mediation module in it, which primary goal was to seamlessly include user in the process of decision making and learning of the system. The knowledge acquisition and dissemination layer of our system is currently used as an integration platform for research aiming at unifying psychophysical context acquisition.

The future works includes integration of existing systems for building affective models with our architecture. In particular that includes: affective design patterns in computer games [11] and use of virtual reality and wearable sensors in affective computing experiments [12,13].

References

1. Bobek, S.: Methods for modeling self-adaptive mobile context-aware sytems. Ph.D. thesis, AGH University of Science and Technology, April 2016. Supervisor: Grzegorz J. Nalepa
2. Picard, R.W.: Affective Computing. MIT Press, Cambridge (1997)

3. Busso, C., et al.: Analysis of emotion recognition using facial expressions, speech and multimodal information. In: Sharma, R., Darrell, T., Harper, M.P., Lazzari, G., Turk, M. (eds.) Proceedings of the 6th International Conference on Multimodal Interfaces, ICMI 2004, State College, PA, USA, 13–15 October 2004, pp. 205–211. ACM (2004)

4. Alm, C.O., Roth, D., Sproat, R.: Emotions from text: machine learning for text-based emotion prediction. In: Proceedings of the Conference on HLT/EMNLP 2005, Human Language Technology Conference and Conference on Empirical Methods in Natural Language Processing, 6–8 October 2005, Vancouver, British Columbia, Canada, pp. 579–586. The Association for Computational Linguistics (2005)

5. Gunes, H., Piccardi, M.: Bi-modal emotion recognition from expressive face and body gestures. J. Netw. Comput. Appl. **30**(4), 1334–1345 (2007)

6. Kreibig, S.D.: Autonomic nervous system activity in emotion: a review. Biol. Psychol. **84**(3), 394–421 (2010). The biopsychology of emotion: Current theoretical and empirical perspectives

7. Ip, H.H.S., Kwong, B.: A conceptual framework of affective context-aware interactive learning media. In: Hui, K., et al. (eds.) Edutainment 2007. LNCS, vol. 4469, pp. 391–400. Springer, Heidelberg (2007). https://doi.org/10.1007/978-3-540-73011-8_39

8. Bahreini, K., Nadolski, R., Westera, W.: FILTWAM - a framework for online affective computing in serious games. In: Gloria, A.D., de Freitas, S. (eds.) Fourth International Conference on Games and Virtual Worlds for Serious Applications, VS-GAMES 2012, Genoa, Italy, 29–31 October 2012, Vol. 15, pp. 45–52. Procedia Computer Science, Elsevier (2012)

9. Salber, D., Dey, A.K., Abowd, G.D.: The context toolkit: aiding the development of context-enabled applications. In: Proceedings of the SIGCHI Conference on Human Factors in Computing Systems, CHI 1999, pp. 434–441. ACM, New York (1999)

10. Damasio, A.: The Feeling of What Happens: Body and Emotion in the Making of Consciousness. Harcourt, Boston (1999)

11. Nalepa, G.J., Gizycka, B., Kutt, K., Argasinski, J.K.: Affective design patterns in computer games. Scrollrunner case study. In: Communication Papers of the 2017 Federated Conference on Computer Science and Information Systems, FedCSIS 2017, pp. 345–352 (2017)

12. Nalepa, G.J., Argasinski, J.K., Kutt, K., Wegrzyn, P., Bobek, S., Lepicki, M.Z.: Affective computing experiments in virtual reality with wearable sensors: methodological considerations and preliminary results. In: Ezquerro, M.T.H., Nalepa, G.J., Mendez, J.T.P. (eds.) Proceedings of the Workshop on Affective Computing and Context Awareness in Ambient Intelligence (AfCAI 2016), vol. 1794. CEUR Workshop Proceedings (2016)

13. Rincon, J.A., Costa, Â., Novais, P., Julian, V., Carrascosa, C.: Using non-invasive wearables for detecting emotions with intelligent agents. In: Graña, M., López-Guede, J.M., Etxaniz, O., Herrero, Á., Quintián, H., Corchado, E. (eds.) ICEUTE/SOCO/CISIS -2016. AISC, vol. 527, pp. 73–84. Springer, Cham (2017). https://doi.org/10.1007/978-3-319-47364-2_8

RDFM: Resilient Distributed Factorization Machines

André Rodrigo da Silva[✉], Leonardo M. Rodrigues, Luciana de Oliveira Rech, and Aldelir Fernando Luiz

Department of Informatics and Statistics (INE),
Federal University of Santa Catarina (UFSC), Florianópolis, SC 88040-900, Brazil
{andre.rodrigo.silva,l.m.rodrigues}@posgrad.ufsc.br,
luciana.rech@ufsc.br,aldelir.luiz@ifc.edu.br

Abstract. Factorization Machines algorithms have been successfully applied to recommender systems due to their ability to handle data sparsity and the cold-start problem. Their scalability makes it suitable to produce evergrowing complex predictive models, which are based on Big Data without performance degradation. The algorithm has been scaled to contexts of distributed and parallel computation, but in general with the strong assumption that those environments are safe and are not subject to arbitrary errors, malicious attacks, and hardware failures. In this work, we show that a distributed average consensus strategy is capable to deal with unsafe and dynamic learning environments.

Keywords: Distributed average consensus · Factorization Machines · Fault tolerance

1 Introduction

Factorization Machines algorithms were initially designed and successfully used in ranking tasks within recommender systems [11,12], capturing characteristics of both similarity measures and regression [9]. Besides, these algorithms were powerful enough to address issues of previous recommender system algorithms, such as the cold-start problem. In recent years, Factorization Machines works proved to be useful in toxicogenomics [15], stock returns [6], student performance [13], microblog information retrieval [10], and many other applications. Particularly, Factorization Machines algorithms have been also successfully used in big data problems [6,8] due to their characteristics of linear time complexity, and the capacity to estimate parameters in high-dimensional and very sparse data.

Conversely, Factorization Machines do have one major weakness. While feature matrix memory consumption can be highly alleviated during training, by using specific data-structures for sparse matrix representations, the algorithm yields dense models that cost too much memory for real-world big data scenarios as each feature needs to be embedded into a low-dimensional vector space.

Supported by CAPES/Brazil and CNPq/Brazil.

L. Rutkowski et al. (Eds.): ICAISC 2019, LNAI 11509, pp. 585–594, 2019.
https://doi.org/10.1007/978-3-030-20915-5_52

To deal with those limitations in training, which are imposed by the memory consumption of the algorithm, distributed and parallel training strategies are proposed in this paper. We believe that this is the first work to make Factorization Machines cope with arbitrary failures. In this context, we run our algorithm in a network with arbitrary failures in its nodes and show that our distributed algorithm is able to learn a regression task nonetheless.

The major contributions of this paper can be summarised as follows:

- A Fault-Tolerant Factorization Machine Algorithm;
- Determination of the number of reliable nodes for it to withstand byzantine failures as $2F$;
- The Tardigrade subroutine to grade parameter matrices.

2   Background

This sections of this paper will briefly discuss relevant concepts to the development and understanding of this work.

2.1   Fault Tolerance in Distributed Systems

One of the greatest challenges of modern computing is to build more robust, reliable and safe systems since computer systems are impaired by vulnerabilities of many natures (e.g. benign or malicious). These vulnerabilities cannot be ignored, particularly as people and organizations have become increasingly dependent on the large-scale distributed computer systems, which are constant targets of vulnerabilities of different natures. In this context, a fault occurs if some system component is successfully affected in such a way that causes its behaviour to depart from its specification. Thus, it is relevant to develop techniques for building robust distributed systems that are capable of detecting and reacting to faults, guaranteeing that services are correctly provided for their users.

Fault tolerance consists of an approach focussed to design and build reliable computer systems to avoid their behaviour being deviated from the corresponding specification. This approach relies on a set of properties, such as availability, reliability, safety, integrity, and maintainability. The most severe fault model is Byzantine [7] since this fault model asserts that a faulty component can exhibit a completely arbitrary benign or malicious behaviour. Note that Byzantine faults are common in modern systems. Fault behaviours, such as data corruption in disk or RAM due to physical effects or in software due to bugs or due to malicious attacks, sometimes, do not affect only the availability. Since these components may or may not resume their normal behaviour after presenting a faulty behaviour, they may affect also application state, i.e. its semantics.

Moreover, the dependability and security properties of a system could be impaired by a system failure or by an opponent that exploits its vulnerabilities, respectively. An alternative to mitigate this risk is the implementation of Byzantine Fault Tolerant (BFT) systems, in which the system properties are ensured even if some of its components fail or are compromised by a successful attack. Byzantine fault tolerance can be seen as a collection of effective methods and techniques to improve cyber-security, maintaining basic security properties of a computer system, e.g. integrity and availability.

2.2 Consensus Strategies

Consensus strategies are commonly used by distributed systems which are resilient. An example of consensus strategy would be in the presence of $f > 0$ components with failures, require of the remaining components to elect which components they believe are trustworthy, requiring the parts to vote [7]. On machine learning the values to be agreed upon, are the parameters of the model being learned, [4] and [14] shows that consensus need not to be exact, the values can be approximately equal this concept is called **distributed average consensus**.

2.3 Factorization Machines

Factorization Machines achieves good prediction metrics in scenarios of sparsity by representing feature interations weights in a $\mathbb{R}^{k \times n}$ dimensional latent feature space, where n represent the features in the dataset, the model equation for Factorization Machines with second order interactions is

$$\hat{y} := w_0 + \sum_{i=1}^{n} w_i x_i + \frac{1}{2} \sum_{f=1}^{k} \left(\left(\sum_{i=1}^{n} v_{i,f} x_i \right)^2 - \sum_{i=1}^{n} v_{i,f}^2 x_i^2 \right) \tag{1}$$

a polynomial regression model of the same order would be

$$\hat{y}(x) := w_0 + \sum_{i=1}^{d} w_i x_i + \frac{1}{2} \sum_{i=1}^{d} \sum_{j=i+1}^{d} w_{i,j} x_i x_j \tag{2}$$

The main advantage of 1 over 2 is the fact that in 2 the second order weight matrix $W := w_{ij} \ldots w_{nn}$ is represented by a factorized matrix of the form $V * V^T$, where $W \in \mathbb{R}^{n^2}$ and $V \in \mathbb{R}^{k \times n}$, assuming $k \ll n$ model interation parameters in 1 will grown linearly w.r.t features, while 2 would show quadratic growth.

3 Related Work

In this section, a review of the literature is carried out with the purpose of serving as theoretical support for the work in hand. The first related work presents Difacto [8], which is a framework for large scale Factoring Machines. This work evolves the model of the Factoring Machines, making it simpler through the individual regularization of each characteristic of the data. In addition, it has become relevant because of its importance in terms of frequency and impact on predictions. Difacto generates a model that is up to 100x more compact than that obtained by the factoring machines, adding gains in the accuracy metric. This framework also uses an asynchronous stochastic gradient descent algorithm to operate in a distributed way and proves that the learning cost function converges to a minimum. The algorithm relies on the Parameter Server architecture to update the model parameters estimation and to distribute the training examples for each node in the network.

Another work of particular interest is the RD-SVM (*Resilient Distributed Support Vector Machines*), which stands out for its ability to tolerate up to F faulty nodes with a minimum of $2F+1$ correct nodes. In this case, the algorithm maintains the convergence to a global minimum of the cost function, without requiring a central control – which could become a single point of failure – and with reduced information traffic between the parts [16]. RD-SVM was inspired by earlier work focused on Wireless Sensor Networks [4]. Although thought for sensors, both the architecture and implementation have proved to be useful to other domains that have limited communication and need to tolerate Byzantine faults. The RD-SMV's success in fault tolerance is largely due to the fact that the objective function (i.e. maximize the distance of classes to a hyperplane) is convex, that is, it has only one global optimum point. Then, the algorithm applies an average consensus strategy leading all computational nodes to an agreement in terms of having approximately the same support vectors.

Another work worth mentioning is the Krum algorithm [1]. This algorithm has been proposed as an approach capable of aggregating vector parameter estimates, drawing on both majority approaches – i.e. approaches that observe, for example, $n-f$ vectors (where f is the number of Byzantine nodes expected to be tolerated in the system), and in approaches based simply on distance between vectors. This algorithm chooses the vector in the vector subset $n-f$ which reduces the quadratic euclidean distance of its neighbours, or the vector closest to all other vectors. In total, the Krum algorithm is able to tolerate $2f+2<n$ Byzantine nodes, with its complexity $O(n^2 \cdot d)$, where n is the number of vectors and d is the number of dimensions of the gradient. Experiments have shown that although this approach performs poorly, aggregation on average is able to withstand Byzantine faults, in which case classical aggregations no longer work.

Finally, derived from the Krum algorithm, the algorithm denominated Multi-Krum does aggregation by average. The aggregation selects the m vectors closest to the centroid of the $n-f$ vectors. The results verified for this algorithm demonstrated that it is able to converge with such rapidity on the aggregation by average without the provision of tolerance to faults.

4   RDFM: Resilient Distributed Factorization Machines

Our distributed algorithm is placed to learn a model in a unsafe distributed environment, subject to arbitrary faults. The goal of the model is to correct predict the rating an user would give to a unseen movie given its features (cast, genre etc.) and the user own features (age, sex, movies ranked in the past etc). Those predictions could then be used to rank movies and do personalised recommendations. The feature vector x_i denotes an user and a movie characteristics

RDFM should correctly predict a movie rating y_i using a model 1 given x_i. The model is learned by iteratively minimising RMSE (Root Mean Squared Error) with Adagrad [3].

Formalisation: The RDFM is a distributed learning algorithm, supposed to work on a interconnected network of computers. The network can be represented by a connected undirected and static graph $G(J, E)$, with M vertices, where the set of vertices $J := \{1, \ldots, M\}$ denotes the computing nodes in the network, and the set of edges $J := \{1, \ldots, M\}$ represents bidirectional communication between the nodes $(j, i) \in E$, only if the nodes i and j are directly connected. Each individual node j has access to a local set of observations (or datasets) given by $B_j := \{(x^1, y^1), (x^2, y^2), \ldots\}$, of predictor variables, to some function denoted by $y : \mathbb{R}^n \mapsto T$, this function maps an observation to a target domain (eg. $T = \mathbb{R}$, for regression, or $T = \{+1, -1\}$, for classification). Through the algorithm execution, each reliable node learns a function $\hat{y}_j(x) : x \mapsto T$ such that $\forall j, \hat{y}_j(x) \approx g(x)$, where $\hat{y}(x)$ describes a function that would be learned in a non-distributed environment.

Strategy: We propose a distributed average consensus subroutine, to promote fault tolerant learning. The subroutine supposes the indication of a parameter F *a priori* that sets the maximum number of expected fault nodes on the neighbourhood, the best $\hat{y}_j^k / |\hat{G}_j^k| - F + 1$ models are used to get an average model parameter matrix, the neighbourhood models are evaluated with a special subset of the validation set, this subset is composed of the top-n observations for which the local machine model showed the lowest cost, as well as the top-n higher cost, this selection of observations is made to prevent malicious agents from shifting the local model, eg. by sending to reliable nodes, models that predictions are very accurate in some specific cases, while still degrading overall cost.

Tardigrade - Byzantine Fault Tolerance: Each node optimizes its own model's parameter matrix $\hat{y}_j$ over the observations in the local dataset B_j, and evaluates the local model performance on a validation subset. The resulting parameter matrix is sent to all the nodes in the neighbourhood, the *Tardigrade* routine proceeds to grade received parameter matrices, accordingly to their performance on a special subset of constant size, the $\hat{y}_j^k / |\hat{G}_j^k| - F + 1$ best models are assumed to come from reliable nodes, the new local model parameter matrix $\hat{y}_j$ is calculated by the average of those parameter models received from local neighbourhood and possibly its own previous model. Algorithm 1 describes this process.

Algorithm 1. – Tardigrade

C mini-batch size;
F number of expected byzantine nodes in the neighbourhood;
B_j^k training examples for model validation;

procedure Tardigrade(k)
1: **for** $index < C$ **do**
2:   Gets a random example from B_j
3:   Updates parameters of the model $\hat{y}_j^k$ to minimize regression error with ADAGRAD.
4:   Evaluates if the current example is eligible to the B_j^k subset – If so, removes one example of B_j^k and adds the current example.
5: **end for**
6: Sends the current model matrix $\hat{y}_j^k$ to the neighbour nodes.
7: **for** index ¡ $|\hat{G}_j^k|$ **do** {Iterates over the set of its own model and models received from the immediate neighbourhood}
8:   **for** index ¡ $|B_j^k|$ **do** {Iters over the validation example cases}
9:     Gets one random case from B_j^k
10:     Qualifies the current model $\hat{g}_j^k$ parameter matrix with a cost function.
11:   **end for**
12: **end for**
13: $SelectedG$ = gets the best $|\hat{G}_j^k| - F$ model estimations in terms of cost.
14: $\hat{y}_j^k = \text{Sum}(\text{SelectedG}) + \hat{y}_j^k / |\hat{G}_j^k| - F + 1$ Gets the average parameter model, discarding the F lowest performing neighbour models.

---

5   Evaluation

In this section we describe our experimental settings, and analyze our empirical results running RDFM.

5.1   Data Preprocessing

To evaluate our work we use the MovieLens1M dataset [5], which is a common benchmark for recommender systems, and has been studied many times, it consists of a set of descriptive variables about items (movies) to be recommended to users, as well as variables about the users who had any interaction with those items. On our experiments we choose to use a subset of the dataset predictive variables, which were the movies, genres, year of release, users including its age and occupation, as well the rating they gave to each movie, which is the target variable or the one we intend to predict. For the MovieLens1M dataset is mostly composed of categorical variables, we opted to encode the data using the *One-Hot-Encoding*. In this encoding, each categorical variable level is treated as one independent factor, and is represented by one single column in the observation matrix, in this column the predictive variable has only two levels: 0 which represents the absence of given factor, and 1 which means the presence of given factor (eg. identifies if the current observation belongs to the "comedy" genre). *One-hot-encoding* of variables may reduce dataset overall variance.

5.2 Experiments

The experiments were run on an Intel Teska K-80 machine, with 61 GB of RAM, 12 GB of hard-disk storage, with Ubuntu Operational System, hosted by a cloud computing service, the parameters of the Adagrad algorithm were kept constant during the experiment, both the *learning rate* and *regularization* were $1e - 05$, $F = 2$ was assumed to be the max number of fault nodes on the neighbourhood. At the beginning of every experiment, the preprocessed version of the MovieLens1M dataset was randomly split between six simulated machines, each machine counts exactly the same number of observations, and the observations where further split in one-hundred learning turns. Once an observation was assigned to a machine, no other machine was able to access it. At every turn 70% of the observations were used for training, and 30% were used in model validation. When training was complete at every turn, the models learnt were used to predict the ratings in the validation dataset, then their Random Mean Squared Error (RMSE) were collected, the *Tardigrade* subroutine was run before the next learning turn.

The learning environment simulated three different types of failures:

- **Hardware failures:** Also known as a "crash failure", a computing node (machine) hardware fatally ceases to work. In this algorithm architecture this means that the system as a whole, loses access to the exclusive data observations in that machine and its model optimising capabilities.
- **Arbitrary failures:** When a computing goes through a failure of arbitrary nature, it will behave in unexpected and incorrect ways, not intended on the system design. This was simulated by making the affected node to send random model parameter matrices to its neighbourhood.
- **Malicious failures:** Those failures are caused by malicious agents, who actively seek to disrupt a system's functionality, such a malicious agent may corrupt data or change the system functionality. We simulated a malicious agent who corrupts data, by inverting or changing the values of the predictor variables, but which maintains the target variable unchanged (rating to a movie, by an user). Effectively making the stochastic gradient descent optimisation to minimise error in an incorrect direction.

To test our algorithm functionality, we made eleven different scenarios, featuring learning with and without fault tolerance (simple averaging parameter matrices), Table 1. enumerates those cases, and shows the mean RMSE for the reliable nodes through all turns.

The experiments verified the learning algorithm convergence, and evidenced the mean RMSE of the reliable nodes at every iteration was not compatible with a normal distribution, as seen in Fig. 1.

Table 1. Experiments with reliable and fault nodes.

#	Reliable	Byzantine	Crash	Malicious	Mean RMSE (reliable nodes)	Tardigrade
1	6	0	0	0	0.5496109	No
2	4	2	0	0	0.8385106	No
3	4	0	2	0	0.5487853	No
4	4	0	0	2	0.8637815	No
5	6	0	0	0	0.5480453	Yes
6	4	2	0	0	0.5489279	Yes
7	4	0	2	0	0.5475024	Yes
8	4	0	0	2	0.5479778	Yes
9	2	4	0	0	0.8464018	Yes
10	2	0	4	0	0.5540041	Yes
11	2	0	0	4	0.8647291	Yes

Plot of experimental results

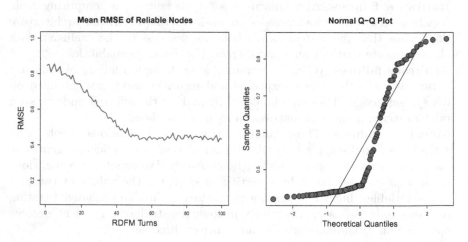

Fig. 1. Convergence of the nodes under RDFM, and RMSE non-normality evidence

To test our hypothesis we choose the Wilcoxon paired test for difference of means. Wilcoxon tests are non-parametric, and work for variables not normally distributed, the observations were not independent as RMSE will lower till convergence, so we used paired observations to verify if there is any difference between treatments. We tested seven statistical hypothesis as seen on Table 2 to explore our algorithm limitations and capabilities, and best understand how it is affected by failures.

Table 2. Statistical tests

#	Null Hypothesis	Alternative Hypothesis	p-value	Region of Rejection	Rejects H_0 (at p=0.01)
1	H_0:There are no difference in mean RMSE between RDFM and model averaging,with no fault nodes.	H_1:There are differences in mean RMSE between RDFM and parameter averaging, with no fault nodes.	0.4181	Two-sides	No
2	H_0:RDFM is not superior in terms of mean RMSE than parameter averaging, with $2F$ reliable nodes, and $F = 2$ byzantine nodes.	H_1: RDFM is superior in terms of mean RMSE than parameter averaging, with $2F$ realiable nodes and $F = 2$ byzantine nodes.	2.2e-16	Right-side	Yes
3	H_0:RDFM is not superior in terms of mean RMSE than parameter averaging, with $2F$ reliable nodes, and $F = 2$ nodes with crash failures.	H_1: RDFM is superior in terms of mean RMSE than parameter averaging, with $2F$ realiable nodes and $F = 2$ crash failures.	0.2399	Right-side	No
4	H_0:RDFM is not superior in terms of mean RMSE than parameter averaging, with $2F$ reliable nodes, and $F = 2$ malicious nodes.	H_1: RDFM is superior in terms of mean RMSE than parameter averaging, with $2F$ realiable nodes and $F = 2$ malicious nodes.	2.2e-16	Right-side	Yes
5	H_0:RDFM is not superior in terms of mean RMSE than parameter averaging, with $1/2F$ reliable nodes, and $F = 4$ byzantine nodes.	H_1: RDFM is superior in terms of mean RMSE than parameter averaging, with $1/2F$ realiable nodes and $F = 4$ byzantine nodes.	0.6037	Right-side	No
6	H_0:RDFM is not superior in terms of mean RMSE than parameter averaging, with $1/2F$ reliable nodes, and $F = 4$ nodes with crash failures.	H_1: RDFM is superior in terms of mean RMSE than parameter averaging, with $1/2F$ realiable nodes and $F = 4$ crash failures.	0.9988	Right-side	No
7	H_0:RDFM is not superior in terms of mean RMSE than parameter averaging, with $1/2F$ reliable nodes, and $F = 4$ malicious nodes.	H_1: RDFM is superior in terms of mean RMSE than parameter averaging, with $1/2F$ realiable nodes and $F = 4$ malicious nodes.	0.5251	Right-side	No

Our results confirm that the fault-tolerance subroutine does not affect convergence when all nodes on the neighbourhood are in a correct state. The statistical tests show that RDFM is superior to parameter model averaging while dealing with malicious, or arbitrary faults with a minimum of $2F$ reliable nodes, while non-fault tolerant alternatives can be disrupted by a single arbitrary failure. Since its a consensus algorithm, RDFM performance will quickly degrade when it loses majority. RDFM convergence under crash failures is not superior to parameter averaging, in both treatments convergence was reached until enough training data was lost due crash failures. In practical settings this kind of failure is expected to be rare.

6 Conclusion

In this paper, we propose a byzantine fault tolerant algorithm for distributed learning with Factorization Machines called RDFM. Our fault tolerant subroutine Tardigrade is based on distributed average consensus. The proposed algorithm is able to learn and converge with $2F$ fault nodes, shows very competitive RMSE metrics and is easy to implement and adapt. Paired Wilcoxon tests confirms and measure RDFM efficacy under the presence of arbitrary and malicious nodes, crash failures, while its architecture avoids single points of failure. Future works may exploit dataset variance between nodes, to better withstand crash failures. The code used in this work is available online [2].

References

1. Blanchard, P., Guerraoui, R., Stainer, J., et al.: Machine learning with adversaries: Byzantine tolerant gradient descent. In: Advances in Neural Information Processing Systems. pp. 119–129 (2017)
2. Da Silva, A.R.: Rdfm - resilient distributed factorization machines. https://github.com/andreblumenau/RDFM (2018)
3. Duchi, J., Hazan, E., Singer, Y.: Adaptive subgradient methods for online learning and stochastic optimization. Journal of Machine Learning Research 12(Jul), 2121–2159 (2011)
4. Flouri, K., Beferull-Lozano, B., Tsakalides, P.: Distributed consensus algorithms for svm training in wireless sensor networks. In: Signal Processing Conference, 2008 16th European. pp. 1–5. IEEE (2008)
5. Harper, F.M., Konstan, J.A.: The movielens datasets: History and context. Acm transactions on interactive intelligent systems (tiis) 5(4), 19 (2016)
6. Knoll, J., Stübinger, J., Grottke, M.: Exploiting social media with higher-order factorization machines: Statistical arbitrage on high-frequency data of the s&p 500. Tech. rep., FAU Discussion Papers in Economics (2017)
7. Lamport, L., Shostak, R., Pease, M.: The Byzantine Generals Problem. ACM Transactions on Programming Languages and Systems 4(3), 382–401 (1982)
8. Li, M., Liu, Z., Smola, A.J., Wang, Y.X.: Difacto: Distributed factorization machines. In: Proceedings of the Ninth ACM International Conference on Web Search and Data Mining. pp. 377–386. ACM (2016)
9. Prillo, S.: An elementary view on factorization machines. In: Proceedings of the Eleventh ACM Conference on Recommender Systems. pp. 179–183. ACM (2017)
10. Qiang, R., Liang, F., Yang, J.: Exploiting ranking factorization machines for microblog retrieval. In: Proceedings of the 22nd ACM international conference on Conference on information & knowledge management. pp. 1783–1788. ACM (2013)
11. Rendle, S.: Factorization machines. In: Data Mining (ICDM), 2010 IEEE 10th International Conference on. pp. 995–1000. IEEE (2010)
12. Rendle, S.: Social network and click-through prediction with factorization machines. In: KDD-Cup Workshop (2012)
13. Thai-Nghe, N., Drumond, L., Horváth, T., Schmidt-Thieme, L.: Using factorization machines for student modeling
14. Xiao, L., Boyd, S., Kim, S.J.: Distributed average consensus with least-mean-square deviation. Journal of parallel and distributed computing 67(1), 33–46 (2007)
15. Yamada, M., Lian, W., Goyal, A., Chen, J., Wimalawarne, K., Khan, S.A., Kaski, S., Mamitsuka, H., Chang, Y.: Convex factorization machine for toxicogenomics prediction. In: Proceedings of the 23rd ACM SIGKDD International Conference on Knowledge Discovery and Data Mining. pp. 1215–1224. ACM (2017)
16. Yang, Z., Bajwa, W.U.: Rd-svm: A resilient distributed support vector machine. In: ICASSP. pp. 2444–2448 (2016)

How Implicit Negative Evidence Improve Weighted Context-Free Grammar Induction

Olgierd Unold[(✉)] and Mateusz Gabor

Department of Computer Engineering,
Wrocław University of Science and Technology,
Wyb. Wyspiańskiego 27, 50-370 Wrocław, Poland
olgierd.unold@pwr.edu.pl

Abstract. Probabilistic context-free grammars (PCFGs) or in general a
weighted context-free grammars (WCFGs) are widely used in many areas
of syntactic pattern matching, especially in statistical natural language
parsing or biological modeling. For a given a fixed set of context–free
grammar rules, probabilities of its rules can be estimated by using the
Inside-Outside algorithm (IO), which is a special case of an expectation-
maximization method. The IO algorithm implies only positive examples
in the data given. In this paper a modified IO algorithm to estimate probabilistic parameters over implicit positive and also negative evidence is
proposed. We demonstrate that a Contrastive Estimation based method
outperforms a standard IO algorithm in terms of Precision, without any
loss of Recall.

Keywords: Grammatical inference · Weighted grammar ·
Probabilistic grammar · Implicit negative evidence ·
Contrastive Estimation

1 Introduction

Weighted or probabilistic context-free grammars (WCFGs or PCFGs) are
applied successfully to natural language (NL) and biological sequences modeling
from the early 90s [19]. Some, but not all, attempts in both areas are listed in
[6,15]. Moreover, it has been proved that weighted and probabilistic context-free
grammars are equally expressive [22].

Given a task, for example, biological or NL sequences to be modeled, the
question then arises how to induce PCFG from data given. The task of learning
PCFGs from data consists of two subproblems: determining a discrete structure
of the target grammar and estimating probabilistic parameters in the grammar.
Given the fixed topology of the grammar, the Inside-Outside algorithm [3,13] is
the standard method used to estimate the probabilistic parameters of a PCFG.
This procedure is an expectation-maximization (EM [5]) method for obtaining
the maximum likelihood of the grammar's parameters. However, it requires the

© Springer Nature Switzerland AG 2019
L. Rutkowski et al. (Eds.): ICAISC 2019, LNAI 11509, pp. 595–606, 2019.
https://doi.org/10.1007/978-3-030-20915-5_53

grammar to be in Chomsky normal form, and it accepts only positive examples in the learning data. Note that in 1969 Horning proved [11] that for effective PCFG induction no negative evidence are obligatory. Using only positive data in learning PCFG has one significant disadvantage of inducing grammars which are not specific for a given language, i.e. not able to distinguish negative examples.

To overcome that problem we propose a novelty modified Inside-Outside algorithm to estimate probabilistic (weighted) parameters over implicit positive and negative evidence in learning data. We employ the concept of Contrastive Estimation (CE) [20], a method that provides a way to use implicit negative evidence. In contrast to the original proposal, the modified IO algorithm has been applied to (a) generative language model, (b) for parsing task. Moreover, the concept of a cost function in CE was implemented.

The rest of this paper is organized as follows. Section 2 introduces some related works, and some significant concepts and definitions are described in Sect. 3. Then, our introduced algorithms are expounded in Sect. 4. After that, experimental protocol, training and test sets, metrics are given and in detail explained in Sect. 5, and the results are summarized in Sect. 6. At last, Sect. 7 gives some concluding remarks and points out further research directions.

2   Related Works

The Contrastive Estimation seems to be the only one method which improves learning of WCFGs with negative examples. The idea of CE is to generate a given positive sentence s, a large neighborhood $\mathcal{N}(s)$ of ungrammatical sentences as negative evidence, by perturbing s with certain operations. Note that EM can be seen as a specific case of CE, where the neighborhood $\mathcal{N}(s)$ is the entire set of learned sentences. It should be noted that instead of the PCFG, CE uses weighted context–free grammar. A complete description of the Contrastive Estimation approach are to be found in [20–22].

In [21] CE was used in a log-linear model on the task of inducing dependency grammars to match linguistic annotations over unlabeled data. In [20] the efficiency of this method was proved for part-of-speech (POS) tagging. Gimpel with co-author enriched this method with cost-augmented function [8] and tested the method in POS induction. Te method has found applications in morphological segmentation [17], bilingual part-of-speech induction [4], and machine translation [27].

Recently, Dyrka et al. used CE to estimate PCFG parameters for grammatical modeling of proteins structures [7].

3   Learning Probabilistic Context–Free Grammars

A Probabilistic Context Free Grammar (PCFG) G consists of [10]:

- a Context–Free Grammar CFG $(\mathcal{V}, \mathcal{T}, \mathcal{R}, \mathcal{S})$ with no useless productions, where
  - $\mathcal{V}$, a finite set of non-terminals disjoint from $\mathcal{T}$,
  - $\mathcal{T}$, a finite set of terminals,
  - $\mathcal{R}$, a finite set of productions,
  - $\mathcal{S} \in \mathcal{V}$ is called the start symbol,

  and
- production probabilities $p(A \rightarrow \beta) = \mathrm{P}(\beta|A)$ for each $A \rightarrow \beta \in \mathcal{R}$, the conditional probability of an A expanding to β.

A production $A \rightarrow \beta$ is useless iff it is not used in any terminating derivation, i.e., there are no derivations of the form $S \Rightarrow^* \gamma A \delta \Rightarrow \gamma \beta \delta \Rightarrow^* w$ for any $\gamma, \delta \in (\mathcal{V} \cup \mathcal{T})^*$ and $w \in \mathcal{T}^*$.

If $r_1 \ldots r_n$ is a sequence of productions used to generate a tree ψ, then

$$\mathrm{P}_G(\psi) = p(r_1) \ldots p(r_n)$$
$$= \prod_{r \in \mathcal{R}} p(r)^{f_r(\psi)},$$

where $f_r(\psi)$ is the number of times r is used in deriving ψ.

$\sum_\psi \mathrm{P}_G(\psi) = 1$ if p satisfies suitable constraints.

3.1 Learning Structure

Gold proved in the middle 1960s one of the main results in language learning theory, that CFGs are not learnable from positive examples only [9]. However, Gold's theorem does not cover all kinds of CFGs, such as for example PCFGs and finite grammars [2,11].

Taking into account the kind of presentation and the type of information, methods of learning CFG's topology can be divided into informant-based and text-based methods, and supervised, unsupervised, and semi-supervised methods, respectively [6]. From several methods available we may mention here ADIOS [23], EMILE [1], Synapse [14], e-GRIDS [16], or GCS [24].

3.2 Learning Production Probabilities

Learning of PCFG is the problem not only of inducing a CFG structure, but also learning rule probabilities from the corpus. Typically, this problem is described as a search in a grammar space where the objective function is the likelihood of the data given the grammar (maximum likelihood estimation):

$$\hat{t}(W) = \arg \max_{t \in T(W)} p(t), \tag{1}$$

where:

- t - left-most derivation,

- W - sentence $(w_1 w_2 \ldots w_n)$,
- $\hat{t}(W)$ - the most likely left-most derivation for sentence W,
- $T(W)$ - set of left-most derivations for sentence W,
- $p(t)$ - probability of left-most derivation.

The Inside-Outside (IO) algorithm [3,13], which is an example of the expectation-maximization method, is the most used method to estimate the production probabilities of a PCFG.

First, we introduce some notation.

Probability of the Rule. This is the probability with which the rule appears in grammar:

- for nonterminal symbols:

$$\varphi(A \longrightarrow BC), \tag{2}$$

- for terminal symbols:

$$\varphi(A \longrightarrow a). \tag{3}$$

Probability of Deriving a Sentence.

$$P(W) = P(S \longrightarrow w_1 w_2 \ldots w_n) \tag{4}$$

Inside Probability. This is the probability of deriving a particular substring from the given sentence $w_i \ldots w_j$ from a given left-side symbol and is presented as:

$$\alpha_{ij}(A) = P(A \longrightarrow w_i \ldots w_j), \tag{5}$$

where A is any non-terminal symbol.

Outside Probability. This is the probability of deriving from the start symbol of the substring $w_i \ldots w_{i-1} A w_{j+1} \ldots w_n$ and is presented as:

$$\beta_{ij}(A) = P(S \longrightarrow w_1 \ldots w_{i-1} A w_{j+1} \ldots w_n). \tag{6}$$

Expected Counts in Sentence. This is the parameter that counts the occurrences of a given rule for a single sentence:

- for nonterminal symbols:

$$c_\varphi(A \longrightarrow BC, W) = \frac{\varphi(A \longrightarrow BC)}{P(W)} \sum_{1 \leq i \leq j \leq k \leq n} \beta_{ik}(A)\alpha_{ij}(B)\alpha_{j+1,k}(C), \tag{7}$$

- for terminal symbols:

$$c_\varphi(A \longrightarrow w, W) = \frac{\varphi(A \longrightarrow w)}{P(W)} \sum_{i \leq 1} \beta_{ii}(A). \tag{8}$$

Total Expected Counts for the Rule in the Corpus. This means the sum of rule counts in the whole corpus:

$$count(A \longrightarrow \alpha) = \sum_{i=1}^{n} c_{\varphi}(A \longrightarrow \alpha, W_i), \tag{9}$$

where $count(A \longrightarrow \alpha)$ means any terminal or non-terminal rule and W_i subsequent sentences in the corpus.

New Probability of the Rule. It is presented as:

$$\varphi'(A \longrightarrow \alpha) = \frac{count(A \longrightarrow \alpha)}{\sum_{\lambda} count(A \longrightarrow \lambda)}, \tag{10}$$

where $count(A \longrightarrow \lambda)$ is as rule with the same left-hand symbol.

The Inside-Outside algorithm consists of the following steps. In the first step (expectation) some random parameters φ are chosen and all of the counts $count(A \longrightarrow \alpha)$ are set to zero. Next, for every sentence W_i in training corpus the Inside probabilities α and the Outside probabilities β are computed. Then the expected number of times that each rule $A \longrightarrow \alpha$ is used in generating sentence W_i is calculated ($c_{\varphi}(A \longrightarrow \alpha, W_i)$). For each rule $A \longrightarrow \alpha$ the number $c_{\varphi}(A \longrightarrow \alpha, W_i)$ is added to the total count $count(A \longrightarrow \alpha)$ and then proceed to the next sentence. After processing each sentence in this way the parameters are re-estimated to obtain new probability of the rule (maximization). Then, the process is repeated and $\varphi = \varphi'$.

4   Improving Learning with Implicit Negative Evidence

Note that Inside-Outside algorithm, or generally speaking EM-style likelihood-based approach, implies only positive examples in a corpus. Such an approach attempts to move the probability mass to a set of production rules supported by the (positive) sentences observed but without identifying the rules from which the probability mass should be moved. At the same time, research in language acquisition in children [18] showed that indirect negative evidence can improve the learning. We can extend this analogy to EM-style approach by using implicit negative evidence, which could help the EM to move from the rules covering the negative evidence to the rules used by the positive examples. Contrastive Estimation introduced by Smith and Eisner [20] exploits this idea of implicit negative evidence available in a sentence for the grammar induction task.

4.1   Contrastive Estimation

The main idea of CE is to move probability mass from the neighborhood of an observed sentence $\mathcal{N}(s)$ to s itself, where the neighborhood $\mathcal{N}(s)$ contains examples that are perturbations of s. Smith and Eisner tested different neighborhoods of sequences, all in the frame of log-linear models.

We explore the idea of CE using randomly generated sentences not belonging to the target language in the task of learning production weights. Moreover, this approach has been applied in the generative model.

We tested the neighborhood $\mathcal{N}(s)$ called Length10, in which for every positive sentence in a corpus, 10 random negative sentences of exactly the same length as the positive sentence have been taken.

In a proposed approach, called IOCE (Inside–Outside CE), we introduce the CE factor of the rule [25]:

$$\psi_{CE}(A \longrightarrow \alpha) = \frac{count(A \longrightarrow \alpha)}{count(A \longrightarrow \alpha) + count_{ng}(A \longrightarrow \alpha)}, \tag{11}$$

where: $count_{ng}(A \longrightarrow \alpha)$–the estimated counts that a particular rule is used in a neighborhood.

The probability of the rule is calculated as follows:

$$\varphi'(A \longrightarrow \alpha) = \frac{count(A \longrightarrow \alpha)}{\sum_{\beta} count(A \longrightarrow \beta)} \cdot \psi_{CE}(A \longrightarrow \alpha). \tag{12}$$

4.2 Cost-Augmented Contrastive Estimation

In 2014 CE was extended to Cost-augmented CE (CCE) by adding specialized cost functions (observation and output) that penalize some part of the structured input/output pair [8]. The new approach was tested over POS induction problem.

In our approach, called IOCE COST, we applied an idea of a cost function to support weaker rules. Among the rules with the same left-hand symbol, the rules with the smaller expected counts should have smaller cost π. The cost function is calculated as follows:

$$\pi(A \longrightarrow \alpha) = \frac{count(A \longrightarrow \alpha)}{\max(count(A \longrightarrow \lambda))}, \tag{13}$$

where: $\max(count(A \longrightarrow \lambda))$–the biggest estimated counts from all rules with the same left-hand symbol.

The probability of the rule is calculated as follows:

$$\varphi'(A \longrightarrow \alpha) = \frac{count(A \longrightarrow \alpha) - \pi(A \longrightarrow \alpha)}{\sum_{\lambda} count(A \longrightarrow \lambda) + \pi(A \longrightarrow \alpha)} \cdot \psi_{CE}(A \longrightarrow \alpha). \tag{14}$$

5 Experiments

We compare IO with CE (with the neighborhood called Length10) and Cost-augmented CE (with the cost function (9)) on learning parameters of weighted grammar in a framework of the generative model. The experiments were carried out according to the experimental protocol described in Algorithm 1, using pyGCS library [26] dedicated to the stochastic version of Grammar-based Classifier System [24]. The standard IO was trained only on positive examples.

Algorithm 1. Experiment protocol

```
1: Load CFG, training set and test set
2: Assign random probabilities to grammar rules
3: For all rules set count(A ⟶ α) = 0
4: Set the stochastic procedure type                    ▷ IO, IOCE, IOCE COST
5: Set the number of iterations
6:
7: for i ← 1 to iterations do
8:     Run CKY+ algorithm with stochastic procedure on the training set
9:     Run CKY+ algorithm without stochastic procedure on the test set
10:    Calculate the metrics
11: end for
12:
13: return PCFG and results                    ▷ The induced PCFG/WCFG and metrics
```

Table 1. Training sets metrics

Set	Size	Positive sentences	Negative sentences	Max. length of sentence
ab	57	34	23	10
anbn	126	5	121	11
bra1	39	17	32	10
pal2	99	64	35	10

Table 2. Test sets metrics

Set	Size	Positive sentences	Negative sentences	Max. length of sentence
ab	102	51	51	15
anbn	100	2	98	15
bra1	102	51	51	15
pal2	102	51	51	15

The experiment were performed over not-overlapping training and test sets, containing both positive and negative sentences taken from four context–free languages [12], ie. **ab** - the language of all strings consisting of equal numbers of as and bs, **anbn** - the language $a^n b^n$, **bra1** - the language of balanced brackets, and **pal2** - palindromes over $\{a, b, c\}$. Metrics of training and test sets are given in Tables 1 and 2, respectively.

To evaluate the quality classification of the compared methods, we use the classification results stored in a confusion matrix. The following four scores were defined as tp, fp, fn, and tn, representing the numbers of true positives (correctly recognized positive sentences), false positives (negatives recognized as positives), false negatives (positives recognized as negatives), and true negatives (correctly recognized negatives), respectively. Based on the values stored in the confusion matrix, we calculate the widely used Precision, Recall (Sensitivity), and combined metric F1-score.

Precision is defined as

$$P = tp/(tp + fp),$$

Recall (Sensitivity) as

$$R = tp/(tp + fn),$$

F1 as the harmonic mean of Precision and Sensitivity

$$F1 = 2 \cdot (P \cdot R/(P + R)).$$

To reduce bias in evaluating the learning, we calculate the average of the classification metrics of the 10 independent runs over training and test sets. The inner loop of expectation-maximization steps were repeated 150 times, the threshold of accepting the sentence as a positive was set to 0.01.

6   Results

Table 3 and Figs. 1, 2, 3, 4 summarize the performance of the three compared methods used to learn weights of WCFG: the standard Inside–Outside method (IO), and two methods make use of implicit negative evidence: Contrastive Estimation (IOCE), and Contrastive Estimation with Length10 cost (IOCE COST).

Note that the IOCE method with Length10 neighborhood gained the highest Precision among tested methods and languages, and thanks to that also the highest F1 metric. Cost-augmented CE approach achieved similar results to the standard Inside-Outside method. We believe that the results obtained by IOCE COST can be improved by introducing more task-dedicated cost functions.

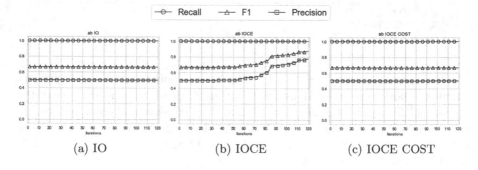

(a) IO   (b) IOCE   (c) IOCE COST

Fig. 1. Induction of ab language

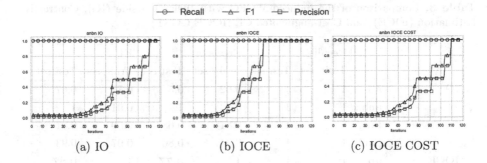

(a) IO   (b) IOCE   (c) IOCE COST

Fig. 2. Induction of anbn language

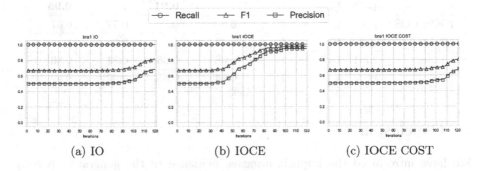

(a) IO   (b) IOCE   (c) IOCE COST

Fig. 3. Induction of bra1 language

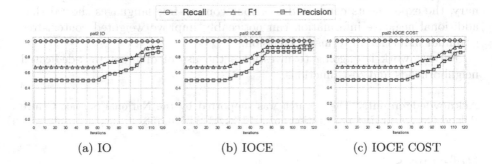

(a) IO   (b) IOCE   (c) IOCE COST

Fig. 4. Induction of pal2 language

Table 3. Comparison of the induced WCFG with Inside-Outside (IO), Contrastive Estimation (IOCE), and Cost-augmented CE (IOCE COST)

		Recall		Precision		F1	
		Train set	Test set	Train set	Test set	Train set	Test set
IO	ab	1	1	0.62	0.5	0.77	0.67
	anbn	1	1	0.83	1	0.91	1
	bra1	1	1	0.81	0.68	0.89	0.81
	pal2	1	1	0.94	0.86	0.97	0.93
IOCE	ab	1	1	**1**	**0.77**	**1**	**0.87**
	anbn	1	1	**1**	**1**	**1**	**1**
	bra1	1	1	**1**	**0.94**	**1**	**0.97**
	pal2	1	1	**1**	**0.91**	**1**	**0.95**
IOCE COST	ab	1	1	0.62	0.5	0.77	0.67
	anbn	1	1	0.83	1	0.91	1
	bra1	1	1	0.68	0.66	0.81	0.80
	pal2	1	1	0.94	0.85	0.97	0.92

7 Conclusion

We have introduced the implicit negative evidence to the generative parsing model by modification of the standard Inside-Outside procedure. Implicit negative evidence has been applied in the frame of Contrastive Estimation and Cost-augmented CE. Though the results presented here seems to be preliminary, the experiments conducted over four context-free languages showed that additional negative information can noticeably improve weighted context-free grammar induction in terms of Precision.

Further work is ongoing to investigate the use of different task-dedicated neighborhoods and cost functions.

Acknowledgements. The research was supported by the National Science Centre Poland (NCN), project registration no. 2016/21/B/ST6/02158.

References

1. Adriaans, P., Vervoort, M.: The EMILE 4.1 grammar induction toolbox. In: Adriaans, P., Fernau, H., van Zaanen, M. (eds.) ICGI 2002. LNCS (LNAI), vol. 2484, pp. 293–295. Springer, Heidelberg (2002). https://doi.org/10.1007/3-540-45790-9_24
2. Adriaans, P.W.: Language learning from a categorial perspective. Ph.D. thesis, Universiteit van Amsterdam (1992)
3. Baker, J.K.: Trainable grammars for speech recognition. J. Acoust. Soc. Am. **65**(S1), S132 (1979)

4. Chen, D., Dyer, C., Cohen, S.B., Smith, N.A.: Unsupervised bilingual POS tagging with Markov random fields. In: Proceedings of the First Workshop on Unsupervised Learning in NLP, pp. 64–71. Association for Computational Linguistics (2011)
5. Dempster, A.P., Laird, N.M., Rubin, D.B.: Maximum likelihood from incomplete data via the EM algorithm. J. R. Stat. Soc. Ser. B (Methodol.) **39**(1), 1–38 (1977)
6. D'Ulizia, A., Ferri, F., Grifoni, P.: A survey of grammatical inference methods for natural language learning. Artif. Intell. Rev. **36**(1), 1–27 (2011)
7. Dyrka, W., Pyzik, M., Coste, F., Talibart, H.: Estimating probabilistic context-free grammars for proteins using contact map constraints. PeerJ **7**, e6559 (2019)
8. Gimpel, K., Bansal, M.: Weakly-supervised learning with cost-augmented contrastive estimation. In: Proceedings of the 2014 Conference on Empirical Methods in Natural Language Processing (EMNLP), pp. 1329–1341 (2014)
9. Gold, E.M., Corporation, T.R.: Language identification in the limit. Inf. Control **10**(5), 447–474 (1967)
10. Hopcroft, J.E.: Introduction to Automata Theory, Languages, and Computation. Pearson Education, Chennai (2008)
11. Horning, J.J.: A study of grammatical inference. Technical report, Department of Computer Science, Stanford University of California (1969)
12. Keller, B., Lutz, R.: Evolving stochastic context-free grammars from examples using a minimum description length principle. In: Workshop on Automatic Induction, Grammatical Inference and Language Acquisition (1997)
13. Lari, K., Young, S.J.: The estimation of stochastic context-free grammars using the inside-outside algorithm. Comput. Speech Lang. **4**(1), 35–56 (1990)
14. Nakamura, K.: Incremental learning of context free grammars by extended inductive CYK algorithm. In: Proceedings of the 2003 European Conference on Learning Context-Free Grammars, pp. 53–64. Ruder Boskovic Institute (2003)
15. Park, H.S., Galbadrakh, B., Kim, Y.M.: Recent progresses in the linguistic modeling of biological sequences based on formal language theory. Genomics Inform. **9**(1), 5–11 (2011)
16. Petasis, G., Paliouras, G., Karkaletsis, V., Halatsis, C., Spyropoulos, C.D.: e-GRIDS: computationally efficient gramatical inference from positive examples. Grammars **7**, 69–110 (2004)
17. Poon, H., Cherry, C., Toutanova, K.: Unsupervised morphological segmentation with log-linear models. In: Proceedings of Human Language Technologies: The 2009 Annual Conference of the North American Chapter of the Association for Computational Linguistics, pp. 209–217. Association for Computational Linguistics (2009)
18. Pullum, G.K., Scholz, B.C.: Empirical assessment of stimulus poverty arguments. Linguist. Rev. **18**(1–2), 9–50 (2002)
19. Sakakibara, Y., Brown, M., Hughey, R., Mian, I.S., Sjölander, K., Underwood, R.C., Haussler, D.: Stochastic context-free grammers for tRNA modeling. Nucleic Acids Res. **22**(23), 5112–5120 (1994)
20. Smith, N.A., Eisner, J.: Contrastive estimation: training log-linear models on unlabeled data. In: Proceedings of the 43rd Annual Meeting on Association for Computational Linguistics, pp. 354–362. Association for Computational Linguistics (2005)
21. Smith, N.A., Eisner, J.: Guiding unsupervised grammar induction using contrastive estimation. In: Proceedings of IJCAI Workshop on Grammatical Inference Applications, pp. 73–82 (2005)
22. Smith, N.A., Johnson, M.: Weighted and probabilistic context-free grammars are equally expressive. Comput. Linguist. **33**(4), 477–491 (2007)

23. Solan, Z., Horn, D., Ruppin, E., Edelman, S.: Unsupervised learning of natural languages. Proc. Nat. Acad. Sci. **102**(33), 11629–11634 (2005)
24. Unold, O.: Grammar-based classifier system: a universal tool for grammatical inference. WSEAS Trans. Comput. **7**(10), 1584–1593 (2008)
25. Unold, O., Rorbach, G.: How implicit negative evidence improve probabilistic grammar induction. In: Extended Abstracts of ICGI2018 (2018). http://icgi2018.pwr.edu.pl/public/ex-abstracts/rorbach18.pdf
26. Unold, O., Rorbach, G., Fislak, M., Czarnecki, M., Cieszko, D.: pyGCS (2018). https://github.com/ounold/pyGCS
27. Xiao, X., Liu, Y., Liu, Q., Lin, S.: Fast generation of translation forest for large-scale SMT discriminative training. In: Proceedings of the Conference on Empirical Methods in Natural Language Processing, pp. 880–888. Association for Computational Linguistics (2011)

Agent Systems, Robotics and Control

Tasks Allocation for Rescue Robotics: A Replicator Dynamics Approach

Sindy Amaya$^{(\boxtimes)}$ and Armando Mateus$^{(\boxtimes)}$

Santo Tomás University, Bogotá, Colombia
{sindyamaya,armandomateus}@usantotomas.edu.co

Abstract. Tasks allocation on homogeneous rescue robots has been an important research field in recent years due to the advance in both robotics and artificial intelligence. Nevertheless, catastrophic scenarios still represent a hard challenge because of the complexity and uncertainty of their characteristics and parameters which produce highly heterogeneous tasks as a result of the different nature of problems they are intended for. We propose hereby an approach to the catastrophic condition exposed above by solving the replicator dynamics equation to reduce the effects of uncertainty. A standard metric based on tasks progress is defined and the main elements of game theory like payoff matrix and allocation ratios are computed in order to obtain the number of robots assigned to each task. Finally, software was built for simulation; by using this software some scenarios were defined and simulations were run to compare and validate our approach.

Keywords: Rescue robotics · Tasks allocation · Game theory · Replicator dynamics equation

1 Introduction

The use of robots in catastrophic scenarios is one of the main research fields in robotics, due to both the need to support people after a disaster and scientific and technical opportunities therein. Previous works on rescue robotics have been developed from specific disciplinary approaches; however, after a catastrophic event it is necessary to perform several tasks such as mapping, navigation, structural health inspection (SHI), life supporting, etc. All these tasks are heterogeneous as a result of the objectives they aim, the operations they perform and the methodology established for their metrics. Game theory is a meta-heuristic method commonly used for negotiation and tasks allocation in multi - agent systems providing optimal solutions for a wide range of disciplines. Nevertheless, there are two great challenges when facing rescue tasks allocation with game theory: the intrinsic uncertainty in the tasks (objectives, resources, size, etc.) and the definition of an appropriate payoff function to compute with. In

© Springer Nature Switzerland AG 2019
L. Rutkowski et al. (Eds.): ICAISC 2019, LNAI 11509, pp. 609–621, 2019.
https://doi.org/10.1007/978-3-030-20915-5_54

Table 1. Summary of rescue tasks for robotics [13], their objective and the main metric proposed in this work.

Task	Objective	Main metrics
Search	Search victims	Number of found victims
Mapping	Map of the disaster zone	Covered area
Rubble removal	Clean and secure	Clean area
Structural inspection	Determine safe structures	Number of structures
In situ medical assessment	First aid assistance	Number of supported victims
Extraction and evacuation	Telemedicine	Number of transported victims
Mobile repeater	Enlarge communications coverage	Coverage area
Serving as a surrogate	Support human tasks	Number of functions
Adaptively shoring	Secure structures	Number of structures
Providing logistics support	Automation in the supply chain	Number of provisions

Sect. 2, a summary and description of the main tasks involved in rescue robotics is shown with a proposed method for normalization based on the type and size of the catastrophic event. In Sect. 3 we summarize the game theory and replicator dynamics fundamentals necessary for our formulation of a solution. In Sect. 4 we propose the reward model along with necessary parameters taking into account Nash equilibria considerations. Section 5 presents simulations and results which validate our proposal. Finally, we discuss conclusions and future work in Sect. 6.

2   Normalization of Heterogeneous Tasks in Rescue Robotics

There exist 10 rescue tasks which can be assigned to robots as presented in [13]; these tasks can be linked to one or more of the 7 rescue phases also presented in the referred document. In order to allocate rescue tasks in teams of robots, it is necessary to face the problem of having heterogeneity in tasks: objectives, variables, processes, communication requirements, autonomy and control; these are some functions and characteristics which differ among rescue tasks for robots. Table 1 summarizes tasks and the main metric variable for each; note that metrics are different in the way they are calculated and the input parameters they require.

2.1   Brief Description of Robotic Rescue Tasks

Tasks in Table 1 include several sub - tasks, e.g., "acting as a mobile repeater" involves the setup tasks, positioning according to available maps and the optimization of power transmission [18]. Reconnaissance and mapping task is one of the most addressed subjects in researching: in [3], coordination of homogeneous robots is achieved by defining "frontier cells" and "exploredness cells" in an optimization problem stated to minimize the exploration time; on the contrary [9] proposes distributed autonomous coordination and centralized semi - autonomous coordination for exploration. [1,6] also work on exploratory tasks

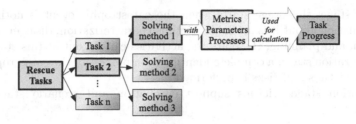

Fig. 1. Perspective of rescue tasks and their characteristics used in this work for tasks progress calculation.

with different approaches. In general, simultaneous localization and mapping (SLAM) techniques are the most adopted method for exploratory tasks.

SHI, structure shoring and rubble removal are tasks involving robotics engineering and civil engineering [5,7,10]. "Logistic support" and "serving as surrogate" tasks are not directly seen as a topic in rescue robotics but they are in service robotics as presented in [16], [8] and [12]. In Fig. 1 a relation chart shows the perspective used in this work: for task 2 of the n rescue tasks, three methods can be used, each one with particular metrics, parameters and processes (used for task progress calculation). For instance, search victims (task 1) could be done by image processing (solving method 1), speech recognition (solving method 2) or a mixed method of both (solving method 3); each method requires specific parameters as input (image, audio, etc) and produces results (probability of a person in a photo, text, etc) having a number of victims as a target. On the contrary, mapping (task) may require LIDAR maps as input and a 3d map as output.

2.2   Normalization of Tasks Metrics

We point out that a set of methods for each rescue task can be selected for carrying it out. Every method, due to the working principle, has its own requirements, algorithms and techniques which lead to specific metrics. This is a problem for tasks allocation because of the need for comparison of tasks which are defined in different dimensions. To deal with the problem above described we propose to normalize metrics, i.e., to assess the performance of the set of robots assigned to a task in a scale [0, 1] insofar as the advance in execution and the progress of the task is performed. The response in catastrophic scenarios is a race against time, then the performance metric should be an appropriate (and linear as far as possible) indicator of completeness per time. As indicated in [11,13] after a disaster event there is a general pattern in which rescue tasks are executed. This issue introduces an additional consideration: to prioritize. We gather tasks in three stages (in the beginning not directly linked to phases) and assign priorities for each group in a stage; note that stages are sequential as follows:

- Early stage: this stage starts when the catastrophic event is notified and information about it is available; victims characterization, disaster zone definition and planning, these are the activities carried out at this stage.
- Stabilization stage: a complete identification process of the catastrophic scenario, victims and risks is performed.
- Operation stage: victims support/evacuation and scenario stabilization tasks.

Length of the stages is directly linked to the scale and nature of the event then it is not possible to set a priori; this is the main reason to use a task progress metric.

3   Game Theory for Tasks Allocation

The evolutionary game theory studies the behavior of a population of agents that interact strategically and reevaluate their choices according to payoff opportunities [15]. By using this approach, a large number of applications have been developed in economics, social sciences, biology (where the evolutionary game theory was originated), engineering, control theory and computer science [2], [17] and [4]. Although different, these scenarios have several characteristics in common: first, they contain a large number of agents that can make decisions; second, each agent is small, that is, their choices have a low impact on the decisions of others and third, agents are anonymous, which means that the outcome of an agent depends on its own strategy and the distribution of the strategies of others. To model scenarios from the perspective of evolutionary game theory, two elements are necessary: first, to define the population game and the second one is the choice of a review protocol [14].

In population games, it must be defined at least one population of agents or players, which are grouped in a mass noted as $m \in \mathbb{R}^{+}$. Then, each individual of the population corresponds to a quantum of that mass. Agents can choose their actions to play from a finite set of available pure strategies denoted as S. In general, the strategies are listed by using natural numbers, i.e., a set with n available strategies, the set of strategies is given by $S = \{1, .., n\}$. Thus, all players have the same set of strategies.

During the game, each player selects a pure strategy from S. The population states are the result of the distribution of the m players mass among the available strategies. The state of the population is defined with the non-negative scalars $p_1, ..., p_n$, where p_i indicates the mass portion of players choosing the strategy $i \in S$. The vector $\mathbf{p} = [p_1, ..., p_n]$ denotes the state of the population. The set of possible population states, which corresponds to all the possible distributions of the agents between the strategies, this is given by the simplex in the Eq. (1):

$$\Delta = \left\{ \mathbf{p} \in \mathbb{R}^n_{\geq 0} : \sum_{i \in S} p_i = m \right\} \tag{1}$$

Individuals, who choose the i th strategy to play get a payment that depends on the state of the population. This payment is characterized by a payoff function $f_i : \Delta \rightarrow \mathbb{R}$. For a given population state $\mathbf{p}$, $f_i(\mathbf{p})$ determines the reward associated with the strategy $i \in S$. A population game is completely defined by the payment vector $\mathbf{f} : \Delta \rightarrow \mathbb{R}^n$, where $\mathbf{f}(\mathbf{p}) = [f_1(\mathbf{p}), ..., f_n(\mathbf{p})]$.

The average fitness represents the average payment obtained by the members of the population:

$$\bar{f}(p) = \frac{\sum_{i \in S} p_i f_i(\mathbf{p})}{m} \tag{2}$$

A population state $\mathbf{p}$ is a *Nash Equilibria*, if in each population no agent can improve their payment unilaterally by changing strategy.

Under a game theory approach, the problem of tasks allocation in a system of multiple robots can be seen as a strategic game, where the set of robots is considered as the population of agents and the set of tasks is the set of strategies, which has the game. The objective is to assign a portion of the population of agents to each one of the strategies so that some index of performance of the complete system can be minimized or maximized. The theory of evolutionary games is proposed to achieve an optimal plan of assignment of tasks for each robot.

3.1 Mean Dynamic and Revision Protocol

The function $\rho : \mathbb{R}^n \times \Delta \rightarrow \mathbb{R}_+^{n \times n}$ is known as the review protocol that describes the times and the result of the decisions made by the agents about how to behave in a repetitive strategic interaction. The scalar ρ_{ij} captures the switch from the i strategy to j strategy.

Mean Dynamics allows to obtain population dynamics that describe the evolution of behavior in each population, programmed with an specific *protocol of revision*. The Eq. (3), know as *Mean Dynamic*, is:

$$\dot{p}_i = \sum_{j \in S} p_j \rho_{ji} - p_i \sum_{i \in S} \rho_{ij} \tag{3}$$

The *Replicator Dynamic equation* (RD) can be deduced from the Eq. (3) and the Pairwise Proportional Imitation. Each agent imitates the strategy of an opponent previously selected, as long as the utility for that opponent is bigger than its own; this is done with a proportional probability to the difference of the utilities.

$$\dot{p}_i = p_i \left(f_i(p) - \bar{f}(p) \right) \tag{4}$$

4 Defining the Payoff Function

For using game theory here inside, the set of robots is represented as agents and the set tasks as strategies so our main concern is to find an optimal allocation of robots for each task to reduce uncertainty effects.

Choosing a payoff function to represent the payment for specific player's strategy is one of the difficult topics in game theory. Next, we will discuss the methodology put into practice in this work.

4.1   Classic Definition of Payoff Matrix

Classic game theory problems like rock - scissors - paper are solved by applying Nash Equilibria. These following steps define how to obtain the portion in which each strategy must be selected for agents on a infinite time-line of game repetitions (iterations).

1. Compute expected value for player i for each strategy j; expected value is calculated.
2. State and solve the $n+1$ linear system by applying Nash Equilibria (same expected value for every player).
3. Obtained results indicate the portion of choosing strategies apart from j for a number of game repetitions which ensures Nash Equilibria and optimal values.
4. To compute the portion of agents choosing strategy it is necessary to get the complement of the obtained value in step 2.

For a given payoff matrix $\mathbf{f}$ of n strategies, the optimal set of agents playing strategies is found by solving the $n + 1$ linear system produced by steps above. For

$$\mathbf{f} = \left\{ \begin{matrix} f_0^0 & f_1^0 & \cdots & f_n^0 \\ f_0^1 & f_1^1 & \cdots & f_n^1 \\ \vdots & \vdots & \ddots & \vdots \\ f_0^n & f_1^n & \cdots & f_n^n \end{matrix} \right\}$$

Where f_j^i represents the payoff for agent i playing strategy j. For a diagonal payment matrix, the linear system produced by applying Nash Equilibria leads to the optimal assignment $\mathbf{p}$ for each agent:

$$p_i^j = \frac{\frac{\prod_{k=1}^n f_k^k}{f_i^j}}{\sum_{i=1}^n \frac{\prod_{k=1}^n f_k^k}{f_i^j}} \tag{5}$$

The last expression is the basis for the development of the payoff function that is proposed below.

4.2   Proposal of Metrics to Evaluate Progress

As previously mentioned, we defined three metrics for task progress evaluation:

1. Advance percentage

$$a_i(\%) = \frac{N_i * T_s}{w_i} * 100 \tag{6}$$

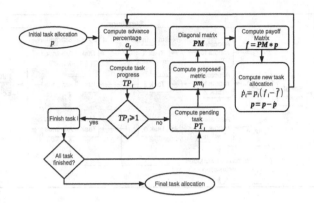

Fig. 2. Proposed flow chart for computing the allocation vector **p**

  a_i: Advance for task i
  N_i: Number of agents dedicated to task i
  T_s: Sample time
  w_i: Total robot hour of the task
2. Task pogress percentage

$$TP_i(\%) = TP_i + a_i(\%) \tag{7}$$

3. Pending task

$$PT_i(\%) = 1 - TP_i(\%) \tag{8}$$

Above metrics define a linear model of the tasks which in most cases is inaccurate. We propose as payoff function the diagonal matrix constructed with elements by computing Eq. (9), PM; this expression is based on Eq. (5). For each task there is an exact set of robots assigned to execute it; it is possible for that to be an empty set. On Figure 2, we depict the algorithm we used to compute the payoff function which is computed using the Eq. 10.

$$pm_i = \frac{\frac{\prod_{j=1}^{n} w_j}{w_i}}{\sum_{k=1}^{n} \frac{\prod_{j=1}^{n} w_j}{w_k}} * PT_i \tag{9}$$

$$\mathbf{f}(\mathbf{p}) = PM * \mathbf{p} \tag{10}$$

5 Simulations and Results

In order to validate the approach, a simulator software with structure as depicted in Fig. 3 was built. Two scenarios are presented here to validate the proposed approach. The first one is intended for validation under ideal conditions, i.e., no stochastic behavior and no modification on the workload. In contrast, the second scenario includes an stochastic behavior for the tasks progress represented by an

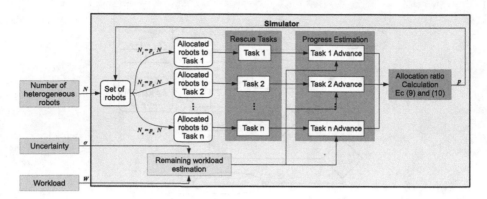

Fig. 3. Overall structure of the built simulator software.

additive random function v(t) (disturbance variable) modeled as a normal continuous probability distribution with parameters in Table 2. A modification on the workload is also programmed to take place at iteration 50; this modification reflects the availability of new information about tasks from that iteration.

For both, scenarios 1 and 2, the initial allocation ratio p[0] is set according to Table 2.

All scenarios are simulated with a sample time (T_s) of 1 h, an integer number of robots and allocated robots. A quantity of 100 homogeneous robots is set to be divided in the three tasks.

5.1   Scenario 1: Ideal Conditions

With the settings described above for scenario 1, the workload for tasks was defined as shown in Fig. 4 (left). After simulation was run, tasks progress, payoff function and robots allocation percentage were computed producing the results in Figs. 4 (right) and 6 (left and right).

On simulation, tasks were finished on iterations (hours) 68, 85 and 79. Note that, because in this work we define workload in robot-hours, the last iteration it_{last} for ideal conditions can be calculated as follows:

$$it_{last} = \frac{\sum w_i * T_s}{N} \tag{11}$$

For settings in Table 2 for scenario 1 $it_{last} = 85$.

Table 2. Parameters used for simulation (* only used for scenario 2).

Task	W (in robot hours)	W[50] (in robot hours)*	v(t)*	p[0]
0	800	1000	$N(\mu = 0, \sigma = 1)$	0,7
1	5300	500	$N(\mu = 0, \sigma = 1)$	0,1
2	2400	4000	$N(\mu = 0, \sigma = 1)$	0,2

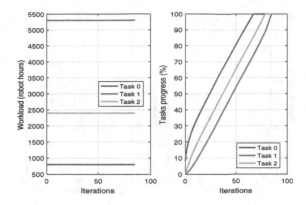

Fig. 4. Workload as income (left) and tasks progress as outcome (right).

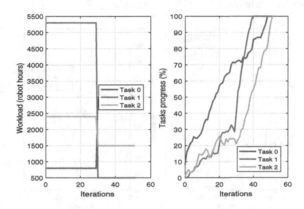

Fig. 5. Workload with change due to new information of tasks on iteration 50 (left) and tasks progress with stochastic behavior (right).

5.2 Scenario 2: Change on Workload and Stochastic

On iteration 50, due to new information about tasks workload, W is redefined as indicated in Table 2. In addition, a stochastic behavior (disturbance variable) is introduced in the model as described in Eq. 12.

$$a_i = \frac{N_i * T_s}{w_i} + v_i(t) \tag{12}$$

Figures 5 and 7 present the results of simulation for this scenario with a particular realization; tasks are finished on iterations 48, 40 and 51.

5.3 Results

From Figs. 4, 5, 6 and 7 it is possible to point out the following:

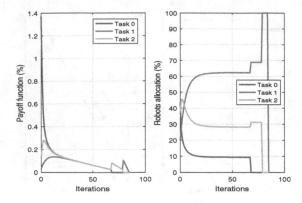

Fig. 6. Payoff computed for each task based on (left) and the obtained robot allocation percentage per tasks (right).

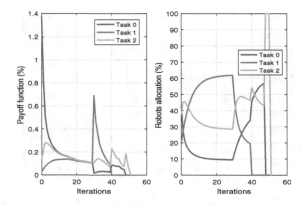

Fig. 7. Payoff computed for each task based on (left) and the obtained robot allocation percentage per tasks (right).

1. Payoff function of every task becomes the same as time goes by; this produces that tasks progress has the same relative speed for each task.
2. There is a lag in iterations for tasks which can be explained by the initial allocation p[0].
3. After all the payoff functions corresponding to tasks equals their values, they rapidly decrease to 0. This confirms conditions defined for Nash Equilibria and Replicator Dynamics ensuring the common variation in the payoff function.
4. Robots allocation goes from the initial p to the optimal. Note that after every tasks is finished all allocation must go to 0.
5. Stochastic behavior added to the task advance is not reflected in the task allocation, but in the payoff function. This is the desired result which holds the number of allocated robots independent of random advances.

6. In addition, the proposed approach is able to react to workload change by adjusting payoff functions and robots allocation ratios. This can be also observed by the change of Payoff function and robots allocation after a task is finished.

6 Conclusions

Tasks allocation in rescue robotics is characterized for the lack of solutions which integrate highly heterogeneous tasks. It is possible to divide a full set of tasks into phases according to the different times in which each task is required (related to the time from the catastrophic event occurrence). The use of advance and progress in task execution was proposed here as a common metric for tasks and the definition of workloads (necessary robot time to finish a task) as cost for every task. Other possible definitions can be done as well in future works adding uncertainty and new information availability.

We proposed a linear behavior for task progresses but real ones can be defined in other ways as exponential behaviors. Another topic to improve for the method here proposed is the inclusion of task - changing costs to represent the lost in time and energy produced when a robot is re-allocated for a different task; in this work we have supposed that robots can immediately stop to advance in a task and start to move on to another so the re-allocation cost is null.

We have taken advantage of the replicator dynamics equation to find the optimal allocation of homogeneous robots into sets of heterogeneous rescue tasks; we also obtained a reduction in the impact of uncertainty in the allocation. This method has proved to be flexible because it does not need a formal mathematical model but only available information. It is necessary the definition of a payoff function for which we propose here as a diagonal matrix, in which the payment for the portion robots dedicated to the execution of task i is a reciprocal function of the task progress.

It is objective of an additional work to test and propose other payoff definitions for non linear scenarios which are closer to real ones. We have proposed for this work a metric which allows a relatively fast equalization of payoff functions for tasks, producing low uncertainty in robot allocation ratios. Obtained results encourage the definition of metrics and more payoff functions in order to have a wide range of choices which can be used to fit real scenarios requirements.

A formal convergence and stability study is encouraged after the results of the work. Some issues like Karush Kuhn Tucker conditions should be ensured for convergence. We have supposed an enormous number of robots so the allocations, quantities between 0 and 1, are not problematic, however for a lower number of robots this could lead to an integer allocation problem which can cause not convergence or instability.

References

1. Amigoni, F., Basilico, N., Quattrini Li, A.: How much worth is coordination of mobile robots for exploration in search and rescue? In: Chen, X., Stone, P., Sucar, L.E., van der Zant, T. (eds.) RoboCup 2012. LNCS (LNAI), vol. 7500, pp. 106–117. Springer, Heidelberg (2013). https://doi.org/10.1007/978-3-642-39250-4_11
2. Arif, M.U., Haider, S.: An evolutionary traveling salesman approach for multi-robot task allocation. In: ICAART, no. 2, pp. 567–574 (2017)
3. Burgard, W., Moors, M., Stachniss, C., Schneider, F.E.: Coordinated multi-robot exploration. IEEE Trans. Robot. 21(3), 376–386 (2005). https://doi.org/10.1109/TRO.2004.839232
4. Chen, R., Julian, G., Bernd, M.: Social learning in a simple task allocation game. arXiv preprint arXiv:1702.05739 (2017)
5. Chen, Y., Dai, J., Mao, X., Liu, Y., Jiang, X.: Image registration between visible and infrared images for electrical equipment inspection robots based on quadrilateral features. In: 2017 2nd International Conference on Robotics and Automation Engineering (ICRAE), December, pp. 126–130 (2017). https://doi.org/10.1109/ICRAE.2017.8291366
6. Grayson, S.: Search & rescue using multi-robot systems (2014)
7. Jeon, H., Bang, Y., Myung, H.: Structural inspection robot for displacement measurement. In: 5th IEEE International Conference on Digital Ecosystems and Technologies (IEEE DEST 2011), May, pp. 188–191 (2011). https://doi.org/10.1109/DEST.2011.5936623
8. Koubaa, A. (ed.): Robot Operating System (ROS): The Complete Reference (Volume 2). SCI, vol. 707. Springer, Cham (2017). https://doi.org/10.1007/978-3-319-54927-9
9. La Cesa, S., Farinelli, A., Iocchi, L., Nardi, D., Sbarigia, M., Zaratti, M.: Semi-autonomous coordinated exploration in rescue scenarios. In: Visser, U., Ribeiro, F., Ohashi, T., Dellaert, F. (eds.) RoboCup 2007. LNCS (LNAI), vol. 5001, pp. 286–293. Springer, Heidelberg (2008). https://doi.org/10.1007/978-3-540-68847-1_27
10. Lins, R.G., Givigi, S.N., Freitas, A.D.M., Beaulieu, A.: Autonomous robot system for inspection of defects in civil infrastructures. IEEE Syst. J. 12(2), 1414–1422 (2018). https://doi.org/10.1109/JSYST.2016.2611244
11. Luo, L., Chakraborty, N., Sycara, K.: Distributed algorithms for multirobot task assignment with task deadline constraints. IEEE Trans. Autom. Sci. Eng. 12(3), 876–888 (2015). https://doi.org/10.1109/TASE.2015.2438032
12. Murphy, R.R., Tadokoro, S., Kleiner, A.: Disaster robotics. In: Siciliano, B., Khatib, O. (eds.) Springer Handbook of Robotics, pp. 1577–1604. Springer, Cham (2016). https://doi.org/10.1007/978-3-319-32552-1_60
13. Murphy, R.R., et al.: Search and rescue robotics. In: Siciliano, B., Khatib, O. (eds.) Springer Handbook of Robotics, pp. 1151–1173. Springer, Berlin (2008). https://doi.org/10.1007/978-3-540-30301-5_51
14. Quijano, N., Ocampo-Martinez, C., Barreiro-Gomez, J., Obando, G., Pantoja, A., Mojica-Nava, E.: The role of population games and evolutionary dynamics in distributed control systems: the advantages of evolutionary game theory. IEEE Control Syst. Mag. 37(1), 70–97 (2017). https://doi.org/10.1109/MCS.2016.2621479
15. Sandholm, W.H.: Population Games and Evolutionary Dynamics. MIT Press, Cambridge (2010)

16. Siciliano, B., Khatib, O. (eds.): Springer Handbook of Robotics. Springer, Cham (2016). https://doi.org/10.1007/978-3-319-32552-1
17. Sun, C., Wang, X., Liu, J.: Evolutionary game theoretic approach for optimal resource allocation in multi-agent systems. In: 2017 Chinese Automation Congress (CAC), October, pp. 5588–5592 (2017). https://doi.org/10.1109/CAC.2017.8243778
18. Zheng, Y., Ling, H., Xue, J.: Disaster rescue task scheduling: An evolutionary multiobjective optimization approach. IEEE Trans. Emerg. Top. Comput. **6**(2), 288–300 (2018). https://doi.org/10.1109/TETC.2014.2369957

Enhancing Cognitive Virtual Maps for Domestic Service Robots by Adapting the User's Perception on Uncertain Information Based on the Robot Experience: A Neural Network Approach

H. M. Ravindu T. Bandara$^{(\boxtimes)}$, B. M. S. S. Basnayake,
A. G. Buddhika P. Jayasekara, and D. P. Chandima

University of Moratuwa, Moratuwa 10400, Sri Lanka
ravitharaka11@gmail.com, basnayake.bmss@gmail.com,
{buddhika,chandima}@uom.lk

Abstract. Assistive robots possess the competency to provide companionship to the human beings. Navigation is an essential factor of the robot. The robot should have the capability to virtually imagine the description of an unknown environment to prove that it possesses a better navigation skill. Subsequently they should improve the capability in relevance to the imagining with its experience. Therefore this paper proposes a method to improve the virtual imagining capability of a service robot while understanding the uncertain information about an object size using the artificial neural network. The proposed method possesses the capability to create a virtual map of an environment and enhances it using the actual sensory data. The Virtual Map Modeler (VOM) has been introduced in order to create the improved virtual maps. The capabilities of the robots have been demonstrated and evaluated for the performance.

Keywords: Assistive robots · Cognitive maps · Virtual maps

1 Introduction

Assistive robot technology is a rapidly developing field in the recent times. Researchers are experimenting and exploring new techniques to make the assistive robots more human friendly [10]. Assistive robots are expected to work with the elderly people and disabled people in order to uplift their living standards [1,5,6]. Hence a robot should be able to make a better companionship for a human in order to connect their lives both physically and emotionally, which makes it a very difficult task. Caretakers are expected to be friendly and understanding the behavior of the care-receivers. If a robot expects to possess such cognitive abilities it should be able to perform navigation tasks in a similar behavior as same as human beings. Researches are developing various techniques

© Springer Nature Switzerland AG 2019
L. Rutkowski et al. (Eds.): ICAISC 2019, LNAI 11509, pp. 622–632, 2019.
https://doi.org/10.1007/978-3-030-20915-5_55

in different approaches such as navigation, object manipulation and robot vision to make the assistive robots more human like. Moreover robot navigation plays an important role in assistive robot technology.

Humans possess cognitive ability to navigate in unknown environments based on a description or navigation commands given by another person. As an example if a person is asked to bring something from an unknown environment based on a given description such as "there is a parcel on a small chair in the left corner of the kitchen", the person should be able to identify that specific chair in the kitchen which he has no visual information about. In a situation like that a human possesses the capability to create a virtual spatial cognitive map based on a given description or conversation. When the person actually perceives the spatial information about the environment he is capable of amalgamating actual sensory information with virtual cognitive map in order to identify the required object. Furthermore, humans can distinguish similar objects based on the object attributes. As an example if there were more than one chair in the room and the person was asked to check on the smallest chair it wouldn't be a difficult task to identify the particular chair in the room. Moreover humans possess the ability to learn and improve their knowledge base, based on the experience which will help to improve the capability in virtual imagination. Therefore the robot should be able to create a virtual map of an unknown environment in order to perform the navigation tasks more human like. Human tends to use uncertain terms such as "small", "medium", "large", "near", "far" and "little" in conversations. Numerical interpretation of the uncertain information may also vary with the perspective view of a person. As an example for a same object two people can have two opinions such as one may say it is a large table and another one can express the same table as a medium size table. In a situation like this a robot should be able to interpret the spatial information from the uncertain term while adapting to the users perspective of view. Moreover, when the robot is creating the virtual map it needs to be comprised with the object attributes such as shape and dimensions which should depend on previous experience. This implies that a robot should be capable of learning during operation process. Learning capability can be used to enhance virtual map by including more details about environment. Such capability will be efficacious in navigation tasks to identify a position precisely [11]. Therefore the assistive robot should be able to adapt to users perspective and learn while assistive tasks in order to make human friendly companion.

A method has been proposed to create a spatial cognitive map based on an interactive conversation between a robot and a user [3]. The system is capable of understanding spatial relationships among objects in an unknown environment and creating or describing virtual cognitive map based on spatial data. However system is not capable of improving virtual map according to user's perspective. A method has been proposed to create cognitive map considering relationship between object attributes which allow robot to identify objects without actually perceiving visual information about objects [4]. It also introduced a conversational management module (CMM) to create an interactive discussion between the robot and a the user in order to perceive information. However the system does not support for spatial information or navigation tasks. A method has been introduced in [7] to navigate robot using navigation commands with uncertain terms such as "close", "near", "far" and "little". The system does not possess the ability to navigate in previously unknown environment or create virtual maps. A virtual spatial representation method for domestic environment has been explained in [8]. A method to decode spatial information communicated through symbolic language phrases by achieving previously unknown symbolic goals has been proposed [9]. However system is lacking ability to visualize the environment before actually perceive it. Therefore this paper proposes a method to improve virtual maps considering object sizes while adapting to users perspective and interpret uncertain terms such as "small", "large", and "medium" in order to enhance human robot interaction.

2   System Overview

Overall functionalities of the proposed system is shown in Fig. 1. The system is capable of creating virtual maps and cognitive maps of unknown environment based on information from the user which is conveyed through interactive discussion. Constructed virtual maps are improved through a learning process using the actual sensory data perceived through laser scanner in order to adapt to the users perspective. System is also capable of understanding uncertain terms related to object size such as "small", "medium", and "large" and use that knowledge to enhance virtual map creating capability. Information Processor (IP) identifies uncertain terms and object type with the aid of language memory which contains linguistic data such as uncertain terms, object names and other articles. Uncertain Data Interpreting Module (UDIM) interprets uncertain information containing terms such as "small", "medium", "large" and convert those data into numerical values. Spatial Data Processing Module (SDPM) identifies positioning of objects based on cognitive maps constructed using vocal information and updates virtual maps based on data perceived by analyzing actual spatial map. Conversation Management Module (CMM) controls the conversation flow between user and the robot in order to acquire more information and maintain a human friendly interaction. Virtual Object Modeler (VOM) identifies the size of an object through a process to enhance the output of Virtual Map Creator (VMC) which creates virtual maps of unknown environment based on information given by Spatial Information Processor (SIP). Conceptual Map creator (ConMaC) combines constructed virtual map with cognitive map to create spatial map with identified object details. Cognitive spatial maps are created by Cognitive Map Creator (CMC) using information received through conversation between the user and the robot.

Creation of virtual and cognitive maps and conversational management module (CMM) are explained in [3]. Same conversational module was used in the proposed system. Uncertain terms were modified to "small", "medium" and "large".

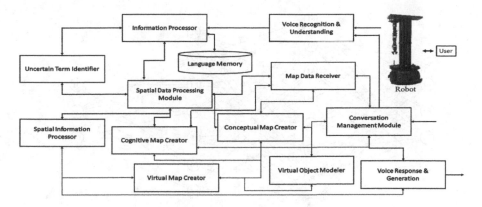

Fig. 1. System overview

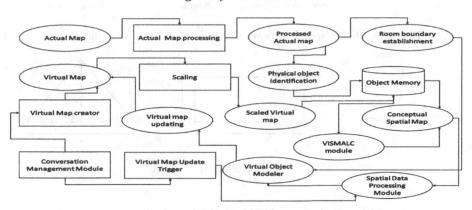

Fig. 2. Process flow of map creation

Figure 2 shows process flow of the proposed system. The robot accrues information via conversation model and sends gathered data to virtual map creator. If the robot is required to gather more information during operations the *virtual map update trigger* activates the CMM. After construction of the virtual map robot perceive an actual map through a sensory inputs from laser scanner. SDPM create links between VOM and conceptual map creator in order to update constructed virtual map. VOM identifies actual sizes of objects based on conceptual map and updates the virtual map according to acquired data.

3   Virtual Object Modeler-VOM

A Virtual Object Modeler (VOM) has been developed to create virtual objects for the Virtual Map. A sub module of the Conversation Model extracts the attributes of a particular object (Uncertain term which describes the size of the object, shape of the object and category of the object) from the conversation and

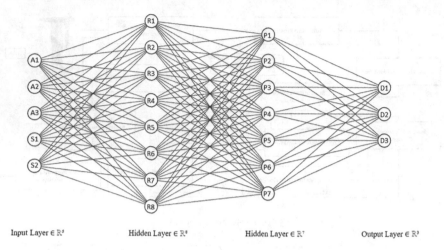

Fig. 3. Artificial Neural Network for object dimension identification

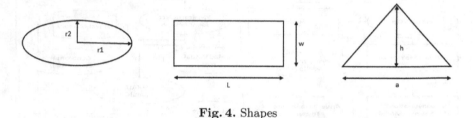

Fig. 4. Shapes

transmits the object attributes to VOM. VOM models the received attributes as follows. Objects are allowed to be identified even though the attributes such as object shape and the object size are not mentioned in the conversation. VOM links to the Cognitive Spatial Map (CSM) to retrieve object shape if the particular object shape is not given by the conversation model output (Figs. 3 and 4).

A = {A1, A2, A3}
A3 = {0, 1, 2}
S = {S1, S2}
S1 = Room length
S2 = Room width

Object sizes set A1 = {1, 2, 3} has been defined as shown in the Table 1. The uncertain terms "small", "medium" and "large" has been considered to interpret the object sizes.

Object category set A2 = {0, 1, 2, 3, 4, 5, ...} has been defined as shown in the Table 2. In the Virtual Object Modeler, an option has been provided to add more categories to the list according to the requirement and the reference value is increased incrementally for each addition.

Table 1. ANN input table

Input type	Input data	Assigned value
Object size	Small	1
	Medium	2
	Large	3
Object category	Chair	0
	Table	1
	Cupboard	2
	Stool	3
	Box	4
	Photocopy machine	5
Object shape	Shape A	0
	Shape B	1
	Shape C	2

Table 2. ANN input table

Shape	Constrains	special case
Shape A	r1, r2 >0 & r1 >=r2	r1 = r2 (Circle)
Shape B	L,W >0 & L >= W	L = W (Squire)
Shape C	h, a >0	-

Shape	D1	D2	D3
Shape A	r1	r2	-100
Shape B	L	W	0
Shape C	H	A	100

All the shapes identified on the map has been approximated to following shapes which are represented by two parameters. Shape A, the oval shape has been represented by parameter $r1$ and $r2$ where $r1$ is the larger radius and $r2$ is the smaller radius. The Circle can be obtained at the special case where $r1 = r2$. Shape B, the rectangle shape has been represented by the length (L) and the width (W). The Squire shape can be obtained as a special case of Shape B where $L = W$. Shape C, the triangle shape has been represented by length of the base (a) and the perpendicular height (h). In this case, all the triangle shapes are approximated to symmetrical triangles.

The values $S1$, $S2$ are obtained from the Room Boundary Establisher (RBE) [2]. An Artificial Neural Network (ANN) has been developed to generate dimensional parameters of the virtual objects as follows. ANN input layer consists of five inputs i.e. {A1, A2, A3, S1, S2} as described previously. Two hidden layers have been used in ANN and the output layer has three outputs i.e. {D1, D2, D3}. Only D1 and D2 are allocated for object dimensional parameters. The third output D3 has been used to generate a value according the object shape i.e. the target value when training are −100 for round shapes, 0 for rectangular shapes and +100 for triangular shapes (Fig. 5).

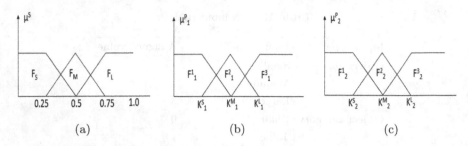

Fig. 5. (a)-Fuzzy sets for first dimensional parameter: generated based on the values K_1^S, K_1^M, K_1^L which are generated by ANN as described, (b)-Fuzzy sets for second dimensional parameter: generated based on the values K_2^S, K_2^M, K_2^L which are generated by ANN as described, (c)-Fuzzy output to give a combine result for an object size based on two object dimensional parameters.

Parameters for "Small" objects.

$$K_1^S = \{K_n = D1|\quad where \quad A1 = 1 \quad \& A2 = T_{SDPM}$$
$$\&\quad A3 = S_{SDPM} \quad \& \quad S1 = S'1 \quad \& \quad S2 = S'2\}$$
$$K_2^S = \{K_n = D2|\quad where \quad A1 = 1 \quad \& A2 = T_{SDPM}$$
$$\&\quad A3 = S_{SDPM} \quad \& \ S1 = S'1 \quad \& \quad S2 = S'2\}$$

Parameters for "medium" objects.

$$K_1^M = \{K_n = D1|\quad \forall n \ \epsilon \ A2, \quad where \quad A1 = 2$$
$$\&\quad A3 = S_{SDPM} \quad \& \quad S1 = S'1 \quad \& \quad S2 = S'2\}$$
$$K_2^M = \{K_n = D2|\quad \forall n \ \epsilon \ A2, \quad where \quad A1 = 2$$
$$\&\quad A3 = S_{SDPM} \quad \& \quad S1 = S'1 \quad \& \quad S2 = S'2\}$$

Parameters for "large" objects.

$$KL1 = \{K_n = D1|\quad \forall n \ \epsilon \ A2, \quad where \quad A1 = 3$$
$$\&\quad A3 = S_{SDPM} \quad \& \quad S1 = S'1 \quad \& \quad S2 = S'2\}$$
$$KL2 = \{K_n = D2|\quad \forall n \ \epsilon \ A2, \quad where \quad A1 = 3$$
$$\&\quad A3 = S_{SDPM} \quad \& \quad S1 = S'1 \quad \& \quad S2 = S'2\}$$

A sigmoidal function has been used as the activation function (f^{act}) for the ANN. When an object location confirmation is identified by the virtual map update trigger module, VOM updates the ANN weights by running the back-propagation with actual D1, D2, D3 parameters. The parameter values are calculated by Spatial Data Processing Module (SDPM) the linked objects from Conceptual Spatial Map (CSM). SDPM detects the objects which does not include uncertain size information (ϵ A1) and then identified objects are approximated to a shape (SSDPM) mentioned above (S_{SDPM} ϵ A3). SDPM retrieve object type T_{SDPM} (ϵ A2) from the Conceptual Spatial Map and sends S_{SDPM}, T_{SDPM} details to VOM and ANN outputs are calculated by VOM with following inputs.

Object dimensional parameters D1 and D2 are calculated by SDPM from CSM according to the Table 2. D1 is used with μ_1^P and D2 is used with μ_2^P with following rule base.

$$If \quad D1 \quad is \quad F_1^1 \quad and \quad D2 \quad IS \quad F_2^1 \quad then \quad O \quad is \quad F_S$$
$$If \quad D1 \quad is \quad F_1^1 \quad and \quad D2 \quad IS \quad F_2^2 \quad then \quad O \quad is \quad F_S$$
$$If \quad D1 \quad is \quad F_1^1 \quad and \quad D2 \quad IS \quad F_2^3 \quad then \quad O \quad is \quad F_M$$
$$If \quad D1 \quad is \quad F_1^2 \quad and \quad D2 \quad IS \quad F_2^1 \quad then \quad O \quad is \quad F_S$$
$$If \quad D1 \quad is \quad F_1^2 \quad and \quad D2 \quad IS \quad F_2^2 \quad then \quad O \quad is \quad F_M$$
$$If \quad D1 \quad is \quad F_1^2 \quad and \quad D2 \quad IS \quad F_2^3 \quad then \quad O \quad is \quad F_M$$
$$If \quad D1 \quad is \quad F_1^3 \quad and \quad D2 \quad IS \quad F_2^1 \quad then \quad O \quad is \quad F_M$$
$$If \quad D1 \quad is \quad F_1^3 \quad and \quad D2 \quad IS \quad F_2^2 \quad then \quad O \quad is \quad F_L$$
$$If \quad D1 \quad is \quad F_1^3 \quad and \quad D2 \quad IS \quad F_2^3 \quad then \quad O \quad is \quad F_L$$

The fuzzy rule base was constructed based on a human study. Defuzzification is done by centroid of area method on μ^S and crisp output (S_{CRSP}) is obtained. The value is considered with μ^S again to calculate values of F_S, F_M, F_L which are

$$F_S^{FZ}, \quad F_M^{FZ}, \quad F_L^{FZ} \quad respectively \quad related \quad to \quad S_{CRSP}.$$
$$V_{SZ} = \text{"Small"} \quad if \quad F_S^{FZ} = MAX \quad \{F_S^{FZ}, F_M^{FZ}, F_L^{FZ}\}$$
$$V_{SZ} = \text{"Medium"} \quad if \quad F_M^{FZ} = MAX \quad \{F_S^{FZ}, F_M^{FZ}, F_L^{FZ}\}$$
$$V_{SZ} = \text{"Large"} \quad if \quad F_L^{FZ} = MAX \quad \{F_S^{FZ}, F_M^{FZ}, F_L^{FZ}\}$$

Then V_{SZ} is updated on virtual map by VOM.

To link the Virtual Map and the Actual Map a Shape Overlap Linker (SOL) has been included with following functions. Object shapes in both maps are approximated to the common shapes using the Aforge.net library. Algorithm 1 is used to link objects in virtual map to objects in actual map.

4   Result and Discussion

The proposed system has been implemented on MIRob [7] platform. Experiment has been carried out to evaluate system capabilities. Figure 6(a), (b) and (c) shows processed actual map, virtual map and identified object map.

Figure 7 shows the enhanced virtual map of the environment after the experiment.

Algorithm 1. Map overlapping for object identification

Require: : Actual map , Virtual map
Ensure: : spatial map

O^A = Objects in actual Map
O^V = Objects in Virtual Map
P^A = Pixels in Actual Map
P^V = Pixels in Virtual Map
$COLOR_F$ = Filling color of maps
Color (P_I^A) = Color of Ith pixel
OVLP [] - Array Overlapping
O^V(Pixel) - retunes the Object Number which includes the pixel.
Link (Object1, Object2) - Links objects

for O_Y^V in O^V do
    Fill $(O_Y^V, COLOR_F)$
end for

for O_X^A in O^A do
    for P_I^A = in O_X^A do
        if Color $(P_I^V) = COLOR_F$ then
            $Y = O^V(P_I^V)$
            OVLP[Y] ++
        end if
    end for
M = Max [OVLP]

    if (MAX >0) then
        Link (O_M^V, O_X^A)
    end if
end for

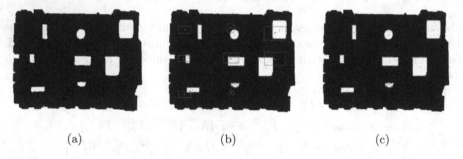

(a)   (b)   (c)

Fig. 6. (a) Actual map of environment, (b) Actual map after overlaped with virtual map, (c) Processed map with identified objects

Fig. 7. Enhanced virtual map

5 Conclusion

A method has been proposed to identify object based on virtual cognitive map and improve the robots knowledge about object size with experience. A method has been introduced to identify object sizes based on uncertain information.

The system is capable of understanding and interpreting uncertain information related to object sizes and create virtual map of unknown environment in a more similar manner to humans which makes the robot more human friendly and effective in navigation tasks. Moreover the robot shows capability to improve virtual map based on experience.

References

1. Abdollahi, H., Mollahosseini, A., Lane, J.T., Mahoor, M.H.: A pilot study on using an intelligent life-like robot as a companion for elderly individuals with dementia and depression. arXiv preprint arXiv:1712.02881 (2017)
2. Bandara, H.M.R.T., Basnayake, B.S., Buddhika, A., Jayasekara, P., Chandima, D.: Enhancing conceptual spatial map by amalgamating spatial and virtual cognitive maps for domestic service robots. In: 2018 2nd International Conference On Electrical Engineering (EECon), pp. 150–155. IEEE (2018)
3. Bandara, H.M.R.T., Muthugala, M.A.V., Jayasekara, A.G.B.P., Chandima, D.P.: Cognitive spatial representative map for interactive conversational model of service robot. In: RO-MAN 2018 - IEEE International Conference on Robot and Human Interactive Communication. IEEE (2018)
4. Bandara, H.M.R.T., Muthugala, M.A.V.J., Jayasekara, A.G.B.P., Chandima, D.P.: Grounding object attributes through interactive discussion for building cognitive maps in service robots. In: 2018 IEEE International Conference on, Systems, Man, and Cybernetics (SMC). IEEE (2018)
5. Hoffman, G., Zuckerman, O., Hirschberger, G., Luria, M., Shani Sherman, T.: Design and evaluation of a peripheral robotic conversation companion. In: Proceedings of the Tenth Annual ACM/IEEE International Conference on Human-Robot Interaction, pp. 3–10. ACM (2015)
6. Muramatsu, M., et al.: Development and evaluation of an interactive therapy robot. In: Cheok, A.D., Inami, M., Romão, T. (eds.) ACE 2017. LNCS, vol. 10714, pp. 66–83. Springer, Cham (2018). https://doi.org/10.1007/978-3-319-76270-8_6
7. Muthugala, M.V.J., Jayasekara, A.B.P.: Enhancing human-robot interaction by interpreting uncertain information in navigational commands based on experience and environment. In: 2016 IEEE International Conference on Robotics and Automation (ICRA), pp. 2915–2921. IEEE (2016)
8. Muthugala, M.V.J., Jayasekara, A.B.P.: MIRob: an intelligent service robot that learns from interactive discussions while handling uncertain information in user instructions. In: 2016 Moratuwa Engineering Research Conference (MERCon), pp. 397–402. IEEE (2016)
9. Talbot, B., Lam, O., Schulz, R., Dayoub, F., Upcroft, B., Wyeth, G.: Find my office: navigating real space from semantic descriptions. In: 2016 IEEE International Conference on Robotics and Automation (ICRA), pp. 5782–5787. IEEE (2016)

10. Nguyen, V., Jayawardena, C.: A technical review of motion prediction methods for indoor robot navigation. Technical Report, July, Unitec Institute of Technology, New Zealand (2015)
11. Zender, H., Mozos, O.M., Jensfelt, P., Kruijff, G.J., Burgard, W.: Conceptual spatial representations for indoor mobile robots. Robot. Auton. Syst. **56**(6), 493–502 (2008)

Enhancing Human-Robot Interaction by Amalgamating Spatial and Attribute Based Cognitive Maps of Assistive Robot

H. M. Ravindu T. Bandara(✉), K. S. Priyanayana,
A. G. Buddhika P. Jayasekara, and D. P. Chandima

University of Moratuwa, Moratuwa 10400, Sri Lanka
ravitharaka11@gmail.com, sahan.priyanayanarr@gmail.com,
{buddhika,chandima}@uom.lk

Abstract. Assistive robot technology is rapidly developing over the time. The assistive robots are expected to use in many areas such as medical, educational and assistive tasks. Assistive robots are mostly used for caretakers of elderly people. Further it is essential to be succoured by a human friendly robot in order to take care the elderly people in the domestic environments. The assistive robots should be friendly, reliable, active, and comprehensible in order to be a friendly companion for humans. Humans tend to include uncertain terms related to the direction and the distance to describe or express ideas. Therefore the assistive robot should be capable of analyzing and understanding numerical meaning of uncertain terms for the purpose of creating conceptual map for effective navigation in three dimensional space. Furthermore assistive robot should be able to identify the objects based on their attributes and distinguish one object from another object based on that knowledge. Therefore this paper proposes a method to understand the spatial information and object attributes in conversations and constructs a cognitive maps based on that information to improve human robot interaction. The proposed method has been implemented on MIRob platform. The experiments have been carried out in an artificially created domestic environment and the results have been analyzed to identify the behaviors of the proposed concept.

Keywords: Social robotics · Cognitive map · Human robot interaction

1 Introduction

Assistive robots have been manufactured in different varieties. Researchers are enhancing capabilities of assistive robots in different aspect in order to make it more human friendly. Assistive robot technology is expected to use in different applications. Moreover assistive robots can be considered as better substitution for caretakers for rapidly increasing elderly population [1]. However humans prefer more human-like companion than a machine without consciousness [2].

© Springer Nature Switzerland AG 2019
L. Rutkowski et al. (Eds.): ICAISC 2019, LNAI 11509, pp. 633–642, 2019.
https://doi.org/10.1007/978-3-030-20915-5_56

Therefore robots needs to have human-like behavior in order to be more close to human beings [8,16]. Therefore robots cognitive capabilities such as communication, navigation, natural command understanding, and intelligent decision making skills should be improved [5,7,14]. Such improvement will be make assistive robot technology a step closer to human-like companion.

Human possess cognitive capabilities of remembering objects based on the spatial and attributional relationships which are considered as very important in domestic navigation systems. Subsequently humans are capable of imagining an environment based on the vocal description or information conveyed through a conversation without having visual information which allows them to navigate in a previously unknown environment. In consideration to a scenario where a dialogue happens between two parties, a human will be explaining the things in a room such as "there is a cupboard in the right side corner of the room". Moreover "there is a table near to that cupboard". The presence of the objects which are on the table is then explained. Among that it was explained about a red color object in sphere shape which is shining and asked to bring it. As in the case of above mentioned scenario the description doesn't imply about the exact object. Nevertheless in consideration of the attributes of the object featuring to the shape, color and the qualities the person possesses the proficiency to select the object which was mentioned in the description. Human beings are capable of understanding the objects through the imaginations even without having the visual information. Moreover they possess the cognitive capability. Further the above mentioned description includes both the spatial information and the attributes about the object. Humans are capable of identifying these objects through the amalgamation of attributional information and the spatial information. This capability plays a vital role in the assistive task. In the application of the above mentioned competency within a robot makes it capable to recognize an object in an unknown environment through the imaginations [10,15,17].

Combining capabilities of identifying the relationship between both spatial and attributional information in order to locate or distinguish a specific object from other objects make the assistive capability more interactive [11]. Human beings are attracted by such abilities. Therefore the robot should be able to store objects in a manner which allows it to categorize objects according to attributes and to establish spatial links to clarify whereabouts of the object without having an actual map of an environment. This facilitates the user to manipulate the robot more human-friendly. A method has been proposed in [4] to create a cognitive map for a service robot based on attributes and used the interest about object attributes. Proposed system is capable of facilitating the cognitive object map and able to amalgamate those cognitive maps in order to create an object memory. Furthermore, it can identify the relationship among the objects based on the attributes and expands the knowledge base about objects through the interactive conversation with the user. However system was more focused on creating the object memory and does not have the capability to identify the spatial information about the objects. A method to create spatial cognitive maps has been proposed in [3]. The system is capable of identifying the spatial relationship between the objects using the vocal information through conversations between the user and robot and creates a cognitive spatial map of an environment. However the system capabilities are limited to spatial information. A method has been proposed in [12] to store robots knowledge about an environment in hierarchically organized manner. The proposed method is called Robot Experience Model (REM). REM consist with 3 main layers and one of them is environment. The layer which seems like an object memory that stores the spatial information of the objects are available in a particular environment. The environment layer also consisted of 3 layers. In those sub layers objects are categorized into 2 distinguished layers based on the spatial location of the objects. Only the spatial attributes and relationships are considered in those layers. The proposed method is not capable of identifying non spatial attributes such as *colour, shape* and *status of an object* which makes the object memory obsolete [6,9,13].

2   System Overview

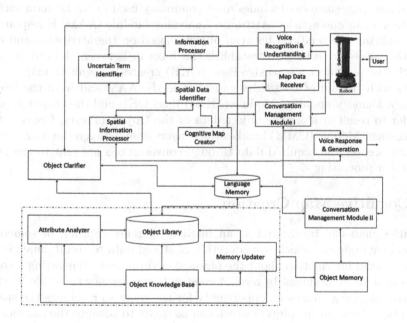

Fig. 1. System overview

Overall functionality of the proposed system is shown in Fig. 1. The proposed system is capable of identifying objects based on attributes and establishing relation between attributes to map objects thus it can be used to store, recall, manipulate, identify and distinguish objects based on similarities. Furthermore, system is capable of identifying spatial information conveyed through interactive conversation model to establish spatial relation between objects. Moreover, spatial and object attribute maps are amalgamated for better human robot interaction.

Information Processor (IP) understands the users instructions using the language Memory and the Conversation Management Module (CMM). IP identifies the uncertain terms defined in the language memory and the extracted data is sent to the respective modules for further processing. Language memory includes the most commonly used linguistic data such as lexical symbols of objects, uncertain terms and articles. Uncertain Term Identifier (UTI), spatial information Processor (SIP) and the Spatial Data Interpreter (SDI) work together in real time to interpret spatial data into the uncertain terms and other way around. Cognitive Map Creator (CMC) creates the cognitive network between the virtual objects based on the spatial data conveyed through the Map Data Receiver (MDR) and through the conversation between the user and the robot. Further CMM manages the interaction between the user and the robot. CMM controls the flow of the conversation between the user and the robot by selecting the voice responses with the help of CMC and SIP. Object library contains the object attributes and other linguistic data related to the objects such as object names. Language memory includes most commonly used linguistic data such as uncertain terms and articles. Attribute Analyzing Module (AAM) is responsible for identifying the relations between objects based on the attributes and conveys the gained knowledge to establish the links in between the objects in a cognitive map. Object Knowledge Base (OKB) creates a cognitive map for the objects with the aid of knowledge gained from the AAM and from the Object Memory. Memory updating Module (MUM) links OKB and the Object Library in order to recall or store the object data in the Object Library. Conversation Management Module (CMM) handles the conversation between the user and the robot. Moreover the acquired data through conversations are sent to the OKB for further processing

3   Cognitive Map Creation

Cognitive map can be derived as an intellectual representation of someone's physical environment which is a collection of stored data to recall, analyse and decode spatial information about the physical environment. Generating a cognitive map of an environment by a robot creates its competency to decide. Further cognitive mapping creates an opportunity for the robot to recognize the spatial connections between the objects which can be useful to advance the interactions with the user.

3.1   Object Map

Object categorization succour to visualize the relationship between the objects. Categorization process helps to categorize the object which is used in AAM. As an example Fig. 2 denotes the cognitive map of the object memory after the categorization. Object map creation was explained in [4].

3.2   Spatial Map

The proposed system will assist the spatial data about a given environment through the aid of the cognitive map. Moreover it will use that information to amplify the interactive conversation through boosting the ability of the robot to describe an environment. Spatial map creation process was explained in [3].

3.3   Amalgamating of the Maps

Both spatial and object cognitive maps are constructed and developed during conversation. For each new object the system encounters during the conversation will be given a unique ID for both maps as an attribute. Objects in spatial and objects in cognitive maps are linked based on this ID. Therefore the system can search for both spatial and attributional data for the same object through the ID.

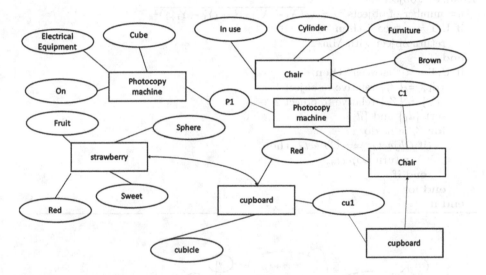

Fig. 2. Graphical representation of example cognitive Map constructed by robot based on both spatial and object attributes.

CMM controls the conversation flow between the robot and the user. CMM was designed by amalgamating CMM from [4] and [3].

Figure 2 shows sample cognitive map of an environment. In this cognitive map there are 4 objects. Cupboard and the strawberry is linked due to the same colour and it can be seen that the photocopy machine is on. According to spatial relations cupboard is near to the chair and chair is near to photocopy machine.

4   Result and Discussion

The proposed system has been implemented in MIRob platform. 20 scenarios with 20 participants have been executed to validate the performance of the proposed system. Each participant was assigned to ask 10 conversation steps from conversation model from robot. System capability of identifying spatial relationship between objects and object categorisation based on attributes are evaluated. Constructed cognitive maps are shown in Figs. 3 and 4 and spatial representation of environment is shown in Fig. 5.

After each scenario participants were asked to give a number on scale of 1 to 10 based on their satisfaction about conversation with robot. 1 implies poor and 10 is for good. Evaluated satisfaction rates are given in Fig. 6.

Algorithm 1. Spatial data Interpretation

Require: : Uncertain term, reference objects coordination X, Y
Ensure: : object ID

    n= number of objects $z_i = \sqrt{(X_i - X_{i+1})^2 - (Y_i - Y_{i+1})^2}$
    if U.T == "near" **then**
        return object with Min$\{z_i\}$
    end if
    if U.T == "between" **then**
        $\{d_1\} = \{Z_i\}$ relative to object 1
        $\{d_2\} = \{Z_i\}$ relative to object 2
        sort $\{d_1\}$ and $\{d_2\}$
        for Z_i in n **do**
            if $Object_{d_1}$ == $Object_{d_2}$ **then**
                return $Object_{d_2}$
            end if
        end for
    end if

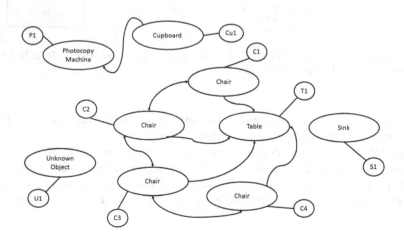

Fig. 3. Spatial cognitive map

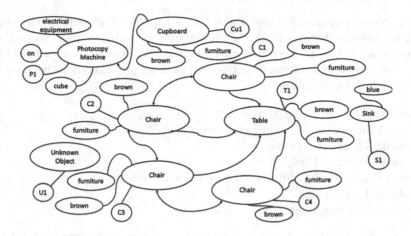

Fig. 4. Cognitive map constructed by the robot based on object attributes

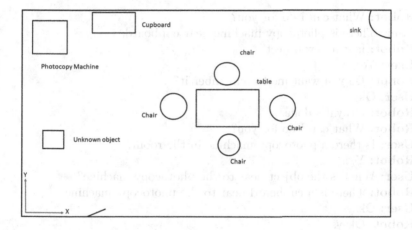

Fig. 5. Spatial data representation of the experiment area

1. **Robot:** How can I help You?
2. **User:** Can you tell me furniture with brown colour?
3. **Robot:** There are chairs, table, cupboard.
4. **Robot:** How can I help You?
5. **User:** What are the fruits do you know of ?
6. **Robot:** There is strawberry.
7. **Robot:** How can I help You?

This conversation shows that the robot is capable of identifying the object based on the attributes and it can distinguish one object from another one by analysing attributes. Even though strawberry was not in constructed object map robot was capable of recalling that object from previous cognitive map and linking with the new information.

1. **Robot:** How can I help You?
2. **User:** Can you tell me fruits with sweet taste?
3. **Robot:** There are strawberry.
4. **Robot:** How can I help You?
5. **User:** What are the object with blue colour ?
6. **Robot:** There is sink.
7. **Robot:** How can I help You?

In this conversation robot shows that its capability on identifying the objects based on the attributes which implying that the robot is successfully categorising objects in the constructed cognitive map.

1. **Robot:** What can I do for you?
2. **User:** There is photocopy machine near cupboard.
3. **Robot:** Is it a new object?
4. **User:** Yes.
5. **Robot:** Do you want me to remember it?
6. **User:** Okay.
7. **Robot:** Okay.it's done.
8. **Robot:** What can I do for you?
9. **User:** Is there a photocopy machine in the room?
10. **Robot:** Yes.
11. **User:** What is the object near to the photocopy machine?
12. **Robot:** There is a cupboard near to the photocopy machine.
13. **User:** Okay.
14. **Robot:** Okay.
15. **Robot:**What can I do for you?

This conversation shows robots capability on identifying and updating cognitive maps. Moreover this conversation includes both spatial information and object attributes which implies the conversation was built by amalgamating spatial cognitive map and object map in robots memory.

Moreover user satisfaction level shows that robot have capability to create interactive conversation between user and the robot using both spatial information about the environment and object attributes.

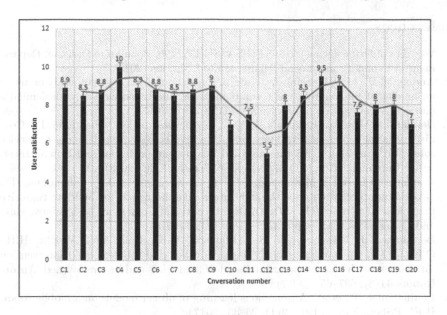

Fig. 6. User satisfaction level

5 Conclusions

A method has been introduced to amalgamate cognitive spatial maps and object maps of a given environment to identify the spatial and attributional information between the objects. The system is capable of creating cognitive spatial map and the object map based on the vocal information conveyed through an interactive conversation between the robot and the user and amalgamate those maps to identify the relationships between the objects and uses such information to make conversations more interactive. Further the conversation between the user and the robot is managed by the Conversation Management Module (CMM) and the Spatial Information Processor (SIP) manages the uncertain information identification and interpretation of the spatial data into uncertain terms for the cognitive map creation. Subsequently an experiment has been carried out in order to validate the robot performance in interactive conversations and the results show that the robot is capable of having interactive conversations with the user through successfully describing the environment while analysing object attributes in order to make the conversation more interactive and informable. Furthermore the system can be further improved by using more attributes in a cognitive map with more sensory inputs that can be acquired by the robot.

References

1. World population ageing 2015: ST/ESA/SER.A/390, Population Division, Department of Economic and Social Affairs, United Nations (2015)
2. Abdollahi, H., Mollahosseini, A., Lane, J.T., Mahoor, M.H.: A pilot study on using an intelligent life-like robot as a companion for elderly individuals with dementia and depression. arXiv preprint arXiv:1712.02881 (2017)
3. Bandara, H.M.R.T., Muthugala, M.V.J., Jayasekara, A.B.P., Chandima, D.: Cognitive spatial representative map for interactive conversational model of service robot. In: 2018 27th IEEE International Symposium on Robot and Human Interactive Communication (RO-MAN), pp. 686–691. IEEE (2018)
4. Bandara, H.M.R.T., Muthugala, M.V.J., Jayasekara, A.B.P., Chandima, D.: Grounding object attributes through interactive discussion for building cognitive maps in service robots. In: 2018 IEEE International Conference on Systems, Man, and Cybernetics (SMC), pp. 3775–3780. IEEE (2018)
5. Boccanfuso, L., Scarborough, S., Abramson, R.K., Hall, A.V., Wright, H.H., O'Kane, J.M.: A low-cost socially assistive robot and robot-assisted intervention for children with autism spectrum disorder: field trials and lessons learned. Auton. Robots 41(3), 637–655 (2017)
6. Fäulhammer, T., et al.: Autonomous learning of object models on a mobile robot. IEEE Robot. Autom. Lett. 2(1), 26–33 (2017)
7. Kanda, T., Ishiguro, H.: Human-Robot Interaction in Social Robotics. CRC Press, Boca Raton (2016)
8. Koceski, S., Koceska, N.: Evaluation of an assistive telepresence robot for elderly healthcare. J. Med. Syst. 40(5), 121 (2016)
9. Konolige, K., Rajkumar, N., Hinterstoisser, S.: Generating a model for an object encountered by a robot, US Patent App. 15/227,612, 8 February 2018
10. Leite, I., Pereira, A., Lehman, J.F.: Persistent memory in repeated child-robot conversations. In: Proceedings of the 2017 Conference on Interaction Design and Children, pp. 238–247. ACM (2017)
11. Mast, M., et al.: Design of the human-robot interaction for a semi-autonomous service robot to assist elderly people. In: Wichert, R., Klausing, H. (eds.) Ambient Assisted Living. ATSC, pp. 15–29. Springer, Cham (2015). https://doi.org/10.1007/978-3-319-11866-6_2
12. Muthugala, M.V.J., Jayasekara, A.B.P.: MIRob: an intelligent service robot that learns from interactive discussions while handling uncertain information in user instructions. In: 2016 Moratuwa Engineering Research Conference (MERCon), pp. 397–402. IEEE (2016)
13. Ruiz-Sarmiento, J.R., Galindo, C., Gonzalez-Jimenez, J.: Exploiting semantic knowledge for robot object recognition. Knowl.-Based Syst. 86, 131–142 (2015)
14. Sheridan, T.B.: Human-robot interaction: status and challenges. Hum. Factors 58(4), 525–532 (2016)
15. Talbot, B., Lam, O., Schulz, R., Dayoub, F., Upcroft, B., Wyeth, G.: Find my office: navigating real space from semantic descriptions. In: 2016 IEEE International Conference on Robotics and Automation (ICRA), pp. 5782–5787. IEEE (2016)
16. Wu, Y.H., Cristancho-Lacroix, V., Fassert, C., Faucounau, V., de Rotrou, J., Rigaud, A.S.: The attitudes and perceptions of older adults with mild cognitive impairment toward an assistive robot. J. Appl. Gerontol. 35(1), 3–17 (2016)
17. Zender, H., Mozos, O.M., Jensfelt, P., Kruijff, G.J., Burgard, W.: Conceptual spatial representations for indoor mobile robots. Robot. Auton. Syst. 56(6), 493–502 (2008)

Proactive Middleware for Fault Detection and Advanced Conflict Handling in Sensor Fusion

Gilles Neyens[✉] and Denis Zampunieris

University of Luxembourg,
2, avenue de l'Université, 4365 Esch-sur-Alzette, Luxembourg
{gilles.neyens,denis.zampunieris}@uni.lu

Abstract. Robots traditionally have a wide array of sensors that allow them to react to the environment and make appropriate decisions. These sensors can give incorrect or imprecise data due to malfunctioning or noise. Sensor fusion methods try to overcome some of these issues by using the data coming from different sensors and combining it. However, they often don't take sensor malfunctioning and a priori knowledge about the sensors and the environment into account, which can produce conflicting information for the robot to work with. In this paper, we present an architecture and process in order to overcome some of these limitations based on a proactive rule-based system.

Keywords: Rule-based systems · Sensor fusion · Conflict handling

1 Introduction

Sensor fusion is used in IT and robotic systems to combine the data coming from different sensors in order to reduce the uncertainty the resulting information would have in case the sensors were used individually.

A lot of the existing work in sensor fusion is carried out on a set of homogeneous sensors and while there exist multi-sensor fusion techniques that are used on heterogeneous sensors, used for example to calculate a more accurate position of the robot [6,21], most do not take into account the known relations between sensors of different types. Also often they do not provide means for handling noise, malfunctioning or corrupted sensors.

Similarly, there exists work on integrating a trust model into the data fusion process [8]. The approach is calculating trust values for each sensor based on historical data of a sensor, the current data, and a threshold representing the upper bound of the maximum allowed difference between the current data and the historical data.

While the previous method gives trust or confidence values to sensors based on historical data, it is only based on data of the same sensor. Other methods try to improve this by taking context into account like [29] or [1] in which they use rules to adapt the parameters of a Kalman filter based on the current context.

© Springer Nature Switzerland AG 2019
L. Rutkowski et al. (Eds.): ICAISC 2019, LNAI 11509, pp. 643–653, 2019.
https://doi.org/10.1007/978-3-030-20915-5_57

The model we propose in this paper will be set between the sensors and the final decision making of the robot and will work together with other fusion methods in order to improve the information that the robot receives. The goal is to reduce the probability of malfunctioning or corrupted sensors negatively affecting the robot. The system will in a first step use classification algorithms tailored for each sensor in order to obtain confidence/trust values for each sensor and in a second step use a priori knowledge about relations between sensors and a proactive rule-based system to reason about the current context of the system, and further refine the confidence for each sensor and potentially improve the data. The notion of proactive computing has been introduced in 2000 [28] for systems that work for and on behalf of the user on their own initiative [24]. In this case, the robot will be the user and the proactive system can be tailored to handle a range of different scenarios in which data coming from different sensors is conflicting with each other.

In the next section, we are going to present related work in the domain of classification algorithms, sensor fusion, and conflict handling as well as the concept of proactive computing that our rule-engine is based on. In Sect. 3, we introduce the general architecture of our system along as the structure for the a priori knowledge that is required by our system. Section 4 contains the method for resolving the conflicts between different sensors. In Sect. 5 the evaluation of our system is described, and we will finish with a conclusion and possible future work.

2　Related Work

2.1　Time Series Classification Algorithms

In our system, we are going to mainly use 2 approaches for time series classification: Hidden Markov Models (HMMs) and Artificial Neural Networks (ANNs).

The mathematical foundations for HMMs have been developed in 1966 and the following years by Baum [3–5]. Over the years they have been used in a lot of different fields, be it speech recognition [11,14,22], failure detection [23] or healthcare applications [13]. More recent studies also have successfully used them for the diagnosis of industrial components [7].

The beginnings of ANNs go back to 1943 [19]. Their use in sensor failure detection started in the 90s [20]. During the last years they have been successfully used in failure detection for gyroscopes, either on their own [15] or in combination with a fuzzy voter and fuzzy rules [18].

While the work in failure detection for some sensors already gave good results, it did not take other sensors of different types into account that could have provided necessary information to detect if something was wrong. In our system, we will, therefore, use the described approaches only as a first step of a whole sensor fault detection, sensor fusion, and conflict handling process.

2.2   Sensor Fusion and Conflict Handling

In the past years, several sensor fusion methods have been used to aggregate data coming from different sensors. Depending on the level of fusion, different techniques have been used. In robotics the most popular method for low-level data is the Kalman filter which was developed in 1960 [16] along with its variants the extended Kalman filter or the unscented Kalman filter who are often used in navigation systems [12,25], but also other methods like the particle filter. On a decision level other methods like the Dempster Shafer theory [9,26] is used.

In this work, we are going to focus on work done on Kalman and particle filters. Studies that used either of these often did not take sensor failures and noise into account, which made these solutions vulnerable in harsh and uncertain environments. A recent study partly addressed these issues by using a particle filter method in combination with recurrent neural networks [30]. This solution managed to correctly identify situations in which sensors were failing but did not yet take sensor noise into account. In [2] the authors propose a fault-tolerant architecture for sensor fusion using Kalman filters for mobile robot localization. The detection rate of the faults injected was 100%, however, the diagnosis and recovery rate is lower at 60%. The study in [32] proposed two new extensions to the Kalman filter, the Fuzzy Adaptive Iterated Extended Kalman Filter and the Fuzzy Adaptive Unscented Kalman Filter in order to make the fusion process more resistant to noise. In [17], the authors used the extended Kalman filter in combination with Bayesian method and managed to detect and predict not only individual failures but also simultaneous occurring failures, however, no fault handling was proposed.

Our system will provide this fault handling in order to provide better data for the robot, by using a proactive system in combination with classification algorithms.

2.3   Proactive Computing

The concept of proactive computing was introduced in 2000 by Tennenhouse [28] as systems working for and on behalf of the user on their own initiative [24]. Based on this concept a proactive engine (PE) which is a rule-based system was developed [33]. The rules running on the engine can be conceptually regrouped into scenarios with each scenario regrouping rules that achieve a common goal [27,34]. A Proactive Scenario is the high-level representation of a set of Proactive Rules that is meant to be executed on the PE. It describes a situation and a set of actions to be taken in case some conditions are met [10].

The PE executes these rules periodically. The system consists of two FIFO queues called currentQueue and nextQueue. The currentQueue contains the rules that need to be executed at the current iteration, while the nextQueue contains the rules that were generated during the current iteration. At the end of each iteration, the rules from the nextQueue will be added to the currentQueue and the next Queue will be emptied.

A rule consists of any number of input parameters and five execution steps [33]. These five steps have each a different role in the execution of the rule.

```
data=getData(dataRequest);
activated=false;
if(checkActivationGuards()){
        activated=true;
        if(checkConditions()){
                executeActions();
        }
}
generateNewRules();
discardRuleFromSystem(currentRule);
```

Fig. 1. The algorithm to run a rule

1. Data acquisition
   During this step, the rule gathers data that is important for its subsequent steps. This data is provided by the context manager of the proactive engine, which can obtain this data from different sources such as sensors or a simple database.
2. Activation guards
   The activation guards will perform checks based on the context information whether or not the conditions and actions part of the rule should be executed. If the checks are true, the activated variable of this rule will be set to true.
3. Conditions
   The objective of the conditions is to evaluate the context in greater detail than the activation guards. If all the conditions are met as well, the Actions part of the rule is unlocked.
4. Actions
   This part consists of a list of instructions that will be performed if the activation guards and condition tests are passed.
5. Rule generation
   The rule generation part will be executed independently whether the activation guards and condition checks were passed or not. I this section the rule creates other rules in the engine or in some cases just clones itself.

During an iteration of the PE, each rule is executed one by one. The algorithm to execute a rule is presented in Fig. 1. The data acquisition part of the rule is run first and if it fails none of the other parts of the rule is executed. The rules can then be regrouped into scenarios. Multiple scenarios can be run at the same time and can trigger the activation of other scenarios and rules.

3   System Architecture

The general architecture of the system is shown in Fig. 2. The sensors of the robot send their data to our system where the classifiers attribute a confidence value for each sensor individually. The proactive engine then uses the results from the classifiers as well as the data in the knowledge base in order to further check the trustworthiness of the different sensors by detecting and resolving potential conflicts between sensors.

The robot itself will pass the data coming from the sensors to our system where it will get processed. It then will get enhanced data along with information on which sensors to trust from our system, which it will then use to make a decision.

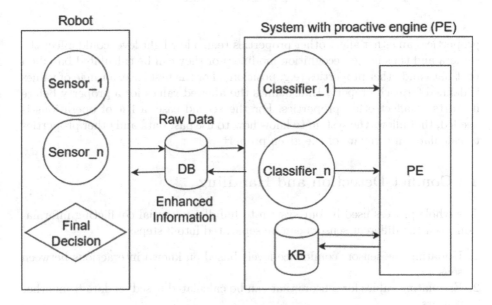

Fig. 2. System structure

In our system, the data will first get processed by some classification algorithms, like for example Hidden Markov Models or Neural Networks, in order to determine if a sensor is failing or still working correctly, along with a confidence value for each sensor. The results from the classification will then be passed to our rule-based engine to detect and handle potential conflicting information. This process will be described in Sect. 4.

First, we will describe what information our system needs in order to fulfill its tasks. For every sensor, we need to know different variables as shown in Table 1. The name of the sensor is the identifier for a given sensor and will be unique. The list of properties are the properties that can be computed from the data from a given sensor, for example for a GPS it would be position and speed. The minimum confidence is the minimum value for the confidence computed based on the classifiers for a sensor in order to trust a sensor. Grace period is the time a sensor will still be used for computations after deemed as untrustworthy. The history length is the amount of past data kept for a given sensor.

In order for the system to know how different properties affect each other or how they can be calculated we need a knowledge base for these properties. The

Table 1. Sensor registration table

Sensor name	List of properties	Minimum confidence	Grace period	History length
GPS	Position, speed	0.8	15 s	1000
Accelerometer	Acceleration	0.8	12 s	800
Light	Light level	0.5	30 s	50
...	...	...	...	...

properties can either affect other properties (e.g. a low light level could affect the camera and thus image recognition modules) or they can be calculated based on past data and other properties (e.g. position). For the first case, a range of values is defined for each property that defines the allowed values for a property before it starts to affect other properties. For the second case, a list of operations is needed, that allows the system to know how to use past data and other properties to calculate an estimate of the given property.

4   Conflict Detection and Handling

The whole process used by our system to handles potential conflicting information from the different sensors can be separated into 3 steps:

1. Updating the sensors confidence levels based on known interactions between sensors
2. Estimating values for sensors that can be calculated based on data from other sensors.
3. Deciding which sensors to trust

The first step is described in the pseudo code shown in Fig. 3. For every sensor, we fetch the property or list of properties they provide. For each of these properties, we then check whether this property can be influenced by other properties. If this is the case we fetch the sensor with the currently highest confidence that provides this property. This sensor also has to have a greater confidence value than its specified minimum confidence. Finally, we check if the data for this sensor is outside the acceptable range defined in the knowledge base and if this is the case we update the confidence for the initial sensor.

The second step is described in the pseudo code in Fig. 4. For every sensor, we again get the list of properties they provide along with the last known data. The system then checks in the knowledge base whether it is possible to calculate an estimate of this property based on data from other sensors. If this is the case it does so based on the past data of the sensor and the current data of related sensors and saves the results.

Finally, Table 2 shows the results from the 2 previous steps. In the last step, we compare the estimates to the actually delivered data from the sensors. If the difference between the two is larger than the predefined error margin we check which data should be trusted based on the current confidence values of the sensor

```
for sensor in sensorList{
        propertyList=GetListOfProperties(sensor, DB);
        for property in propertyList{
                relationList=CheckRelations(property, KB);
                for relation in relationList{
                        updateConfidence(sensor, relation, DB);
                }
        }
}
```

Fig. 3. Update confidence (KB = Knowledge base, DB = Data base)

```
for sensor in sensorList{
        propertyList=GetListOfProperties(sensor, DB);
        currentData=getCurrentData(sensor, DB);
        for property in propertyList{
                relatedPropList=getRelatedProperties(property
                        ,KB);
                action=getAction(property, KB);
                for relatedProp in relatedPropList{
                        relatedSensorWithHighestConfidence=
                                getMostTrustedSensor(relatedProp,
                                DB);
                        dataRelatedProp.add(
                                relatedSensorWithHighestConfidence
                                .getData());
                }
                pastDataOfProperty=getPastData(property, DB);
                estimate=calculateEstimate(action,
                        pastDataOfProperty, dataRelatedProp);
                saveEstimate(sensor, property, currentData,
                        estimate, DB);
        }
}
```

Fig. 4. Estimate calculation (KB = Knowledge base, DB = Data base)

and of the related sensors used to calculate the estimate. For the related sensors, we first check whether all of them meet their minimum confidence criteria. If this is the case we take the average of the confidences and check whether it is higher than the current confidence of the initial sensor. The information passed to the robot will then include the final confidence level for every sensor and either the original raw data or the estimated data based on the previous computation.

5   Experimental Evaluation

The evaluation for our system is work under development via a proof of concept in the robotics simulation software Webots [31] (Fig. 5) which provides us with

Table 2. Estimate calculation results table

Sensor name	Property	Confidence	Estimate	Related sensors confidence
GPS	Position	0.2	49.82, 6.13, 321.36	0.8, 0.9, 0.78
...	...	...	...	...

a range of different sensors (GPS, Accelerometer, Sonar, etc.) and gives us the possibility to add custom sensors to the robot. The robot will be evaluated for a specific scenario in which it has to mow the lawn in an efficient way while avoiding obstacles and keeping itself safe. In the scenario the robot will be confronted with a range of random dynamic events that can happen, e.g. rain, animals running over the lawn, etc. Two versions of the robot will be compared: one without our system that takes its decisions based on the aggregated data from sensor fusion techniques and one with our system in addition to these sensor fusion techniques. Both versions of the robot will be tested for a list of parameters:

1. Speed
   The robot should mow the lawn as fast as possible.
2. Efficiency
   The robot should mow the lawn with as little battery usage as possible. This will be split into two parts: The distance traveled by the robot and the internal performance of the systems.
3. Safety
   The robot should keep itself safe and avoid any danger while also not endangering people and animals crossing the lawn while it is trying to fulfill its task.

For both versions of the robot, we will inject faults and noise for the different sensors. In a first step, we will only inject fault for sensors individually and then, progressively, we will inject faults for more and more sensors in order to detect

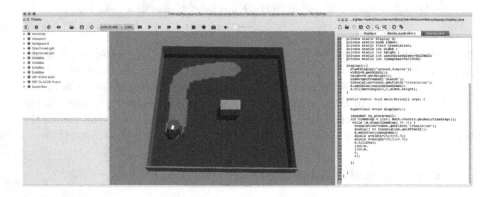

Fig. 5. Webots example

how many simultaneous faults the system can handle. This will also allow us to verify different properties like robustness and resilience for the system.

It was also considered to compare our system to other similar systems, but a lack of very precise information on the implementation of other systems would make this comparison unreliable.

6 Conclusion

In this paper, we have introduced a generic middleware model for handling conflicting data coming from heterogeneous and possibly defective sensors in a robotic system. The process is used alongside state-of-the-art sensor fusion techniques in order to improve the information the robot receives from its sensors. This allows the robot to make better decisions overall. We also have presented our ongoing experiment to test and evaluate this model.

7 Future Work

In the future, we would like to extend this system in different ways. First, as it is important for robots to dynamically adapt to the environment, we want to add self-learning capabilities to our system in order to improve the conflict handling done.

Secondly, we want to provide additional information to the robot in order for it to be able to make even better decisions. This could be done by providing virtual sensors that will provide more abstract information to the robot based on the data received from the sensors, like for example a virtual sensor for the danger level. These virtual sensors would behave in the same way as the normal sensors from the perspective of the robot.

References

1. Akbari, A., Thomas, X., Jafari, R.: Automatic noise estimation and context-enhanced data fusion of IMU and Kinect for human motion measurement. In: 2017 IEEE 14th International Conference on Wearable and Implantable Body Sensor Networks (BSN), pp. 178–182. IEEE (2017)
2. Bader, K., Lussier, B., Schön, W.: A fault tolerant architecture for data fusion: a real application of Kalman filters for mobile robot localization. Robot. Auton. Syst. **88**, 11–23 (2017). https://doi.org/10.1016/j.robot.2016.11.015. http://www.sciencedirect.com/science/article/pii/S0921889015302943
3. Baum, L.E., Eagon, J.A.: An inequality with applications to statistical estimation for probabilistic functions of markov processes and to a model for ecology. Bull. Am. Math. Soc. **73**(3), 360–363 (1967). https://projecteuclid.org:443/euclid.bams/1183528841
4. Baum, L.E., Petrie, T.: Statistical inference for probabilistic functions of finite state Markov chains. Ann. Math. Stat. **37**(6), 1554–1563 (1966). https://doi.org/10.1214/aoms/1177699147

5. Baum, L.E., Petrie, T., Soules, G., Weiss, N.: A maximization technique occurring in the statistical analysis of probabilistic functions of Markov chains. Ann. Math. Stat. **41**(1), 164–171 (1970). https://doi.org/10.1214/aoms/1177697196
6. Bostanci, E., Bostanci, B., Kanwal, N., Clark, A.F.: Sensor fusion of camera, GPS and IMU using fuzzy adaptive multiple motion models. Soft Comput. **22**(8), 2619–2632 (2018)
7. Cannarile, F., Compare, M., Baraldi, P., Di Maio, F., Zio, E.: Homogeneous continuous-time, finite-state hidden semi-Markov modeling for enhancing empirical classification system diagnostics of industrial components. Machines **6**(3), 34 (2018)
8. Chen, Z., Tian, L., Lin, C.: Trust model of wireless sensor networks and its application in data fusion. Sensors **17**(4), 703 (2017)
9. Dempster, A.P.: A generalization of bayesian inference. J. Roy. Stat. Soc. Ser. B (Methodol.) **30**(2), 205–247 (1968). http://www.jstor.org/stable/2984504
10. Dobrican, R.A., Neyens, G., Zampunieris, D.: A context-aware collaborative mobile application for silencing the smartphone during meetings or important events. Int. J. Adv. Intell. Syst. **9**(1&2), 171–180 (2016)
11. Gales, M., Young, S.: The application of hidden Markov models in speech recognition. Found. Trends Signal Process. **1**(3), 195–304 (2008)
12. Hide, C., Moore, T., Smith, M.: Adaptive kalman filtering for low-cost INS/GPS. J. Navig. **56**(1), 143–152 (2003)
13. Hu, S., Shao, Z., Tan, J.: A real-time cardiac arrhythmia classification system with wearable electrocardiogram. In: 2011 International Conference on Body Sensor Networks (BSN), pp. 119–124. IEEE (2011)
14. Huang, X.D., Ariki, Y., Jack, M.A.: Hidden Markov Models for Speech Recognition, vol. 2004. Edinburgh University Press, Edinburgh (1990)
15. Hussain, S., Mokhtar, M., Howe, J.M.: Sensor failure detection, identification, and accommodation using fully connected cascade neural network. IEEE Trans. Ind. Electron. **62**(3), 1683–1692 (2015). https://doi.org/10.1109/TIE.2014.2361600
16. Kalman, R.E.: A new approach to linear filtering and prediction problems. Trans. ASME-J. Basic Eng. **82**(Series D), 35–45 (1960)
17. Kordestani, M., Samadi, M.F., Saif, M., Khorasani, K.: A new fault prognosis of MFS system using integrated extended Kalman filter and Bayesian method. IEEE Trans. Ind. Inform., 1 (2018). https://doi.org/10.1109/TII.2018.2815036
18. Kwon, S., Ahn, H.: Sensor failure detection, identification and accommodation using neural network and fuzzy voter. In: 2017 17th International Conference on Control, Automation and Systems (ICCAS), pp. 139–144, October 2017. https://doi.org/10.23919/ICCAS.2017.8204431
19. McCulloch, W.S., Pitts, W.: A logical calculus of the ideas immanent in nervous activity. Bull. Math. Biophys. **5**(4), 115–133 (1943)
20. Naidu, S.R., Zafiriou, E., McAvoy, T.J.: Use of neural networks for sensor failure detection in a control system. IEEE Control Syst. Mag. **10**(3), 49–55 (1990). https://doi.org/10.1109/37.55124
21. Nemra, A., Aouf, N.: Robust INS/GPS sensor fusion for UAV localization using SDRE nonlinear filtering. IEEE Sens. J. **10**(4), 789–798 (2010)
22. Rabiner, L.R.: A tutorial on hidden Markov models and selected applications in speech recognition. Proc. IEEE **77**(2), 257–286 (1989)
23. Salfner, F., Malek, M.: Using hidden semi-Markov models for effective online failure prediction. In: 2007 26th IEEE International Symposium on Reliable Distributed Systems, SRDS 2007, pp. 161–174. IEEE (2007)

24. Salovaara, A., Oulasvirta, A.: Six modes of proactive resource management: a user-centric typology for proactive behaviors. In: Proceedings of the Third Nordic Conference on Human-Computer Interaction, pp. 57–60. ACM (2004)

25. Sasiadek, J., Wang, Q.: Sensor fusion based on fuzzy Kalman filtering for autonomous robot vehicle. In: 1999 Proceedings of IEEE International Conference on Robotics and Automation, vol. 4, pp. 2970–2975. IEEE (1999)

26. Shafer, G.: A Mathematical Theory of Evidence. Princeton University Press, Princeton (1976)

27. Shirnin, D., Reis, S., Zampunieris, D.: Design of proactive scenarios and rules for enhanced e-learning. In: Proceedings of the 4th International Conference on Computer Supported Education, Porto, Portugal, 16–18 April 2012, pp. 253–258. SciTePress-Science and Technology Publications (2012)

28. Tennenhouse, D.: Proactive computing. Commun. ACM **43**(5), 43–50 (2000)

29. Tom, K., Han, A.: Context-based sensor selection, 14 October 2014, US Patent 8,862,715

30. Turan, M., Almalioglu, Y., Gilbert, H., Araujo, H., Cemgil, T., Sitti, M.: Endosensorfusion: particle filtering-based multi-sensory data fusion with switching state-space model for endoscopic capsule robots. In: 2018 IEEE International Conference on Robotics and Automation (ICRA), pp. 1–8. IEEE (2018)

31. Webots: http://www.cyberbotics.com, commercial Mobile Robot Simulation Software

32. Yazdkhasti, S., Sasiadek, J.Z.: Multi sensor fusion based on adaptive Kalman filtering. In: Dołęga, B., Głębocki, R., Kordos, D., Żugaj, M. (eds.) Advances in Aerospace Guidance, Navigation and Control, pp. 317–333. Springer, Cham (2018). https://doi.org/10.1007/978-3-319-65283-2_17

33. Zampunieris, D.: Implementation of a proactive learning management system. In: Proceedings of "E-Learn-World Conference on E-Learning in Corporate, Government, Healthcare & Higher Education", pp. 3145–3151 (2006)

34. Zampunieris, D.: Implementation of efficient proactive computing using lazy evaluation in a learning management system (extended version). Int. J. Web-Based Learn. Teach. Technol. **3**, 103–109 (2008)

Indoor Robot Navigation Using Graph Models Based on BIM/IFC

Wojciech Palacz(✉), Grażyna Ślusarczyk, Barbara Strug, and Ewa Grabska

The Faculty of Physics, Astronomy and Applied Computer Science,
Jagiellonian University, ul. Łojasiewicza 11, 30-348 Kraków, Poland
wojciech.palacz@uj.edu.pl

Abstract. This paper deals with a method of path planning for indoor robots in buildings which is based on the building-related knowledge. Knowledge extracted from the IFC data model is used to construct a hypergraph model of the building layout. Information needed for route planning, e.g., room dimensions, directionality and types of doors, is stored in attributes attached to the hypergraph. As the declarative knowledge is represented by a graph-based structure, an artificial intelligence method in the form of a heuristic search of this structure is applied. A modified shortest-path search algorithm used to calculate the optimal route with regard to costs incurred by the robot during passing through different spaces and opening doors is proposed.

Keywords: Mobile robots · Route planning · Graph models ·
Knowledge representation · BIM/IFC

1 Introduction

This paper introduces a method of path planning for indoor robots in public buildings which is based on the building-related knowledge. The accessibility of different routes for robots depends both on the building structure and on the semantics of component elements (e.g., widths of corridors and door types). In order to perform complex and important tasks robots should be able to move without human assistance [11]. The suitable representation of the knowledge about the environment in which mobile robots operate is very important for their effective functioning. The most common representations, which allow for finding and following effective paths to targets, are metric, topological and hybrid representations [12,15,18].

Nowadays, when Building Information Modelling (BIM) is becoming a standard, information about spatial layouts of buildings and characteristics of their component elements can be extracted from Industry Foundation Classes (IFC) models. Spatial and non-spatial building-specific knowledge obtained from an IFC file can be stored in a graph. Therefore, for various types of self-sufficient mobile indoor robots graphs constitute an adequate representation which can be used to improve planning methods applied for them. Attributes assigned to

© Springer Nature Switzerland AG 2019
L. Rutkowski et al. (Eds.): ICAISC 2019, LNAI 11509, pp. 654–665, 2019.
https://doi.org/10.1007/978-3-030-20915-5_58

graph nodes store types of building elements and their sizes. Attributes of graph edges represent costs of moving between spaces, which depend on width of openings, existence of lifts, distances between spaces, and door types. On this graph, an AI method in the form of heuristic search is applied.

This paper contributes to the field of artificial intelligence methods applied to robot path planning theory and practice. It is known that knowledge about the building specified with the BIM/IFC files can be used for development of the planning space [5, 9, 17]. The proposed approach offers intelligent knowledge-based path planning for robots, which is based on the graph representation of buildings. While computing the lengths of accessible indoor routes, costs of passing through large open spaces like halls, lobbies and corridors, as well as costs of opening doors are taken into account.

The BIM/IFC files and graph models derived from them contain information about construction elements of a building. Elements like chairs, packages left on the floor and other movable obstacles are not represented. For this reason routes selected by the proposed algorithm can only be an approximate, high-level paths. The task of driving a robot through a room (or a segment of a corridor) while getting past unexpected obstacles has to be delegated to a low-level navigation algorithm. This paper assumes that mobile robots have such algorithms built in.

2 Related Work

Autonomous mobile robots must have three abilities: an ability to gain information about the environment, an ability for working for an extended period without human intervention, and an ability to move without human assistance. A suitable representation of the knowledge about the environment in which they operate is very important for their effective functioning. Robots must be able to recognize encountered objects as well as plan and follow paths to their targets.

The optimal path to follow is usually defined as the shortest one and calculated by an appropriate graph algorithm, e.g., the Dijkstra's one or A*. This means that a robot must have (or be able to construct at a moment's notice) a map of the building in the form of a graph, where nodes represent doors and other important points, and edges represent possible movements from one point to another [2]. In [8] a reduced visibility graph is used to reflect possible route choices and the Fastest-Path Algorithm finds the fastest path for travelers [4]. In [16] metrical-topological models constructed from labelled floor plan geometry are used to describe the shape and connectivity of space, and constitute useful underlying tools for wayfinding. However, for almost all current navigation applications complex building interiors with large open spaces and vertical communication means present challenges.

In this paper, graphs are used as the knowledge representation for the building data. Graphs are commonly used to model relations in many systems. They can be used in design systems to model topological relations between components, in databases to model logical relations between objects as well as to model data and control flow or specification and analysis of software systems. Majority of the research is focused on simple graphs, but many different types of graphs have also been developed. An extension of simple graphs, called CP-graphs, uses an additional notion of bonds which specify points of attachment for edges [13]. Hypergraphs extend simple graphs by allowing for hyperedges which connect multiple nodes instead of just two [10]. This paper uses hypergraphs, as they allow us to represent relations among specified fragments of building components.

One of the very important issues related to buildings is designing and maintaining their accessibility [1]. There is a lot of research related to searching for evacuation routes. In particular, the problem of searching for best routes for disabled people in public buildings is considered in [14]. The solution proposed in [14] creates a graph model of the considered building on the basis of information retrieved from IFC files, and then applies a modified version of the Dijkstra's algorithm. It, however, requires assigning to each graph node a lookup table containing the costs of passing through the space represented by this node.

This paper proposes an alternative method, in which such lookup tables are not necessary. The costs of passing from one door to another in the same space are calculated during the search, on the basis of node attributes. Also, a modified version of the A* algorithm is used instead of the Dijkstra's algorithm.

3   Graph Models Based on IFC Files

The IFC file format [3] provides an object-oriented semantic data model for storing and exchanging building information. It is an interoperable standard for CAD applications, which supports the exchange of information in Architecture, Engineering and Construction (AEC) industry in order to improve collaboration among different disciplines and applications. As is explained in [6], an IFC model is composed of IFC entities arranged in a hierarchical manner. Each entity includes a fixed number of attributes and any number of properties.

An IFC model includes information on floor layouts, accessibility between spaces, sizes of spaces, stairs and doors. [14] and [7] describe how this data can be extracted from a given IFC file. This paper proposes using their method in order to gather information required to construct an attributed hypergraph which models the building layout. Such hypergraphs have two types of hyperedges. Hyperedges of the first type, called component hyperedges, represent spaces. Fragments of components represented by hypergraph nodes correspond to the walls of spaces. Hyperedges of the second type, called relational hyperedges, represent relations among fragments of components and can be either directed or non-directed depending on the symmetry of relations.

Let us consider an example of the layout hypergraph in Fig. 2 representing the floor layout of the first floor of an office building shown in Fig. 1. The hypergraph contains eleven component hyperedges representing spaces. Each component hyperedge is connected with nodes representing walls of the corresponding area. Relational hyperedges labelled "acc" correspond to accessibility relations between the spaces and represent accessibility through doors, openings or through stairs between storeys.

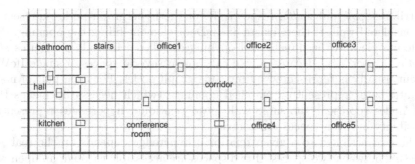

Fig. 1. A layout of the first floor of an office building

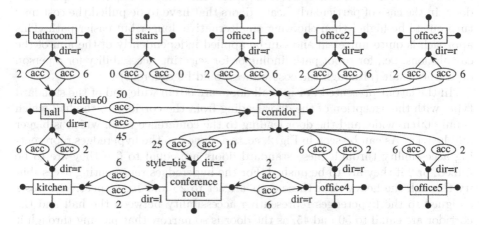

Fig. 2. A layout hypergraph corresponding to the floor layout from Fig. 1

Attributes of relational hyperedges store costs of moving between spaces, which depend on width of openings, equipping stairs with ramps, door types and their opening directions. The cost of passing from one accessible space to the other one can be different in respect to the passing direction, as for example pushing or pulling the door requires a different effort, similarly as going up and down the stairs. So, hyperedges representing the accessibility relation have to be directed with each of them representing passing between spaces in one direction. Labels of component hyperedges store names of spaces, while their attributes store other properties of spaces, like their types (rooms, corridors, stairs, etc.) and sizes. Node attributes store properties of openings.

Information provided by the extraction algorithm [7,14] is used to construct such a hypergraph model. For each IfcSpace or IfcStairs element, a component hyperedge representing this space is created. Then for each space all its bounding IfcWall elements are found, nodes representing them are created, and assigned as target nodes to the hyperedge representing the considered space. For each IfcWall element its openings are collected and their positions and widths saved in attributes *pos* and *width*, respectively, of the hypergraph node representing the considered wall. If there exists an IfcDoor element filling the opening, then the door style and the direction of opening are stored in node attributes *style* and *dir*, respectively. Because a wall can bound several spaces, a single IfcWall element usually is represented by multiple graph nodes. For each pair of nodes with attributes representing matched openings (which necessarily means that these nodes represent the same wall), two relational hyperedges representing accessibility between spaces are added.

The cost assigned to a given relational hyperedge depends on the real cost of passing between two spaces. If two spaces are accessible through an open wall then the hyperedge cost is set to 0. In the case of a door it is calculated as the number of meters that can be covered in the same time as required to pass that door. In the case of particularly heavy doors that have to be pulled the cost may turn out to be higher than choosing an alternative, longer but easier path. This approach is quite universal and can be applied independently of the aim of the calculations, i.e., for robot path finding or for selecting accessibility for a person on a wheelchair (although the cost values would be different).

In the layout presented in Fig. 1 all doors are 80 cm wide and of the standard type, with the exception of the door leading from the corridor to the hall which is only 60 cm wide, and the door leading to the conference room which is bigger and heavier. As can be seen in Fig. 2, costs assigned to the hyperedges representing accessibility through these standard doors are equal to 6 if they are to be pulled, or 2 if they are to be pushed. For the hyperedges representing accessibility through the heavy door these costs are set to 25 and 10, respectively. Costs assigned to the hyperedges representing accessibility between the hall and the corridor are equal to 50 and 45, as the door is so narrow that passing through it requires much effort from a robot. Costs of passing between the stairs and the corridor are equal to 0 as there is an opening between these spaces without a door to open.

4   Robot Path Planning Problem

The layout hypergraph representing building-specific knowledge, including positions and widths of openings and doors, styles and opening directions of doors, which influence the costs of moving between spaces and through them, is used to compute the optimal routes for robots. It should be noted that in the layout hypergraph the accessibility relation is defined between doors (or openings) in walls which bound spaces, not between whole spaces. Costs stored in the hyperedge attributes take into account only time required to open and pass doors. Time required to cross spaces is not represented at all. Therefore, the costs of passing from one door to another in the same space (each space can have several entry/exit points, especially the ones like halls or corridors) need to be calculated separately, on the basis of the distances between these doors which can be determined on the basis of the *pos* attributes assigned to hypergraph nodes that specify door locations (see appendix).

Inputs:
    layout_graph : hypergraph
    starting_room, target_room : hyperedge
Outputs:
    path_as_rooms : list<hyperedges>
    path_as_points : list<coordinates>
    path_cost : number
Temporary data generated on the fly:
    waypoint_graph : directed_graph
    starting_point, target_point : waypoint
                // "waypoint" means "a node in the waypoint_graph"
    waypoints_for_wall : map<node, set<waypoint>>
                // also serves as a "this wall was already processed" set
    waypoints_for_room : map<hyperedge, set<waypoint>>

Fig. 3. Data structures used by the algorithm from Fig. 4

At the first step of the search process, start and destination component hyperedges are defined. Then, in order to lower the computational cost, all component hyperedges representing spaces which are connected only by one entry/exit with other spaces, and are neither the start nor the destination one, are discarded from the hypergraph, as there is no possibility of passing through the spaces they represent. The optimal routes are computed using a modified single-source minimum-cost graph paths search algorithm. The modification allows for taking into account not only costs assigned to the relational hyperedges, but also distances between openings/doors. These distances are calculated when the search algorithm visits a given space for a first time. For spaces which are never reached no calculations are done—this lowers the computational cost even further.

Minimum cost path search algorithms, like Dijkstra's or A*, need a graph where nodes represent waypoints and the costs of moving between them are attached to edges. So, the discussed layout hypergraph cannot be used directly, but it contains information sufficient to construct a waypoint graph on the fly, during the run of the algorithm. To simplify this process we assume that all spaces are convex polygons which contain no obstacles.

For each space represented by a component hyperedge, a set of waypoints can be determined on the basis of attributes in the attached wall nodes. For each door leading in or out of this space, a single waypoint placed just in front of that door is constructed. For walls which are only partially solid (like the northern wall of the corridor in Fig. 1) or are fully void (the southern wall of the staircase) locations of openings are extracted, then for each opening three waypoints are constructed—two at the sides and third in the middle of the opening.

Waypoint nodes constructed for a given space are connected by edges (they form a complete subgraph), with costs proportional to the Euclidean distance between them. These edges will be denoted as "internal", as they represent movements internal to a single space. The waypoint graph needs to have "external"

```
function find_path
    starting_waypoint :=
            create_room_subgraph_return_centerpoint(starting_room)
    target_waypoint :=
            create_room_subgraph_return_centerpoint(target_room)
    open_set.add(starting_waypoint)
    g_score[starting_waypoint] := 0
    f_score[starting_waypoint] :=
                distance(starting_waypoint.coords, target_waypoint.coords)
    current := null
    while open_set is not empty
        previous := current
        current := element in open_set with the lowest f_score
        if current = target_waypoint
            calculate_outputs()
            return     // a path to the target was found!
        if previous is not null
            if waypoint_graph.edge(previous, current) is internal
                acc_walls := nodes connected to current.wall by "acc" edges
                foreach w in acc_walls
                    extract_waypoints_for_wall(w)
                    create_external_edges(current.wall, w)
            else
                // (previous, current) is external
                r := component hyperedge attached to current.wall
                create_room_subgraph(r)
        open_set.remove(current)
        closed_set.add(current)
        foreach neighbor of current
            if neighbor in closed_set
                continue
            if neighbor not in open_set
                open_set.add(neighbor)
            sc := g_score[current] + waypoint_graph.edge(current, neighbor).cost
            if sc >= g_score[neighbor]
                continue
            came_from[neighbor] := currrent
            g_score[neighbor] := sc
            f_score[neighbor] := g_score[neighbor] +
                        + distance(neighbor.coords, target_waypoint.coords)
```

Fig. 4. A modified A* algorithm

edges, too. They represent movements through a door or through an opening. Costs associated with them are the same as for the corresponding relational hyperedges in the layout hypergraph. Let us also assume that the robot starts and ends its path in the middle of a space. This adds two more waypoint nodes

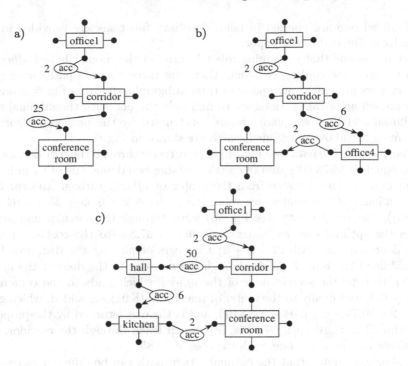

Fig. 5. Three subgraphs representing routes with different costs

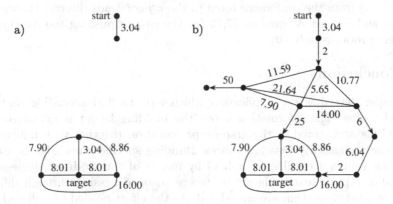

Fig. 6. Initial (a) and final (b) waypoint graphs

and their sets of "internal" edges. While computing the cost of moving from
the starting room to the target one, the costs assigned to "internal" edges are
summed up with costs assigned to "external" edges.

An enhanced version of the A* algorithm which includes these modifications
is presented in Fig. 4. The differences between the standard version of A* and

the modified one are marked in bold. Auxiliary functions are provided in the appendix at the end of the paper.

Let us assume that a cleaning robot located in the room labelled *office1* is to go to clean the conference room. There are three possible paths leading to the target room, which correspond to three subgraphs shown in Fig. 5; however, the proposed algorithm is designed to find only the one with the minimal cost. The initial and final waypoint graphs constructed by the proposed algorithm performing the above mentioned search are shown in Fig. 6.

The first possible path (see Fig. 5a) leads directly through the corridor, and its cost is equal to 38.73 (the sum of costs of passing two doors, one of them heavy, and of crossing the distance from the center of *office1*, through the corridor, to the middle of the conference room, i.e., $3.04 + 2 + 5.65 + 25 + 3.04$ (see Fig. 6b)). The second path (see Fig. 5b) leads through the corridor and *office4* and is the optimal one, as its cost is equal to 37.86 (to the cost of opening three doors on this path $(2 + 6 + 2)$ the costs of passing the distances from the middle of the *office1* (3.04) through the corridor to the door of the *office4* (10.77), then to the second door of the *office4* which leads to the conference room (6.04), and finally to the center of that room (8.01) are added, which gives $3.04 + 2 + 10.77 + 6 + 6.04 + 2 + 8.01$), and is the one returned by the proposed algorithm. The third path (see Fig. 5c), which leads through the corridor, hall and kitchen is the worst one, with the cost of 89.85.

It should be noted that the optimal return path can be different as costs of passing doors in opposite directions are different. In the running example the optimal way from the conference room to the *office1* leads directly through the corridor and its cost is equal to 27.73 (as the cost of pushing the doors of the conference room is only 10).

5   Conclusions

This paper describes the application which aids to find accessible routes to selected rooms. The information about the building layout is extracted from the IFC file and stored in the graph representation together with information about the accessibility between spaces. Building-specific knowledge is used to search for routes accessible for robots by means of the modified single-source minimal-cost path search algorithm, where costs of passing through different spaces and between them are considered. As the effort needed to pull and push doors is different, the cost of the route can depend on its direction, so the directed hypergraphs are used to represent layouts. The nodes of these hypergraphs represent walls surrounding spaces and attributes assigned to them allow us to store information about types of doors, their width and directions of opening.

In future the proposed algorithm will be modified to find not only the shortest but also other accessible routes and store them for emergency use, e.g., for situations when obstacles can block the shortest path or when one of the doors on this path are out of order or some spaces are temporarily inaccessible. In this approach, the hypergraph representation of building floor plans will be searched by the modified DFS method.

Appendix

Auxiliary functions invoked by the path finding algorithm from Fig. 4.

```
function create_room_subgraph(room : hyperedge)
    extract_waypoints_for_room(room)
    create_internal_edges(room)

function create_room_subgraph_return_centerpoint(room : hyperedge)
    extract_waypoints_for_room(room)
    centerpoint := waypoint_graph.new_node()
    centerpoint.coords := center of room
    waypoints_for_room[room].add(centerpoint)
    create_internal_edges(room)
    return centerpoint

function create_internal_edges(room : hyperedge)
    foreach s in waypoints_for_room[room]
        foreach t in waypoints_for_room[room]
            if s = t
                continue
            e := waypoint_graph.new_edge(s, t)
            e.cost := distance(s.coords, t.coords)
            e.internal := true

function create_external_edges(starting_wall, target_wall : node)
    foreach rel in "acc" edges outgoing from starting_wall to target_wall
        foreach s in waypoints_for_wall[starting_wall] which correspond to rel
            t := waypoint closest to s from waypoints_for_wall[target_wall]
            e := waypoint_graph.new_edge(s, t)
            e.cost := according to attributes of rel
            e.internal := false

function extract_waypoints_for_room(room : hyperedge)
    if room is in waypoints_for_room
        return waypoints_for_room[room]
    var results : set<waypoint>
    foreach x in nodes attached to room
        y := extract_waypoints_for_wall(x)
        results.add(y)
    waypoints_for_room[room] := result
    return results
```

```
function extract_waypoints_for_wall(wall : node)
    if wall is in waypoints_for_wall
        return waypoints_for_wall[wall]
    var results : set<waypoint>
    foreach attr in wall.attributes
        if attr describes a door
            n := waypoint_graph.new_node()
            n.wall := wall
            n.coords := middle of door
            results.add(n)
        elif attr describes an opening
            n1 := waypoint_graph.new_node()
            n1.wall := wall
            n1.coords := south-western end of opening
            n2 := waypoint_graph.new_node()
            n2.wall := wall
            n2.coords := middle of opening
            n3 := waypoint_graph.new_node()
            n3.wall := wall
            n3.coords := north-eastern end of opening
            results.add(n1, n2, n3)
    waypoints_for_wall[wall] := result
    return results

function calculate_outputs()
    path_as_rooms.push_front(target_room)
    path_as_points.push_front(target_waypoint.coords)
    current = target_waypoint
    while current in came_from
        path_cost += waypoint_graph.edge(came_from[current], current).cost
        current := came_from[current]
        r := room associated with current.wall
        if path_as_rooms.front() != r
            path_as_rooms.push_front(r)
        path_as_points.push_front(current.coords)
```

References

1. Bright, K., Di Giulio, R.: Inclusive Buildings: Designing and Managing an Accessible Environment. Blackwell Science, London (2002)
2. Büchel, D., Gilliéron, P.Y.: Pedestrian navigation inside buildings. Géomatique Suisse **11/2004**, 664–668 (2004). (in French)
3. buildingSMART International: IFC introduction. https://www.buildingsmart.org/about/what-is-openbim/ifc-introduction/. Accessed 10 Dec 2018
4. Höcker, M., Berkhahn, V., Kneidl, A., Borrmann, A., Klein, W.: Graph-based approaches for simulating pedestrian dynamics in building models. In: Menzel, K., Scherer, R. (eds.) Proceedings of the ECPPM 2010, pp. 389–394. CRC Press, Boca Raton (2010)

5. Isikdag, U., Zlatanova, S., Underwood, J.: A BIM-oriented model for supporting indoor navigation requirements. Comput. Environ. Urban Syst. **41**, 112–123 (2013)
6. Ismail, A., Nahar, A., Scherer, R.: Application of graph databases and graph theory concepts for advanced analysing of BIM models based on IFC standard. In: Proceedings of the 24th EG-ICE International Workshop, Nottingham, UK (2017)
7. Ismail, A., Strug, B., Ślusarczyk, G.: Building knowledge extraction from BIM/IFC data for analysis in graph databases. In: Rutkowski, L., Scherer, R., Korytkowski, M., Pedrycz, W., Tadeusiewicz, R., Zurada, J.M. (eds.) ICAISC 2018. LNCS (LNAI), vol. 10842, pp. 652–664. Springer, Cham (2018). https://doi.org/10.1007/978-3-319-91262-2_57
8. Kneidl, A., Borrmann, A., Hartmann, D.: Generating sparse navigation graphs for microscopic pedestrian simulation models. In: Proceedings of the 18th EG-ICE International Workshop. Twente, Netherlands (2011)
9. Lin, Y.H., Liu, Y.S., Gao, G., Han, X.G., Lai, C.Y., Gu, M.: The IFC-based path planning for 3D indoor spaces. Adv. Eng. Inform. **27**(2), 189–205 (2013)
10. Minas, M.: Concepts and realization of a diagram editor generator based on hypergraph transformation. Sci. Comput. Program. **44**(2), 157–180 (2002)
11. Siegwart, R., Nourbakhsh, I.R., Scaramuzza, D.: Introduction to Autonomous Mobile Robots, 2nd edn. The MIT Press, Cambridge (2011)
12. Ślusarczyk, G., Łachwa, A., Palacz, W., Strug, B., Paszyńska, A., Grabska, E.: An extended hierarchical graph-based building model for design and engineering problems. Autom. Constr. **74**, 95–102 (2017)
13. Strug, B., Paszyńska, A., Paszyński, M., Grabska, E.: Using a graph grammar system in the finite element method. Int. J. Appl. Math. Comput. Sci. **23**(4), 839–853 (2013)
14. Strug, B., Ślusarczyk, G.: Reasoning about accessibility for disabled using building graph models based on BIM/IFC. Vis. Eng. **5**(10), 1–12 (2017)
15. Tomatis, N.: Hybrid, metric-topological representation for localization and mapping. In: Jefferies, M.E., Yeap, W.K. (eds.) Robotics and Cognitive Approaches to Spatial Mapping. Springer Tracts in Advanced Robotics, vol. 38, pp. 43–63. Springer, Heidelberg (2007). https://doi.org/10.1007/978-3-540-75388-9_4
16. Whiting, E., Battat, J., Teller, S.: Topology of urban environments: graph construction from multi-building floor plan data. In: Dong, A., Vande Moere, A., Riitahuhta, A. (eds.) Computer-Aided Architectural Design Futures (CAADFutures) 2007, pp. 115–128. Springer, Dordrecht (2007). https://doi.org/10.1007/978-1-4020-6528-6_9
17. Xu, M., Wei, S., Zlatanova, S., Zhang, R.: BIM-based indoor path planning considering obstacles. ISPRS Ann. Photogramm. Remote Sens. Spat. Inf. Sci. **IV−2/W4**, 417–423 (2017)
18. Zender, H., Martínez Mozos, Ó., Jensfelt, P., Kruijff, G.J.M., Burgard, W.: Conceptual spatial representations for indoor mobile robots. Robot. Auton. Syst. **56**(6), 493–502 (2008)

An Algorithm for Swarm Robot to Avoid Multiple Dynamic Obstacles and to Catch the Moving Target

Quoc Bao Diep[1], Ivan Zelinka[1(✉)], and Roman Senkerik[2]

[1] Faculty of Electrical Engineering and Computer Science,
Technical University of Ostrava, 17. listopadu 15, Ostrava, Czech Republic
diepquocbao@gmail.com, ivan.zelinka@vsb.cz
[2] Department of Informatics and Artificial Intelligence,
Faculty of Applied Informatics, Tomas Bata University in Zlín,
Nad Stráněmi 4511, 76005 Zlín, Czech Republic
senkerik@utb.cz

Abstract. This paper presents a method for swarm robot to catch the moving target and to avoid multiple dynamic obstacles in the unknown environment. An imaginary map is built, including the highest mountain, some small hills, and a lowest lying land, respectively corresponding to the starting position of the robot, the detected obstacles, and the target. The robot is considered as a flow of water flowing from high to low. The flow of water is the robot trajectory that is divided into a set of points created by an algorithm called Self-organizing migrating algorithm. Simulation results are also presented to show that the obstacle avoidance and catching target task can be reached using this method.

Keywords: Self-organizing migrating algorithm · Obstacle avoidance ·
Swarm robot · Path planning

1 Introduction

One of the most important issues for swarm robotics applications is catching up with moving targets and avoiding multiple dynamic obstacles. It's complicated in that it requires an algorithm to work in real time to avoid obstacles that are standing or moving in an unknown environment where the robot does not know their position until detecting them by sensors arranged on the robot.

Besides the long-standing methods such as potential field method [8], and the vector field histogram [1], several new methods such as follow the gap method [10], and barrier function [2], or artificial intelligence methods such as genetic algorithm [7], and neural network [6] also demonstrate their effectiveness. Among the methods of artificial intelligence used to solve the problem as a function optimization problem, the self-organizing migrating algorithm (SOMA) emerges as a fast, powerful and efficient algorithm [4,12,13].

© Springer Nature Switzerland AG 2019
L. Rutkowski et al. (Eds.): ICAISC 2019, LNAI 11509, pp. 666–675, 2019.
https://doi.org/10.1007/978-3-030-20915-5_59

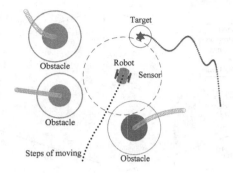

Fig. 1. The robot model and obstacles.

In this paper, the authors propose a method to guide the robot to catch the moving target without colliding with any dynamic obstacles based on the construction of an imaginary map and application of the SOMA.

2 Techniques

2.1 The Principle

The final goal of the robot is catching the moving target without colliding with any dynamic obstacles in the unknown environment. The assumptions outlined below ensure that the robot can work well under certain circumstances to ensure that the goal is achieved.

– *Robot*: For simplicity, all the physical dimensions of the robot are enclosed by a circle of radius r_{robot}. The sensors on the robot can accurately measure the distance to the obstacles within the sensors range, see Fig. 1. The robot is offered about the position of the target and can be controlled to reach a furthest desired position called moving step, i.e., the robot moves from the current position to a given furthest position without any difficulty. Moving step is a given parameter depending on the physical structure of the robot.
– *Obstacles*: Obstacles are considered as circles of radius r_{obs}. The obstacles can move at any speed and the robot does not know about the obstacles position until they are detected by the sensors.
– *Velocity*: The velocity of the robot must be greater than the velocity of each obstacle because if the opposite happens, the robot will not be able to avoid these dynamic obstacles. Similarly, to catch the target, the robot must move with the velocity greater than the target's velocity.

A method that can be visualized as *high mountain flowing water* is proposed to solve the issue. In this method, an imaginary map is built, in which the starting position of the robot considered as the top of the high mountain, the target considered as the lowest lying land, the obstacles considered as small hills,

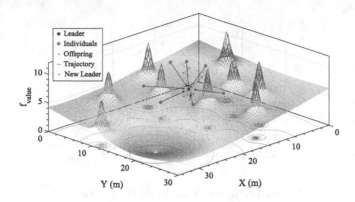

Fig. 2. The imaginary map.

and the robot considered as water, flowing from the top of the mountain to the lowest lying land, flowing around small hills without flowing back into them as natural law, see Fig. 2. When the target and obstacles move, the small hills and the lowest lying land also move respectively.

To build this map, a mathematical model will be shown in the next subsection.

2.2 The Imaginary Map

The starting position of the robot, the moving target, and the dynamic obstacles are three components that build the map, respectively corresponding to the top of the mountain, the lowest lying land, and the small hills. The lowest lying land and the small hills are not fixed things, but they will move based on the location of the target and the detected obstacles with the size of small hills depending on the distance and the size of obstacles.

The map is constructed using (1). Based on the idea presented above, the equation will contain two components: a sunken zone of the target created by the first component, depending on the distance (location) of the target that robot known; a raised zone of obstacles created by the second component, depending on the size and location of the obstacle.

$$f_{value} = \alpha \; dis_{tar} + \sum_{n=0}^{num_{obs}} \frac{c + r_{obs}}{b + dis_{obs}^2} \tag{1}$$

where:

- f_{value}: the fitness value,
- α: the sunken coefficient of the target,
- b: the influential coefficient of obstacle,
- c: the dynamic influential coefficient of obstacle,
- num_{obs}: the number of obstacles,

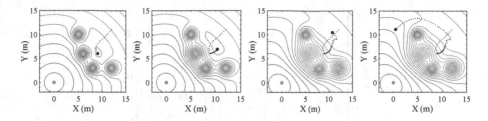

Fig. 3. The robot is trapped between obstacles.

- r_{obs}: the radius of obstacle,
- dis_{tar}: the distance from robot to target,
- dis_{obs}: the distance from robot to each detected obstacle.

The obstacles avoidance problem and catching target have now become an optimization problem, in which the optimal value is the fitness value in (1). At each processing times, SOMA will create a next point that robot must pass through. Two successive points are called moving step of robot, in which the distance from the current point to the next point must be less than or equal to the moving step, predetermined based on the physical structure of robot, see Sect. 2.1.

In case the robot is held by surrounding obstacles and the gaps between the obstacles is not enough for the robot to pass as shown in Fig. 3, the coefficient c will be changed to move the robot away from the hold. This coefficient plays the same role as the coefficient c in [5].

The robot trajectory is considered as a set of points created by SOMA that are presented in the next section.

3 Self-organizing Migrating Algorithm

SOMA was inspired by the competition-cooperation behavior of a group of intelligent insects while looking for food [12,13]. This algorithm has been applied to solve many different problems such as [9,11]. In the obstacles avoidance problem, SOMA acts as an algorithm that creates the next point for the robot move to. In other words, each individual in a population of SOMA is an imaginary point on the map.

At the start of the algorithm, a population containing all individuals is initialized around the current position of the robot based on (2). The population is then evaluated by the fitness function (1). A leader that contains the best fitness value is chosen for the current migration loop.

$$Pos_i = Pos_{actual} + rand_{-1 \to 1} Pos_{max} \tag{2}$$

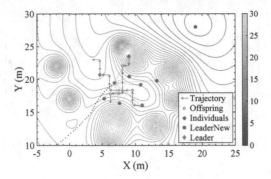

Fig. 4. The principle of SOMA.

where:

- Pos_i: the position of the ith individual,
- Pos_{actual}: the actual position of the robot,
- Pos_{max}: the maximum position,
- $rand_{-1 \to 1}$: random number from -1 to 1.

Then, the mutation process takes place in preparation for the perturbation movement of individuals [12,13]. A random number created in $[0,1]$ is compared with a given number of SOMA (called PRT) to perform the perturbation movement, see (3). Different from other evolutionary algorithms, the mutation process is performed before the crossover process. In order words, the $PRTVector$ is created and changed at each individual jump, before an individual performs its movement to ensure diversity of the population and increase the efficiency of the algorithm. Therefore, the individual trajectory is not straight, but the ladder, see Figs. 2 and 4.

$$if \ rand < PRT; \ PRTVector = 1; \ else, \ 0. \tag{3}$$

The offspring in SOMA are generated by the crossover process to create a set of new individuals by moving the parent individual perturbatively [3,12,13]. In other words, parents move towards the leader in trajectories created earlier by $PRTVector$ in the mutation process, see (4).

$$P_{os}^{new} = P_{current} + (P_{leader} - P_{current}) \ t \ PRTVector \tag{4}$$

where:

- P_{os}^{new}: the offspring position in new migration loop,
- $P_{current}$: the offspring position in current migration loop,
- P_{leader}: the leader position in current migration loop,
- t: jumping step, from 0 to $PathLength$.

Finally, the new leader is chosen not only to have the lowest fitness value but also to have the distance between the actual position of the robot and new leader must be smaller than the moving step given before.

4   Simulation Results

4.1   Setup

Matlab has been used to implement the proposed algorithm with the environment presented below.

- The robot used in the simulation was placed at the position $(1,1)$m, with a radius $r_{robot} = 0.8$ m. The sensors can detect obstacles within a radius $r_{sensor} = 3.5$ m. The moving step of the robot $r_{movingstep} = 0.3$ m.
- The size and the initial positions of the obstacles are given in Table 1. In this simulation, the obstacles were placed in 9 different positions, including three standing obstacles (from 7th to 9th), six remaining dynamic obstacles moving in different trajectory and given in Table 2.
- The trajectory of the target is given in Table 2.
- The parameters of SOMA are given in Table 3.

Table 1. The initial position and radius of obstacles

$Obstacle_i$	1	2	3	4	5	6	7	8	9
x_i (m)	03	17	08	34	15	15	08	25	13
y_i (m)	10	08	22	10	03	17	16	04	26
r_i (m)	2.1	2.4	2.0	2.3	2.0	1.8	2.2	2.5	2.3

Table 2. The trajectory of obstacles and the target

$Obstacle_i$	$x(m)$	$y(m)$
1	$2sin(t/13)^2 + t/20$	$-t/10$
2	$t/22$	$sin(t/19) + t/11$
3	$t/15$	$-t/110$
4	$-sin(t/19) - t/11$	$cos(t/20)$
5	$-t/13$	$-sin(t/13) + t/11$
6	$t/60$	$0t$
$Target$	$-t/900$	$0.25sin(t/13)^2 - t/750$

Table 3. The parameters of SOMA

PopSize	Migration	PathLength	PRT	Step
40	10	2.7	0.1	0.11

4.2   Results

Figure 5 shows the simulation results. The dark color circles represent the dynamic obstacles, numbered 1 through 9 respectively, and they turn red to indicate that they are detected by the sensor of the robot. The black and blue dotted line show the trajectories of the robot and the target respectively. The green circle dotted line shows the trajectory of the obstacles. The figures were captured at 15th, 30th, 50th, 69th, 100th and 123rd s.

At the beginning of time, no obstacles were detected, so in the map, there was only an element of the sunken zone of the target. At the 15th s, the first obstacle

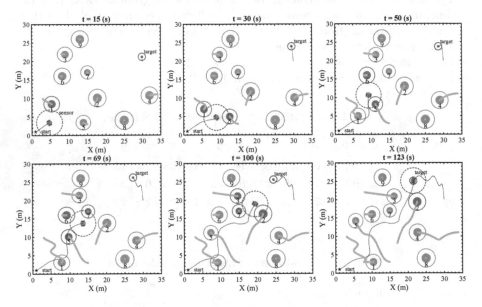

Fig. 5. The moving process of robot at different times. (Color figure online)

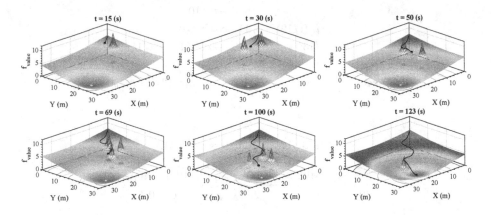

Fig. 6. The detailed trajectory of the robot in 3D map.

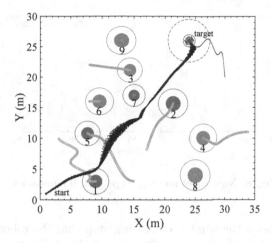

Fig. 7. Simulations were repeated 100 times.

was detected, a small hill appeared on the map (see Fig. 6), which influenced the trajectory of robot. At 30th s, two obstacles were detected, the 1st and the 5th, so two small hills appeared in the map. Since the gap between the two obstacles is wide enough, the robot moves through the gap to catch the target, as can be seen in Fig. 6. This process continues until the robot catches the moving target. Since the speed of the robot is greater than the speed of the obstacles (assumed in Sect. 2.1), the robot can completely avoid them. In case the robot is trapped by surrounding obstacles, the coefficient c will be changed, and the size of the small hill will become larger, leading the robot away from the hold, as shown in Fig. 3 and [5].

In this simulation, it took 123 s for the robot to reach the target. During the movement of the robot, the 4th, 8th, and 9th obstacles were undetected, in other words, they did not affect the movement of the robot, not appear on the map, although they still existed in reality.

Figure 6 shows the entire process of moving the robot in the form of a 3D map at the same time as shown in Fig. 5. The small hills rising upwards indicate that obstacles have been detected. The black dot is the position of the robot, the yellow dot is the position of the target, and it moves with the trajectory given in Table 2, the sunken zone also changes accordingly. In this map, the robot as a stream flows from high to low, moving round the small hills. When the hills change their position and size, the water is pushed to a lower land, as natural law. It means that the robot always tends to move to the target and not move into the obstacles.

To ensure the stability of the algorithm, the simulation was repeated 100 times, in which, the moving step of the robot changed to $r_{movingstep} = 0.4$ m, the parameters of simulation were preserved.

Figure 7 shows the trajectories of the robot, target, and obstacles after 100 simulation times. The black dotted line demonstrates the stability of the algo-

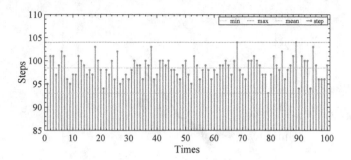

Fig. 8. Number of moving steps in 100 simulations.

rithm. Figure 8 shows the number of moving step that the robot needs to reach the target. The minimum number is 93 steps at the 79th simulation, maximum number is 104 steps at the 68th and the 89th simulation.

5   Conclusion

The paper has solved the whole problem of catching the moving targets and avoiding multiple dynamic obstacles. The paper also successfully built a 3D map which depicts the robot, target, obstacles corresponding to the top of the mountains, small hills, and the lowest lying land. The trajectory of the robot was divided into a set of points, and the SOMA algorithm was proposed to find a reasonable trajectory for the robot. The paper also suggested ways leaving the robot moving away from the trapped area when the robot be held by the surrounding obstacles. The simulation results have been shown to demonstrate that the method is effective.

Acknowledgment. The following grants are acknowledged for the financial support provided for this research: Grant of SGS 2019/137, VSB-Technical University of Ostrava. The Author Roman Senkerik would like to acknowledge the support of the Ministry of Education, Youth and Sports of the Czech Republic within the National Sustainability Programme Project no. LO1303 (MSMT-7778/2014), further the European Regional Development Fund under the Project CEBIA-Tech no. CZ.1.05/2.1.00/03.0089.

References

1. Borenstein, J., Koren, Y.: The vector field histogram-fast obstacle avoidance for mobile robots. IEEE Trans. Robot. Autom. **7**(3), 278–288 (1991)
2. Chen, Y., Peng, H., Grizzle, J.: Obstacle avoidance for low-speed autonomous vehicles with barrier function. IEEE Trans. Control Syst. Technol. **99**, 1–13 (2017)
3. Davendra, D., Zelinka, I.: Optimization of quadratic assignment problem using self organising migrating algorithm. Comput. Inform. **28**(2), 169–180 (2012)

4. Davendra, D., Zelinka, I., et al.: Self-organizing migrating algorithm. New Optimization Techniques in Engineering (2016)
5. Diep, Q.B., Zelinka, I.: Obstacle avoidance for swarm robot based on self-organizing migrating algorithm. In: XIIIth International Symposium Intelligent Systems, INTELS 2008, St. Petersburg, Russia (2018, accepted, in print)
6. Duguleana, M., Mogan, G.: Neural networks based reinforcement learning for mobile robots obstacle avoidance. Expert Syst. Appl. **62**, 104–115 (2016)
7. Hu, Y., Yang, S.X.: A knowledge based genetic algorithm for path planning of a mobile robot. In: 2004 Proceedings of IEEE International Conference on Robotics and Automation, ICRA 2004, vol. 5, pp. 4350–4355. IEEE (2004)
8. Koren, Y., Borenstein, J.: Potential field methods and their inherent limitations for mobile robot navigation. In: 1991 Proceedings of IEEE International Conference on Robotics and Automation, pp. 1398–1404. IEEE (1991)
9. Senkerik, R., Zelinka, I., Davendra, D., Oplatkova, Z.: Utilization of SOMA and differential evolution for robust stabilization of chaotic logistic equation. Comput. Math. Appl. **60**(4), 1026–1037 (2010)
10. Sezer, V., Gokasan, M.: A novel obstacle avoidance algorithm: "follow the gap method". Robot. Auton. Syst. **60**(9), 1123–1134 (2012)
11. Tomaszek, L., Zelinka, I.: Analysis of SOMA algorithm using complex network. In: Zelinka, I., Chen, G. (eds.) Evolutionary Algorithms, Swarm Dynamics and Complex Networks. ECC, vol. 26, pp. 115–129. Springer, Heidelberg (2018). https:// doi.org/10.1007/978-3-662-55663-4_5
12. Zelinka, I.: SOMA-self-organizing migrating algorithm. New Optimization Techniques in Engineering. Studies in Fuzziness and Soft Computing, vol. 141, pp. 167–217. Springer, Heidelberg (2004). https://doi.org/10.1007/978-3-540-39930-8_7
13. Zelinka, I.: SOMA—self-organizing migrating algorithm. In: Davendra, D., Zelinka, I. (eds.) Self-Organizing Migrating Algorithm. SCI, vol. 626, pp. 3–49. Springer, Cham (2016). https://doi.org/10.1007/978-3-319-28161-2_1

Emergence of Collective Behavior in Large Cellular Automata-Based Multi-agent Systems

Franciszek Seredyński and Jakub Gąsior[✉]

Department of Mathematics and Natural Sciences,
Cardinal Stefan Wyszyński University, Warsaw, Poland
{f.seredynski,j.gasior}@uksw.edu.pl

Abstract. We study conditions of emergence of collective behavior of agents acting in the two-dimensional (2D) Cellular Automata (CA) space, where each agent takes part in spatial Prisoner's Dilemma (PD) game. The system is modeled by 2D CA evolving in discrete moments of time, where each cell-agent changes its state according to a currently assigned to its rule. Rules are initially assigned randomly to cells-agents, but during iterated game agents may replace their current rules by rules used by their neighbors. While each agent is oriented on maximization of its own profit in the game, we are interested in answering the question if and when a phenomenon of global cooperation in a large set of agents is possible. We present results of the experimental study showing conditions and degree of such cooperation.

Keywords: Collective behavior · Multi-agent systems ·
Spatial prisoner's dilemma game · Second order cellular automata

1 Introduction

The emergence of cooperation between members of human teams is a subject of study for a number of years. Understanding the mechanisms and conditions of emerging cooperation is important for different areas of science, including computer science, in particular in parallel and distributed computing. Phenomena of competition and cooperation can be seen, e.g. in cloud computing [4], where a huge number of users compete for distributed computational resources or in the Internet of Things [3], where tiny sensors should cooperate to conserve their batteries.

The Prisoner's Dilemma (PD) game [9] is one of the most accepted game-theoretical models where both *cooperation* and *defection* of humans can be observed. A. Tucker was a scientist who first formalized the game as the 2-person game around 1950. At the beginning of 1980s, R. Axelrod organized the first tournament [1] to recognize competitive strategies in the 2-person Iterated Prisoner's Dilemma (IPD) game and the winner was a strategy Tit-For-Tat

© Springer Nature Switzerland AG 2019
L. Rutkowski et al. (Eds.): ICAISC 2019, LNAI 11509, pp. 676–688, 2019.
https://doi.org/10.1007/978-3-030-20915-5_60

(TFT). TFT assumes cooperation of a player on the first move and subsequent repeating actions of the opponent player used in the previous move. Because Genetic Algorithms (GAs) became at that time a popular search technique in solving optimization problems, Axelrod proposed [2] to apply GAs to discover strategies enabling cooperation in the 2-person PD game. GAs were able to discover TFT strategy and a number of other interesting strategies specific for humans.

While discovering cooperating strategies in the 2-person PD game was relatively easy, discovering strategies of cooperation in N-person PD games ($N > 2$) is not easy problem. The approach proposed by Axelrod to code an individual of GA was not effective in this case, therefore Yao and Darwen proposed in [12] another approach where GAs are still applied but the payoff function of the game was simplified, which enabled to reduce the size of an individual of GA. The main idea of the simplified payoff function was that a payoff of a given player in the game depends on a number of cooperating players among the remaining $N - 1$ participants of the game. Under these assumptions, GA was able to find strategies of players enabling global cooperation for a number of players equal to around 10. For more players, such strategies were not discovered by GA. One of the main reasons of that is the form of the payoff function which in fact assumes participation of a player in a game with a "crowd" - a large number of anonymous persons without any structural relations between them. It is rather difficult to imagine a reasonable behavior in such a crowd.

A concept of spatial games in 2D space with a neighbor relation between players is a solution of the crowd problem. Among the first concepts related to spatial IPD was a game on the ring considered by Tsetlin [10] in the context of games of Learning Automata (LA), where a payoff of a given player depends on its action and actions of two immediate neighbors.

A number of spatial IPD games on 2D grids has been studied recently. Nowak and May proposed [8] an original spatial IPD game on a 2D grid with two types of players - players who always cooperate (all-C) and players who always defect (all-D). Players occupy cells of 2D space and each of them plays PD game with all neighbors and depending on the total score is replaced by the best performing player in the neighborhood. They show that both types of players persist indefinitely in chaotically changing local structures.

Ishibuschi and Namikawa studied in [6] a variant of spatial IPD game with two neighborhoods: one for playing locally defined PD game with randomly selected neighbors, and the second one for mating strategies of the game by a locally defined GA. Howley and O'Riordan considered in [5] N-person IPD game with all-to-all interactions between players and existence of a tagging mechanisms structure in subgroups of players. Katsumata and Ishida in [7] extended the model of spatial IPD games proposed by [8] by considering 2D space as the 2D CA and introducing an additional strategy called k-D, which tolerates at most k defections in local neighborhood. They showed emergence of specific spatial structures called membranes created by players using k-D strategies, which separate cooperating and defecting players.

In this paper we consider the model proposed in [7] but we focus on the study of the issue of emerging collective behavior in large teams of players. The structure of the paper is following. In the next Section some background concerning CA is given. Section 3 contains details of the studied spatial IPD game. Section 4 contains the results of the experimental study, and the last Section contains Conclusions.

2   Cellular Automata

CA are spatially and temporally discrete computational systems originally proposed by Ulam and von Neumann in the late 1940s to study processes of self-reproduction of machines. Today they are powerful tools used in computer science, mathematics and natural science to model different phenomena and develop parallel and distributed algorithms [11].

One-dimensional (1D) CA is in the simplest case a collection of two-state elementary cells arranged in a lattice of the length n, which locally interact and evolve in a discrete time t.

For each cell $i\,(0 \leq i \leq n-1)$ called a central cell, a neighborhood of a radius r is defined. The neighborhood consists of $n_i = 2r + 1$ cells, including the cell i (sometimes a central cell is not included). A cyclic boundary condition is applied to a finite size of CA, which results is in a circle grid.

It is assumed that a state q_i^{t+1} of the i-th cell at the time $t+1$ depends only on states of its neighbors at the time t, and a transition function f called also a rule defines the way of updating the cell i. If CA updates states of its cells according to a single rule assigned to all cells, such CA is called a uniform CA. If two or more different rules are assigned to update cells, such CA is called a non-uniform CA.

Two dimensional (2D) CA is 2D lattice consisting of $n \times n$ elementary cells. For each cell a local 2D neighborhood of a radius r is defined. At a given discrete moment of time t each cell (i, j) is in some state $q_{i,j}^t$, in the simplest case it is a binary number 0 or 1.

At discrete moments of time, all cells synchronously update their states according to the local rules (transition functions), which depend on states of their neighborhood. A cyclic boundary condition is also applied to the finite size of 2D CA. 2D CA can be also uniform or non-uniform. In classical CA rules assigned to cells are not changed during evolving CA cells.

3   Iterated Spatial Prisoner's Dilemma Game

We consider 2D CA of the size $n \times n$. Each cell of CA has a Moore neighborhood of radius r, and also a rule assigned to it which depends on the state of its neighborhood.

Each cell of 2D CA will be considered as an agent (player) participating in the iterated spatial Prisoner's Dilemma (ISPD) game. Each player (a cell of CA) has two possible actions: C (cooperate) and D (defect). It means that at a given moment of time each cell is either in the state C or the state D. Payoff function of the game is given in Table 1.

Table 1. Payoff function of a row player participating in ISPD game.

Action	Cooperate (C)	Defect (D)
Cooperate (C)	$R = 1$	$S = 0$
Defect (D)	$T = b$	$P = 0$

Each player playing a game with an opponent player in a single round (iteration) receives a payoff equal to R, T, S or P. Values of these payoffs used in this study are specified in Table 1, where $P = S = 0$, $R = 1$, and $T = b \, (1.1 < b < 1.8)$. If a player takes action C and the opponent player also takes action C than the player receives payoff equal to $R = 1$. However, if a player takes action D and the opponent player still takes action C, the defecting player receives payoff equal to $T = b$. In two remaining cases, a player receives a payoff equal to 0. This payoff function was originally proposed in [8] and later also used by [7]. It slightly differs from a standard PD game [1,9], where the assumption is that $T > R > P > S$. It preserves the essentials of PD $(T > R > P)$ and by keeping $P = S$ simplifies the model making the parameter b the only parameter in the model.

In fact, each player associated with a given cell plays in a single round a game with each of his 8 neighbors and this way collects some total score. After q number of rounds (iterations of CA) each cell (agent) of CA can change its rule (strategy). We assume that considered 2D CA is non-uniform CA, and to each cell one of the following rules can be assigned: *all-C* (always cooperate), *all-D* (always defect), and *k-D* (cooperate until not more than $k \, (0 \le k \le 7)$ neighbors defect). The strategy *k-D* is a generalized strategy TFT, and when $k = 0$ it is exactly the strategy TFT.

A player changes its current strategy into another one comparing collected during q rounds total score with scores collected by his neighbors. He selects as his new strategy the strategy of the best performing neighbor, i.e. the player whose the collected total score is the highest. This new strategy is used by a cell (player) to change its current state, and the value of the state is used in games during the next q rounds.

It is worth to notice that the considered 2D CA differs from a classical CA, where rules assigned to cells do not change during evolving CA in time. CA with a possibility of changing rules is called the second order CA. In opposite to classical CA, the second-order CA has potentials to solve optimization problems.

The concept of a dynamic changing of CA rules during evolving in time was proposed by [8] who used only two strategies *all-C* and *all-D* and was interested in observing sequences of spatial patterns - dynamic fractals, and studying their mathematical properties. In [7] the model proposed by [8] was extended by adding additional strategy *k-D*, and the main research issue was to study conditions of appearing of specific structures called membranes created by cells using *k-D* rules which protected cooperated players from defected players. In this study we follow the main assumptions of the model considered in [7] but we are interested in the collective behavior of a large team of players, in particular in conditions of emerging global cooperation in such teams.

4   Experimental Results

4.1   Experimental Parameters Settings

The following settings were used in the experiments:

- 2D CA with a size of 100×100 was used, i.e. with a total number of agents equal to 10000.
- An initial state (C or D) of each cell was set with probability $p_1 = 0.5$.
- To each cell one of 3 rules (*all-C*, *all-D*, *k-D*) was assigned with probability $p_2 = 0.33$; for a given run a constant value of k from the range $[0, \dots, 7]$ was set, but for a cell to which rule *k-D* was assigned, the value of k was an integer number randomly generated from the range $[0, \dots, k]$.
- A neighborhood of each cell was set to $r = 1$.
- For a given run, the value of b was selected from the range $[1.1, \dots, 1.8]$.
- Updating of rules assigned to cells was conducted after $q = 1$ rounds (iterations).
- During a single run of an experiment, depending on values of b, a number of rounds ranged from 100 to 500.
- If averaging of results was applied it was done on the base of 30 single runs.

4.2   Experiment #1: Sample Runs of ISPD Game

The purpose of the first set of experiments was to observe the dynamics of the game for some values of the main parameter of the payoff function b and strategies *all-C*, *all-D* and *k-D* $k = 0, 1, 2, 3$ used by players. Figure 1 shows 10 sample runs for a given value of $b = 1.4$.

One can see that in 1 run over 10 the team of players achieves a level of cooperation close to 100% of cooperating players after around 40 iterations. Global cooperation on the level around 90% is achieved after near 350 iterations in 4 out of 10 runs. In remaining runs cooperation on the level around of 70% is observed and achieving this state requires around 380 iterations. All runs can be classified into one of three classes of behavior. We observe the first class of behavior when after reaching a peak level of cooperation it is continued in a stable way. The second class of behavior is characterized by reaching a peak of cooperation which next is decreasing during some number of iteration, and in the final phase players slowly return to the previous peak of cooperation. The third class of cooperation is similar to the previous one but after decreasing phase of cooperation, the players stabilize their behavior providing a level cooperation lover that in the peak phase.

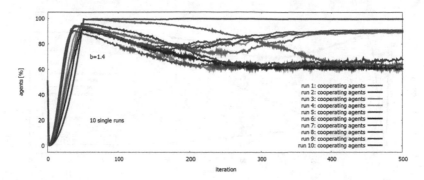

Fig. 1. Ten sample runs for the value of parameter $b = 1.4$ and k-D strategy with $k = 0, 1, 2, 3$.

Figure 2 shows more details of a single run of the game with the parameters like in Fig. 1. One can see (Fig. 2(a)) that the behavior of the players in the game corresponds to the second class of behavior, according to the classification given above. In the beginning phase of the game, players achieve a peak level of cooperation close to 90% (red color). In the next phase the level of cooperation is slowly decreasing to return back to the level of cooperation close to the peak one. Figure 2(a) explains also the behavior of players in terms of distribution of strategies between players during the game. The peak level of the cooperation achieved in the first phase of the game is a result of increasing number of players who use *all-C* strategy (yellow color). Exploiting *all-C* strategy finds its limit because more and more players discover that k-D strategy (color green) or even *all-D* strategy are more profitable when surrendering players mainly cooperate (the second phase of the game). It results in a decreasing of the level of global cooperation. Players using *all-D* strategy find in around 150 iteration that more profitable strategy is k-D, and this strategy becomes dominating during the third phase of the game. We can observe some equilibrium of distribution of strategies between players. About 75% of the players use k-D, about 23% use *all-C* strategy and remaining 2% of the players use *all-D*.

Figure 2(b) gives more detailed information about k-D strategy mainly use in this run. We can see that about 70% of players use *3-D* strategy and remaining players use other k-D strategy ($k = 0, 1, 2$ but their frequencies are low.

4.3 Experiment #2: Sample Runs of ISPD Game Under Different Values of Parameters b and k

The purpose of the second set of experiments was to observe the dynamics of the game for different values of the parameter b and strategies *all-C*, *all-D* and k-D $k = 0, 1, 2, 3$. Figure 3 shows typical single runs of the game under values of the parameter $b = 1.2$ and $b = 1.6$ with use of k-D, $k = 0, 1, 2, 3$. One can see (Fig. 3a) that for the game with the parameter $b = 1.2$ players very quickly achieve the level of cooperation equal to 95% (in red). Prevailing number of players (about

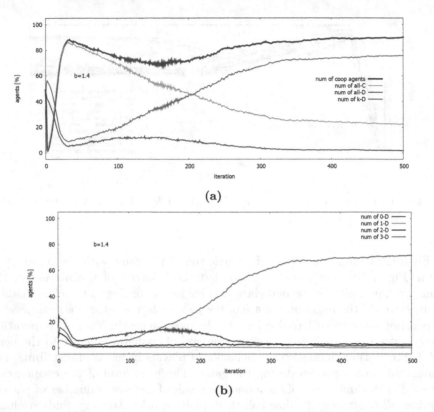

Fig. 2. A single run for the value of parameter $b = 1.4$ and $k - D$ strategy with $k = 0, 1.2, 3$: (a) a number of cooperating agents and applied strategies as a function of a number of iteration, (b) development of strategy $all\text{-}D$, $k = 0, 1, 2, 3$. (Color figure online)

90%) use $all\text{-}C$ strategy (yellow color), about 7% use $k\text{-}D$ strategy (green color) and about 3% use $all\text{-}D$ strategy (black color). When the parameter $b = 1.6$ (see, (Fig. 3b)) the team of players achieves much lover level of cooperation, about 47%. This level of cooperation is the result of using by about 46% of players the strategy $all\text{-}C$, by another 46% of players the strategy $k\text{-}D$, and about by 7% the strategy $all\text{-}D$.

Figure 4 shows single runs of the game played during 100 iterations for the range $[1.1, \ldots, 1.7]$ of the parameter b, and TFT strategy ($k = 0$). We do not show results of experiments with another value of k because the behavior of the team of players does not depend too much on the value of k used in the strategy of $k\text{-}D$ but sufficiently depends on the parameter of b.

One can see that players team achieves the level of near 95% cooperation in the range of values of b between 1.1 and 1.3. When the value of b is in the range $[1.4, \ldots, 1.5]$ a high level of cooperation is possible. When $b = 1.6$

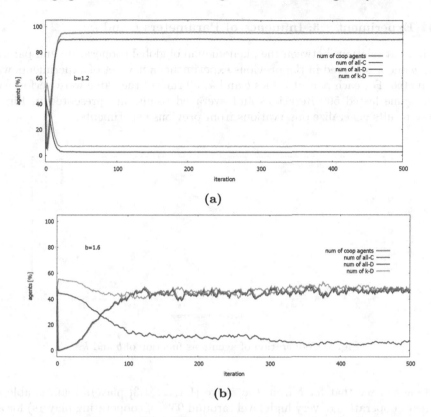

Fig. 3. A single run with *all-D*, $k = 0, 1, 2, 3$ for: (a) the value of parameter $b = 1.2$, (b) the value of parameter $b = 1.6$ (Color figure online)

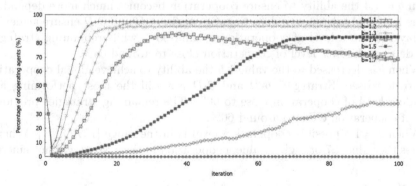

Fig. 4. Sample runs for a range of values b and TFT strategy.

cooperation emerges very slowly and the players' team is not able to cooperate for values of $b \geq 1.7$.

4.4   Experiment #3: Influence of Parameters b and k

To find out relations between the phenomenon of global cooperation and parameters b and k observed in the previous experiments a new set of experiments was conducted. For each pair of values b and k, 30 runs of the game were performed. Each game lasted 500 iterations and averaged results are presented in Fig. 5. These results generalize observations from previous experiments.

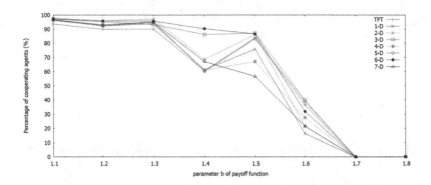

Fig. 5. Cooperation of agents as function of b and k.

One can see that for b from the range $[1.1, \ldots, 1.3]$ players team is able to achieve cooperation of very high level (around 95% of cooperating players) for all strategies k-D. Small differences are visible: *TFT* strategy is slightly less effective than other strategies, while the best performing strategies are *6-D* and next *3-D*. When $b = 1.4$ the ability to ensure cooperation becomes much more dependent on the level k of tolerance of defecting. Strategies *6-D* and *3-D* ensure achieving by players team a level of cooperation around 90%, while remaining strategies provide a much lower level of cooperation close to around 65%.

When b is decreased to the value 1.5 the ability to achieve global cooperation is also decreased. Strategies *6-D* and *3-D* are still the most performing and provide a level of cooperation close to 90%. The remaining strategies provide a level of cooperation close to around 60%.

When $b = 1.6$ possible cooperation level is in the range [15%–40%]. When b reaches the value 1.7 or higher value, cooperation in the system will not emerge.

4.5   Experiment #4: Patterns of Agents' Actions and Strategies

For presented in Fig. 5 dependencies between the level of global cooperation and parameters b and k accompany spatial patterns of actions taken by players and patterns of strategies used by them. Because the main factor influencing these dependencies is the parameter b presented patterns are shown for a constant value of $k = 3$.

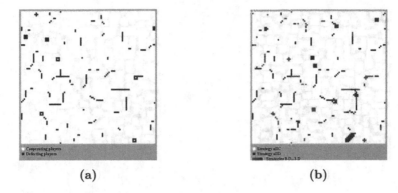

(a)   **(b)**

Fig. 6. $b = 1.1$, *3-D*: agents' actions (a) and strategies (b).

Figure 6 shows corresponding patterns of players' actions and strategies used by them for a game with parameter $b = 1.1$. One can see that dominating action used by players (see, Fig. 6a) is action C (white color), and rarely action D (black color) is used. Actions of players which defect create short, isolated, sometimes vertical or horizontal regular structures. Dominating strategy used by players (see, Fig. 6b) is strategy *all-C* (white color), and some players use strategies *all-D* and *k-D*. Spatial structure of strategies assignment is similar to actions structure.

For games with values $b = 1.2$ and $b = 1.3$ (not shown) spatial structures of actions and strategies are similar like for the game with $b = 1.1$, but we can observe an increasing length of regular vertical and horizontal structures, which are still isolated for $b = 1.2$, but mostly connected for $b = 1.3$. We can see also an increasing number of strategies *k-D* which replace strategy $all - D$.

For $b = 1.4$ (see, Fig. 7) spatial structures of both actions and strategies are created by different sizes connected rectangles. For the actions pattern (see, Fig. 7a) rectangles are created by increasing number of action D, and for the strategies pattern (see, Fig. 7b) by similar number of strategies *all-D* and strategies *k-D*.

When $b = 1.5$ (see, Fig. 8) both actions and strategies spatial structures are created by irregular isolated chains, wherein the strategies pattern more than half of strategies *all-D* was replaced by strategies *k-D*.

When $b = 1.6$ we can see (see, Fig. 9a) that players playing action C create isolated structures surrounded by prevailing number of players playing action D. However, when we look at the strategies pattern (Fig. 9b) we notice that most strategies *all-D* were replaced by strategy *k-D*.

Finally, when $b = 1.7$ we can notice (not shown) that except a tiny island of players playing C, near 100% of players selects action D. However, dominating strategy performed by players is not strategy *all-D* but strategy *k-D*.

(a)   (b)

Fig. 7. $b = 1.4$, *3-D*: agents' actions (a) and strategies (b).

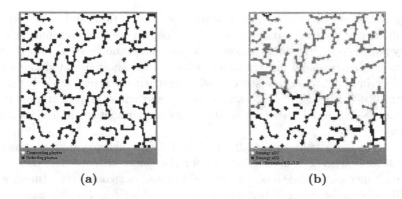

(a)   (b)

Fig. 8. $b = 1.5$, *3-D*: agents' actions (a) and strategies (b).

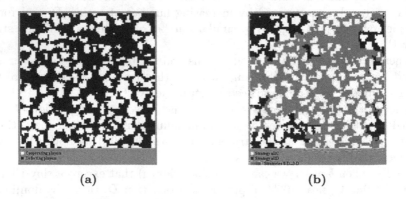

(a)   (b)

Fig. 9. $b = 1.6$, *3-D*: agents' actions (a) and strategies (b).

5   Conclusions

We have studied the conditions of emergence of global cooperation in large CA-based agent teams. We have shown that the phenomenon of global cooperation depends on values of two parameters: the parameter b of payoff function reflecting a gain of a player who defects while the other player still cooperates and on the value k of tolerance of defecting by a player. We can point four regions of values of these two parameters, each of them characterizing possibilities of the emergence of global cooperation.

For the values of b between 1.1 and 1.3 near 95% of agents are willing to cooperate and this ability a little depends on a value of k. When b is between 1.4 and 1.5, global cooperation level is in the range 60%–90% and this ability much larger depends on the value of k. When b is close to 1.6, only 15% to 40% of agents is able to cooperate and the level of cooperation depends on the parameter k. When b reaches 1.7 or more, no cooperation is observed in the system.

If someone is planning an application of a game-theoretic approach to design distributed management system and expects to profit from the phenomenon of global cooperation he should be aware that more tight requirements concerning the payoff function parameters should be fulfilled.

References

1. Axelrod, R.: The Evolution of Cooperation. Basic Books Publishing, New York (1984)
2. Axelrod, R.: The evolution of strategies in the iterated prisoner's dilemma. Dyn. Norms (1987)
3. Gąsior, J., Seredyński, F., Hoffmann, R.: Towards self-organizing sensor networks: game-theoretic ε-learning automata-based approach. In: Mauri, G., El Yacoubi, S., Dennunzio, A., Nishinari, K., Manzoni, L. (eds.) ACRI 2018. LNCS, vol. 11115, pp. 125–136. Springer, Cham (2018). https://doi.org/10.1007/978-3-319-99813-8_11
4. Gąsior, J., Seredyński, F., Tchernykh, A.: A security-driven approach to online job scheduling in IaaS cloud computing systems. In: Wyrzykowski, R., Dongarra, J., Deelman, E., Karczewski, K. (eds.) PPAM 2017. LNCS, vol. 10778, pp. 156–165. Springer, Cham (2018). https://doi.org/10.1007/978-3-319-78054-2_15
5. Howley, E., O'Riordan, C.: The emergence of cooperation among agents using simple fixed bias tagging. In: 2005 IEEE Congress on Evolutionary Computation, vol. 2, pp. 1011–1016, September 2005
6. Ishibuchi, H., Namikawa, N.: Evolution of iterated prisoner's dilemma game strategies in structured demes under random pairing in game playing. IEEE Trans. Evol. Comput. 9(6), 552–561 (2005)
7. Katsumata, Y., Ishida, Y.: On a membrane formation in a spatio-temporally generalized prisoner's dilemma. In: Umeo, H., Morishita, S., Nishinari, K., Komatsuzaki, T., Bandini, S. (eds.) ACRI 2008. LNCS, vol. 5191, pp. 60–66. Springer, Heidelberg (2008). https://doi.org/10.1007/978-3-540-79992-4_8
8. Nowak, M.A., May, R.M.: Evolutionary games and spatial chaos. Nature 359, 826 (1992)

9. Osborne, M.: An Introduction to Game Theory. Oxford University Press, New York (2009)
10. Tsetlin, M., Scitran: Automaton Theory and Modeling of Biological Systems. Academic Press, New York (1973)
11. Wolfram, S.: A New Kind of Science. Wolfram Media, Utrecht (2002)
12. Yao, X., Darwen, P.J.: An experimental study of N-person iterated prisoner's dilemma games. In: Yao, X. (ed.) EvoWorkshops 1993-1994. LNCS, vol. 956, pp. 90–108. Springer, Heidelberg (1995). https://doi.org/10.1007/3-540-60154-6_50

A Multi-demand Negotiation Model with Fuzzy Concession Strategies

Yufeng Yang[1] and Xudong Luo[2(✉)]

[1] Department of Philosophy, Institute of Logic and Cognition,
Sun Yat-sen University, 135 Xingang West Road,
Guangzhou 510275, People's Republic of China
yangyuf3@mail2.sysu.edu.cn

[2] Department of Information and Management Science,
College of Computer Science and Information Technology,
Guangxi Normal University, 15 Yucai Road,
Guilin 541004, People's Republic of China
luoxd@mailbox.gxnu.edu.cn

Abstract. This paper proposes a multi-demand negotiation model in discrete domain. To make the bargaining more realistic, we equip our negotiating agents with fuzzy concession strategies modelled by fuzzy rules. Specifically, while keeping the preference on agent's demands unchanged during the course of negotiation, negotiating agents keep can give up several demands in each round at their will. In addition, we experimentally studied our fuzzy negotiation model and reveal the relationships among various factors involved and different concession strategies.

Keywords: Automated negotiation · Multi-demand · Bargaining ·
Fuzzy concession · Fuzzy logic · Negotiation strategies · Game theory ·
Incomplete information

1 Introduction

Negotiation is a communication process among a group of agents, which aims to reach an agreement on some matter [6,11,12]. In a broad sense, negotiations are ubiquitous in our daily lives, ranging from shopping in a small grocery to large-scale national diplomacy. The research on negotiation is carried out mainly in three domains: game theory [4,14,17], business and management science [3,16], and computer science [2,12,15]. In computer science, researchers focus more on the automated negotiation, because of its advantages such as more effective, more efficient and more stable [11].

In real life, there are a sort of negotiation problems concerned with discrete issues. For example, diplomatic negotiations between two countries involve many issues in discrete domain; two parties in congress often need to reach an agreement in a number of discrete political demands; and a husband and his wife may

© Springer Nature Switzerland AG 2019
L. Rutkowski et al. (Eds.): ICAISC 2019, LNAI 11509, pp. 689–707, 2019.
https://doi.org/10.1007/978-3-030-20915-5_61

also bargain on housework assignments, such as who does laundry, cleaning and cooking, which are also non-continuous demands. To address this sort of negotiation problems, Zhang [21] proposed an axiomatic bargaining model in discrete domains. The solution to his bargaining problem holds very good properties: it can be uniquely characterized by five normal logical axioms, and satisfies Weak Pareto optimality. However, his model assumed that the agents concede one demand in each round and so negotiation strategy is in need. However, in real life, normally people who negotiate with each other do not concede only one demand in each round considering efficiency, and the number of demands that they want to give up in each round may vary during the process of negotiation.

To tackle these problems, in this paper we employ fuzzy logic to build a model in which the negotiating agents can concede the number of the demands at their will. Unlike Zhan's work [18] that assesses human users' psychological characteristics through changing negotiating agent's preference order, our model keeps the preference order unchanged during the negotiation which may be more reasonable. In Zhan's work [18], the user's psychological characteristics involved are all about the user himself and they do not consider the opponents in negotiation. In our paper, in each round the reaction of agent's strategy is based on the action of its opponent in the previous round.

The rest of the paper is organized as follows. Section 2 recaps some basic notations of fuzzy logic. Section 3 presents our negotiation model. Section 4 experimentally analyses our negotiation model. Section 5 discusses the related work to see clearly how our work advances the state-of-art in the area of automated negotiation. Finally, Sect. 6 concludes the paper and discusses some ideas for further work.

2   Preliminaries

This section recaps some notations in fuzzy logic, which we will use in this paper.

The following definition is about the implication of the Mamdani method [13].

Definition 1. *Suppose that A_i is a Boolean combination of fuzzy sets $A_{i,1}$, $\cdots, A_{i,m}$, where $A_{i,j}$ is a fuzzy set defined on $X_{i,j}$ $(i = 1, \cdots, n; j = 1, \cdots, m)$, and B_i is a fuzzy set on Y $(i = 1, \cdots, n)$. Then when the inputs are $\mu_{A_{i,1}}(x_{i,1}), \cdots, \mu_{A_{i,m}}(x_{i,m})$, the output of all rules $A_1 \to B_1, \cdots, A_n \to B_n$ is a fuzzy set C, which is defined as:*

$$\forall y \in Y, \mu_C(y) = \max\{\mu_1(y), \cdots, \mu_n(y)\}, \tag{1}$$

where

$$\mu_i(y) = \min\{f(\mu_{A_{i,1}}(x_{i,1}), \cdots, \mu_{A_{i,m}}(x_{i,m})), \mu_{B_i}(y)\}, \tag{2}$$

where $\mu_{A_{i,j}}(x_{i,j})$ is the membership degree of $x_{i,j}$ in fuzzy set $A_{i,j}$, f is obtained through replacing $A_{i,j}$ in A_i by $\mu_{A_{i,j}}(x_{i,j})$ and replacing "and", "or", "not" in A_i by "min", "max", "$1 - \mu$", respectively.

The result that we get is still a fuzzy set. To defuzzify the fuzzy set, C, we need the following centroid method [13]:

Definition 2. *The centroid point u_{cen} of the fuzzy set C defined in Definition 1 is:*

$$u_{cen} = \frac{\int_Y y\mu_C(y)dy}{\int_Y \mu_C(y)dy}. \tag{3}$$

Actually, u_{cen} is the centroid of the area covered by the curve of membership function μ_C and the x-coordinate.

Next, we introduce the concept of total pre-order [21] used in the next section.

Definition 3. *D is a non-empty set. We say that $\geqslant$ is a total pre-order on D if it is a binary relation and satisfies the following properties: (i) completeness: $\forall a, b \in D$, $a \geqslant b$ or $b \geqslant a$; (ii) reflexivity: $\forall a \in D$, $a \geqslant a$; and (iii) transitivity: $\forall a, b, c \in D$, if $a \geqslant b$ and $b \geqslant c$, then $a \geqslant c$. For any ρ, γ and a total pre-order $\geqslant$ on D, if $\rho \geqslant \gamma$ and $\gamma \geqslant \rho$, we say $\rho = \gamma$; and if $\rho \geqslant \gamma$ and $\gamma \not\geqslant \rho$, we say $\rho > \gamma$.*

3 Negotiation Model

In this section, we will present our negotiation model.

3.1 Basic Concepts

Definition 4. *Our negotiation model is a three tuple $(N, \{DL_i\}_{i \in N}, S)$, where:*

(i) $N = \{1, 2, ..., n\}$ is a set of negotiating agents.

(ii) $DL_i = \{(DS_i, \geqslant_i) \mid i \in N\}$ is the demand list of each negotiating agent i, where DS_i is a non-empty demand set of agent i, which is represented by a finite set of literals in propositional language L, and $\geqslant_i$ is a total pre-order on each DS_i, representing the preference ordering of each negotiating agent on their demands set, DS_i. Each DS_i is a logically consistent set, but $DS_i \bigcup DS_j$ may have conflict demands. The number of demands in the demand list DL_i is denoted by l_i.

(iii) $S = \{s_i \mid i \in N\}$ is the set of negotiation strategies, negotiating agent i can use only one strategy in the set S in one negotiation.

In the above definition, each agent's demand set DS_i is a set of logical literals with only one connective $\neg$, rather than a set of compound propositions with connectives $\neg, \vee, \wedge, \rightarrow$, and $\leftrightarrow$, because j it is more convenient for people to express their requirements or demands as simple propositions rather than compound propositions [18].

Example 1. Negotiating agent A has demands which can be written as $DS_A = \{\omega, \neg\tau, \theta, \beta, \alpha, \lambda, \neg\rho, \phi, \neg\gamma, \zeta\}$, and negotiating agent B has demands which can be written as $DS_B = \{\neg\zeta, \phi, \rho, \gamma, \beta, \neg\alpha, \neg\delta, \lambda, \neg\omega, \theta\}$. Agent A's preference ordering, denoted as $\geqslant_A$, on demands is defined as:

$$\alpha >_A \lambda >_A \omega =_A \beta >_A \phi >_A \neg\rho >_A \neg\gamma =_A \neg\tau >_A \theta >_A \zeta,$$

and agent B's preference ordering, denoted as $\geqslant_B$, of demands is defined as:

$$\beta >_B \neg\delta =_B \lambda >_B \neg\alpha >_B \neg\omega >_B \neg\zeta >_B \gamma >_B \theta >_B \phi >_B \rho.$$

Then we can denote negotiating agent A's demand list DL_A as $<\alpha, \lambda, \omega =_A \beta, \phi, \neg\rho, \neg\gamma =_A \neg\tau, \theta, \zeta>$, and denote negotiating agent B's demand list DL_B as $<\beta, \neg\delta =_B \lambda, \neg\alpha, \neg\omega, \neg\zeta, \gamma, \theta, \phi, \rho>$. The number of demands of DL_A and DL_B, denoted as l_A and l_B, are both equal to 10. Clearly, we can see that the union of DS_A and DS_B is not a logically consistent set, denoted as $DS_A \bigcup DS_B \vdash \bot$. So they have to make concessions to reach an agreement. The negotiation process will be shown in Example 2.

Definition 5. *Given a demand list $DL_i = (DS_i, \geqslant_i)$, a subset X_i of DL_i is comprehensive if $\forall p \in X_i$, $q \in DL_i$, we have $q \geqslant p \implies q \in X_i$.*

This means that if an element e is in a comprehensive subset X_i of DL_i, any element $b \in DL_i$ with higher preference than e is in X_i.

Definition 6. *Given a DL_i in language L, $DL_i^{(r)}$, a comprehensive subset of DL_i, is the demand list of negotiating agent i at the beginning of round r.*

We use $l_i^{(r)}$ to represent the length of the demand list $DL_i^{(r)}$ or the number of demands in $DL_i^{(r)}$. So, $DL_i^{(1)}$ is the initial demand list of negotiating agent i before the negotiation. $l_i^{(1)}$ is the length of the initial demand list $DL_i^{(1)}$.

Definition 7. *Suppose in round r negotiating agent i decides to give up $CN_i^{(r)}$ demands in the tail of $DL_i^{(r)}$, which are the least preferred by the negotiating agent i. Then negotiation procedure is a sequence of tuples: $\{(DL_i^{(1)}, CN_i^{(1)}), \cdots, (DL_i^{(r)}, CN_i^{(r)}), \cdots\}_{i \in N}$, where $r \in [1, N]$ and satisfies: (i) $DL_i^{(1)}$ and $CN_i^{(1)}$ are the initial demand list and the initial concession number of negotiating agent i respectively; and (ii) $DL_i^{(r)}$ and $CN_i^{(r)}$ are the demand list at the beginning of round r and the concession number of negotiating agent i, respectively. for all $i \in N$, each $DL_i^{(r+1)}$ is a comprehensive subset of each $DL_i^{(r)}$ and we have: $l_i^{(r+1)} = l_i^{(r)} - CN_i^{(r)}$.*

Definition 8. *An agreement of the negotiation is $\bigcup_{i \in N} DL_i^{(f)}$, if: (i) for any $i \in N$, $DL_i^{(f)} \neq \emptyset$ and (ii) for all $i \in N$, $\bigcup_{i \in N} DS_i^{(f)} \nvdash \bot$, where $DL_i^{(f)} = (DS_i^{(f)}, \geqslant_i)$ and $\bigcup_{i \in N} DS_i^{(f)}$ is the union of demand set of each negotiating agent i in round f. A disagreement of the negotiation is that there is $i \in N$ and r, such that $DL_i^{(r)} = \emptyset$.*

In the above definition, condition (i) means that the demand set of each agent i should not be empty, and condition (ii) means that the union of demands sets of all agents is logically consistent in round f. The disagreement means that at least one agent hold no demands in round r.

Definition 9. *Each negotiation strategy s_p in the strategy set S is a function:* $CN_p^{(r)} = s_p(..., CN_q^{(r-1)}, ...)$, *where $CN_p^{(r)}$ is the concession number in round r of negotiating agent using the strategy s_p and $CN_q^{(r-1)}$ is the concession number of the other negotiating agents in round $r - 1$. That is $q \in [1, n]$ and $q \neq p$.*

That is, the agent's concession number in the current round is decided by the opponent's concession number in the previous round. In this paper, we just consider the strategy function with one variable. Those with multi-variables will be studied in future.

Algorithm 1. The specification of our negotiation process

Input:
    n: The number of negotiating agents participating the negotiation;
    $a \in \{0, 1\}$: To mark whether the negotiation ended with an agreement;
    $DL_i^{(1)}$: The initial demand list of negotiating agent i;
    $CN_i^{(1)}$: The initial concession number of negotiating agent i;
    s_i: The strategy used by negotiating agent i;
    $r = 0$: The negotiation round;
Output:
    a: Reaching an agreement or not;
    r: The round when agents reach an agreement;
    $l_i^{(a)}$: The length of left demands of negotiating agent i reaching an agreement;
1: **while** $\bigcup DL_i \vdash \perp$ **do**
2:   $r = r + 1$;
3:   **for** $i = 1; i \leqslant n$ **do**
4:     **if** $l_i^{(r)} > CN_i^{(r)}$ **then**
5:       $DL_i^{(r+1)} = DL_i^{(r)} - CN_i^{(r)}$;
6:     **else**
7:       $DL_i^{(r+1)} = \varnothing$;
8:     **end if**
9:     **if** $DL_i^{(r+1)}$ is $\varnothing$ **then**
10:       **return** $a = 0$;
11:     **else**
12:       $CN_i^{(r+1)} = s_i(.., CN_j^{(r)}, ...), j \neq i$;
13:     **end if**
14:   **end for**
15: **end while**
16: **return** $a = 1, r, l_i^{(r)}$;

3.2   Negotiation Process

Our negotiation process is specified in Algorithm 1. Its line 5 means that the negotiating agent i's demand list in the round $r + 1$, $DL_i^{(r+1)}$, gets from the demand list in the round r, $DL_i^{(r)}$, by giving up $CN_i^{(r)}$ demands, which are the least preferred by agent i.

In the experiments (see the next section), we just consider negotiation between two agents (*i.e.*, $n = 2$ in Algorithm 1) with the same number of demands (logical literals) in their demand list, which are generated randomly and over which the preference ordering of each agent is represented by the order of these demands. Each demand list itself is logically consistent, but some conflicting demands may exist between two demand lists. To reach an agreement, they need to give up some less preferred demands in each negotiation round until no conflicting demands exist between them. In each round, different agents may give up different number of demands according to their strategies. If one of the agents' demand list becomes empty in one negotiation round, the negotiation ended with a disagreement. In this paper, we assume that an agent knows its opponent's last concession number of demands, but does not know its opponent's demand preference, initial conflicting demands' number, and concession history and strategy.

Table 1. The negotiation process between the negotiating agent A and B from Example 1

Initial		Round1		Round2		Round3	
DL_A	DL_B	DL_A	DL_B	DL_A	DL_B	DL_A	DL_B
α	β	α	β	α	β	α	β
λ	$\neg\delta$	λ	$\neg\delta$	λ	$\neg\delta$	λ	$\neg\delta$
ω	λ	ω	λ	ω	λ	ω	
β	$\neg\alpha$	β	$\neg\alpha$	β	$\neg\alpha$	β	
ϕ	$\neg\omega$	ϕ	$\neg\omega$	ϕ	$\neg\omega$		
$\neg\rho$	$\neg\zeta$	$\neg\rho$	$\neg\zeta$	$\neg\rho$			
$\neg\gamma$	γ	$\neg\gamma$	γ	$\neg\gamma$			
$\neg\tau$	θ	$\neg\tau$	θ				
θ	ϕ	θ					
ζ	ρ						

Example 2. (Example 1 continued). From the demand lists of agent A and B in Example 1, we can see that the demand numbers of DL_A and DL_B both equal to 10, and $DS_A \bigcup DS_B \vdash \bot$. The left demands of each agent after each negotiation round is clearly shown in Table 1. *Firstly,* from the union of the demand lists of agents A and B, we can see that there are five pairs of conflicting

demands: $\{\alpha, \neg\alpha\}$, $\{\omega, \neg\omega\}$, $\{\rho, \neg\rho\}$, $\{\gamma, \neg\gamma\}$ and $\{\zeta, \neg\zeta\}$. So, the number of initial conflicting demands in the negotiation is 5. *Second*, we suppose the initial concession numbers of agents A and B are 1 and 2, respectively. So, they will concede 1 and 2 least preferred demands, respectively. The result of the first round is showed in columns 3 and 4 in Table 1. *Third*, agent B may be a generous person or one who is eager to reach an agreement as soon as possible. Although realising that agent A just conceded one demand in the previous round, agent B still wants to concede more, saying 3 demands in the second round. Agent A, however, may be a 'tit for tat' person who concedes the same number of demands as agent B. So, in the second round, they concede 2 and 3 least preferred demands, respectively, as shown in columns 5 and 6 in Table 1. But there are still conflicting demands in the union of their left demand lists: $\{\alpha, \neg\alpha\}$ and $\{\omega, \neg\omega\}$. *Fourth*, since agent B gives up 3 demands in the second round, agent A is also willing to give up 3 demands. And agent B keeps giving up 3 demands. In the third round, finally they reach an agreement with left demands showed in columns 7 and 8 in Table 1. Namely, there are no conflicting demands in the union of demand lists left by the two agents. The round number of this example is 3 and their left demands' numbers are 4 and 2, respectively.

There are several variables in our model, such as strategic combination, the number of initial conflicting demands and initial concession rate combination. We will see how these variables influence the negotiation success rate, negotiation rounds and the number of left demands in the simulation experiments in Sect. 4.

3.3 Fuzzy Concession Strategies

In this work, we just consider three kinds of fuzzy concession strategies: *titForTatSmaller*, *titForTatNormal*, and *titForTatLarger*, which input variables are opponent's concession number in the last negotiation round, and output variables are their own concession number in the current round. The three fuzzy concession strategies are showed in Tables 2, 3 and 4. Agent using 'titForTatNormal' strategy gives up the same number of demands as his opponent did in the previous round. Agent using 'titForTatSmaller' strategy gives up less demands than his opponent did in the previous round. Agent using 'titForTatLarger' strategy will give up more demands than his opponent did in the previous round. The agent using 'random' strategy randomly gives up 0 to 10 demands.

Table 2. Fuzzy rules for titForTatSmaller strategy

If *last concession number of opponent* is *very small* then *my concession number* is *very small*.
If *last concession number of opponent* is *small* then *my concession number* is *very small*.
If *last concession number of opponent* is *medium* then *my concession number* is *small*.
If *last concession number of opponent* is *large* then *my concession number* is *medium*.
If *last concession number of opponent* is *very large* then *my concession number* is *large*.

Table 3. Fuzzy rules for titForTatNormal strategy

If *last concession number of opponent* is *very small* then *my concession number* is *very small*.
If *last concession number of opponent* is *small* then *my concession number* is *small*.
If *last concession number of opponent* is *medium* then *my concession number* is *medium*.
If *last concession number of opponent* is *large* then *my concession number* is *large*.
If *last concession number of opponent* is *very large* then *my concession number* is *very large*.

Table 4. Fuzzy rules for titForTatLarger strategy

If *last concession number of opponent* is *very small* then *my concession number* is *small*.
If *last concession number of opponent* is *small* then *my concession number* is *medium*.
If *last concession number of opponent* is *medium* then *my concession number* is *large*.
If *last concession number of opponent* is *large* then *my concession number* is *very large*.
If *last concession number of opponent* is *very large* then *my concession number* is *very large*.

In this paper, we assume that the membership function of input and output variable are the same, meaning that the same number of demands given up by two agents are viewed as the same degree to the two agents. Figure 1 is the membership function with five linguistic terms of output variable, my concession number. Here we assume that the number of demands given up by an agent in one round is in the range of 0 to 10.

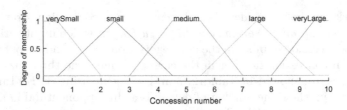

Fig. 1. The membership function of the five linguistic terms of output variable

4   Experimental Analyses

This section will experimentally analyse how the initial concession numbers of agents and their initial conflicting demands impact the performance of concession strategies.

4.1   Experiment Settings

First, in the experiments below, we choose two demand lists randomly with fixed number of initial conflicting demands (*i.e.*, 70 in 100). Two negotiating agents' initial concession number pair is denoted as (x, y) where x and y are chosen from $\{1, 5, 9\}$.

Second, each agent can choose one concession strategy from the strategy set, S. In our experiments, S contains 4 strategies: 'titForTatSmaller', 'titForTatNormal', 'titForTatLarger', 'random'. The first three strategies are all fuzzy concession strategies as shown in Sect. 3.3. Agents using the 'random' strategy (also called Zero Intelligence strategy [5]) will concede demands randomly between 1 and 10 after initial concession. Two kinds of strategies used by two agents in the same negotiation are called strategy pair. For each initial concession number pair of each strategy pair, we will do the simulation experiments 1,000 times under a fixed number of initial conflicting demands.

Third, the results of the experiments are evaluated by three criteria: *success rate*, *average negotiation rounds* and *average number of left demands in agreements*. The success rate is the percentage of negotiations ending with agreements. As we defined in Definition 8, a negotiation ended with a disagreement if at least one agent has no demands left. The average negotiation rounds is the average number of rounds spent in the successful negotiations. This criterion reflects the efficiency of the negotiations, which also means the average time that agents need to reach agreements. The average number of left demands in agreements is the average demand number of agents left in agreements. In the same negotiation, the number of left demands of different agents can be different. This criterion reflects the agreement quality of negotiations. The more demands are left in the agreement, the higher utility the agent gets from the negotiation.

The experimental results for the setting above are showed in Figs. 2, 3, 4, 5, 6 and 7, where ICD is the abbreviation for the number of initial conflicting demands, ICNP is for the initial concession number pair, NR is for negotiation rounds and NLDIA is for the number of left demands in agreements. We can use Fig. 2 as an example to illustrate the meaning of some common things in these 6 figures. Figure 2 shows how the success rate of negotiation is influenced by the initial concession number pair and the different strategy pair when the number of initial conflicting demands is 70. The labels on the x-axis in sub-figures represent strategy names and each line also represents one kind of strategy showed in the legend.[1] Each point on the particular line indicates the success rate of agents using the strategy of the line to negotiate with agents using the strategy of the x-axis coordinate of the point. In each sub-figure, the left number of the initial concession number pair is the initial concession number of agents using the strategy of particular line. The right number of the initial concession number pair is the initial concession number of agents using the strategy of the x-axis coordinate of the point. For example, in Fig. 2(d) the first point of the 'random' strategy line (-x-) represents the success rate of the negotiations between agents using 'random' strategy and ones using 'titForTatSmaller' strategy with their

---

[1] '-+-' line is 'titForTatSmaller' strategy(S1). '-o ' line is 'titForTatNormal' strategy(S2). '-*.' line is 'titForTitLarger' strategy(S3). And '-x-' line is 'random' strategy(S4).

initial concession numbers being 5 and 1, respectively. The basic things of Figs. 3, 4, 5, 6 and 7 are the same as those of Fig. 2, except ones we discuss particularly.

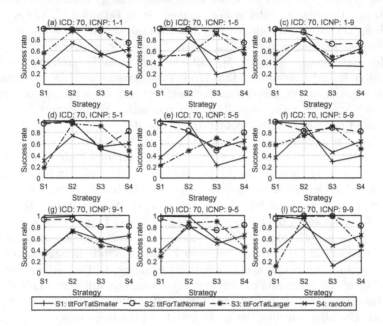

Fig. 2. Success rate of negotiations between agents using different strategies with different initial concession numbers when the number of initial conflicting demands is 70.

4.2 Success Rate

From Fig. 2, we can see:

(i) The initial concession number impacts little on the success rate of the agents using 'random' strategy. The points on the 'random' line (-x-) are the success rate of negotiations between agents using 'random' strategy and ones using other strategies. From Fig. 2 (a)–(i), we can find that the 'random' line is relatively stable. Its first point always stays between 30% and 40%. Its second point is between 75% and 80%. Its third point keeps around 50%. Its fourth point paces up and down 65%. This means that the agents using 'random' strategy like the opponents using 'titForTatNormal' strategy most since their negotiation success rate is the highest. And they may not like the opponents using 'titForTatSmaller' strategy since the success rate of their negotiation is the lowest.

(ii) The initial concession number pair also impacts little on the success rate of agents using 'titForTatSmaller' strategy unless negotiating with agents using 'titForTatLarger' strategy. The points on the 'titForTatSmaller' line (-+-) indicate the success rate of negotiations between the agents using 'titForTatSmaller' strategy and the ones using other strategies. The agents using 'titForTatSmaller' strategy like the opponents using 'titForTatNormal' strategy or the same strategy as theirs for their negotiation success rates are always higher than 95%. The third on the line indicates the success rate of the negotiations between agents using 'titForTatSmaller' strategy and ones using 'titForTatLarger' strategy, changing between 10% (when the initial concession number pairs is $(9,9)$) and 60% (when the initial concession number pair is $(9,5)$). So, the agents using 'titForTatSmaller' strategy do not like to meet opponents using 'titForTatLarger' strategy with a larger initial concession number. The fourth point on the 'titForTatSmaller' line is the same as the first point on the 'random' line.

(iii) The success rate of the agents using 'titForTatNormal' strategy to negotiate with the ones using 'titForTatLarger' strategy also varies with initial concession number pair. The points on the 'titForTatNormal' line (-o) are the success rate of the agent using the strategy to negotiate with ones using each kind of strategy. Its first and second points represent the success rate of negotiations with ones using 'titForTatSmaller' strategy and the ones using the same strategy, respectively, always staying higher than 80%. Its third is its success rate when negotiating with the ones using 'titForTatLarger' strategy. It reaches 45% and 55% when the initial concession number pair of two agents are $(5,5)$ and $(5,1)$, respectively. In the other sub-figures, it is at least 70%. Its fourth is the same as the second point on the 'titForTatSmaller' strategy line (-+-).

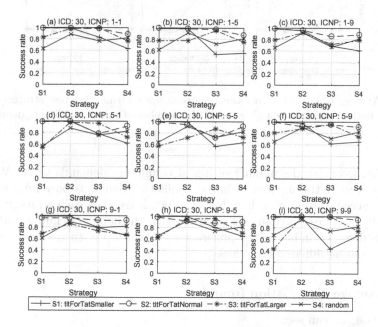

Fig. 3. Success rate of negotiations between agents using different strategies with different initial concession numbers when the number of initial conflicting demands is 30.

(iv) As the initial concession number changes, the success rate of negotiations between the agents using 'titForTatLarger' strategy and other strategies varies greatly. The third point on the 'titForTatLarger' line (-*.) is the success rate of negotiations between two agents both using 'titForTatLarger' strategy. It reaches the lowest position 50% when the initial concession number pair is $(1, 9)$ or $(9, 1)$. In others, it is higher than 70%. The other points on the line are the same as the third points on the other lines.

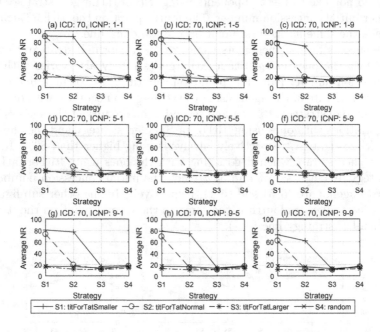

Fig. 4. Average rounds of negotiations between agents using different strategies with different initial concession numbers when the number of initial conflicting demands is 70.

In Fig. 3, we set the number of initial conflicting demands to 30. We find that the drop of the number of initial conflicting demands only improves the average success rate of each line, but the overall trend of each strategy line in the sub-figures does not change. This means that the number of initial conflicting demands does not influence the preference relationship in success rate between the agents using different strategies.

4.3   Average Negotiation Rounds

From Fig. 4, we can see:

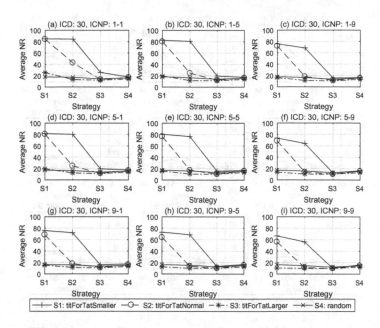

Fig. 5. Average negotiation rounds of negotiations between agents using different strategies with different initial concession numbers when the number of initial conflicting demands is 30.

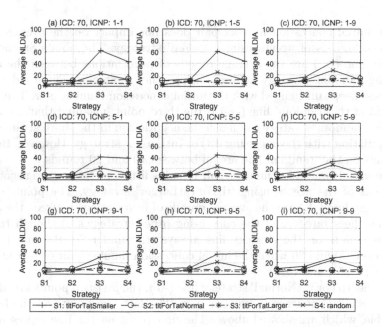

Fig. 6. Average number of left demands in agreements of agents using different strategies with different initial concession numbers when the number of initial conflicting demands is 70.

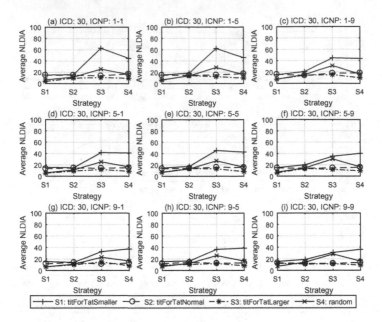

Fig. 7. Average number of left demands in agreements of agents using different strategies with different initial concession numbers when the number of initial conflicting demands is 30.

(i) The initial concession number pair does not impact on the average negotiation rounds of agents using 'random' strategy. The points on the 'random' line (-x-) are the average rounds of negotiations between the agents using 'random' strategy and ones using other strategies. The 'random' line almost keeps unchanged with the initial concession number pair. The lowest point of the 'random' line (-x-) is the third point, meaning that the agents using 'random' strategy can finish the negotiation in the shortest time when negotiating with the one using 'titForTatLarger' strategy. However, the four points on the 'random' line are all between 10 and 20 rounds.

(ii) The initial concession number pair impacts little on the average negotiation rounds of the agents using 'titForTatLarger' strategy. The points on the strategy line (-*.) are the average rounds of negotiations between the agents using the strategy and the ones using other strategies. Although the last three points on the strategy line always stay under 20, the first point is between 20 and 30 when the initial concession number pair of two agents is (1, 1), (1, 5), and (5, 1).

(iii) For the 'titForTatNormal' strategy line (-o), the first two points are affected by the initial concession number pair. The last two points on the line are stable, which are showed above. The first point on the line represents the average rounds of negotiations between the agents using 'titForTatNormal' strategy and the ones using 'titForTatSmaller' strategy. It is the highest among the four points on the line (-o) in each sub-figure and always stays higher than 60. From the sub-figures in the order of Fig. 4(a)–(c), (f) and (i) (or (a), (d), and (g)–(i)), we can see that the point decreases from around 90 to about 60 when the initial concession number of one agent goes up. The second point of the line (-o) represents the average rounds of the negotiations between two agents both using 'titForTatNormal' strategy. Like the first point, the second point decreases from about 45 to about 10 when one agent's initial concession number increases from the sub-figures in the order of Fig. 4(a)–(c), (f) and (i) (or (a), (d), and (g)–(i)). From the 9 sub-figures, we can see that the third point of the line (-o) is the lowest point and the first point is the highest. This means that agents using 'titForTatNormal' strategy prefer agents using 'titForTatLarger' strategy most since their negotiations take the shortest rounds in average. Similarly, the agents using 'titForTatNormal' strategy dislike the ones using 'titForTatSmaller' strategy most.

(iv) On the 'titForTatSmaller' strategy line (-+-), the first three points are influenced by two agents' initial concession number pair, but the last point is not. The first point on the line (-+-) stands for the average rounds of the negotiations between two agents both using 'titForTatSmaller' strategy. It is the highest point (always higher than 70) in each sub-figure. In the order of Figs. 4(a)–(c), (f) and (i) (or (a), (d), and (g)–(i)), we can see that the point decreases from 90 to about 70 with one agent's initial concession number. The second point on the line (-+-) stands for the average rounds of negotiations between the agents using 'titForTatSmaller' strategy and the ones using 'titForTatNormal' strategy. It is just slightly lower than the first point in the 9 sub-figures. And it has a similar trend with the first point, but ranges from 90 to 60. The third point on the line (-+-) stands for the average rounds of negotiations between the agents using 'titForTatSmaller' strategy and the ones using 'titForTatLarger' strategy. Its trend is also similar to the first two points except the range is 30 to 10.

In Fig. 5, we set the number of initial conflicting demands to 30. Then we find that the drop of the number only has some effect on the first two points on the 'titForTatSmaller' strategy line (-+-) and the first point on the 'titForTatNormal' strategy line (-o), but little on other points. Compared with negotiation success rate, the average negotiation round is more regular as the initial concession number pair of two agents increases, but it is influenced little by the number of initial conflicting demands.

4.4   The Average Number of Left Demands in Agreements

From Fig. 6, we can see that only the third and fourth points of the 'titForTatSmaller' line (-+-) and the third point of the 'random' line (-x-) is higher than 20. The third point on the 'titForTatSmaller' line (-+-) stands for the average number of left demands of the agents using 'titForTatSmaller' strategy when reaching agreements with the ones using 'titForTatLarger' strategy. From Figs. 6 (a)–(c), (f) and (i), we can see that the point decreases from 60 to about 30 with

Table 5. Relationship between negotiating agents using different strategies

Strategy name	Variables	titForTatSmaller	titForTatNormal	titForTatLarger	Random
titForTatSmaller	Success rate	Very high	Very high	Low	Low
	Average rounds	Very high	Very high	Very low	Very low
	ANLDIA	Very low	Very low	Medium	Medium
titForTatNormal	Success rate	Very high	Very high	High	High
	Average rounds	Very high	Low	Very low	Very low
	ANLDIA	Very low	Very low	Very low	Very low
titForTatLarger	Success rate	Low	High	High	Medium
	Average rounds	Low	Very low	Very low	Very low
	ANLDIA	Very low	Very low	Very low	Very low
random	Success rate	Low	High	Medium	High
	Average rounds	Low	Low	Very low	Low
	ANLDIA	Very low	Very low	Low	Very low

each agent's initial concession number. And the value of the point in Fig. 6 (e) is between those of the points in Figs. 6 (b) and (h). The fourth point on line (-+-) stands for the average number of left demands of the agents using 'titForTatSmaller' strategy when reaching agreements with the agents using 'random' strategy. In Figs. 6 (a)–(c), the point is between 40 and 45, but between about 35 and 40 in the other sub-figures. The third point on line (-x-) stands for the average number of left demands of the agents using 'random' strategy when reaching agreements with the ones using 'titForTatLarger' strategy. It is between 20 and 30.

In Fig. 7, we set the number of initial conflicting demands to 30. Then we find that its drop only has very small improvement on all the points but does not change the overall trend of the strategy lines. Three points higher than 20 are the same points when the number of initial conflicting demands is 70. This means that the number of initial conflicting demands does not influence the relationship in the average number of left demands in agreements between the agents using different concession strategies.

4.5   Relationship Between Agents Using Different Strategies

From the analysis above, we can summarise the relationship between different concession strategies in Table 5, where ANLDIA stands for the average number of left demands in agreements. The value in column 4 and row 1 is very high, which means that the preference degree of agents using 'titForTatSmaller' strategy to negotiate with agents using 'titForTatNormal' strategy is very high in terms of success rate.

5   Related Work

This section will show how our work advances the state-of-art in the field of negotiation.

Fuzzy logic can be used for an agent to decide how to respond to opponent's offers. Kolomvatsos et al. [10] use fuzzy logic to decide what the buyer agent should respond to the seller's offers according to its belief in the seller's deadline, the remaining time to the deadline, and the valuation of the product. However, their model is only built for buyer and they consider little about the average negotiation rounds; while our model involves the both sides of negotiation, and we also experimentally analyse our model's success rate, average rounds, and the number of left demand in agreements. Zhan et al. [20] build a negotiation model for policy making, in which fuzzy logic and uniform operator are employed to evaluate the proposal consisting of several policies and accordingly decide how to respond to the opponent's proposal. Their experiments show that the global utility of a proposal and the negotiation rounds can be influenced by the discount factor. Nonetheless, unlike our model, in their model the policies in a proposal are not ordinal and they consider little about any negotiation strategies.

Also fuzzy rules can be used to generate offers. He et al. [5] use fuzzy rules to help buyer and seller agents to make the best bid in a double auction. They show that their fuzzy bidding strategies outperform four other previous ones. However, their model is in continuous domain, involving only one demand (price of the product). Rather, our negotiation model involves many demands in discrete domain. Costantino and Gravio [1] proposed a multistage bilateral bargaining model, in which the inputs of their fuzzy inference system are the offer in the last negotiation round, the current contractual power and market penetration; and the output is a degree to which the agent should concede. However, they did little experimental analysis. Instead, we did extensive experiments, showing how the negotiation results are influenced by the initial concession number, the number of initial conflicting demands, and the combination of different strategies.

Moreover, fuzzy constraints are used to handle multi-issue negotiation. Luo et al. [11] propose such a model, in which prioritised fuzzy constraints are mainly used to help agents trade-off between multiple issues. Their model can find a Pareto-optimal solution for both sides of negotiation, and minimise the amount of their private information revealed. Karim and Pierluissi [8] also develop one of this kind, in which a mediator knows data of both buyer and seller and matches them according to historical data. However, they consider little about the negotiation strategy. Although our model also has a mediator that accepts the demand lists of both agents, it just checks whether conflicting demands exist in two input demand lists, but does not elicit any information of agents except the number of demands that an agent concede in the previous round. Moreover, our agents can choose different negotiation strategies. Zhan et al. [19] build a negotiation model based on prioritised Atanassov intuitionistic fuzzy constraint, which covers the model of Luo et at. [11] as their special case. However, they consider little about negotiation strategy. Rather, we get four fuzzy concession strategies involved.

All the models above are in the continuous domains, but there exist some in discrete domain. Zhang [21] propose an axiomatic bargaining model. Later on, Jing et al. [7] improve it by considering integrity constraints. Zhan et al.

[18] also improve it by using fuzzy rules to change the preference structures of agents during negotiation. Their agents only concede one demand in a negotiation round. It seems fair, but in reality the number of demands that people are willing to give up in one round of negotiation is different. Our model reflect the natural of human negotiation. Further, they do not pay attention to the negotiation strategies, as we did. Based on fuzzy reasoning with a regression approach, Kaur et al. [9] design bidding strategies for buyers to predict the bid amounts at a particular moment in the eBay-style auction. Nonetheless, unlike ours, the eBay-style auction only concerns one demand (the price) in continuous domain.

6   Conclusion

This paper proposes a novel negotiation model in the discrete domain, in which agents can concede a number of demands according to its will in each negotiation round. And their concession strategies is modelled by fuzzy rules. Through simulation experiments, we discover the relationship among different fuzzy concession strategies and their advantages and disadvantages with respect to our negotiation model. In the future work, it is interesting to use the machine learning algorithm to improve our agents or compare the differences among strategies using different algorithms according to game theory.

Acknowledgements. This work was partly supported by Natural Science Foundation of Guangdong Province (No. 2016A030313231), National Social Science Foundation of China (NSSFC) (No. 14ZDB015), and National Natural Science Foundation of China (No. 6197024010).

References

1. Costantino, F., Di Gravio, G.: Multistage bilateral bargaining model with incomplete information-a fuzzy approach. Int. J. Prod. Econ. **117**(2), 235–243 (2009)
2. de la Hoz, E., Lopez-Carmona, M.A., Klein, M., Marsa-Maestre, I.: Hierarchical clustering and linguistic mediation rules for multiagent negotiation. In: Proceedings of the Eleventh International Conference on Autonomous Agents and Multiagent Systems, vol. 3, pp. 1259–1260 (2012)
3. Fisher, R., Ury, W., Patton, B.: Getting to Yes: Negotiating an Agreement Without Giving in. Penguin Books, London (1991). (This is the revised, 2nd edition. While the first edition, unrevised, is published by Houghton Mifflin, 1981)
4. Fujita, K., Ito, T., Klein, M.: A secure and fair protocol that addresses weaknesses of the Nash bargaining solution in nonlinear negotiation. Group Decis. Negot. **21**(1), 29–47 (2012)
5. He, M., Leung, H.-F., Jennings, N.R.: A fuzzy-logic based bidding strategy for autonomous agents in continuous double auctions. IEEE Trans. Knowl. Data Eng. **15**(6), 1345–1363 (2003)
6. Jennings, N.R., Faratin, P., Lomuscio, A.R., Parsons, S., Wooldridge, M.J., Sierra, C.: Automated negotiation: prospects, methods and challenges. Group Decis. Negot. **10**(2), 199–215 (2001)

7. Jing, X., Zhang, D., Luo, X., Zhan, J.: A logical multidemand bargaining model with integrity constraints. Int. J. Intell. Syst. **31**(7), 673–697 (2016)
8. Karim, M.S., Pierluissi, J.: Fuzzy driven multi-issue agent negotiation on electronic marketplace. In: Meghanathan, N., Nagamalai, D., Chaki, N. (eds.) Advances in Computing and Information Technology. Advances in Intelligent Systems and Computing, vol. 178, pp. 239–248. Springer, Berlin (2013). https://doi.org/10.1007/978-3-642-31600-5_24
9. Kaur, P., Goyal, M.L., Lu, J.: A comparison of bidding strategies for online auctions using fuzzy reasoning and negotiation decision functions. IEEE Trans. Fuzzy Syst. **25**(2), 425–438 (2017)
10. Kolomvatsos, K., Anagnostopoulos, C., Hadjiefthymiades, S.: A fuzzy logic system for bargaining in information markets. ACM Trans. Intell. Syst. Technol. **3**(2), 32 (2012)
11. Luo, X., Jennings, N.R., Shadbolt, N., Leung, H.-F., Lee, J.H.-M.: A fuzzy constraint based model for bilateral multi-issue negotiations in semi-competitive environments. Artif. Intell. **148**(1–2), 53–102 (2003)
12. Luo, X., Miao, C., Jennings, N.R., He, M., Shen, Z., Zhang, M.: KEMNAD: a knowledge engineering methodology for negotiating agent development. Comput. Intell. **28**(1), 51–105 (2012)
13. Mamdani, E.H., Assilian, S.: An experiment in linguistic synthesis with a fuzzy logic controller. Int. J. Man-Mach. Stud. **7**(1), 1–13 (1975)
14. Nash Jr., J.F.: The bargaining problem. Econometrica: J. Econ. Soc. **18**(2), 155–162 (1950)
15. Pan, L., Luo, X., Meng, M., Maio, C., He, M., Guo, X.: A two-stage win-win multiattribute negotiation model: optimazationa and then concession. Comput. Intell. **29**(4), 577–626 (2013)
16. Raiffa, H.: The Art and Science of Negotiation. Harvard University Press, Cambridge (1982)
17. Rubinstein, A.: Perfect equilibrium in a bargaining model. Econometrica **50**(1), 97–109 (1982)
18. Zhan, J., Luo, X., Feng, C., He, M.: A multi-demand negotiation model based on fuzzy rules elicited via psychological experiments. Appl. Soft Comput. **67**, 840–864 (2018)
19. Zhan, J., Luo, X., Jiang, Y.: An atanassov intuitionistic fuzzy constraint based method for offer evaluation and trade-off making in automated negotiation. Knowl.-Based Syst. **139**, 170–188 (2018)
20. Zhan, J., Luo, X., Jiang, Y., Ma, W., Cao, M.: A fuzzy logic based policy negotiation model. In: Li, G., Ge, Y., Zhang, Z., Jin, Z., Blumenstein, M. (eds.) KSEM 2017. LNCS (LNAI), vol. 10412, pp. 79–92. Springer, Cham (2017). https://doi.org/10.1007/978-3-319-63558-3_7
21. Zhang, D.: A logic-based axiomatic model of bargaining. Artif. Intell. **174**(16–17), 1307–1322 (2010)

Author Index

Printed in the United States
By Bookmasters